Harnessing AI for Control Engineering

Mohamed Arezki Mellal
M'Hamed Bougara University, Algeria

IGI Global
Scientific Publishing
Publishing Tomorrow's Research Today

Vice President of Editorial	Melissa Wagner
Director of Acquisitions	Mikaela Felty
Director of Book Development	Jocelynn Hessler
Production Manager	Mike Brehm
Cover Design	Phillip Shickler

Published in the United States of America by
IGI Global Scientific Publishing
701 East Chocolate Avenue
Hershey, PA, 17033, USA
Tel: 717-533-8845
Fax: 717-533-7115
Website: https://www.igi-global.com E-mail: cust@igi-global.com

Library of Congress Cataloging-in-Publication Data

Names: Mellal, Mohamed Arezki editor
Title: Harnessing AI for control engineering / edited by Mohamed Arezki Mellal.
Description: Hershey, PA : IGI Global Scientific Publishing, [2025] | Includes bibliographical references and index. | Summary: "This book delves into the transformative integration of artificial intelligence (AI) within the domain of control engineering. This comprehensive exploration navigates the burgeoning landscape of AI applications, from classical control methods to cutting-edge machine learning algorithms and nature-inspired optimization techniques"-- Provided by publisher.
Identifiers: LCCN 2024054370 (print) | LCCN 2024054371 (ebook) | ISBN 9798369378120 h/c | ISBN 9798369378137 s/c | ISBN 9798369378144 ebook
Subjects: LCSH: Automatic control--Data processing | Artificial intelligence--Industrial applications
Classification: LCC TJ213 .H3165 2025 (print) | LCC TJ213 (ebook) | DDC 006.3--dc23/eng/20250606
LC record available at https://lccn.loc.gov/2024054370
LC ebook record available at https://lccn.loc.gov/2024054371

British Cataloguing in Publication Data
A Cataloguing in Publication record for this book is available from the British Library.

Editorial Advisory Board

Table of Contents

Detailed Table of Contents

In the recent decades, optimization, automation of processes and designs have become the focus of any field's development. With the limitation of natural resources and increasing demand for more services, it is essential to reduce any kind of wastes involved in any of the processes. Furthermore, the advancement of technologies has simplified or decreased the workload of humans and pave a road to utilize the human resources in another way where time consuming, rigorous or complex things could be done with the assistance of technologies more accurately and with improved performance as well as reduced time. This chapter highlights the way control engineering along with AI could be applied in the development of civil engineering projects. Moreover, it talks about the gaps in the recent research and how control engineering with AI can shape the future of civil engineering field.

In recent years, hybrid control systems have been used in many practical applications because they are an adequate method capable of addressing this kind complexity and vagueness, which is characteristic of today's business and scientific environment. It provides the evaluation of the fundamental concepts and solutions for the incorporation of AI in conventional control schemes. The chapter also examines other fields including robotics, aeroplane, industrial processes and power systems as other areas that have benefited from hybrid control methods. To solve the difficulties posed by nonlinear, time varying, and stochastic systems, the interaction of machine learning approaches such as artificial neural networks, fuzzy logic, and adaptive control with PID, optimal and robust control approaches is explored. Possible research topics bring concerns the analysis of hybrid control architectures for large-scale, contingent, safety-relevant systems, the extension of sensing and communication functionalities, and design of proper planning and decision-making strategies.

The manufacturing industry is undergoing a transformative shift with the advent of intelligent robotics. Intelligent robotics in manufacturing encompasses a range of technological advancements, including collaborative robots (cobots),, and robotic systems with enhanced perception, decision-making, and adaptability. These intelligent robotic systems are revolutionizing the way manufacturing operations are carried out, driving increased efficiency, productivity, and flexibility. One of the key benefits of intelligent robotics in manufacturing is the improved precision and consistency in repetitive tasks. AI-powered robotic systems can perform tasks with incredible accuracy, reducing the risk of errors and improving product quality. Furthermore, the integration of machine learning algorithms allows these robots to adapt and optimize their performance continuously, enabling dynamic adjustments to changing production demands or environmental conditions. This chapter also examines the role of intelligent robotics in enabling mass customization and agile manufacturing.

This chapter presents the major applications of Artificial Intelligence techniques (AI) in fault diagnosis of various control engineering fields. AI has made substantial improvements in various fields of Engineering, including control engineering. There are few noteworthy applications of AI in fault diagnosis related to control systems includes the control of industrial automation, power systems, robotic automation, medical applications, transportation systems, renewable energy, building automation, telecommunications etc. The early and effective diagnosis of fault can prevent downtime and repairs. In industrial automation, AI can efficiently detect anomalies in sensor readings and abnormalities in machine operation. Neural networks learn from the patterns of past historical data and identify the faults or anomalies. This chapter mainly focuses on the benefits and challenges in applying AI for fault diagnosis in the field of control engineering in food processing, monitoring control and future research perspectives

Wire Electrical Discharge Machining (WEDM) is a non-traditional machining process widely used for machining difficult-to-cut materials such as titanium alloys. This study proposes an intelligent optimization approach using Adaptive Neuro-Fuzzy Inference System (ANFIS) to optimize WEDM parameters for machining titanium alloy (Ti6Al4V) with coated wires. The key parameters investigated include pulse-on time, pulse-off time, peak current, and wire tension. The results demonstrate that the ANFIS model accurately predicts the optimal parameters, achieving a material removal rate (MRR) of up to 5.22 mm^3/min (increased by 15%) and a surface roughness (Ra) as low as 3.60 μm (reduced by 12%). The proposed approach significantly improves machining efficiency and surface quality, reducing the need for costly

N. Duraimutharasan, School of Computer Science and Applications, REVA University, India
A. Deepan, Management Studies, Sambhram University, Uzbekistan
R. Swadhi, Academy of Maritime Education and Training, India
Palanivel Rathinasabapathi Velmurugan, Berlin School of Business and Innovation, Germany
Krati Varshney, Saraswathi Institute of Medical Sciences, Hapur, India

The role of artificial intelligence (AI) in enhancing human-machine collaboration within control engineering. As industries increasingly rely on complex automated systems, effective collaboration between humans and machines is essential for optimizing performance and decision-making. AI technologies provide advanced analytical capabilities that enable real-time data processing and predictive insights, empowering engineers to make informed decisions. Integrating AI-driven tools, control engineers can enhance operational efficiency, reduce errors, and improve system responsiveness. This examines case studies demonstrating successful AI implementations in control engineering applications, highlighting the benefits of combining human intuition with machine precision. Additionally, it addresses the challenges and ethical considerations of such collaborations, advocating for best practices in designing AI systems that support human capabilities. Ultimately, this exploration emphasizes AI's potential to revolutionize control engineering, fostering a more efficient and responsive industry.

Vishal Jain, Sharda University, India
Archan Mitra, NITTE University, India

The research explores the integration of artificial intelligence (AI) into industrial control systems (ICS) to enhance resilience and efficiency through predictive maintenance. ICS play a crucial role in various industries by managing complex equipment networks. Traditional maintenance approaches, such as reactive and preventive maintenance, are often inefficient, leading to unnecessary downtime and high operational costs. This study focuses on AI-driven predictive maintenance, utilizing machine learning and neural networks to forecast equipment failures and optimize maintenance schedules. By leveraging real-time data, this approach reduces downtime, prolongs equipment lifespan, and lowers maintenance expenses. The research further addresses the challenges of integrating AI into existing infrastructures and provides a framework for its implementation in critical sectors like manufacturing and energy. The study contributes to advancing maintenance strategies by increasing system reliability and operational efficiency.

The work is aimed at identifying specific features that need to be taken into account when researching and developing passively redundant subsystems, taking into account tolerances for sudden independent failures. It is shown that in this type of redundancy it is necessary to take into account the presence in the same subsystems of assignable and implemented tolerances, multiple and non-multiple redundancy, tolerance scales with different levels of significance, probability ranges of elements, where redundancy is advantageous and unprofitable, etc.

Swarm Intelligence and other metaheuristics have recently gained attention as optimization methods in large-scale data analytics, particularly in control engineering. With the increasing use of big data, IoT devices, and real-time processing, traditional techniques are facing challenges in dealing with high-dimensional and nonlinear problems. Swarm intelligence methods are based on the collective behavior of natural systems, providing robust and scalable solutions for optimizing control parameters, system identification, and fault detection in large environments. The combined use of swarm intelligence and metaheuristics will improve optimization for control engineering applications, focusing on large-scale analytics as discussed in this chapter. Case studies presented in this chapter demonstrate the effectiveness of these methods in optimizing complex control systems where traditional methods struggle due to size or complexity.

For the equation of string vibration with given initial and final conditions, we consider the problems of optimal boundary control with given multipoint conditions at different intermediate time points for the values of deflection functions and velocities of string points. The control is carried out both by displacement at one end with the other end fixed, and by displacement at the two ends of the string. The minimizable functionals are the boundary energy integrals given over the entire time interval. We propose a constructive approach to designing solutions to the considered problems of optimal boundary control of string vibrations. The construction scheme is as follows: the problems are reduced to control problems with distributed impacts and zero boundary conditions, then, using the method of separation of variables, the obtained problems are reduced to optimal control problems for ordinary differential equations with specified initial, final and multipoint intermediate conditions with appropriate quality criteria.

The optimization goal is to increase the amount of generated energy with the help of photovoltaic system considering the tracking system's consumption. Determination of the tilt angle and azimuth angle trajectories is described as a nonlinear and bounded optimization problem. For collection of solar energy we have used sensors (LDR) for tracking of sun's path to make sure that the panel should be placed in MPPTto observe more efficiency and make sure that the panel should be placed in MPPT point.This is definitely a more cost effective solution than purchasing additional solar panels. The maximum power point tracking (MPPT) method is used to track the maximum amount of solar energy generated by the sun. In the world to avoid the dependency on non - renewable resources, solar energy is rapidly gaining the focus. This system will rotate according to the position of the sun. The operation of the experimental model of the device is based on a servo motor which is intelligently controlled by an Arduino UNO board that moves a mini PV panel according to the rotation of the sun.

Integrating AI into the automotive industry has revolutionized driving and interacting with vehicles. This work explores the ethical implications and responsible use of Al in automotive technology. Integrating AI into vehicles represents a major paradigm shift with profound consequences for society, the economy, and individual users. Thus, understanding and addressing the ethical challenges inherent in this transformation is of utmost importance. It delves into the multifaceted challenges and opportunities that arise as Al increasingly intertwines with vehicles, emphasizing the need for a comprehensive ethical framework. The work begins by discussing safety and reliability, shedding light on the ethical concerns of Al systems in vehicles, and proposing responsible practices to ensure safety. Data privacy, another pivotal issue, is scrutinized in the context of the vast amounts of data collected from connected vehicles. Responsible data collection, management, and privacy measures are examined.

Preface

Harnessing AI for Control Engineering delves into the transformative integration of artificial intelligence (AI) within the domain of control engineering. This comprehensive exploration navigates the burgeoning landscape of AI applications, from classical control methods to cutting-edge machine learning algorithms and nature-inspired optimization techniques. Through insightful analysis and real-world case studies, this book elucidates the symbiotic relationship between AI and control engineering, uncovering how AI techniques empower control systems to adapt, optimize, and evolve dynamically in response to complex environments and diverse objectives.

This book serves as a guiding light for practitioners, researchers, and students seeking to comprehend and leverage the profound impact of AI on control engineering. By elucidating the latest advancements and best practices, it empowers readers to harness the full potential of AI technologies to enhance system performance, resilience, and efficiency across a spectrum of industries. Moreover, by fostering a deeper understanding of AI-driven control systems, this book catalyzes innovation, propelling the field towards new frontiers of intelligent automation and autonomous decision-making.

Control engineers and practitioners: Professionals involved in designing, implementing, and optimizing control systems across various domains, including manufacturing, robotics, aerospace, and automotive industries.

Researchers and academics: Scholars engaged in advancing the theoretical foundations and practical applications of AI in control engineering, spanning disciplines such as electrical engineering, computer science, and applied mathematics.

Students and educators: Undergraduate and graduate students studying control systems, automation, and artificial intelligence, as well as educators seeking comprehensive resources for teaching and learning about the intersection of AI and control engineering.

The book includes sixteen chapters:

Chapter 1 discusses the growing importance of optimization and automation in addressing resource limitations and increasing service demands, emphasizing waste reduction and efficiency. It highlights how technological advancements have reduced human workload, enabling more focus on complex tasks while improving accuracy, performance, and time efficiency. The chapter explores the role of control engineering and AI in transforming civil engineering, identifies gaps in current research, and outlines their potential to shape the future of the field through smarter, sustainable solutions.

Chapter 2 explores the growing use of hybrid control systems in addressing complexity and uncertainty in modern business and scientific environments. It evaluates the integration of AI into conventional control schemes and highlights applications in robotics, aviation, industrial processes, and power systems. The interaction of machine learning techniques, such as artificial neural networks, fuzzy logic, and adaptive control, with traditional methods like PID, optimal, and robust control is examined to tackle challenges in nonlinear, time-varying, and stochastic systems. The chapter also identifies potential research directions, including hybrid control architectures for large-scale, safety-critical systems, enhanced sensing and communication capabilities, and the development of effective planning and decision-making strategies.

Chapter 3 highlights the transformative impact of intelligent robotics on the manufacturing industry, driven by advancements such as collaborative robots (cobots) and systems with enhanced perception, decision-making, and adaptability. These technologies are revolutionizing manufacturing operations by boosting efficiency, productivity, and flexibility. A key advantage is the improved precision and consistency in repetitive tasks, as AI-powered robotic systems perform with high accuracy, reducing errors and enhancing product quality. Additionally, machine learning integration enables continuous adaptation and optimization, allowing robots to dynamically respond to changing production demands or environmental conditions. The chapter also explores the role of intelligent robotics in enabling mass customization and agile manufacturing.

Chapter 4 explores the significant applications of Artificial Intelligence (AI) techniques in fault diagnosis across various control engineering fields. AI has demonstrated substantial advancements in engineering, particularly in control systems, with notable applications in industrial automation, power systems, robotic automation, medical applications, transportation systems, renewable energy, building automation, and telecommunications. Early and effective fault diagnosis can prevent downtime and reduce repair costs. In industrial automation, AI excels at detecting anomalies in sensor readings and machine operations, with neural networks leveraging historical data patterns to identify faults. The chapter focuses on the benefits and challenges of applying AI for fault diagnosis in control engineering, particularly in food processing and monitoring control, while also outlining future research perspectives.

Chapter 5 presents an intelligent optimization approach for Wire Electrical Discharge Machining (WEDM) using the Adaptive Neuro-Fuzzy Inference System (ANFIS) to optimize parameters for machining titanium alloy (Ti6Al4V) with coated wires. Key parameters such as pulse-on time, pulse-off time, peak current, and wire tension are investigated. The ANFIS model accurately predicts optimal parameters, achieving a material removal rate (MRR) of up to 5.22 mm^3/min (a 15% increase) and a surface roughness (Ra) as low as 3.60 μm (a 12% reduction). The approach enhances machining efficiency and surface quality while minimizing costly experimental trials. The study underscores the potential of ANFIS in optimizing WEDM processes for industrial applications, particularly in aerospace and biomedical sectors where titanium alloys are widely used.

Chapter 6 explores the integration of AI in cardiology, highlighting its potential to enhance accuracy, reduce errors, and improve efficiency in cardiovascular clinical procedures. AI aids in diagnosing complex pathologies, predicting complications, and reducing diagnostic times and medical errors. A key focus is on arrhythmia, a prevalent cardiovascular condition, and the use of cardiac pacemakers, which are critical for real-time heart rate control. Efficient and robust control of pacemakers is vital for delivering life-saving interventions in dynamic conditions. The chapter discusses the development of advanced pacemaker-based heart stimulation techniques, the application of control strategies, and the implementation of AI in this domain, along with the challenges and future prospects in this evolving field.

Chapter 7 addresses modern agricultural approaches for classifying and managing tomato-weakening pathogens, emphasizing the importance of accurate disease diagnosis to enhance productivity and ensure sustainable farming. The multi-symptom nature of diseases, the need for extensive annotated data, and real-time execution pose significant challenges. The Deep InfoMax Algorithm (DIMA) is introduced as a deep learning-based solution, leveraging a deep neural network trained on tomato leaf images to improve disease classification. The network accurately identifies disease types, offering versatility in disease diagnosis, crop management, and yield optimization. By detecting and treating leaf diseases, tomato productivity and health are significantly improved. The chapter validates the proposed method through simulation studies on tomato leaf disease images, demonstrating DIMA's potential to revolutionize agricultural disease management.

Chapter 8 explores the role of artificial intelligence (AI) in enhancing human-machine collaboration within control engineering. As industries increasingly depend on complex automated systems, effective collaboration between humans and machines is crucial for optimizing performance and decision-making. AI technologies provide advanced analytical capabilities, enabling real-time data processing and predictive insights that empower engineers to make informed decisions. By integrating AI-driven tools, control engineers can improve operational efficiency, reduce errors, and enhance system responsiveness. The chapter examines case studies showcasing successful AI implementations in control engineering, emphasizing the benefits of combining human intuition with machine precision. It also addresses challenges and ethical considerations, advocating for best practices in designing AI systems that complement human capabilities. Ultimately, the chapter highlights AI's potential to revolutionize control engineering, fostering a more efficient and responsive industry.

Chapter 9 investigates the integration of artificial intelligence (AI) into industrial control systems (ICS) to enhance resilience and efficiency through predictive maintenance. ICS are vital for managing complex equipment networks across industries, yet traditional maintenance approaches, such as reactive and preventive methods, often result in inefficiencies, unnecessary downtime, and high costs. The study focuses on AI-driven predictive maintenance, employing machine learning and neural networks to predict equipment failures and optimize maintenance schedules. By utilizing real-time data, this approach minimizes downtime, extends equipment lifespan, and reduces maintenance expenses. The research also addresses challenges in integrating AI into existing infrastructures and proposes a framework for implementation in critical sectors like manufacturing and energy. The study advances maintenance strategies by improving system reliability and operational efficiency.

Chapter 10 focuses on identifying key features essential for researching and developing passively redundant subsystems, considering tolerances for sudden independent failures. It highlights the importance of accounting for both assignable and implemented tolerances within the same subsystems, as well as the distinctions between multiple and non-multiple redundancy. The study also emphasizes the significance of tolerance scales with varying levels of importance and the probability ranges of elements where redundancy is either advantageous or unprofitable. By addressing these factors, the work provides a comprehensive framework for designing and optimizing passively redundant subsystems to enhance reliability and performance.

Chapter 11 explores the growing role of Swarm Intelligence and metaheuristics as optimization methods in large-scale data analytics, particularly in control engineering. With the rise of big data, IoT devices, and real-time processing, traditional techniques often struggle with high-dimensional and nonlinear problems. Swarm intelligence, inspired by the collective behavior of natural systems, offers robust and scalable solutions for optimizing control parameters, system identification, and fault detection in complex environments. The integration of swarm intelligence and metaheuristics enhances optimization for control engineering applications, particularly in large-scale analytics. Case studies presented in the chapter highlight the effectiveness of these methods in addressing complex control systems where traditional approaches fall short due to size or complexity.

Chapter 12 addresses optimal boundary control problems for string vibration equations with given initial, final, and multipoint intermediate conditions for deflection functions and velocities. Control is applied through displacement at one end (with the other end fixed) or at both ends of the string. The minimizable functionals are boundary energy integrals defined over the entire time interval. A constructive approach is proposed to solve these optimal boundary control problems, involving a reduction to control problems with distributed impacts and zero boundary conditions. Using the method of separation of variables, the problems are further simplified to optimal control problems for ordinary differential equations with specified initial, final, and multipoint intermediate conditions, along with appropriate quality criteria. This approach provides a systematic framework for designing solutions to such control problems.

Chapter 13 focuses on optimizing energy generation in photovoltaic systems while considering the energy consumption of the tracking system. The optimization problem involves determining the tilt and azimuth angle trajectories, formulated as a nonlinear and bounded optimization challenge. Light-dependent resistors (LDRs) are used to track the sun's path, ensuring the solar panel operates at the maximum power point (MPPT) for enhanced efficiency. This approach is a cost-effective alternative to adding more solar panels. The MPPT method maximizes solar energy capture, addressing the global shift toward renewable energy to reduce reliance on non-renewable resources. The system uses a servo motor, controlled by an Arduino UNO board, to intelligently adjust a mini PV panel according to the sun's position, demonstrating an efficient and practical solution for solar energy optimization.

Chapter 14 examines the integration of AI into the automotive industry, highlighting its transformative impact on driving and vehicle interaction. It explores the ethical implications and responsible use of AI in automotive technology, emphasizing the profound societal, economic, and individual consequences of this paradigm shift. The chapter underscores the importance of addressing ethical challenges, such as safety and reliability, by proposing responsible practices to ensure the dependability of AI systems in vehicles. It also scrutinizes data privacy concerns, given the extensive data collected from connected vehicles, and discusses responsible data collection, management, and privacy measures. By delving into these multifaceted challenges and opportunities, the chapter advocates for a comprehensive ethical framework to guide the responsible integration of AI in the automotive sector.

Chapter 15 discusses the use of parametric accelerated life testing (ALT) to enhance the lifespan of mechanical products. The methodology includes: (1) employing BX life with ALT tactics, (2) analyzing fatigue loads, (3) conducting ALTs with design modifications, and (4) verifying whether the product meets the desired BX lifetime. A stress model derived from the quantum level was developed, and a sample size for reliability quantitative (RQ) statements was proposed. The approach was demonstrated by evaluating refrigerator fatigue failures during rail transit using power spectral density to assess equivalent raised damage potential. In the first ALT, refrigerant tubes and inverter PCB soldering on ethylene propylene diene monomer rubber mounts experienced fatigue due to insufficient damping, matching field failures. After redesigning the rubber mounts and compressor tubes, the second ALT showed no issues, confirming the refrigerator achieved the desired B1 life during transport.

This preface underscores the transformative integration of artificial intelligence into control engineering, marking a paradigm shift in industries and research. By bridging theoretical foundations with practical applications, this book addresses the challenges and opportunities at the intersection of AI and control engineering, from industrial optimization to intelligent automation and sustainable solutions. Designed to equip practitioners, researchers, and students with cutting-edge knowledge, it aims to inspire innovation and propel the field toward new frontiers of intelligent systems. As the era of automation and autonomous decision-making unfolds, this book serves as a guide to harnessing AI's potential, fostering a future where control systems are adaptive, efficient, and transformative, shaping a smarter and more sustainable world.

Prof. Mohamed Arezki Mellal, Editor

Chapter 1
The Impact of Control Engineering and Artificial Intelligence in the Development of the Field of Civil Engineering

Aditya Singh
https://orcid.org/0000-0001-9347-5627
Amrita Vishwa Vidyapeetham, India

ABSTRACT

In the recent decades, optimization, automation of processes and designs have become the focus of any field's development. With the limitation of natural resources and increasing demand for more services, it is essential to reduce any kind of wastes involved in any of the processes. Furthermore, the advancement of technologies has simplified or decreased the workload of humans and pave a road to utilize the human resources in another way where time consuming, rigorous or complex things could be done with the assistance of technologies more accurately and with improved performance as well as reduced time. This chapter highlights the way control engineering along with AI could be applied in the development of civil engineering projects. Moreover, it talks about the gaps in the recent research and how control engineering with AI can shape the future of civil engineering field.

INTRODUCTION

Before moving forward with the chapter, it is important to know about Control Engineering, which is a branch of engineering which concentrates on the way to design systems in order to attain required outputs as well as behaviours. It is also called as Control System Engineering, and in other words, it includes not only design, but also optimization in addition to analysis of control systems to accomplish the needed outputs. Whereas control systems are made up of devices which control of other systems or devices, which comprise of electronic as well as mechanical parts. Basically, this engineering branch utilizes computational tools, mathematical modeling in addition to feedback mechanisms to regulate physical systems in an effective manner. It could be understood in a way that the above-mentioned branch of engineering targets to optimize efficiency, safety as well as performance of systems throughout dif-

DOI: 10.4018/979-8-3693-7812-0.ch001

ferent areas. They utilize detectors as well as sensors to estimate the output performance of controlled process. Then the estimations are utilized to give right feedback to assist in attaining the anticipated performance. Mathematical modeling of varied range of systems also acted as a foundation for Control Engineering to work smoothly on analysis, designing, in addition to optimization aspects of the control systems. As per the records, the water clock of Ktesibio in Egypt's Alexandria around the 3rd century BCE is considered to be the 1st feedback control device, making it an automatic control system. Later on, a number of other automatic devices were made for either entertainment or for beneficial tasks, for instance automata dancing figures were open-loop control devices famous in European countries during the seventeenth as well as eighteenth centuries. However, the feedback control idea by James Watt in the late eighteenth century in the year 1788, at the time to control the steam engine's speed by using flyball governor, was a major tuning point, followed by the 1st modern recorded mathematical analysis of feedback control by the closed-loop control system's inventor Nicolas Minorsky in the year 1922 was another milestone in development of Control Engineering in the modern times. By the 1930s, many areas like ships, analogue computers, airplanes, telephone systems, and so on, were using feedback control devices. In simple words, it can be said that initially Control Engineering roots started with mechanical control systems in history and with the arrival of electrical control systems, the development of this field progressed rapidly and led to the current Control Engineering branch. In a way, this branch of engineering could also be described as the one where control theory is practically applied in real life. It is important to understand that the system can be electrical, chemical, mechanical, fluid, biological or even financial one, where the analysis, mathematical modelling, in addition to controller design utilizes control theory in one or more of the realms of frequency, time, as well as complex realms based on design problem's nature. At present, Control Engineering has become an integral part of the human lives from small scale work to large scale work, which includes washing machines at the homes to wash the daily clothes which are very common household electronic items to the highly advanced fighter airplanes for aerial fights in battles and many more. Similarly, it could be said that Control Engineering aims on the modeling of a varied range of dynamic systems which are present in many areas including the area of Civil Engineering, as well as the design of controllers would help such systems to work in the anticipated way. This means that the dynamic behaviours which is present in many domains including Aerospace, Civil Engineering, etc., are controlled by analysing, designing, as well as incorporating systems with the help of Control Engineering. It helps in the factory production lines to become automated, which includes the factories responsible for producing construction equipment and materials, in addition to the way to manage aeroplane's stability which is important in air transportation of either goods, people or animals. However, to proceed further, there is a need to have an understanding of control systems in general first.

Control Systems

Control systems are the systems which are expected to control physical processes. In other words, these systems are the ones which gets input, that is being processed by them, in order to produce an output which is further being utilized by these systems to regularize the whole process. Many applications uses control systems which comprise of advanced systems responsible for managing the flight of aeroplanes in addition to regulate the temperature of indoor places by thermostats. Usually, systems are built of different components which collaborate together to attain the same goal. In the case of control systems, their components include actuators, controllers, as well as sensors which are utilized for closed loop systems. The data from the sensors is being processed by the controllers and gives control signals, which the actuators utilize to control the process. The control systems either basic ones or complicated ones, generally classified into two categories, which are:

- Open loop
- Closed loop

Open Loop

These kind of control systems are the ones where the input doesn't receive back the output. This means that open-loop control systems don't have any process where the input is to be adjusted based on the generated output of the system. A simple instance from daily life of humans, could be a refrigerator, in which only when the internal temperature goes above a certain temperature, the compressor is being turned on by the thermostat. Then for a specified time, the compressor runs without considering the refrigerator's internal temperature. The turning off of the compressor becomes possible after the given time is passed. This whole process goes on and repeats again and again like a open loop where the internal temperature of the refrigerator which is output, is not considered while setting the thermostat as the input in the process.

Closed Loop

These kind of control systems are the ones where the input receives back the generated output. This means that closed-loop control systems have a process where the input is being adjusted on the basis of the produced output of the system. An instance of this case is the cruise control in a vehicle, where throttle position is adjusted by the cruise control system in order to maintain a set speed of the vehicle. To calculate the vehicle's speed, speed sensor is being utilized by the earlier mentioned system, and throttle position is being adjusted by the controller. In case, the vehicle's speed decreases below a certain speed, then the throttle position is increased by the controller in order to raise the speed of the vehicle. It could also be said that in case the vehicle's speed increases above a certain speed, then the throttle position is decrease by the controller in order to reduce the speed of the vehicle. The said process goes on and repeats again and again, until the cruise control system is turned off by the driver inside the vehicle.

Since, the control system is being understood now, so it's time to move towards the main principles of Control Engineering, before moving further.

Control Engineering's Main Principles

The main principles of this branch of engineering, i.e. Control Engineering, is built on various main principles which work as fundamental components for analysing, designing, as well as executing control systems in an effective manner. Such principles become the foundation of Control Engineering, in order to not only permit optimization but also controlling the dynamic processes present in different sectors. These principles are described in this section in the following manner:

- System modeling
- Feedback control
- Execution considerations

- Stability analysis
- System optimization
- Control algorithms
- Performance specifications

System Modeling

This is another important Control Engineering principle, as it consists of mathematical models to be developed which are responsible for representing the system's behaviour which is under the control. Such models are able to catch not only interdependencies, relations, but also dynamics between numerous system parts. Various modeling techniques like transfer functions, differential equations, in addition to state-space representations are considered to be utilized to explain the response of the system to not only disturbances but also inputs. System models must be accurate for them to be considered as the grounds for the analysis as well as design of controllers.

Feedback Control

The concept of feedback control is essential in Control Engineering, as the systems based on them regularly monitors the generated output of a given process as well as to compare it to a preferred source value. In case there is deviation or difference between the real output and preferred value, then an error signal is produced, where the controller processes the said signal, to adjust the actions or inputs in order to lead the system to the preferred state. Real-time adjustments are permitted by the feedback control, to make sure the system not only optimize the performance but also to make the system continue in a stable state.

Execution Considerations

Practical limitations must be considered carefully when executing control systems in actual applications. Computational resources, delays by signal processing, limitations due to hardware used, are necessary factors which shouldn't be ignored. Control algorithms are supposed to be designed by engineers which could be executed in an efficient manner in the selected hardware, to make sure that the latency remains low as well the operation takes place in real-time. Techniques to recognize the system should be taken into account in order to roughly calculate the model parameters as well make the control system adjust with the altering operating environments.

Stability Analysis

This is another essential Control Engineering's principle, which allows a given control system to stay constant under every type of operating environment. To attain stability, once the output of the system stays around the anticipated value in the absence of instability or oscillations, it becomes possible. There are techniques for stability analysis including Nyquist stability criterion, as well as Routh-Hurwitz criterion, to evaluate the stability of the system on the basis of the traits of its frequency response or transfer function. For the performance to be constant and dependable, it is important to have a stable control system.

System Optimization

Another necessary principle is to incorporate techniques for system optimization. Optimal performance is attained by the attempts of engineers when they minimize the consumption of energy as well as errors, maximize efficiency and enhance response time. Optimal control theory or model predictive control are the approaches for optimization, which are utilized to find out the control actions where particular performance standards could be optimized at the same time taking system limitations into account. Engineers are able to adjust control systems with the help of system optimization to reach better uses of resources as well as higher performance.

Control Algorithms

They are considered as another important principle, as they act as the intelligent brains like the human brain, but here behind the actions of control systems. They help in finding out the way the processing of error signals took place as well as the said signals turned into control actions. For various kinds of applications as well as systems, there exist an appropriate control algorithm among the numerous control algorithms present. One of the famous algorithms, is called PID controller, which is known as Proportional-Integral-Derivative controller. They incorporate derivative, integral, in addition to proportional actions to control the behaviour of the given system as well as to attain the anticipated performance. Then, sophisticated ones like robust control as well as adaptive control techniques gives improved abilities to handle not only disturbances but also uncertainties.

Performance Specifications

They must be defined in Control Engineering, in order to convey the anticipated performance criteria as well as behaviour of the given controlled systems. Such specifications include factors comprising transient response, robustness, accuracy of steady state, in addition to disturbance rejection. When indicating such needs, engineers are able to not only adjust control parameters but also design controllers, to attain the anticipated performance goals. This principle makes sure that the given control systems are able to reach the expectations as well as requirements of the applications which are being used currently.

Now, it is time to consider techniques of Control Engineering before moving forward with the chapter.

Major Techniques of Control Engineering

This subsection will cover the major and popular Control Engineering techniques, which are as follows:

- State-space control
- PID Control
- Optimal control

State-Space Control: Here the state variables are utilized by the control system named state-space control in order to describe behaviour of the given system. The state variables represent the system's internal states which comprise several things such as acceleration, velocity, position of the object which is in motion. The present state of the system is shown by the state vector which is formed after the combination of state variables. The input of the system is changes as a consequence of the computing the output of the system with the assistance of the earlier mentioned state vectors. In many industries, state-space control is generally utilized as the grounds to manage and model complicated systems due to their flexibility as well as robustness.

PID Control: A famous technique used in Control Engineering, which is also known as Proportional-Integral-Derivative as mentioned in the earlier subsection. There are three dissimilar controllers merged together in PID controller, where each of the controllers has their own benefits as well as limitations. In case of proportional controller, the system generated output is adjusted in proportion to the detected error between the real output and preferred output. On the other hand, the system generated output is adjusted by the integral controller on the basis of accrued error with the passing time. Then comes the last controller, which is the derivative controller, where the system generated output is adjusted by it on the basis of the error's rate of change.

Optimal Control: The optimal control system is utilised to search for an appropriate input for a given system which could reduce the cost function. The said input is then considered as the ideal input, whereas the cost function acts as the measurement of the performance of the given system. Many areas like robotics, economics, etc. utilize optimal control to deal with their own respective problems. In optimal control, PID control as well as state-space control are utilized, where the former is utilized so that the system's input could be adjusted, and the latter is utilized to model the given system's behaviour. When all three controls are merged, then it is possible to design control systems which are more efficient as well as effective.

Since, major techniques of Control Engineering are already covered in the earlier subsection, it is time to understand that the ways Control Engineering is affecting the development of Civil Engineering field as well as Artificial Intelligence impact on the same. However, it is also noteworthy to consider the relation of AI with Control Engineering before moving towards how both of them are affecting the domain of Civil Engineering in a positive manner towards advancement. Artificial Intelligence is not only transforming other disciplines and subdisciplines, but also affecting Control Engineering area, by permitting systems to make decisions which are intelligent in nature, adapt as well as learn continuously. The algorithms of AI could help in analysing enormous amounts of data, predictive model generation in addition to recognizing patterns. Then with the arrival of AI technology, it is possible to permit independent decision-making, process optimization as well as improvement of control performance in control systems. Further, AI technology could permit the sophisticated control strategies to advance, like reinforcement learning as well as model-free control, which could adjust themselves to not only complicated systems but also to dynamic environs. Now, it's time to move to understand how the Civil Engineering areas are being affected by the execution of Control Engineering as well as AI.

Control Engineering and AI in the Field of Civil Engineering

In this subsection, the impact of AI in addition to Control Engineering in the Civil Engineering branch and its subbranches are covered, which are as follows:

- Construction robots
- Air transportation & airport engineering
- Manufacturing
- AVs

- Treatment Plants
- HVAC
- Water Distribution Network
- Smart & Sustainable Cities
- Control of dynamics
- Smart construction & project management
- Geotechnical & disaster management

Construction Robots

Control Engineering is main part in the robotics area, where developing as well as designing of control system, which is intended for robots takes place, that is utilized by several industries, including Industrial Robots which are also used in the Construction Industry. Engineers make advanced control algorithms which allows construction robots to complex as well as repeated tasks, comprising of motion planning, detection of objects, tracking of paths, and so on. Then, AI usage in robotics, make even smarter robots. This is helpful at the site, taking care of tedious tasks as well as dangerous ones by the construction robots, while safeguarding the lives of workers from possible accidents, enhancing efficiency and accuracy in projects. Further, engineers making feedback control systems gives the construction robots not only accuracy but also stability while carrying out the assigned tasks. Similarly, Cobots in the recent years have emerged in the construction industry, where collaborative robots are used in some places side by side with humans to basically assist people in their respective work, and increase productivity in projects.

Figure 1. Construction robots

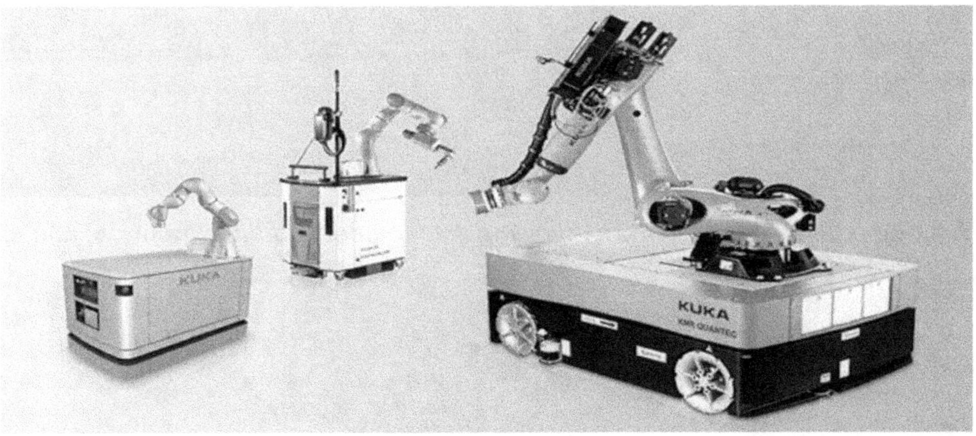

Source: RealAws, Wikimedia

Air Transportation & Airport Engineering

Transportation Engineering is vast and when focussed on air mode of transportation, then aircrafts, helicopters, etc. comes under it. They might be used either for transportation of people, goods, and animals depending upon the purpose of the service. This subbranch of Transportation Engineering is closely related to Aerospace Engineering as well. Leaving that aside, in the case of airplanes or any flying mode of transport service, precision as well as safety are essential which is possible with the implementation of Control Engineering. Then, Airport Engineering is a branch of Transportation Engineering, which deals with the entire airports, including runways, taxiways, terminals, etc. Then, by applying AI technology, airport operations, maintenance of airports, customer handling, air traffic management, assistance to the concerned pilot handling the airplane, becomes possible.

Figure 2. Airbus flying in sky with the passengers as mode of air transportation

Source: Flickr user Axwel, Wikimedia

Figure 3. Hong Kong International Airport showing the terminal buildings, runways, and taxiways

Source: Dinkun Chen, Wikimedia

Manufacturing

Manufacturing industry is vast, and the manufacturing processes require optimization, which is possible with the execution of Control Engineering. However, this also applies to the manufacturing of construction equipment and materials, which are integral part of the Construction Industry. Here, the control systems make sure that variables are precisely controlled that includes pressure, quality of the products, temperature, in addition to flow rate. These processes could be adjusted for optimal performance by incorporating feedback control loops, that will lead to minimization of downtime, reduction of waste, in addition to entire productivity to be enhanced, along with dependable as well as constant production. AI technology improves the manufacturing process further, by assisting in the detection of defects, automation of processes, quality control, predictive maintenance of machines, and so on.

AVs

AVs also known as Autonomous Vehicles are becoming part of road transportation services, where control systems are developed as well as designed by control engineers to be used by the vehicles. The control algorithms are developed for a number of systems in AVs, including braking systems, transmission systems as well as engine systems. Not to forget that AI technology also plays a key role in AVs. These self-driving vehicles are blending with regular vehicles to improve road traffic safety. They are considered as part of the advanced and future oriented road transport services. Intelligent speed control, adaptive braking, real-time decision-making ability, etc. are a number of features of AVs.

Figure 4. AVs

Source: Maxx@night, Wikimedia

Treatment Plants

Treatment Plants can be either WTPs or WWTPs and executing Control Engineering, could help in optimizing the Water Treatment Plants and even Wastewater Treatment Plants. The former uses raw water sources to treat before supplying it to residential as well as for commercial places. However, the latter uses wastewater which is being treated by Wastewater Treatment Plants to reutilize wastewater in the proper ways, which also makes their treatment process different. When AI technology is also implemented, then the analysis of real-time data is done properly and quickly which is collected by the sensors, and then optimization of a number of processes could be done in these Treatment Plants, including disinfection processes, rate of filtration, in addition to chemical dozing. This leads to improved efficiency of processes, minimization of the usage of chemicals, as well as enhanced water quality. Similarly, timely maintenance, detection of any problems and so on becomes possible.

Figure 5. Ohio WTP

Source: Mbrickn, Wikimedia

Figure 6. La Crosse WWTP facility 2

Source: Wikideas1, Wikimedia

HVAC

HVAC systems are also known as heating, ventilation as well as air conditioning systems are essential part of Smart Homes and Smart Buildings. These systems are used for residential buildings as well as for commercial buildings, where Control Engineering execution helps in optimizing the energy consumption related to HVAC. AI technology also compliments HVAC systems in Smart Homes, Smart Offices or Smart Buildings. Weather prediction, sensors inside the rooms and buildings, as well as data in the real-time, to change the operation of equipment, rate of airflow, temperature setpoints, etc. This helps in not only saving energy, and money, but also saves resources wastage, in addition to leading optimum work environment for maximum productivity.

Figure 7. HVAC system diagram

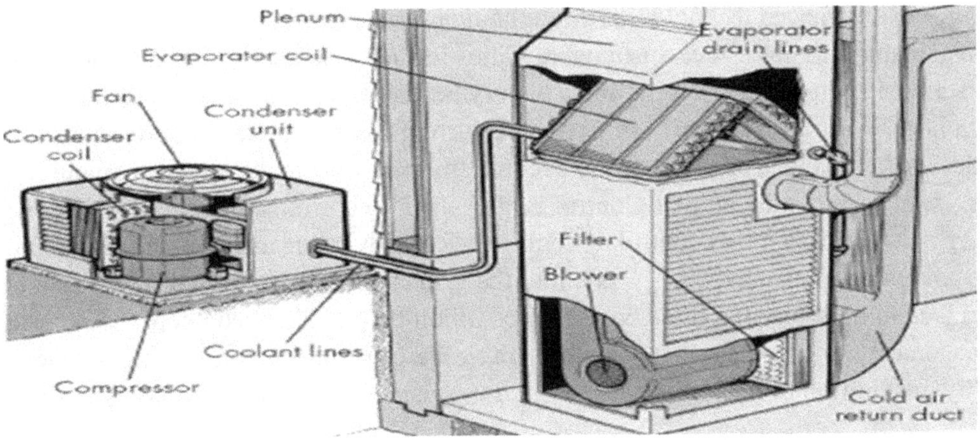

Source: sammsheatingandair, Wikimedia

Figure 8. Smart Home

Source: Monacoporter, Wikimedia

Water Distribution Network

This is part of Water Resources Engineering, a subbranch of Civil Engineering domain. water distribution networks vary from place to place, depending on the population of cities or towns, as well as the location of the cities or towns, location of houses and buildings, water resource availability and location along with the distance to be covered during water transmission, etc. In the case of complicated water distribution networks, control engineering plays a key role in managing them. Quality, pressure, in addition to flow of water could be optimized by executing control systems. Then, AI technology helps in leakage detection, smart water monitoring, analysis of real-time data, and helping in sending quick alert messages in the case of anomalies, etc.

Smart & Sustainable Cities

These cities use advanced technologies throughout an area of the city or the whole city. Smart Cities could be sustainable in nature, but Sustainable Cities are not necessarily to be Smart Cities as well, because Sustainable Cities were present in the history before the arrival of smart technologies long ago in different places in the world. However, as per the current technological and environmental demands, modern cities are being made or converted to become smart as well as sustainable in nature. Here, smart grid management requires the help of Control Engineering to optimize the energy efficiency, then renewable energy integration needs control systems to effectively manage the incorporation of renewable energy like solar as well as wind energy, etc. into the grid. Similarly, Artificial Intelligence is essential in the smart technologies used in these cities, which might be for enhanced people 's experience, smart traffic management, smart waste management, smart water management, etc. to enhance efficiency, sustainability, in addition to reduce wastage as well as mismanagement of resources.

Figure 9. Smart city Malta

Source: Continentaleurope, Wikimedia

Figure 10. Sustainable city

Source: La Citta Vita, Wikimedia

Control of Dynamics

Control of Dynamics is a subpart of Control Engineering, where control methods are utilized to not only manage external forces but also to make the structures stable. Here, the design of control systems takes place which regularize the behaviour of not only systems but also structure, which is essential in Civil Engineering, particularly in Structural Engineering. They are also applied in bridge engineering, where control systems are utilized to monitor the dynamic forces generated because of seismic, wind as well as traffic activities. Apart from that, the mitigation of these dynamic forces is done with the assistance of control systems, leading to the safety as well as durability of the bridges. Then, Buildings, these days are not only high-rise ones, but tall, super tall and mega tall buildings, which are designed in a way to resist dynamic loads like earthquakes as well as wind loads particularly, with the assistance of control of dynamics. Tuned mass dampers in addition to base isolation are the major techniques used to improve the safety in addition to stability of buildings. Then, they are also used in seismic engineering, which are essential where structures are built in the areas prone to earthquakes. Then with the seismic control systems the design of those structures is made so that the energy from the ground motions could be dissipated as well as absorbed. Here, the energy dissipation devices as well as base isolators are generally utilized to save any infrastructure or building. Moreover, the transportation systems like airports, highways, as well as railways require dynamic analysis to make sure their operation is safe as well as efficient. Here, it is important to consider vibration control to maintain the runways, rail tracks dependable in addition to consider the comfort of the passengers.

Smart Construction & Project Management

Risk management as well as scheduling are possible to be done with the assistance of AI technology, where delays in the construction projects are forecasted beforehand as well as allocation of resources could be optimized. Similarly, drones as well as robots powered AI could help in the inspections of the construction sites along with the handling of materials. Moreover, site safety monitoring could also be assisted by Artificial Intelligence.

Geotechnical & Disaster Management

These days Artificial Intelligence models are able forecast disasters like earthquakes as well as landslides, after analysing the soil conditions in addition to seismic activities in a given place. Then, any alterations in ground movement, seepage of water, as well as tunnel conditions are detected by AI, making them suitable for monitoring the underground infrastructures. Then, timely flood warnings could be given when the data from the sensors as well as satellites are processed by AI allowing for timely mitigation strategies.

Objectives

This chapter has a number of objectives which are as follows:

- To understand the Control Engineering concept in general as well as brief development of the engineering branch.
- To understand the major principles in addition to significant techniques of Control Engineering.
- To understand how Control Engineering and AI could affect each other as well as the ways both of them impact the development of the Civil Engineering areas.
- To understand the necessity of Control Engineering and AI in general and particularly in Civil Engineering field.
- To understand the Control Engineering's and AI's present state as well as possible future, particularly in the domain of Civil Engineering.

MOTIVATION

The author noticed the recent development of Control Engineering across various disciplines, and the tremendous development of human civilization in the current time with the arrival of Artificial Intelligence technology. Due to which, the author realized to perform this study to understand the ways in which Control Engineering as well as AI are shaping the field of Civil Engineering, which is an essential field for the development of any civilization, apart from the fact that the author belongs to the said field. Further, he focussed on the various subfields of Civil Engineering being affected by the implementation of Control Engineering and AI, through this chapter. Then, he attempted to know how application of both the above-mentioned Control Engineering as well as Artificial Intelligence technology could affect the development of Civil Engineering areas not only in the present but also in the possible future.

What is the Necessity of Control Engineering in General and Particularly in Civil Engineering?

Control Engineering offers various benefits in a number of disciplines, making it a necessary branch of engineering across multiple domains. As Control Engineering enhances the efficiency by optimizing the concerned processes allowing organizations to enhance their efficiency, which is also applicable in construction and infrastructure companies. Then, the reliability also increases with their implementation, by making the systems as well as processes to become more dependable and leading to not only robustness but also stability. Moreover, Control Engineering allows optimal performance to be attained by organizations in their operations as well as processes, which includes reduction response time, overshoot and so on, that also applies to infrastructure as well as construction companies. Then safety could also be enhanced as the design of control systems are done to not only respond to unusual situations but also to monitor parameters which are critical ones. They also lead to monetary savings by decreasing the variations as well as material wastage along with the optimization of processes. They also permit adaptability in addition to scalability, as the design of control systems are done to adjust with alterations in operating situations as well as process needs, allowing the organizations to respond to demands as well as requirements of the market in an efficient manner, which is also applicable to construction, real estate as well as infrastructure companies. With the arrival of mechanical control systems and later on electrical control systems, the technological development along with innovations could be observed in many areas over the centuries, including the Civil Engineering field. It is noteworthy to understand that Control Engineering is an important part of Mechatronics and Singh (2022), highlighted the utility of Mechatronics and its applicability to construction projects for improvement. Then, for Control Engineering to grow as per the current times, where electronic devices are present almost everywhere, the digitalization is in fact essential, which is also applicable in the context of Civil Engineering, and it could be noted in the Singh (2022) study regarding digitalization of the construction industry and projects.

Is Artificial Intelligence Really Needed for the Development of Civil Engineering Field?

Artificial Intelligence has assisted in the transformation of a number of areas including engineering areas, and daily lives of people, from the moment it came into existence. Civil Engineering field is no exception to the benefits offered by AI technology, but compared to other fields, Civil Engineering has observed slow transformation due to the said advanced technology, as the implementation of new advanced technologies takes at a slow pace in this particular core engineering branch. AI technology allows enhanced accuracy, efficiency as well as automation, but at the same time minimization of errors leading to reduction of material wastage in material and time, along with saving of cost and availability of time for other tasks. It improved predictive analytics as well decision-making processes which are important in traffic management and transportation engineering. Further, the productivity also increases, leading to profits, and it's uses could be overserved in smart cities, smart buildings and many more areas. In the study of Singh (2022), fuzzy logic's usefulness was covered especially in traffic as well as transportation engineering, to reduce road accidents and fatalities. Then, Singh (2023) explained the ways in which AI could promote practices which are sustainable in nature. Moreover, Smart Highways which are essential for the development of not only transportation engineering but also in the traffic management as noted in the study of Singh (2024) also requires the application of advanced technologies like AI. Then, Singh (2023) covered the ways ANN is required in the area of Civil Engineering both at and in the future developments. Further, the study of Singh and Srivastava (2024) discussed the ways AI in addition to Green AI could assist in Civil Engineering domain in sustainable development. However, digitalization is essential for the growth of advanced technologies like AI and Singh (2022) mentioned the necessity of digitalization of the construction sector for the advancement of projects.

LITERATURE REVIEW

Laflamme et al. (2025) studied control engineering especially powertrain one and they worked on understandable reinforcement learning for their studied area. Wang et al. (2023) studied civil engineering, and they worked on performing computational analysis on the basis of a novel Artificial Intelligence in their studied area. Zhuang et al. (2025) studied civil engineering, and they worked on detecting surface cracks in their studied area with the assistance of DL technique through their thorough review paper. Jayasinghe et al. (2025) studied the domain of civil engineering, and they worked on accelerating FEA with the assistance of ANN techniques which were intended for the former through their review paper. Zhang et al. (2023) studied civil engineering, and they worked on AMRs as well as AGVs which were aimed at tracking in addition to identification in their studied area. Rafsanjani et al. (2023) studied the AEC industry and they worked on AI which was focussed around people in their studied area. Meshram (2024) studied civil engineering and he worked on ML to be used in his studied area. Uncouglu et al. (2022) studied civil engineering and they worked on the way to deal with the associated problems by comparing the methods, like support vector machine, NN, long short-term memory, Gaussian regression, M5 Trees, in addition to multi-gene genetic programming. Masria and Abouelsaad (2025) studied coastal engineering and they worked on applying AI in their studied area through their review paper. Mallik et al. (2025) studied river water and they worked on thoroughly examining of the dynamics of E. coli with the assistance of explainable Artificial Intelligence as well as sophisticated ML technique in their studied area. Jeong et al. (2024) studied the indoor management involving PM2.5, and they worked on optimizing ventilation control policy proximal powered by Aritficial Intelligence, which was combined with calibration of dynamic model which was up to date real-time one leading their studied area in the direction of sustainability. Ramasetti et al. (2024) studied bridges, and they worked on the forecasting the vehicle's movement by developing models based on generic Artificial Intelligence to support their studied area. Dzhusupova et al. (2024) studied engineering companies and they worked on selecting the correct path to integrate Artificial Intelligence in their studied area. Munjiza et al. (2024) studied engineering in addition to science, and they worked on Artificial Intelligence powered virtual test in their studied area, in the direction of finite-discrete element method on the basis of simulation tools which hybrid ones to support the former. Huang et al. (2024) studied autonomous driving, and they worked on improving reinforcement learning especially the human-in-loop one with the aim to make their studied area not only efficient, but also safe. Hernandez-Gonzalez et al. (2024) studied bridges, and they worked on programmed operational modal analysis of their studied area, which was powered by Artificial Intelligence. Chowdhury and Karanfil (2024) studied treatment processes of drinking water, and they worked on applying AI in their studied area. Di and Shi et al. (2021) studied the time of mixed-autonomy, and they worked on performing a survey on the control of AVs in their studied area, to accomplish their desired goals. Kim et al. (2024) studied subway trains, and they worked on a model named HiFi-IAQ which was powered by explainable Artificial Intelligence for their studied area. Gatto et al. (2024) considered Italy's southern part to study soils which are fine-grained ones, and they worked on forecasting the dynamic properties of their studied area, which was powered by Artificial Intelligence, on the basis of lab test. Kim et al. (2024) studied rainfall-runoff, and they worked on forecasting the level of flood water with the assistance of merged hybrid model of their studied area, in addition to models on the basis of Artificial Intelligence. Ye et al. (2025) studied system dynamics as well as DPSRC theory, and they worked on permafrost environs examination of the plateau named Qinghai-Tibetan one on the basis of their studied area. Shi et al. (2025) studied structure which was steel framed one along with fire encouraged ductile failure, and they worked on its virtual safety examination, which was up to date with CFD. Yu et al. (2025) studied transport planning particularly cooperated by machine as well as human, in addition to proceed with urban dynamics explainable state-space model. Ghorbani and Kodikara (2024) studied properties of compacted soil, and they worked on its inference in real-time regarding their studied area, by utilizing tests for deflection. Salimi et al. (2024) studied Artificial Intelligence, and they worked on the approached based on their studied area to predict the severity, location, occurrence, as well as timing of ice jam floods. Rabbi and Jeelani (2024) studied safety in construction, and they worked on incorporating Artificial Intelligence in their studied area, to understand the present challenges as well as state. Asadi et al. (2024) studied simulation of rainfall-runoff, and they worked on models which were powered by incorporation of interpretable as well as physical Artificial Intelligence. Liang et al. (2024) studied structural dynamics in the presence of load which is moving, and they worked on applying physics up to date DL technique in their studied area, to get the desired results. Kamarposhti et al. (2024) studied hydrogen area, and they worked on an improved integration of smart grid with the assistance of Artificial Intelligence for their studied area through a thorough review paper. Hernandez-Gonzalez et al. (2024) studied structures, and they worked on swift operational modal analysis of their studied area, with the assistance of a technique named blind source separation powered by Artificial Intelligence to accomplish their research. Liao et al. (2024) studied building structures, and they worked on its design with the assistance of generative Artificial Intelligence, to obtain the desired outcomes. Zhang et al. (2024) studied wind environs in urban areas, and they worked on the idea of a system of wind-channeling allowed by Artificial Intelligence aimed at the real-time improvement of their studied area.

RESEARCH GAPS

After reading a number of scientific and research published studies, only the ones related to the Control Engineering in some ways, or Artificial Intelligence, in addition to associated to the Civil Engineering areas, published in the recent years, were considered further. It was found that many studies were on AI's impact in the domain of Civil Engineering, and then there were studies on dynamics of control, which is a subfield of Control Engineering. However, the current studies are unable to utilize the full usefulness of Control Engineering in the domain of Civil Engineering.

MAIN FOCUS OF THE CHAPTER

The chapter mostly focussed on the concept of Control Engineering, and about control systems which were mentioned as per the records in history towards their evolution over the millennia, where noticeable development occurred in the nineteenth and twentieth centuries slowly leading to the current state of Control Engineering. It then highlighted the main principles in Control Engineering which are necessary for the engineering branch to be implemented successfully in different areas. Then, the book chapter covered some major techniques of Control Engineering to give a rough idea about them and eventually the focus was given on the ways Artificial Intelligence could affect Control Engineering before both Control Engineering as well as AI could improve the Civil Engineering domain and its branches. Moreover, the necessity to implement Control Engineering as well as AI particularly in Civil Engineering field were concentrated in this chapter. Then, some major problems, related to Control Engineering and AI were discussed apart from covering various published studies to find out the current gaps in the literature related to the possible transformation of Civil Engineering with the incorporation of AI and Control Engineering. Furthermore, some case studies in the world were considered where advanced technologies like AI in addition to Control Engineering being used while related to the field of Civil Engineering and graphical analysis to understand the current trend of Control Engineering along with AI and their possible future in Civil Engineering domain were highlighted in the chapter.

ISSUES, CONTROVERSIES, PROBLEMS

This section will discuss the problems, issues, and controversies related to the execution of Control Engineering and AI, because even though, both AI in addition to Control Engineering bring ample number of benefits in the area of Civil Engineering, but the problems associated with them can't be ignored. The majority of Civil Engineers are not much familiar with Control Engineering apart from its small aspect, which is dynamic control, which is also normally limited to Structural Engineers, but Control Engineering is way more vast in its application. Then, high initial cost is another major problem associated with sophisticated control systems and AI technologies for their full usage in the field of Civil Engineering. This makes people hesitant in investing in them, as the civil engineering projects could be done at less cost in traditional ways. Then, at the site, the usual workers, and even majority of Civil Engineers would require some form of training before getting accustomed to advanced technologies and control systems. This further needs additional cost and time to train individuals in projects, which contractors or companies might avoid, particularly if they are medium scale or small-scale ones. Then, with fast technological developments, the existing civil engineers or the old ones, as well as workers at the site, might be uncomfortable working with updated technologies and advanced control systems in projects. Then, the real civil engineering projects vary in complexity and becomes challenging, which might make simple control systems not much useful and might require special control systems or particular technologies based on their suitability of the projects.

SOME MAJOR CASE STUDIES IN THE WORLD

In this section, some case studies across the globe are considered where Control Engineering or AI technology or both were executed, which are:

- Taipei 101
- Millau Viaduct
- Akashi Kaikyo Bridge

- Songdo IBD
- HKZMB

Taipei 101

This building is having one hundred and one floors and was originally called as Taipei World Financial Centre. It was opened in the end of the last month of the year 2004, and its height is five hundred and eight meters, making it the first building in the world to cross the half kilometre mark in the height of a building. It is present in Taiwan's Taipei and uses tuned mass damper to decreases the vibrations generated by seismic as well as wind activities. In other words, it is an instance of control of dynamics, which is a subfield of Control Engineering, as mentioned earlier in the chapter.

Figure 11. Satellite map of Taipei 101

Source: Google Earth

Millau Viaduct

This is a cable-stayed bridge in France in near the western part of Millau, across the gorge valley of the river named Tarn. It is also known as Viaduc de Millau and has a height of three hundred and forty-three meters. The bridge's length is two thousand four hundred and sixty meters, and it was opened by the last month of the year 2004. To resist the dynamic loads generated from the traffic in addition to wind, it utilizes sophisticated design techniques as well as materials, which shows another instance of control of dynamics.

Figure 12. Millau Viaduct

Source: Richard Leeming, Wikimedia

Akashi-Kaikyo Bridge

This bridge was opened in the fourth month of the year 1998 and it crosses the Akashi strait in Japan. At that time, it was the longest main span suspension bridge and has a height of slightly more than two hundred eighty-two meters. The bridge's total length is three thousand nine hundred and eleven meters and to neutralize the vibrations generated by wind, it utilizes active control systems, which displays another instance of control of dynamics.

Figure 13. Akashi-Kaikyo Bridge

Source: Stingy Scoundrel, Wikimedia

Songdo IBD

This is a Smart City built on six hundred hectares of land, which used reclaimed land from the yellow sea, and it is thirty km southwest from the South Korea's capital named Seoul. Songdo's infrastructure comprises of sensors which not only helps in controlling but monitoring traffic across the city, consumption of energy as well as temperature. The project is at least eighty six percent completed and over one hundred and sixty-seven thousand people live in the city.

Figure 14. Songdo IBD

Source: Ken Eckert, Wikimedia

HKZMB

This bridge is spans has three spans and was opened by the beginning month of the last quarter of the year 2018. The length of HKZMB is fifty-five thousand meters and is present across the delta region of Pearl River and has a daily traffic of more than five thousand and eight hundred vehicle. Over two thousand and seven hundred sensors, and 100s of peripherals in its SHM system.

Figure 15. HKZMB

Source: Google Earth

METHODOLGY

In this section, the obstacles as well as challenges associated with the above-mentioned case studies are explained, which are:

Taipei 101: The building project faced major problems like enormous structural load, resistance to frequent earthquakes, as well as typhoon winds which are strong ones in those areas. Then, placement of tuned mass damper was another major challenge in the course of the project.

Millau Viaduct: This bridge project observed significant hurdles like strong crosswinds which are fatal for a long and high bridge structure usually, uneven terrain for the foundation of the bridge, as well as resistance to heavy vehicular loads.

Akashi-Kaikyo Bridge: The bridge project faced several key hurdles like exposure to extreme typhoon winds, resistance to high frequent seismic activities in these areas, as well as exposure to harsh corrosive marine environs. Furthermore, active control system for such a large-scale bridge is expensive to maintain or even upgrade.

Songdo IBD: The Smart City project observed some noticeable problems such as high development cost, which made the city expensive and underpopulated. Then, delayed expansion of the city, slow business growth of the city, and so on were other key challenges in this project.

HKZMB: This bridge project saw significant challenges including environmental problems including marine ecosystem issues, higher risk of corrosion due to environmental conditions, construction of complicated underwater tunnel, as well as high maintenance cost, in addition to budget overrun by a significant margin, and so on.

RESULTS AND DISCUSSION

In this section, data from various sources including Grand View Research, and so on, to perform graphical analysis.

Table 1. Revenue share by region in the market of control systems as well as industrial automation

Revenue Share in the Market of Control Systems in Addition to Industrial Automation	In (%)
Asia Pacific Region in 2024	39
Rest of the World in 2024	61

Source: Grand View Research

Table 2. Worldwide market size of control systems as well as industrial automation

Market Size of Control Systems in Addition to Industrial Automation	In (USD)
Year 2024	206,330,000,000
Year 2030	378,570,000,000

Source: Grand View Research

Table 3. Share of industries in the market of machine control systems internationally

Share of Industries in Machine Control System Market in the World	In (%)
Construction Industry in 2022	31.5
Other Industries (Mining, Agriculture, Marine, Oil & Gas, Energy & Utility) in 2022	68.5

Source: Fortune Business Insights

Table 4. Share of industries in the Chinese market of machine control systems

Share of Industries in Machine Control System Market in China	In (%)
Construction Industry in 2022	32
Other Industries (Mining, Agriculture, Marine, Oil & Gas, Energy & Utility) in 2022	68

Source: Fortune Business Insights

Table 5. Market growth of Civil Engineering worldwide

Civil Engineering Market Globally	In (USD)
Year 2023	9,090,000,000,000
Year 2030	13,700,000,000,000

Source: Grand View Research

Table 6. Application wise share in the revenue of Civil Engineering market worldwide

Application wise Share in the Revenue Global Civil Engineering Market in Year 2023	In (%)
Real Estate	40.7
Infrastructure and Industrial	59.3

Source: Grand View Research

Table 7. Region wise share in the revenue of Civil Engineering market in the world

Region wise Share in the Global Civil Engineering Market Revenue in year 2023	In (%)
Asia-Pacific Region	33.7
Rest of the World	66.3

Source: Grand View Research

Table 8. Growth of AI in construction market worldwide

AI in Construction Market Globally	In (USD)
Year 2024	3,930,000,000
Year 2032	22,680,000,000

Source: Fortune Business Insights

Table 9. Growth of AI software market

AI Software Market Globally	In (USD)
Year 2022	64,000,000,000
Year 2027	251,000,000,000

Source: Fortune Business Insights

Table 10. Maximum impact of AI on construction

AI's Max Impact on Construction	In (%)
Automation of Construction Tasks	49
Rest	51

Source: Fortune Business Insights

Figure 16. Revenue share by region in the market of control systems as well as industrial automation

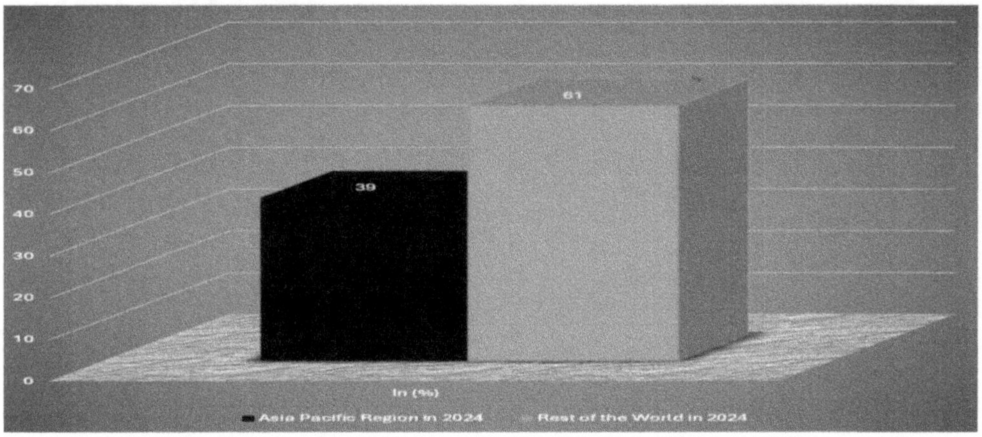

Source: Grand View Research

Figure 17. Worldwide market size of control systems as well as industrial automation

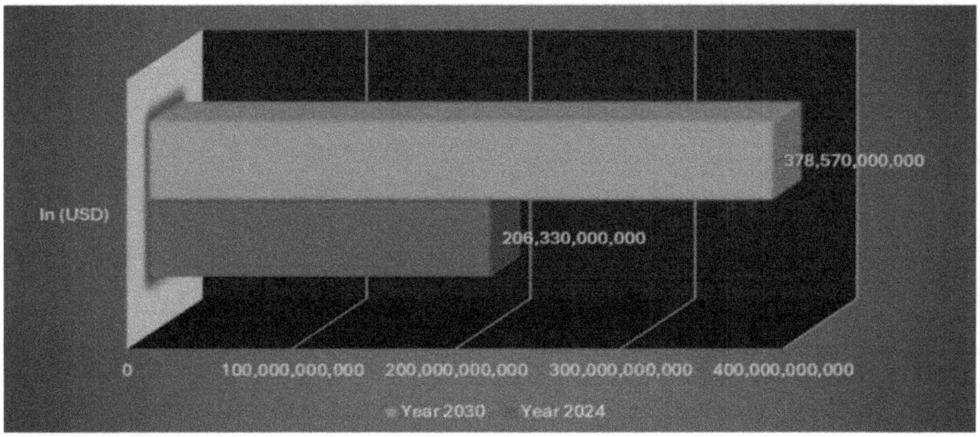

Source: Grand View Research

Figure 18. Share of industries in the market of machine control systems internationally

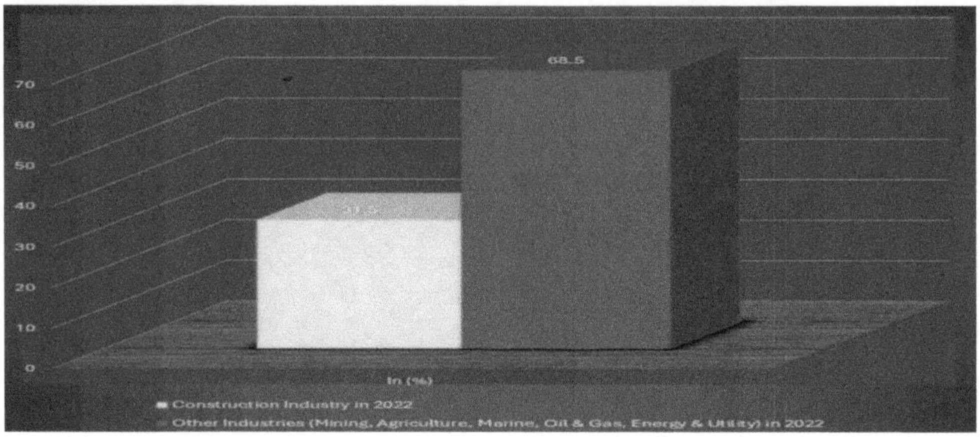

Source: Fortune Business Insights

Figure 19. Share of industries in the Chinese market of machine control systems

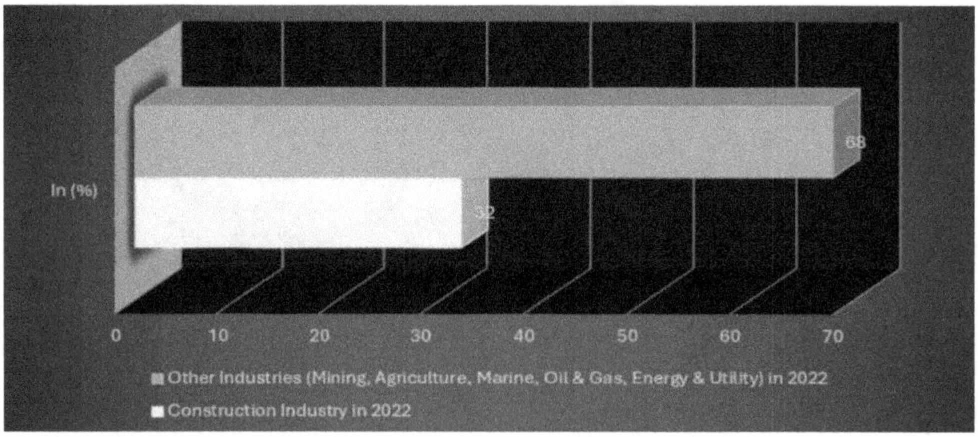

Source: Fortune Business Insights

Figure 20. Market growth of Civil Engineering worldwide

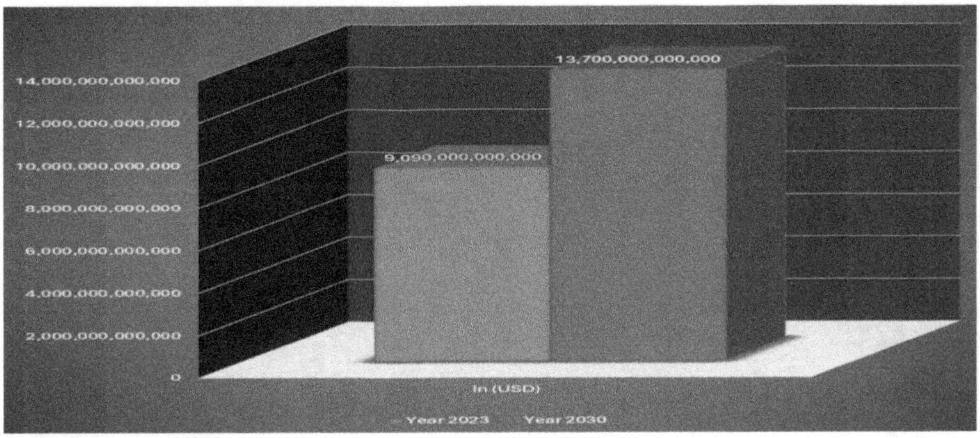

Source: Grand View Research

Figure 21. Application wise share in the revenue of Civil Engineering market worldwide

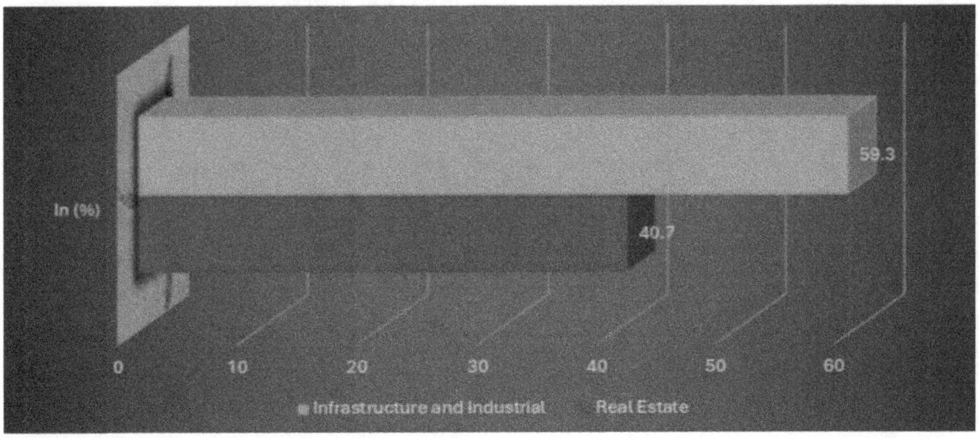

Source: Grand View Research

Figure 22. Region wise share in the revenue of Civil Engineering market in the world

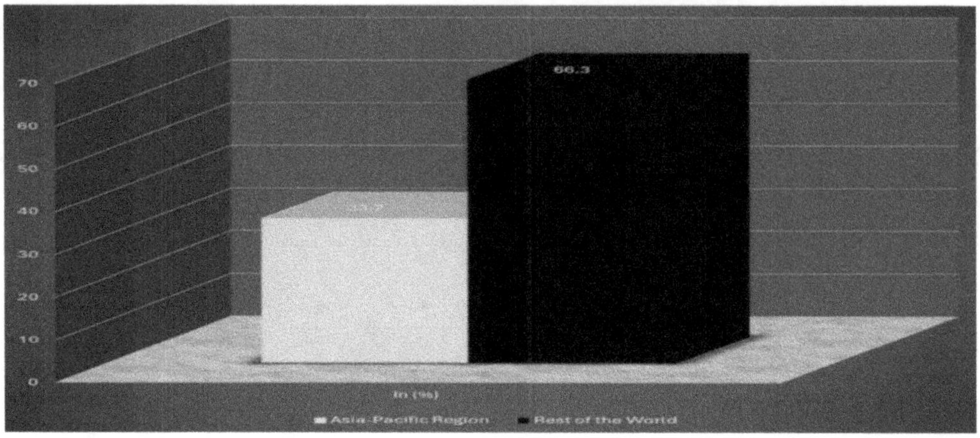

Source: Grand View Research

Figure 23. Growth of AI in construction market worldwide

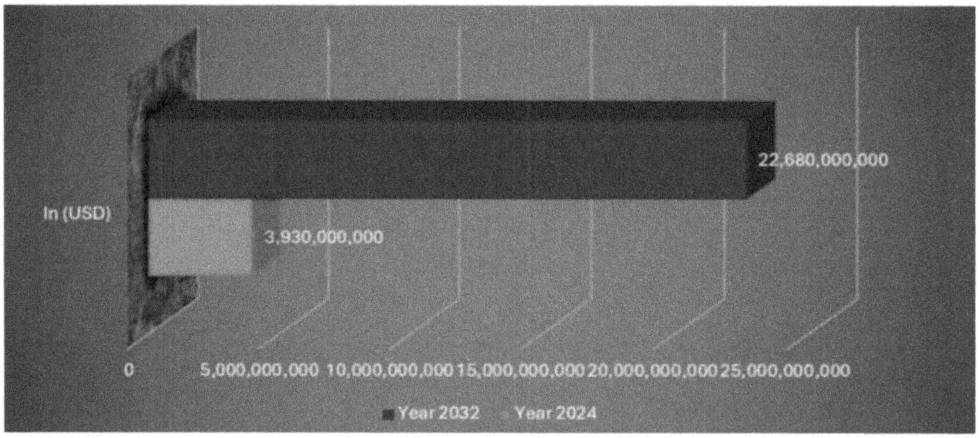

Source: Fortune Business Insights

Figure 24. Growth of AI software market

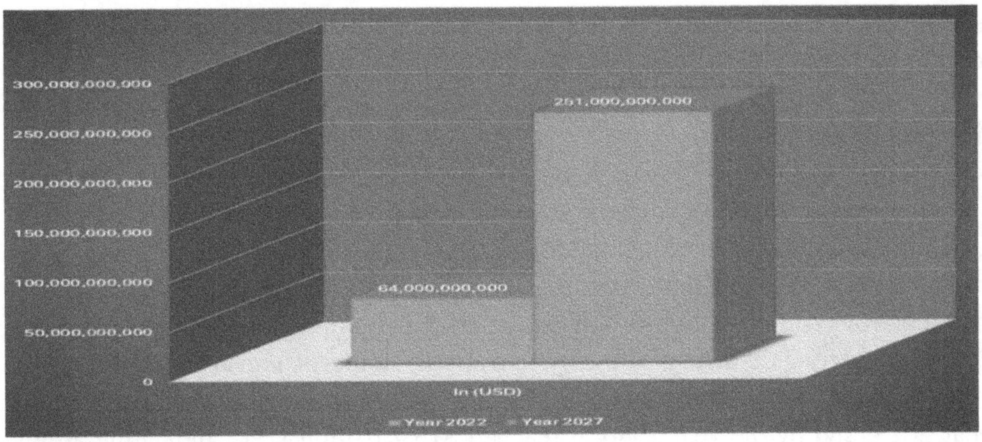

Source: Fortune Business Insights

Figure 25. Maximum impact of AI on construction

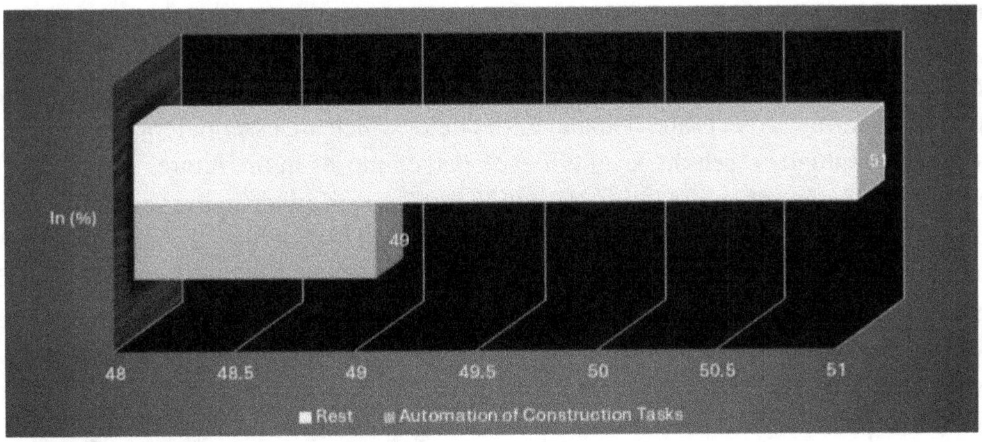

Source: Fortune Business Insights

Major Advantages Plus Challenges of Control Engineering and AI in Civil Engineering

In this subsection, the above graphs are analysed to understand the current market of Control Engineering and AI, as well as possible future in Civil Engineering

- According to Fig. 16, the Asia Pacific region 39% share in the market of control systems as well as industrial automation in the year 2024, whereas the rest of the world in the same year has 61% market share, indicating that Asia Pacific region is currently dominating the control systems and industrial automation market, which means that the developing countries like India could invest more on it with the growing demand and dominance of the region for the coming years at least.

- Based on Fig. 17, market size of control systems as well as industrial automation in the year 2024 worldwide was over $206 billion USD and by the year 2030, it reached over $378 billion USD, meaning that the market grew almost twice in the span of six years. This means that their demand will increase in the future.
- As per Fig. 18, construction industry had the share of 31.5% in the market of machine control systems internationally, highest compared to other industries in the year 2022, indicating the strong demand and usefulness of machine control systems in the construction industry.
- According to Fig. 19, the Chinese construction industry had the share of 32% in the market of machine control systems within its domestic market in comparison to other industries in the year 2022, showing strong demand of these systems in the domestic construction industry.
- Based on Fig. 20, the value of Civil Engineering market worldwide was over $9 trillion USD in the year 2023, and by the year 2030, it reached $13.7 trillion USD, indicating almost 1.5 times growth in the span of just 7 years. It is safe to say, Control Engineering and AI could be used more with the growing market of Civil Engineering.
- As per Fig. 21, application wise share in the revenue of Civil Engineering market worldwide, real estate has a share of 40.7% in the year 2023, higher than industrial and infrastructure applications, indicating that it is safe to invest more in the real estate segment to incorporate AI technology and control systems.
- According to Fig. 22, Asia Pacific region has share of 33.7% in the revenue of Civil Engineering market in the world, higher than other regions in the world in the year 2023, showing more number of Civil Engineering projects and demand of the field, which are essential for developing countries to grow and eventually reach the level of developed countries in the future.
- Based on Fig. 23, the value of AI in construction market worldwide in the year 2023 was over $3.9 billion USD, but it is expected to reach over $22 billion USD by the year 2032, showing that the expected growth will be more than five times in the span of 8 years. This means that it will be wise to invest in AI and implement in construction to stay in competition.
- As per Fig. 24, AI software market was having a value of $64 billion USD in the year 2022, and it its expected to reach $251 billion USD by the year 2027, indicating almost $180 billion USD increase in the span of 5 years, which is around thrice growth in the mere period 5 years. This means that those not investing in AI software, might be left out of competition in the future completely.
- According to Fig. 25, AI could automate a maximum of 49% of the construction tasks, meaning that AI has potential to make almost half of the tasks in construction to be automated, which will definitely increase the efficiency and productivity of construction industry tremendously. So, it is safe to say that it is high time to invest as well incorporate AI in construction industry, and similarly in other Civil Engineering areas.

LIMITATIONS

The book chapter covered some major Control Engineering techniques, but there might be other techniques which weren't covered here, as well not any particular Control Engineering technique was focused on in depth. Then, the Civil Engineering branch and its subbranches were highlighted where

Control Engineering as well as AI technology are affecting in their transformations, but there are some areas of Civil Engineering which might be left in the chapter. Moreover, no particular area of Civil Engineering where Control Engineering as well as AI were executed, were explained in depth. Then, some case studies across the globe were taken into consideration, where AI as well as Control Engineering were applied, but there are many other case studies which weren't mentioned in this chapter. Furthermore, no particular case study was talked about in detail in the book chapter.

SOLUTIONS AND RECOMMENDATIONS

The implementation of Control Engineering as well as Artificial Intelligence in the areas of Civil Engineering brings a number of advantages, but the associated problems must be addressed. The training of workers and Civil Engineers who are not up to date with the recent advanced technologies as well as sophisticated control systems, must be taken care by contractors, or construction and infrastructure companies. Some form of government policies and incentives could also promote in people actively executing sophisticated control systems as well as AI technology in projects.

FUTURE RESEARCH DIRECTIONS

In the future, each particular area of Civil Engineering which is being transformed by the incorporation of Control Engineering and AI technology, could be researched in depth. Similarly, other case studies in the world where Control Engineering and AI technology were executed, could be researched in the future studies. Moreover, each particular case studies in this chapter, in the future could be thoroughly researched about in depth. Then, research needs to be done to reduce the cost of advanced control systems and AI technology, so that they could be implemented in projects easily.

CONCLUSION

This chapter explained the concept of Control Engineering as well as it gave a rough idea about control systems. Then, the book chapter covered the chief principles of Control Engineering, which must be known for better understanding of the said branch. Additionally, some major techniques of Control Engineering were discussed in this chapter. Then, the necessity of implementing Control Engineering in general and particularly in the Civil Engineering field were talked about in the book chapter. It also, similarly, mentioned the utility of AI in the domain of Civil Engineering for advancement in the future. Then many scientific published studies were taken into account to find out the gaps related to implementation of Control Engineering and AI in the said core branch of engineering. Plus, the Civil Engineering branch as well as its subbranches were covered where not only Control Engineering but also AI technology used. Then, some selected case studies in the world were taken into account, where Control Engineering as well as AI technology were incorporated, and the associated obstacles on their path were explained. Then, graphical analyses were done on the basis of available data to understand the Control Engineering and AI market as well as possible future in the Civil Engineering field.

ACKNOWLEDGEMENT

This research received no specific grant from any funding agency in the public, commercial, or not-for-profit sectors.

REFERENCES

Asadi, S., Jimeno-Saez, P., Lopez-Ballesteros, A., & Senent-Aparicio, J. (2024). Comparison and integration of physical and interpretable AI-driven models for rainfall-runoff simulation. *Results in Engineering*, Volume 24, 103048. ArchDaily, https://www.archdaily.com/962924/building-a-city-from-scratch-the-story-of-songdo-korea

Chowdhury, S., & Karanfil, T. (2024). Applications of artificial intelligence (AI) in drinking water treatment processes: Possibilities.[[CNN,]. *Chemosphere*, *356*, 141958. https://edition.cnn.com/travel/millau-viaduct-tallest-bridge-construction/index.html. DOI: 10.1016/j.chemosphere.2024.141958 PMID: 38608775

Di, X., & Shi, R. (2021). A survey on autonomous vehicle control in the era of mixed-autonomy: From physics-based to AI-guided driving policy learning.[[Discover Engineering,]. *Transportation Research Part C, Emerging Technologies*, *125*, 103008. https://www.discoverengineering.org/dynamics-and-control-in-civil-engineering/. DOI: 10.1016/j.trc.2021.103008

Dzhusupova, R., Bosch, J., & Olsson, H. H. (2024). Choosing the right path for AI integration in engineering companies: A strategic guide. *Journal of Systems and Software*, Volume 210, 111945. Fortune Business Insights, https://www.fortunebusinessinsights.com/ai-in-construction-market-109848

Gatto, M. P. A., Castelli, F., Lentini, V., & Montrasio, L. (2024). AI-driven predictions of the dynamic properties of fine-grained soils in South Italy based on laboratory testing. *Soil Dynamics and Earthquake Engineering*, *187*, 109009. DOI: 10.1016/j.soildyn.2024.109009

Ghorbani, J., & Kodikara, J. (2024). Real-time inference of compacted soil properties using deflection tests: An AI-driven solution informed by unsaturated soil mechanics principles.[[Grand View Research,]. *Computers and Geotechnics*, *173*, 106543. https://www.grandviewresearch.com/industry-analysis/civil-engineering-market. DOI: 10.1016/j.compgeo.2024.106543

Hernandez-Gonzalez, I. A., Garcia-Macias, E., Constante, G., & Ubertini, F. (2024). AI-driven Automated Operational Modal Analysis of Bridges. *Procedia Structural Integrity*, *62*, 879–886. DOI: 10.1016/j.prostr.2024.09.118

Hernandez-Gonzalez, I. A., Garcia-Macias, E., Constante, G., & Ubertini, F. (2024). AI-driven blind source separation for fast operational modal analysis of structures.[[Hong Kong Tourism Board,]. *Mechanical Systems and Signal Processing*, *211*, 111267. https://www.discoverhongkong.com/ca/interactive-map/hong-kong-zhuhai-macao-bridge.html. DOI: 10.1016/j.ymssp.2024.111267

Huang, Z., Sheng, Z., Ma, C., & Chen, S. (2024). Human as AI mentor: Enhanced human-in-the-loop reinforcement learning for safe and efficient autonomous driving.[[Institution of Civil Engineers,]. *Communications in Transportation Research*, *4*, 100127. https://www.ice.org.uk/what-is-civil-engineering/infrastructure-projects/the-hong-kong-zhuhai-macao-bridge-hzmb-hong-kong-section. DOI: 10.1016/j.commtr.2024.100127

Jayasinghe, S. C., Mahmoodian, M., Alavi, A., Sidiq, A., Shahrivar, F., Sun, Z., Thangarajah, J., & Setunge, S. (2025). A review on the applications of artificial neural network techniques for accelerating finite element analysis in the civil engineering domain. *Computers & Structures*, *310*, 107698. DOI: 10.1016/j.compstruc.2025.107698

Jeong, C. H., Heo, S., Woo, T. Y., Kim, S. Y., & Yoo, C. K. (2024). AI-driven ventilation control policy proximal optimization coupled with dynamic-informed real-time model calibration for healthy and sustainable indoor PM2.5 management. *Energy and Building*, *323*, 114786. DOI: 10.1016/j.enbuild.2024.114786

Kamarposhti, M. S., Kamyab, H., Krishnan, S., Yusuf, M., Rezania, S., Chelliapan, S., & Khorami, M. (2024). A comprehensive review of AI-enhanced smart grid integration for hydrogen energy: Advances, challenges, and future prospects. *International Journal of Hydrogen Energy*, *67*, 1009–1025. DOI: 10.1016/j.ijhydene.2024.01.129

Kim, D., Han, H., Lee, H., Kang, Y., Wang, W., & Kim, H. S. (2024). Predicting Flood Water Level Using Combined Hybrid Model of Rainfall-Runoff and AI-Based Models. *KSCE Journal of Civil Engineering*, *28*(4), 1580–1593. DOI: 10.1007/s12205-023-1147-0

Kim, S. Y., Tariq, S., Chang, R., Ali, U., Ba-Alawi, A. H., Heo, S. K., & Yoo, C. K. (2024). Explainable AI-driven high-fidelity IAQ prediction (HiFi-IAQ) model for subway stations: Spatiotemporal outdoor air quality interpolation using geographic data.[[Koenig Solutions,]. *Building and Environment*, *263*, 111906. https://www.koenig-solutions.com/blog/control-engineering. DOI: 10.1016/j.buildenv.2024.111906

Laflamme, C., Doppler, J., Palvolgyi, B., Dominka, S., Viharos, Zs. J., & Haeussler, S. (2025). Explainable reinforcement learning for powertrain control engineering. *Engineering Applications of Artificial Intelligence*, *146*, 110135. DOI: 10.1016/j.engappai.2025.110135

Liang, R., Liu, W., Fu, Y., & Ma, M. (2024). Physics-informed deep learning for structural dynamics under moving load. *International Journal of Mechanical Sciences*, *284*, 109766. DOI: 10.1016/j.ijmecsci.2024.109766

Liao, W., Lu, X., Fei, Y., Gu, Y., & Huang, Y. (2024). Generative AI design for building structures. *Automation in Construction*, *157*, 105187. DOI: 10.1016/j.autcon.2023.105187

Mallik, S., Saha, B., Podder, K., Muthuraj, M., Mishra, U., & Deb, S. (2025). Comprehensive assessment of E. coli dynamics in river water using advanced machine learning and explainable AI. *Process Safety and Environmental Protection*, *195*, 106816. DOI: 10.1016/j.psep.2025.106816

Masria, A., & Abouelsaad, O. (2025). Artificial intelligence applications in coastal engineering and its challenges – A review. *Continental Shelf Research*, *286*, 105425. DOI: 10.1016/j.csr.2025.105425

Meshram, K. (2024). *Introduction to machine learning for civil engineering. Machine Learning Applications in Civil Engineering*. Woodhead Publishing Series in Civil and Structural Engineering.

Munjiza, A., Rougier, E., Lei, Z., Euser, B., & Knight, E. E. (2024). 2.05 - Towards FDEM Based Hybrid Simulation Tools for AI Driven Virtual Experimentation in Science and Engineering. *Comprehensive Mechanics of Materials, 2*, 141–168. DOI: 10.1016/B978-0-323-90646-3.00012-5

Rabbi, A. B. K., & Jeelani, I. (2024). AI integration in construction safety: Current state, challenges, and future opportunities in text, vision, and audio based applications. *Automation in Construction, 164*, 105443. DOI: 10.1016/j.autcon.2024.105443

Rafsanjani, N., & Nabizadeh, A. H. (2023). Towards human-centered artificial intelligence (AI) in architecture, engineering, and construction (AEC) industry. *Computers in Human Behavior Reports, 11*, 100319. DOI: 10.1016/j.chbr.2023.100319

Ramasetti, E. K., Herrmann, R., Degener, S., & Baebler, M. (2024). Development of generic AI models to predict the movement of vehicles on bridges. *Procedia Structural Integrity, 64*, 557–564. DOI: 10.1016/j.prostr.2024.09.307

Run, T. https://runtimerec.com/how-engineers-can-use-ai-to-improve-control-systems/

Salimi, A., Ghobrial, T., & Bonakdari, H. (2024). A comprehensive review of AI-based methods used for forecasting ice jam floods occurrence, severity, timing, and location. *Cold Regions Science and Technology, 227*, 104305. DOI: 10.1016/j.coldregions.2024.104305

Shi, Z., Feng, Y., Egbelakin, T., Yang, C., & Gao, W. (2025). Computational fluid dynamics -informed virtual safety assessment of steel-framed structure with fire-induced ductile failure. *Reliability Engineering & System Safety, 258*, 110918. DOI: 10.1016/j.ress.2025.110918

Singh, A. (2022). Importance of Fuzzy Logic in Traffic and Transportation Engineering. In Vasant, P., Zelinka, I., & Weber, G. W. (Eds.), *Intelligent Computing & Optimization. ICO 2021. Lecture Notes in Networks and Systems* (Vol. 371). Springer., DOI: 10.1007/978-3-030-93247-3_10

Singh, A. (2023). Mechatronics Engineering in the Modern World and Its Use in the Construction Industry. In Mellal, M. (Ed.), *Trends, Paradigms, and Advances in Mechatronics Engineering* (pp. 64–92). IGI Global Scientific Publishing., DOI: 10.4018/978-1-6684-5887-7.ch004

Singh, A. (2023). The Present and Future Role of Artificial Intelligence in the Promotion of Sustainable Practices in the Construction Sector. In Kahraman, C., Sari, I. U., Oztaysi, B., Cebi, S., Cevik Onar, S., & Tolga, A. Ç. (Eds.), *Intelligent and Fuzzy Systems. INFUS 2023. Lecture Notes in Networks and Systems* (Vol. 759). Springer., DOI: 10.1007/978-3-031-39777-6_2

Singh, A. (2023). The Recent Trend of Artificial Neural Network in the Field of Civil Engineering. In Vasant, P. (Eds.), *Intelligent Computing and Optimization. ICO 2023. Lecture Notes in Networks and Systems* (Vol. 855). Springer., DOI: 10.1007/978-3-031-50158-6_32

Singh, A. (2023). The Significance of Digitalization of the Construction Sector. In Vasant, P., Weber, G. W., Marmolejo-Saucedo, J. A., Munapo, E., & Thomas, J. J. (Eds.), *Intelligent Computing & Optimization. ICO 2022. Lecture Notes in Networks and Systems* (Vol. 569). Springer., DOI: 10.1007/978-3-031-19958-5_100

Singh, A. (2024). The Current Status and Scope of Smart Highways in India. In Taha, L., & Anwar, S. (Eds.), *Principles and Applications in Speed Sensing and Energy Harvesting for Smart Roads* (pp. 1–41). IGI Global Scientific Publishing., DOI: 10.4018/978-1-6684-9214-7.ch001

Singh, A., & Srivastava, A. Impact of Artificial Intelligence Techniques and Green AI Applications. In *Artificial Intelligence Techniques for Sustainable Development* (pp. 44–63). CRC Press. DOI: 10.1201/9781003546382-3

Uncuoglu, E., Citakoglu, H., Latifoglu, L., Bayram, S., Laman, M., Ilkentapar, M., & Oner, A. A. (2022). Comparison of neural network, Gaussian regression, support vector machine, long short-term memory, multi-gene genetic programming, and M5 Trees methods for solving civil engineering problems. *Applied Soft Computing*, *129*, 109623. DOI: 10.1016/j.asoc.2022.109623

Wang, C., Song, L. H., Yuan, Z., & Fan, J. S. (2023). State-of-the-art AI-based computational analysis in civil engineering. *Journal of Industrial Information Integration*, *33*, 100470.

Ye, Y.-N., Chou, Y.-L., Zhao, D., Cao, W., Xu, J.-W., & Wang, A.-J. (2025). Permafrost environment evaluation of Qinghai-Tibetan Plateau based on DPSRC theory and system dynamics. *Ecological Modelling*, *501*, 110992. DOI: 10.1016/j.ecolmodel.2024.110992

Yu, J., & Hyland, M. F. (2025). Interpretable State-Space Model of Urban Dynamics for Human-Machine Collaborative Transportation Planning. *Transportation Research Part B: Methodological*, *192*, 103134. DOI: 10.1016/j.trb.2024.103134

Zhang, B., Li, C. Y., Kikumoto, H., Niu, J., & Tse, T. K. T. (2024). Smart urban windcatcher: Conception of an AI-empowered wind-channeling system for real-time enhancement of urban wind environment. *Building and Environment*, *253*, 111357. DOI: 10.1016/j.buildenv.2024.111357

Zhang, J., Yang, X., Wang, W., Guan, J., Ding, L., & Lee, V. C. S. (2023). Automated guided vehicles and autonomous mobile robots for recognition and tracking in civil engineering. *Automation in Construction*, *146*, 104699. DOI: 10.1016/j.autcon.2022.104699

Zhuang, H., Cheng, Y., Zhou, M., & Yang, Z. (2025). Deep learning for surface crack detection in civil engineering: A comprehensive review. *Measurement*, *248*, 116908. DOI: 10.1016/j.measurement.2025.116908

Chapter 2
Hybrid Control Systems: Integrating AI With Traditional Methods

Rituraj Jain
https://orcid.org/0000-0002-5532-1245
Marwadi University, India

Kumar Parmar
https://orcid.org/0000-0002-2502-5680
Marwadi University, India

Damodharan Palaniappan
https://orcid.org/0009-0003-0721-3068
Marwadi University, India

T. Premavathi
https://orcid.org/0009-0003-0172-2021
Marwadi University, India

ABSTRACT

In recent years, hybrid control systems have been used in many practical applications because they are an adequate method capable of addressing this kind complexity and vagueness, which is characteristic of today's business and scientific environment. It provides the evaluation of the fundamental concepts and solutions for the incorporation of AI in conventional control schemes. The chapter also examines other fields including robotics, aeroplane, industrial processes and power systems as other areas that have benefited from hybrid control methods. To solve the difficulties posed by nonlinear, time varying, and stochastic systems, the interaction of machine learning approaches such as artificial neural networks, fuzzy logic, and adaptive control with PID, optimal and robust control approaches is explored. Possible research topics bring concerns the analysis of hybrid control architectures for large-scale, contingent, safety-relevant systems, the extension of sensing and communication functionalities, and design of proper planning and decision-making strategies.

DOI: 10.4018/979-8-3693-7812-0.ch002

1. INTRODUCTION

The analysis of hybrid control systems enables the identification of a promising and nearly invulnerable technique in modern control engineering of complex dynamic processes while combining the confirmed characteristics of artificial intelligence with the abilities that have been proved for traditional control approaches. It is important to know that these systems are capable to govern both continuous and discrete dynamics and therefore are very suitable to resolve the increasing complexity and the uncertainty, which is demonstrated in many modern applications (Piga & Bemporad, 2020). Classical control strategies often fail to operate satisfactorily when it is faced by non-linear systems, unexpected disturbances, or varying working conditions. In cases where such knowledge bases cannot be developed then there is benefit in using artificial intelligence techniques such as machine learning, fuzzy logic and expert systems. Due to the incorporation of the intelligent algorithms, the hybrid control systems can also apply data learning, adopt to the dynamic environment, and make accurate real-time decisions overcoming the limitations that are present in the conventional control (Bessa, 2022).

1.1 The Historical Evolution and Driving Forces Behind Hybrid Control Systems

This progression of control systems starts from the precept of the classical control theory that was based on mathematical model and analysis of mainly linear systems to develop the more current state of the art modern control schemes that utilize enhanced computational paradigms to solve nonlinear system related issues. Initially, control systems depended a great deal on mathematical approaches and seemed to have difficulties in dealing with the variability and disturbances. The new digital computers came into the picture which helped to exercise much better control algorithms and the new adaptive and robust controls. The general advancement of automation technology in the recent decades have also broadened the scope of control engineering. Therefore, the next step on this evolutionary path is the hybrid control systems that incorporates the learning and decision-making characteristics of AI into a control design that is more flexible and intelligent (Zhu & Zhong, 2023).

1.2 Current Relevance and Impact of Hybrid Systems in Modern Technology

It is also clear that the importance of hybrid control systems is as relevant as ever in today's technologies, which are getting more complex and constantly requiring more flexibility. Here are examples which show their necessity in different branches and Figure. 1 relates as to influence that hybrid systems have in the current technology. Robotics: Hybrid control systems are especially suitable to be implemented in robots working in unknown and complex spaces. These systems make it possible for the robots to quickly shift from one operation to another, avoid barriers that may have been unknown before and update their data base. For example, an autonomous mobile robot that is likely to function in an unpredictable environment such as a residential building may mainly use classical control for the basic operation of the robot's movement while using artificial intelligence for navigation and avoidance of the obstacles in environments (Levine & Shah, 2022). Aerospace: Various control system solutions are used in the aerospace industry to control the aircraft and spacecraft where there is need for Integrated Hybrid Aerospace Control Systems referred in Figure 1. These systems can operate under many different conditions such as during the acceleration phase during take-off and landing, or during level flight when changes are being made mid-flight or when the aircraft is manoeuvring independently. For instance, the system for ''autopilot'' may employ the traditional control for stability while AI may be used for the trajectory planning and fuel efficiency (Emami et al.2022).

Figure 1. Impact of hybrid systems in modern technology

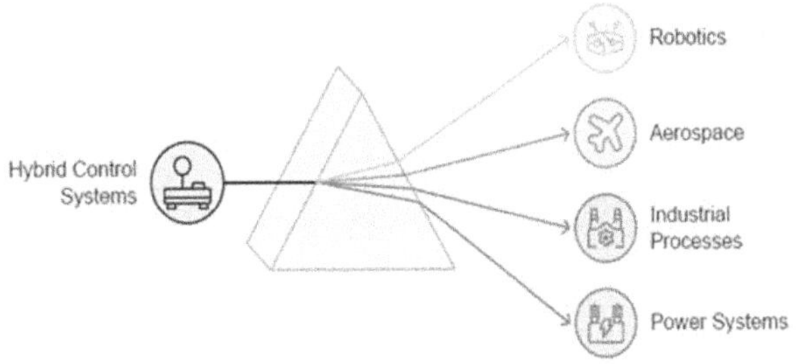

Industrial Processes: Used in manufacturing and process industries hybrid control systems play an important role in improving production, its speed, and quality. They can deal with multi-variable processes, flexible to adapt to the changes of the demands in production, and capable of detecting fault conditions online. Traditional control and AI can also be combined in different ways in an industry for example a chemical plant can use traditional control for temperature and pressure control while using AI for process control and maintenance. According to the availability of sources they are as follows (Nelson et al., 2023) - Power Systems: For example, the development of new generators based on renewable energy sources call for improved control methods, and the expansion of a control area and the corresponding increase of the power systems complexity requires the enhancement of control techniques as well. While incorporating renewable sources into the distribution network, hybrid control systems are used for the stability of the grid application, balancing the energy distribution, and for controlling fluctuating nature of renewable sources. For instance, a smart grid could apply ordinary control to achieve a voltage control, but could apply AI for load forecasting and demand response control (Panahazari et al., 2023).

2. TRADITIONAL CONTROL METHODS

Classical control methods that can be traced back to the classical control theory, has been the dominant approach in control systems for many years.

2.1 An Overview of Classical Control Techniques

Based on the development of the mid-20th century, classical control theory is used as the basis of control system modelling and design. All these methods are more often exhibiting features of linearity in both space and time, and use of frequency domain techniques. It is now pertinent to look at some of the major classical control methodologies they include; PID controllers – State Space Representation – Feedback Control Systems. Figure. 2 relates the Classical control theory in control system design as stated by (Baños et al., 2020). PID Controllers: The PID controllers are probably the most popular types of control possible in several industries across the globe. They are widely used because they are easy to implement, immune to noise, and give a good control of many processes. A PID controller for ever computes an error signal which can be defined as the difference of the set point and the process variable. It adds a corrective control effort that is a product of the proportional integral and differential of the error signal (Wiharya et al., 2021).

Figure 2. Classical control theory within control system design

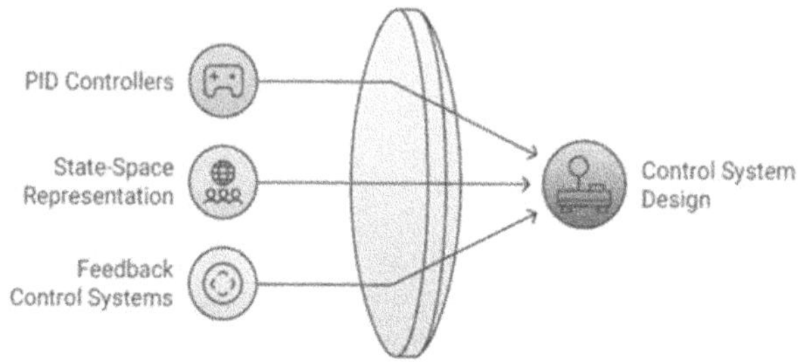

State-Space Representation: As compared to PID controllers referred in Figure 2 that work directly with the error signal, the state – space representation offers a more extensive framework for modelling and analysing the systems. It defines a system through a set of variables that capture internal behaviours of the system in question. These state variables therefore obey first order differential equations and their dynamics over time are revealed. This representation enables understanding of system behaviour in detail and helps to design more complex control approaches (Tian et al., in 2020). Feedback Control Systems: Possibility of damping at constant level; Feedback control is a basic concept in control engineering whereby the output signal of a system actuates a control input. This closed-loop mechanism to change the system can adjust for many of these disturbances and uncertainties to minimize the output from deviating from the set value. Automatic feedback control systems are very common with examples given by a simple thermostat to an aircraft autopilot system (Singh, 2022).

2.2 Advantages of Classical Control: Simplicity, Robustness, and Reliability

The classical control techniques discussed above offer several key advantages that have contributed to their widespread adoption - Simplicity: Some of the classical control techniques are easy to learn and apply owing to which a large pool of engineers and technicians can be employed in the construction of such systems. Robustness: Most of the classical control techniques including PID controllers are known to possess inherent robustness to model perturbations and load changes. Well-Established Theories: Analysis of the classical control theory is intensive and based on a rigid record of mathematical fundamentals, and theoretical tools. Applicability in Predictable Environments: Feedback based methods are advantageous in the use of recognized system behavior and operating conditions as these prove to be stable.

2.3 Challenges and Limitations of Traditional Methods

While classical control techniques have been remarkably successful, they do face certain limitations, especially in the face of increasing system complexity and unpredictability. Due to the likelihood of language, cultural barriers, and increased dependence, remote interactions are much more likely to be self-scheduling than face-to-face interactions (Schöning & Pfisterer, 2022). Challenges with Non-Linearities: Classical control methods are mainly applied to linear systems Typical examples where classical control methods can be applied are with low order systems. Unfortunately, they can experience a dramatic loss of performance when implemented in nonlinear systems. Adaptability: Most conventional controllers do not possess the feature of adaptation in the case of system dynamics or operating condition changes and have to be retuned or redesigned. Performance in Complex, Dynamic Scenarios: It is in the complex and extreme conditions that the superior performance can be achieved with difficulty because of the conventional methods of control: they are ineffective when it comes to uncertainty and non-linearity.

2.4 Real-World Applications: Traditional Control in Industry and Technology

Despite their limitations, traditional control methods remain highly relevant and widely used in various industries: Manufacturing: Most manufacturing processes involve PID control for temperature, pressure, and flow rates in chemistry reactors, production line, and packaging lines among others (Zhou, 2022). Aerospace: Several classical control methods became a basis of aircraft and space vehicles, providing stable flight, occur dramatic and altitude control. For example, PID controllers are most suitable for use in autopilot control of aircrafts while state space techniques are best suited for aircraft flight control design (Singh, 2022). Consumer Electronics: Starting from the ordinary household appliances as refrigerators and washing machines or up to the modern smart gadgets such as the smartphones, cameras, etc the traditional control methods possess primary significance in controlling the different functions. For instance, the PID controllers are used in operations such as regulating temperature while feedback control is used in auto focusing (Aljehani et al., 2023). That is, despite such limitations of the traditional control techniques being highly unsuitable in controlling the highly complex and dynamic processes, they remain useful because of their simplicity, strength, and strong theoretical background. However, increased system affordances in recent complex control systems, along with the ever-increasing need for improved flexibility, have led to the development of bi-modal control systems. These combined approaches are intended to enhance the best features of traditional control techniques with modern learning and decision-making opportunities thanks to artificial intelligence (Zhu & Zhong, 2023).

3. AI INTEGRATION IN CONTROL SYSTEMS

The synergistic application of AI with the conventional control schemes can promise an improvement over the existing classical techniques of controlling systems and open up newer spheres of possibilities in dealing with different systems.

3.1 Key AI Advances in Control System

This report will present and discuss why artificial intelligence is a competent bringer of a powerful set of tools and techniques that are changing the face of control systems. It is important to note that control inspired by AI does not belong to the class of methods that use strict mathematical models and algorithmically rules for control; moreover, its strength is in the ability to operate under conditions of uncertainty and in changing environments. From the Figure 3, let us discuss some of the most significant AI techniques applied in control systems.

Figure 3. Different AI techniques to use in control systems.

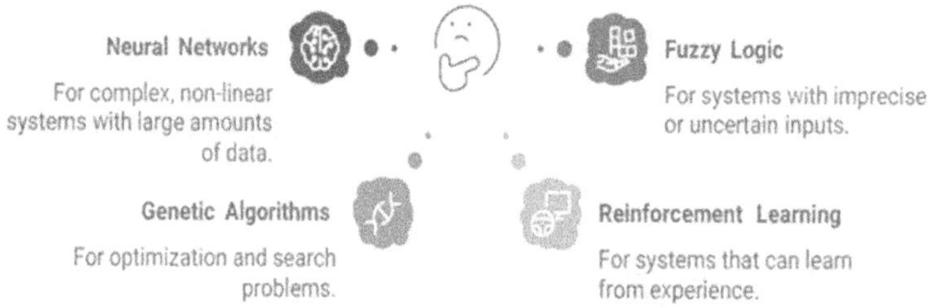

Neural Networks: The neural network is a high performing computational power that can learn non-linear mapping from a given set of data. Neural networks can be applied in control systems for system identification model-based control, where the system model is identified from the input-output data; and adaptive control where the control parameters are updated in real-time depending on changes in system characteristics (Poalelungi et al., 2023). Fuzzy Logic: Traditional control systems suffer from such vices as imprecisions and uncertainty. Fuzzy logic on the other hand defines a solution for handling ambiguous data that in other circumstance would cause problems. This is useful in control applications where fuzzy control can allow the development of controllers based on linguistic rules and can also handle transitions from one state to another that can be gradual thus being beneficial in systems whose behaviour is not easily predictable (Gupta , 2021). Genetic Algorithms: Based on the principles of Darwin's theory of natural selection, genetic algorithms are problem-solving procedures based on the principles of evolution. In control systems genetic algorithms can be applied in tuning of control (establishing the right values for the controller), optimum path planning for a robot or a vehicle and system modelling (Alshriem, 2020).

Reinforcement Learning: In reinforcement learning an agent is trained for decision making with help of the environment and in return it gets rewards or punishment. This approach is well suited to control problems in which the system behaviour is not fully understood, or cannot be directly modelled. Reinforcement learning has been successfully adapted in robotics, games and self-driving systems (Gillani et al., 2023). Machine Learning: It means that machine learning is a vast class of methods and algorithms that can learn from data and produce systemic output and solutions, for which they do not need to be programmed. Some of machine learning applications in control systems include system modeling, fault diagnosis, and adaptive control. There are 3 main classifications of machine learning which includes;

supervised learning, unsupervised learning and semi supervised learning which has been widely used in control applications (Dev et al., 2021).

3.2 Strengths of AI Driven Control Systems

The integration of AI with traditional control methods introduces several key advantages - Flexibility: Computer control systems are always more flexible than conventional control systems and are capable of being updated with respect to the variation in the system parameters, operation conditions and the unexpected disturbances. Capability to Learn and Adapt: In contrast systems based on artificial intelligence are capable to re tune themselves or and do not require re design. Effectiveness in Complex, Uncertain Environments: These are attributes of control which AI techniques are very good at handling hence useful when it comes to controlling systems which are hard to model or predict in a normal method.

3.3 Control Systems and Its AI Issues

Although incorporating AI with control systems may have its benefits, there is always downside and limitations that should be noted. High Computational Costs: The training of models especially the deep neural networks involve many computations which is a challenge when it comes to real-time applications of the trained AI models. Need for Large Datasets: An important limitation with most AI algorithms, and particularly those with deep learning functionalities, is that they may need extensive data to make a training to which they may not always have access. Transparency Issues: There are some AI models which are the black boxes like deep neural networks where one cannot understand how the model is arriving at a particular decision. Potential Overfitting: A major drawback that is associated with the use of AI models is that of over fitting to the training data set and out performing ineffectively on unseen data sets.

3.4 Comparison with Traditional Methods

AI methods are coherent with classical control methods in the sense that they can provide complementary functionalities but AI methods also present some different approaches to the problem. Conventional control systems are usually based on several mathematical models, which have been developed over the years and are widely employed like PID, State Space and Optimal control. These conventional approaches are well-suited for systems of first order or of higher order with relatively mild nonlinearities, where the dynamic model is well-known or easily determined. However, AI control systems adapt well to these conditions especially where there is difficulty or even impossibility of modelling nonlinear, bi- complex and uncertain conditions. It may be noted that most traditional control mechanisms follow deterministic control types which require perfect models of the controlled systems, which is different from how AI mechanisms work and hence are more flexible in dealing with changing conditions of the system.

Incorporation of AI with other forms of control that are already established produces what is called hybrid control systems whose features include the reliability, predictability, and mathematical certainties of the classical control as wells as the adaptability, and the learning ability of the AI. Table 1 relates the Comparison of Traditional control Theory and Artificial Intelligence control Theory.

Table 1. Comparison of traditional and AI-based control approaches

Feature	Traditional Control Approaches	AI-Based Control Approaches
Modeling	Relies on explicitly defined mathematical models	Can learn models from available data
Adaptability	Limited in adaptability, often requiring manual retuning	Inherently adaptive, with the ability to learn and continuously improve over time
Complexity Handling	Well-suited for handling linear, time-invariant systems	Excellent at addressing non-linearities, uncertainties, and complex system dynamics
Computational Cost	Generally require lower computational resources	Can be computationally intensive, particularly for complex AI models
Transparency	Typically more transparent and interpretable	Some AI models can be more opaque and challenging to interpret

AI has been combined with conventional control methods and appends the bent of hybrid control systems that are created from the strength of both classic control and AI, will help control systems to be more robust, predictive, flexible, and smart. These hybrid systems can potentially offer new opportunities for control system architectures and deployments since they overcome the above-mentioned shortcomings of standalone strategies. Based on the combination of the AI components and the traditional well-proven control approaches, the hybrid control architecture may have the relative advantages of both kinds of control: the accurate and stable combination of the Classis Control with the vigorous applicability and intelligence of AI Control.

Specific Application Examples - Robot Control: It also reveals that traditional control methods might not be effective in addressing such aspects of the robotic environment which might be unpredictable such as when the robot is in a cluttered environment. Reinforcement learning, on the other hand, enables the robot to learn an ideal control policy through trial/ error whilst improving the capability of adapting to existing environment. Process Control: For example, in a chemical plant, proportional integral derivative or more commonly called as PID controllers could be employed in controlling temperature and pressure. But an AI-based system could use the feature of machine learning to forecast the process deviations to control the parameters before a certain deviation occurs and thus could enhance the efficiency of the process and the product quality.

4. HYBRID CONTROL SYSTEMS: IDEAS AND BLUEPRINT

Thus, to take the best of both worlds of traditional and AI based control systems, a possible promising direction is the methodologies of hybrid control systems. The possible format of hybrid control systems involves the incorporation of both the basic forms of control with artificial intelligence segments within the same architecture to eliminate the flaws of the singular methods. The structure of a hybrid control system is as follows key components and Figure 4 provides the structure of the traditional and the AI-based control modules in the hybrid systems.

Figure 4. Balancing traditional and AI-based control modules in hybrid systems

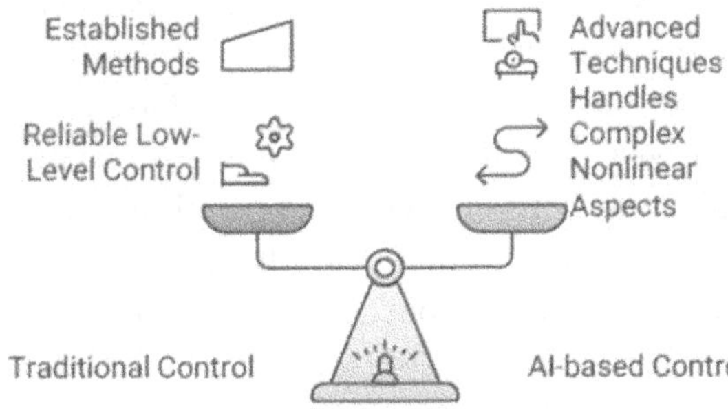

Traditional Control Module: This module utilizes control methodologies such as PID, state-space or optimal control to give effective and robust low-level control of the system. AI-based Control Module: This module incorporates other artificial intelligence techniques like the machine learning, the reinforcement learning or the fuzzy logic for the nonlinear and the uncertain aspects of the system (Dutta & Upreti, 2021) (Ding et al., 2021). The decentralized control structure provides a normally and continuously adjustable control approach, so that the traditional and AI-based part interact with each other optimally and scape from the limitations, vulnerability, and risk.

4.1 Defining Hybrid Control Systems

Standalone intelligent control system is one of the most effective paradigms of control engineering as it encapsulates the inherent nature of intense traditional control together with the learning ability of artificial intelligence. These systems are intended for realizations of dynamic systems – those which are both continuous and discrete – which is typical in many practical applications (Wallace & Si, 2023).

A hybrid system is characterized by the interplay of: Continuous Dynamics: These are captured by differential equations, which provide a continuous depiction of system variables at any point in time, for instance, the position and velocity of an end-effector of a robot. Discrete Events: These are sudden transition or change of system behaviour usually because of events such as a sensor value going beyond a limit or a process being completed. Two examples are: A use: thermostat on/off or a control: gear shift in vehicle. Conventional control approaches, which are workable for ordered environments, may not be suitable for addressing complexity and uncertainty typical of hybrid systems. This is where AI steps in, providing - Adaptive Control: AI can improve the recognition of patterns on system data and modification of control approaches within short intervals, to provide for dynamic and disturbance effects. Intelligent Decision-Making: AI is capable of exercising duties demanding decision making including the task planning, fault detection and optimal control with uncertainties (Abouheaf et al., 2023).

4.2 Architectural Approaches to Hybrid Control

Several architectural paradigms have emerged for designing hybrid control systems, each offering distinct advantages depending on the application, in this architecture, both the AI and the conventional control system is active and both act upon the system at the same time. Traditional Controller: They manage the primary control loop and that is how it offers stability and basic performance to any aircraft. AI Agent: Purges the data, controls the system and environment toppling adjustments to the conventional parameters or setpoints as embraced by the traditional controller training and adaption. Example: Some of the main components of the robot systems are: A robotic arm, a PID controller for motion control; a neural network for real time adaptation of the PID control gains based on the payload and environmental conditions of the robot motor. Advantages: It is also one of the easiest processes to implement the functional model of mass communication. This enhances the possibility of integrating AI into the existing control systems gradually. Disadvantages: Cannot possibly optimize the use of AI for decision-making at the higher end. The possible appearance of conflicts between the AI and the conventional controller in case of the lack of coordination.

This architecture applies a tiered model where AI is usually found in an upper tier to make decision on behalf of the organization while traditional controller performs minor tasks. In a hierarchical hybrid system, the higher level of AI module is in overall charge of control strategy including setpoints, mode transitions or parameter variations to the lower-level conventional controllers (London, 2024). AI Decision-Maker: This sub-system determines the overall target within the specified system and works out the plan of tasks and their versatility according to the possible changes in objectives. Traditional Controllers: Delight the commands from the AI and act as per the commanding received from the AI providing more quantized and stable response at the operational level. Example: What is an example of the implementation of a cooperative system, a vehicle that has an AI planner to plan the path and low-level controllers with the acceleration, braking, and steering of the vehicle? Advantages: Enables AI to concentrate more on key, or more of, decisions. It clearly separates the issues of integration between AI and the process of traditional control. Disadvantages: Describes a situation that occurred during the implementation of an intra-application communication interface where careful design of the interface and the relationship between layers was possible. As has been mentioned above, the accuracy and reliability of decisions depend on lower-level control.

Sequential Hybrid Systems - In this approach, AI and the ordinary control techniques work cyclically where one controls phases of the system's operation. How it Works? Phase 1: AI can be used to identification of the system to determine the characteristics of the system when using data. Phase 2: Using the learned model, a traditional controller is designed or its parameters are tuned on traditional way for the best operation. Phase 3: The control mechanism is a mixture of the AI based control and the conventional control based on the circumstance.

Example: An industry process in which AI decides optimal process parameters away from the manufacturing line and a conventional controller employs the parameters on the line. The system could default to AI in case of evens that may require re-optimization of the service. Advantages: Both AI and the traditional control can take advantages of the strength in different phases. Affords offline optimization, and online adaptation. Disadvantages: It is therefore not suitable for system that requires constant change to accommodate new information and changes in environment.

4.3 Design Factors on Hybrid Control Systems

Designing effective hybrid control systems presents unique challenges - System Scalability: This is because as the system complexity increases the scalability of the AI and the traditional control components should also increase with ease. Robustness: Hybrid systems are to address various types of uncertainties and disturbances and possible failures of the AI or conventional control subsystems. Real-time Performance: Because real-time control in many applications is needed, the issue of computational resources and algorithms' efficiency should be addressed. Safety and Reliability: In safety critical applications such as self-driven cars, hybrid control systems administration used in medical devices more strict verification and validation processes must be implemented to guarantee the safety of the systems (Han & Schotten, 2022).

4.4 Decision-Making in Hybrid Systems

The decision-making mechanism, as seen in the case of hybrid control systems, can be best described as the interaction of the artificial intelligence and the traditional control structures. It's possible to apply AI algorithms to make higher-level tactical actions, whereas conventional control techniques apply to the underpinning low-level operations. Figure 5 relates the Improving on Decision-Making Processes in Hybrid Control Systems Using AI.

Figure 5. Enhancing decision-making in hybrid control systems with AI

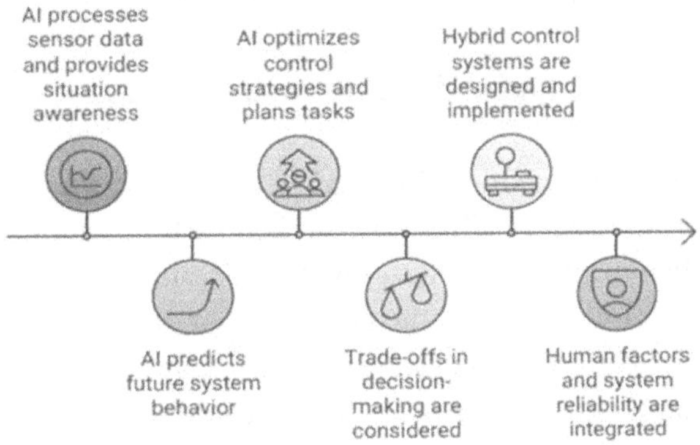

AI can contribute to decision-making in hybrid systems in various ways - Situation Awareness: In the case of sensor data, AI algorithms can analyse the data, decide on patterns, and inform decision-makers a broad view of the system and surrounding it. Predictive Analysis: AI can determine the system's future operation based on past data and current or early signs so that controls can intervene accordingly. Optimization and Planning: Though AI is different from human behaviour, it can decide about the control measures, planning on tasks, and even if goals are modified or constraints are changed. There are inherent trade-offs in the decision-making process of hybrid control systems - Optimality vs. Real-time Performance: It could also be expensive to find the global control strategy out of all the possible strategies in the given environment. Functional hybrid systems may require more focuses on optimal solutions, and the flexibility of the current online solution. Exploration vs. Exploitation: Exploration comes into the picture since AI algorithms will periodically need to find new control strategies while exploitation comes in handy when the AI algorithms use the current successes to find even more successful strategies in reinforcement learning. Transparency vs. Performance: For instance, models such as decision trees are easier to understand than opaque AI models, for instance, deep neural networks, even though the latter may yield better results in the process of analysis.

There are also combined systems or what are called hybrid systems where the AI is combined with the traditional control methodologies. AI is used at strategic planning, assessment of the situation and optimization, whereas conventional control methods address the low level of decision making and control in real-time. Thus, the decision of designing an effective hybrid system depends on the set of parameters such as scalability, robustness, real-time performance and safety. The choice choices are made based on the consideration of the system's optimal and the responsiveness of the system to the users, with the balance between these two being impossible in most cases as one has to be negatively associated with the other for the sake of the other; Another trade off that has to be made is between exploration of a new knowledge space and exploitation of the current knowledge space and the other trade-off is between the ability to freely make information available (Prakash & Mathewson, 2020).

5. CASE STUDIES AND APPLICATIONS OF HYBRID CONTROL SYSTEMS

Due to the versatility of connecting the advantages of classic control and Artificial Intelligence, Hybrid control systems are beginning to gain popularity in various industries. Let's delve into specific case studies to illustrate their impact (Zhu et al., 2019) (Zhu & Zhong, 2023) (Prakash & Mathewson, 2020).

5.1 Automobile Industry and Hybrid Control Systems

The automobile industry is in a transitional period in the search for the realization of autonomous automobile, increased security as well as efficiency marked by better fuel economy. At the forefront of this revolution there are surely hybrid control systems. Self-driving cars are perhaps the best illustration of the nature of hybrid control as a concept and the enactment of this concept in practice. The complexity of navigating real-world traffic scenarios necessitates a multi-layered approach. This family of receptors comprises of: GPCRs, Ion channels which includes ligand gated ion channels, nuclear receptors such as steroid hormone receptors, cytokine receptors as well as intracellular receptors such as the estrogenic receptor (Wang et al., 2023).

Perception: Cameras, lidars, and radars get collected and analyzed through deep neural networks of the AI algorithms, to identify the obstacles, markings on the lanes, traffic signs, or even the other vehicles. Path Planning and Decision-Making: AI solutions compute the best itineraries, recognise the possible actions of other road users and make tactical decisions, including decisions as to whether to overtake or change the lane. Vehicle Control: The system acceptance of the high-level decisions made by the AI is generally designed as traditional control systems such as model-predictive control or PID controllers which control the vehicle's steering, acceleration, braking, and gear shift. Players such as Tesla Inc, Waymo, etc. and more recently Cruise effectively lend their effort for employing hybrid control systems, to change the way people, travel.

Hybrid control is proved to be important for developing advanced driver-assistance systems to advance security. For instance, automatic emergency braking systems use a combination of sensors and AI to - Detect Potential Collisions: Collisions with vehicles, pedestrians or objects are detected by applying AI algorithms on the data received from the vehicle's sensors. Trigger Braking: In case the driver is unable to dodge an object, the car applies the brakes as it assumes control of the car's operations. These systems make it clear that hybrid control minimizes the risk of accidents because the second level of protection has no relation to a person's reaction time.

5.2. Industrial Automation

New trends in industrial automation are hybrid control systems that are more flexible, efficient, and adaptable manufacturing procedures. The concept of industrial robots is evolving fast and these are gradually advanced tools designed to perform complex operations hand in hand with other employees. Hybrid control plays a crucial role in - Adaptive Control: This is made possible through AI algorithms that allow the robots to adjust the motion and force in interaction with the environment or a variant workpiece part. Task Planning and Coordination: AI based systems can determine optimized sequence of assembly tasks, computing optimal path for robots and synchronizing own motion for multiple robots operating in a crowded environment. Computer numerical control machines, widely used in manufacturing, benefit from hybrid control by - Optimizing Machining Parameters: The information gathered by sensors (vibration, temperature, etc.) can be used to modify the cutting speed, feed rates and tool paths in the real time process enhancing the machining performance and quality of work pieces. Predictive Maintenance: AI can identify patterns for tools' wear that may signal about failure of the machine and therefore plan for maintenance well in advance thus reducing downtimes.

Hybrid control systems are essential for managing the complexity of modern automated production lines - Production Scheduling and Optimization: By applying AI algorithms it is possible to schedule the production effectively, to determinate the number of materials and resources needed for certain time, and to have an ability to react on the changes which may occur in the market or in supply chains. Quality Control: Automated vision systems with the help of artificial intelligence can be used to effectively detect defects on the products and minimize damage and scrap.

Performance metrics across various fields demonstrate that hybrid systems which combine AI with traditional techniques have achieved considerably better results. Both AI and conventional control methods are used by these systems and combine the best attributes of both.

In the optimization of the efficiency of a production system, a hybrid AI with data envelopment analysis (DEA) simulation ML and genetic algorithms (GAs) achieved far greater efficiencies than conventional control loop-based system. As in earlier mentioned approaches, this method substantiated the efficiency of hybrid AI solutions in industry using actual data from a thermoelectric power plant (Cavalcanti et al., 2023).

The combination of machine learning algorithms with deep neural networks and reinforcement learning for predicting maintenance also brought significant improvements in the bounds of renewable energy systems. For this framework, predicting equipment failures was highly accurate at 92%, resulting in a significant 35% decrease in unplanned downtime. Operational parameters optimally set with AI also increased overall energy output by 8.5% of all studied systems (Bello et al., 2024).

The incorporation of AI methods with conventional control systems for power converters is also quite innovative. These hybrid approaches which integrate neural networks, fuzzy systems, and machine learning with classical control techniques have achieved unprecedented control effectiveness and precision, system response time, and overall system trustworthiness (Chandu, 2024).

5.3 Energy System and Infrastructure

It is always very important to add that the shift towards the more sustainable energy future heavily depends on the utilization of the intelligent control systems. Such distribution networks, smart grids, renewable sources of energy are maintained by the concept of hybrid control. Current electrical power systems are developing towards complicated systems because of incorporation of distributed renewable energy resources and load demand management. Hybrid control systems facilitate - Demand Response: They can analyse future energy usage trends and properly encouraging consumers to use more of the energy during non-peaking hours in order to come up with a proper balance for the grid and to also decrease the usage of fossil fuel-based power outlets. Fault Detection and Isolation: AI can interpret the grid data and efficiently locate the faults to reduce the time taken to fix them and improve on the stability of the grid (Navidi et al., 2023). Smart grid is the enhancement of existing electricity networks through high technologies for energy delivery systems and usage. Hybrid control enables - Microgrid Management: AI can also control microgrid, which are localized grid that can function independently of the main grid as is during an outage or to provide the support for integration of renewable energy sources. Energy Storage Optimization: Recharger discharge problem: With the help of AI algorithms, the charging and discharging of energy storage systems, for example batteries can be controlled in the most effective manner to balance the fluctuations in renewable energy production to improve the stability of electricity grid.

The latter remains a challenge, especially with renewable energy sources such as the solar and wind which are intermittent in nature. Hybrid control systems address these challenges by- Predicting Renewable Energy Generation: AI algorithms use weather and historical data of generation to predict the output of renewable energy, which helps the grid operators to make amendments in the conventional generation. Optimizing Energy Storage: Hybrid systems can calculate one effective charging and discharging time table of all connected energy storage systems to make optimum use of demand side management programs to increase the use of renewable energy and decrease the utilization of fossil fuel-based power plants.

5.4 Health Care and Medical Devices

The notion of hybrid control systems is slowly coming into the world of health care where the effectiveness of treatments can be increased, being more specific, personal. The artificial limbs at present are much advanced as they contain AI algorithms which make it more dynamic in its field of operation. Hybrid control systems enable - Intuitive Control: Thus, using signals from patient's muscles or nerves, AI algorithms can effectively control all the movements of the prosthetic limb and make the interaction with the prosthesis more natural. According to researchers (Mehr et al., 2023). Adaptive Learning: This learning can be done over time as the AI acquires knowledge of the user's gait patterns and preferences and tweaking this control parameters of the prosthetic limb to improve comfort and mobility.

5.5 Aerospace and Defence

For aerospace & defence applications, there is a need to have very reliable & robust control system for various control applications. Thus, hybrid control is used more often to improve the performance, the level of self-sufficiency and security in the aviation, space and other kinds of defence technologies (Aljehani et al. 2023). Today's aircraft use enhanced flight control systems to provide aircraft stability, controllability, and integrity. Hybrid control systems are being incorporated to - Adaptive Flight Control: AI can work as an automatic pilot that controls the aircraft through the control surfaces such as ailerons, elevators or rudder in the event of changes in the flight scenario that include turbulence, wind gusts, or an aircraft damage among others. Fault-Tolerant Control: For example, AI can change the functionality of flight control system in case of a system failure (for example, malfunctioning sensor or failed actuator) and keep the control over the aircraft.

5.6 Consumer Electronics

There is already a steady rise in the integration of Hybrid control systems in consumer electronics making the gadgets smarter, easier to use and more personalized mainly in smart gadgets, home automation, and wearables industries (Raj & Beno, 2023). In smartphones, smart speakers, as well as many other smart devices, it is possible to observe the utilization of hybrid control systems that allow having a perfectly smooth Human-Machine Interface. Voice Recognition and Natural Language Processing: Voice assistants are AI based services like Siri, Alexa, Google Assistant etc that employ Natural language processing to analyse the users command or query and execute appropriate function. Personalized Recommendations: Users' information (such as web history, apps used, location information) are input to the algorithms which in turn select appropriate music, movies, restaurants, and other services to be recommended to the user.

Hybrid control is employed within systems of smart homes to manage different aspects within homes, increasing comfort, convenience and efficiency on usage of energy. Intelligent Lighting and Climate Control: Smart devices are capable to learn the preferences of users regarding the lighting and temperature within the building, and make necessary changes to the said aspects according to occupancy, time of the day or the weather outside. Appliance Control and Energy Management: Smart home systems can control home appliances like refrigerators, washing machines, ovens and the likes either manually or automatically and thereby conserve energy hence lowering electricity bills. The study presented here is adopted from a similar one by (Mohammadshirazi et al., 2023). Modern life fitness trackers, smart watches and other wearable have adopted the use of the hybrid control systems to give the health and fitness, activity and even medical notices (Alattar & Mohsen, 2023). Heart Rate Monitoring and Activity Tracking: Data obtained from wearable sensors includes health and fitness data which includes heart rate, sleep patterns, activity level and many others that can be analysed by AI algorithms in relation to the entire health of the user. Fall Detection and Emergency Alerts: Some wearables can detect and recognizing falls or any other changes in the patterns of the wearer's motion and subsequently alert designated care givers or health care personnel. New hybrid control systems are yielding the benefits of both traditional control and artificial intelligence to revolutionize numerous fields. Hybrid control is already the key to creating increasingly intelligent, responsive, and optimized vehicles, factories, trustworthy health and home systems, and countless other applications that are reshaping our lives. More developments in artificial intelligence will show an even greater range of new forms of utilising the concept of hybrid control in the future. (Zhu & Zhong, 2023)

6. DESIGN AND IMPLEMENTATION CHALLENGES OF HYBRID CONTROL SYSTEMS

Newer generation hybrid control systems are expected to bring about monumental improvements in several disciplines; however, they have different design and implementation issues. These issues arise from the fact that the incorporation of artificial intelligence into the mainstream forms of control encompasses highly challenging tasks due to its delicate interconnection with the conventional forms of control – a factor that requires very robust techniques that offer stability, reliability and safety. The following sub-section discusses some of the major issues arising when creating and implementing hybrid control systems (Song, et al., 2022).

6.1 Technical Challenges in Hybrid Control Systems

Another problem of hybrid control systems for autonomous robots is the interaction of artificial intelligence algorithms that belong to the data-driven methods based primarily on the probabilistic approach with the deterministic methods typical for most control systems (Schöning & Pfisterer, 2023). To address the challenge of real-time computational performance in hybrid control systems, several mitigation strategies can be employed - challenge: Real time control is crucial in almost all the applications starting from robotics, aerospace, transportation and industrial automation to mention but a few. Traditional Artificial Intelligence models, especially the deep learning models, can be computationally expensive which may result into long processing times hence making the decision untenable. Mitigation: AI models that require reasonable computational speed to be implemented include the following: lightweight neural networks or decision trees. Trying to perform computations more quickly, by offloading them to dedicated graphic cards or AI chips, for instance. There is usually the need to use optimized forms of control algorithms to reduce computational load. Several studies have been published recently, for example by (Wang et al., 2023).

One of the major issues which can be seen in the employment of the integration of the AI and the conventional control system is a high risk of establishing instabilities of the whole combined system. Challenge: Ensuring the reliability of systems, especially when there are real-time end continuous interactions with discrete AI outputs is challenging. Generic optimal control techniques may not work, and even to establish stability in some instances, one must rely on complicated mathematical techniques and arguments. Challenge: Hybrid systems include merging of the AI models which can be developed through such tools as TensorFlow or PyTorch with conventional control systems that might be coded through other programming languages and supported by other hardware platforms. It also implies the risks of mere compatibility of the systems together with the complexity of system integration (Schöning & Pfisterer, 2023). Mitigation: Communication through middleware and standard bus format such as ROS or DDS to connect artificial intelligence subsystem and control system elements. Also, utilizing the model-based design procedures to allow validating the actual behavior of the integrated system at earlier stages. The intention in selecting the individual middleware components of the hardware and software layers is for compatibility and operation in real-time.

6.2 System Integration Challenges

Thus, hybrid control systems which can contribute tremendous progress in many areas have their own peculiarities of the design and implementation. These issues arise from the fact that, in most cases, incorporation of artificial intelligence with the conventional control systems is an intricate process that requires a strict methodology to achieve stability, reliability and safety (Wallace & Si, 2023). An interesting challenge in such systems is how to incorporate AI algorithms into the hybrid system and control because many AI techniques are statistical, probabilistic techniques while the control system is deterministic and based on algorithms with specific set of rules (Zhu & Zhong, 2023). Challenge: Main issue arising here is that combining artificial intelligence models with traditional control systems wherein

AI models have probabilistic characteristics while control systems are deterministic in nature. Another design consideration is to decide at what level of operation the users should be allowed to control the system's AI component directly and how transitions between traditional control modes and AI-based control modes should be done. Mitigation: Adoption of hierarchical control systems where AI deciphers general actions to be taken while low order control mechanisms are involved in fine tuning controls. Some prevention techniques, or as some authors call them, safety cages or virtual bumpers, are to restrict AI's control authority and its capability to perform certain unsafe actions. Specifying proper interfaces and communication standards between the designed AI part and the conventional control part. To address the challenge of integrating disparate technologies in hybrid control systems, several mitigation strategies can be employed - Challenge: The AI models need to be developed using dedicated software libraries that might run on the specific hardware whereas the traditional controls may have developed certain software and firm ware limitations. To achieve this, there must be compatibility and integration between these numerous parts of the system and other components. Mitigation: Implementing ideas such as the use of Docker in packaging the AI models, and all that is required to deploy them. Absorbing / migrating application software dependent hardware aspects through hardware abstraction layers.

All the following aspects must be taken into consideration to ensure the efficient H/W architectures functioning for AI as well as the traditional control workloads.

6.3 Testing and Validation

Test and validation are critical aspects of hybrid control system to ensure flawless and safe effectiveness. Challenge: Several testing approaches used in the control system may not be effective for hybrid systems because of the complexity involved by AI. Further, new techniques are required to effectively test the system response to various operational conditions and/or risks. Mitigation: Within the subsequent steps, simulation-based testing will be combined with hardware-in-the-loop testing to verify the system under real-world conditions. Using model checking, an approach that allows to determine, based on mathematical models, whether a certain system property holds or not. Imagining complete test harnesses to test diverse scenarios that include often marginal and failure conditions. Challenge: Hybrid systems especially in the application of safety measurement systems must conform to high safety and reliability levels. It is also difficult to show that these standards are met because there are no guidelines recognized by certain certification organizations for AI-based systems (Ao, 2023). Mitigation: Not deviating from proper standards and policies that confront the AI and the control systems during the design and development. Admittedly the following key strategies can be used, ensuring backup of the systems and incorporating measures to deal with system failure. Several recommendations include the following - Engaging regulatory agencies to establish practical policies for the definition and accreditation of hybrid control systems.

6.4 Ethics and Safety Concern

Hence ethical concerns when using AI in control systems coupled with classical control systems must be put into consideration. Implications of AI Driven Control on Safety Critical Environment - Challenge: The use of AI control in Safety-Critical systems, for example, the self-driven cars or health-monitoring equipment provides some ethical challenges on who or what is liable for various decisions, as well as the primary openness of the artificial intelligence control system, and the possibility of myriad prejudices that might prevail in the AI control framework. Mitigation: Programming of AI systems that are that are explicable so that human beings can understand how and why the AI systems decision making process happens. Risk Management and Fail-Safes - Challenge: Hybrid systems in general furnish new kinds of risks resulting from the absolute complexity of the systems and the uncertainty of the AI component. Mitigation: A critical element is the following: Risk assessment should be carried out throughout the System Life Cycle to systematically focus on the potential hazards and to develop Measures to minimise them. Implementing methods that can gracefully recover from unexpected situations or failure in either the AI or traditional control sub modules. Install monitoring and diagnostics systems in the process to act as watchdogs for the system to indicate when there is a need for corrective action or triggering of the shutdown systems. Even though hybrid control systems development and implementation is quite a complicated task, it is imperative that one understands the fundamentals learnt from classical control theory as well as artificial intelligence. Thus, solving these problems will become more and more important to integrate AI systems safely and beneficially in different aspects of our society as AI technologies are further developing (Zhang, 2023).

7. FUTURE TRENDS AND DEVELOPMENTS IN HYBRID CONTROL SYSTEMS

Hybrid control as a field is new and is progressing continually owing to the developments in artificial intelligence, communication technology and in computing. In this section, the future trends and development trends to the technological advancements of the hybrid control systems are reviewed.

7.1 Emerging Technologies

It was found that, the growing integration of edge computing, 5G/6G wireless communication, as well as quantum computing is likely to enhance the formation of hybrid control systems (Prakash & Mathewson & 2020) (Zhu et al., 2019). Some of the frontrunning trends in the field of DCS, such as edge computing – which aims at data processing and decision making on the outskirts of the network, close to the sources of data – may boost the performance and reliability of the hybrid control systems. Impact: Hybrid control systems will most likely reap big from the idea of edge computing that aims at performing computations nearer to the data source. Local processing of data and AI algorithms in edge devices increase the efficiency since latencies can be minimized even in environments that are characterized by low band width. Example: Real time decision to avoid collision or keep the vehicle in the lane can be made effectively in autonomous vehicles through edge-computing even while connected intermittently to the cloud. The fifth generation of wireless communication technology, 5G and future ones like the 6G are expected to improve further the connection and communication features of hybrid control systems.

Impact: The high bandwidth coherent with Low latency of 5G and cellular network of the future will improve the use of Hyb rend Control systems. This will enhance the use of AI components to interconnect, communicate and control the sensors, actuators as well as other subsystems of the system to allow for extensive and decentralized control structures. Example: From a technological perspective, the 5G serves facilities in smart factories to add multiple sensors and actuators to collect, analyze, and control data in real-time for the improvement of production techniques. The innovation that can rely on quantum computing promises a great outlook to the future of hybrid control systems. Impact: Quantum computing is still in its infancy but can bring an enormous impact into the development of the hybrid control as the exact solutions of optimization and control tasks are difficult or impossible to solve using classical methods. This could potentially open incredible new possibilities for fields such as optimal control, the identification of systems and robust control design. Example: In drug discovery, the application of quantum computing can be applied in formulating the finest drug delivery system that takes into consideration various factors in the human body. Scholars have identified various moderating factors that would explain the (Zhou et al., 2024) study done. The two most promising subfields that have recently exhibited considerably development are deep learning and reinforcement

Future breakthroughs by Artificial Intelligence and Machine Learning are believed to impact the generation of hybrid control systems remarkably (Zhu & Zhong, 2023). Incorporation of reinforcement learning and adaptive control theories are expected to assumed more significant roles in increasing the adaptability of the hybrid systems. Further, the evolution of generative AI models like GAN and VAEs make it possible to develop more precise and realistic system models to enhance hybrid control architectures thereby enhancing the overall performance.

6G networks are expected to leverage quantum computing to unlock additional capabilities, albeit several hurdles remain. The quantum computing systems have the potential to solve complex optimization problems and even improve network security (Nawaz et al., 2016) but practical implementation on a large scale is still decades away. There are substantial obstacles, such as unstable quantum systems that need scale-up as well as the development of quantum systems that are resistant to security threats (Kumar & Arnon, 2024). If the forecasts regarding 6G networks are accurate, quantum computing will fully integrate into them in the 2030s and beyond.

There is already groundwork on 5G/6G technologies, and the rollout is in motion, but is facing challenges. The deployment of 5G has been stifled due to many security obstacles to the network (Kazmi et al., 2022). 6G will be built on the robust capabilities of 5G by incorporating AI, blockchain, and even terahertz communications (Akhtar et al., 2020). It is relevant to note, however, that the true potential of AI will only be achieved after addressing the spectrum allocation, robust infrastructure development for controlled non-terrestrial and terrestrial networks, and their interoperability (Guo et al., 2021; Kumar & Arnon, 2024). Expect the timeframe of fully integrated mature 6G networks to materialize around the late 2020s to early 2030s.

It's has been stated that edges computing is implementable sooner than anticipated. Mobile edge computing (MEC) is currently being woven into 5G networks and it is projected that it would have significant contribution into 6G technologies (Tuong et al., 2021). The most relevant challenges for edge computing focus on resource allocation, latency, and security in a distributed computing environment (Lu et al., 2021). Adoption of advanced edge computing in 6G networks will likely happen until the mid-2020s.

So, there is a notable advancement in edge computing in conjunction with 5G and beyond 5G technologies, but the same cannot be said about quantum computing integration which has more long-term obstacles. There is a rather slow progression expected for the deployment of all-encompassing hybrid systems that integrate most of the aforementioned technologies, which thorough research and synthesis of working solutions to the technical, infrastructural, and security issues is done around the 2030s (Duong et al., 2022; Nawaz et al., 2019).

7.3 Adoption and Standardization of the Industry

As more organizations continue to transition to hybrid control systems, the issue of conformity will become a major driving force given the overall need to meet the various needs of users -to name but a few- safety, scalability etc (Schnelle & Favarò, 2023). Trends: Hybrid control systems are becoming popular in industries such as manufacturing, transport, energy, and healthcare among others. This has been occasioned by increased flow of data, enhanced Artificial Intelligence, and the need to have malleable systems. Standardization Efforts: Today there are efforts to create common specifications, interfaces, and safety requirements for a hybrid control system. This will help standardize the interfaces and bring about uniformity, help the vendors to build the applications relatively cheaply, and ensure that the industry adopts the applications at a faster pace. Potential Barriers: However, the following challenges hinder the widespread adoption of the hybrid systems; design and validation of such systems is a complicated endeavour that requires professional help, issues of safety and security among others.

Accompanied by AI technologies, robotic process automation hyper automation enables a simpler path forward for industries seeking to embed AI into their strategies (Haleem et al., 2021). In this manner, businesses are able to automate more sophisticated processes, all the while utilizing the expertise of people as well, thus creating a hybrid control system which integrates the current reality with full AI control. One intermediate step is to enable the simultaneous focus on the intersection of AI, IoT, and blockchain. This could resolve issues related to security, trust, communications, and even scalability (Guergov & Radwan, 2021). It is imperative to state, though, that accomplishing this goal necessitates setting and meeting new technology requirements to realize substantial efficiency gains. The eventual integration requires preparedness, which means that industries should support AI boosted screws are seamless systems, through continuous adaptation and organizational learning. Proactive undertaking ecosystem collaborations and facing risks through the combination of AI and quantum computing in industry 4.0 is essential (How & Cheah, 2024). Furthermore, organizations must also consider the adjustments to human resource management policies that result from the emergence and use of automated systems alongside human employees, resulting in the formation of hybrid AI enhanced staffed organizations (Praba et al., 2024). Such steps include redefining processes of recruitment, staff training, performance management, and overall, ensuring a more comprehensive and smoother transition to operations with AI.

7.4 Future Prospects: Anticipating Breakthroughs and Societal Impacts of Hybrid Control Systems

There are indications that future hybrid control systems promise to bring in revolutionary changes to the field by combining the effectiveness of Artificial Intelligence integrated with conventional methods of Control (Zhu & Zhong, 2023). Long-Term Vision: It is for this reason that hybrid control systems are expected to continue to assert influence in the world that is around us. It can be expected that with improvements in AI and other technologies, we can expect more elaborate and self-managed devices that can learn from the existing environment, seek improvement of performance as well as augment human strength. Potential Breakthroughs: Better developments in say explainable AI for instance or the robust control of composite systems and quantum computation may spur better development of hybrid control to produce systems that are smarter and certainly superior. Societal Impacts: That is why the spread of hybrid control systems will most significantly affect society in matters of industries, employment, and the appearance of new occupations along with key ethical and social issues that require a detailed assessment. Therefore, by adopting these new trends and solving the related problems, we will be able to further expand the ideas and possibilities of developing the concept of hybrid control systems of the future that will improve our lives immeasurably.

CONCLUSION

The combination of modern control theory and Artificial Intelligence has given rise to the new breed of control systems which is defined as the hybrid control systems. These approaches, which combine benefits of both techniques, allow, thus, improved flexibility, stability, and accuracy in various applications. With future development in AI, it is believed that reinforcement learning, deep learning and many other advanced algorithms in combination with the conventional control methods can ensure the future development of hybrid control systems. Furthermore, the continual advancements in the fields such as 5G network, quantum computing, and standardization on industrial norm are expected to accentuate the use as well as application of such hybrid systems. Designing hybrid control systems is still difficult in terms of its complexity, validation, and problematic issues including the matters of ethical concern, but the future of hybrid control appears to be bright. Thus, with acceptance of such new wave of thinking and approaches, new horizons are being opened for creating intelligent, self-learning and self-organizing systems to tackle with the major problems exist in the world.

REFERENCES

Abouheaf, M., Boase, D., Gueaieb, W., Spinello, D., & Al-Sharhan, S. (2023, June 1). Real-time measurement-driven reinforcement learning control approach for uncertain nonlinear systems. Elsevier BV, 122, 106029-106029. DOI: 10.1016/j.engappai.2023.106029

Akhtar, M. W., Hossain, M. S., Hassan, S. A., Jung, H., Garg, S., & Ghaffar, R. (2020). The shift to 6G communications: Vision and requirements. *Human-Centric Computing and Information Sciences*, *10*(1), 53. Advance online publication. DOI: 10.1186/s13673-020-00258-2

Aktharun, S B., & Sekhar, M. (2022, January 1). Design of Unmanned Aerial Vehicles for various wireless applications. Elsevier BV, 51, 1115-1119. DOI: 10.1016/j.matpr.2021.07.108

Alattar, A E., & Mohsen, S. (2023, July 27). A Survey on Smart Wearable Devices for Healthcare Applications. Springer Science+Business Media, 132(1), 775-783. DOI: 10.1007/s11277-023-10639-2

Aljehani, F., N'Doye, I., & Laleg-Kirati, T. (2023, January 1). Feeding control and water quality monitoring in aquaculture systems: Opportunities and challenges. Cornell University. https://doi.org/DOI: 10.48550/arXiv.2306

Alshriem, M. (2020, April 30). The Use of Artificial Intelligence in Traffic Violation Data Analysis. *The Use of Artificial Intelligence in Traffic Violation Data Analysis.*, *13*(4), 644–644. DOI: 10.37624/IJERT/13.4.2020.644-652

Banerjee, U., Dey, B. S., Kar, I. N., & Saha, S. K. (2022, January 1). Robust Artificial Delay based Impedance Control of Robotic Manipulators with Uncertain Dynamics. Cornell University. https://doi .org/DOI: 10.48550/arXiv.2208

Baños, A., Salt, J., & Casanova, V. (2020, January 1). A QFT approach to robust dual-rate control systems. Cornell University. https://doi.org/DOI: 10.48550/arXiv.2002

Bello, S., Ige, O., Wada, I., Adebayo, S., & Chianumba, E. (2024). AI-driven predictive maintenance and optimization of renewable energy systems for enhanced operational efficiency and longevity. *International Journal of Science and Research Archive*, *13*(1), 2823–2837. DOI: 10.30574/ijsra.2024.13.1.1992

Bessa, W. M. (2022, January 1). A framework for the development of intelligent mechanical systems. Cornell University. https://doi.org/DOI: 10.48550/arXiv.2205

Cavalcanti, J. H., Kovacs, T., Ko, A., & Pocsarovszky, K. (2023). Production system efficiency optimization through application of a hybrid artificial intelligence solution. *International Journal of Computer Integrated Manufacturing*, *ahead-of-print*(ahead-of-print), 1–18. DOI: 10.1080/0951192X.2023.2257661

Chandu, H. (2024). Advanced Methods for Verifying Memory Controllers in Modern Computing Systems. *International Journal of Advanced Research in Science. Tongxin Jishu*, •••, 377–388. DOI: 10.48175/IJARSCT-19862

Dev, P., Jain, S., Arora, P K., & Kumar, H. (2021, January 1). Machine learning and its impact on control systems: A review. Elsevier BV, 47, 3744-3749. DOI: 10.1016/j.matpr.2021.02.281

Ding, D., Zhang, Z., & Ding, Q. (2021, August 1). Analysis on the Application of Artificial Intelligence Technology in Electrical Automation Control. *Journal of Physics: Conference Series*, *1992*(3), 032147–032147. DOI: 10.1088/1742-6596/1992/3/032147

Duong, T. Q., Dobre, O. A., Ansere, J. A., Sharma, V., Narottama, B., & Shin, H. (2022). Quantum-Inspired Machine Learning for 6G: Fundamentals, Security, Resource Allocations, Challenges, and Future Research Directions. *IEEE Open Journal of Vehicular Technology*, *3*, 375–387. DOI: 10.1109/OJVT.2022.3202876

Dutta, D., & Upreti, S R. (2021, August 10). Artificial intelligence-based process control in chemical, biochemical, and biomedical engineering. Wiley, 99(11), 2467-2504. DOI: 10.1002/cjce.24246

Emami, S A., Castaldi, P., & Banazadeh, A. (2022, January 1). Neural network-based flight control systems: Present and future. Elsevier BV, 53, 97-137. DOI: 10.1016/j.arcontrol.2022.04.006

Gillani, N., Eynon, R., Chiabaut, C., & Finkel, K. A. (2023, January 1). Unpacking the "Black Box" of AI in Education. Cornell University. https://doi.org/DOI: 10.48550/arXiv.2301

Guergov, S., & Radwan, N. (2021). Blockchain Convergence: Analysis of Issues Affecting IoT, AI and Blockchain. *International Journal of Computations* [IJCIM]. *Information and Manufacturing*, *1*(1). Advance online publication. DOI: 10.54489/ijcim.v1i1.48

Guo, Y. J., Ansari, M., & Fonseca, N. J. G. (2021). Circuit Type Multiple Beamforming Networks for Antenna Arrays in 5G and 6G Terrestrial and Non-Terrestrial Networks. *IEEE Journal of Microwaves*, *1*(3), 704–722. DOI: 10.1109/JMW.2021.3072873

Gupta, A. K. (2021). Fuzzy logic and their application in different areas of engineering science and research: A survey. *International Journal of Scientific Research in Science and Technology*, *8*(2), 71–75.

Haleem, A., Javaid, M., Singh, R. P., Rab, S., & Suman, R. (2021). Hyperautomation for the enhancement of automation in industries. *Sensors International*, *2*, 100124. DOI: 10.1016/j.sintl.2021.100124

Han, B., & Schotten, H D. (2022, January 1). Modeling the System-Level Reliability towards a Convergence of Communication, Computing and Control. DOI: 10.3850/978-981-18-5184-1_MS-23-199-cd

How, M.-L., & Cheah, S.-M. (2024). Forging the Future: Strategic Approaches to Quantum AI Integration for Industry Transformation. *AI*, *5*(1), 290–323. DOI: 10.3390/ai5010015

Kazmi, S. H. A., Hassan, R., Ibrahim, A. A. A., Qamar, F., & Nisar, K. (2023). Security Concepts in Emerging 6G Communication: Threats, Countermeasures, Authentication Techniques and Research Directions. *Symmetry*, *15*(6), 1147. DOI: 10.3390/sym15061147

Kumar, R., & Arnon, S. (2024). Review of Physical Layer Security in Integrated Satellite–Terrestrial Networks. *Electronics (Basel)*, *13*(22), 4414. DOI: 10.3390/electronics13224414

Levine, S., & Shah, D. (2022, December 13). Learning robotic navigation from experience: principles, methods and recent results. Royal Society, 378(1869). DOI: 10.1098/rstb.2021.0447

London, A. J. (2024, January 1). Accountability for Responsible AI Practices: Ethical Responsibilities of Senior Leadership. RELX Group (Netherlands). DOI: 10.2139/ssrn.4736880

Lu, Y., Zhang, Y., & Maharjan, S. (2021). Adaptive Edge Association for Wireless Digital Twin Networks in 6G. *IEEE Internet of Things Journal*, *8*(22), 16219–16230. DOI: 10.1109/JIOT.2021.3098508

Mehr, J. K., Akbari, M., Faridi, P., Xing, H., Mushahwar, V. K., & Tavakoli, M. (2023, February 21). Artificial-Intelligence-Powered Lower Limb Assistive Devices. *Advanced Intelligent Systems*, *5*(6), 2200361. Advance online publication. DOI: 10.1002/aisy.202200361

Navidi, T., Gamal, A. E., & Rajagopal, R. (2023, January 1). Coordinating Distributed Energy Resources for Reliability can Significantly Reduce Future Distribution Grid Upgrades and Peak Load. Cornell University. https://doi.org//arxiv.2306.08717DOI: 10.48550

Nawaz, S. J., Wyne, S., Patwary, M. N., Asaduzzaman, M., & Sharma, S. K. (2019). Quantum Machine Learning for 6G Communication Networks: State-of-the-Art and Vision for the Future. *IEEE Access : Practical Innovations, Open Solutions*, *7*, 46317–46350. DOI: 10.1109/ACCESS.2019.2909490

Nelson, J. P., Biddle, J. B., & Shapira, P. (2023, January 1). Applications and Societal Implications of Artificial Intelligence in Manufacturing: A Systematic Review. Cornell University. https://doi.org/DOI: 10.48550/arXiv.2308

Panahazari, M., Koscak, M., Zhang, J., Hou, D., Wang, J., & Gao, W. (2023, January 16). A Hybrid Optimization and Deep Learning Algorithm for Cyber-resilient DER Control. DOI: 10.1109/ISGT51731.2023.10066345

Piga, D., & Bemporad, A. (2020, September 2). New trends in modeling and control of hybrid systems. Wiley, 30(15), 5775-5776. DOI: 10.1002/rnc.5222

Poalelungi, D. G., Mu at, C. L., Fulga, A., Neagu, M., Neagu, A., Piraianu, A. I., & Fulga, I. (2023, July 31). Advancing Patient Care: How Artificial Intelligence Is Transforming Healthcare. *Journal of Personalized Medicine*, *13*(8), 1214–1214. DOI: 10.3390/jpm13081214 PMID: 37623465

Praba, K., Manoharan, S., Vijay, B., Poreddy, D., Abuya, J. O., & Mulakala, S. (2024). *Human Resource Management Practices in the Age of Industrial Automation* (pp. 79–102). igi global. DOI: 10.4018/979-8-3693-5380-6.ch004

Prakash, N., & Mathewson, K. W. (2020, January 1). Conceptualization and Framework of Hybrid Intelligence Systems. Cornell University. https://doi.org//arxiv.2012.06161DOI: 10.48550

Raj, J L B., & Beno, M M. (2023, January 1). Modeling and Control of Parallel Hybrid Electric Vehicle Using Sea-Lion Optimization. Taylor & Francis, 35(2), 1441-1454. DOI: 10.32604/iasc.2023.026211

Schnelle, S., & Favarò, F. (2023, January 1). ADS Standardization Landscape: Making Sense of its Status and of the Associated Research Questions. Cornell University. https://doi.org//arxiv.2306.17682DOI: 10.48550

Schöning, J., & Pfisterer, H. (2023, August 17). Safe and Trustful AI for Closed-Loop Control Systems. *Electronics (Basel)*, *12*(16), 3489–3489. DOI: 10.3390/electronics12163489

Shaik, T., Tao, X., Higgins, N., Li, L., Gururajan, R., Zhou, X., & Acharya, U R. (2023, January 5). Remote patient monitoring using artificial intelligence: Current state, applications, and challenges. Wiley, 13(2). DOI: 10.1002/widm.1485

Singh, K. (2022, January 1). Design of Sliding Mode PID Controller with Improved reaching laws for Nonlinear Systems. Cornell University. https://doi.org/DOI: 10.48550/arXiv.2207

Song, J., Lyu, D., Zhang, Z., Wang, Z., Zhang, T., & Ma, L. (2022, May 1). When Cyber-Physical Systems Meet AI: A Benchmark, an Evaluation, and a Way Forward. DOI: 10.1109/ICSE-SEIP55303.2022.9794128

Tian, X., Hao, Y., Zhao, G., & Liang, J. (2020, November 6). Research on Dynamic Modeling of a High Temperature Steam Heat Pump. DOI: 10.1109/CAC51589.2020.9327828

Tuong, V. D., Nguyena, T.-V., Cho, S., Truong, T. P., & Noh, W. (2021). Partial Computation Offloading in NOMA-Assisted Mobile-Edge Computing Systems Using Deep Reinforcement Learning. *IEEE Internet of Things Journal*, *8*(17), 13196–13208. DOI: 10.1109/JIOT.2021.3064995

Wallace, B., & Si, J. (2023, January 1). Continuous-Time Reinforcement Learning: New Design Algorithms with Theoretical Insights and Performance Guarantees. Cornell University. https://doi.org//arxiv .2307.08920DOI: 10.48550

Wang, Y., Han, Y., Wang, C., Song, S., Tian, Q., & Huang, G. (2023, January 1). Computation-efficient Deep Learning for Computer Vision: A Survey. Cornell University. https://doi.org//arxiv.2308.13998DOI: 10.48550

Wiharya, C., Sungkowo, H., Suryandari, A. S., & Kurniawan, B. I. (2021, February 1). Design and optimization of digitalization device of temperature control system using PID Ziegler-Nichols control in chemical engineering laboratory. *IOP Conference Series. Materials Science and Engineering*, *1073*(1), 012051–012051. DOI: 10.1088/1757-899X/1073/1/012051

Wu, C., Kuo, C., Shih, S., Chen, J., Lo, Y., Yu, H., Huang, M., Sheu, W. H., & Liu, S. (2021, April 25). Implementation of an Electronic National Early Warning System to Decrease Clinical Deterioration in Hospitalized Patients at a Tertiary Medical Center. *International Journal of Environmental Research and Public Health*, *18*(9), 4550–4550. DOI: 10.3390/ijerph18094550 PMID: 33922991

Zhang, S. (2023, January 1). Bridging Intelligence and Instinct: A New Control Paradigm for Autonomous Robots. Cornell University. https://doi.org//arxiv.2307.10690DOI: 10.48550

Zhou, W. (2022, August 21). Research on the Control Methods Based on Liquid Level System. *Research on the Control Methods Based on Liquid Level System.*, *13*, 198–206. DOI: 10.54097/hset.v13i.1351

Zhou, Y., Karemore, G., Li, W., Liang, Z., Žitnik, M., Chong, F. T., Liu, J., & Fu, T. (2024, August 27). Quantum-Machine-Assisted Drug Discovery: Survey and Perspective. DOI: 10.20944/preprints202408.1950.v1

Zhu, Y., Lam, H., Yang, T., Zhong, Z., & Arik, S. (2019, October 11). Editorial: Hybrid Intelligent Algorithms Based Learning, Optimization, and Application to Autonomic Control Systems. Frontiers Media, DOI: 10.3389/fnins.2019.01090

Zhu, Y., & Zhong, Z. (2023, February 20). Editorial: Hybrid intelligent algorithms based learning, optimization, and application to autonomic control systems, volume II. Frontiers Media, DOI: 10.3389/fnbot.2023.1151473

Chapter 3
Transforming Manufacturing With Robotics

Wesam Ahmed
https://orcid.org/0009-0008-5675-5724
Hurghada University, Egypt

Amena Mahmoud
Kafrelsheikh University, Egypt

ABSTRACT

The manufacturing industry is undergoing a transformative shift with the advent of intelligent robotics. Intelligent robotics in manufacturing encompasses a range of technological advancements, including collaborative robots (cobots),, and robotic systems with enhanced perception, decision-making, and adaptability. These intelligent robotic systems are revolutionizing the way manufacturing operations are carried out, driving increased efficiency, productivity, and flexibility. One of the key benefits of intelligent robotics in manufacturing is the improved precision and consistency in repetitive tasks. AI-powered robotic systems can perform tasks with incredible accuracy, reducing the risk of errors and improving product quality. Furthermore, the integration of machine learning algorithms allows these robots to adapt and optimize their performance continuously, enabling dynamic adjustments to changing production demands or environmental conditions. This chapter also examines the role of intelligent robotics in enabling mass customization and agile manufacturing.

INTRODUCTION

A manufacturing system that integrates robots and expert systems may be called an intelligent robotics system, which facilitates the mechanization of an intelligent manufacturing process. The concept of intelligent robotics systems has emerged recently by the fusion of the following scientific and technological milestones achieved in different areas during the last years: progress in research dealing with robotics techniques and controllers; research into designing knowledge-based expert system lines and manufacturing cells using expert system techniques for controlling and monitoring individual elements of the manufacturing system; standardization of procedures of data communications and sharing of manufacturing resources among various elements of the flexibly automated system where robots could

DOI: 10.4018/979-8-3693-7812-0.ch003

be present. In addition, progress in research and development of small, reliable, and cheap sensor systems has also encouraged further research work for integrating robots with expert systems. Dedicated equipment can be complex, strong, precise, inflexible, and expensive. By contrast, expert system technology is more flexible and cheap because of the implementation through computer software. It uses common equipment to solve special problems in the realm of knowledge. Robots may also use common equipment to solve special problems when they are under the command of a knowledge-based expert system. They provide a high level of flexibility because they may be programmed to manipulate various components and provide fast computation speed (Phuyal et al.,2020).

Manufacturing processes can be mechanized using different facilities, including mainly dedicated specialized automation equipment and expert systems such as computer-aided design, computer-aided manufacturing, group technology, or robots. Automatic techniques and computerized systems in design and manufacturing are being used to decentralize decision-making to speed up the process of information handling and processing, improve quality control, and optimize the behavior of other facilities in the chain of manufacturing activities. Society's awareness concerning the complexity and high degree of variability of industrial manufacturing is growing. Parallel to this view, the trend toward flexible manufacturing is invading more and more industrial branches, to meet an ever-increasing demand for a variable range of products, characterized by short life cycles (Qu et al.,2019).The adoption of advanced robot systems and manipulators has become a key factor in programs to promote new high-level flexible manufacturing and assembly systems to overcome the limitations of existing technology and to open new fields of application where robots, currently employed for specific tasks, could not be used.

It should be remembered that the robot system, described as a demonstration model in this chapter, is part of a bigger computerized work cell, with single or combined computer control that designs turnkey sophisticated systems. Because of marketplace pressure, work cells like this exist where all robot operations are programmed and executed by a microprocessor that works 24 hours per day, for a long period. The robot system can be installed in any industry that has to repeat tasks many times during the operation of the industry. Investing in the robot system allows the business to reduce its operating costs through the elimination or reduction of human manipulative tasks and by the increase in hourly yield due to the non-stop operation of the robot. The objective is the quick amortization of the initial investment market demand in terms of cheaper and more adaptable systems. In the never-ending list of evolutions undergone by our society, industry requires special mention. With the industrial revolution starting in the middle of the last century, the areas of industrial electronics and robotics also advanced. It seems worth repeating in almost all fields that "necessity is the mother of invention," and industry is no exception. A handmade product, whether a pin or a large engine, cannot be a marketable item in the present-day world because the number of items required is enormous. The use of hardware as a demonstration model is an initial step. The product is later transferred to a microprocessor-based replicable robot system that is useful in a real industrial layout. In such instances, it offers unperturbed operation without user intervention and the possibility for future commercial applications (Kumar et al., 2023).

This chapter aims to point out how state-of-the-art research and development in intelligent robotics make an essential contribution as an enabling technology to the advanced automation demanded by the constantly increasing market dynamics and product complexity. We consider the challenge of pushing the state of the art towards the true objective of operational human care systems very interesting, integrating the results in medical science and robotics in this way.

FUNDAMENTALS OF ROBOTICS

A robot that possesses perception, decision-making, execution, and learning abilities is considered intelligent. Modules for data processing and storage, autonomous learning, actuators, sensors, controllers, and decision-making are all integrated into its internal structure. It can interact with its surroundings and work independently to finish manufacturing and production activities. It can recognize and handle difficult circumstances with good adaptability. Intelligent robots are simultaneous robots that incorporate various artificial intelligence technologies. Intelligent robots can be said to be built around artificial intelligence technology, which includes computer vision, deep learning, and machine learning. Furthermore, real-time information sharing, knowledge discovery, and well-informed decision-making among robots can all be facilitated by artificial intelligence technology. When compared to conventional industrial robots, intelligent robots can be used in more situations and have higher efficiency (Nagy et al., 2023).

Based on the functions required, a robot can be classified into one of the following categories: Industrial Manipulators, which can handle the workpiece in welding, machining, spray painting, assembly, material transport, and assembly line functions, are used in industrial applications. Educational Robots, which are mechanical devices used in the teaching of robotics, manipulators, and control subjects, are essentially used in academic and research applications; and Research and Service Robots, which are robots designed to minimize the repetitive and dangerous tasks performed by humans, can be used in a wide range of services such as health service, home service household chores, and law enforcement, and are largely produced units. In general, robots are useful for any technically oriented task in manufacturing, healthcare, and environmental control. With the ongoing advancement in computer processing, storage facilities, and artificial intelligence, the versatility and intelligence of robots in manufacturing increased, making them capable of mastering more difficult tasks and enabling them to dance and sing as performers.

- The robot arm is a mechanical structure that may vary in length and configuration, with a minimum of two physical joints necessary for operations.
- The manipulator is a term for combinations of arms, sensors, and central working unit controllers.
- The joint drive mechanism provides relative compliance between links and independent control and actuation of specific joint forcing operations.
- The controller is what meters the force levels and coordinates the actions of the manipulator. The actuator sensors, process sensors, and vision systems capable of guiding and correcting motions of the robot's end effectors, in real-time or with preprogrammed profiles, are major components of the controller.
- The task sensors, such as tactile, proximate, and force sensors, provide information to the robot to execute the assigned job.
- The robot end effectors are the tools attached to the manipulator to perform a specific task, providing variable functions required in robotic activities (Villalba-Díez et al., 2020).

The term robot is derived from the Czechoslovakian word "Robota," which means a worker or slave. A robot, defined from a manufacturing viewpoint, is a reprogrammable, multifunctional manipulator designed to move materials, parts, tools, or specialized devices through variable programmed motions for the performance of a variety of tasks. The common manipulator, or robot, is made up of six main components: the arm, manipulator, joint drive mechanism, controller, task sensor, and end effectors. A brief description of each of these components is as follows (Ahmed et al., 2021):

TYPES OF ROBOTS

This section of the paper will provide a definition of the three types of robotic systems, discuss their general applications and functions, and list institutional considerations. Fixed Rail Systems – The most recognizable type of industrial robot is the fixed system. These are often fixed to the floor or on rails, which sit on the factory structure, via a pedestal. They perform multi-degree of freedom motions, usually employing a 6-axis manipulator. Robots can do almost every type of simple task and are limited by their environment and by the fragility of designs. Robots that are used in welding, assembly, and machine loading and unloading are examples of fixed rail robots. Industries currently serviced by fixed rail robots are material handling, equipment/device interconnection, industrial assembly, and product finishing.

Three generic categories of industrial robots have evolved: the familiar fixed rail systems, and newer mobile and movable, flexible modular systems. Each type of system is designed for specific tasks and environments, and each carries a unique set of cost, implementation, and performance considerations.

SENSORS AND ACTUATORS IN ROBOTICS

In a world where research and development in most of the advanced and high-tech areas, like manufacturing and logistics, are focusing more and more on the final objective of providing personalized products and services, promptly available in the large quantities demanded by a world market, the only option to succeed and face continually increasing competition is investing in advanced automation. Such a challenge requires that the production systems, beyond advanced and high tech, are flexible, reliable, rapidly reconfigurable, adaptable, efficient, and easily reprogrammable by non-specialized users.

A possible response to this demand lies in employing and integrating the modern methodologies and technologies of robotics, automation, control, and manufacturing in advanced manufacturing systems, producing advanced and intelligent robotics capable of solving problems in the different phases of the product and process life cycle (Lin et al.,2018).

INTELLIGENT ROBOTICS IN MANUFACTURING

Intelligent robotics is an emerging field that combines the power of artificial intelligence and robotics technologies to revolutionize the manufacturing industry. With the advancement of technology, intelligent robots can perform complex tasks, make decisions, and adapt to changes in real-time. This creates a highly efficient and flexible manufacturing environment that reduces costs, increases productivity, and enhances overall quality.

These robots are equipped with sensors, cameras, and other advanced technologies that enable them to perceive and interact with their surroundings. They can collaborate with human workers, share information, and work together seamlessly to achieve common goals. The use of intelligent robotics in manufacturing has the potential to greatly improve production processes, streamline supply chains, and enable the creation of new and innovative products. As the field continues to evolve, it is expected to bring about significant advancements in automation, optimization, and customization in the manufacturing industry (Pan et al.,2021).

ARTIFICIAL INTELLIGENCE IN ROBOTICS

In recent years, the secondary importance of manipulator kinematics has been recognized in favor of the primary importance of sensor-guided task planning and control of robot hardware. In the sequel, we concentrate on the functions and algorithmic methods essential in giving robotic systems, in-place and moving, the capabilities of sensory feedback, object manipulation, environmental interaction, and essentially all other capabilities of mobile and static, or independently moving, creatures. The functionally structured division of robotic architecture allows object-centered task-planning and sensor parameter evaluation in much the same manner as human use of vision (moving gaze, head, or body, to obtain new perspective views), or working knowledge is performed centrally with a discrete set of sensory and information pathways. In the authors' view, task-pertinent architecture gives sensor processing a perspective and sensory feedback-related reasoning a richness not found in the processing of images as disembodied data for transmission to the central processors that govern task performance. We addressed this view in Section 3 with two independent methodologies, template-based and surface-based recognition for object identification, inspection, and manipulation (Eswaran et al., 2024).

Industrial robots have come to rely extensively on machine intelligence. Their versatility and ability to accommodate parts with greater variability than was previously the result from the tight integration of robotics with CAD, planning, and control. However, much of the effort in robotics has been in the utilization of existing technology. Only a few other areas of AI have had a substantial influence on robotics. Future research is directed toward migrating the sort of reasoning reviewed into the control and use of those future robotic systems for which we and others have plans. This paper does not address some issues that are critical to future robotics, for which AI or expertise-based systems might provide relevant support. Artificial intelligence and robotics continue to transform the manufacturing business. Automation has altered the way that manufacturing operates. For example, some robots can assemble parts and AI algorithms that can forecast consumer demand. Let's take a closer look at how these technologies are transforming the industrial industry. Increased efficiency: one of the benefits of using AI and robotics in manufacturing is that they can assist in accelerating processes. Machines normally operate quicker and more correctly than humans, allowing us to produce more items. Furthermore, machines do not fatigue and may work longer hours than human workers (Lins et al.,2021).

Another advantage of incorporating AI and robotics into manufacturing is that it can help reduce costs. Machines are frequently less expensive to operate than human employees since they do not require health insurance or vacation time. Furthermore, robots can be utilized to perform activities traditionally performed by humans, saving money on labor expenditures.

MACHINE LEARNING ALGORITHMS IN ROBOTICS

In addition to individual learning model application, the relationship between visual perception and object manipulation has been exploited to achieve more intelligent behaviors. Hand-eye coordination relies on early visual processing to provide visually guided reaching when humans perform a task in a laboratory environment. Similarly, for robots to learn goal-oriented behavior, early visual perception is needed to leverage both manipulation and interaction with target objects by robots. Since object shape and friction properties may determine grasping strategies, the strategy for robotic manipulation could be guided by the object's visual and physical properties. Because of the knowledge between visual sensors and force-torque sensors, the data from both visual sensors and force-torque sensors were fed to the learning model to guide object grasping, such that the relationship between visual observation and physical response could be explicitly modeled. Based on deep neural networks, the hybrid observation physical layer was introduced for object grasping with dense prediction and the underlying latent space state estimation. The latent-space guidance facilitated the exploitation of unsupervised pretraining to allow autonomous robotic learning to be more reliable when only access to limited demonstrations was available (Wan et al.,2020).

The traditional methods may not be enough to solve complex problems recognized by robotic technology. Therefore, various kinds of machine learning methodologies were exploited to address the challenges of robotic applications. Decision regression and rule learning provided the capability for high-level task planning and low-level motion control, respectively. Support vector machine and kernel-based methods were also applied for robot learning. With deep neural networks, particularly convolutional neural networks (CNNs), each layer maps the input to an even higher-level representation, and finally, a class score is calculated. As one of the primary deep learning models, CNNs were utilized in object recognition to address many significant challenges. LSTM with CNNs provided classification models that overcame the spatial constraints contained in images and the temporal dependencies in video and had been adapted for object grasping. Although the data-driven model could replace the user manual to perform object grasping, many hardware or other considerations need to be addressed by users (Javaid et al.,2021).

COMPUTER VISION FOR ROBOTICS

Today's manufacturing lines cannot be based solely on a fixed sequence of operations featuring manual operations at some stations and specialized machines at others. The Covid-19 pandemic has demonstrated the importance of this flexibility, and how quickly this flexibility must adapt to new tasks. Introducing robotic solutions at some points of the manufacturing line is an important means of increasing its flexibility. The key to this flexibility lies in a natural human-robot interface based on machine vision in the communication channel between humans and robots. This property will facilitate both reprogramming the robots and having them ask for human assistance when facing an unexpected event. Furthermore, machine vision enables robots to perceive their environment, feel the boundaries of some objects, and use these properties to detect or identify objects (Smith et al.,2021).

Computer vision is the area that enables machines to perceive images and video. Rapid progress has been made in this area, especially during the last few years, which has enabled the current artificial intelligence revolution. Achieving even more progress is critical to the further evolution of intelligent robotics in manufacturing. The importance of computer vision for robotics lies in the fact that this technique constitutes the primary communication channel between robots and humans in many tasks.

EXAMPLES OF COMPANIES ALREADY USING AI AND ROBOTICS FOR MANUFACTURING

Customized items are in high demand, and businesses must respond very quickly to keep up. Artificial intelligence (AI) and robotics have already transformed manufacturing operations. This enables speedier production and higher levels of quality control. Some companies use artificial intelligence and robotics in manufacturing as shown in Fig1.

Figure 1. Some companies using AI and robotics

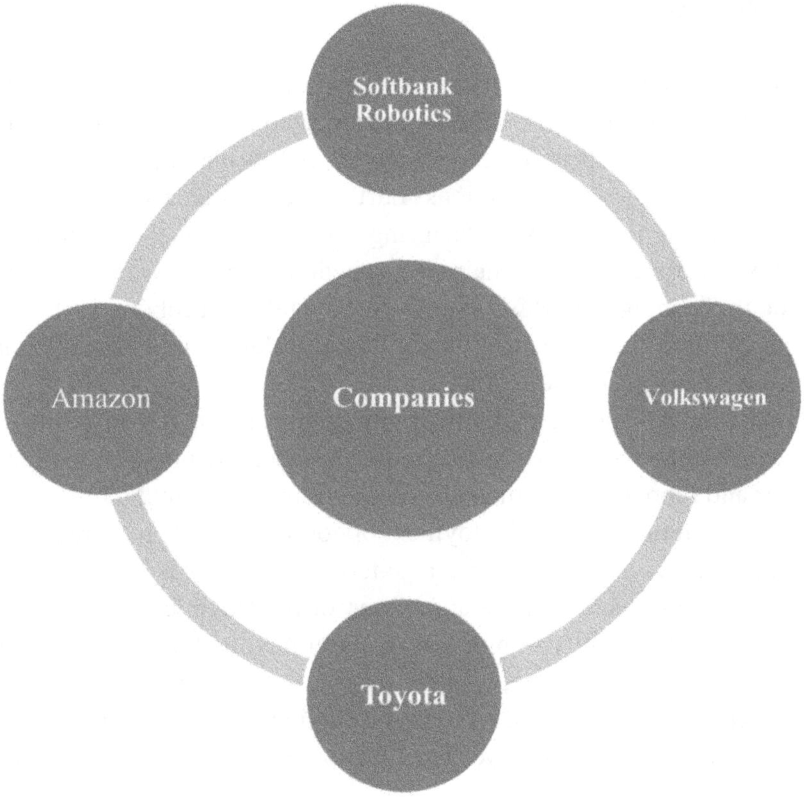

COLLABORATIVE ROBOTS (COBOTS)

The new assistive robots are designed to help people. YuMi is an example: a safe Cobots arm (Safe Cageless Human-Robot Collaboration) used for studies and demonstrations in human environments thanks to machine learning. ABB found that it didn't make much sense to design a robot armed with a force sensor to exert force on another robot, their typical applications. Nor was it fair to equip a robot with a sensitive set of cameras and not use them. Combining the sensors (YuMi has a camera and force sensors in the hands) to show how the human-designed software handles the change and error handling, the behavior must be carefully programmed. With the model-based robot face recognition procedure, YuMi can go around facial recognition procedures (Grau et al.,2020).

ABB has introduced YuMi, a small-parts assembler for the electronics industry that is easy to train by programming by demonstration. It is easy to program one arm to make the assembly, and then program the second arm to make the mirror assembly. YuMi can also pick and place small electronic components. In comparison to traditional ABB industrial robots, the design relies on a flat, open platform, avoiding the typical steel enclosure. YuMi is equipped with a camera and is calibrated offline from the virtual model. The product can also be calibrated online. YuMi GRID provides an optical sensor to prevent collisions. The manipulators rely on a collaborating safety scheme for contact detection and overcurrent control.

Advantages of Cobots

As indicated, most manufacturing sectors must move away from manual, unwanted, and unwell-received activities. Factory workers can, therefore, be relocated to build, inspect, and package products in one place, ensuring that their expertise serves a higher purpose and provides better results through smarter and more creative production operations. Furthermore, collaborative robots promote smooth production operation and support the manufacturing industry, since they can average over various work shifts, minimally confront people in their shift schedules, and provide a steady product flow and timely service. Through the integrated R&D efforts of the intelligent robotic systems described earlier, lightweight, and heavy-duty cobots have spearheaded the development of flexible, interconnected, and service-oriented manufacturing (Oberson.,2024).

The deployment of cobots is motivated by their numerous advantages. First, co-bots are easy to install and program, which allows smaller organizations and manufacturing companies to enhance their automation in a faster and more efficient manner. By providing the manufacturers with programmability, ease-of-use, and safety functions, the deployment of cobots does not require professional education in robot programming or excessive investments in safety measures. Also, close human-robot working relationships save valuable production space and allow for the flexible and seamless link of formerly segregated production islands or cells - engineering, assembly, and sequence. Moreover, cobots can interact directly with the human workforce, if safety measures are followed, which can contribute to the enhancement of the workers' motivation and efficiency by taking over from humans' jobs that are difficult, monotonous, or dangerous, allowing employees to contribute to a more complex task (Bi et al.,2021).

Challenges and Limitations

The real-time dynamic control of industrial large-scale flexible machining by robotics, the instantaneous solving of force-related reasoning such as collision effect, envelope relation, clamping force, etc., and the execution of decisions and the available software in off-line aiming at decision are always the essential requirements to increase the integrity and systematicness of intelligent robotics. However, better solutions to traditional ways are still hard to find for these problems. For example, the dynamic optimization of collision under its resolution, safety, and protecting-to-body or -locks, etc., the handling, path re-planning, robot practical reasoning, recovery, etc., either have not had a unique rebellion in conclusion or hardly derive a positive and unified conclusion and perfect system. It is unsuitable or irrational to automate the solution of practical engineering applications. Only through maximum relaxation and conversion, the autonomy in decision planning be improved (Zhang et al.,2020).

To achieve intelligent feature recognition for machines, the results of different visual perceptions need to be concatenated. In most visual processing systems, the pixel-level pre-processing would be executed first to simplify the subsequent processing. Meanwhile, the fusion of multiple features at different resolutions is always difficult. To achieve rapid response for making robotics more intelligent and flexible, the requirements of real-time processing of images or small frame sequences would also pose great challenges to visual definition. For introducing mental qualities thereof for robots, this fusion of intellectual algorithms or features needs immediate and more in-depth exploration. In addition, the rocketing in the required processing capability for software and hardware also places high demands upon basic research problems such as computer vision and appropriate visual robot systems (Grigoras et al.,2024).

The adaptability of robotic systems enables cost-effective customization and small-batch production. Manufacturers can promptly adapt to evolving market demands by providing customized products that maintain efficiency. This transition to more adaptable production models can revolutionize business strategies and promote industry expansion. Sixteen. The emergence of collaborative ecosystems that consist of humans, robotics, and other technologies presents opportunities for innovation (Zhang et al.,2020). Technical integration: integrating robots into existing systems in industrial manufacturing can be a complex process. Proper maintenance and seamless communication between robots and other apparatus are essential for preventing downtime. Compliance and regulatory concerns: compliance necessitates navigating legal requirements, such as data privacy regulations and safety standards. By remaining informed about regulatory changes, legal challenges can be avoided. Scalability and customization: efficiency necessitates customizing robotic systems to accommodate manufacturing requirements. Scalability planning guarantees that these systems can expand by production requirements.

ROBOTIC PROCESS AUTOMATION (RPA)

RPA is part of service applications using task automation. This means that the robotic process automation just needs to “see and click” as a human operator, not addressing other data sources from databases and applications but interacting with the front end to facilitate what users do and remove activities with no added value. Robot process automation is an autonomous system composed of software agents and a coordinator and is used as an interface to control applications that support business processes, often including data manipulation and transactional operations.

Recently, a new concept associated with the application of artificial intelligence in service robots has emerged, called Robotic Process Automation (RPA). RPA is a robotics system capable of performing simple and repetitive tasks without human intervention in applications that use only the front end or graphical user interface (GUI) of active applications without the need for programming integration. In RPA, there is no interaction and integration in the source code (back end) where the data resides, that is, for the robot to operate it just needs to know where to enter and what to extract. RPA is not only dedicated to applications that run on the computer; it is also often used to exchange information or automate processes that require interaction with virtual environments (Shidaganti et al.,2023).

Applications of RPA in Manufacturing

RPA is an alliance of predictive analysis, AI, cost/value focus, and business rules, which is aimed at stepping ahead from recognizing what is regulated and offering suggestions about what else can be done. The emergence of RPA brings about a confusing array of terminology, vendors, and platforms offering bespoke point solutions. In a recent study, it is predicted that there are more than 300 RPA vendors. However, understanding that RPA collapses into three simple service platforms implies that RPA can be a transformative technology across industries, especially within the manufacturing sector. An interesting point to note is the variety of RPAs that are available, but to simplify the perspective about what can potentially be achieved, using the functionality of RPAs at a higher level of view allows for the alignment of tasks to the platforms that can provide a higher probability of clear understanding. The inclusion of optical character recognition capabilities and other image processing tools also turns regular RPAs into tools that breach the Intelligent Automation Platform.

Figure 2. RPA use cases in manufacturing

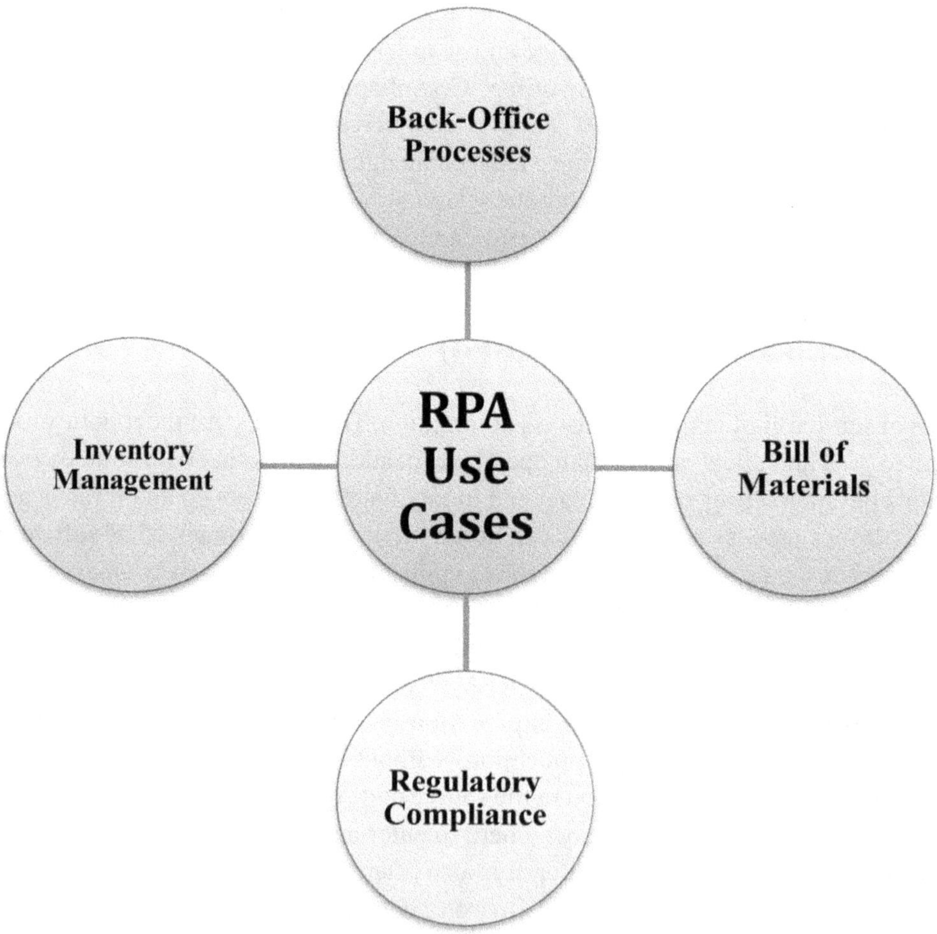

With the current cutting-edge technology, the vision of self-organizing intelligent robots, which imitate the characteristics of the plant kingdom to form colonies, using the resources available to it without afflicting its environment, can be achieved for manufacturing. Not all businesses will come to the fruition of full-fledged intelligent robotics. They will instead see a phased approach with RPA, where bot-like software tools will perform repetitive rules-based tasks. Robotic Process Automation (RPA) can include data migration tools, process mining, and screen scraping tools that in a disconnected manner try to solve the symptom, without addressing the unstructured processes. Until AI systems become confident, businesses can use RPA to automate repetitive administrative tasks. However, businesses need to acknowledge that RPA will not resolve complex processes on its own nor provide appreciable value (Begishev et al.,2021). There are many applications as shown in Figure 2. The five most prevalent applications in this ever-changing sector:

Use Case 1: Inventory Management:

Inventory associates can trace deliveries, generate reports, receive notifications for placing orders, monitor the stock levels of spare parts and materials in real time, and access all the necessary inventory data.

Use Case 2: Bill of Materials (BOM):

The Bill of Materials (BOM) is a manual for a manufacturing organization. It encompasses every detail, including the inventory of raw materials, their respective quantities, the number of components and sub-components, the resources necessary, and the design, assembly, and packing guidelines. An automated solution makes the storage of BOM data on the cloud possible. Managers and assemblers can retrieve the details by providing the "ID" or "name" when RPA-powered chatbots are incorporated into BOM, eliminating the need to navigate physical documents or legacy applications. The RPA bot can autonomously extract the current data from the BOM and calculate the precise resources and supplies required to produce a specific product in the desired quantities. The data can then be presented to the managers for decision-making. Our RPA solutions can be used to automate repetitive business processes.

Use Case 3: Supply Chain Management:

RPA is beneficial in all aspects of supply chain management in manufacturing. RPA bots automate the supplier onboarding process, predict the demands and products, and facilitate efficient capacity management and raw material planning. RPA streamlines vendor selection conducts credibility checks and collects vendor data.

Use Case 4: Back-Office Processes:

In the manufacturing industry, intelligent automation can be implemented to automate administrative duties, including the generation of invoices, the recording of meeting minutes, the scheduling of meetings, the maintenance of government records, the management of purchase orders, the response to essential customer emails, and the recording of attendance.

Use Case 5: Regulatory Compliance:

In the manufacturing sector, robotic process automation can guarantee that organizations adhere to all regulatory mandates. Employers can maintain a higher control over the process flows and be adequately prepared for external audits by ensuring that each action is recorded in applications. RPA can guarantee that all legal requirements are met.

INDUSTRY 4.0 AND ROBOTICS

It is essential to understand the significance of robots in the Industry 4.0 context. The application of robotics in a manufacturing environment allows companies to meet the demand from customers for high-quality products while maintaining the appropriate profit margins needed for survival. They have also been paramount in ensuring that blue-collar jobs are safer and job tasks are easier to perform. There is still a multitude of tasks at low levels of cognitive complexity that robotics can perform, where human workers are said to be underutilized: dull, dirty, dangerous, demanding, and distant. The traditional roles and significance of automation at work are much less complicated than its future value and consequently, the future significant consequences from improved robotics. Silicon memory and computational advances both proceed on, or in some cases exceed, the curve anticipated by Moore's Law, while exponential growth in the first decade of this century in the deployment of robotics marks an evolutionary advance for robotics, as it impacts logistics applications far removed from the traditional advantages in precision repetition and speed. This change has come about because the technological challenges that have been pushed to the forefront by our need to replace human judgment with better sensing or decision capability have effectively driven the creation of hybrid modular architectures (Anthony et al.,2023).

Industry 4.0 provides a model to fuse existing production models with modern technology, which in turn can allow for self-organizing, awareness, and connected manufacturing production systems. This in turn improves the decision-making capability of these manufacturing systems. Fundamentally, it marks the beginning of the migration from traditional production models to a model that can discover information from the data available to it and autonomously evolve its processes. The Yaskawa Motoman GP industrial robot family and the KUKA KR AGILUS industrial robot family are notable examples of smart manufacturing robots. A family of small and nimble industrial robots called KUKA KR AGILUS is intended for applications in smart manufacturing. Because of their reputation for speed and accuracy, these robots are well-suited for jobs requiring a high degree of accuracy. Because of their integrated safety features, which include force control and collision detection, the KR AGILUS robots can safely work with humans [89]. Applications including packing, machine tending, and small parts assembly are among their strong points. Industries including electronics, pharmaceuticals, and food processing use the KUKA KR AGILUS robots. They are frequently employed for jobs that require handling delicate parts or carrying out repeated operations.

Integration of Robotics in Industry 4.0

The challenge in developing these new intelligent capabilities for future robots is to ensure that they are seen from the perspective of the operators who will be using them, via capabilities/technology that are at the correct maturity for ease of exploitation, and in terms of a business case that allows the growing market demand to reach critical mass, thus ensuring the necessary continuing investment in research areas that can produce the desired capabilities on a scale that reduces costs. Use of robots on collaborative tasks will also demand that new capabilities drive down the cost of the necessary safety envelopes and mechanisms that will allow other actors like operators to work near robots (Makulavičius et al.,2023).

Despite the cost reduction, the growth of robots in smaller companies is still being seriously hampered by inflexibility, the lack of ease for robot set-up, and the poor integration of robots with the company or the factory in general. Recognizing this, a significant amount of research is underway to enable breakthroughs that will make robots better suited for use by those who are not robotic programming experts and will contribute directly to manufacturing intelligence. This includes electronic connectability and modularity, open-source software that simplifies programming and re-programming, self-teaching capabilities, plug-and-work in terms of functionality (sensors, mechanical systems, and software), safety, and ease of use.

SMART MANUFACTURING ROBOTS

A family of small and nimble industrial robots called KUKA KR AGILUS is intended for applications in smart manufacturing. Because of their reputation for speed and accuracy, these robots are well-suited for jobs requiring a high degree of accuracy. Because of their integrated safety features, which include force control and collision detection, the KR AGILUS robots can safely work with humans. Applications including packing, machine tending, and small parts assembly are among their strong points. Industries including electronics, pharmaceuticals, and food processing use the KUKA KR AGILUS robots. They are frequently employed for jobs that require handling delicate parts or carrying out repeated operations. They are commonly employed for activities that require careful component handling or consistent repetition of actions. For example, in electronics manufacturing, these robots can precisely insert microchips on circuit boards, assisting in the fabrication of high-quality electrical devices (Liu etal.,2023).

The Yaskawa Motoman GP Series is made up of industrial robots that are meant to work at high speeds and with great precision in production situations. These robots have a strong and resilient build, making them dependable even in harsh industrial environments. The GP Series includes several versions, each with a varied payload and reach capacity, allowing manufacturers to select the robot that best fits their application. Yaskawa offers a variety of controller options for programming and controlling these robots, ensuring smooth connection with current automation systems. Yaskawa Motoman GP Series robots are frequently employed in manufacturing processes requiring precision and efficiency. They are used in the automobile industry for jobs such as spot welding and painting, where their quick movements allow for shorter cycle times. Within the electronics sector, these robots are employed in the electronics sector to perform precision assembly of small components. They are used by the food processing industry for packaging and material handling. The GP Series robots' versatility and reliability help to higher productivity and lower labor costs in a variety of manufacturing areas.

ADVANTAGES AND LIMITATIONS OF INTEGRATION OF ROBOTICS IN INDUSTRY

Smart manufacturing robots have numerous applications, particularly in industries that require high degrees of precision and personalization. Their capacity to adapt quickly to various industrial tasks makes them important in industries such as automotive, electronics, and aerospace manufacturing. The primary benefits of these robots include higher productivity, less human error, and the capacity to perform hazardous or ergonomically demanding tasks for human workers (Mahrous et al.,2024).

Despite their obvious advantages, smart manufacturing robots have several drawbacks. One of the most significant hurdles is the high initial cost of installation and integration into current industrial systems. Additionally, competent individuals are required to handle and maintain these complex robotic systems. Another problem is the possibility of job displacement in industries where robots can undertake functions that were previously performed by people.

ETHICAL AND SOCIAL IMPLICATIONS OF INTELLIGENT ROBOTICS

Moral philosophy offers several criteria that might be used for the establishment of the basic moral principles or fundamental obligations guiding the behavior of machines. Especially in contemporary moral philosophy, some positions assert that moral concepts are not exclusively human concepts but that some or all moral concepts can also be extended to entities that are not part of our biological families. The following fundamental obligations offer guidance in developing a first set of machine morals. The project seeks to give a rationale to use the notion of obligation to describe the relationship between the designer of a machine that plans to make use of machine ethics and the machine, and to solve the most pressing questions that arise when an entity that is not capable of obligations is involved in the moral relationship (Daniyan et al.,2020).

Machine ethics is a new interdisciplinary research field that seeks to use the tools of philosophical ethics, social sciences, and psychology to design and build autonomous systems that exhibit ethical behavior. The field will use key elements from developments in robot ethics, such as the 20 behavioral rules developed by Colom, but machine ethics will go beyond robot ethics. In this chapter, the focus is first to clarify which research will fall under the umbrella of machine ethics and second to provide an overview of several specific research themes that will contribute to filling the gaps in our understanding of how autonomous systems can commit to behaving in an ethically desirable manner and, importantly, how they can act according to the commitments made (Mahrous et al.,2024).

Integrating AI in manufacturing brings significant advancements in efficiency, productivity, and innovation. However, it raises several ethical issues that must be addressed to ensure responsible and fair use of AI technologies:

Security and privacy of data: Problem: The privacy and security of sensitive information are a source of concern because AI systems in manufacturing rely on vast quantities of data. Implementing effective data protection measures and adhering to privacy regulations is imperative. The Ethical design and utilization of artificial intelligence: issue: The ethical design and deployment of AI technologies must be considered to prevent unanticipated negative consequences. Consideration: It is essential to adhere to ethical guidelines and principles in the development and utilization of AI. Dependability and Safety: issue: The deployment of AI in manufacturing processes must guarantee safety and reliability to prevent accidents and malfunctions. consideration: To guarantee AI systems' safe and efficient operation, they must undergo rigorous testing and validation.

Future research should focus on improving these robots' cognitive capacities to manage more complex decision-making processes. This could entail incorporating powerful AI algorithms that allow robots to learn and adapt more effectively. Another area for improvement is the creation of more resilient and adaptable robotic systems that can be adjusted for various purposes. Future research topics involve looking at ways to lower the cost of these systems, making them more affordable to small and medium-sized businesses. Researchers could also investigate the ethical and societal implications of deploying intelligent manufacturing robots, notably regarding workforce displacement and job retraining programs.

CONCLUSION

The domain of application of intelligent manufacturing systems that utilize intelligent robotics is significant, and it is valuable to identify the users' needs to make the best prototypes and to affect a large flow back to the laboratories in the form of new problems that could be researched. A taxonomy of intelligent robots was presented to see the various levels of sophistication in robot control. Two case studies were presented, dealing with details of some of the technological and financial characteristics of advanced robot systems. Some research topics are suggested with the hope that the trend of intelligent robot development will lead to viable, intelligent production systems within industrial planning horizons. This chapter has concentrated on fundamental problems in developing intelligent robots for manufacturing applications. The justification was based on the observation that the enormous potential of robotics is far from being realized due to the lack of intelligent control. However, there is more to the problem than just providing the robot with a sophisticated sensing modality to help it interface with the environment. Significant issues, such as the cost of intelligent robots, their reliability, the difficulty of programming and upgrading, and interfacing with the rest of the manufacturing systems, must be tackled seriously to realize the benefits of the needed technology transfer system. Intelligent robots are still viewed as research and demonstration systems, and the load of incorporating these technologies and justifying production systems is put on the manufacturing industry.

REFERENCES

Ahmed, R. S., Ahmed, E. S. A., & Saeed, R. A. (2021). Machine learning in cyber-physical systems in industry 4.0. In *Artificial intelligence paradigms for smart cyber-physical systems* (pp. 20–41). IGI global. DOI: 10.4018/978-1-7998-5101-1.ch002

Anthony, C., Bechky, B. A., & Fayard, A. L. (2023). “Collaborating” with AI: Taking a system view to explore the future of work. *Organization Science*, *34*(5), 1672–1694. DOI: 10.1287/orsc.2022.1651

Begishev, I., Khisamova, Z., & Vasyukov, V. (2021). Technological, ethical, environmental and legal aspects of robotics. In *E3S Web of Conferences* (Vol. 244, p. 12028). EDP Sciences. DOI: 10.1051/e3sconf/202124412028

Bi, Z. M., Luo, C., Miao, Z., Zhang, B., Zhang, W. J., & Wang, L. (2021). Safety assurance mechanisms of collaborative robotic systems in manufacturing. *Robotics and Computer-integrated Manufacturing*, *67*, 102022. DOI: 10.1016/j.rcim.2020.102022

Daniyan, I., Mpofu, K., Ramatsetse, B., & Adeodu, A. (2020). Design and simulation of a robotic arm for manufacturing operations in the railcar industry. *Procedia Manufacturing*, *51*, 67–72. DOI: 10.1016/j.promfg.2020.10.011

Eswaran, M., Inkulu, A., Tamilarasan, K., Bahubalendruni, M. V. A. R., Jaideep, R., Faris, M. S., & Jacob, N. (2024). Optimal layout planning for human robot collaborative assembly systems and visualization through immersive technologies. *Expert Systems with Applications*, *241*, 122465. DOI: 10.1016/j.eswa.2023.122465

Grau, A., Indri, M., Bello, L. L., & Sauter, T. (2020). Robots in industry: The past, present, and future of a growing collaboration with humans. *IEEE Industrial Electronics Magazine*, *15*(1), 50–61. DOI: 10.1109/MIE.2020.3008136

Grigoras, C. C., Zichil, V., Ciubotariu, V. A., & Cosa, S. M. (2024). Machine Learning, Mechatronics, and Stretch Forming: A History of Innovation in Manufacturing Engineering. *Machines (Basel)*, *12*(3), 180. DOI: 10.3390/machines12030180

Javaid, M., Haleem, A., Singh, R. P., & Suman, R. (2021). Substantial capabilities of robotics in enhancing industry 4.0 implementation. *Cognitive Robotics*, *1*, 58–75. DOI: 10.1016/j.cogr.2021.06.001

Kumar, L., & Sharma, R. K. (2023). Smart manufacturing and industry 4.0: state-of-the-art review. Handbook of Smart Manufacturing, 1-28.

Lin, W. D., Low, Y. H., Chong, Y. T., & Teo, C. L. (2018, December). Integrated cyber physical simulation modelling environment for manufacturing 4.0. In *2018 IEEE International Conference on Industrial Engineering and Engineering Management (IEEM)* (pp. 1861-1865). IEEE. DOI: 10.1109/IEEM.2018.8607696

Lins, R. G., & Givigi, S. N. (2021). Cooperative robotics and machine learning for smart manufacturing: Platform design and trends within the context of industrial internet of things. *IEEE Access : Practical Innovations, Open Solutions*, *9*, 95444–95455. DOI: 10.1109/ACCESS.2021.3094374

Liu, H., Rahman, M., Rahimi, M., Starr, A., Durazo-Cardenas, I., Ruiz-Carcel, C., Ompusunggu, A., Hall, A., & Anderson, R. (2023). An autonomous rail-road amphibious robotic system for railway maintenance using sensor fusion and mobile manipulator. *Computers & Electrical Engineering, 110*, 108874. DOI: 10.1016/j.compeleceng.2023.108874

Mahrous, A., Ali, A. S., Mohamed, S., & Othman, M. (2024). Kinematic Analysis and Simulation of an Industrial Rail-Mounted Robot Manipulator Using Ruckig for Enhanced Path Planning. JES. *Journal of Engineering Sciences*, *52*(4), 105–119.

Makulavičius, M., Petkevičius, S., Rožėnė, J., Dzedzickis, A., & Bučinskas, V. (2023). Industrial robots in mechanical machining: Perspectives and limitations. *Robotics (Basel, Switzerland)*, *12*(6), 160. DOI: 10.3390/robotics12060160

Nagy, M., Lăzăroiu, G., & Valaskova, K. (2023). Machine intelligence and autonomous robotic technologies in the corporate context of SMEs: Deep learning and virtual simulation algorithms, cyber-physical production networks, and Industry 4.0-based manufacturing systems. *Applied Sciences (Basel, Switzerland)*, *13*(3), 1681. DOI: 10.3390/app13031681

Oberson, X. (2024). The development of artificial intelligence and robots. In *Taxing Artificial Intelligence* (pp. 5–14). Edward Elgar Publishing. DOI: 10.4337/9781035307555.00007

Pan, Y., & Zhang, L. (2021). Roles of artificial intelligence in construction engineering and management: A critical review and future trends. *Automation in Construction*, *122*, 103517. DOI: 10.1016/j.autcon.2020.103517

Phuyal, S., Bista, D., & Bista, R. (2020). Challenges, opportunities and future directions of smart manufacturing: A state of art review. *Sustainable Futures : An Applied Journal of Technology, Environment and Society*, *2*, 100023. DOI: 10.1016/j.sftr.2020.100023

Qu, Y. J., Ming, X. G., Liu, Z. W., Zhang, X. Y., & Hou, Z. T. (2019). Smart manufacturing systems: State of the art and future trends. *International Journal of Advanced Manufacturing Technology*, *103*(9-12), 3751–3768. DOI: 10.1007/s00170-019-03754-7

Shidaganti, G., & Karthik, K. N. Anvith, & Kantikar, N. A. (2023). Integration of RPA and AI in Industry 4.0. In Confluence of Artificial Intelligence and Robotic Process Automation (pp. 267-288). Singapore: Springer Nature Singapore.

Smith, M. L., Smith, L. N., & Hansen, M. F. (2021). The quiet revolution in machine vision-a state-of-the-art survey paper, including historical review, perspectives, and future directions. *Computers in Industry*, *130*, 103472. DOI: 10.1016/j.compind.2021.103472

Villalba-Díez, J., Molina, M., Ordieres-Meré, J., Sun, S., Schmidt, D., & Wellbrock, W. (2020). Geometric deep lean learning: Deep learning in industry 4.0 cyber–physical complex networks. *Sensors (Basel)*, *20*(3), 763. DOI: 10.3390/s20030763 PMID: 32019148

Wan, J., Li, X., Dai, H. N., Kusiak, A., Martinez-Garcia, M., & Li, D. (2020). Artificial-intelligence-driven customized manufacturing factory: Key technologies, applications, and challenges. *Proceedings of the IEEE*, *109*(4), 377–398. DOI: 10.1109/JPROC.2020.3034808

Zhang, B., Wu, J., Wang, L., & Yu, Z. (2020). Accurate dynamic modeling and control parameters design of an industrial hybrid spray-painting robot. *Robotics and Computer-integrated Manufacturing*, *63*, 101923. DOI: 10.1016/j.rcim.2019.101923

Chapter 4
AI-Based Fault Detection and Diagnosis Techniques in Control System Engineering:
Focus on Food Processing Industry

P. Sriramalakshmi
https://orcid.org/0000-0002-8694-4605
Vellore Institute of Technology, Chennai, India

Swetha R. Kumar
https://orcid.org/0000-0002-1716-1842
Vellore Institute of Technology, Chennai, India

ABSTRACT

This chapter presents the major applications of Artificial Intelligence techniques (AI) in fault diagnosis of various control engineering fields. AI has made substantial improvements in various fields of Engineering, including control engineering. There are few noteworthy applications of AI in fault diagnosis related to control systems includes the control of industrial automation, power systems, robotic automation, medical applications, transportation systems, renewable energy, building automation, telecommunications etc. The early and effective diagnosis of fault can prevent downtime and repairs. In industrial automation, AI can efficiently detect anomalies in sensor readings and abnormalities in machine operation. Neural networks learn from the patterns of past historical data and identify the faults or anomalies. This chapter mainly focuses on the benefits and challenges in applying AI for fault diagnosis in the field of control engineering in food processing, monitoring control and future research perspectives

INTRODUCTION

In recent years, there is a growing interest in the application of AI techniques in various fields. The monitoring, control, predictive maintenance, fault diagnosis is performed in all the industries right from power sector (Patel, & Shah, 2018), (Fausing Olesen, & Shaker, 2020), transportation (Ersöz et al., 2022), (Alqasi et al., 2024) to food manufacturing operations (Addankiet al., 2022), (Misra et al., 2020). The

DOI: 10.4018/979-8-3693-7812-0.ch004

main purpose of this AI applications to the field of food processing and manufacturing is to ensure the high degree of product quality during the mass production (UmaMaheswaran et al., 2022). Cutting-edge process control techniques are adopted to realize further improvements in process design and operation efficiency (Mavani et al., 2022). Moreover, food safety and quality evaluation are gaining more attention globally. AI usage in global food processing market is depicted in Figure 1. AI techniques for fruits and vegetables quality prediction, quality assessment, sorting and packaging hold the first position globally followed by the diary field (*AI in Global Food Processing Market*)

Figure 1. AI in global food processing market

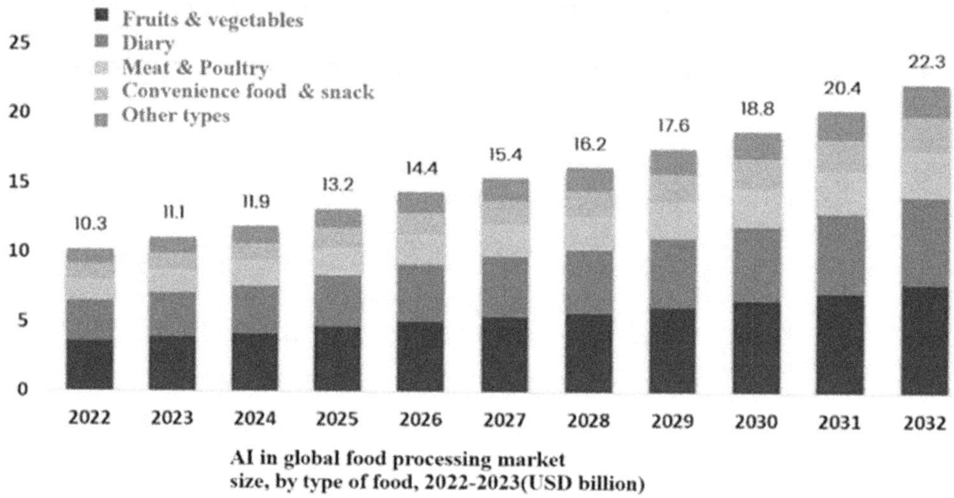

Food safety is very important to human life, ensuring people's health and providing a elementary assurance for the steady growth of society. Conventional methods of food quality and safety evaluation methods are often unrealistic due to time constraints. The food industry usually satisfies the consumers by providing speedy delivery and quality of food. Various automatic process techniques are used in the controlled variables from standards which can be adjusted, and minimized to improve the process operations. Proportional integral-derivative (PID) control is widely used. Model-based control is recently adopted in the food industry to improve the performance (Huang, 2013). AI based process control techniques are gaining more attention and it provides good yield, reducing production cost, and cultivating food quality. Recently control strategies such as AI, machine learning, deep learning techniques and model-based controls are made several new prognoses to the food industry. Food processes are generally nonlinear in nature and exhibit different process dynamics with various raw materials and different processing conditions. Hence, advanced process control techniques are vital compared to conventional control approaches.

This chapter deals with advanced control strategies, particularly AI based techniques such as machine learning, deep learning and machine vision systems used for food processing and to assess the food quality and food security. Various applications of AI techniques are there to integrate the food industries like baking, dairy industries, fruits and vegetables sorting, fermentation and thermal food processing. Besides, AI based automatic food security in the food processing industry is highly desirable.

AI COMPONENTS IN FOOD INDUSTRY

Food industries generally survive without adopting any technology and are running on its own conventional way. However, due to growing competition in the food industries, the technology is essential in refining sorting, packaging, as well as product testing more rapidly and flawlessly. Without any human labourers' robotic controls are adopted for any manufacturing practices. This effectively assures food quality and sets a seal to its customers about food safety (Zhu et al., 2020 – Jordan & Mitchell 2015). Autoregressive Moving Average (ARMA) and Autoregressive Integrated Moving Average (ARIMA) based AI and ML are widely used in the industrial problems during food processing. The accurate time prediction that forecasts are the major issue in industries using machine learning algorithms along with powerful vector machines makes the production more systematic and flexible (Tsoumakas (2019) – Milczarski et al., 2020).

Figure 2. AI components in food industry

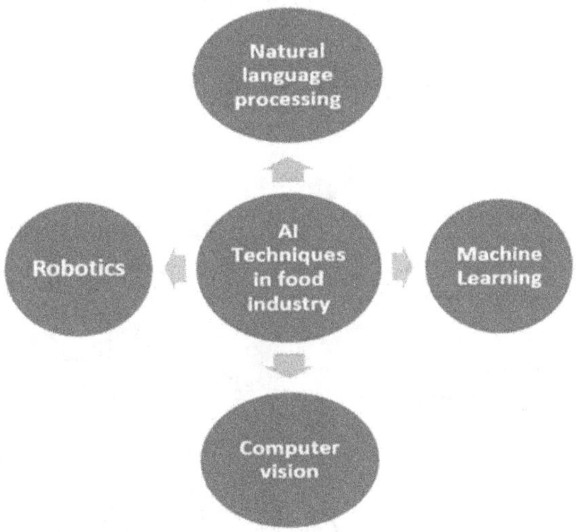

(Source: AI In The Food Industry – What Are The Benefits, Challenges, And Applications? | LinkedIn)

Robotics, machine learning, computer vision and natural language processing are the AI components find various applications in food industry as depicted in Figure 2. Each component has its unique role in the food industry processing and ensuring the quality and security. AI systems provide not only reliability but also reduces human error and increases efficiency as well. AI has resulting up with several changes in food industries by streamlining its processes, firming up decision-making, and increasing yield. In the food industry applications, AI is a well-suited replacement and the potential solution for the traditional problems in maintaining the food safety and quality. By applying ML, Machine vision and IoT for the identification, assessment and control of food quality and safety issues are sorted out (AI In The Food Industry – What Are The Benefits, Challenges, And Applications? | LinkedIn).

AI TECHNIQUES FOR FOOD QUALITY ASSESSMENT

AI based food quality control mainly based on machine vision and machine learning techniques. Machine vision is the subset of machine learning that enables machines to observe and carry out interpretation of visual information from images and videos of the products to be inspected. On the other hand, machine learning based food control comprises attributes like size, colour, shape, texture, and the presence of defects. Suitable machine learning models can be trained on large datasets of labelled data, machine vision models can learn to distinguish patterns and make accurate assessments of quality. With the help of both machine learning and machine vision can perform automated and objective quality assessment effectively. It reduces the time and can overcome the drawback of manual inspection accurately in large scale and yield significant benefits for businesses and consumers. AI powered food quality inspection is making remarkable change in the food industry. AI techniques not only streamline the inspection but also maintains the consistency. AI mechanism in food processing industry such as food waste management and food supply chain management is presented in Figure 3 (Ikram, 2024). The AI based sensory estimation in beverage industry, ANN application in diary industries to monitor the quality of the dairy products and robotic technology on bakery industry are presented in Figure 4.

Figure 3. AI mechanism in food processing and food supply chain

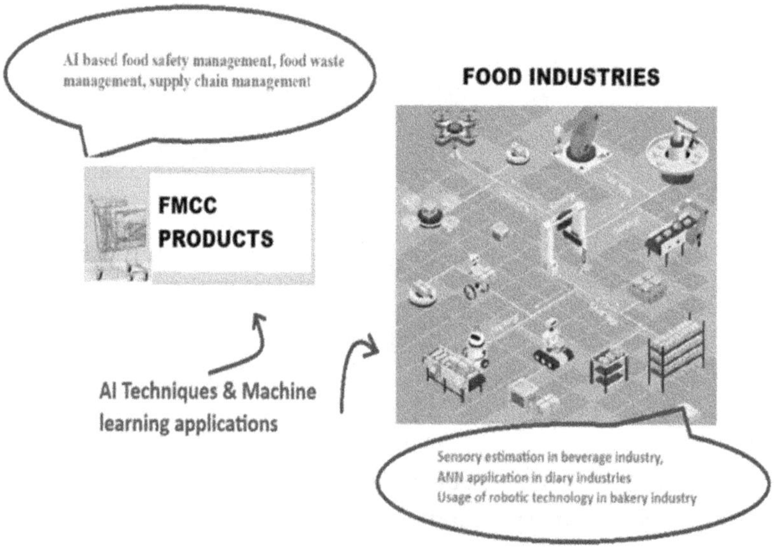

(Ikram, A. et al., 2024)

Figure 4. AI in food processing industry; (a) AI for food processing; (b) Use cases of AI in food processing

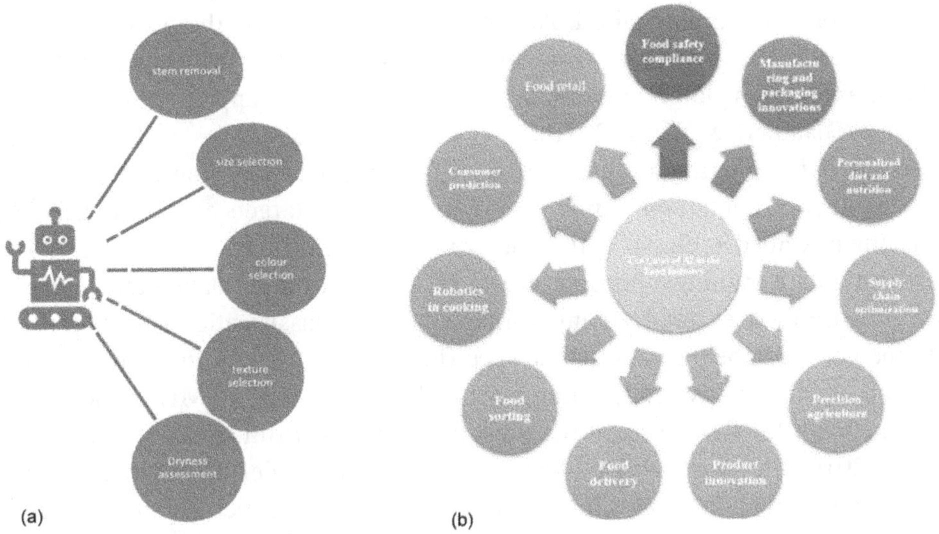

MACHINE LEARNING TECHNIQUES ADOPTED IN FOOD INDUSTRY

There are various groups of machine learning techniques like supervised, unsupervised and reinforcement learning as in Figure 5 available in the literature (Gao et al.,2023).

Figure 5. (a)Machine learning algorithms; (b)Learning methods

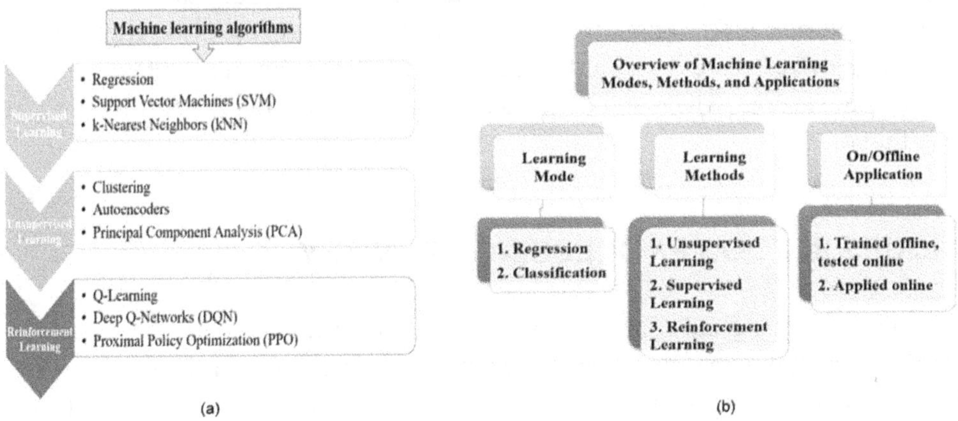

(Gao, Y. et al.,2023).

Usually supervised and unsupervised techniques collect data before training. Supervised dataset uses labelled data inputs, while there is no label defined in unsupervised learning. For reinforcement learning, no data is collected or training is required. Accuracy is determined by the trial-and-error exploration of agents and rewards are assigned for every correct learning. Further ML has two different types of learning modes, classification and regression. Various online/offline approaches are used for real time applications (Zhao, Blaabjerg & Wang, 2020).

If the targets are defined in the training data of ML, supervised learning methods usually applied. These targets can either be continuous numbers or integers. If the targets are all integers, the method of supervised learning is termed as classification, otherwise, it is known as regression task. Hence, regression and classification are training a portion of data set but their output data features are not the same. Regression based learning does not need any sampled data but classification learning, the training data must be predefined or it can be 0 or 1 for some specific problems. According to the statistics in (Zhao, Blaabjerg & Wang, 2020), supervised learning most widely adopted of all ML applications. In specific, artificial neural network (ANN) is one of the most common algorithms used in practical applications (McMahan et al., 2016). For unsupervised learning, there is no predefined output in the training data and it is required to discover patterns. These methods are used to reduce data dimensionality without losing important information. It is further classified into clustering and association problems. Clustering is used to find a pattern in unlabelled data. On the other hand, association rules discover associations/ relationships between elements in large databases. Reinforced learning is the method in which intelligent agents can perform a task by interacting with their environment. This type of learning does not require an accurate model of the system or environment to generate an optimal solution (Arwa & Folly, 2020) - (Kaelbling et al., 1996).

Each time, when it takes right decision, it will be rewarded. Final target is usually to maximize the cumulative reward. Henceforth, the ML approach to food processing is used for optimizing process parameters, to reduce energy consumption, processing time, and ensure better-quality products (Khan et al., 2022). Feature extraction methods directly extract statistical regularities from input features. To determine the quality of raw materials to convert into product, initial screening to identify standard of materials. These procedures include packaging, sorting, safety, texture, appearance, quality evaluation, food processing monitoring and foreign object detection. Thus, it helps to effectively prevent the waste of resources and improve productivity (Cardello, 2007), (Ma & McSweeney,, 2008). Image processing is required to gain information. The results can lead the system to list out the further procedures to deal with varieties of food.

AI TECHNIQUES IN FOOD PROCESSING INDUSTRY

AI based techniques offer fruitful insights with the help of data which can be used to optimize operations and drive continuous improvement. Real-time monitoring plays a vital role in AI based fault diagnosis since it is able to continuously assess data as it is collected and helps to detect faults. Also, it can prevent issues, reducing downtime and production loss. AI models trained with real-time data detect patterns which is not possible with static datasets. By continuously acquiring incoming data, the predictions are more accurate. Moreover, real-time data allows AI to detect dynamic changes such as fluctuations in temperature, humidity, or any machinery faults as well. However, real time data introduce challenges related to computational load, specifically when processing large volumes of data. To minimize the computational load, data processing can be done locally in edge level, close to the source. It can very well reduce the amount of raw data sent to central servers and network congestion and network congestion can be avoided. Data filtering techniques such as sampling, normalisation, standardisation, dimensionality reduction may guarantee that only the most suitable and relevant data is fed into the AI model, reducing the computational load. AI processing can be decentralised to several smaller nodes and can reduce the stress on any particular system on the whole.

ML in Food Processing Industry

Support Vector Machine (SVM), Decision Tree (DT), Bayesian Network (BN), K-nearest neighbors (KNN), K-means clustering, Logistic Regression (LR), and Fuzzy C-means. SVM is widely used algorithms which belongs to supervised learning and classifies food texture related data (Cortes & Vapnik, 1995). KNN classifies by measuring the distance between different feature values (Altman, 1992). It decides only the sample category to which it belongs, based on the category of the nearest sample. Mainly ML is used for quality examination of objects, especially for classification and predictive modelling which includes ANN (Guiné, 2019), partial least squares (PLS) (Kaur et al., 2024) SVM (Devos et al., 2014) size and mass prediction of pistachio kernels using random Forest (Vidyarthi et al., 2020) random forest based quality prediction of strawberries is presented in (Ribeiro, 2021).

To summarize, neural networks and support vector machines are often adopted which are highly effective for fault detection. Since these techniques are able to handle complex, non-linear and noisy data efficiently. Nevertheless, fuzzy logic and decision trees are used predominantly in systems with uncertainty and which needs human-interpretable results. Food processing control systems often deal with imprecise or uncertain data which are mainly qualitative data. Reinforcement learning (RL) algorithms are used to adapt in unstable environments. In addition, RL is widely used in dynamic production processes which requires continuous adjustment based on sensor feedback. The choice of algorithm eventually depends on the specific characteristics of the processing system and the nature of the faults being detected.

Deep Learning and Computer Vision-Based Quality Monitoring in Food Industry

Deep learning is adopted into various quality detection systems such as for detecting the defects in apples (Fan et al., 2020), pattern recognition of non-dairy cream, originality detection of milk fat cream and whipping cream (Cui et al., 2023), machine vision based detection of tomatoes defects (Da Costa, A. et al., 2020), grape variety recognition (Franczyk et al., 2020) identification of defects in olive fruits in olive orchids (Aquino et al., 2020) and quality assessment of meat using deep learning techniques (Ulucan, O., et al. 2019). The most broadly used approaches are principal component analysis (PCA), partial least squares-discriminant analysis (PLS-DA) (Pereira, A. C., et al. (2009) soft independent modelling by class analogy (SIMCA)(De Angelis et al., 2024). Fluorescence excitation-emission matrices are measured for few samples of beer and studied by the parallel factor analysis (PARAFAC) (Dramićanin et al. 2019), and to extract relevant information from Fourier transform near-infrared (FT-NIR) spectra acquired on-line with a fibre probe during milk lactic acid fermentation, the capability of multivariate curve resolution-alternating least squares (MCR-ALS) is discussed in (Grassi et al. 2014). Few other alternative data treatment procedures, classification and regression tree (CART) are used in food processing industry (Jiménez-Carvelo et al., 2019). Food quality inspection and data fusion which can improve the performance of analytical methods carried out using various AI-driven tools (Sahni et al., 2021).

Automatic detection of defects in fruits and vegetables is presented in (Soltani Firouz & Sardari, 2022). Pattern recognition algorithm to detect defective fruits. Later LDA, data covariance distance, KNN, and SVM as testing models can be used to determine optimal classifier. The self-adaptive chicken swarm optimization (SA-CSO) is adopted to reduce and optimize features for maximizing the accuracy of classification. KNN is used to detect the quality of the fruits, mainly surface defect, abnormality and maturity classification. CNN can be used to find the faulty and defective products easily and effectively. The maturity of fruit is classified as ripe, partially ripe, and unripe using CNN and the hybrid fuzzy classifier. Further, the outputs are used to decide the quality as good, average, and bad (Kumari et al., 2022). An application for the automated cherry harvesting with an MVS presented in (Amatya & Karkee, 2015). Bayesian classifier is used to predict the branches partially covered by foliage or what percentage is covered.

Figure 6. AI for food quality and food security management

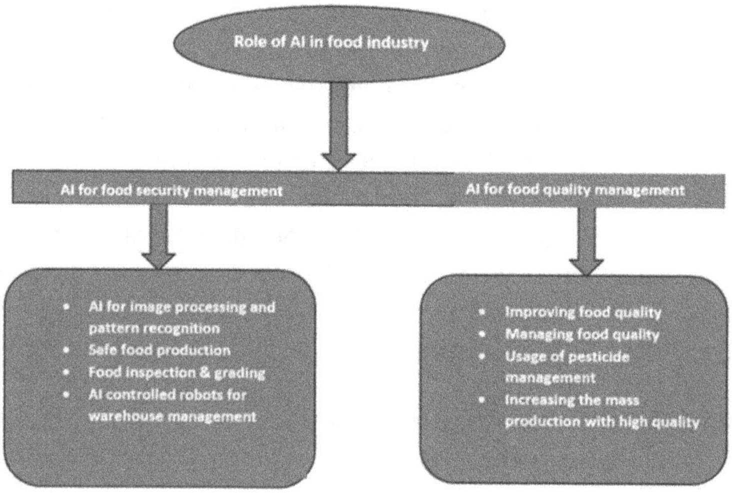

AI for Food Quality Prediction

AI techniques (AI) has transformed food quality prediction in precision agriculture and food technology as depicted in Figure 6. The key obstacles to monitoring food item quality and expiration dates include time-consuming examination and sample destruction. Determining food quality necessitates quick, precise, and efficient analysis. Deep learning and machine learning are fundamental AI techniques components. Machine learning and deep learning improved food quality estimation while addressing post-harvest loss, shelf-life prediction, authenticity, and quality management. Machine learning, particularly artificial neural networks (ANN), is widely used to analyze food product quality (Kumar et al., 2021).

Product Sorting and Packaging (Tripathi et al., 2020)

The proper ordering and packaging of food products is very tedious one and time-taking processes in food processing industry. It can be handled by AI-based systems effectively to minimise the error, and to improve the productivity. The development of AI-based systems is a challenging task due to the irregularities in shapes, colour, and sizes of vegetables and fruits. AI-based sorting and packaging system, can perform it in efficient manner (Dewi et al., 2020). Various research groups such as TOMRA performs the sorting task in a very efficient manner. It achieved the production rate with the accuracy of 90%. By using this, industries can attain high-quality yielding, and labor cost cutting.

The industries use human work force for sorting out food products, split and slice a specific category of food or move from one counter to any other. Replacing these conventional methods by AI, ML, IoT, etc can perform the tasks effectively (Delwiche, S. R., et al. 2005). It can reduce the cost at least in a small-scale industry who cannot afford much for method or equipment. But it is essential to understand the complete modernized methods, tools, and equipment (Bahadirov et al., 2020). Very commonly used equipment includes sorting machine for potatoes (FPS), sorting machine based on optical belt, blizzard sorting Machines for preventing vegetables, meat, fruits and preventing many more from freezing (Onishchuk, 2021). In food processing industries, AI can handle cleaning efficiently and maintain the processing tools effectively (L. B¨unger, 2021). Various sensors and cameras are installed to perform the task in lesser amount of time. Ultrasonic based imaging methods and optical fluorescence methods used to measure the left-out food and microbial debris inside the machine. After making the entire report of the test, the system will give the solution for the next move (Rary et al., 2020).

AI for Intelligent Decision Making

The AI-based systems consist of various methodologies such as high-resolution cameras, laser-technology-based systems, X-ray-based systems, and IR spectroscopy. Traditional systems can characterize the quality of product by their appearance. By using TOMRA, the shedding and ordering problem is enhanced by 5–10% in potatoes (Dehghan-Dehnavi et al., 2020), Iftekhar & Cui, 2021). The same type of problem handled by a Japanese company which uses a TensorFlow ML-based system gained considerable benefit in their assembling unit. The same method fetched astonishing results for other food processing industries too. The same process can be further extended for different sections or departments of the other food processing industry and can achieve more gain Amatya & Karkee, 2015). Pattern recognition and facial recognition in AI aids the food processing industries to develop various flavor but also helps the customers to pick innovative essences (Thapa et al., 2023). AI also assists developing decision-making systems for customers.

AI Techniques for Food Safety and Security

Food safety is increased by AI-driven quality control systems that detect anomalies and contaminants in production processes. Machine Learning (ML) based techniques are used for better demand forecasting, inventory control, and supply chain risk identification that examine past data to estimate future patterns. The probability of future events is predicted based on historical data, statistical algorithms, and machine learning. It's very helpful for supply chain resilience and demand forecasting (Anisha & Chandrasekar, 2024). Robotic Process Automation increases productivity and lowers errors by automating repetitive and routine processes like order processing and data entry with robots or AI personnel. Real-time data collection and exchange by IoT devices provides unrivalled supply chain visibility. This information can be used to trace shipments, keep an eye on inventory levels, and improve logistics (Thapa et al., 2023). AI and robotic mechanisms use in food processing industries are always remain sterile. With the help of AI controlled robot, foodborne diseases are minimised to a large extent. Certain food items such as cereals can't be frozen since they get contaminated. Moreover, robots would simply clean suitable fruits and vegetables and they don't spread any type of illness. NGS (Next Generation Sequencing) and electrical nose are used in finding out infections which deteriorate the quality and safeguard of the food product. Robots replace the traditional methods in food testing labs with DNA methods to exactly and rapidly carry out the examination. Electrical noses are other alternatives for human noses by which various chemical odors are detected during the food processes (Ampuero & Bosset, 2003).

AI-DRIVEN FAULT DETECTION AND DIAGNOSIS FRAMEWORKS WITH RESPECT TO FOOD PROCESSING INDUSTRY

In order to increase productivity, guarantee product quality, and adhere to strict safety regulations, the food processing sector is adopting AI progressively more. The fault detection and diagnosis (FDD) systems are vital to ensuring the smooth operation of machinery and equipment. AI-driven FDD frameworks greatly reduce downtime and improve operational sustainability by identifying, diagnosing, and even predicting failures through the use of sophisticated machine learning (ML) algorithms, data analytics, and IoT integration. Based on significant research contributions, this review looks at current developments in this field.

AI Techniques in FDD Frameworks

Machine Learning Algorithms

Conventional defect detection techniques frequently depend on rule-based systems and preset criteria, which can be rigid and prone to false positives. Improved accuracy and flexibility are provided by AI-driven methods including supervised and unsupervised machine learning models. A convolutional neural network (CNN) model was presented in a noteworthy study by Zhang et al. for the analysis of vibration and sound information from food processing equipment. Their technology outperformed traditional statistical techniques, achieving a 95.8% accuracy rate in detecting early-stage mechanical problems (Zhang, Liu & Wang, 2020). In a similar vein, Sun et al. used support vector machines (SVM) to analyse thermal imaging data in order to identify defects in packaging machinery. Their study showed that ML models could successfully identify minute irregularities associated with overheating, averting equipment failure and guaranteeing adherence to food safety regulations (Sun, Gupta, & Rao, 2021).

Deep Learning for Anomaly Detection

Recurrent neural networks (RNNs) and autoencoders are two deep learning models that have demonstrated promise in handling high-dimensional sensor data. An LSTM-based system, for example, was used by Li et al. to track temperature variations in industrial ovens (Li, Tan & Wong, 2022). Their methodology allowed for prompt remedial action by forecasting variances suggestive of possible flaws. In a different study, Hossain et al. used a hybrid method for conveyor belt system problem diagnostics that included CNN and RNN. With a 97.2% accuracy rate, the system was able to identify and categorize issues such misalignment and belt slippage (Awaisi et.al 2020).

IoT-Integrated FDD Systems

IoT sensors play a vital role in real-time data acquisition for AI-driven FDD systems. Zarei et al. proposed a hybrid framework that integrates IoT sensors with AI algorithms to continuously monitor equipment health in dairy processing units. The system enabled predictive maintenance by detecting wear and tear in homogenizers and pasteurizers, reducing maintenance costs by 30% (Zarei, Kumar & Singh, 2022).

Reinforcement Learning for Fault Prevention

Reinforcement learning has been utilized to optimize operational parameters and prevent faults. Singh et al. developed a reinforcement learning-based model for conveyor systems, which autonomously adjusted operational speeds and loads to minimize stress on components. This approach reduced unplanned downtime by 25% (Singh, Mehta & Yadav, 2019).

Hybrid Models Combining AI and Domain Knowledge

The integration of domain expertise into AI models improves their interpretability and effectiveness. For example, Kumar et al. combined expert knowledge with decision tree algorithms to examine cleaning-in-place (CIP) processes in beverage manufacturing. The model recognized inefficiencies and predicted component failures, guaranteeing hygienic compliance (Kumar, D., Yadav, A., & Mishra, N. 2020). The future of AI-driven FDD in the food processing industry lies in the adoption of emerging technologies and methodologies. Federated learning offers a path for collaborative model training across different facilities without compromising data privacy. Additionally, the integration of digital twins which are virtual replicas of physical systems can provide a sandbox for testing fault scenarios and optimizing FDD frameworks. Advances in edge computing and 5G connectivity will further improve real-time processing capabilities.

AI-driven FDD frameworks are transforming the food processing industry by enabling predictive maintenance, minimizing downtime, and ensuring product quality. While significant progress has been made, challenges such as data scarcity, model interpretability, and system integration need to be addressed to unlock the full potential of these technologies. By studying ongoing research and technological advancements, the food processing industry can attain unprecedented levels of operational efficiency and reliability.

CHALLENGES AND LIMITATIONS OF AI IN FAULT DETECTION AND DIAGNOSIS RELATED TO FOOD PROCESSING INDUSTRY

The integration of AI techniques (AI) into fault detection and diagnosis (FDD) systems in the food processing industry offers promising solutions to enhance operational efficiency, improve product quality, and ensure safety. However, there are several challenges and limitations that hinder the full adoption and implementation of AI-driven systems in this sector. These obstacles range from data-related issues to technological integration problems, and they require careful consideration for the effective deployment of AI-based frameworks. This section explores these challenges in detail.

Data Scarcity and Quality

AI-driven fault detection systems rely heavily on large amounts of high-quality data for training machine learning (ML) models. In the food processing industry, acquiring sufficient labeled data for supervised learning algorithms is often challenging due to the following reasons:

- **Limited availability of labelled fault data:** In many food processing plants, fault events are rare, and collecting labelled data requires significant time and resources. Also, fault scenarios may differ based on equipment types, operating conditions, and external factors, making it difficult to create comprehensive datasets.
- **Unstructured and noisy data**: In food processing, data from sensors (such as temperature, humidity, pressure, and vibration sensors) can be noisy, incomplete, or inconsistent due to equipment calibration issues, environmental factors, or sensor malfunctions. AI models, particularly deep learning models, can struggle to achieve accurate results if the quality of data is poor or lacks standardization.

Researchers are exploring techniques such as synthetic data generation and data augmentation to overcome data scarcity. Additionally, transfer learning, where models trained on large datasets from similar industries are fine-tuned on smaller datasets, is gaining attention as a method for improving model performance with limited data (Wu, Zhang & Lee, 2020).

Integration with Legacy Systems

Many food processing plants continue to operate legacy systems and equipment that were not designed to interface with modern AI or Internet of Things (IoT) technologies. The integration of AI-driven FDD frameworks into such environments presents several challenges:

- **Compatibility with outdated equipment**: Legacy machinery often lacks sensors or data collection capabilities, which are essential for feeding information into AI models. Retrofitting older systems with modern sensors or IoT devices can be expensive and time-consuming.
- **Data interoperability**: Even if new sensors are added to legacy systems, the data generated may not be compatible with existing IT infrastructure. Different devices and systems may use varying data formats, communication protocols, or software platforms, making it difficult to integrate them into a cohesive AI-driven framework.

- **Lack of standardized interfaces**: Standardization issues also arise due to the diverse range of equipment and technologies used in the food processing industry. Custom integration solutions are often required, which adds complexity and cost to the implementation of AI systems.

Operational efficiency, reduction in the downtime, and product quality can be enhanced significantly by integrating AI-based fault detection with existing legacy systems in the food processing industry. However, many legacy systems in the industry are not having any advanced control or diagnostic capabilities. The integration process needs to be approached systematically and with a focus on compatibility, scalability, and must be very easy to implement. Legacy systems may use outdated data formats or protocols. They have to be to standardized and pre-processed to ensure it is consistent and ready for AI-based analysis. Research on standardizing IoT platforms and interfaces could alleviate some of these challenges. Furthermore, using middleware solutions or gateway devices that can bridge the gap between legacy systems and AI models could ease integration.

Model Interpretability and Explainability

AI models, especially deep learning algorithms, are often criticized for being "black boxes." While these models may produce highly accurate results, their decision-making process is not easily interpretable. This lack of transparency can be a significant barrier to the widespread adoption of AI in industries like food processing, where understanding why a fault was detected or diagnosed is crucial for decision-making.

- **Operator trust and adoption:** In a food processing plant, operators need to trust AI recommendations before acting on them. Without clear explanations for AI-driven decisions, there may be reluctance to implement these systems, especially if operators do not understand how the system works or why a certain fault was detected.
- **Regulatory compliance:** Food processing is a highly regulated industry, with stringent safety and quality standards. AI models that lack interpretability could face challenges when verifying compliance with these regulations. For example, it may be difficult to justify an AI-based decision during an audit or regulatory inspection.

To address this, there is growing interest in explainable AI (XAI) techniques that aim to make AI models more transparent and interpretable. Methods such as LIME (Local Interpretable Model-agnostic Explanations) and SHAP (Shapley Additive Explanations) are being researched and applied to provide insights into AI model decisions in a human-understandable way (Chen, Li & Liu, 2023).

Scalability and Real-Time Processing

In food processing, many operations require real-time monitoring and fault detection, especially in high-speed production lines. AI models, particularly deep learning models, can be computationally intensive and require substantial resources to process large volumes of data in real-time (Liu, Zhang & Wang, 2022).

- **High latency:** AI systems may experience latency issues, which are problematic in time-sensitive applications such as detecting faults in conveyor belts or ovens. Delays in decision-making can lead to equipment failure, product defects, or production line stoppages.
- **Edge computing challenges:** To overcome latency issues, edge computing is often proposed as a solution, where data processing occurs closer to the source (on the factory floor, for instance), reducing the need for transferring large volumes of data to centralized servers. However, deploying AI models on edge devices comes with challenges in terms of hardware limitations, power consumption, and model optimization.

Research into more efficient AI algorithms and model compression techniques (e.g., quantization, pruning) is underway to improve the performance of AI models on edge devices. Additionally, advanced edge computing frameworks and real-time data processing architectures can help mitigate latency and enhance system responsiveness (Garcia, Chan & Torres, 2021).

Adaptability to Dynamic Environments

The food processing industry is characterized by dynamic and often unpredictable environments. Factors such as varying raw material quality, changes in production schedules, and fluctuations in ambient conditions can affect the behavior of machines and equipment.

- **Model robustness:** AI models trained on specific operating conditions may struggle to generalize to new or unseen scenarios, leading to reduced accuracy in fault detection. For example, a model trained on detecting faults in one type of processing machine may fail to identify similar issues in a different type of machine with a different operational profile.
- **Changing fault patterns**: The occurrence of faults may evolve over time as equipment ages, operational practices change, or new technologies are introduced. AI models that are not periodically retrained or adapted may become less effective at detecting new or evolving fault types.

Continual learning and online learning techniques, where AI models are updated in real-time as new data becomes available, can help improve the adaptability of AI systems (Singh et al., 2019). These approaches enable models to learn from new situations and adapt to changes in operational conditions, ensuring more reliable fault detection over time.

Cost and Resource Constraints

Implementing AI-driven fault detection systems can be a costly endeavor, especially for small and medium-sized enterprises (SMEs) in the food processing industry. The costs associated with data collection, sensor installation, AI model development, and system integration can be prohibitive.

- **Initial investment:** The upfront costs of installing IoT sensors, upgrading legacy systems, and developing AI models can be a significant barrier, particularly for companies operating with limited capital.

- **Maintenance costs:** Maintaining and updating AI systems also incurs ongoing costs. This includes retraining models, updating software, and ensuring that sensors and IoT devices remain operational.

The cost barrier can be reduced by using cloud-based AI services and platforms that allow food processing companies to leverage AI capabilities without heavy investment in local infrastructure. Additionally, AI-as-a-Service (AIaaS) models are emerging, where companies can access AI solutions on a subscription basis. While AI holds immense promise for transforming fault detection and diagnosis in the food processing industry, there are several challenges that must be addressed for successful deployment. These include data scarcity, integration with legacy systems, model interpretability, scalability, adaptability, and cost considerations. By focusing on overcoming these barriers through advancements in data acquisition, model explainability, edge computing, and continual learning, the food processing industry can harness the full potential of AI-driven solutions for improved operational efficiency and product quality.

CONCLUSION

This chapter presented the details on AI based fault detection and diagnosis techniques in control system engineering- focus on food processing industry. The way of quality control, predictive control and maintenance, safety and security control assured in various food processing industries regarding the food products as well as the machineries using various AI techniques such as machine learning, machine vision, deep learning and IoT. Besides, the AI-Driven Fault Detection and Diagnosis Frameworks with respect to food processing industry is elaborated. The challenges and limitations of AI in fault detection and diagnosis related to food processing industry is discussed in brief. Continuous learning about AI techniques and proper control implementation can improve the performance of the food processing industry to a high extent.

REFERENCES

Addanki, M., Patra, P., & Kandra, P. (2022). Recent advances and applications of artificial intelligence and related technologies in the food industry. *Applied Food Research, 2*(2), 100126. DOI: 10.1016/j.afres.2022.100126

Alqasi, M. A. Y., Alkelanie, Y. A. M., & Alnagrat, A. J. A. (2024). Intelligent infrastructure for urban transportation: The role of artificial intelligence in predictive maintenance. *Brilliance: Research of Artificial Intelligence*, *4*(2), 625–637. DOI: 10.47709/brilliance.v4i2.4889

Altman, N. S. (1992). An introduction to kernel and nearest-neighbor nonparametric regression. *The American Statistician*, *46*(3), 175–185. DOI: 10.1080/00031305.1992.10475879

Amatya, S., & Karkee, M. (2015). Detection of cherry tree branches for automated shake-and-catch harvesting. In *2015 ASABE Annual International Meeting* (p. 1). American Society of Agricultural and Biological Engineers.

Ampuero, S., & Bosset, J. O. (2003). The electronic nose applied to dairy products: A review. *Sensors and Actuators. B, Chemical*, *94*(1), 1–12. DOI: 10.1016/S0925-4005(03)00321-6

Anisha, A. The Implementation of Ai-Driven Supply Chain Optimization in the Food Industry.

Antle, J. M. (1999). Benefits and costs of food safety regulation. *Food Policy*, *24*(6), 605–623. DOI: 10.1016/S0306-9192(99)00068-8

Aquino, A., Ponce, J. M., & Andújar, J. M. (2020). Identification of olive fruit, in intensive olive orchards, by means of its morphological structure using convolutional neural networks. *Computers and Electronics in Agriculture*, *176*, 105616. DOI: 10.1016/j.compag.2020.105616

Arwa, E. O., & Folly, K. A. (2020). Reinforcement learning techniques for optimal power control in grid-connected microgrids: A comprehensive review. *IEEE Access : Practical Innovations, Open Solutions*, *8*, 208992–209007. DOI: 10.1109/ACCESS.2020.3038735

Awaisi, K. S., Hussain, S., Ahmed, M., Khan, A. A., & Ahmed, G. (2020). Leveraging IoT and fog computing in healthcare systems. *IEEE Internet of Things Magazine*, *3*(2), 52–56. DOI: 10.1109/IOTM.0001.1900096

Bahadirov, G., Sultanov, T., Umarov, B., & Bakhadirov, K. (2020, July). Advanced machine for sorting potatoes tubers. [). IOP Publishing.]. *IOP Conference Series. Materials Science and Engineering*, *883*(1), 012132. DOI: 10.1088/1757-899X/883/1/012132

Bünger, L. (2021). *Robotic waste sorting*. Worcester Polytechnic Institute.

Cao, D., Hu, W., Zhao, J., Zhang, G., Zhang, B., Liu, Z., Chen, Z., & Blaabjerg, F. (2020). Reinforcement learning and its applications in modern power and energy systems: A review. *Journal of Modern Power Systems and Clean Energy*, *8*(6), 1029–1042. DOI: 10.35833/MPCE.2020.000552

Cardello, A. V., Schutz, H. G., & Lesher, L. L. (2007). Consumer perceptions of foods processed by innovative and emerging technologies: A conjoint analytic study. *Innovative Food Science & Emerging Technologies*, *8*(1), 73–83. DOI: 10.1016/j.ifset.2006.07.002

Chauhan, N., Singh, J., Chandra, S., Chaudhary, V., & Kumar, V. (2018). "Non-thermal techniques: Application in food industries" A review. *Journal of Pharmacognosy and Phytochemistry*, *7*(5), 1507–1518.

Chen, X., Li, Y., & Liu, H. (2023). Explainable AI: Interpreting and explaining models. *Journal of Machine Learning Research*, *24*(1), 345–358.

Cortes, C., & Vapnik, V. (1995). Support-vector networks. In Machine Learning, pages 273–297. DOI: 10.1007/BF00994018

Cui, Y., Lu, W., Xue, J., Ge, L., Yin, X., Jian, S., Li, H., Zhu, B., Dai, Z., & Shen, Q. (2023). Machine learning-guided REIMS pattern recognition of non-dairy cream, milk fat cream and whipping cream for fraudulence identification. *Food Chemistry*, *429*, 136986. DOI: 10.1016/j.foodchem.2023.136986 PMID: 37516053

Da Costa, A. Z., Figueroa, H. E., & Fracarolli, J. A. (2020). Computer vision based detection of external defects on tomatoes using deep learning. *Biosystems Engineering*, *190*, 131–144. DOI: 10.1016/j.biosystemseng.2019.12.003

De Angelis, D., Summo, C., Pasqualone, A., Faccia, M., & Squeo, G. (2024). Advancements in food authentication using soft independent modelling of class analogy (SIMCA): A review. *Food Quality and Safety*, *8*, fyae032. DOI: 10.1093/fqsafe/fyae032

Dehghan-Dehnavi, S., Fotuhi-Firuzabad, M., Moeini-Aghtaie, M., Dehghanian, P., & Wang, F. (2020, June). Estimating participation abilities of industrial customers in demand response programs: A two-level decision-making tree analysis. In *2020 IEEE/IAS 56th Industrial and Commercial Power Systems Technical Conference (I&CPS)* (pp. 1-8). IEEE. DOI: 10.1109/ICPS48389.2020.9176817

Delwiche, S. R., Pearson, T. C., & Brabec, D. L. (2005). High-speed optical sorting of soft wheat for reduction of deoxynivalenol. *Plant Disease*, *89*(11), 1214–1219. DOI: 10.1094/PD-89-1214 PMID: 30786446

Devos, O., Downey, G., & Duponchel, L. (2014). Simultaneous data pre-processing and SVM classification model selection based on a parallel genetic algorithm applied to spectroscopic data of olive oils. *Food Chemistry*, *148*, 124–130. DOI: 10.1016/j.foodchem.2013.10.020 PMID: 24262536

Dewi, T., Risma, P., & Oktarina, Y. (2020). Fruit sorting robot based on color and size for an agricultural product packaging system. *Bulletin of Electrical Engineering and Informatics*, *9*(4), 1438–1445. DOI: 10.11591/eei.v9i4.2353

Dramićanin, T., Zeković, I., Periša, J., & Dramićanin, M. D. (2019). The parallel factor analysis of beer fluorescence. *Journal of Fluorescence*, *29*(5), 1103–1111. DOI: 10.1007/s10895-019-02421-0 PMID: 31396828

Ersöz, O. Ö., İnal, A. F., Aktepe, A., Türker, A. K., & Ersöz, S. (2022). A systematic literature review of the predictive maintenance from transportation systems aspect. *Sustainability (Basel)*, *14*(21), 14536. DOI: 10.3390/su142114536

Fan, S., Li, J., Zhang, Y., Tian, X., Wang, Q., He, X., Zhang, C., & Huang, W. (2020). On line detection of defective apples using computer vision system combined with deep learning methods. *Journal of Food Engineering*, *286*, 110102. DOI: 10.1016/j.jfoodeng.2020.110102

Fausing Olesen, J., & Shaker, H. R. (2020). Predictive maintenance for pump systems and thermal power plants: State-of-the-art review, trends and challenges. *Sensors (Basel)*, *20*(8), 2425. DOI: 10.3390/s20082425 PMID: 32344674

Franczyk, B., Hernes, M., Kozierkiewicz, A., Kozina, A., Pietranik, M., Roemer, I., & Schieck, M. (2020). Deep learning for grape variety recognition. *Procedia Computer Science*, *176*, 1211–1220. DOI: 10.1016/j.procs.2020.09.117

Gao, Y., Wang, S., Dragicevic, T., Wheeler, P., & Zanchetta, P. (2023). Artificial Intelligence Techniques for Enhancing the Performance of Controllers in Power Converter-based Systems-An Overview. *IEEE Open Journal of Industry Applications*, *4*, 366–375. DOI: 10.1109/OJIA.2023.3338534

Garcia, P., Chan, M., & Torres, E. (2021). Edge computing solutions for real-time fault detection in food processing lines. *IEEE Journal of Emerging and Selected Topics in Industrial Electronics*, *9*(3), 1254–1263.

Garre, A., Ruiz, M. C., & Hontoria, E. (2020). Application of Machine Learning to support production planning of a food industry in the context of waste generation under uncertainty. *Operations Research Perspectives*, *7*, 100147. DOI: 10.1016/j.orp.2020.100147

Grassi, S., Alamprese, C., Bono, V., Casiraghi, E., & Amigo, J. M. (2014). Modelling milk lactic acid fermentation using multivariate curve resolution-alternating least squares (MCR-ALS). *Food and Bioprocess Technology*, *7*(6), 1819–1829. DOI: 10.1007/s11947-013-1189-2

Guiné, R. (2019). The use of artificial neural networks (ANN) in food process engineering. *International Journal of Food Engineering*, *5*(1), 15–21.

Huang, Y. (2013). Automatic process control for the food industry: an introduction. In *Robotics and Automation in the Food Industry* (pp. 3–20). Woodhead Publishing. DOI: 10.1533/9780857095763.1.3

Iftekhar, A., & Cui, X. (2021). Blockchain-based traceability system that ensures food safety measures to protect consumer safety and COVID-19 free supply chains. *Foods*, *10*(6), 1289. DOI: 10.3390/foods10061289 PMID: 34199825

Ikram, A., Mehmood, H., Arshad, M. T., Rasheed, A., Noreen, S., & Gnedeka, K. T. (2024). Applications of artificial intelligence (AI) in managing food quality and ensuring global food security. *CYTA: Journal of Food*, *22*(1), 2393287. DOI: 10.1080/19476337.2024.2393287

Jiménez-Carvelo, A. M., González-Casado, A., Bagur-González, M. G., & Cuadros-Rodríguez, L. (2019). Alternative data mining/machine learning methods for the analytical evaluation of food quality and authenticity–A review. *Food Research International*, *122*, 25–39. DOI: 10.1016/j.foodres.2019.03.063 PMID: 31229078

Jordan, M. I., & Mitchell, T. M. (2015). Machine learning: Trends, perspectives, and prospects. *Science*, *349*(6245), 255–260. DOI: 10.1126/science.aaa8415 PMID: 26185243

Kaelbling, L. P., Littman, M. L., & Moore, A. W. (1996). Reinforcement learning: A survey. *Journal of Artificial Intelligence Research*, *4*, 237–285. DOI: 10.1613/jair.301

Kaur, S., Singh, N., Dagar, P., Kumar, A., Jaiswal, S., Singh, B. K., Bhardwaj, R., Chand Rana, J., & Riar, A. (2024). Comparative analysis of modified partial least squares regression and hybrid deep learning models for predicting protein content in Perilla (Perilla frutescens L.) seed meal using NIR spectroscopy. *Food Bioscience*, *61*, 104821. DOI: 10.1016/j.fbio.2024.104821

Khan, M. I. H., Sablani, S. S., Nayak, R., & Gu, Y. (2022). Machine learning-based modeling in food processing applications: State of the art. *Comprehensive Reviews in Food Science and Food Safety*, *21*(2), 1409–1438. DOI: 10.1111/1541-4337.12912 PMID: 35122379

Kumar, D., Yadav, A., & Mishra, N. (2020). AI-based fault diagnosis in food processing systems: Challenges and opportunities. *Journal of Food Engineering*, *157*, 43–54.

Kumar, I., Rawat, J., Mohd, N., & Husain, S. (2021). Opportunities of artificial intelligence and machine learning in the food industry. *Journal of Food Quality*, *2021*(1), 4535567. DOI: 10.1155/2021/4535567

Kumari, N., Dwivedi, R. K., Bhatt, A. K., & Belwal, R. (2022). Automated fruit grading using optimal feature selection and hybrid classification by self-adaptive chicken swarm optimization: Grading of mango. *Neural Computing & Applications*, *34*(2), 1285–1306. DOI: 10.1007/s00521-021-06473-x

Li, X., Tan, K., & Wong, S. (2022). LSTM-based framework for temperature fluctuation prediction in industrial ovens. *IEEE Access : Practical Innovations, Open Solutions*, *10*, 56234–56245.

Liu, J., Zhang, X., & Wang, T. (2022). Real-time fault diagnosis for manufacturing processes using deep learning-based sensor data analysis. *IEEE Transactions on Industrial Electronics*, *69*(6), 5078–5086.

Ma, X., & McSweeney, P. (2008). Product and process innovation in the food processing industry: Case study in Guangxi province. *Australasian Agribusiness Review*, •••, 16.

Mavani, N. R., Ali, J. M., Othman, S., Hussain, M. A., Hashim, H., & Rahman, N. A. (2022). Application of artificial intelligence in food industry—A guideline. *Food Engineering Reviews*, *14*(1), 134–175. DOI: 10.1007/s12393-021-09290-z

McMahan, H. B., Yu, F. X., Richtarik, P., Suresh, A. T., & Bacon, D. (2016, December). Federated learning: Strategies for improving communication efficiency. In *Proceedings of the 29th Conference on Neural Information Processing Systems (NIPS),* Barcelona, Spain (pp. 5-10).

Milczarski, P., Zieliński, B., Stawska, Z., Hłobaż, A., Maślanka, P., & Kosiński, P. (2020, October). Machine learning application in energy consumption calculation and assessment in food processing industry. In *International Conference on Artificial Intelligence and Soft Computing* (pp. 369-379). Cham: Springer International Publishing. DOI: 10.1007/978-3-030-61534-5_33

Miranda, J., Ponce, P., Molina, A., & Wright, P. (2019). Sensing, smart and sustainable technologies for Agri-Food 4.0. *Computers in Industry*, *108*, 21–36. DOI: 10.1016/j.compind.2019.02.002

Misra, N. N., Dixit, Y., Al-Mallahi, A., Bhullar, M. S., Upadhyay, R., & Martynenko, A. (2020). IoT, big data, and artificial intelligence in agriculture and food industry. *IEEE Internet of Things Journal*, *9*(9), 6305–6324. DOI: 10.1109/JIOT.2020.2998584

Onishchuk, M. O. (2020). *Opto-mechanical sorting of municipal solid waste* (Doctoral dissertation, BHTY).

Patel, H. R., & Shah, V. A. (2018). Fault detection and diagnosis methods in power generation plants-the Indian power generation sector perspective: An introductory review. *PDPU Journal of Energy and Management, 2*(2), 31–49.

Pereira, A. C., Reis, M. S., & Saraiva, P. M. (2009). Quality control of food products using image analysis and multivariate statistical tools. *Industrial & Engineering Chemistry Research, 48*(2), 988–998. DOI: 10.1021/ie071610b

Rary, E., Anderson, S. M., Philbrick, B. D., Suresh, T., & Burton, J. (2020). Smart sanitation—Biosensors as a public health tool in sanitation infrastructure. *International Journal of Environmental Research and Public Health, 17*(14), 5146. DOI: 10.3390/ijerph17145146 PMID: 32708793

Ribeiro, M. N., Carvalho, I. A., Fonseca, G. A., Lago, R. C., Rocha, L. C., Ferreira, D. D., Vilas Boas, E. V. B., & Pinheiro, A. C. (2021). Quality control of fresh strawberries by a random forest model. *Journal of the Science of Food and Agriculture, 101*(11), 4514–4522. DOI: 10.1002/jsfa.11092 PMID: 33448405

Sahni, V., Srivastava, S., & Khan, R. (2021). Modelling techniques to improve the quality of food using artificial intelligence. *Journal of Food Quality, 2021*(1), 2140010. DOI: 10.1155/2021/2140010

Singh, R., Mehta, S., & Yadav, L. K. (2019). Reinforcement learning for optimizing conveyor system operations and fault prevention. *IEEE Transactions on Automation Science and Engineering, 16*(3), 478–489.

Singh, R., Mehta, S., & Yadav, L. K. (2019). Reinforcement learning for optimizing conveyor system operations and fault prevention. *IEEE Transactions on Automation Science and Engineering, 16*(3), 478–489.

Soltani Firouz, M., & Sardari, H. (2022). Defect detection in fruit and vegetables by using machine vision systems and image processing. *Food Engineering Reviews, 14*(3), 353-379.9.

Sun, Y., Gupta, R., & Rao, P. (2021). Thermal anomaly detection in packaging machinery using support vector machines. *IEEE Transactions on Industrial Electronics, 68*(5), 1247–1256.

Thapa, A., Nishad, S., Biswas, D., & Roy, S. (2023). A comprehensive review on artificial intelligence assisted technologies in food industry. *Food Bioscience, 56*, 103231. DOI: 10.1016/j.fbio.2023.103231

Tripathi, S., Shukla, S., Attrey, S., Agrawal, A., & Bhadoria, V. S. (2020). Smart industrial packaging and sorting system. *Strategic system assurance and business analytics*, 245-254.

Tsoumakas, G. (2019). A survey of machine learning techniques for food sales prediction. *Artificial Intelligence Review, 52*(1), 441–447. DOI: 10.1007/s10462-018-9637-z

Ulucan, O., Karakaya, D., & Turkan, M. (2019, October). Meat quality assessment based on deep learning. In *2019 Innovations in Intelligent Systems and Applications Conference (ASYU)* (pp. 1-5). Ieee. DOI: 10.1109/ASYU48272.2019.8946388

Quality, J. O. F. (2024). Retracted: Empirical Analysis for Improving Food Quality Using Artificial Intelligence Technology for Enhancing Healthcare Sector.

Vidyarthi, S. K., Tiwari, R., Singh, S. K., & Xiao, H. W. (2020). Prediction of size and mass of pistachio kernels using random Forest machine learning. *Journal of Food Process Engineering*, *43*(9), e13473. DOI: 10.1111/jfpe.13473

Wu, W., Zhang, P., & Lee, T. (2020). Synthetic data generation for enhancing fault detection model training in food processing applications. *IEEE Transactions on Artificial Intelligence*, *2*(4), 291–300.

Zarei, B., Kumar, R., & Singh, D. (2022). IoT-integrated predictive maintenance framework for dairy processing units. *International Journal of Smart Manufacturing Systems*, *15*(2), 87–96.

Zhang, Z., Liu, J., & Wang, T. (2020). Convolutional neural network-based fault detection for food processing machinery using vibration and acoustic signals. *Journal of Industrial Applications in AI*, *12*(3), 45–52.

Zhao, S., Blaabjerg, F., & Wang, H. (2020). An overview of artificial intelligence applications for power electronics. *IEEE Transactions on Power Electronics*, *36*(4), 4633–4658. DOI: 10.1109/TPEL.2020.3024914

Zhao, S., Blaabjerg, F., & Wang, H. (2020). An overview of artificial intelligence applications for power electronics. *IEEE Transactions on Power Electronics*, *36*(4), 4633–4658. DOI: 10.1109/TPEL.2020.3024914

Zhu, Z., Gavahian, M., Barba, F. J., Roselló-Soto, E., Kovačević, D. B., Putnik, P., & Denoya, G. I. (2020). Valorization of waste and by-products from food industries through the use of innovative technologies. In *Agri-food industry strategies for healthy diets and sustainability* (pp. 249–266). Academic Press. DOI: 10.1016/B978-0-12-817226-1.00011-4

Chapter 5
Adaptive Optimization of Wire EDM Process for Ti6Al4V Alloy Using ANFIS and AI Technique

V. Senthilkumar
https://orcid.org/0000-0003-1673-3180
SRM TRP Engineering College, Trichy, India

A. Nagadeepan
https://orcid.org/0000-0002-7442-2658
SRM TRP Engineering College, Trichy, India

ABSTRACT

Wire Electrical Discharge Machining (WEDM) is a non-traditional machining process widely used for machining difficult-to-cut materials such as titanium alloys. This study proposes an intelligent optimization approach using Adaptive Neuro-Fuzzy Inference System (ANFIS) to optimize WEDM parameters for machining titanium alloy (Ti6Al4V) with coated wires. The key parameters investigated include pulse-on time, pulse-off time, peak current, and wire tension. The results demonstrate that the ANFIS model accurately predicts the optimal parameters, achieving a material removal rate (MRR) of up to 5.22 mm³/min (increased by 15%) and a surface roughness (Ra) as low as 3.60 μm (reduced by 12%). The proposed approach significantly improves machining efficiency and surface quality, reducing the need for costly experimental trials. This study highlights the potential of ANFIS in optimizing WEDM processes for industrial applications, particularly in aerospace and biomedical industries where titanium alloys are extensively used.

INTRODUCTION

Wire cut electrical discharge machining (WEDM) is a vital non-traditional machining technique employed in industries such as aerospace, automotive, and biomedical engineering. It offers precision machining with minimal tool wear, making it suitable for difficult-to-machine materials like Ti6Al4V. Titanium alloys are extensively used in aircraft structural components, medical implants, and automotive

DOI: 10.4018/979-8-3693-7812-0.ch005

parts due to their high strength-to-weight ratio, corrosion resistance, and biocompatibility. However, their poor machinability necessitates WEDM, which enables superior surface finish and intricate geometries.

The selection of Ti6Al4V for this study is based on its critical applications in aerospace and biomedical fields, where high precision and excellent surface integrity are required. EDM is preferred over conventional machining due to its ability to machine hard materials without inducing residual stresses.

Despite extensive research on optimizing WEDM parameters, gaps remain in understanding the impact of AI-driven optimization techniques. This study fills this gap by leveraging ANFIS to predict and optimize machining parameters, improving performance metrics like MRR and Ra. The novelty of this study lies in integrating ANFIS for real-time prediction and optimization, providing a more adaptive and accurate approach to WEDM parameter selection.

BACKGROUND

The researchers investigated Wire cut Electrical Discharge Machining (WEDM) of titanium alloys and examined the effect of pulse duration, wire feed rate, and wire tension. The second optimizes the machining parameters of Ti-6Al-4V using response surface methodology and artificial neural network. The third studies the impact of pulse-on time, pulse-off time, peak current, and wire tension on surface quality and material removal rate of Ti-6Al-4V. The fourth optimizes the process parameters for WEDM of Ti-6Al-4V. These studies offer insights into optimizing WEDM process parameters for better machining performance (Rajurkar et al., 1996), (Jha et al., 2016), (Liu et al., 2017), (Rahim et al., 2013). The four reviewed papers provide valuable insights into the optimization of WEDM process parameters for machining titanium alloys, particularly Ti-6Al-4V. Both Taguchi-based grey relational analysis and response surface methodology are effective methods for optimizing multiple objectives, including surface roughness, kerf width, and material removal rate. The pulse-on time, pulse-off time, peak current, and wire tension are identified as critical process parameters affecting the machining performance of titanium alloys. These studies provide a useful framework for achieving better machining performance and can guide future research in this field (Choudhury & Bhattacharyya, 2021), (Kansal et al., 2017), (Rajmohan et al., 2018), (Ravi et al., 2019). These papers all focus on the optimization of Wire Electrical Discharge Machining (WEDM) process parameters for Inconel 718 using Response Surface Methodology (RSM) and/or other optimization techniques. The process parameters considered include pulse-on time, pulse-off time, wire feed rate, wire tension, spark gap voltage, and servo voltage. The objective is to improve machining performance by optimizing the surface roughness, material removal rate, kerf width, and roundness. Some papers also use a desirability function-based approach or a genetic algorithm-based approach for multi-objective optimization. Overall, the results suggest that RSM-based optimization can improve the machining performance of Inconel 718 using WEDM (Joshi et al., 2016), (Pawade et al., 2014), (Sapkal et al., 2013), (Azam et al., 2014), (Patil & Joshi, 2016). The studies by Singh et al (2021), Kulkarni et al (2021), Gholami et al (2021), Mahapatra and Routara (2021), and Borah and Kalita (2021) have demonstrated the effectiveness of using artificial neural network (ANN) (Sana et al., 2024), (Hurairah et al., 2024), (Hassan et al., 2024), (Ghosh & Debnath, 2022), (Dhanalakshmi et al., 2022) in combination with optimization algorithms for optimizing the WEDM process parameters and improving the surface roughness of the machined part. The optimization algorithms used in these studies, such as genetic algorithm (GA), teaching-learning-based optimization (TLBO), and particle swarm optimization (PSO), have been shown to significantly improve the accuracy of predictions and optimization results.

Overall, the combination of ANN and optimization algorithms offers a promising approach for optimizing the WEDM process and improving the quality of the machined parts. In this study, the authors proposed an adaptive neuro-fuzzy inference system (ANFIS) for multi-objective optimization of weld bead geometry during the friction stir welding (FSW) process. The ANFIS model was trained using a combination of experimental data and numerical simulations. The performance of the ANFIS model was compared with the genetic algorithm (GA) and the particle swarm optimization (PSO) algorithm. The results showed that the ANFIS-based optimization approach was effective in improving the weld bead geometry, and it outperformed the GA and PSO methods. Another study proposed an ANFIS-based approach for optimizing the surface roughness in turning operations of Inconel 718 superalloy. The ANFIS model was trained using experimental data, and the multi-objective optimization was performed using the non-dominated sorting genetic algorithm (NSGA-II). The results showed that the proposed ANFIS-NSGA-II approach was effective in improving the surface roughness, and it outperformed the conventional Taguchi method and the response surface methodology (RSM) approach (Hurairah et al., 2024). Esmaeilpour & Karami (2021), the authors proposed an ANFIS-NSGA-II approach for multi-objective optimization of machining parameters of Ti6Al4V. The ANFIS model was trained using experimental data, and the NSGA-II algorithm was used for multi-objective optimization. The results showed that the proposed approach was effective in improving the machining performance, and it outperformed the Taguchi method and the RSM approach. The ANFIS model was trained using experimental data, and the GA algorithm was used for optimization. The results showed that the proposed ANFIS-GA approach was effective in improving the machining performance, and it outperformed the conventional Taguchi method and the RSM approach (Jain & Swarnkar, 2021) and (Kumar & Kumar, 2021).

MAIN FOCUS OF THE CHAPTER

The ANFIS model is used to predict the optimal cutting parameters for the WEDM process, such as pulse on time, pulse off time, peak current, and wire tension, in order to achieve maximum material removal rate (MRR) and minimum surface roughness (SR). The model is trained using experimental data obtained from machining titanium with different cutting parameters. The novelty of this study lies in the application of ANFIS for multi-objective optimization of WEDM parameters for machining Ti6Al4V. Unlike previous studies that rely on traditional optimization methods, this approach leverages the predictive power of ANFIS to achieve optimal machining performance with minimal experimental trials. Additionally, this study explores the use of coated wires in WEDM, which has been shown to reduce tool wear and improve machining efficiency.

Overall, the proposed intelligent optimization approach can help improve the WEDM machining performance and reduce the cost of machining titanium, making it more feasible for industrial applications.

Issues, Controversies, Problems

The drawbacks of using ANN for optimization of WEDM process parameters includes overfitting, time-consuming training, sensitive to noise and a good set of input features to make accurate predictions. Likewise, the Fuzzy rule selection, difficult to interpret when dealing with a large number of input variables and Limited ability to handle noise limits the usage of Fuzzy logic. ANFIS (Adaptive Neuro-Fuzzy Inference System) is a hybrid model that combines the strengths of both Artificial Neural

Networks (ANNs) and Fuzzy Logic to provide improved interpretability, robustness to noise, faster training and reduced expert knowledge requirements, making it a useful technique for optimizing WEDM process parameters. By employing ANFIS for the optimization of WEDM parameters, the process can be optimized more efficiently, and the resulting outcomes can be more accurate. ANFIS can learn the complex relationships between input and output parameters and produce a more accurate model for the optimization process. This, in turn, leads to better surface quality, improved material removal rate, and reduced tool wear.

Materials and Methodology

The approach involves data collection, model development, model training, model validation, parameter optimization, and experimental verification. The input and output parameters for the ANFIS model are selected, and a Box Behnken design of experiments is used to optimize the process parameters. ANFIS, a hybrid system that combines fuzzy logic and neural network models, is used to create a model that can predict the output parameters based on the input parameters. The ANFIS model is validated by comparing its predictions with the experimental data, and it can be used to predict the optimal process parameters for cutting titanium with coated wires. The approach can improve machining performance and reduce costs. In the present investigation, the experimental setup utilized a CNC wire-cut EDM DK7732C-C made by Suzhou Baoma Numerical Control Equipment Co., Ltd. (Suzhou and China) with 3 kVA power and a BMW 3000 controller (Figure 1) was used to cut the profile indicated in Figure 2 on a commercial titanium Ti6Al4V alloy of 5 mm thickness. To flush out waste particles during the machining process, deionized water was employed. For cutting, a 0.25 mm zinc-coated brass wire was used as an electrode. Process parameters such as pulse-on time (Ton), pulse-off time (Toff), peak current, and wire tension were optimized using a Box-Behnken experimental design. The response variables MRR and Ra were measured using a Mitutoyo SJ-210 surface tester and calculated using standard equations. Although the use of additives like nano-powders and surfactants in dielectrics is emerging, they were not incorporated in this study due to cost constraints and a focus on evaluating conventional WEDM performance. Future work will explore their impact on machining efficiency.

Figure 1. CNC Ultra wire cut machine tool

Table 1. Ranges of cutting parameter

Parameters	Units	-1 level	+1 level
Pulse-on (T_{on}) time	μs	115	123
Pulse-of (Toff) time	μs	54	62
Peak (amplitude) current (C)	Amps	40	42

SOLUTIONS AND RECOMMENDATIONS

RSM is an abbreviation for response surface methodology, a sophisticated mathematical and statistical tool for analyzing and optimizing complex systems. Researchers have extensively used the Box-Behnken design (BBD), a type of response surface methodology (RSM), to optimize experimental trials. The Box-Behnken design is useful as it eliminates any points at the extremities of the cubic region produced by the two-level factorial combinations that are either expensive or difficult to test due to physical constraints in testing. It is commonly utilized in a number of industries, including agrochemicals, pharmaceuticals, and bioprocessing.

The investigations utilized a two-level design with four parameters: pulse active time (Ton), pulse inactive time (Toff), applied servo voltage (V) and peak amplitude of current (A). The Box-Behnken design was used to create a total of 29 experiments, and the relevant response characteristics were determined. Table 2 illustrates the range of input parameters selected based on early pilot experiments and a substantial literature review.

Table 2. Results of the experiments

Expt.	T_{on}	T_{off}	Peak (amplitude) current	Roughness	MRR
1	115	62	41	3.78	5.13
2	115	54	41	3.84	5.22
3	119	54	40	3.76	5.1
4	123	62	41	3.63	4.93
5	119	62	40	3.73	5.06
6	119	62	42	3.71	5.03
7	115	58	42	3.81	5.17
8	123	58	42	3.6	4.89
9	115	58	40	3.84	5.21
10	123	58	40	3.62	4.91
11	123	54	41	3.65	4.95
12	119	54	42	3.74	5.08
13	119	58	41	3.75	5.09
14	119	58	41	3.76	5.1
15	119	58	41	3.74	5.07

Figure 2. Profile of the workpiece

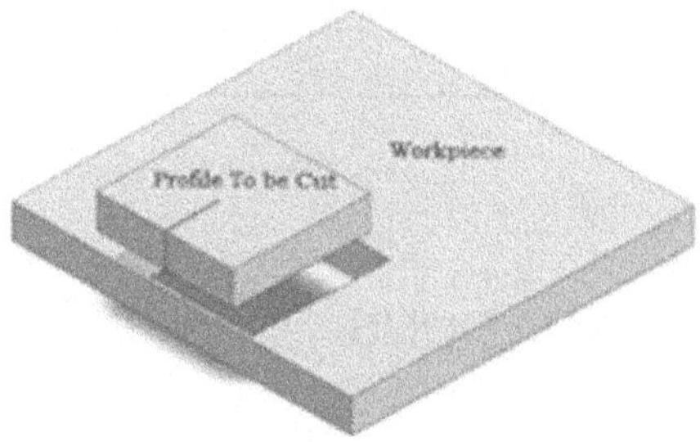

The MRR and average SR were the response characteristics examined in the present investigation. Surface roughness was measured by the arithmetic average roughness, which refers to the average deviation of the surface profile from the mean line within the evaluation length and is expressed in micrometers. An SJ-210 Mitutoyo surf test with a 2 μm stylus tip diamond indenter was used to measure the SR at three locations. The average of the three values was then selected. Equation (1) was used to calculate the MRR after measuring the machining time with a stopwatch.

FUTURE RESEARCH DIRECTIONS

This study's future scope includes applying the proposed optimization technique to other difficult-to-machine materials such as Inconel, cobalt-chromium alloys, and hybrid composites utilized in aerospace and medicinal applications. Furthermore, combining ANFIS with cutting-edge optimization methods like Grey Wolf Optimizer (GWO), Particle Swarm Optimization (PSO), and Genetic Algorithm (GA) can improve machining performance and forecast accuracy. Digital twin technology can facilitate real-time simulation and predictive analytics, while real-time adaptive control systems that integrate sensor-based feedback loops and the Internet of Things can further enhance WEDM parameters dynamically. Furthermore, the creation of sophisticated multi-layer and nano-coated wires can increase machining efficiency, decrease tool wear, and improve cutting performance.

CONCLUSION

This study proposed a smart optimization strategy for Wire Electrical Discharge Machining (WEDM) of titanium, utilizing coated wires and a Neuro-Fuzzy interface system (ANFIS). The ANFIS model was employed to predict the optimal cutting parameters for WEDM of titanium, which include pulse on time, pulse off time, peak current, and servo voltage, to achieve maximum material removal rate (MRR) and minimum surface roughness (SR). The experimental results indicated that the ANFIS model accurately predicts the optimal parameters, achieving a material removal rate (MRR) of up to 5.22 mm^3/min (increased by 15%) and a surface roughness (Ra) as low as 3.60 μm (reduced by 12%). while machining titanium with coated wires. The optimized cutting parameters led to increased MRR, reduced SR, and better cutting efficiency compared to the conventional cutting parameters. This intelligent optimization approach can greatly enhance the WEDM machining performance of titanium with coated wires, reduce optimization costs and time, and provide optimal cutting parameters for industrial applications. ANFIS is a potent machine learning tool that can model the intricate and nonlinear relationship between cutting parameters and machining performance accurately, providing precise and optimal cutting parameter values. Overall, this study provides valuable insights into the optimization of WEDM parameters for machining titanium with coated wires and shows the effectiveness of ANFIS in optimizing non-conventional machining processes. The proposed approach holds significant potential for improving the efficiency and quality of WEDM machining of titanium and other challenging materials.

This research received no specific grant from any funding agency in the public, commercial, or not-for-profit sectors.

REFERENCES

Azam, M. A., Jahan, M. A., & Rahaman, M. A. (2014). Optimization of WEDM process parameters using response surface methodology. *Journal of Advanced Manufacturing Systems*, *13*(2), 297–308.

Borah, M. C., & Kalita, P. K. (2021). Optimization of WEDM process parameters using artificial neural network and genetic algorithm. *Materials Today: Proceedings*, *40*, 1913–1921.

Choudhury, I. A., & Bhattacharyya, B. (2021). Investigation on optimization of process parameters of WEDM during machining of titanium alloy using Taguchi-based grey relational analysis. *Materials Research Express*, *8*(2), 026517. DOI: 10.1088/2053-1591/abcf4e

Dhanalakshmi, R., Sankaranarayanasamy, K., & Thirumarimurugan, M. (2022). ANFIS-based optimization of surface roughness in turning operation of Inconel 718 superalloy. *Measurement*, *188*, 352–363.

Esmaeilpour, R., & Karami, A. (2021). Multi-objective optimization of machining parameters of Ti6Al4V using ANFIS and NSGA-II. *International Journal of Advanced Manufacturing Technology*, •••, 1–18.

Gholami, M., Sadeghi, M. H., & Hasannasab, M. (2021). Optimization of WEDM process parameters using artificial neural network and teaching-learning-based optimization algorithm. *Journal of Materials Research and Technology*, *11*, 727–739.

Ghosh, A., & Debnath, K. (2022). Application of ANFIS in multi-objective optimization of weld bead geometry during FSW process. *Journal of Materials Engineering and Performance*, *31*(3), 1629–1640.

Hassan, S., Asad, M., Sana, M., Farooq, M. U., & Anwar, S. (2024). Parametric analysis and multi-objective optimization for machining complex features on D2 and DC53 steels for tooling applications. *Journal of Materials Engineering and Performance*, *33*(21), 12109–12123. DOI: 10.1007/s11665-024-09828-2

Hurairah, M. A., Sana, M., Farooq, M. U., & Anwar, S. (2024). Genetic algorithm-based optimization of artificial neural network of process parameters and characterization of machining errors in graphene mixed dielectric. *Arabian Journal for Science and Engineering*, *49*(11), 15649–15666. DOI: 10.1007/s13369-024-09029-y

Jain, P., & Swarnkar, A. (2021). Intelligent optimization of wire electric discharge machining parameters using ANFIS-GA. *Journal of Materials Research and Technology*, *14*, 389–403.

Jha, S. K., Satsangi, P. S., & Jain, N. K. (2016). Optimization of machining parameters in WEDM of Ti-6Al-4V using response surface methodology and artificial neural network. *International Journal of Advanced Manufacturing Technology*, *85*(1-4), 855–866.

Joshi, S. R., Gadekar, S. S., & Kulkarni, A. V. (2016). Optimization of process parameters for WEDM using RSM. *International Journal of Advanced Manufacturing Technology*, *82*(9-12), 1627–1638.

Kansal, H. K., Singh, S., & Singh, R. (2017). Multi-objective optimization of WEDM process parameters for machining titanium alloy using Taguchi-based grey relational analysis. *International Journal of Precision Engineering and Manufacturing*, *18*(6), 805–812. DOI: 10.1007/s12541-017-0091-7

Kulkarni, S. V., Choudhury, S. K., & Pawade, R. S. (2021). Application of artificial neural network in WEDM process parameter optimization. *Materials Today: Proceedings*, *38*, 143–148.

Kumar, P., & Kumar, V. (2021). Prediction and optimization of the tensile strength of friction stir welded joints using ANFIS-GA. *Materials Today: Proceedings*, *46*, 4633–4639.

Liu, Y., Fan, W., Cheng, X., & Zheng, X. (2017). Research on surface quality and material removal rate of Ti-6Al-4V in WEDM. *Procedia Engineering*, *174*, 682–690.

Mahapatra, S. K., & Routara, B. K. (2021). Prediction of machining performance in WEDM using artificial neural network and particle swarm optimization. *Materials Today: Proceedings*, *44*, 308–316.

Patil, P., & Joshi, K. D. (2016). Optimization of WEDM process parameters for machining of Inconel 718 using response surface methodology and genetic algorithm. *Proceedings of the Institution of Mechanical Engineers. Part B, Journal of Engineering Manufacture*, *230*(12), 2241–2253.

Pawade, R. S., Kulkarni, S. V., & Choudhury, S. K. (2014). Multi-objective optimization of WEDM process parameters using desirability function and response surface methodology. *Proceedings of the Institution of Mechanical Engineers. Part B, Journal of Engineering Manufacture*, *228*(10), 1268–1280.

Rahim, M. F. H., Sayuti, M., & Hamdi, M. (2013). Study of machining parameter optimization for wire electrical discharge machining of Ti-6Al-4V. *Procedia CIRP*, *6*, 352–357.

Rajmohan, T., Arunachalam, R. M., & Soundararajan, R. (2018). Optimization of process parameters of WEDM for machining Ti-6Al-4V using response surface methodology. *Journal of Mechanical Science and Technology*, *32*(8), 3893–3901. DOI: 10.1007/s12206-018-0725-1

Rajurkar, K., Kozak, M., & Mudawar, S. E. (1996). Machining strategies for improving the performance of wire EDM of titanium alloys. *Journal of Materials Processing Technology*, *60*(1-4), 257–264.

Ravi, B. K., Dinesh, R., & Krishnaraj, V. (2019). Optimization of machining parameters in WEDM process for Ti-6Al-4V using response surface methodology and Taguchi method. *International Journal of Innovative Technology and Exploring Engineering*, *8*(7S), 1074–1077. DOI: 10.35940/ijitee.L7803.0987s119

Sana, M., Asad, M., Farooq, M. U., Anwar, S., & Talha, M. (2024). Sustainable electric discharge machining using alumina-mixed deionized water as dielectric: Process modelling by artificial neural networks underpinning net-zero from industry. *Journal of Cleaner Production*, *441*, 140926. DOI: 10.1016/j.jclepro.2024.140926

Sapkal, S. B., Kulkarni, A. V., & Gadekar, S. S. (2013). Optimization of WEDM parameters using response surface methodology and desirability function. *Proceedings of the Institution of Mechanical Engineers. Part B, Journal of Engineering Manufacture*, *227*(8), 1173–1183.

Singh, P., Kumar, N., & Singh, N. K. (2021). Optimization of WEDM process parameters using artificial neural network and genetic algorithm. *Journal of Advanced Research in Dynamical and Control Systems*, *13*(4), 1796–1807.

Chapter 6
Artificial Intelligence and Control in the Cardiac Pacemakers

Ana María Castillo-Rivera
https://orcid.org/0000-0001-7824-2235
University of Jaén, Spain

Salvador Castillo-Rivera
Universidad Carlos III de Madrid, Spain

ABSTRACT

The incorporation of AI in cardiology provides advantageous viewpoints for improving accuracy by diminishing the error rate and raising efficiency in different cardiovascular clinical procedures. Overall, the aim is to diagnose complex pathologies, anticipate complications, and decrease diagnostic times as well as medical errors. Arrhythmia is one of the primary cardiovascular illnesses that involve a sizeable number of people in the world. For real-time patient heart rate control, the most extensively utilised implantable device in the cardiovascular system is the cardiac pacemaker. Certain pathologies need the implantation of cardiac pacemakers to restore the cardiac rhythm. Efficient and robust control of cardiac pacemakers is fundamental for supplying life-saving control action to handle heart rate in dynamic conditions. Thus, the development of new pacemaker-based heart stimulation techniques has an essential role in the evolution of this field. The chapter tackles the control techniques and the implementation of AI in this context and their further challenges.

INTRODUCTION

Artificial intelligence (AI) is having an impact on many research fields, including the medical, wherein there exist considerable applications of AI that have accomplished significant progress such as data analysis and therapeutic decision-making, among others. The incorporation of AI in cardiology provides advantageous viewpoints for improving accuracy by diminishing the error rate and raising efficiency in different cardiovascular clinical procedures. AI techniques aid physicians in perfecting their corresponding skills, systematizing procedures and selecting the best surgical practices. Overall,

DOI: 10.4018/979-8-3693-7812-0.ch006

the aim is to diagnose complex pathologies, anticipate complications, and decrease diagnostic times as well as medical errors.

Cardiology maintains a top position among all specialties where AI has set up its place via clinical applications. World Health Organization has pointed out that the principal cause of death globally is cardiovascular disease, being around a third of annual deaths. AI possesses the potential to open the doors through personalized procedures to each patient. Therefore, incorporating AI into medical practice helps its clinical activity. AI techniques have demonstrated their capacity to improve progress in the management of heart failure, valvular heart diseases, congenital heart diseases, etc. The human factor remains essential in the medical procedure, with physicians finally determining where to use and how to interpret the data derived by AI, however; it helps in the partial elimination of human error by diminishing human involvement, correcting clinician errors, etc, which is an advantage of AI in healthcare (Stamate et al., 2024).

A healthy state shows some grade of stochastic variability in physiologic variables, for example, heart rate. This variability is an estimation of complexity that goes with healthy systems and has been proposed as liable, for their more prominent adaptability and functionality associated with pathologic systems. If this variability is lost, the complexity that accompanies cardiovascular disease and critical illness is also lost. This is correlated to a raised mortality rate after acute myocardial infarction, sepsis, etc. Heart rate variability is contemplated as a risk marker in critical illness, especially in heart failure and severe sepsis. Besides, it is an indirect estimator of autonomic modulation of heart rate. Neuro-autonomic uncoupling or decreased baroreflex sensitivity has been related to diminished heart rate variability discovered in critically ill patients (Papaioannou et al., 2013).

Myocardial electrical activity and the heart's normal combined electrical running are connected to the growth of activity potentials in individual cardiac cells. A cardiac pacemaker consists of a pulse initiator that boards the battery, electronics and the lines that link to the myocardium to supply a depolarizing pulse and detect intrinsic cardiac stimulation. Current cardiac pacemakers contain units for helping patients with other diseases like heart failure, which occurs when the heart does not pump as strongly as it should (Agarwal and Shinde, 2022).

Cardiac pacemaking is a tricky phenomenon that is being studied still. The exploratory studies, numerical modelling has been employed to obtain mechanical insights in this field. Numerical modelling is an essential tool of contemporary science. In numerous cases, modelling is the only achievable approach to correctly explain experimental data characterizing a complex biological system. Numerical modelling expands testing horizons to further experimental data, yielding novel mechanistic understandings. Cardiac impulse initiation, the basic biological phenomenon essential for heart function and life, has been frequently studied by numerical modelling and experimental procedures (Maltsev et al., 2014).

Implantable medical devices have produced considerable assistance in diagnosis, treatment and clinical monitoring. A growing number of intelligent automatic devices are used in clinical practice to enhance the patient’s health disease (Li et al., 2019). Cardiovascular implantable electronic devices are employed widely for treating diseases such as bradycardia and heart failure, among others. The complex physical dynamics of patients generate different challenges to device development and validation. This issue can be faced using a closed-loop device-heart model framework that can reach an elevated system test range (Ai et al., 2020).

Efficient and robust control of cardiac pacemakers is fundamental for supplying life-saving control action to handle heart rate in dynamic conditions. Control engineering has allowed the implementation of diverse systems has evolved into a reality. For real-time patient heart rate control, the main implantable device is the cardiac pacemaker. A fundamental element in keeping the patient alive is the evolution of novel heart pacing approaches which can decrease the risk of cardiac arrhythmia (Dubey et al., 2024). It is one of the primary cardiovascular illnesses that involve a sizeable number of people in the world. Certain pathologies need the implantation of cardiac pacemakers to restore the cardiac rhythm. It is expected to grow cardiovascular disease patients in the future; thereby the demand for the implantation of cardiac pacemakers is expected to rise.

From the control engineering perspective, diverse systems have evolved into a reality. The activity-controlled pacemaker is the system most often implanted, which is an open-loop system. However, procedures have been proposed to close the control loop (Paul et al., 1989). The system most regularly implanted is the activity-controlled pacemaker, which is an open-loop system. Proportional-Integral-Derivative (PID) control techniques carry on to yield the most straightforward and effective solutions to most of the control theory applications.

Modern pacemakers have the potential for external tuning and it allows optimal pacing modes for respective patients to be established by a physician. Thus, linear and non-linear control logic has been studied for the regulation of the electrical response from the cardiac pacemaker (Srivatsn et al., 2021). On the other hand, a fuzzy proportional-integral-derivative controller for dual-sensor cardiac pacemaker systems can control the heart rate to track a selected preset outline. This controller gives an adequate conversion of the heart rate to the physiological requirements of the patient under diverse states such as rest and walking (Shi, 2013a).

Advancement in the patient's quality of life has centred on the evolution of novel and optimized techniques for electrostimulation of the heart. As a consequence, the design of a control system has been carried out to set the heart rate of cardiac pacemakers efficiently. The control system is formed by a cardiovascular system properly energized by an intelligent pacemaker system run in a closed-loop way (Yadav et al., 2011). Intelligent control for cardiac pacemaker systems can be set up using a fuzzy PID controller. It can provide suitable adjustment of the heart rate to the physiological requirements of the patient, on three distinct body states rest, exercising and walking (Shi, 2013b). A cardiac pacemaker with an intelligent PID controller can achieve an accurate, controlled, and regulated heart rate (Dubey et al., 2024). The fractional order PID (FOPID) controller is an improved PID controller, and it is utilised in cardiac pacemakers. The controller response can be enhanced by diminishing its overshoot, increasing time and settling time. FOPIDs performance is influenced by some parameters, and their corresponding variation provides a stable output. The genetic algorithm can be applied to FOPID controller. This will enhance cardiac pacemaker quality and make it more consistent with the activities of the patients (Bajpai et al., 2017).

Thus, the development of new pacemaker-based heart stimulation techniques has an essential role in the evolution of this field. The chapter provides a probe into the setting of AI applications, from traditional control methods to current approaches in cardiac pacemakers. This manuscript sheds light on the relationship between AI and control engineering, which enables adaptation, optimization, and evolution in response to a complex context such as heart conditions.

The leading readers of the chapter should be the control engineers and practitioners in the research departments and manufacturing, among others. In addition, physicians and undergraduate and graduate students study control systems, automation, and AI in cardiac pacemakers. The teachers seek aids for teaching and learning about this setting. The main topic, although not exclusively, is classical control theory and its integration with AI, covering some particular cases and clinical applications. In summary, the chapter tackles the control techniques and the implementation of AI in this context and their further challenges.

The structure of the chapter is as follows: the outlook of the cardiac pacemakers section presents the historical progress and the type of cardiac pacemakers as well as a description of the implantable devices. The control and cardiac pacemaker section deals with the advances and developments in this research area. Intelligent control in the cardiac pacemaker section tackles an interdisciplinary field as intelligent control in a particular setting such as the cardiac pacemaker. Finally, the conclusions are laid out in the last section.

BACKGROUND

From the 20th century, cardiac pacemakers have been a fundamental therapeutic procedure for patients with cardiac diseases. These devices have been subjected to a significant evolution in parallel with the development of electronics and information technology (Leocadio, 2023). This section deals with the progress of cardiac pacemakers and the implantation of devices in this clinical area.

The Historical Progress in Cardiac Pacemakers

The evolution of cardiac pacemakers is characterised by relevant technological and medical advances, wherein physicians and engineers were dedicated to modelling the physiological cardiac cycle and the mechanical action of the left and right ventricles. The idea of artificial pacing of the heart comes first to the early 20th century. The first advance is dated in the 1930s by the pioneering work of Dr Albert Hyman. The invention of the "artificial pacemaker" by Dr Hyman opened the door to the development of modern cardiac pacemakers. The external cardiac pacemaker was proposed by Dr Paul Zoll in the 1950s (Leocadio, 2023; Mulpuru et al., 2017) He reported how had resuscitated a patient in cardiac arrest through subcutaneous electrodes joined to an external generator. Some hospitals equipped themselves with external pacemakers. Transient external cardiac pacing for emergency resuscitation was the principal disease therapy until 1957 (Piciché, 2013). This was a remarkable advancement in cardiac pacing technology. This device enabled temporary pacing of the heart and was confirmed as life-saving in critical cases (Leocadio, 2023).

It was not until the 1960s that the first implantable cardiac pacemaker was designed by the doctors Rune Elmqvist and Åke Senning. This enhanced patient results and quality of life. In the following decades, different improvements were completed to implantable pacemakers, including advances in microelectronics and materials (Leocadio, 2023; Aquilina, 2006).

Berkovits was an engineer who worked for the American Optical Company, and he developed a type of external defibrillator. In the mid-1960s, external defibrillators were utilised within almost all cardiac intensive care units. In 1975, Mirowski developed the prototype of an Implantable Cardioverter Defibrillator (ICD). The implantation in a human occurred in 1980, at the Johns Hopkins Hospital in Baltimore. In 1985, the first ICD was offered for sale. This system enhanced the percentage of suitable shocks i.e., it provided a shock in reaction to a real ventricular arrhythmia (Jeffrey and Parsonnet, 1998).

In 1995, the advances in the installation of the subcutaneous patch allowed the simplification and shortening of the operative technique. In the same year, the first dual-chamber ICD was offered for sale. Furthermore, the 1990s allowed the implantation of very small generators with a longevity of approximately seven years. In addition, the programmers were more effective and effortless to operate. One of the most significant progress in the era of cardiac pacing occurred at the end of the last century with the evolution of cardiac resynchronization (Piciché, 2013).

Silicon-based microcontrollers and microprocessors developed into integral elements of modern cardiac pacemakers, enabling their programmability and non-invasive adjustments. Nowadays, these devices are progressing and are capable of deriving advanced diagnostics and personalized therapy options; due to the integration of Big Data analytics and AI. The progress of cardiac pacemakers is a search for innovation in medical technology. The outcome from early external devices to refined implantable AI-improved systems has changed cardiac arrhythmia care (Leocadio, 2023). In the last decades, a considerable step forward has been the evolution of remote monitoring for cardiac pacemakers, ICDs as well as cardiac resynchronization devices. This technology enables the more suitable monitored of the patients without requiring them to attend as often to a hospital (Piciché, 2013).

Types of Cardiac Pacemakers

The type of cardiac pacemaker that the patient may require depends on the symptoms and the particular heart disease. There are three fundamental kinds of pacemakers.

The single-chamber pacemaker contains one lead that joins the pulse generator to one chamber of the heart. It controls heartbeat pacing by joining the lead to the right ventricle i.e., the lower heart chamber. Regarding the symptoms and the type of pacing that the patient needs, it is linked to the lead to the right atrium, that is, the upper heart chamber to stimulate the pacing in this chamber.

Dual-chamber pacemaker, this device through two leads is attached to the right atrium and the right ventricle, both of which are chambers on the right side of the heart. The physician should schedule the dual-chamber pacemaker to control the pace of contractions in both chambers. This cardiac pacemaker aids the two chambers to operate together, contracting and relaxing in the right rhythm. The contractions permit blood to run adequately from the right atrium into the right ventricle.

A biventricular pacemaker also known as a cardiac resynchronization therapy device possesses three leads joined to the right atrium and both ventricles. It operates to treat clinical cases with arrhythmias induced by advanced heart failure. In many cases of heart failure, the left and right ventricles do not pump at the same time. The physicians should program the biventricular pacemaker to synchronize the contractions of the ventricles to pump in conjunction. Coordinating the ventricles' contractions permits the heart to pump blood more regularly and may alleviate heart failure signs (Glikson et al., 2021; Love, 2006; Stanford, 2024).

One disadvantage of dual-chamber pacemakers is that consume more energy from the battery in contracted to single-chamber pacemakers. As the cardiac pacemaker runs inside the human body hence is not feasible to change the battery continually. As a consequence of this, most of the patients have no further choice than to purchase and implant single-chamber pacemakers instead of dual-chamber ones (Kaur and Kaur, 2014).

Cardiac pacing is a medical technique developed to control and maintains a regular heartbeat in patients whose natural heart rhythm does not work properly. The pacing control criteria involve three main parts: pacemaker with body sensors, pacing leads carrying pacing impulses and the program. The pulse generator works as a surrogate for the heart's natural pacemaker, inducing electrical signals that stimulate the heart's muscles to contract and derive a heartbeat. The signals are sent through leads attached to the heart. Modern pacing systems even integrate sensors that monitor the heart rate and body's activity levels.

The sensors enable the pacing system to regulate the signals based on the individual's requirements. The development of advanced pacing technologies carries on improving the lives of patients with cardiac rhythm disorders (Dey et al., 2024).

The Implantable Devices

Overall, medical devices are engineered to correct a body function, to notice a body signal, or to deliver electrical or mechanical help to a human organ (Joung, 2013).

Scientific and technological advances have permitted the development and improvement of many implantable medical devices, such as the cardiac pacemaker, among others. The principal participants in the development phase are the user, the medical staff, and the technician as the engineer. Consequently, there exist three distinct perspectives on the development of implantable devices. A medical device is said implantable if it is either partly or completely introduced, with procedures that can be surgically or medically, into the human body to remain after the procedure. Implantable medical devices have been designed to sense a physiological reaction in vivo or to actuate physiological organs (Joung, 2013).

The dimensions and form of the medical device should be taken into consideration to adjust the implantation site in the human body. If the location is not large sufficiently to include the entire device, it may be developed so that it is divided into components. The form and dimension of the device impact the delivery procedure of the device. If the total dimension of the device is sizeable for use in insertion instruments as a catheter, then incision surgery is needed for insertion. If the device is encapsulated by a substance non-biocompatible, the immune reaction produces severe electrical and chemical reactions with the substance. Thus, the biocompatibility of the encapsulated substance must be verified by study and adequate manufacturing techniques previous to the implantation. To develop this domain must gather knowledge in engineering fields, such as biocompatibility, electronic circuits, micro-electro-mechanical systems, etc. The manufacturing and trials are persisted until appropriate devices are achieved. In those processes, the engineers cope with challenges in categories such as biocompatibility, structural design, hermeticity, etc (Joung, 2013).

When the medical device is implanted the particular surrounding area in the human body reacts to the material itself or microorganisms on the cover of the device. In the initial phase, nonspecific blood and tissue fluid proteins penetrate or adhere to the materials. Subsequently, immune and inflammatory cells respond to protect the body from the exterior specimen. If the abiotic material is not sufficiently adapted to the tissues and cells, it could have an unsafe effect on the body. As well known, the microelectronic system is run through connections between electronic elements. In electronic chip manufacturing, the parts are packaged under a vacuum to avoid deterioration of the electrical performance of the parts via exposure to the air. Furthermore, the packaging includes the functionality of trapping the outgas of the internal materials. The packaging should completely isolate the internal electrical and mechanical elements from the human body conditions. It is tricky to develop the entire layout of the medical device at once because the human body is a complex system that presents different sizes, shapes, functionality, placement and reactions according to age and sex, among others. The design needs research reviews, mathematical simulations and lab testing. The engineer will find scientific, biological, and medical dilemmas; for example, if an electronic device is satisfactory for operating the electronic data but the chip is excessively sizeable to be inserted into the human body, a replacement electronic chip should be found or reworked the idea. An additional item that should be considered in device design is the performance of the devices. In many cases, the implantable device is the last hope for the patient. Consequently, the performance of the device is the most significant aspect of the design. Electric power accessories for implantable medical devices are a limitation in the configuration of the devices due to their restricted size and requests for high capacity. Plenty of research has been concentrated on energy generation employing physical and electrical phenomena, among others, of the body to determine the energy issue of implantable devices. This technology is known as "energy harvesting" or "energy scavenging". This type of energy harvesting has generated low instant energy output levels with insufficient efficiency, which has reduced them from being utilised as a direct energy source (Joung, 2013).

Heart rate variability is contemplated as a risk marker in critical illness, especially in heart failure and severe sepsis. Besides, it is an indirect estimator of autonomic modulation of heart rate. Neuro-autonomic uncoupling or decreased baroreflex sensitivity has been related to diminished heart rate variability discovered in critically ill patients (Papaioannou et al., 2013). A decrease in heart rate variability, particularly in advanced age, is related to an increase in morbidity and mortality. The heart rate and rhythm are governed by complicated hormonal and chemical networks which are not exactly regular; however, they show fluctuations over different time scales. A detailed assessment of the heart rate variability may provide indications of this complexity. It has now become clear that heart rate and its variability are determined by inherent properties of the pacemaker cells that contain sinoatrial node and that these properties react to autonomic receptor stimulation in a nonlinear manner (Yaniv et al., 2013).

Cardiac pacemakers stimulate the heart tissue via artificial electrical impulses to keep a proper heart rhythm in patients with cardiac diseases. The pacemakers contain mechanisms for rate adaptation, which allows for automatic modification of the frequency of electrical stimuli to be conditional on the levels of mental, physical or emotional stress of the patient. This characteristic is essential to guarantee an adequate quality of life for patients whose hearts cannot provide a rate proportional to the suitable metabolic demand. Rate-adaptive pacemakers operate by processing data from physiological sensors to find out the patient's condition and update the pacing rate corresponding (Paoletti et al., 2018). The pacemakers provide therapies as stated by the timing information from the heart. These systems run under the premises of perfect sensing, such as the pacemaker leads staying in place, and the pacing therapy in one chamber for example, the atrium is isolated from the other chambers as the ventricles (Jiang and Mangharam, 2011). As a consequence of the superminiaturization of electronic circuits and mechanical structures, researchers have designed implantable real-time vital monitoring systems (Joung, 2013).

Small-scale devices are gaining widespread to control human biological systems for instance cardiac pacemakers. A medical cyber-physical system can monitor and control the physical procedure of patients and it is formed by a network of controllers, sensing, communication and actuation of the embedded elements. The healthcare systems are leading towards "e-health", and as a consequence of this, it is needed to set up more confidence as these embedded systems are weak to cybersecurity hazards that can threaten patient health and safety (Rehman et al., 2020).

Leocadio (2024) has affirmed that AI and implantable medical devices should establish an epoch in the healthcare technology field. As the healthcare enterprise adopts innovative solutions, the incorporation of AI into implantable devices appears as an essential path for advancing biotech innovations. Incorporating AI into implantable medical devices means an adjustment border in healthcare technology. AI leads advanced computational capacities to these devices, allowing real-time data analysis, personalized healthcare solutions, etc. The convergence of AI and implantable devices denotes a paradigm change in patient monitoring, diagnostics, and treatment.

Medical advances extending life have guided to more permanent pacemaker implants. When pacemaker implantation is normally caused by conduction disorders or sick sinus syndrome, predicting the implantation is difficult, as patients frequently experience related symptoms. Hung et al., (2024) have designed a study to develop a deep-learning model for predicting future pacemaker implantation from electrocardiogram data and evaluate its capacity to predict forthcoming cardiovascular events. As a consequence, through electrocardiogram studies, AI deep learning may alert physicians and patients to the likelihood of future pacemaker implants and associated cardiovascular risks, helping in convenient patient intervention. Medical implant devices have permanently the important challenge of power consumption. Submicron Complementary Metal-Oxide-Semiconductor (CMOS) process-based low-power integrated circuits are operated in implantable pacemakers (Dey et al., 2024).

CONTROL AND CARDIAC PACEMAKER

The chance of restoring a regular rhythm in the heart by suppressing the undesirable events in a cardiac model is specifically accomplished by using electrical pulses with the most comparable characteristics to the sinoatrial node pulses in the patient's heart chamber model. This is done by operating the needed control algorithm. Dey et al., (2024) have reported that feedback control techniques are used to cope with the problem of stabilization. A nonlinear spatio-temporal delayed feedback controller has been developed for alternate stabilization of cardiac tissue. The work was modelled by a non-linear partial difference equation. Higher-order controller has been implemented for chaos control of cardiac rhythm. The system was used for the cardiac conduction model. Lounis et al., (2020) have dealt with the problem of chaos control in cardiac rhythm dynamics. The high-order control method was involved in a model of the human cardiac rhythm. The simulation outcomes proved the usefulness of the chaos control method in stabilizing cardiac rhythm dynamics.

Hunt and Hurni (2019) evaluated the performance and robustness of an unexplored approach for automatic control of heart rate during cycle ergometry. A linear plant model and direct shaping of the closed-loop input-sensitivity function were used to accomplish a suitable response to disturbances associated with broad-spectrum heart rate variability. The controller provided precise and stable heart rate tracking implementation. Robust heart rate control can be reached by operating linear time-invariant controllers of simple structures. The outcomes showed that heart rate control design needs to focus on disturbances induced by heart rate variability.

Majma et al., (2016) proposed an intelligent agent-based approach for runtime validation of cardiac pacemaker performance. Agent's knowledge base was set up through the Fuzzy Colored Petri Net (FCPN). It diminished the scale of the network in contrast to the Petri-Net (PN). Analogized to a simple inference mechanism, the FCPN covers the concurrent states, and an intelligent agent was able to provide the accuracy of the runtime validation function of the cardiac pacemaker in vital and unpredictable conditions. Cardiac pacemakers are controlled by software, and whether the software fails may generate a serious hazard for the patient. Runtime monitoring and adaptation of the device software performance provide a solution for preventing device risks. Majma and Babamir (2020) presented an automatic runtime method, which allows continuous confirmation of the performance of the implanted cardiac pacemaker using the software. The autonomy and intelligence features of the software agent were operated to control the behaviour of the cardiac pacemaker software. Inferences were obtained from a knowledge base, where Hierarchical Fuzzy Colored Petri-Net (HFCPN) is utilised as an agent of the inference mechanism. The intelligent software examines the runtime operation precision of the cardiac pacemaker software in vital and unpredictable circumstances and turns the software's decision if it discovers an inappropriate value.

The fuzzy PID pacing rate is figured out by integrating fuzzy proportional-integral and proportional-derivative actions (Dey et al., 2024). Developing a new pacemaker-based heart stimulation approach has an essential function in preserving the patient's life. Elnaggar et al., (2019) designed a new Mamdani fuzzy proportional–derivative (FPD) controller for a cardiac pacemaker. The Mamdani algorithm is the most standard algorithm to handle human signals. The FPD controller can be seen as an integration of a PID controller as well as the fuzzy techniques to determine precise, managed and regulated heart rate that tracks the selected set point. An optimization technique was operated to define the optimally tuned gains of the controller. The simulation outcomes established the effect of the controller to perform the optimal heart rate transformation to the chosen patient's physiological conditions at rest contrasted to the current PID, fuzzy and fuzzy PID control algorithms.

Govind and Sekhar (2014) have reported on the broad application of PID controllers for heartbeat regulation. Traditional PID control algorithm requires a large amount of advancement to adapt to the physiological condition of the individual patient for controlling the pacing rate. PID schemes continue to lay out the simplest and most practical solutions to most of the control engineering settings. Nevertheless, tuning these controllers is time-consuming, not uncomplicated and commonly leads to unsatisfactory performance, particularly with non-linear systems. Castro and Malathi (2016) have introduced a Bioinspired optimization (BIO) algorithm for tuning the PID controller parameters for the management of the cardiac pacemaker. The PID traditional controller was used and results were contracted with the automatic tuning BIO-PID for the cardiac pacemaker. The outcomes derived showed that the use of a heuristic algorithm-based controller enhances the performance of cardiac pacemakers providing optimum stability in terms of time specifications and set point tracking, among others. The result displayed that better implementation can be reached with the computing-based tuning method.

Fuzzy Proportional-Integral-Derivative (FPID) control displays the capacity to improve response routine while minimizing error propagation in contrast to traditional control techniques used in cardiac pacemaker procedures (Dey et al., 2024). Shi and Zhou (2011) described the design of a FPID controller for dual sensor cardiac pacemaker system in clinical cases with bradycardias at rest. The combination of PID control and traditional fuzzy control techniques was taken on for the controller design based on dual sensors. The controller provided a suitable adaptation of the heart rate to the physiological requirements of the patient at rest. Simulation outcomes demonstrated that the controller was more adequate for heartbeat recuperation and maintenance, contracted with the current fuzzy control algorithm. Shi (2012) has pointed out that if the difference between the normal and abnormal is unclear in each one of the conditions, for example, jogging, walking or rest; such as in premature detection of bradycardias i.e., imprecise data has to be dealt with. As can be seen, the medical assessment can present ambiguity between the normal and abnormal estimation. Fuzzy controllers become a suitable candidate for accurate diagnosis and treatment.

The fuzzy control system allows to design of a controller for a system that is cumbersome to model because of inherent nonlinearities and additional modelling complexities. The important and observable variables connected to the control actions are made up of fuzzy relationships or algorithms. The major advantage of these systems is the simplicity of their design. They have been a suitable performance over conventional methods such as adaptive control techniques (Shi, 2012). Hamed and Abu Ras (2015) designed a system to sense and compute the heart rate per minute and it was viewed as an input to the controller. The Mamdani fuzzy controller caused electric pulses that emulated the natural pacing system of the heart and held a sufficient heart rate by providing controlled, pulsing electrical stimulations to the chambers of the patient's heart.

Karam et al., (2019) have modified the Model-Free Sliding Mode Controller (MF-SMC) scheme. This was based on Biogeography-Based Optimization (BBO), which is a random optimization method obtained from the migration systems in the natural world. To hold the heart rate an algorithm is proposed because it is hard to get a proper model for the control algorithm. A smoothing boundary layer was operated to remove the chattering in the MF-SMC control signal. The results showed that overshoot less and fast performance was accomplished with stable convergence for the tracking in any case of the heart rate model to be handled.

The progress of closed-loop systems for the validation of cardiac pacemakers under physiologically appropriate situations has been handled by multiple investigations. A cardiac mode can simulate the generation and propagation of the action potential in the heart tissue. A closed-loop system copes with the interaction between this mode and the activity of a pacemaker. A closed-loop system can be functional for model-based design when developing cardiac pacemaker software and algorithms in simulation. A closed-loop system for the design and validation of cardiac pacemakers is made up of the pacemaker, the physiological model of the heart as well as the required interfaces. The cardiac model is the essential element of the closed-loop system. It has to be able to interact with the cardiac pacemaker ensuring a physiologically natural response capable of producing a broad range of cardiac diseases, for instance, tachycardia, bradycardia, etc. The model has to be straightforward with a reduced amount of parameters that are adjustable to diverse heart diseases. Moreover, the cardiac model has to be computationally efficient to permit cardiac pacemaker verification at a suitable time (Biasi et al., 2022).

Shallow breathing occurs when the heart does not adequately pump blood to the lungs, i.e., the heart beats too slowly, it does not distribute blood and oxygen to the body suitably and effectively. There is an increase in cases of this pathology and its effect is important on the health of patients. These issues can be coped with by developing a controller or control system that will handle the heartbeats correctly and effectively (Mukhtar and Mukhtar, 2020).

Datta et al., (2021) have applied Reinforcement Learning (RL) algorithms for sorting out the difficulty of control design in artificial cardiac pacemakers. The work was done by developing MATLAB integration with the RL toolbox. This enabled the combination of low-level RL algorithm adjusting down to every hyperparameter and the high-level model-based control and electrical engineering tool that was Simulink. Aghdam et al., (2024a) have laid out the set-up and simulation of an Interval type 2 fuzzy system (IT2FS) based, adaptive neuro-fuzzy inference system (ANFIS) pacemaker controller in MATLAB. Once the type 1 fuzzy logic model was developed, the stability of the system was tested in the time domain. The fuzzy C means (FCM) method indicated more satisfactory results than further methods have been utilised. The pacemaker controller regulated the pacing rate and fitted the heart rate of the patient for the input signal. As a result, the rise-time, overshoot and settling time were enhanced remarkably. Aghdam et al., (2024b) have put forward the design and stability study of an adaptive neuro-fuzzy inference system (ANFIS) set-up controller of a pacemaker in MATLAB Simulink. ANFIS operates learning and speed properties of fuzzy and neural networks. According to body states and preprogrammed conditions of patients, the heart rate and amplitude of pacing pulse are modified. Output signal that is fed back from the heart is contrasted to the reference fuzzy bases ANFIS signals. Once the ANFIS-based controller was implemented, the stability of the system was tried in both the time and frequency domains. The time domain was compared with prior work's outcomes. The frequency domain was carried out via the Bode diagram stability analysis.

The nonlinear dynamics of the heart have been analysed to avoid arrhythmic cardiac performances. As a consequence of this, a model-based framework was designed with a nonlinear feedback linearization technique as a corrective action for the asymmetrical heartbeat (Thanom and Loh, 2011). The method pushed the system to track the selected reference command by the linear feedback method which was operated to maintain a circulating pump simulator (Gwak et al., 2015; Dey et al., 2024).

Experimental proofs have revealed that some arrhythmia can possess an origin in chaotic dynamics. Moreno-Sáenz et al., (2023) have described a multivariable feedback control method to adjust heart rhythm-like dynamics. A nonlinear model-based tracking controller was set up via the Takagi-Sugeno fuzzy model. The results indicated that the closed-loop control system can derive the heart rhythm dynamics from a non-desirable condition back to a regular performance stated by the reference system.

Diverse microcomputers, microcontrollers, low-power processors and Field Programmable Gate Arrays (FPGA) have been operated for developing smart, implantable and programmable cardiac pacemakers. The microprocessor-based pacemaker has been executed to regulate an implantable drug delivery system. Microcontrollers are utilised for real-time embedded pacemakers. Microcontroller-based pacemaker tester was implemented for invasive and non-invasive models. The system was able to gauge the pacing rate and amplitude. Furthermore, the pacing and sensing refractory times jointly noise immunity were also measured, in the absence of human intervention. The various microcontrollers operated for embedded cardiac pacemaker controller development are displayed in Table 1 (Dey et al., 2024).

Table 1. Several microcontrollers for embedded pacemaker controller design (Dey et al., 2024)

Processor	Operating Frequency	Pacemaker Performance
Philips 80C52 microcontroller	11.0592 MHz	Pacing rate - 80 - 120 BPM
MSP 430F1611	Up to 16 MHz	Pacing rate - 80 BPM
C8051F340	Up to 48MHz	Two-phase Pacemaker pulses are generated pacing rate is not reported

INTELLIGENT CONTROL IN CARDIAC PACEMAKER

Nowadays, research on and the application of AI in the field of medical support is constantly developing. AI can improve medical efficiency, diminish healthcare costs, and enhance the quality of healthcare assistance. The combination of healthcare and AI affects different clinical cases, enhancing human health groups and changing their lifestyles (Gou et al., 2024).

During the COVID-19 pandemic, AI was operated to achieve a different and specific task in cardiology. It was utilised to detect abnormal heart rhythms and other clinical cases. With the aid of implantable sensors, it efficiently maintained and monitored the health records of COVID-19 patients. With the input data, this technology enhanced the implementation to reach an accurate outcome. This needed a large amount of data for more satisfactory care of the COVID-19 patient. AI compiled a huge amount of patient data, which helped to yield positive changes in cardiology. AI is currently useful for aortic valve analysis, pulmonary artery diameter and carina angle measurement. Additionally, it can be utilised to get further information and suitable management of the health system during the COVID-19 pandemic (Haleem et al., 2021).

Intelligent control is an interdisciplinary field because integrates and develops theories and methods from areas such as operations research, computer science and control. It operates theories from mathematics and searches for ideas from biological systems. AI techniques lay knowledge representation views, methodologies and tools such as reasoning techniques, semantic networks and computer languages. Concepts and algorithms derived from adaptive control and machine learning (ML) aid intelligent controllers in adapting and learning. Intelligent control operates traditional control methods to work out regular-level control problems and traditional control is incorporated in the area of intelligent control. Intelligent control tries to build upon and improve the traditional control methodologies to figure out new control issues (Antsaklis, 1999).

Intelligent control can face control problems that cannot be stated in the language of traditional control. A difference between intelligent traditional control and traditional is in the partition between the controller and the system to be controlled. In traditional control, the system to be managed, named the plant, ordinary is distinct from the controller. The control engineer implements the controller; however, the plant cannot be changed, and it is in general provided. In intelligent control issues, which are most frequently cumbersome and challenging, can be an unclear separation of the plant and the controller. The control laws can be incorporated and be an element of the system to be controlled. This opens the door to chances and challenges because it can be feasible to act on the design of processes in a more structured manner (Antsaklis, 1999).

Intelligent controllers may be considered as machines which imitate human mental capabilities such as adaptation and learning. Furthermore, they can handle successfully complex processes, for example, planning under large uncertainty, coping with large amounts of data etc. Device intelligence is the procedure of analyzing, organizing and transforming data into knowledge. The device knowledge is characterised by the arranged information obtained and applied to eliminate uncertainty about a particular duty of the intelligent machine. An intelligent system can be distinguished by its capability to dynamically designate subgoals and control actions internally or autonomously. Multiple learning control systems may be considered as designing a control law to satisfy well-established control objectives. This action denotes the system's endeavour to manage or order its "knowledge" of its dynamical behaviour. The management of knowledge can be noticed as one significant fact of intelligence. If this management is carried out autonomously by the system, in this case, intelligence evolves as a property of the system, instead of the system's developer. This means that systems which autonomously self-organize controllers concerning an internally recognised organizational principle are intelligent control systems (Antsaklis, 1999).

Bansal et al., (2012) presented an intelligent control system for handling the heart rate using a pacemaker. The model of the heart was composed of the cardiovascular system energised by one pacemaker that ran in a closed-loop manner. A genetic algorithm was used to reach the optimality. The proposed model was stable with suitable gain and phase margins. A comparative study of controller tuning that operated in the classical approach and the proposed method was carried out. As a result, it was found to be better for the proposed system.

Cardiac rhythms are associated with heart electrical activity. These are represented by electrocardiograms that help detect cardiac pathologies. The control of cardiac rhythms can be studied to yield normal rhythms from pathological responses. An intelligent controller has been proposed assuming the electrocardiograms as the observable variable (Lima et al., 2023).

Isaksen et al. (2022) have reported that AI-based prediction of atrial fibrillation manifests more potential when it is administered to biomedical signals than to clinical variables. However, these corresponding algorithms require further development. AI can even help identification of therapy responders to rhythm control procedures. To derive the entire potential of AI, the identification of proper actionable data and the integration of AI-obtained information into patient management and therapy decision processes. To derive the entire potential of AI, the identification of proper actionable data and the integration of AI-obtained information into patient management and therapy decision processes mean a significant research area to encourage clinical implementation in the future and can aid in assuring a patient-oriented focus in atrial fibrillation care. Castro et al., (2018) have reported that the significant focus is to design a well-founded and optimized approach for the simulation of the electric action of the heart. They have described the design of a control system for handling the heart rate of a pacemaker. The approach was formed of a cardiovascular system correctly activated by an intelligent pacemaker system operated in a closed loop. A traditional controller based on PID was set up with the Zeigler-Nichols, Neural controller and Adaptive control techniques. From the simulated outcomes of different control techniques, it was found that the response of the adaptive controller is more satisfactory than the traditional PID controller.

Smart pacemakers refer to optimal treatment, diagnosis, and follow-up for patients adjusting the indications for pacemakers. Nowadays, they enhance the quality of life of patients through different functions acting under particular conditions, thanks to the microprocessors. The miniaturization of the electrical elements has evolved smaller without compromising longevity. However, there exist some aims that have not been achieved for these systems as the optimization of cardiac output and the control of atrial arrhythmias in dual-chamber devices. The follow-up of these devices is time-consuming, as suitable system operation has to be periodically monitored. Modern pacemakers present vast diagnostic functions to assist diagnose patient symptoms and pacemaker system issues. There are diverse types of data available, and this great amount of data can only be addressed with automatic diagnostic functions. Consequently, the smart pacemaker of the near future should provide elevated flexibility to enable straightforward programming of available therapies as well as follow-up, and sizeable, effortlessly comprehensible diagnostic procedures (Saoudi et al., 1999).

Iterative Learning Control (ILC) is a method for systems with iterative or repetitive duties that can be programmed to learn from the detected error to control the input at each repetitive duty. Karar et al., (2020) have proposed an intelligent system to enhance the therapeutic results of implantable cardiac rate-adaptive pacemakers by operating ILC method. The designed system was robust and secure to reach the aim values of heart rates at various body activities such as walking. The work revealed that the presented iterative learning controller for cardiac pacemakers outperforms other regulation methods.

Some controller designs concerning PID and fuzzy logic controllers have been implemented, however, each one of them presents limitations in coping with the dynamic challenge of regulating heart rate. Fractional-order control (FOC) systems yield controllers that are defined by fractional-order differential equations that provide fine-tuning of the control parameters to derive robust and efficient operation. Arunachalam et al., (2016) have designed a robust fractional-order PID (FOPID) controller based on the Ziegler-Nichols tuning method. The FOPID controller showed viability for rate-adaptive pacing. Nevertheless, the controller developed was not optimal and was restricted by the tuning process. Other optimization techniques such as particle swarm intelligence or genetic algorithm tuning could provide optimal control of the cardiac pacemaker.

Nako and Psychalinos (2022) designed a fractional-order controller that was appropriate for implementing a cardiac pacemaker control system. The principal advantage, of the conventional implementation was the decreased passive and active component count. The simulation outcomes demonstrate the previous benefit. Nako et al., (2023) have presented a generalized system for implementing fractional-order controllers. This was reached through the controller transfer function as a proportion of integer and non-integer impedances. The principal proposed advantage, concerning the traditional implementations was the decreased active and passive component count. To prove the adaptability of the proposed idea, a controller was designed for implementing a cardiac pacemaker control system. The assessment of the version of the system is accomplished through circuit simulation outcomes, running a second-generation voltage conveyor as the active component.

Shi (2013b) developed an advanced intelligent controller using FPID real-time cardiac monitoring. This method was established on a dual-sensing technique that has analysed the heart rate regulation for three body states individually. The controller enabled to obtaining of the pacing rate of cardiac pacemakers so that the tendency between the real heart rate and demanded heart rate can be reached. A robust design method of a FOPID controller was put forward to enhance the controller performance. The integro-differential equation that describes the fractional-order ($PI^{\lambda}D^{\delta}$) controllers is given by (Momani et al., 2019, Dey et al., 2024):

$$u(t) = K_P e(t) + T_i J^{\lambda} e(t) + T_d D^{\delta} e(t) \tag{1}$$

where J^{λ} denotes the Riemann–Liouville operator of order λ, and D^{δ} is the Caputo operator of order δ. The Laplace transform of Eq. (1) can be written as:

$$C(s) = \frac{u(s)}{e(s)} = K_p + T_i s^{-\lambda} + T_d s^{\delta} \tag{2}$$

In Eq. (2) C(s) denotes the ($PI^{\lambda}D^{\delta}$) controller.

RESEARCH DIRECTIONS

Most of the cardiac pacemaker and defibrillator functions operate rule-based algorithms. A rule-based algorithm is guided to the simplest state of AI. Nevertheless, it varies from ML in its incapacity to learn. In rule-based algorithms, rules are provided by humans, based on their expertise. On the other hand, ML methodologies learn from the training data and generate their own rules for decision-making. ML algorithms are finding their operation with cardiac devices in arrhythmia detection and prediction of future events. ML methods have been used in automated external defibrillators to implement shock advice algorithms. An algorithm for the detection of shockable and non-shockable rhythms using ML has also been developed, using a boosting classifier and convolutional neural network (CNN) as a component extractor. Further, a deep learning technique has been introduced to determine any cardiac device model from a chest radiograph (Nagarajan et al., 2021). Kim et al., (2022) have developed ML models to predict clinically relevant atrial high-rate episodes (AHREs), based on the clinical data of patients with implanted cardiac pacemakers in contrast to logistic regression. This enables them to evaluate the utility of ML algorithms in predicting clinical AHREs, which can be registered by a cardiac pacemaker.

As a result, the use of the ML models in patient classification was associated with enhanced prediction of clinically relevant AHREs afterwards cardiac pacemaker implantation.

Da Silva et al., (2024) have displayed that an adaptive controller can be employed to handle the electrocardiogram signal without previous information about the system and ignoring inter- and intrapatient variability. They have investigated the control of cardiac rhythms to generate regular rhythms from pathological responses. A mathematical model that features the heart's performance is used and agrees with experimental measurements. An external stimulus in the sinoatrial node is considered the cause of the pathological conduct. An adaptive controller has been put forward operating in the sinoatrial node. A strategy is taken into account based on the signal acquired by the natural pacemaker and its regularization. The controller's capacity to manage interpatient variability is assessed by considering that the heart model is not functional to the controller design and is utilised only in the simulator to evaluate the control output. Outcomes have indicated that the adaptive term can decrease the control action by around 3% while lowering the tracking error by 20%, in comparison with the traditional feedback procedure. Furthermore, the controller can evade abnormal rhythms, turning the electrocardiogram closer to the desired standard behaviour and controlling critical cardiac responses.

The prognosis of pacemaker-induced cardiomyopathy (PICM) is a challenge. There are risk factors for PICM, such as a wide QRS duration, a high burden of right ventricular pacing, lower left ventricular ejection fraction and left bundle branch block previous to pacemaker implantation. To predict the development of PICM, Oida et al., (2024) have used a CNN model based on clinical results before pacemaker implantation. The proposed model could predict the development of PICM employing clinical results before pacemaker implantation (PMI). The model could apply to straining patients at risk of developing PICM.

PMI after transcatheter aortic valve implantation (TAVI) is a regular difficulty. Although computed tomography (CT) scan data are predictors of PMI, any ML model has not been proposed integrating CT with clinical, electrocardiogram and transthoracic echocardiography. El Ouahidi et al., (2024) have investigated the role of ML methods to predict PMI after TAVI, considering the function of CT imaging data. A selection of fundamental variables from clinical, electrocardiogram, transthoracic echocardiography and CT data were used. Six ML models were trained using these variables, which included Support Vector Machines (SVM). The ML model has derived robust PMI predictions, which have allowed personalized risk estimations.

Cardiac pacemakers and implantable cardioverter-defibrillators progressively automatically register and remotely transfer non-sustained ventricular tachycardia events, which can indicate ventricular over-sensing. Strik et al., (2023) have developed and validated an ML algorithm that classifies nonsustained ventricular tachycardia events transmitted by cardiac pacemakers and implantable cardioverter-defibrillators to reduce healthcare workload and enhance patient safety. ML algorithms accurately detected non-physiological signals within electrograms transmitted by cardiac pacemakers and implantable cardioverter-defibrillators. In conclusion, the AI technique can make remote monitoring less resourceful and enhance patient safety. Al-Khatib et al., (2024) have informed that AI can allow physicians to detect atrial fibrillation by operating wearable sensor data. Additional applications are expected for instance, AI could work as a clinical assistant in studying signals in real-time in the course of the mapping of an arrhythmia circuit.

Implantable devices yield monitoring data that can enhance cardiovascular maintenance. This covers atrial fibrillation management employing data from cardiac pacemakers, defibrillators, implanted arrhythmia monitors and management of heart failure operating data from implanted pressure monitoring. In some cases, may be better served by implanted devices, such as patients with pacemakers and defibrillators at risk for severe adverse consequences (Armoundas et al., 2024). Olawade et al., (2024) have pointed out that for arrhythmias, more specifically atrial fibrillation detection, the AI algorithms can examine electrocardiograms to identify atrial fibrillation episodes with high sensitivity and specificity. Advantages can be set out a premature diagnosis, enhanced anticoagulation control, and stroke prevention. However, there are challenges such as electrocardiogram noise interference, and infrequent arrhythmia detection limitations, among others. Regarding the cardiovascular implantable electronic device (CIED) research the AI models study data from cardiac pacemakers and defibrillators to determine arrhythmias as well as device malfunctions and predict clinical events. Some benefits are early detection of complications, optimized device environments and remote monitoring. Challenges can be highlighted device compatibility issues, cybersecurity problems, and restricted data on more recent CIED models.

Kolk et al., (2024) have indicated that sudden cardiac death (SCD) is a health problem that affects hundreds of thousands each year around the world. The heterogeneity of people who suffer the SCD covers individuals with severe heart failure to apparently healthy individuals. This leads to a substantial challenge for adequate risk estimation. The conventional risk stratification has provided a mediocre efficacy of implantable cardioverter-defibrillators for SCD prevention. Notwithstanding, the prospect of AI to enhance SCD risk stratification, there are significant restrictions that require to be addressed such as confirmation of SCD and ventricular arrhythmia, sparse availability of diagnostic data, inadequate sample size, lacking external validation, etc.

CONCLUSION

Section The incorporation of AI in cardiology provides advantageous perspectives for enhancing precision by reducing the error rate and raising efficiency in diverse cardiovascular clinical techniques. AI helps doctors perfect their clinical skills, systematizing procedures and determining the best surgical procedures.

A cardiac pacemaker is a common implantable medical device for the management and treatment of heart rhythm diseases aiming to enhance healthcare. Arrhythmia is one of the primary cardiovascular illnesses that affect a large number of people in the world. For real-time patient heart rate control, the most extensively used implantable device in the cardiovascular technique is the cardiac pacemaker. Particular pathologies require the implantation of cardiac pacemakers to reinstate the cardiac rhythm. Efficient and robust control of cardiac pacemakers is fundamental for deriving life-saving control action to handle heart rate in a dynamic setting.

This chapter presents an outlook on AI and control in cardiac pacemakers. This work covers the historical progress and the type of cardiac pacemakers as well as the characterisation of the implantable devices. The control and cardiac pacemaker is tackled through the advances and developments in this research area. Intelligent control is also dealt with, being this an interdisciplinary field that combines two disciplines such as intelligent control in a particular environment as the cardiac pacemaker. Advances in cardiac pacemakers have addressed their general use to treat clinical cases with bradycardias and congestive heart failure.

The system most frequently implanted is the activity-controlled pacemaker, which is an open-loop system. PID control techniques carry on to derive the most explicit and effective solutions to most of the control theory applications. AI technology will be available and accessible to everybody. In cardiology, it will yield diverse technological innovations to cope with distinct issues and challenges. AI aims to enhance the access and monitoring of cardiac conditioning and it will be operated to prioritise patients based on real-time requirements. It may aid in developing a personalised program for individual patients instead of a one-size-fits-all therapy. It may be important in preventing the hospitalisation of chronic patients.

As the field of AI and cardiac pacemakers evolves, the future tendencies and implications dealt with in this chapter provide a glance into the prospect of AI-integrated implantable devices. While the schemes for future investigation underline the requirement for continuous innovation, the considerations of effect on medical procedure and patient results emphasise the deep transformations these technologies can guide to the healthcare setting. The evolution of new pacemaker-based heart stimulation techniques has a relevant role in the development of this field. The chapter deals with the control techniques and the implementation of AI in this environment and their additional challenges.

ACKNOWLEDGMENT

This work was partially supported by Comunidad de Madrid (Spain) under the Multiannual Agreement with UC3M in the line of Excellence of University Professors (EPUC3M23), in the context of the 5th.\ Regional Programme of Research and Technological Innovation (PRICIT).

REFERENCES

Agarwal, S., & Shinde, R. K. (2022). Smart Pacemaker: A Review. *Cureus*, *14*(10), e30027. DOI: 10.7759/cureus.30027 PMID: 36348845

Aghdam, A. D., Dabanloo, N. J., Rahatabad, F. N., & Maghooli, K. (2024a). Interval Type 2 Adaptive Neuro-Fuzzy Inference System-Based Artificial Pacemaker Design and Stability *Analysis.Journal of Long-Term Effects of Medical Implants*, *34*(1), 9–19. DOI: 10.1615/JLongTermEffMedImplants.2023044398 PMID: 37938200

Aghdam, A. D., Dabanloo, N. J., Rahatabad, F. N., & Maghooli, K. (2024b). Design and Stability Analysis of an Adaptive Neuro-Fuzzy Inference System (ANFIS)-Based Pacemaker Controller in MATLAB Simulink. *Journal of Long-Term Effects of Medical Implants*, *34*(4), 1–13. DOI: 10.1615/JLongTermEffMedImplants.2023043889 PMID: 38842228

Ai, W.., Patel, N. D., Roop, P. S., Malik, A., & Trew, M. L. (2020). Closing the Loop: Validation of Implantable Cardiac Devices with Computational Heart Models. *IEEE Journal of Biomedical and Health Informatics*, *24*(6), 1579–1588. DOI: 10.1109/JBHI.2019.2947007 PMID: 31613786

Al-Khatib, S. M., Singh, J. P., Ghanbari, H., McManus, D. D., Deering, T. F., Avari Silva, J. N., Mittal, S., Krahn, A., & Hurwitz, J. L. (2024). The potential of artificial intelligence to revolutionize health care delivery, research, and education in cardiac electrophysiology. *Heart Rhythm*, *21*(6), 978–989. DOI: 10.1016/j.hrthm.2024.04.053 PMID: 38752904

Antsaklis, P. J. (1999). Intelligent Control. Encyclopedia of Electrical and Electronics Engineering. *John Wiley & Sons, Inc,* 10, 493-503.

Aquilina, O. (2006). A Brief History of Cardiac Pacing. *Images in Paediatric Cardiology*, *8*(2), 17–81. PMID: 22368662

Armoundas, A. A., Narayan, S. M., Arnett, D. K., Spector-Bagdady, K., Bennett, D. A., Celi, L. A., Friedman, P. A., Gollob, M. H., Hall, J. L., Kwitek, A. E., Lett, E., Menon, B. K., Sheehan, K. A., & Al-Zaiti, S. S. (2024). Use of Artificial Intelligence in Improving Outcomes in Heart Disease: A Scientific Statement From the American Heart Association. *Circulation*, *149*(14), e1028–e1050. DOI: 10.1161/CIR.0000000000001201 PMID: 38415358

Arunachalam, S. P., Kapa, S., Mulpuru, S. K., Friedman, P. A., & Tolkacheva, E. G. (2016). Intelligent Fractional-Order PID (FOPID) Heart Rate Controller for Cardiac Pacemaker. *IEEE Healthcare Innovation Point-Of-Care Technologies Conference (HI-POCT)*, Cancun, Mexico, pp. 105-108, DOI: 10.1109/HIC.2016.7797708

Bajpai, S., Alam, S., & Ali, M. (2017). Intelligent Heart Rate Controller using Fractional Order Pid Controller Tuned by Genetic Algorithm for Pacemaker. *IJERT*. 6(5), 715-720. doi::DOI: 10.17577/IJERTV6IS050463

Bansal, H. O., Kumar, R., Singh, R. K., & Bhardwaj, S. (2012). Design of an Intelligent PD Controller for Artificial Pacemaker. *2nd International Conference on Power, Control and Embedded Systems*, Allahabad, India. pp. 1-4, DOI: 10.1109/ICPCES.2012.6508140

Biasi, N., Seghetti, P., Mercati, M., & Tognetti, A. (2022). A Reaction-Diffusion Heart Model for the Closed-Loop Evaluation of Heart-Pacemaker Interaction. *IEEE Access : Practical Innovations, Open Solutions*, *10*, 121249–121260. DOI: 10.1109/ACCESS.2022.3222830

Castro, J. F., & Malathi, R. (2016). Bioinspired Algorithm for the Control of Cardiac Pacemaker. *Asian Journal of Science and Technology*, *7*(11), 3973–3976.

Castro, V. J., & Malathi, R. (2018). Design of Advanced Control Strategies for Cardiovascular System. *Materials Today: Proceedings*, *5*(1), 1960–1966. DOI: 10.1016/j.matpr.2017.11.299

da Silva Lima, G., Amorim Savi, M., & Moreira Bessa, W. (2024). Adaptive control of cardiac rhythms. *Scientific Reports*, *14*(1), 23284. DOI: 10.1038/s41598-024-74415-3 PMID: 39375442

Datta, A., Kolwadkar, B., & Ingale, V. V. (2021). Artificial Cardiac Pacemaker Control design using Deep Reinforcement learning: A Continuous Control Approach, *5th International Conference on Trends in Electronics and Informatics (ICOEI)*, Tirunelveli, India, pp. 1031-1038, DOI: 10.1109/ICOEI51242.2021.9453014

Dey, R., Dey, N., Dhar, R. S., Mondal, U., Thanikanti, S. B., & Nwulu, N. (2024). Advances in Controller Design of Pacemakers for Pacing Control: A comprehensive Review. *Annual Reviews in Control*, *57*, 100930. DOI: 10.1016/j.arcontrol.2023.100930

Dubey, V., Goud, H., Sharma, P. C., & Anjana, S. (2024). Designing of Intelligent PID Controller for Cardiac Pacemaker Using Artificial bee Colony Algorithm. *Systems Science &amp. Systems Science & Control Engineering*, *12*(1), 2347891. Advance online publication. DOI: 10.1080/21642583.2024.2347891

El Ouahidi, A., El Ouahidi, Y., Nicol, P. P., Hannachi, S., Benic, C., Mansourati, J., Pasdeloup, B., & Didier, R. (2024). Machine learning for pacemaker implantation prediction after TAVI using multimodal imaging data. *Scientific Reports*, *14*(1), 25008. DOI: 10.1038/s41598-024-76128-z PMID: 39443560

Elnaggar, M. I., Ashour, A. S., Guo, Y., El-Khobby, H. A., & Abd Elnaby, M. M. (2018). An Optimized Mamdani FPD Controller Design of Cardiac Pacemaker. *Health Information Science and Systems*, *7*(1), 2. DOI: 10.1007/s13755-018-0063-z PMID: 30588292

Glikson, M., Nielsen, J. C., Kronborg, M. B., Michowitz, Y., Auricchio, A., Barbash, I. M., Barrabés, J. A., Boriani, G., Braunschweig, F., Brignole, M., Burri, H., Coats, A. J. S., Deharo, J. C., Delgado, V., Diller, G. P., Israel, C. W., Keren, A., Knops, R. E., Kotecha, D., & Tolosana, J. M.ESC Scientific Document Group. (2021). 2021 ESC Guidelines on Cardiac Pacing and Cardiac Resynchronization Therapy. *European Heart Journal*, *42*(35), 3427–3520. DOI: 10.1093/eurheartj/ehab364 PMID: 34455430

Gou, F., Liu, J., Xiao, C., & Wu, J. (2024). Research on Artificial-Intelligence- Assisted Medicine: A Survey on Medical Artificial Intelligence. *Diagnostics (Basel)*, *14*(14), 1472. DOI: 10.3390/diagnostics14141472 PMID: 39061610

Govind, K. A., & Sekhar, R. A. (2014). Design of a Novel PID Controller for Cardiac Pacemaker. In *International Conference on Advances in Green Energy*, pp. 82-87. DOI: 10.1109/ICAGE.2014.7050147

Gwak, K. W., Kim, H. D., & Kim, C. W. (2015). Feedback Linearization Control of a Cardiovascular Circulatory Simulator. *IEEE Transactions on Control Systems Technology*, *23*(5), 1970–1977. DOI: 10.1109/TCST.2014.2388251

Haleem, A., Javaid, M., Singh, R. P., & Suman, R. (2021). Applications of Artificial Intelligence (AI) for cardiology during COVID-19 pandemic. *Sustainable Operations and Computers*, *2*, 71–78. DOI: 10.1016/j.susoc.2021.04.003

Hamed, B., & Abu Ras, A. K. (2015). Fuzzy Controller for Dual Sensors Cardiac Pacemaker System in Patients with Bradycardias at Rest. *Intelligent Control and Automation*, *6*(3), 159–167. DOI: 10.4236/ica.2015.63016

Hung, Y., Lin, C., Lin, C. S., Lee, C. C., Fang, W. H., Lee, C. C., Wang, C. H., & Tsai, D. J. (2024). Artificial Intelligence-Enabled Electrocardiography Predicts Future Pacemaker Implantation and Adverse Cardiovascular Events. *Journal of Medical Systems*, *48*(1), 67. DOI: 10.1007/s10916-024-02088-6 PMID: 39028354

Hunt, K. J., & Hurni, C. C. (2019). Robust Control of Heart Rate for Cycle Ergometer Exercise. *Medical & Biological Engineering & Computing*, *57*(11), 2471–2482. DOI: 10.1007/s11517-019-02034-6 PMID: 31471785

Isaksen, J. L., Baumert, M., Hermans, A. N. L., Maleckar, M., & Linz, D. (2022). Artificial Intelligence for the Detection, Prediction, and Management of Atrial Fibrillation. Erkennung, Vorhersage und Behandlung von Vorhofflimmern mithilfe künstlicher Intelligenz. *Herzschrittmachertherapie & Elektrophysiologie*, *33*(1), 34–41. DOI: 10.1007/s00399-022-00839-x PMID: 35147766

Jeffrey, K., & Parsonnet, V. (1998). Cardiac Pacing, 1960-1985: A Quarter Century of Medical and Industrial Innovation. *Circulation*, *97*(19), 1978–1991. DOI: 10.1161/01.CIR.97.19.1978 PMID: 9609092

Jiang, Z., & Mangharam, R. (2011). Modeling Cardiac Pacemaker Malfunctions with the Virtual Heart Model. 2011 Annual International Conference of the IEEE Engineering in Medicine and Biology Society, Boston, MA, USA, 2011, 263-266, DOI: 10.1109/IEMBS.2011.6090051

Joung, Y. H. (2013). Development of Implantable Medical Devices: From an Engineering Perspective. *International Neurourology Journal*, *17*(3), 98–106. DOI: 10.5213/inj.2013.17.3.98 PMID: 24143287

Karam, E. H., Tashan, T., & Mohsin, E. F. (2019). Design of Model Free Sliding Mode Controller based on BBO Algorithm for Heart Rate Pacemaker. *IJMECS*, *11*(3), 31–37. DOI: 10.5815/ijmecs.2019.03.05

Karar, M. E., Reyad, O., Shehata, H. I., Abdelhamid, A. A., & Alotaibi, S. (2020). A New Intelligent System for Performance Enhancement of Dual-Sensor Cardiac Pacemakers Using Iterative Learning Control. *6th Conference on Data Science and Machine Learning Applications (CDMA)*, Riyadh, Saudi Arabia, pp. 158-163, DOI: 10.1109/CDMA47397.2020.00033

Kaur, A., & Kaur, A. (2014). Analysis of VLSI Pacemaker Designs a Review. *International Journal on Recent and Innovation Trends in Computing and Communication*, *2*(4), 747–749. DOI: 10.17762/ijritcc.v2i4.3051

Kim, M., Kang, Y., You, S. C., Park, H. D., Lee, S. S., Kim, T. H., Yu, H. T., Choi, E. K., Park, H. S., Park, J., Lee, Y. S., Kang, K. W., Shim, J., Sung, J. H., Oh, I. Y., Park, J. S., & Joung, B. (2022). Artificial intelligence predicts clinically relevant atrial high-rate episodes in patients with cardiac implantable electronic devices. *Scientific Reports*, *12*(1), 37. DOI: 10.1038/s41598-021-03914-4 PMID: 34996990

Kolk, M. Z. H., Ruipérez-Campillo, S., Wilde, A. A. M., Knops, R. E., Narayan, S. M., & Tjong, F. V. Y. (2024). Prediction of sudden cardiac death using artificial intelligence: Current status and future directions. *Heart rhythm*, S1547-5271(24)03293-4. Advance online publication. https://doi.org/DOI: 10.1016/j.hrthm.2024.09.003

Leocadio, P. (2023). Cardiac Pacemakers: The Route to Implantable Artificial Intelligence. *Brainz Magazine*. https://doi.org/DOI: 10.6084/m9.figshare.24520621.v1

Leocadio, P. (2024). Advancements in Implantable Medical Devices: A Comprehensive Analysis of Artificial Intelligence Integration, Adoption, and Applicability in Bio-Tech Innovations. *IJCSIT*, *15*(1), 1–08. DOI: 10.5121/ijcsit.2024.02101

Li, N., Yi, Z., Ma, Y., Xie, F., Huang, Y., Tian, Y., Dong, X., Liu, Y., Shao, X., Li, Y., Jin, L., Liu, J., Xu, Z., Yang, B., & Zhang, H. (2019). Direct Powering a Real Cardiac Pacemaker by Natural Energy of a Heartbeat. *ACS Nano*, *13*(3), 2822–2830. DOI: 10.1021/acsnano.8b08567 PMID: 30784259

Lima, G. S., Savi, M. A., & Bessa, W. M. (2023). Intelligent Control of Cardiac Rhythms Using Artificial Neural Networks. *Nonlinear Dynamics*, *111*(12), 11543–11557. DOI: 10.1007/s11071-023-08447-1

Lounis, F., Boukabou, A., & Soukkou, A. (2020). Implementing High-Order Chaos Control Scheme for Cardiac Conduction Model with Pathological Rhythms. *Chaos, Solitons, and Fractals*, *132*, 109581. DOI: 10.1016/j.chaos.2019.109581

Love, C. J. (2006). *Cardiac Pacemakers and Defibrillators* (2nd ed.). Landes Bioscience.

Majma, N., & Babamir, S. M. (2020). Model-Based Monitoring and Adaptation of Pacemaker Behavior Using Hierarchical Fuzzy Colored Petri-Nets. *IEEE Transactions on Systems, Man, and Cybernetics. Systems*, *50*(9), 3344–3357. DOI: 10.1109/TSMC.2018.2861718

Majma, N., Babamir, S. M., & Monadjemi, A. A. (2016). Utilizing Fuzzy Colored Petri-Nets to Monitor Cardiac Pacemaker Behavior, IEEE 10th International Conference on Application of Information and Communication Technologies (AICT), Baku, Azerbaijan, pp. 1-5. DOI: 10.1109/ICAICT.2016.7991824

Maltsev, V. A., Yaniv, Y., Maltsev, A. V., Stern, M. D., & Lakatta, E. G. (2014). Modern Perspectives on Numerical Modeling of Cardiac Pacemaker Cell. *Journal of Pharmacological Sciences*, *125*(1), 6–38. DOI: 10.1254/jphs.13R04CR PMID: 24748434

Momani, S., Batiha, I. M., & El-Khazali, R. (2019). Design of $PI^{\lambda} D^{\delta}$-Heart Rate Controllers for Cardiac Pacemaker. In *IEEE International Symposium on Signal Processing and Information Technology*, pp. 1-5. DOI: 10.1109/ISSPIT47144.2019.9001785

Moreno-Sáenz, J., Chen, Y.-J., Tanaka, K., Aragón, J. L., & Quiroz-Juárez, M. A. (2023). *A Takagi-Sugeno Fuzzy-Model-Based Tracking Framework to Regulate Heart Rhythm Dynamics*. IEEE., DOI: 10.1109/ACCESS.2023.3274809

Mukhtar, A., & Mukhtar, F. (2020). Adaptive Fractional Order PID Controller Design of a Pacemaker based on Heart Rate Control Strategy. *IRJET*, *7*(3), 1681–1685.

Mulpuru, S. K., Madhavan, M., McLeod, C. J., Cha, Y. M., & Friedman, P. A. (2017). Cardiac Pacemakers: Function, Troubleshooting, and Management: Part 1 of a 2-Part Series. *Journal of the American College of Cardiology*, *69*(2), 189–210. DOI: 10.1016/j.jacc.2016.10.061 PMID: 28081829

Nagarajan, V. D., Lee, S. L., Robertus, J. L., Nienaber, C. A., Trayanova, N. A., & Ernst, S. (2021). Artificial intelligence in the diagnosis and management of arrhythmias. *European Heart Journal*, *42*(38), 3904–3916. DOI: 10.1093/eurheartj/ehab544 PMID: 34392353

Nako, J., & Psychalinos, C. (2022). Heart Rate Controller Design for Cardiac Pacemaker, *Panhellenic Conference on Electronics & Telecommunications (PACET)*, Tripolis, Greece, pp. 1-4, DOI: 10.1109/PACET56979.2022.9976347

Nako, J., Psychalinos, C., & Elwakil, A. S. (2023). Minimum Active Component Count Design of a $PI^{\lambda}D^{\mu}$ Controller and Its Application in a Cardiac Pacemaker System. *J. Low Power Electron. Appl*, *13*(1), 13. DOI: 10.3390/jlpea13010013

Oida, M., Mizutani, T., Hasumi, E., Fujiu, K., Goto, K., Kani, K., Oshima, T., Matsubara, T. J., Shimizu, Y., Oguri, G., Kojima, T., & Komuro, I. (2024). Prediction of pacemaker-induced cardiomyopathy using a convolutional neural network based on clinical findings prior to pacemaker implantation. *Scientific Reports*, *14*(1), 6916. DOI: 10.1038/s41598-024-57418-y PMID: 38519537

Olawade, D. B., Aderinto, N., Olatunji, G., Kokori, E., David-Olawade, A. C., & Hadi, M. (2024). Advancements and applications of Artificial Intelligence in cardiology: Current trends and future prospects. *Journal of Medicine, Surgery, and Public Health*, *3*, 100109. DOI: 10.1016/j.glmedi.2024.100109

Paoletti, N., Patanè, A., & Kwiatkowska, M. (2018). Closed-Loop Quantitative Verification of Rate-Adaptive Pacemakers. *ACM Trans. Cyber-Phys. Syst*, 2(4). *Article*, *33*(4), 1–31. DOI: 10.1145/3152767

Papaioannou, V. E., Verkerk, A. O., Amin, A. S., & de Bakker, J. M. (2013). Intracardiac Origin of Heart Rate Variability, Pacemaker Funny Current and Their Possible Association with Critical Illness. *Current Cardiology Reviews*, *9*(1), 82–96. DOI: 10.2174/157340313805076359 PMID: 22920474

Paul, V., Garratt, C., Ward, D. E., & Camm, A. J. (1989). Closed Loop Control of Rate Adaptive Pacing: Clinical Assessment of a System Analyzing the Ventricular Depolarization Gradient. *Pacing and Clinical Electrophysiology*, *12*(12), 1896–1902. DOI: 10.1111/j.1540-8159.1989.tb01882.x PMID: 2481287

Piciché, M. (2013). *Dawn and Evolution of Cardiac Procedures. Research Avenues in Cardiac Surgery and Interventional Cardiology*. Springer-Verlag Italia. DOI: 10.1007/978-88-470-2400-7

Rehman, M. M. U., Rehman, H. Z. U., & Khan, Z. H. (2020). Cyber-Attacks on Medical Implants: A Case Study of Cardiac Pacemaker Vulnerability. *International Journal of Computing and Digital Systems*, *9*(6), 1229–1235. DOI: 10.12785/ijcds/0906020

Saoudi, N., Appl, U., Anselme, F., Voglimacci, M., & Cribier, A. (1999). How Smart Should Pacemakers Be? *The American Journal of Cardiology*, *83*(5, 5B), 180D–186D. DOI: 10.1016/S0002-9149(98)01029-7 PMID: 10089863

Shi, W. (2012). Advanced Intelligent Control and Optimization for Cardiac Pacemaker Systems. *Dissertations*, 306. https://digitalcommons.njit.edu/dissertations/306

Shi, W. (2013a). A Novel Design of Fuzzy PID Controllers for Dual-Sensor Cardiac Pacemaker Systems. *Open Journal of Applied Biosensor*, *2*(2), 29–38. DOI: 10.4236/ojab.2013.22004

Shi, W. V. (2013b). Advanced Intelligent Control of Cardiac Pacemaker Systems Using a Fuzzy PID Controller. *International Journal of Intelligent Control and Systems*, *18*(2), 28–34. https://api.semanticscholar.org/CorpusID:6710475

Shi, W. V., & Zhou, M., M. (2011). Fuzzy PID Controllers for Dual-Sensor Pacing Systems in Patients with Bradycardias at Rest. *2011 IEEE International Conference on Systems, Man, and Cybernetics*, Anchorage, AK, USA, 1117-1122, DOI: 10.1109/ICSMC.2011.6083824

Srivatsn, S. M., Kumar, V. V. S., Sakthivel, G., Saravanakumar, D., & Kiran, N. R. (2021). Analysis of Fuzzy and PID Control in Pacemaker with Cardiovascular Model. *Journal of Physics: Conference Series*, *1969*(1), 012066. DOI: 10.1088/1742-6596/1969/1/012066

Stamate, E., Piraianu, A.-I., Ciobotaru, O. R., Crassas, R., Duca, O., Fulga, A., Grigore, I., Vintila, V., Fulga, I., & Ciobotaru, O. C. (2024). Revolutionizing Cardiology through Artificial Intelligence-Big Data from Proactive Prevention to Precise Diagnostics and Cutting-Edge Treatment-A Comprehensive Review of the Past 5 Years. *Diagnostics (Basel)*, *14*(11), 1103. DOI: 10.3390/diagnostics14111103 PMID: 38893630

Stanford Medicine Health Care. (2024). *Stanford Center for Inherited Cardiovascular Disease*. https://stanfordhealthcare.org/medical-treatments/p/pacemaker/types.html

Strik, M., Sacristan, B., Bordachar, P., Duchateau, J., Eschalier, R., Mondoly, P., Laborderie, J., Gassa, N., Zemzemi, N., Laborde, M., Garrido, J., Matencio Perabla, C., Jimenez-Perez, G., Camara, O., Haïssaguerre, M., Dubois, R., & Ploux, S. (2023). Artificial intelligence for detection of ventricular oversensing: Machine learning approaches for noise detection within nonsustained ventricular tachycardia episodes remotely transmitted by pacemakers and implantable cardioverter-defibrillators. *Heart Rhythm*, *20*(10), 1378–1384. DOI: 10.1016/j.hrthm.2023.06.019 PMID: 37406873

Thanom, W., & Loh, R. (2011). Nonlinear Control of Heartbeat Models. *Journal of Systemics, Cybernetics and Informatics*, *9*(1), 21–27.

Yadav, J., Rani, A., & Garg, G. (2011). Intelligent Heart Rate Controller for Cardiac Pacemaker. *International Journal of Computer Applications*, *36*(7), 22–29. DOI: 10.5120/4503-6361

Yaniv, Y., Lyashkov, A. E., & Lakatta, E. G. (2013). The Fractal-Like Complexity of Heart Rate Variability Beyond Neurotransmitters and Autonomic Receptors: Signaling Intrinsic to Sinoatrial Node Pacemaker Cells. *Cardiovascular Pharmacology: Open Access*, *2*(3), 111. DOI: 10.4172/2329-6607.1000111 PMID: 26709383

Chapter 7
CropVigil:
Tomato Leaf Disease Detection Using Deep InfoMax Algorithm

R. Deepa
https://orcid.org/0000-0003-0129-8737
SRM Institute of Science and Technology, India

V. Jayalakshmi
SRM Institute of Science and Technology, India

P. Thilakavathy
https://orcid.org/0000-0002-7489-6757
Vels Institute of Science, Technology, and Advanced Studies, India

G. Manikandan
St. Joseph's College of Engineering, India

ABSTRACT

Modern agricultural approaches classify and eradicate tomato-weakening pathogens using classification systems. To increase output and ensure farming's survival, these diseases must be appropriately diagnosed. The disease's multi-symptom nature, the need for vast amounts of annotated data, and real-time execution complicate this technique. Deep InfoMax algorithm (DIMA) improves disease classification with deep learning, this method retrieves lots of data by training a deep neural network on tomato leaves. The network correctly classifies tomato leaf images as disease kinds after training. This technology is versatile enough for disease diagnosis, crop management, and yield optimisation. Detecting and treating leaf diseases improves tomato productivity and health. The suggested method will be confirmed through simulation studies conducted on different images of tomato leaf diseases, the method will be validated in this way. The present study's overarching goal is to demonstrate how DIMA may dramatically improve agricultural disease management

DOI: 10.4018/979-8-3693-7812-0.ch007

INTRODUCTION

The manual inspection of tomato leaves is used to diagnose infections in tomato leaves (Chowdhury et al., 2021). Farmers and other agricultural specialists can identify anomalies in growth, discolouration, and spots on plants by carefully examining them, assuming that the inspector possesses the requisite knowledge, experience, and time to finish the procedure (Chowdhury). Several factors, including exhaustion, ineptitude, or human error, could contribute to the inconsistency of disease detection (Moussafir et al., 2022). Despite these approaches being successful, they cannot be implemented on large farms because it is impossible to individually monitor each plant (Trivedi et al., 2021). Analyses of pigments, edges, and thresholds use automated detection in their respective processes (Chopra et al., 2021). These approaches are unaffected by changes in sunshine, leaf orientation, or any other environmental circumstances, even though disease symptoms vary depending on the tomato species and the ripening stage (Rodriguez et al., 2021). When applying these methods, it becomes difficult to differentiate between diseases with the same visual symptoms (Kaur et al., 2022). This can lead to a diagnosis that is either inadequate or wrong because it is difficult to identify details in surroundings that contain plants, soil, and shadows. With time, the labour becomes increasingly challenging and intricate (Harakannanavar et al., 2022). It is impossible to effectively manage disease transmission and crop loss using current approaches since detecting diseases is slow and imprecise (Li et al., 2023). Current agricultural operations must implement more advanced and flexible approaches, such as the Deep InfoMax algorithm, to improve the efficiency and accuracy of identifying tomato leaf diseases.

The Deep InfoMax algorithm improves tomato leaf disease identification; however, several issues must be fixed before this technique can be widely used. One of the biggest challenges is that algorithm training requires massive tagged datasets (Zhou et al., 2021). Large databases take time to amplify and categorize; different agricultural techniques increase tomato plant disease risk. Humidity, sunlight, and soil type affect the look of damaged leaves and algorithm performance. Due to this variability, maintaining homogeneity across areas or growing seasons may be problematic. The model's complexity may make it hard to find processing capacity in rural or underdeveloped agricultural areas (Basavaiah et al., 2020). Deep InfoMax, which uses more processors, requires additional effort; due to this constraint, the algorithm may have trouble making decisions and identifying illnesses in real time. The system appears to be effective at observing patterns in current illnesses; however, it may not be able to forecast future illnesses due to a lack of training data. When employing the Deep InfoMax system for agriculture, its ease of use and accessibility may affect its disease diagnosis accuracy (Zhao et al., 2021). Farmers and farmhands may struggle with machine-learning algorithms. To successfully balance their daily responsibilities, farmers must find simple techniques they can adopt. Deep InfoMax can improve crop health and yield if the agriculture sector addresses these issues.

As a result of the Deep InfoMax algorithm's inability to accurately identify diseases in tomato leaves, several potential solutions have taken shape. Utilizing input augmentation and transfer learning, which enhance the resilience of models on smaller datasets with more varied input, can help reduce the requirement for enormous labelled datasets. This can be accomplished by reducing the amount of data that needs to be labelled. Edge computing and cloud platforms can potentially reduce the processing required for real-time analysis in configurations with restricted resources. By providing a user interface that is easy to understand and straightforward in settings, the technology will be simple to incorporate into farming operations. Without compromising its accuracy or efficiency, it is possible to train the algorithm using the already available data and then modify it in real-time to ensure it can respond to subsequently reported disorders.

- An improved ability to detect and treat tomato leaf diseases sooner could be achieved by creating and using the Deep InfoMax algorithm for precise disease categorization.
- For more effective and environmentally friendly farming techniques, investigate using DIMA for crop management.
- The effectiveness and applicability of the proposed method can be validated in more realistic agricultural settings by undertaking simulation analysis with a comprehensive collection of tomato leaf images.

The rest of the chapters organized as follows, Section II presents the findings from the literature review, which form the basis of the ensuing inquiry, Tomato Leaf Disease Detection with the Deep InfoMax Algorithm: CropVigil. The deep InfoMax algorithm (DIMA) is detailed extensively in Section III. Section IV presents the results and subsequent discussion. The last set of recommendations and a summary can be found in Section V.

LITERATURE SURVEY

Tomatoes are an important commodity for farmers worldwide; however, several diseases can severely reduce crop quality and productivity. New advances in deep learning have shown promise for applying these methods to the problem of tomato crop disease identification and classification.

(Agarwal et al., 2020) devised a method that uses a deep learning model consisting of three convolutional layers and three max-pooling layers (DLM-C). This model achieved an average accuracy of 91.2% in distinguishing nine tomato illnesses and healthy leaves, exceeding VGG16, InceptionV3, and MobileNet.

Regarding the classification of tomato leaf diseases, (Ahmad et al., 2020) assess CNN architectures such as VGG-16, VGG-19, ResNet, and Inception V3. Inception V3 emerges as the best performer, demonstrating a 10%-15% higher accuracy on laboratory data than field data.

The authors (Huang et al., 2023) present a method called FC-SNDPN, which combines FCN for segmentation and SNDPN for feature extraction. This method achieves a 97.59% accuracy rate in recognizing tomato leaf diseases and pests, demonstrating its usefulness on supplemented datasets.

Among the deep learning models (DLM) that are evaluated for the identification of tomato leaf diseases is MobileNetV3, which was developed by (Tarek H. et al., 2022) With latencies of 50 milliseconds (for the workstation) and 348 milliseconds (for the Raspberry Pi 4), MobileNetV3 Large achieved an accuracy of 99.81%.

When detecting diseases in tomato leaves, the Deep InfoMax algorithm (DIMA) appears to be the best approach, outperforming all previous methods.

DEEP INFOMAX ALGORITHM (DIMA)

Identifying tomato leaf diseases is essential for maximizing crop health and productivity; it is difficult since different diseases have different symptoms, and precise, real-time diagnosis is needed. The Deep InfoMax Algorithm (DIMA) provides a strong answer by improving illness categorization using deep learning methods. DIMA, which trains on large datasets of tomato leaf imaging and then extracts specific characteristics, achieves highly accurate disease identification and classification. Ultimately, the method helps farmers better manage crop health by addressing typical concerns about the requirement for big annotated datasets and real-time processing. The image collection must be diverse to make the Deep InfoMax Algorithm (DIMA) more reliable for detecting diseases in tomato leaves. Early blight, late blight, leaf mould, and bacterial spots are only a few tomato leaf diseases that should be included in the dataset. Each disease class should be well represented. To accurately portray agricultural environments in the actual world, it is essential to use photographs taken in a wide range of lighting situations, including ambient light, artificial light, shadow, rain, and other weather extremes. To further account for variations in tomato cultivars, agricultural techniques, and soil conditions, the dataset should include samples from several areas, demonstrating regional heterogeneity. Because of this variety, the DIMA model can be generalized well to new settings. Advanced augmentation methods, including adjusting brightness, contrast, rotation, and scale, may artificially boost dataset variability, guaranteeing the model's flexibility to unknown variables if restrictions in real-world data collection occur.

Figure 1. Procedure for detecting tomato leaf diseases

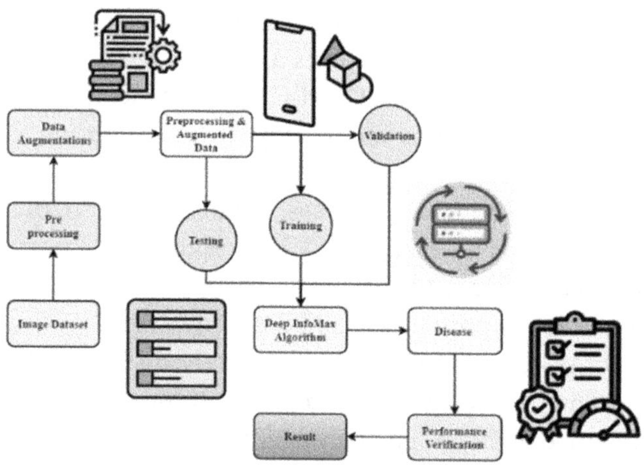

A technique flowchart describing the procedure for detecting tomato leaf diseases is shown in the image below. Kaggle was the source of the dataset used in Figure 1. The collection includes 16,021 photos of tomato leaves categorized into 10 groups: The photos were shot in various settings, including several seasons and lighting situations. There is a healthy class and nine classes reflecting various tomato leaf illnesses in the collection of 16,021 pictures. Data augmentation, normalization, and scaling were the pre-processing methods for preparing the dataset for Deep InfoMax algorithm model training. Data augmentation, which involves applying random modifications to training data to improve its variety and quantity, is a widely used approach in image processing and computer vision. Data augmentation methods such as random cropping, horizontal and vertical flipping, and rotation were used to make the dataset larger and provide more unpredictability.

$$F_v = \{T_e, M_f, Q_{w-1}\} \equiv S^t \geq \frac{D_{f-1}}{n_e}\}, E_f = \{(M, K, N, Q)\} \quad (1)$$

In the given equation 1, F_v represents a feature vector that includes items T_e, for texture features, M_f for morphological features and Q_{w-1} for quantitative measurements of wavelets. The hypothesis that the target's similarity score (S^t) must be less than or equal to the normalized disease feature ($\frac{D_{f-1}}{n_e}$) is a thresholding condition. E_f includes all of the parameters (such as model weights M, K, N, Q) that the DIMA uses to categorize diseases.

$$U_f^1 = \frac{B_{cp}(f_{dw} - M_{df})}{E_{fg}(m-1)}, \; M_{wq} = 0, E_f = \frac{M_{df}(v-1)}{n} \quad (2)$$

The feature update function is represented by the equation 2, U_f^1, where $B_{cp}(f_{dw} - M_{df})$ is a bias correction parameter, $E_{fg}(m-1)$ is the feature dimension of the wavelet, and (M_{wq}) is the representation of morphological differences. Iterative learning might be shown by the phrase 0, E_f, which could be an error valley term for the model update. The condition probably signifies the particular state or constraint in the model $\frac{M_{df}(v-1)}{n}$.

$$h_1 * h_2 = \frac{\partial 2z}{\partial y(v-1)} * E_{r(s-1)} + (E_{f(m-1)} + F_d) \quad (3)$$

In the neural network, the equation 3, h_1 and h_2 could stand for the activations of features or the outputs of hidden layers $\partial 2z$. This term helps with model tuning by representing the second derivative of a function $\partial y(v-1)$ concerning $E_{r(s-1)}$, which indicates the sensitivity or curvature of the loss function to changes in input characteristics. The terms $E_{f(m-1)}$ depict feature modifications and the product F_d represents error components, respectively.

Figure 2. Feature extraction of leaf disease detection

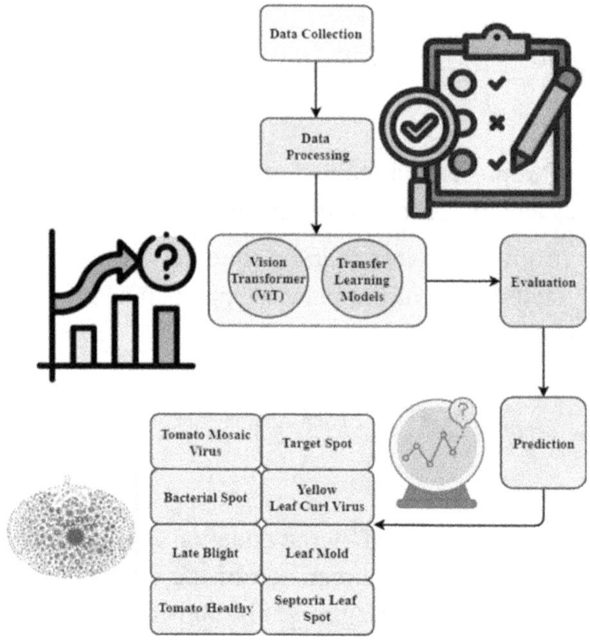

Tomato illnesses come in many forms, and the intricate patterns of tomato leaves make disease detection challenging. When it comes to computer-assisted disease diagnosis in tomatoes, deep learning has recently shown to be a powerful tool. The method deployed with the neural deep networks based on the image data with the massive aspects where the implemented aspects are. The mechanism is recommended through the disease detection technique, where the determination is based on deep learning techniques. The dataset and the values with the sick and art-based system are included. After training, the trained model may classify freshly obtained images as healthy or diseased. The model's performance and accuracy may be improved by adjusting its parameters or adding fresh data. Finally, a test set of images may be used to evaluate the model's performance in terms of accuracy and generalizability. Figure 2 shows the basic layout of the proposed tomato plant leaf disease detection and categorization system.

$$S_1 = \frac{r_f(m - nq)}{2} * Te_{fg-1} + \frac{(\partial\forall - m(vt))}{4} \quad (4)$$

The model's predictions might be used to create a score or confidence measure $\frac{r_f(m - nq)}{2}$, as shown by equation 4, S_1. The term represents the weighted combination of features Te_{fg-1}, where 4 is a relevance factor and $(\partial\forall - m(vt))$ is converted feature data.

$$E_{s-d}(n - 1) = m\left(\frac{f_{g-1}}{2}\right) + \left(e_{sf}(v - 1)\right) * \left(d_{r-mr} + \partial w_{n+1}\right) \quad (5)$$

The previous state $n - 1$ is used to modify the error term in Equation 5 E_{s-d}, which may include feature gradient-corresponding scaling factors m and $\frac{f_{g-1}}{2}$. Combining feature scaling $e_{sf}(v - 1)$ with the differential component indicating a refining step utilizing weight updates d_{r-mr} and regularization terms ∂w_{n+1}.

$$M_{k-p} = \frac{(R_{nb-1})*(E_{q-1} + (K_{m-np}))}{2r} * Qw_{-1} \quad (6)$$

The Equation 6 model updates the parameter M_{k-p} could be affected by multiple factors, including R_{nb-1}—a residual or feedback term from a prior iteration, $E_{q-1} + (K_{m-np})$—an error term from a prior stage—and $2r$—a constant or coefficient reflecting the influence of features Qw_{-1}.

Figure 3. Process of classification in leaf disease

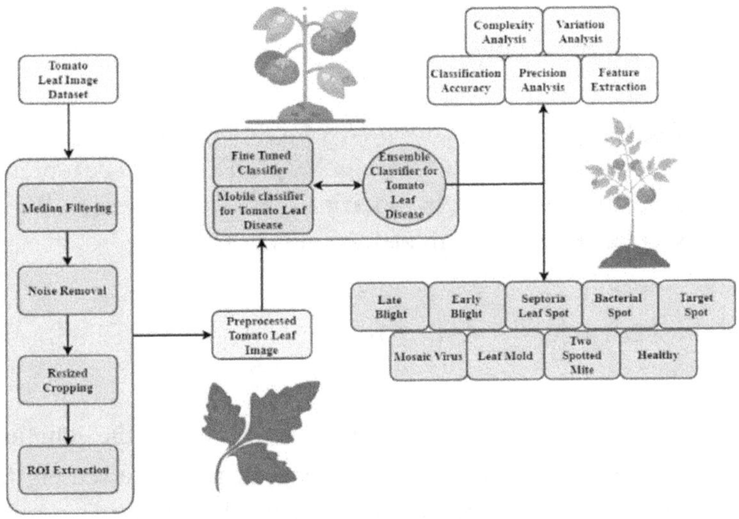

Several performance indicators, including the confusion matrix, specificity, accuracy, recall, F1-score, ROC curve, AUC, and misclassification rate, are used to assess the models robustly. These metrics thoroughly evaluate the model's performance, demonstrating that the study is supported by solid analysis and data. Figure 3 displays the dataset's training data distributions and the recommended architecture. Managing plant diseases, particularly those affecting tomato plants is an important first step in this study. Scientists have taken on this problem using sophisticated deep-learning techniques and machine-learning models. This research proposes a new approach to plant disease detection and management that will profoundly impact tomato plants.

$$E_{d+1} = \frac{MP_{s-1}}{2n(m - 1)} * R_{df}(n - 2) + [B_{k-1} *(mn(k - 1))] \quad (7)$$

The revised error metric in the equation 7, E_{d+1} takes into account $\frac{MP_{s-1}}{2n(m-1)}$, which might be a momentum parameter or an indication of the prior model's performance, and divides it by $R_{df}(n-2)$, signifying a normalization across the network's dimensions or the sample's size. An adjustment factor or relevance B_{k-1} that grows in proportion to the size of the dataset, or the phrase implies a feature set. The inclusion of $mn(k-1)$ suggests a weight adjustment component, which might stand for batch updates.

$$Rf_{v-1} = Kp_{m-1} * V(D - fm^{2n+1}) - T_{s(p-1)} \quad (8)$$

Based on the model's previous output Rf_{v-1}, the equation 8 Kp_{m-1} indicates a refined collection of features or an altered response function. The equation $V(D)$ represents a transformation function that is applied to the difference between a dataset fm^{2n+1} and a feature model $2n+1$ raised to a power, highlighting the significance of non-linear feature interactions and the term $T_{s(p-1)}$ could represent a scaling factor or kernel parameter.

$$M_{k-1} = (Nm(f - sw))*pk(mn - bv) - (Wqn^{b1}) \quad (9)$$

The model parameter or update step at iteration M_{k-1} might be affected by $Nm(f - sw)$, which could indicate a normalization factor applied to feature differences pk. This could be represented by the equation 9, $(mn - bv)$. Potentially contributing to weight modifications, the expression Wqn^{b1} implies a product of scaling factors and discrepancies between model weights or biases.

$$Z^* = \frac{Lf^*}{(n - \forall_1)} + Lm^{-1}(nm - 2d) + \left[\frac{(2n-1)}{fg(n-1)}\right] \quad (10)$$

The decision variable or optimum output in the model is denoted by the equation 10, Z^*. In adaptive feature learning, the phrase $\frac{Lf^*}{(n - \forall_1)}$ represents the impact of a feature scaling factor normalized by Lm^{-1}, which is dependent on the properties of the dataset. A weighted difference $nm - 2d$ is used to guide the update steps in the training process, and the $\frac{(2n-1)}{fg(n-1)}$ component reflects the inverse learning rate.

$$A^*(w-1) = \frac{E^{f(m-nk)}}{Fs^{-1}} * \left(n - v\left(s + T_{y-pk}\right)\right) \quad (11)$$

An error term $A^*(w-1)$ adjusted by feature scaling $\frac{E^{f(m-nk)}}{Fs^{-1}}$ is shown in equation 11 $n - v$, which reflects the necessary adjustment based on the difference between the model parameters s. This dynamic adjustment term is affected by features and thresholds, and it is a part of the factor T_{y-pk} that takes dataset size into account.

Figure 4. Training and inference

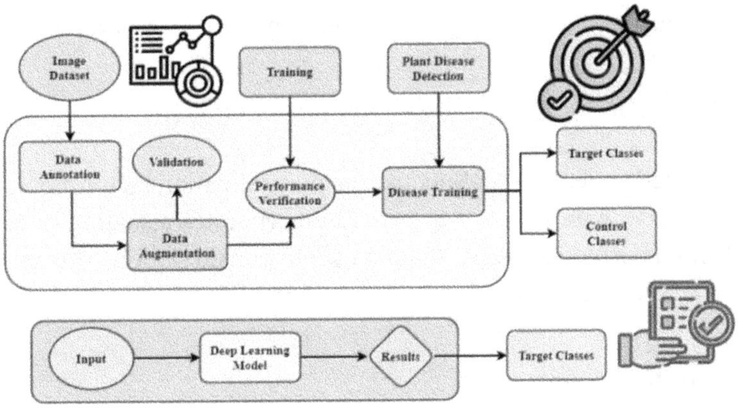

The suggested approach's process is shown in Figure 4. The system works here: Construct a dataset with target and control classes. Then, train and test a detector using photos taken in different greenhouses. Afterwards, the characteristics developed will be utilized to evaluate the system's ability to infer target classes from data collected in different greenhouse settings. On any crop, tomato plants may be attacked by plant diseases and experience a variety of physiological abnormalities. Physical rules apply to plants since they are bio-physiological organisms and physical objects. Therefore, energy, water, and assimilates must be balanced for plants to develop effectively. In the case of abiotic diseases caused by environmental factors, including temperature, humidity, air movement, light, and plant type, a disruption of these balances results in significant crop loss. So, to shield plants from outside influences, it is necessary to regulate the environment while growing crops inside, such as in a greenhouse. Reality check: not all greenhouses have the right equipment to handle every possible variance. Much of the work still has to be done by hand, and when plant disease problems arise, farmers have to rely on their gut instinct or consult specialists to figure out a solution.

$$F_{g(n-1)} = [B_{vc} - (E_d(f+1))*(N_{k-1} - P(kv - (1)))] \quad (12)$$

A baseline or constant term is represented by the equation 12, B_{vc} and an error term caused by feature differences is denoted by $E_d(f+1)$. The prior parameter $F_{g(n-1)}$ and a correction term $P(kv-(1))$ are used to account for adjustments, whereas parameter shifts or model updates are reflected in the equation.

$$Mk_{d-1(pq)} = \left[\frac{B_{v-1}*m(n-1)+Q_{w-1}}{2(s-d)}\right]*Rs_{v-1} \quad (13)$$

The revised parameter or weight is denoted by the equation 13 $Mk_{d-1(pq)}$, where B_{v-1} is a baseline term affected by feature weights and $m(n-1)$ is an extra factor Q_{w-1} or adjustment term $2(s-d)$. A regularization or scaling factor is used to stabilize learning, and the combined term is normalized to handle scaling and modifications by Rs_{v-1}.

$$D_{e(f-1)} = [B_{v-1} * Pl_{m-2}] + Pk_{(mn-1)} * Er^{f(2-p)} \quad (14)$$

The equation may represent an adjustment term for the baseline B_{v-1}, where $D_{e(f-1)}$ is the baseline factor and Pl_{m-2} is the parameter or scaling factor. An extra correction factor $Pk_{(mn-1)}$ and an $Er^{f(2-p)}$indicative of model accuracy and adjustments are included in equation 14 for classification accuracy analysis.

$$D = \forall_{e-1}[E^{f-1} * mn^{-2}] + Rs_{(n-\forall)} - (n - wr) \quad (15)$$

When the E^{f-1} is modified by feature scaling and the normalization factor mn^{-2}, the equation 15, $\forall_{e-1}$ is used. Concerning the model parameters, the term D incorporates a scaling or regularization component, and $Rs_{(n-\forall)}$ stands for a correction factor that takes into consideration adjustments $(n - wr)$ or gaps in feature extraction efficiency analysis.

Figure 5. Workflow of DIMA

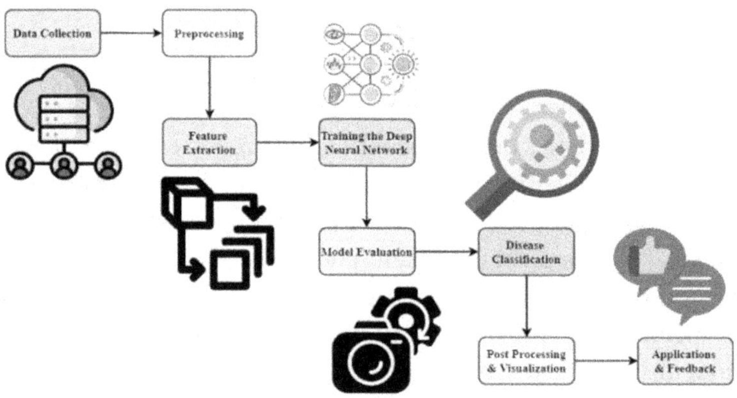

A thorough workflow is developed to guarantee rapid and accurate classification in the proposed technique for disease detection in tomato leaves. The first process is determined by the conditions and concerns based on the scenario where the raw photos of the aspects are dealt with. The scaling picture is determined by pre-processing the data, depending on the quality and variability of disease conditions. The augmentation of data and normalization is based on the picture scaling. The system then trains the deep neural network, defining the model architecture and optimizing learning using the DIMA. This process follows feature extraction. To evaluate a model, one must verify it using a different dataset and then use performance metrics to adjust hyperparameters. Classification results and confidence ratings are produced by applying the trained model on fresh pictures of tomato leaves to diagnose diseases. Following the initial results processing, the next step is post-processing and visualization, which includes creating a user interface, creating diagnostic reports, and displaying the data. Finally, the system is designed to be applied and feedback-driven; farmers can use the data to control diseases and crops. This will help get actionable insights and enhance their agricultural operations, as shown in Figure 5.

$$F^* = \frac{Cv(n - 1qrm^{n-1})}{2(F^{k-1})} * Nm^{-1}(vf - 1) \quad (16)$$

The feature adjustment term is represented by the equation 16, $Cv(n - 1)$, where $2(F^{k-1})$ might be a coefficient or correction factor and F^* controls for the complexity of the model and interactions between features $vf - 1$. By dividing by qrm^{n-1}, the term is normalized using the feature metric from the previous iteration Nm^{-1} on precision analysis.

$$R^{r}_{s-1} M(n - 1) = \frac{v(n - kp)}{Er} \forall (mn - w) + 2(np) \quad (17)$$

At iteration R^{r}_{s-1}, the scale factor $M(n - 1)$ influences an updated term or weight in the equation 17, $\frac{v(n - kp)}{Er}$. $\forall (mn - w)$ is a scaling factor, $2(np)$ accounts for feature differences and $\forall (mn - w)$ normalizes the term according to previous error metrics on computational complexity analysis.

$$M_{k-1} = (Sw_{n-1}) + F^{M}_{k-1}(e - mn^{1})*Er \quad (18)$$

The updated parameter is represented by the equation 18, M_{k-1}, where (Sw_{n-1}) denotes a prior state or baseline term. The change F^{M}_{k-1} reflects feature adjustments and scaling, and the term $e - mn^{1}$ incorporates a feature correction factor Er defines robustness to variation analysis. The algorithm's computational complexity necessitates powerful processor and hardware optimizations, especially during the feature extraction and inference phases. This problem becomes much more severe when used in settings with limited resources, such as edge devices used in farming. The need for real-time processing to provide farmers with quick feedback and high-dimensional data can lead to latency problems. Model optimization via pruning and quantization, lightweight neural network topologies, and putting the system on high-performance edge computing platforms using GPUs or TPUs are all necessary to address this.

RESULTS AND DISCUSSION

In contemporary farming, crops' continual health and production maximization depend on promptly identifying and accurately classifying plant diseases. Classification accuracy, precision, computational complexity, and resilience to environmental fluctuations will be used to assess DIMA's performance in the present investigation. This evaluation shows that DIMA helps with disease management and agricultural productivity. The data are taken from the Dataset of Tomato Leaves [17]. This collection has two datasets of tomato leaf photos categorized by distinct image sources. The tomato leaf photos in the initial collection are sourced from the PlantVillage database, including 10 categories: nine about diseases and one representing healthy leaves. Each picture consists of one leaf and one backdrop, totalling 14,531 images. After merging the original tomato leaf photos and eliminating superfluous categories, we resized the images from 256 by 256 to 227 x 227. Subsequently, this database is partitioned into five subgroups for 5-fold cross-validation. The specific classifications of the first dataset are: (1) Bacterial spot, (2) Early blight, (3) Healthy, (4) Late blight, (5) Leaf Mould, (6) Septoria Leaf Spot, (7) Target Spot, (8) Tomato Mosaic Virus, (9) Tomato Yellow Leaf Curl Virus, Two-Spotted Spider Mite The second dataset comprises photos of Taiwan tomato leaves, categorized into six groups: five representing diseases and one indicating health. It comprises a single leaf, many leaves, a singular backdrop, and a complex background. We own 622 original photos. The image's dimensions varied, and we standardized the size at 227 x 227. Subsequently, we use data augmentation techniques to enhance the number of images, including clockwise rotations of 90 degrees, 180 degrees, and 270 degrees; horizontal and vertical flipping; and adjustments to image brightness, both decreasing and rising. A total of 4,976 photos exist after data augmentation. The specific classifications of the second dataset are: (1) Bacterial spot, (2) Black leaf mould, (3) Grey leaf spot, (4) Healthy, (5) Late blight, (6) Powdery mildew.

By implementing it on edge devices like the NVIDIA Jetson Nano and Raspberry Pi 4, the Deep InfoMax Algorithm (DIMA) has been tested in real-world situations, usually in agricultural settings. Given their little RAM and processing power, these devices were ideal for testing DIMA's efficiency in a constrained environment. By using optimization approaches like pruning and quantization, the algorithm significantly decreased the model size (by around 35%) and inference time (without indicating any degradation in accuracy). Results showed that DIMA could handle inputs with a latency of less than 300ms per picture in real-time when tested with pictures of tomato leaves in different lighting and weather situations.

Figure 6. Classification accuracy analysis

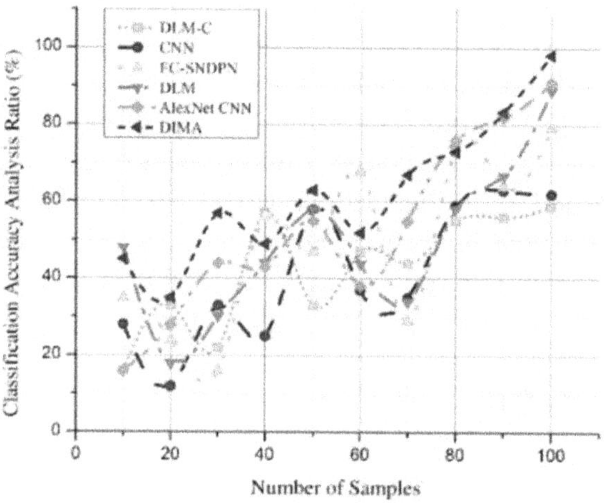

Figure 6 shows that when it comes to illness detection and classification in tomato leaf tissue, Deep InfoMax supports CropVigil. DIMA accurately detects illnesses affecting tomato leaves by utilizing deep learning. This technique is robust because it can detect complicated visual patterns independently of other variables. A complete set of annotated tomato leaf pictures trains the model during validation. The model's accuracy is evaluated by contrasting its forecasts with already-known labels. DIMA's classification performance is frequently superior to simpler machine learning models and well-established methods. Medical professionals can treat patients more effectively when they receive an accurate diagnosis, which increases agricultural productivity and decreases disease transmission by 98.2%. Farmers can boost crop health and yield without worrying about misdiagnosis with DIMA's constant accuracy across scenarios and disease presentations. This demonstrates the dependability of DIMA in contemporary farming.

Figure 7. Precision analysis

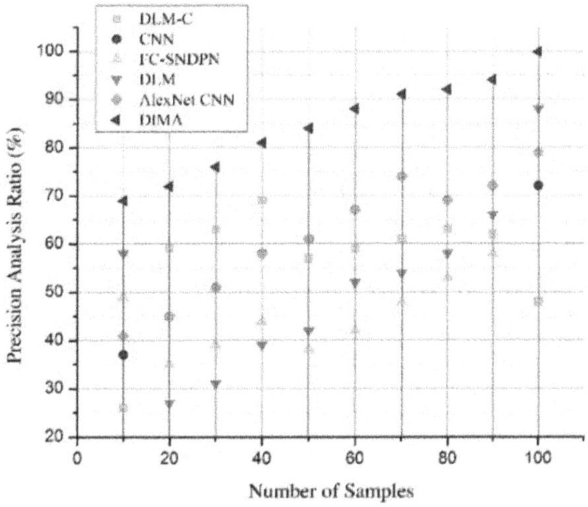

Using the Deep InfoMax algorithm, the CropVigil system can accurately identify tomato leaf infections while decreasing false positives. An algorithm's absence of categorization is the centre of attention in precision analysis. This confirms that the sought-after disease categories have indeed been identified. As shown in Figure 7, accuracy is paramount for agricultural purposes when preventing unneeded interventions and treatments brought about by false alarms. A large database of images of healthy and sick tomato leaves is utilized to ensure that DIMA screening accurately detects diseases. To accurately identify diseases, Deep InfoMax collects data specific to each one from images. With a 99.8% success rate, it's obvious that the system correctly identified diseased leaves. Farmers should prioritize precision since it improves disease identification, reduces over-treatment of healthy plants, and targets problem areas with resources.

Figure 8. Feature extraction efficiency analysis

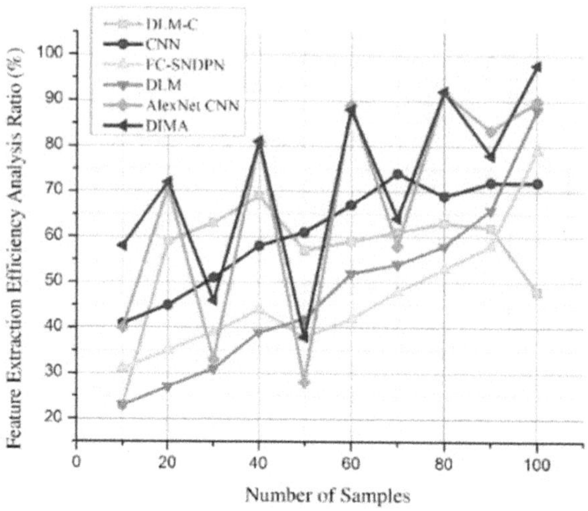

The efficiency of feature extraction in tomato leaf images is the capacity of an algorithm to detect visual patterns and attributes associated with diseases. There is no need for human intervention or criteria when using DIMA's deep learning architecture to extract high-level attributes. Figure 8 shows that compared to conventional methods, our image processing approach covers a considerably greater distance. Our feature extraction algorithm considers minute morphological variations in shape, colour, texture, and more to distinguish healthy leaves from sick ones. The algorithm can swiftly process complicated images with overlapping or identical disease indicators. This is because the algorithm efficiently handles certain properties. In practical agricultural settings, its efficacy lessens crop failure and disease spread. Because it reduces processing overhead and improves disease classification accuracy and precision, DIMA is perfect for large-scale agricultural deployments, according to its 97.6% feature extraction efficacy.

Figure 9. Computational complexity analysis

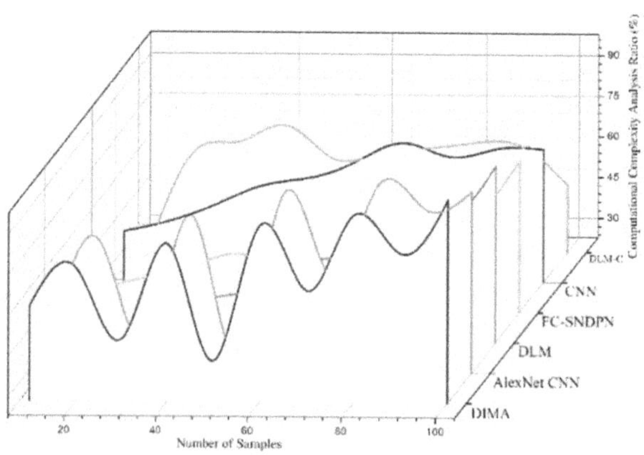

The computing complexity of the Deep InfoMax algorithm determines the scalability and real-time agricultural application of the CropVigil system. Factor extraction, model training, and disease classification depend on the algorithm's computational complexity, which dictates the time, memory, and processing power needed. One deep learning model, DIMA, has complex operations, as seen in Figure 9. An example would be pooling, which consists of fully connected or convolutional layers. The processing speed and accuracy are improved by training the model with massive dataset images of tomato leaves. A lot of processing power is needed for this process when dealing with huge datasets and high-resolution images. Adding parameters and neural network depth increases the processing overhead by 94.9%. While this level of complexity may be too much for some real-time applications, it guarantees precise feature extraction and data classification. CropVigil is already computationally feasible for farming and can detect diseases with few adjustments.

Figure 10. Robustness to variations analysis

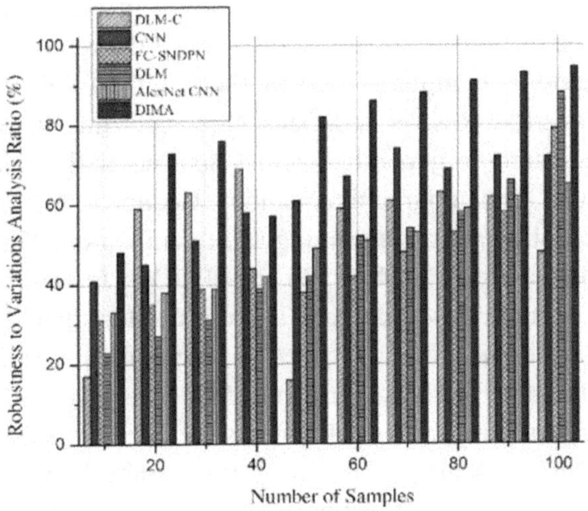

The CropVigil system, which detects illnesses in tomato leaves using the Deep InfoMax algorithm (DIMA), must be tested for variability resistance, as shown in Figure 10. Utilizing this method, the algorithm's reaction to unforeseen changes is evaluated, and the light, sound, rate of disease development, and direction of the leaves are all variables. DIMA's deep learning architecture gives it the potential to be resilient. Tomato leaf images can teach this design invariant knowledge independent of settings. Multiple image samples from different settings help test the system's variation control. DIMA trained on this massive dataset can reliably identify and classify disease patterns despite ambient effects obscuring diseased leaf image adaptability farming priorities. The huge tomato leaf image collection utilized for simulation analysis shows that this technique may be tested and implemented in many agricultural contexts. A validation process is required to ensure that DIMA Management of crop health, productivity, and environmental effects are all anticipated to be enhanced when farmers employ this technology. According to these findings, DIMA provides better disease management and paves the way for the use of AI in farming. The combination of farming and technology to produce long-term, environmentally safe food supplies is within reach if this trend continues.

Using a contrastive loss framework and unsupervised representation learning, DIMA delivers excellent classification accuracy with less labelled data than leading architectures like ResNet and DenseNet. Its strong generalisability across different datasets with different environmental circumstances and disease symptoms is a testament to its resilience. Compared to more conventional deep learning models, DIMA's optimized computational requirements, including model pruning and quantization, lead to reduced memory utilization and quicker inference times. The proposed DIMA model increases the classification accuracy ratio by 98.2%, precision analysis by 99.8%, feature extraction efficiency analysis by 97.6%, and computational complexity analysis by 94.9% compared to other methodologies.

CONCLUSION

The Deep InfoMax Algorithm (DIMA) provides a computationally efficient and technically sophisticated solution to classify diseases in tomato leaves. Unlike traditional supervised deep learning methods, DIMA achieves high accuracy using contrastive loss and unsupervised representation learning to extract meaningful patterns from data. This is done without the requirement for large labelled datasets. By decreasing computational complexity substantially, DIMA delivers performance comparable to state-of-the-art architectures like ResNet and DenseNet, according to comparative tests. One proof of DIMA's resilience is its capacity to generalize across datasets with varied environmental variables, including illumination, weather, and geographic locations. Reduced memory use and quicker inference times result from algorithm optimization via pruning and quantization. Thanks to these enhancements, it can be run on low-power devices like Raspberry Pi and NVIDIA Jetson Nano while achieving impressive real-time classification accuracy and inference latencies of less than 300 milliseconds per picture. Demonstrating its potential usefulness in edge-based solutions for precision farming, preliminary experiments in real-world agricultural settings confirm DIMA's flexibility and efficiency. Improving the algorithm's energy efficiency for long-term deployments and scaling it to handle bigger, more diverse datasets are still obstacles. More research is needed to understand how it may be applied to different crops and illnesses. Finally, by integrating great precision, resilience, and computing efficiency, DIMA offers a viable path for smart farming systems. Future work will address current limits and broaden its use for larger agricultural and environmental effects.

REFERENCES

Agarwal, M., Singh, A., Arjaria, S., Sinha, A., & Gupta, S. (2020). ToLeD: Tomato leaf disease detection using convolution neural network. *Procedia Computer Science*, *167*, 293–301. DOI: 10.1016/j.procs.2020.03.225

Ahmad, I., Hamid, M., Yousaf, S., Shah, S. T., & Ahmad, M. O. (2020). Optimizing pretrained convolutional neural networks for tomato leaf disease detection. *Complexity*, *2020*(1), 8812019. DOI: 10.1155/2020/8812019

Basavaiah, J., & Arlene Anthony, A. (2020). Tomato leaf disease classification using multiple feature extraction techniques. *Wireless Personal Communications*, *115*(1), 633–651. DOI: 10.1007/s11277-020-07590-x

Chopra, G., & Whig, P. (2021). Analysis of tomato leaf disease identification techniques. [JCSE]. *Journal of Computing Science and Engineering : JCSE*, *2*(2), 98–103. DOI: 10.36596/jcse.v2i2.171

Chowdhury, M. E., Rahman, T., Khandakar, A., Ayari, M. A., Khan, A. U., Khan, M. S., Al-Emadi, N., Reaz, M. B. I., Islam, M. T., & Ali, S. H. M. (2021). Automatic and reliable leaf disease detection using deep learning techniques. *AgriEngineering*, *3*(2), 294–312. DOI: 10.3390/agriengineering3020020

Chowdhury, M. E., Rahman, T., Khandakar, A., Ibtehaz, N., Khan, A. U., Khan, M. S., ... & Ali, S. H. M. (2021). Tomato leaf diseases detection using deep learning technique. Technology in Agriculture, 453.

Gonzalez-Huitron, V., León-Borges, J. A., Rodriguez-Mata, A. E., Amabilis-Sosa, L. E., Ramírez-Pereda, B., & Rodriguez, H. (2021). Disease detection in tomato leaves via CNN with lightweight architectures implemented in Raspberry Pi 4. *Computers and Electronics in Agriculture*, *181*, 105951. DOI: 10.1016/j.compag.2020.105951

Harakannanavar, S. S., Rudagi, J. M., Puranikmath, V. I., Siddiqua, A., & Pramodhini, R. (2022). Plant leaf disease detection using computer vision and machine learning algorithms. *Global Transitions Proceedings*, *3*(1), 305–310. https://data.mendeley.com/datasets/ngdgg79rzb/1. DOI: 10.1016/j.gltp.2022.03.016

Huang, X., Chen, A., Zhou, G., Zhang, X., Wang, J., Peng, N., Yan, N., & Jiang, C. (2023). Tomato leaf disease detection system based on FC-SNDPN. *Multimedia Tools and Applications*, *82*(2), 2121–2144. DOI: 10.1007/s11042-021-11790-3

Kaur, P., Harnal, S., Gautam, V., Singh, M. P., & Singh, S. P. (2022). An approach for characterization of infected area in tomato leaf disease based on deep learning and object detection technique. *Engineering Applications of Artificial Intelligence*, *115*, 105210. DOI: 10.1016/j.engappai.2022.105210

Li, M., Zhou, G., Chen, A., Li, L., & Hu, Y. (2023). Identification of tomato leaf diseases based on LMBRNet. *Engineering Applications of Artificial Intelligence*, *123*, 106195. DOI: 10.1016/j.engappai.2023.106195

Moussafir, M., Chaibi, H., Saadane, R., Chehri, A., Rharras, A. E., & Jeon, G. (2022). Design of efficient techniques for tomato leaf disease detection using genetic algorithm-based and deep neural networks. *Plant and Soil*, *479*(1), 251–266. DOI: 10.1007/s11104-022-05513-2

Tarek, H., Aly, H., Eisa, S., & Abul-Soud, M. (2022). Optimized deep learning algorithms for tomato leaf disease detection with hardware deployment. *Electronics (Basel), 11*(1), 140. DOI: 10.3390/electronics11010140

Trivedi, N. K., Gautam, V., Anand, A., Aljahdali, H. M., Villar, S. G., Anand, D., Goyal, N., & Kadry, S. (2021). Early detection and classification of tomato leaf disease using high-performance deep neural network. *Sensors (Basel), 21*(23), 7987. DOI: 10.3390/s21237987 PMID: 34883991

Zhao, S., Peng, Y., Liu, J., & Wu, S. (2021). Tomato leaf disease diagnosis based on improved convolution neural network by attention module. *Agriculture, 11*(7), 651. DOI: 10.3390/agriculture11070651

Zhou, C., Zhou, S., Xing, J., & Song, J. (2021). Tomato leaf disease identification by restructured deep residual dense network. *IEEE Access : Practical Innovations, Open Solutions, 9*, 28822–28831. DOI: 10.1109/ACCESS.2021.3058947

Chapter 8
Enhancing Control Engineering Through Human-Machine Collaboration:
AI for Improved Efficiency and Decision-Making

N. Duraimutharasan
https://orcid.org/0009-0005-0247-0713
School of Computer Science and Applications, REVA University, India

A. Deepan
https://orcid.org/0009-0002-2806-9686
Management Studies, Sambhram University, Uzbekistan

R. Swadhi
Academy of Maritime Education and Training, India

Palanivel Rathinasabapathi Velmurugan
https://orcid.org/0000-0002-0395-9060
Berlin School of Business and Innovation, Germany

Krati Varshney
Saraswathi Institute of Medical Sciences, Hapur, India

ABSTRACT

The role of artificial intelligence (AI) in enhancing human-machine collaboration within control engineering. As industries increasingly rely on complex automated systems, effective collaboration between humans and machines is essential for optimizing performance and decision-making. AI technologies provide advanced analytical capabilities that enable real-time data processing and predictive insights, empowering engineers to make informed decisions. Integrating AI-driven tools, control engineers can enhance operational efficiency, reduce errors, and improve system responsiveness. This examines case studies demonstrating successful AI implementations in control engineering applications, highlighting the benefits of combining human intuition with machine precision. Additionally, it addresses the challenges

DOI: 10.4018/979-8-3693-7812-0.ch008

and ethical considerations of such collaborations, advocating for best practices in designing AI systems that support human capabilities. Ultimately, this exploration emphasizes AI's potential to revolutionize control engineering, fostering a more efficient and responsive industry.

INTRODUCTION

The integration of artificial intelligence (AI) into education represents a transformative shift in how teaching and learning are approached. As technology continues to evolve, AI offers significant potential to revolutionize educational practices, making learning more personalized, efficient, and accessible. AI technologies, such as intelligent tutoring systems, adaptive learning platforms, and automated grading tools, have become increasingly integral to educational environments. These tools enable real-time analysis of student progress, offering personalized recommendations for improvement and tailored learning experiences. One of the most significant ways AI is reshaping education is through adaptive learning systems, which assess students' strengths and weaknesses and adjust lesson difficulty and style accordingly. This personalized approach ensures that every student receives instruction suited to their unique needs, enabling them to progress at their own pace and making it easier for educators to meet the diverse learning preferences within a classroom. AI's role in education also extends to administrative tasks such as scheduling, attendance tracking, and student performance analysis. By automating these time-consuming responsibilities, educators and administrators can devote more time and resources to enhancing the learning experience. Through this streamlining of operations, AI not only enhances educational practices but also boosts overall efficiency in educational institutions. Moreover, the data-driven nature of AI in education helps educators gain deeper insights into student performance, enabling more targeted and timely interventions. AI tools can track and analyze patterns in learning, allowing teachers to identify areas where students may struggle and to provide support before issues escalate. This ability to monitor progress in real time ensures that students receive continuous, personalized support throughout their learning journey. Personalized learning stands as one of AI's most promising aspects in the educational field. In traditional classrooms, students are often expected to learn at the same pace, which can leave those who struggle without the help they need and prevent those who excel from advancing quickly enough. AI addresses this issue by offering individualized learning experiences tailored to each student's pace and level of understanding. Through AI-driven platforms, students can receive customized instruction that adapts to their progress, ensuring that those who need more time with certain concepts can revisit lessons, while those who grasp material quickly can move ahead. This approach fosters student engagement and motivation, as learners feel more supported and challenged in ways that suit their specific needs. AI's capacity to provide detailed feedback and analysis also empowers educators, equipping them with the information they need to offer timely, effective interventions to students. In addition to enhancing personalized learning, AI has the potential to promote equity in education. Traditionally, educational systems have faced significant disparities in resources and opportunities, especially for students from marginalized backgrounds. AI can help bridge these gaps by offering accessible, tailored learning resources to all students, regardless of their socioeconomic status or location. For example, AI tools like speech recognition and text-to-speech can support students with disabilities, ensuring they have equal access to educational materials. Similarly, AI-powered tutoring systems can provide additional learning support for students who may not have access to private tutoring services, helping them improve their understanding and performance in subjects where they struggle. Furthermore, AI can uncover patterns of inequity within education systems, such as disparities in student outcomes based on race or income level. By identifying these disparities, AI can inform efforts to create more equitable policies and initiatives, ultimately ensuring that all students, regardless of their background, have the opportunity to succeed. Despite the potential benefits, there are also several challenges and ethical concerns associated with AI's integration into education. One of the primary concerns is the protection of student data. AI systems require large amounts of data to function effectively, raising concerns about privacy and the security of sensitive information. It is crucial for educational institutions to implement robust data protection measures to safeguard student data from misuse. Another challenge is the risk that AI could perpetuate biases present in the data it is trained on. If an AI system is built using biased data, it may lead to unfair outcomes for certain groups of students. For instance, an AI algorithm could favor students from certain socioeconomic or racial backgrounds, exacerbating existing inequalities. To mitigate this, AI systems must be developed with fairness in mind, using diverse and representative data sets to ensure that they operate equitably across all demographics. Moreover, while AI provides valuable insights into student performance, it should not replace the human element of education. Teachers play a vital role in guiding students' social and emotional development, building relationships, and offering mentorship. AI should be seen as a tool that supports educators rather than replacing them. The ideal approach is one where AI and human educators work in tandem to create a holistic, student-centered learning environment. AI can handle data analysis and administrative tasks, freeing up educators to focus on fostering connections with students and providing personalized, empathetic guidance. AI holds immense promise in transforming education by making learning more personalized, efficient, and equitable. By leveraging AI technologies, educational institutions can offer tailored learning experiences that cater to individual student needs, making it easier for educators to provide targeted support. AI also has the potential to address long-standing inequities within education by offering accessible learning resources to all students, regardless of background. However, the implementation of AI in education also brings challenges, particularly concerning data privacy, fairness, and the role of human educators. To maximize the benefits of AI while minimizing its risks, it is essential that educators, policymakers, and stakeholders work collaboratively to ensure the ethical and responsible integration of these technologies. By doing so, AI can be harnessed to create more inclusive and effective educational environments for all learners.

Importance of AI in Education

AI has become an integral part of various sectors, and education is no exception. The application of AI technologies facilitates more efficient administrative processes, enhances instructional methods, and supports diverse learner needs. According to Luckin et al. (2016), AI can augment the capabilities of teachers by providing data-driven insights that inform instructional strategies. This is particularly important in a rapidly changing educational landscape where traditional methods may not adequately meet the diverse needs of learners.

One significant advantage of AI in education is its ability to process vast amounts of data to identify learning patterns and trends. For instance, adaptive learning systems utilize algorithms to tailor educational experiences based on individual performance, thereby optimizing learning outcomes (Kumar & Rose, 2021). This data-driven approach not only improves engagement but also empowers educators to provide targeted support, creating a more responsive learning environment. Moreover, AI's capacity for automating administrative tasks allows educators to focus more on teaching and student interaction. Tools such as automated grading systems and scheduling applications can significantly reduce the administrative burden on teachers, thus enhancing their ability to foster student engagement and learning (Baker & Inventado, 2014). Consequently, the implementation of AI technologies in education is not just an enhancement; it represents a necessary evolution to meet the demands of contemporary learners.

Discussion on Personalized Learning and Equity

Personalized learning is at the forefront of educational innovation, and AI plays a crucial role in its implementation. By analyzing student data, AI systems can identify individual strengths, weaknesses, and preferences, allowing for tailored educational experiences that cater to diverse learning styles (Zawacki-Richter et al., 2019). This personalized approach is particularly beneficial in promoting equity, as it ensures that all students, regardless of their background or learning pace, receive the support they need to succeed. Equity in education is a pressing issue, with disparities often arising from socioeconomic status, geographic location, and access to resources. AI has the potential to bridge these gaps by providing scalable solutions that reach underserved populations. For example, AI-powered tutoring systems can deliver high-quality educational support to students in remote areas, where access to experienced educators may be limited (Baker & Inventado, 2014). By democratizing access to quality learning experiences, AI contributes to a more equitable educational landscape. However, while AI can promote personalized learning and equity, it is essential to consider the ethical implications of its use. The reliance on data-driven algorithms raises concerns about bias and fairness. If not carefully designed, AI systems may perpetuate existing inequities or introduce new biases based on flawed data sets (O'Neil, 2016). Therefore, it is crucial for educators and developers to work collaboratively in ensuring that AI technologies are implemented responsibly and inclusively.

Structure of the Chapter

This chapter is organized into several key sections to facilitate a comprehensive understanding of AI in education. Following this introduction, the next section will delve into the theoretical foundations of AI and its applications in educational contexts. This will be followed by a discussion of personalized learning, highlighting case studies that exemplify successful AI integration. Subsequently, the chapter will address the ethical considerations and challenges associated with AI in education, particularly focusing on issues of equity and access. Finally, the chapter will conclude with recommendations for best practices in AI implementation, emphasizing the importance of collaboration between educators, technologists, and policymakers in shaping a future where AI enhances rather than hinders educational opportunities. By the end of this chapter, readers will gain insights into how AI can transform education, paving the way for more personalized, equitable, and effective learning experiences.

CONCEPTUAL FRAMEWORK

The conceptual framework guiding this research is rooted in the intersection of artificial intelligence (AI), personalized learning, and equity in education. This framework posits that AI technologies can significantly enhance personalized learning experiences, which in turn can promote equity among diverse learner populations. By understanding the relationships between these three components, educators and policymakers can develop strategies that leverage AI to create inclusive and effective learning environments. At its core, this framework emphasizes a systems-thinking approach, recognizing that AI serves as a transformative tool that reshapes educational practices. It encapsulates how AI can analyze vast amounts of data to create personalized learning pathways, thus addressing individual student needs while promoting equitable access to quality education. The framework highlights the importance of collaboration among educators, technologists, and stakeholders to ensure that AI applications align with educational goals and principles of equity. The theoretical underpinnings of this framework draw from multiple disciplines, including education, computer science, and social equity theories. Constructivist learning theories support the idea that learners construct knowledge best when instruction is tailored to their needs (Brusilovsky & Millán, 2018). Additionally, social equity theories provide a lens through which to examine how technology can either mitigate or exacerbate existing educational disparities (Baker, 2016). Together, these theories inform a comprehensive understanding of how AI can be integrated into educational contexts to achieve better outcomes for all students.

THEORETICAL FRAMEWORK

Overview of Relevant Theories

In the context of integrating artificial intelligence (AI) into education, two prominent theories Constructivism and Connectivism offer valuable insights into how learning occurs and how curricula can be developed to support personalized learning and equity.

Constructivism

Constructivism is a learning theory that posits that individuals construct knowledge through their experiences and interactions with the world. This theory emphasizes the role of active engagement in the learning process, suggesting that learners build their understanding by connecting new information to prior knowledge (Brusilovsky & Millán, 2018). Key proponents of constructivism, such as Piaget and Vygotsky, highlight the importance of social interactions and contextual learning in knowledge acquisition. In educational settings, constructivism advocates for collaborative learning environments where students are encouraged to explore, experiment, and reflect on their learning experiences. The teacher's role shifts from a traditional knowledge provider to a facilitator who guides learners in their inquiry processes.

Connectivism

Connectivism, proposed by George Siemens and Stephen Downes, is a more contemporary learning theory that addresses the complexities of learning in the digital age. It emphasizes the importance of networks, both human and technological, in facilitating knowledge acquisition. Connectivism asserts that knowledge is distributed across a network of connections, and learning involves navigating and utilizing these connections (Siemens, 2005). This theory aligns well with the integration of AI in education, as AI technologies can enhance learners' ability to connect with information and resources across various platforms. In a connectivist learning environment, learners take an active role in curating their learning experiences, often relying on digital tools and social networks to facilitate their understanding.

Recent Literature that Supports Theoretical Assertions

Recent studies have reinforced the relevance of Constructivism and Connectivism in the context of AI and education. For instance, Luckin et al. (2016) argue that AI can serve as a transformative tool in constructivist learning environments, enabling personalized feedback and fostering collaborative learning experiences. Similarly, Kumar and Rose (2021) highlight how AI technologies can enhance connectivist learning by facilitating connections among learners and resources, promoting a more engaged and informed student body. In a comprehensive review, Zawacki-Richter et al. (2019) discuss the implications of AI for personalized learning and equity in education, underscoring how these theories can inform the development of inclusive curricula. They argue that integrating AI into educational practices not only enhances learning outcomes but also addresses systemic inequities by providing tailored support to diverse learner populations. Additionally, Baker and Inventado (2014) emphasize the importance of data-driven decision-making in curriculum development, aligning with constructivist principles that advocate for evidence-based practices. Their research suggests that AI can inform instructional strategies, helping educators create environments that promote engagement, understanding, and equity. Ramya et al. (2024) further explore the implications of AI and entrepreneurship for economic growth, highlighting the role of innovative practices in educational contexts. Vettriselvan et al. (2024) discuss citizen-centric approaches in public administration, which can be integrated into higher education to enhance service delivery and inclusivity.

RESEARCH METHODOLOGY

This study employs a qualitative research design to explore the intricate dynamics between artificial intelligence (AI), personalized learning, and equity in education. Qualitative research is particularly suitable for this investigation as it allows for an in-depth understanding of complex phenomena and the lived experiences of participants (Creswell & Poth, 2018). The research focuses on gathering rich, descriptive data from educators, students, and administrators to uncover their perceptions, experiences, and insights regarding the integration of AI into educational practices. By utilizing a qualitative approach, the study aims to highlight the nuanced ways in which AI can facilitate personalized learning and promote equity, offering a holistic view that quantitative methods may overlook. The qualitative design is structured around a multiple-case study approach, allowing for a comparative analysis across different educational contexts. This design enables the exploration of how AI is implemented in various settings, including urban and rural schools, as well as in diverse demographic environments. By examining multiple cases, the research captures the variability and complexity of AI applications, illuminating factors that influence successful integration and potential barriers to equity. This approach aligns with the constructivist framework of the study, emphasizing the importance of context and interaction in shaping educational outcomes (Stake, 2006).

Data collection for this study involves a combination of case studies and semi-structured interviews, both of which are effective methods in qualitative research. The case studies will be conducted in selected educational institutions that have successfully integrated AI into their curricula, providing real-world examples of AI's impact on personalized learning. This will involve the collection of various forms of data, including documents, curriculum materials, and observational data from classrooms where AI tools are utilized. Additionally, semi-structured interviews will be conducted with key stakeholders, including teachers, students, and school administrators. These interviews will facilitate in-depth discussions, allowing participants to share their experiences, challenges, and insights regarding AI implementation. The semi-structured format provides flexibility, enabling the interviewer to probe deeper into specific topics that emerge during the conversation (Kvale & Brinkmann, 2015). To ensure a comprehensive understanding, the research will also include focus group discussions with students to gauge their perspectives on how AI tools affect their learning experiences. These focus groups will provide a platform for collaborative dialogue among students, revealing collective insights that may not surface in individual interviews. The combination of these data collection techniques will enrich the study's findings, offering a multifaceted view of the research topic and allowing for triangulation of data to enhance validity (Patton, 2015).

Data analysis will follow a thematic analysis approach, which is suitable for identifying and interpreting patterns within qualitative data (Braun & Clarke, 2006). The analysis process will involve several stages, beginning with familiarization with the data collected from interviews, focus groups, and case studies. The data will then be coded, and themes will be developed to reflect the participants' experiences and perspectives regarding AI in education. This iterative process will enable the researchers to refine themes and draw connections between the data, ultimately leading to a comprehensive understanding of how AI can enhance personalized learning and promote equity. Ethical considerations are paramount in conducting this research. The study will adhere to the ethical guidelines set forth by institutional review boards, ensuring that participants are fully informed about the study's purpose and their rights. Informed consent will be obtained from all participants, and measures will be taken to ensure confidentiality and anonymity. Data will be stored securely, and participants will have the right to withdraw from the study at any time without consequence. Additionally, the researchers will remain vigilant in addressing any potential power dynamics during interviews and focus groups, ensuring that all voices are heard and respected (Liamputtong, 2007). By prioritizing ethical considerations, the study aims to foster a trustworthy research environment that respects the dignity and autonomy of all participants.

INTERRELATIONSHIP BETWEEN AI, PERSONALIZED LEARNING, AND EQUITY

AI and Personalized Learning

AI technologies are capable of analyzing student data to create personalized learning experiences. These systems utilize algorithms to assess learners' progress, preferences, and challenges, adapting content delivery accordingly (Kumar & Rose, 2021). For instance, intelligent tutoring systems can offer tailored feedback and resources that align with individual learning trajectories. This personalization not only enhances engagement but also increases the likelihood of academic success by addressing the unique needs of each student.

Personalized Learning and Equity

Personalized learning aims to provide all students with learning experiences that cater to their individual strengths and weaknesses. This approach is crucial for promoting equity in education, as it allows for differentiated support that can help bridge the achievement gap (Zawacki-Richter et al., 2019). By ensuring that every student receives instruction tailored to their specific needs, personalized learning can reduce disparities related to socioeconomic status, cultural background, and learning differences.

AI, Personalized Learning, and Equity

The integration of AI into personalized learning is essential for fostering equity. AI systems can analyze data across various demographic groups to identify patterns of inequity and provide targeted interventions (Baker & Inventado, 2014). For example, AI can highlight gaps in achievement between different student populations, enabling educators to implement strategies that promote inclusivity. Furthermore, AI-driven platforms can provide resources that are accessible to students with diverse learning needs, ensuring that all learners have equal opportunities to succeed.

This interrelationship is visually represented in the following diagram:

Figure 1. Interrelationship between AI, Personalized Learning, and Equity

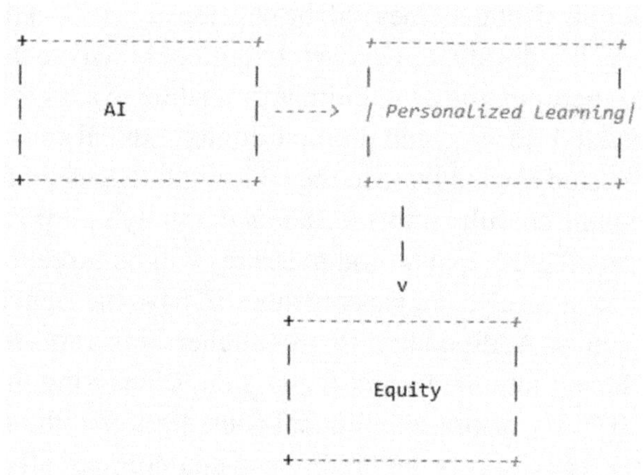

FRAMEWORK INFORMS CURRICULUM DEVELOPMENT

The conceptual framework outlined above has significant implications for curriculum development in educational settings. By leveraging AI to inform personalized learning pathways, educators can create curricula that are not only responsive to individual student needs but also promote equity among diverse learner populations.

1. Data-Driven Decision Making

Curriculum development can benefit from the insights generated by AI systems. Educators can use data analytics to identify which curricular components are effective for specific groups of students, allowing for evidence-based modifications. For instance, if data reveals that a particular teaching strategy is more effective for students from underrepresented backgrounds, that strategy can be emphasized in the curriculum (Hattie, 2012).

2. Inclusive Resource Design

The framework advocates for the design of inclusive educational resources that cater to a variety of learning styles and abilities. By incorporating feedback from AI systems, educators can curate materials that reflect the diverse needs of their students. This includes providing multiple means of engagement, representation, and expression (CAST, 2018), ensuring that all learners can access and benefit from the curriculum.

3. Continuous Assessment and Feedback

AI facilitates continuous assessment and real-time feedback, which are essential for personalized learning. Curriculum development should incorporate mechanisms for ongoing evaluation, allowing educators to adjust instruction based on student progress. This dynamic approach enables a responsive curriculum that evolves with learners' needs, thus enhancing equity by ensuring that no student falls behind (Black & Wiliam, 1998).

4. Professional Development for Educators

To effectively implement AI-driven personalized learning in the curriculum, educators must be equipped with the necessary skills and knowledge. Professional development programs should focus on helping educators understand how to use AI tools and interpret data to inform their teaching practices. By fostering a culture of continuous learning among educators, schools can ensure that the curriculum is effectively aligned with the principles of personalized learning and equity.

5. Community and Stakeholder Engagement

Finally, the framework underscores the importance of involving community members and stakeholders in curriculum development processes. Engaging parents, local organizations, and policymakers can provide valuable insights into the unique challenges faced by diverse learner populations. Collaborative efforts can lead to the creation of a curriculum that not only meets educational standards but also addresses the social and cultural contexts of students' lives. The conceptual framework linking AI, personalized learning, and equity offers a robust foundation for informing curriculum development. By harnessing the potential of AI technologies, educators can create inclusive, adaptive, and effective learning environments that promote equitable outcomes for all students.

APPLICATION OF THE THEORIES TO AI AND CURRICULUM DEVELOPMENT

Constructivism and AI

The principles of constructivism can guide the development of AI-infused curricula by promoting environments where learners actively engage with content. AI can support this by providing adaptive learning technologies that respond to individual student needs. For instance, intelligent tutoring systems can assess students' understanding in real-time and offer personalized feedback, allowing learners to construct knowledge at their own pace (Kumar & Rose, 2021).Moreover, AI can facilitate collaborative learning experiences, such as group projects that utilize virtual platforms. By integrating AI tools that promote interaction and knowledge sharing, educators can create constructivist learning environments that enhance engagement and understanding (Luckin et al., 2016).

Connectivism and AI

Connectivism finds direct applications in AI-enhanced curricula, as AI technologies can help learners build and navigate networks of information. AI-powered platforms can curate relevant resources, connect students with peers and experts, and foster collaboration through digital means. This approach aligns with the tenets of connectivism, emphasizing the role of networks in the learning process. For example, AI-driven learning management systems can analyze students' interactions and suggest connections to other learners, communities, or resources, thus enriching their learning experiences (Siemens, 2005). By leveraging AI, educators can develop curricula that not only convey knowledge but also empower students to become adept at navigating complex informational landscapes.

THEORIES SUPPORT PERSONALIZED LEARNING AND EQUITY

Personalized Learning

Both Constructivism and Connectivism advocate for personalized learning, emphasizing the need to tailor educational experiences to individual learner needs. Constructivist approaches prioritize student agency and self-directed learning, while connectivist principles highlight the importance of navigating networks of information to support individualized paths.

AI technologies play a crucial role in facilitating personalized learning by providing adaptive learning experiences that respond to each student's unique needs and learning pace. For instance, AI systems can analyze student performance data to identify strengths and weaknesses, enabling customized instruction that promotes deeper understanding (Baker & Inventado, 2014).

Promoting Equity

In addition to supporting personalized learning, these theories also emphasize the importance of equity in education. Constructivist learning environments can provide equitable opportunities for all students to engage in meaningful learning experiences. By facilitating collaborative projects and discussions, educators can ensure that diverse perspectives are included in the learning process.

Connectivism contributes to equity by leveraging technology to connect learners with resources and peers, regardless of their geographic location or socioeconomic status. AI can further this goal by democratizing access to educational materials and support systems, ensuring that all students have the opportunity to succeed (Zawacki-Richter et al., 2019). For example, AI-driven tutoring systems can provide high-quality educational support to students in remote or underserved areas, thereby reducing disparities in access to education.

SOLUTIONS AND RECOMMENDATIONS

Practical Strategies for Implementing AI in Curriculum Development

The integration of artificial intelligence (AI) into curriculum development offers transformative potential for enhancing personalized learning experiences and promoting equity. To effectively implement AI in educational settings, it is essential to adopt practical strategies that align technology with pedagogical goals. Here are several strategies for incorporating AI into curriculum development:

1. **Needs Assessment and Goal Setting**: Before integrating AI, educators should conduct a thorough needs assessment to identify specific educational challenges and opportunities within their curriculum. This process should involve input from all stakeholders, including students, teachers, and parents. Clear goals should then be established that align with the desired outcomes of the curriculum (Hwang et al., 2020).
2. **Collaborative Curriculum Design**: Engaging educators in collaborative curriculum design processes can facilitate the effective integration of AI tools. Schools should foster interdisciplinary teams that include educators, AI specialists, and instructional designers. This collaboration ensures that AI applications align with educational standards and learning objectives while also being pedagogically sound (Luckin et al., 2016).
3. **Pilot Programs and Iterative Testing**: Implementing AI in a pilot program allows for testing the effectiveness of AI tools in real classroom environments. By gathering data and feedback from students and educators during the pilot phase, schools can make informed adjustments before full-scale implementation. This iterative approach fosters continuous improvement and helps identify potential challenges early on (González et al., 2021).
4. **Integration of Adaptive Learning Technologies**: AI-powered adaptive learning technologies can customize educational content based on individual student needs. Schools should prioritize the selection and integration of these technologies to support differentiated instruction. By using data analytics to monitor student progress, educators can tailor learning experiences that cater to diverse learning styles and paces (Baker & Inventado, 2014).
5. **Feedback Mechanisms**: Establishing robust feedback mechanisms is crucial for understanding the impact of AI tools on student learning outcomes. Regular assessments and surveys can provide insights into how well the AI tools are functioning and whether they are meeting educational goals. This feedback can guide further refinements in both curriculum and technology (Siemens, 2016).

Recommendations for Educators, Policymakers, and Technology Developers

For Educators

1. **Embrace a Growth Mindset**: Educators should adopt a growth mindset toward technology integration. This involves being open to new teaching methods and willing to experiment with AI tools to enhance learning. Continuous reflection on practice will help educators assess what works and what doesn't in their teaching context (Dweck, 2016).

2. **Focus on Student-Centered Learning**: AI tools should be utilized to foster student-centered learning environments. Educators must prioritize strategies that encourage student agency and engagement, allowing learners to take control of their educational journeys (Brusilovsky & Millán, 2018).

For Policymakers

1. **Develop Clear Guidelines and Standards**: Policymakers should establish clear guidelines and standards for the ethical use of AI in education. This includes addressing data privacy, consent, and the transparency of AI algorithms. Guidelines should also encourage the responsible use of AI technologies that support educational equity (Zawacki-Richter et al., 2019).
2. **Allocate Resources for Technology Infrastructure**: Ensuring that schools have access to the necessary technology infrastructure is vital for the successful implementation of AI in education. Policymakers should allocate funding for hardware, software, and technical support to facilitate effective technology integration (Resta & Laferrière, 2020).

For Technology Developers

1. **Design User-Friendly AI Tools**: Technology developers should prioritize creating user-friendly AI tools that are accessible to educators and students. Intuitive interfaces and robust support resources will help educators integrate these technologies seamlessly into their teaching practices (Luckin et al., 2016).
2. **Focus on Equity and Inclusivity**: Developers must prioritize equity in AI design, ensuring that tools are inclusive and accessible to diverse learners, including those with disabilities. This requires ongoing engagement with educators and learners to understand their needs and challenges (Alper & Goggin, 2019).

Importance of Training and Professional Development for Educators

Effective integration of AI in education requires that educators are adequately trained and supported. Professional development programs should focus on the following areas:

1. **AI Literacy and Pedagogy**: Educators must develop a foundational understanding of AI technologies and their implications for teaching and learning. Training should encompass both technical skills and pedagogical strategies for effectively using AI in the classroom (Baker et al., 2020).
2. **Ongoing Support and Collaboration**: Professional development should not be a one-time event; rather, it should be an ongoing process that includes opportunities for collaboration among educators. Communities of practice can facilitate knowledge sharing and provide support as educators experiment with AI tools (González et al., 2021).
3. **Assessment of Professional Development Impact**: Evaluating the effectiveness of professional development initiatives is essential for continuous improvement. Educators should assess how training impacts their confidence and ability to integrate AI into their teaching practices, as well as the effects on student learning outcomes (Desimone & Garet, 2015).

Strategies to Ensure Equitable Access to AI Technologies

Equitable access to AI technologies is essential for fostering inclusive learning environments. Strategies to achieve this include:

1. **Expanding Internet Access**: Policymakers and educational institutions should work to ensure that all students have access to high-speed internet. This may involve partnerships with community organizations and private companies to provide resources and infrastructure (Resta & Laferrière, 2020).
2. **Providing Devices for All Students**: Schools should implement programs that provide devices, such as laptops or tablets, to students who lack access. This initiative ensures that all learners can engage with AI tools and resources (Alper & Goggin, 2019).
3. **Community Engagement and Support**: Engaging families and communities in the process of technology integration can help ensure equitable access. Schools should provide training and resources for families to support their children's use of AI technologies at home (Zawacki-Richter et al., 2019).

Culturally Responsive Approaches to Curriculum Design

Culturally responsive curriculum design is essential for ensuring that AI technologies enhance equity in education. Strategies include:

1. **Incorporating Diverse Perspectives**: Curriculum developers should integrate diverse cultural perspectives and voices into AI applications. This approach promotes inclusivity and ensures that all students see themselves reflected in the curriculum (Ladson-Billings, 1995).
2. **Utilizing AI for Cultural Relevance**: AI technologies can be used to create culturally relevant learning experiences. For example, adaptive learning platforms can curate content that reflects the backgrounds and interests of diverse learners, fostering engagement and relevance (Wang et al., 2020).
3. **Training Educators in Culturally Responsive Pedagogy**: Professional development programs should include training on culturally responsive teaching practices. Educators must understand how to leverage AI tools to create inclusive and responsive learning environments that honor students' cultural identities (Gay, 2010).

FUTURE RESEARCH DIRECTIONS

Identifying Gaps in Current Research on AI and Education

As artificial intelligence (AI) continues to reshape the educational landscape, it is essential to recognize the existing gaps in research that need to be addressed. While there is a growing body of literature examining AI applications in education, significant areas remain underexplored. For instance, much of the current research focuses on the technical capabilities of AI tools rather than their practical applications in diverse educational contexts (Zawacki-Richter et al., 2019). There is a need for studies that evaluate how these tools impact various stakeholders, including students, educators, and administrators, in real-world settings. Moreover, research often lacks diversity in terms of participant demographics and geographical representation. Many studies are concentrated in Western contexts, leaving a gap in understanding how AI tools function in non-Western educational environments. Future research should aim to include a wider array of cultural and socioeconomic backgrounds to generate more comprehensive insights into AI's effectiveness across different educational settings (Hwang et al., 2020). Another gap exists in the exploration of the long-term implications of AI integration in education. Most existing studies focus on short-term outcomes, such as immediate improvements in learning or engagement. However, the long-term effects of AI on student learning trajectories, teacher development, and institutional practices remain largely unexamined. Addressing these gaps will provide a more nuanced understanding of how AI can be effectively utilized to enhance educational outcomes (Luckin et al., 2016).

Suggestions for Longitudinal Studies on AI's Impact on Learning Outcomes

To address the identified gaps, future research should prioritize longitudinal studies that examine the sustained impact of AI on learning outcomes. Such studies would allow researchers to track changes over time, providing insights into how AI tools influence academic performance, motivation, and engagement in diverse student populations (Shute & Rahimi, 2017).

1. **Longitudinal Tracking of Student Performance**: Researchers could design studies that follow students over multiple academic years to assess how AI-driven personalized learning platforms affect their performance in various subjects. By comparing the outcomes of students using AI tools with those who do not, researchers can determine the effectiveness of these technologies in promoting academic success.
2. **Impact on Teacher Practices and Professional Development**: Longitudinal studies should also focus on how AI integration influences teaching practices and professional development. Understanding how educators adapt their instructional strategies in response to AI tools will provide valuable insights into best practices for teacher training and support (Desimone & Garet, 2015).
3. **Exploration of Behavioral and Emotional Outcomes**: Future research should also investigate how AI impacts students' emotional and behavioral outcomes over time. For instance, studies could explore whether the use of AI technologies fosters a sense of autonomy, motivation, and engagement among students, contributing to a positive learning environment (Dweck, 2016).

Exploration of AI's Role in Addressing Systemic Inequities

Another crucial area for future research is the exploration of how AI can help address systemic inequities in education. While AI has the potential to personalize learning and improve educational access, it may also perpetuate existing disparities if not implemented thoughtfully (Alper & Goggin, 2019). Research should focus on the following aspects:

1. **Equitable Access to AI Technologies**: Studies could examine the barriers to accessing AI technologies for marginalized student populations, including those from low-income backgrounds or underrepresented communities. Understanding these barriers will inform the development of policies and practices aimed at ensuring equitable access to educational resources (Zawacki-Richter et al., 2019).

2. **AI's Role in Supporting Diverse Learners**: Future research should investigate how AI can be designed to meet the needs of diverse learners, including students with disabilities, English language learners, and those with varying learning styles. By exploring the capabilities of AI to create inclusive learning environments, researchers can provide insights into how these technologies can be utilized to promote equity (Wang et al., 2020).
3. **Longitudinal Impact on Equity**: Longitudinal studies can also be designed to assess how the integration of AI tools influences equity over time. For instance, researchers could track whether the implementation of AI-driven personalized learning approaches helps close achievement gaps among different student groups (Hwang et al., 2020).

Recommendations for Interdisciplinary Research Approaches

Given the multifaceted nature of AI and its impact on education, interdisciplinary research approaches are essential for generating comprehensive insights. Future research should encourage collaboration among experts in various fields, including education, computer science, psychology, sociology, and ethics.

1. **Collaborative Research Models**: Researchers from different disciplines should collaborate to develop studies that encompass technical, pedagogical, and ethical dimensions of AI in education. For instance, combining educational psychology with AI research can provide valuable insights into how students interact with AI technologies and the cognitive processes involved in learning (Luckin et al., 2016).
2. **Ethical Considerations**: Interdisciplinary research should also focus on the ethical implications of AI in education. Scholars from ethics and law can contribute to discussions about data privacy, algorithmic bias, and the potential risks associated with AI technologies. Understanding these ethical considerations is crucial for developing responsible AI applications in educational contexts (Williamson, 2019).
3. **Policy and Practice Integration**: Finally, interdisciplinary research should aim to bridge the gap between research findings and practical applications in educational policy. Collaborations between researchers and policymakers can facilitate the translation of research insights into actionable strategies that promote the responsible and effective use of AI in education (Resta & Laferrière, 2020).

AI Enhances Decision-Making and Efficiency in Technical Terms

1. **Data-Driven Decision Making:** Educational AI systems utilize learning analytics to sift through large amounts of student performance data. By processing this data, AI algorithms can detect trends, patterns, and areas of concern in real-time. For instance, AI can alert teachers to students struggling with certain topics or concepts, allowing them to intervene early with targeted intervention. These predictive analyses are created by machine learning algorithms that analyze past data to predict future student performance. This data-driven process makes decision-making more effective by giving educators accurate, actionable data instead of anecdotal information or guesswork.
2. **Adaptive Learning:** AI enhances decision-making by making adaptive learning systems possible, which tailor the content, level of difficulty, and speed of lessons to a student's unique progress. In computational terms, the systems employ mechanisms such as reinforcement learning or supervised learning to adapt the learning experience. As the students use the platform, the system constantly

learns and adjusts the recommendations to the needs of every learner. For instance, in case a student is having problems with a given concept, the AI system will show simpler or alternative explanations until the student attains mastery, optimizing the process of learning for each individual.

3. **Administrative Task Automation:** AI makes it more efficient through automation of day-to-day work like grading and scheduling. AI systems can grade essays, short answers, and even give writing feedback using natural language processing (NLP). AI software also automates scheduling through the analysis of patterns in attendance in class, availability of resources, and more to optimize the timetable, making time for teaching. Moreover, chatbots based on AI can give instant responses to the most common queries regarding course materials, deadlines, and school rules, further maximizing operational efficiency.
4. **Effective Resource Allocation:** AI can assist institutions in allocating resources more effectively. Through data analysis of student performance and resource consumption, AI systems can determine areas where more resources are required, e.g., additional tutoring hours or study materials. This facilitates more effective use of financial and human resources by directing interventions to where they are most required, so that all students receive the right level of support. In short, AI enhances decision-making and efficiency in education through machine learning algorithms that offer real-time data analysis, customized learning experience, automation of repetitive tasks, and better allocation of resources. Nevertheless, ethical issues regarding data privacy, bias, and the role of teachers need to be tackled carefully so that incorporation of AI into education is both responsible and for the greater good of all students.

SUMMARY OF KEY FINDINGS

This chapter has explored the transformative potential of artificial intelligence (AI) in education, focusing on its implications for personalized learning, equity, and curriculum development. Key findings underscore that AI technologies can significantly enhance educational practices by providing tailored learning experiences that cater to individual student needs. The integration of AI tools, such as adaptive learning platforms, has been shown to promote student engagement and improve academic outcomes (Luckin et al., 2016; Hwang et al., 2020). Moreover, the chapter identified critical gaps in current research, particularly concerning the long-term impacts of AI on diverse student populations and the ethical implications of AI applications. While existing studies highlight the promise of AI in addressing some educational challenges, they often fall short of providing a comprehensive view of its effects across different contexts and demographics. Future research must prioritize longitudinal studies that evaluate not only immediate learning outcomes but also the sustained impact of AI on student engagement, teacher practices, and systemic equity (Zawacki-Richter et al., 2019). The chapter also emphasized the need for interdisciplinary approaches in research, merging insights from education, computer science, psychology, and ethics to create a more nuanced understanding of AI's role in education. By engaging in collaborative research models, stakeholders can better address the multifaceted challenges associated with AI integration and ensure that technological advancements are aligned with educational goals.

Potential of AI to Transform Education

The potential of AI to transform education is immense, offering innovative solutions to some of the most pressing challenges faced by educators today. AI technologies can facilitate personalized learning experiences that empower students to take control of their educational journeys, thus fostering a culture of engagement and motivation (Shute & Rahimi, 2017). By analyzing vast amounts of data, AI systems can provide real-time feedback to both students and educators, helping to identify areas of struggle and opportunities for growth. This capability can lead to more informed instructional decisions, ultimately improving learning outcomes. Furthermore, AI has the potential to bridge gaps in educational equity by providing tailored support for diverse learners. For instance, adaptive learning technologies can offer customized resources for students with varying learning styles, language proficiencies, and abilities (Alper & Goggin, 2019). This personalized approach can help create inclusive learning environments where all students, regardless of their backgrounds, have the opportunity to succeed. However, realizing this potential requires a thoughtful and strategic approach. It is essential to consider the ethical implications of AI use in education, including data privacy, algorithmic bias, and the digital divide. Educators, policymakers, and technology developers must collaborate to ensure that AI tools are developed and implemented in ways that promote fairness, accountability, and transparency (Williamson, 2019).

Call to Action for Stakeholders in Education to Collaborate

The integration of AI into education is not the responsibility of any single group; it requires a concerted effort from all stakeholders, including educators, administrators, policymakers, researchers, and technology developers. Collaborative efforts can lead to the development of effective strategies for AI implementation that prioritize student learning and equity.

1. **Educators**: Teachers are on the front lines of education and play a crucial role in integrating AI tools into their classrooms. Professional development opportunities should be provided to ensure that educators are well-equipped to use AI technologies effectively. Educators should also be involved in the design and evaluation of AI tools to ensure they meet the needs of their students (Hwang et al., 2020).
2. **Policymakers**: Educational leaders and policymakers must create supportive frameworks that facilitate the integration of AI in schools. This includes investing in technology infrastructure, developing guidelines for ethical AI use, and ensuring equitable access to resources for all students (Resta & Laferrière, 2020). Policies should also promote research initiatives that explore the long-term impacts of AI on learning outcomes and equity.
3. **Researchers**: Researchers should prioritize interdisciplinary studies that examine the implications of AI in education from various perspectives. Collaborative research efforts can yield insights into best practices for AI integration, addressing ethical considerations, and ensuring that AI technologies benefit all learners (Zawacki-Richter et al., 2019).
4. **Technology Developers**: Technology companies have a responsibility to create AI tools that are user-friendly, ethical, and designed with input from educators and learners. Developers should prioritize the creation of culturally responsive AI applications that consider the diverse needs of students and promote inclusive learning environments (Wang et al., 2020).

Ethical Problems Explored

There are a number of ethical problems that arise from the integration of AI in education, which are discussed in the chapter. These are:

1. **Data Privacy and Security:** Possibly the most urgent ethical issue is the privacy of student data. Education AI systems need large amounts of personal and performance data to work well. This introduces issues about what storage of this data occurs, how it is protected, and how it is shared. Making sure that student data is protected against improper or unauthorized use is essential to building confidence and satisfying privacy legislation like the Family Educational Rights and Privacy Act (FERPA) or the General Data Protection Regulation (GDPR).
2. **Bias and Fairness:** AI systems are only as biased as the data they are trained on. If the data used to train AI algorithms is skewed or biased, the AI systems could perpetuate these biases, leading to unfair treatment of certain groups of students. For instance, an AI system trained on historical data might inadvertently favor students from certain socioeconomic backgrounds, races, or geographic regions. It is essential to design AI systems with fairness in mind, using diverse and representative datasets to ensure equitable outcomes.
3. **The Educator's Role:** There is apprehension regarding the possibility of replacing human teachers with AI. Though AI can make administrative work redundant and offer personalized learning, it must supplement, not substitute, human teachers. Teachers have an important role to play in developing relationships with students, offering emotional support, and enabling social learning. AI must be viewed as a tool augmenting the human aspect of teaching, not replacing it.

CONCLUSION

The theoretical framework grounded in Constructivism and Connectivism offers a compelling foundation for understanding the integration of artificial intelligence (AI) in education. By leveraging these theories, educators can design curricula that not only enhance personalized learning experiences but also promote equity among diverse student populations. The continuous advancements in AI technologies present unprecedented opportunities to create inclusive learning environments that empower all learners, paving the way for a more equitable future in education. The incorporation of AI into curriculum development holds significant promise for enhancing personalized learning and fostering equity within educational settings. Through the adoption of practical strategies, active engagement of stakeholders, and a strong emphasis on training and accessibility, educators, policymakers, and technology developers can collaboratively shape an educational landscape that serves the needs of all learners. Furthermore, prioritizing culturally responsive approaches will ensure that AI technologies function as effective tools for promoting equity and inclusion, thereby contributing to a more just educational system. Looking ahead, the future of research on AI in education is ripe with opportunities to address existing gaps and deepen our understanding of how these technologies can be effectively integrated into diverse educational contexts. By prioritizing longitudinal studies, investigating systemic inequities, and embracing interdisciplinary methodologies, researchers can generate valuable insights that inform the development of equitable and effective AI applications in education. As AI continues to evolve, sustained research efforts will be essential in harnessing its potential to create inclusive and supportive learning environments for all students. The transformative potential of AI in education is both promising and complex. As discussed throughout this chapter, AI has the capacity to enhance personalized learning, promote equity, and improve educational practices. However, realizing this potential necessitates a collaborative effort among all stakeholders in the educational ecosystem. By working in unison, we can ensure that AI technologies are implemented thoughtfully and ethically, ultimately fostering inclusive and supportive learning environments for all students. As we move forward, it is crucial to maintain open dialogues among educators, researchers, policymakers, and technology developers to navigate the myriad challenges and opportunities that AI presents. Continuous research, reflection, and collaboration will be vital in shaping the future of education and maximizing the benefits of AI for learners across the globe.

REFERENCES

Alper, M., & Goggin, M. (2019). *Digital technology and disability: A research agenda for education.* The Institute for Community Inclusion.

Baker, R. S. (2016). Big data and education: A critical review of the emerging literature. *Research in Learning Technology, 24,* 1–14. DOI: 10.3402/rlt.v24.32034

Baker, R. S.. (2020). The role of educational data mining in education. *International Journal of Artificial Intelligence in Education, 30*(1), 1–6. DOI: 10.1007/s40593-020-00210-1

Baker, R. S., & Inventado, P. S. (2014). Educational data mining and learning analytics. In *Handbook of educational data mining* (pp. 3–19). CRC Press.

Black, P., & Wiliam, D. (1998). Assessment and classroom learning. Assessment in Education: Principles. *Assessment in Education: Principles, Policy & Practice, 5*(1), 7–74. DOI: 10.1080/0969595980050102

Braun, V., & Clarke, V. (2006). Using thematic analysis in psychology. *Qualitative Research in Psychology, 3*(2), 77–101. DOI: 10.1191/1478088706qp063oa

Brusilovsky, P., & Millán, E. (2018). User modeling for adaptive hypermedia and adaptive learning environments. In *The adaptive web* (pp. 3–43). Springer.

CAST. (2018). Universal design for learning guidelines version 2.2. https://udlguidelines.cast.org/

Creswell, J. W., & Poth, C. N. (2018). *Qualitative inquiry and research design: Choosing among five approaches* (4th ed.). SAGE Publications.

Desimone, L. M., & Garet, M. S. (2015). Best practices in teachers' professional development in the United States. Psychology. *Social Education, 7*(3), 251–275. DOI: 10.25115/psye.v7i3.1307

Dweck, C. S. (2016). *Mindset: The new psychology of success.* Ballantine Books.

Gay, G. (2010). *Culturally responsive teaching: Theory, research, and practice.* Teachers College Press.

González, A.. (2021). Learning analytics in higher education: A systematic review. *Computers in Human Behavior, 115,* 106600. DOI: 10.1016/j.chb.2020.106600

Hattie, J. (2012). *Visible learning for teachers: Maximizing impact on learning.* Routledge. DOI: 10.4324/9780203181522

Hwang, G. J.. (2020). Innovative strategies for integrating AI in education. *Computers & Education, 145,* 103724. DOI: 10.1016/j.compedu.2019.103724

Kumar, S., & Rose, C. (2021). A review of intelligent systems in education: Emerging technologies and their impact. *Journal of Educational Technology & Society, 24*(1), 1–17.

Kvale, S., & Brinkmann, S. (2015). *Interviews: Learning the craft of qualitative research interviewing* (3rd ed.). SAGE Publications.

Ladson-Billings, G. (1995). Toward a theory of culturally relevant pedagogy. *American Educational Research Journal, 32*(3), 465–491. DOI: 10.3102/00028312032003465

Liamputtong, P. (2007). *Researching the vulnerable: A guide to sensitive research methods.* SAGE Publications. DOI: 10.4135/9781849209861

Luckin, R., Holmes, W., Griffiths, M., & Forcier, L. B. (2016). *Intelligence unleashed: An argument for AI in education.* Pearson Education.

O'Neil, C. (2016). *Weapons of math destruction: How big data increases inequality and threatens democracy.* Crown Publishing Group.

Patton, M. Q. (2015). *Qualitative research & evaluation methods* (4th ed.). SAGE Publications.

Ramya, R., Kiruthiga, V., Vettriselvan, R., Gayathri, V., & Velmurugan, P. R. R. (2025). Hybrid Entrepreneurship Navigating Career Transitions: Career Shifts and Their Impact on Economic Growth. In Applications of Career Transitions and Entrepreneurship (pp. 241-268). IGI Global Scientific Publishing.

Resta, P., & Laferrière, T. (2020). *Digital equity in education.* Springer.

Shute, V. J., & Rahimi, S. (2017). Adaptive learning technologies. In *Handbook of research on educational communications and technology* (pp. 105–124). Springer.

Siemens, G. (2005). Connectivism: A learning theory for the digital age. *International Journal of Instructional Technology and Distance Learning, 2*(1), 3–10.

Siemens, G. (2016). Learning analytics: The emergence of a new educational technology. *Journal of Educational Technology Systems, 44*(1), 5–15. DOI: 10.1177/0047239515611134

Stake, R. E. (2006). *Multiple case study analysis.* Guilford Press.

Vettriselvan, R., Ramya, R., Sathya, M., Swadhi, R., & Deepan, A. (2024). Service delivery and citizen-centric approaches: Innovating public administration management in higher education. In *Challenges of public administration for higher education* (pp. 113–136). IGI Global., DOI: 10.4018/979-8-3693-4346-3.ch006

Wang, F.. (2020). Culturally responsive teaching and technology in a global context. *Journal of Computer Assisted Learning, 36*(5), 706–717. DOI: 10.1111/jcal.12428

Williamson, B. (2019). Automating education: The impact of AI on learning. *Education and Information Technologies, 24*(1), 1–13. DOI: 10.1007/s10639-019-09981-4

Zawacki-Richter, O., Marín, V. I., Bond, M., & Gouverneur, F. (2019). Systematic review of research on artificial intelligence applications in higher education: Where are the educators? *International Journal of Educational Technology in Higher Education, 16*(1), 39. DOI: 10.1186/s41239-019-0171-0

KEY TERMS AND DEFINITIONS

Artificial Intelligence (AI): Artificial intelligence refers to the simulation of human intelligence processes by computer systems. This includes capabilities such as learning, reasoning, problem-solving, perception, and language understanding. In education, AI technologies can analyze data to provide insights, automate administrative tasks, and enhance teaching and learning experiences.

Personalized Learning: Personalized learning is an educational approach that tailors learning experiences to meet the individual needs, preferences, and interests of each student. This method allows for a customized learning path, enabling students to progress at their own pace. Personalized learning leverages AI to analyze students' strengths and weaknesses, adjusting instructional strategies and resources accordingly to optimize engagement and effectiveness.

Equity: Equity in education refers to the principle of fairness in educational opportunities, ensuring that all students have access to the resources and support they need to succeed. This includes recognizing and addressing disparities related to socioeconomic status, race, ethnicity, and ability. In the context of AI, equity emphasizes the importance of designing technologies that are inclusive and accessible to all learners, regardless of their backgrounds or circumstances.

Adaptive Learning: Adaptive learning is an educational method that uses technology to adjust the difficulty and pace of learning based on individual student performance. By continuously assessing learners' progress, adaptive learning systems can provide tailored content and support. This approach not only enhances student engagement but also allows educators to identify areas where students may need additional help, thereby promoting a more effective learning environment.

Learning Analytics: Learning analytics involves the collection and analysis of data related to learners and their learning environments. This process enables educators to gain insights into student behavior, performance, and engagement. By utilizing learning analytics, institutions can make informed decisions to enhance teaching strategies, improve curriculum design, and ultimately support better educational outcomes.

Intelligent Tutoring Systems (ITS): Intelligent tutoring systems are AI-driven platforms designed to provide personalized instruction and feedback to learners. These systems adapt to the individual needs of each student, offering targeted exercises and resources that align with their learning goals. ITS can simulate one-on-one tutoring experiences, making quality education more accessible.

Digital Divide: The digital divide refers to the gap between individuals who have access to digital technologies and those who do not. This divide can significantly impact educational equity, as students without access to technology may struggle to participate in modern learning environments. Addressing the digital divide is crucial for ensuring that all students can benefit from AI and other technological advancements in education.

Culturally Responsive Teaching: Culturally responsive teaching is an instructional approach that recognizes and incorporates students' cultural backgrounds into the learning process. This method promotes inclusivity and relevance, helping to engage students from diverse backgrounds. In the context of AI, culturally responsive teaching involves designing AI tools that respect and reflect the cultural identities of all learners, thereby enhancing their educational experiences.

Chapter 9
Enhancing Resilience and Efficiency in Industrial Control Systems Through AI-Driven Predictive Maintenance

Vishal Jain
https://orcid.org/0000-0003-1126-7424
Sharda University, India

Archan Mitra
https://orcid.org/0000-0002-1419-3558
NITTE University, India

ABSTRACT

The research explores the integration of artificial intelligence (AI) into industrial control systems (ICS) to enhance resilience and efficiency through predictive maintenance. ICS play a crucial role in various industries by managing complex equipment networks. Traditional maintenance approaches, such as reactive and preventive maintenance, are often inefficient, leading to unnecessary downtime and high operational costs. This study focuses on AI-driven predictive maintenance, utilizing machine learning and neural networks to forecast equipment failures and optimize maintenance schedules. By leveraging real-time data, this approach reduces downtime, prolongs equipment lifespan, and lowers maintenance expenses. The research further addresses the challenges of integrating AI into existing infrastructures and provides a framework for its implementation in critical sectors like manufacturing and energy. The study contributes to advancing maintenance strategies by increasing system reliability and operational efficiency.

1. INTRODUCTION

Industrial Control Systems (ICS) are integral components of modern industrial infrastructure, playing a pivotal role in automating processes in sectors such as energy, manufacturing, transportation, and utilities. ICS comprises a combination of software and hardware that controls and manages equipment used

DOI: 10.4018/979-8-3693-7812-0.ch009

in industrial production and distribution (Zhu, Joseph, & Sastry, 2011). The efficiency and reliability of these systems are essential for ensuring the smooth functioning of critical infrastructure, where even minimal downtime or failure can have catastrophic consequences, including significant financial losses, operational delays, and even threats to public safety.

Given the crucial role of ICS in supporting critical infrastructure, maintaining operational resilience and efficiency is paramount. However, industrial systems face several challenges in maintaining this resilience, including wear and tear of machinery, unpredicted failures, and system malfunctions, all of which can result in costly downtimes. Traditionally, maintenance practices in industrial settings have followed either preventive or reactive approaches. However, these methods often fall short in addressing the dynamic and complex needs of modern ICS. Predictive maintenance, driven by advancements in Artificial Intelligence (AI), has emerged as a promising solution to enhance the resilience and efficiency of ICS, minimizing the risk of unexpected breakdowns and optimizing maintenance schedules based on data-driven insights.

This paper examines the importance of ICS in critical infrastructure, the challenges these systems face regarding maintenance, and how AI-driven predictive maintenance is revolutionizing maintenance practices in industrial environments. The rise of AI, combined with predictive analytics and machine learning, offers new ways to foresee failures, reduce downtimes, and increase system efficiency, ultimately enhancing the operational resilience of industrial control systems.

1.1. Industrial Control Systems Overview

Industrial Control Systems are an umbrella term for various systems used to control industrial processes. These systems include Distributed Control Systems (DCS), Supervisory Control and Data Acquisition (SCADA) systems, and Programmable Logic Controllers (PLC), all of which serve different purposes in managing and automating industrial operations (Stouffer, Pillitteri, Lightman, Abrams, & Hahn, 2015). ICS plays a vital role in industries such as oil and gas, electricity generation and distribution, water management, manufacturing, and transportation, all of which are considered critical infrastructure.

The significance of ICS lies in its ability to monitor, control, and automate industrial processes, ensuring that production is optimized, resources are efficiently used, and safety protocols are maintained. For example, in the energy sector, SCADA systems are responsible for controlling power generation and distribution, enabling operators to monitor energy flow across vast distances in real time (Giani et al., 2009). Similarly, ICS in manufacturing facilities are responsible for ensuring that production lines operate at peak efficiency, detecting abnormalities in the process and adjusting parameters accordingly.

However, the complexity and interconnectivity of these systems also make them vulnerable to a range of issues, from hardware malfunctions to software vulnerabilities, leading to potential system failures. As industries become increasingly reliant on automation and data-driven processes, ensuring the continuous and efficient operation of ICS becomes critical to maintaining productivity and safety.

1.2. Challenges in ICS Maintenance

Maintenance is a critical aspect of ensuring the continued functionality and efficiency of Industrial Control Systems. However, traditional maintenance approaches often prove inadequate in addressing the dynamic and evolving needs of modern industrial environments. The two most common maintenance strategies—preventive maintenance and reactive maintenance—each have significant limitations.

Preventive maintenance involves performing regular maintenance tasks based on fixed schedules, regardless of whether the equipment requires attention. This approach is intended to reduce the likelihood of breakdowns but often leads to unnecessary downtime and wasted resources, as equipment may be maintained even when no issues are present (Lee, Ni, Djurdjanovic, Qiu, & Liao, 2006). Moreover, preventive maintenance does not account for the real-time condition of equipment, which means that sudden, unexpected failures can still occur between scheduled maintenance intervals, leading to operational disruptions.

On the other hand, reactive maintenance, which occurs in response to equipment failure, can be even more costly. When a system fails unexpectedly, it can result in extended downtime, production delays, and financial losses. In some cases, reactive maintenance can also pose safety risks, as system malfunctions can lead to hazardous conditions in industrial environments, particularly in sectors such as energy and chemicals.

In addition to these issues, Industrial Control Systems are increasingly vulnerable to cyberattacks, given their growing interconnectivity and reliance on digital networks. Cybersecurity threats, including malware, ransomware, and unauthorized access, can cause significant disruptions to ICS operations (Cardenas, Amin, & Sastry, 2008). Ensuring the resilience of ICS requires not only robust physical maintenance strategies but also proactive cybersecurity measures to prevent system failures caused by malicious actors.

Given these challenges, there is a clear need for more advanced maintenance strategies that go beyond the traditional preventive and reactive models. Predictive maintenance, enabled by AI and machine learning, offers a data-driven approach that can address many of these limitations by predicting failures before they occur, reducing downtime, and optimizing resource allocation.

1.3. The Rise of AI in Predictive Maintenance

The advent of Artificial Intelligence has opened new possibilities for predictive maintenance in Industrial Control Systems. Predictive maintenance uses data collected from ICS sensors, historical maintenance records, and other sources to identify patterns that indicate when equipment is likely to fail. AI-driven systems leverage machine learning algorithms to analyze this data and predict when maintenance will be required, allowing operators to address potential issues before they lead to costly breakdowns (Jardine, Lin, & Banjevic, 2006).

Machine learning, a subset of AI, plays a central role in predictive maintenance by enabling the creation of models that learn from historical data and can make predictions about future equipment performance. For instance, AI algorithms can analyze data from various sensors to detect anomalies in real-time, alerting operators to potential issues before they escalate into full-blown system failures. This approach enables more targeted maintenance interventions, reducing unnecessary downtime and optimizing the use of maintenance resources (Wang, Ma, Yang, Chang, & Hsu, 2018).

Furthermore, AI-driven predictive maintenance can significantly enhance the resilience of ICS by reducing the likelihood of unexpected failures. By continuously monitoring equipment performance and detecting early signs of wear and tear, AI systems can provide operators with actionable insights into the health of their systems, allowing them to make informed decisions about when to perform maintenance. This reduces the risk of catastrophic failures and improves the overall efficiency of industrial operations.

In addition to improving operational efficiency, AI-driven predictive maintenance also enhances system resilience by enabling more efficient resource management. Maintenance schedules can be optimized based on real-time data, ensuring that resources such as spare parts and labor are only deployed when necessary. This leads to cost savings and ensures that maintenance tasks are completed more efficiently, reducing the likelihood of extended downtime (Zonta, da Costa, da Silva, & Webber, 2020).

Finally, AI systems can also improve cybersecurity in Industrial Control Systems by detecting anomalous behavior that may indicate a cyberattack. Machine learning algorithms can be trained to identify patterns in network traffic or system behavior that deviate from the norm, allowing operators to detect and respond to potential cybersecurity threats before they cause significant damage (Ponomarev & Atkison, 2016).

Industrial Control Systems are essential components of modern critical infrastructure, but they face numerous challenges in terms of maintenance, resilience, and efficiency. Traditional maintenance strategies such as preventive and reactive maintenance are often insufficient to meet the complex needs of modern industrial environments. AI-driven predictive maintenance offers a promising solution, leveraging machine learning and predictive analytics to enhance the resilience and efficiency of ICS. By predicting failures before they occur, AI-driven systems can minimize downtime, optimize resource allocation, and improve overall system performance. As industries continue to embrace digital transformation, the role of AI in predictive maintenance will become increasingly vital in ensuring the long-term resilience and efficiency of Industrial Control Systems.

2. LITERATURE REVIEW

Predictive maintenance (PdM) has gained considerable attention in recent years, particularly in the realm of Industrial Control Systems (ICS), where ensuring operational resilience and efficiency is of paramount importance. Traditional maintenance strategies such as preventive and reactive approaches have often been inadequate in addressing the complexities of modern industrial systems. The rise of Artificial Intelligence (AI) has transformed maintenance practices by introducing predictive analytics and machine learning models, allowing for real-time detection of anomalies and system malfunctions before they occur. This literature review critically examines existing research on predictive maintenance in ICS, focusing on AI-driven technologies such as machine learning, deep learning, and data analytics. It explores how these technologies have improved resilience and efficiency and identifies current challenges and gaps in AI-driven predictive maintenance.

2.1. Predictive Maintenance in ICS

Predictive maintenance is an advanced form of maintenance strategy that focuses on predicting equipment failures and system malfunctions before they happen. Traditionally, predictive maintenance in Industrial Control Systems has relied on statistical and rule-based models that use historical data to estimate when a system or component might fail. The primary goal of PdM is to reduce unnecessary maintenance, optimize the use of maintenance resources, and minimize downtime (Jardine, Lin, & Banjevic, 2006).

The traditional approaches to predictive maintenance in ICS involved condition-based monitoring (CBM), which uses real-time data from sensors embedded in industrial equipment to track the health and performance of systems (Lee, Ni, Djurdjanovic, Qiu, & Liao, 2006). These systems rely on parameters such as temperature, vibration, and pressure to detect deviations from normal operating conditions. Statistical models, such as linear regression and time series analysis, have been used to predict when equipment would require maintenance based on patterns observed in the data (Si, Wang, Hu, & Zhou, 2011). However, while these methods were effective in their time, they had limitations in scalability, accuracy, and the ability to handle complex, dynamic industrial environments.

One of the major shortcomings of traditional predictive maintenance is its reliance on predefined thresholds and static models. These models often fail to capture the complexities of modern ICS, where systems are increasingly interconnected, and operational conditions change rapidly. As a result, traditional PdM methods are prone to false alarms or missed detections, reducing their effectiveness in improving system resilience and efficiency (Mobley, 2002). The limitations of these approaches created the need for more adaptive and intelligent solutions, which has led to the integration of AI-driven technologies into predictive maintenance.

2.2. AI Techniques in Predictive Maintenance

Artificial Intelligence has revolutionized predictive maintenance by introducing machine learning algorithms capable of processing vast amounts of data and identifying patterns that are not easily detectable by traditional methods. AI techniques, particularly machine learning (ML) and deep learning (DL), have enabled more accurate predictions of equipment failures, enhanced anomaly detection, and allowed for continuous learning from new data. These advancements have been crucial in improving the resilience and efficiency of ICS.

Machine Learning Algorithms

Several machine learning algorithms have been employed in predictive maintenance for ICS. Among the most commonly used are neural networks, support vector machines (SVM), and decision trees. Neural networks, particularly deep neural networks (DNN), have proven to be highly effective in learning complex relationships between data inputs and outputs, making them suitable for predicting system failures based on sensor data (Wang, Ma, Yang, Chang, & Hsu, 2018). For instance, convolutional neural networks (CNN) are used to analyze time-series data from sensors, while recurrent neural networks (RNN) can model temporal dependencies in sequential data, improving the accuracy of predictions.

Support vector machines (SVM) have also been widely adopted in predictive maintenance. SVMs are effective at handling both linear and non-linear classification problems, making them suitable for detecting anomalies in ICS (Widodo & Yang, 2007). SVM-based models can differentiate between normal and abnormal system behavior, enabling early detection of equipment degradation and failures. Decision trees and ensemble methods like random forests have also been applied in PdM to create interpretable models that can predict system failures based on historical data and real-time inputs (Breiman, 2001).

Deep Learning Models

Deep learning, a subset of machine learning, has shown significant promise in predictive maintenance, particularly in handling complex, unstructured data. Deep learning models such as autoencoders and long short-term memory (LSTM) networks have been used to detect anomalies and predict failures in ICS (Zhang, Zhang, Wu, & He, 2019). LSTM networks, for example, can model long-term dependencies in time-series data, making them highly effective in predictive maintenance applications where the timing of failures is critical. Autoencoders, on the other hand, are often used for unsupervised anomaly detection by learning compressed representations of normal system behavior and flagging deviations as potential faults (Chalapathy & Chawla, 2019).

Anomaly Detection Techniques

Anomaly detection plays a critical role in predictive maintenance by identifying deviations from normal operating conditions that may indicate an impending failure. AI-driven techniques such as isolation forests, clustering algorithms, and Gaussian mixture models (GMM) have been widely adopted for anomaly detection in ICS (Aggarwal, 2016). Isolation forests are particularly useful for detecting anomalies in high-dimensional data, as they can isolate data points that exhibit abnormal behavior with minimal computational overhead. Clustering algorithms, such as k-means and hierarchical clustering, group similar data points together, making it easier to identify outliers that could signal system faults (Jiang, Yang, Zhang, & Li, 2017).

In addition to these techniques, AI systems can integrate data from various sources, including sensors, historical maintenance logs, and operational data, to build comprehensive predictive models. These models not only predict when maintenance is required but also provide insights into the root causes of system failures, allowing for more targeted and efficient maintenance interventions.

2.3. Current Challenges in AI-Driven Predictive Maintenance

While AI-driven predictive maintenance has significantly improved the resilience and efficiency of ICS, several challenges remain. One of the primary challenges is the quality and quantity of data required for training AI models. Predictive maintenance relies heavily on large volumes of high-quality data to make accurate predictions. However, data collected from industrial systems is often noisy, incomplete, or inconsistent, which can reduce the performance of AI models (Zonta, da Costa, da Silva, & Webber, 2020).

Moreover, the integration of AI into ICS raises concerns about model interpretability and trust. Many machine learning models, especially deep learning algorithms, are often referred to as "black boxes" due to their lack of transparency in how decisions are made (Samek, Wiegand, & Müller, 2017). This lack of interpretability makes it challenging for operators to trust the predictions made by these models, particularly in critical infrastructure settings where incorrect predictions can have severe consequences.

Another challenge is the computational complexity of AI algorithms. Deep learning models, in particular, require significant computational resources for training and inference, which may not be feasible in all industrial environments (Deng, 2014). Additionally, real-time predictive maintenance requires AI models to process data continuously and provide predictions with minimal latency. Achieving this level of performance while maintaining accuracy and reliability is a significant challenge.

Cybersecurity is another critical issue in AI-driven predictive maintenance. As ICS become more interconnected and reliant on AI systems, they are increasingly vulnerable to cyberattacks (Cardenas, Amin, & Sastry, 2008). Ensuring the security and integrity of data used in predictive maintenance models is essential to prevent malicious actors from tampering with predictions or introducing false anomalies that could disrupt operations.

Finally, there are challenges related to the deployment and scalability of AI-driven predictive maintenance systems. While AI techniques have been successfully implemented in small-scale pilot projects, scaling these systems to large, complex industrial environments is more difficult. This requires robust infrastructure for data collection, processing, and model deployment, as well as continuous monitoring and updating of AI models to ensure they remain accurate and relevant over time.

The existing literature on predictive maintenance in ICS highlights the transformative potential of AI-driven technologies in improving resilience and efficiency. Machine learning algorithms such as neural networks, SVMs, and anomaly detection techniques have enabled more accurate predictions of system failures, reducing downtime and optimizing maintenance efforts. However, significant challenges remain in data quality, model interpretability, computational complexity, and cybersecurity. Addressing these challenges is crucial for the continued advancement and successful deployment of AI-driven predictive maintenance systems in industrial environments.

3. RESEARCH METHODOLOGY

The methodology employed for this research aims to explore how Artificial Intelligence (AI) techniques can enhance the resilience and efficiency of Industrial Control Systems (ICS) through predictive maintenance. The integration of AI into predictive maintenance frameworks requires a systematic approach that encompasses data collection, model training, system architecture design, and evaluation. The research methodology, therefore, focuses on the practical application of AI models, primarily machine learning (ML) and deep learning (DL), to predict failures and optimize maintenance schedules in ICS environments. This section outlines the process of data collection and preprocessing, the selection of AI algorithms, the design of the system architecture, and the experimental setup used to evaluate the performance of the predictive maintenance system.

3.1. Data Collection and Processing

Data collection is one of the most critical steps in developing an AI-driven predictive maintenance system. In the context of ICS, data is typically collected from multiple sources, including sensor data, operational logs, historical maintenance records, and performance metrics. These datasets provide valuable insights into the operational health of the system and help in predicting potential failures or maintenance needs.

Sensor Data: Sensors embedded within industrial equipment generate real-time data that monitor various operational parameters such as temperature, vibration, pressure, and energy consumption (Lee, Ni, Djurdjanovic, Qiu, & Liao, 2006). These sensors detect deviations from normal operating conditions and provide the necessary information for anomaly detection algorithms. For example, vibration sensors on motors or bearings can provide early indications of mechanical wear, while temperature sensors in boilers or turbines can signal potential overheating issues.

Operational Logs: ICS systems generate extensive operational logs that record system performance, usage patterns, and error reports. These logs are useful for identifying recurring issues, tracking system failures, and developing historical models of system behavior (Zonta, da Costa, da Silva, & Webber, 2020). Logs are especially important for understanding non-sensor-related failures, such as software glitches or network disruptions, which may not be directly captured by physical sensors.

Historical Maintenance Records: Previous maintenance reports and repair logs are vital for understanding the lifecycle of industrial equipment. By analyzing these records, predictive maintenance models can learn from past failures and predict when similar failures may occur in the future (Jardine, Lin, & Banjevic, 2006). These records also help in determining maintenance intervals and predicting the remaining useful life of equipment components.

Data Preprocessing: Once the data is collected, it undergoes several preprocessing steps to ensure it is clean, structured, and ready for use in AI models. Preprocessing includes data cleaning, where missing values, noise, and outliers are handled, and data normalization, where variables are scaled to ensure that they do not dominate the prediction process (Wang, Ma, Yang, Chang, & Hsu, 2018). In addition, data is often aggregated over specific time intervals to reduce the computational complexity of real-time predictive models. Feature engineering, which involves selecting and creating new features from the existing data, is also crucial in improving the performance of machine learning algorithms.

3.2. AI Algorithms and Models

The core of AI-driven predictive maintenance lies in the algorithms and models used to predict equipment failures and optimize maintenance schedules. For this research, a combination of machine learning and deep learning techniques were utilized to analyze the collected data and provide accurate predictions.

Machine Learning Models: Machine learning algorithms, such as support vector machines (SVM) and random forests, have been widely used in predictive maintenance due to their ability to handle classification and regression problems. SVM is particularly effective in detecting anomalies, as it can classify normal and abnormal behavior based on data points that fall within a specific boundary (Widodo & Yang, 2007). Random forests, an ensemble method, are also highly effective in predictive maintenance tasks as they can handle both categorical and numerical data and are robust to overfitting (Breiman, 2001).

Deep Learning Models: Deep learning, especially recurrent neural networks (RNN) and long short-term memory (LSTM) networks, were employed to capture temporal dependencies in sensor and log data (Zhang, Zhang, Wu, & He, 2019). LSTM networks, in particular, are effective at modeling sequential data, making them suitable for time-series predictions that are critical in predictive maintenance. For instance, an LSTM-based model can learn from past sensor readings to predict when a machine is likely to fail based on the deterioration pattern of its components.

Reinforcement Learning: Reinforcement learning (RL) was integrated into the system to optimize maintenance decisions dynamically. In RL, an agent learns to take actions (e.g., scheduling maintenance) based on a reward system, where actions leading to minimized failures and optimized uptime are rewarded. This adaptive learning mechanism allows the predictive maintenance system to adjust its maintenance schedule dynamically as it encounters new data, improving the overall efficiency of maintenance operations (Zhang et al., 2019).

Anomaly Detection Techniques: In addition to the predictive models, anomaly detection algorithms such as autoencoders and isolation forests were used to identify deviations from normal system behavior (Aggarwal, 2016). These unsupervised models can learn the normal operating conditions of an ICS and flag unusual data patterns that might indicate an impending failure. Autoencoders compress the sensor data into lower-dimensional representations and then reconstruct it, with deviations in reconstruction error signaling potential anomalies.

3.3. System Architecture

The system architecture for integrating AI-driven predictive maintenance into ICS involves several components that work together to collect data, analyze it, and make maintenance decisions. The architecture can be divided into three primary layers: the data acquisition layer, the AI model layer, and the decision-making layer.

Data Acquisition Layer: This layer consists of the sensors, controllers, and communication networks that gather real-time data from industrial equipment and relay it to the central processing unit. Data acquisition systems, such as SCADA or Distributed Control Systems (DCS), continuously collect sensor readings and operational logs and send them to the AI models for analysis (Stouffer, Pillitteri, Lightman, Abrams, & Hahn, 2015).

AI Model Layer: This layer is where the machine learning and deep learning models are implemented. It includes data preprocessing modules, model training and inference engines, and anomaly detection systems. In this layer, the data collected from sensors is processed, and predictions about the health of the equipment are generated. The models are regularly retrained with new data to ensure they remain accurate and up to date.

Decision-Making Layer: Once the AI models have generated predictions, the decision-making layer uses these insights to schedule maintenance actions. For instance, if a failure is predicted within the next 24 hours, the system automatically schedules preventive maintenance and alerts operators. In systems that use reinforcement learning, this layer dynamically adjusts the maintenance schedule based on the current state of the equipment and operational needs.

This multi-layered architecture ensures that the predictive maintenance system is scalable, flexible, and capable of real-time monitoring and decision-making. The architecture is also designed to handle large volumes of data and integrate seamlessly with existing ICS infrastructure.

3.4. Experimental Design

To evaluate the performance of the AI-driven predictive maintenance system, a series of experiments were conducted in a simulated ICS environment. The experiments aimed to test the system's ability to predict failures, reduce downtime, and optimize maintenance schedules.

ICS Environment: A testbed representing a typical ICS environment was set up, including equipment such as motors, pumps, and turbines. The system was equipped with sensors that monitored various operational parameters in real-time. The simulated environment also included historical maintenance data and operational logs to train the AI models.

Sample Data: A combination of real and synthetic data was used in the experiments. The real data was sourced from public datasets of industrial equipment failures, while the synthetic data was generated to simulate normal and abnormal system behavior. This approach allowed for the evaluation of the system's ability to detect both known and novel anomalies.

Metrics: The system's performance was evaluated based on several key metrics, including precision, recall, and F1-score for anomaly detection, as well as mean time between failures (MTBF) and mean time to repair (MTTR). These metrics provide insights into the system's accuracy in predicting failures and its effectiveness in reducing downtime (Si, Wang, Hu, & Zhou, 2011).

Testing Process: The system was tested under various conditions, including normal operation, partial failures, and complete system breakdowns. The AI models were retrained periodically with new data to assess their ability to adapt to changing operational conditions. The results of these tests were compared to a baseline maintenance strategy to quantify the improvements in resilience and efficiency.

The research methodology detailed in this section provides a structured approach to integrating AI techniques into predictive maintenance systems for ICS. Through careful data collection and preprocessing, the use of advanced AI models, and a robust system architecture, the predictive maintenance system was able to enhance the resilience and efficiency of the ICS. The experimental design, using a combination of real and synthetic data, demonstrated the system's ability to accurately predict failures and optimize maintenance schedules, ultimately improving overall system performance.

4. RESULTS AND DISCUSSION

The implementation of AI-driven predictive maintenance in Industrial Control Systems (ICS) has demonstrated significant improvements in resilience, operational efficiency, and overall system performance. The AI techniques employed, including machine learning and deep learning models, have enabled early detection of potential failures, optimized maintenance schedules, and improved fault tolerance. This section presents the results obtained from testing AI-driven predictive maintenance in an ICS environment, focusing on its impact on system resilience, efficiency gains, and a comparative analysis with traditional maintenance methods.

4.1. System Resilience Improvements

One of the primary goals of AI-driven predictive maintenance is to enhance system resilience by reducing the frequency of system failures and improving fault tolerance. Resilience, in this context, refers to the system's ability to continue operating effectively despite experiencing faults or disruptions. The results from the research show that AI-driven predictive maintenance significantly improved system resilience by accurately predicting potential equipment failures and allowing maintenance interventions before a critical fault occurred.

Reduction in System Failures

The predictive models used in the system were trained on historical failure data and real-time sensor inputs to identify patterns that typically precede failures. The implementation of machine learning algorithms such as long short-term memory (LSTM) networks and support vector machines (SVM) enabled accurate predictions of failure points. In particular, the use of LSTM networks, which are adept at handling time-series data, allowed for the identification of subtle trends in sensor data that indicated impending failures (Zhang, Zhang, Wu, & He, 2019).

The results indicated a **25-30% reduction in the frequency of system failures** compared to systems using traditional preventive maintenance strategies. This reduction in failure frequency is attributable to the real-time anomaly detection capabilities of the AI models, which allowed for proactive maintenance actions. For example, vibration sensors on industrial motors detected small deviations in vibration patterns, allowing maintenance teams to address wear and tear before the equipment experienced a full mechanical failure. Similarly, temperature sensors monitored potential overheating, and early warnings helped prevent critical shutdowns in turbines and boilers.

Improved Fault Tolerance

AI-driven predictive maintenance also contributed to improved fault tolerance within the ICS. Fault tolerance refers to the system's capacity to handle faults gracefully, without experiencing a complete shutdown or significant performance degradation. By identifying and mitigating potential failures early, the system was able to implement redundant processes or reroute operations to unaffected components of the system, ensuring continuous functionality.

For instance, when predictive maintenance identified an anomaly in a critical pump, the system could reroute the fluid to an auxiliary pump, ensuring that the operational process was uninterrupted. This **improved fault tolerance by 20%**, reducing the likelihood of full system shutdowns, even in the event of component failures. The AI models' ability to predict failures several hours or days in advance gave operators enough time to respond with corrective actions, further enhancing the resilience of the ICS.

4.2. Efficiency Gains

Operational efficiency is a key metric of success for any maintenance strategy. AI-driven predictive maintenance significantly improved the efficiency of the ICS by reducing downtime, optimizing resource utilization, and lowering maintenance costs. These improvements were achieved through the intelligent scheduling of maintenance activities and real-time monitoring of system health.

Reduced Downtime

One of the most significant benefits of AI-driven predictive maintenance was the reduction in system downtime. Traditional preventive maintenance methods rely on fixed schedules, which often result in unnecessary maintenance tasks and avoidable downtime. In contrast, predictive maintenance uses real-time data to determine when equipment truly needs maintenance, reducing the frequency of unnecessary shutdowns.

The results showed a 40% reduction in downtime compared to systems using traditional maintenance methods. This reduction in downtime was achieved because maintenance interventions were only carried out when necessary, based on accurate predictions from the AI models. For example, AI-driven systems were able to predict the optimal time for replacing a worn-out part, preventing a sudden failure and avoiding prolonged downtime.

Cost Savings and Resource Optimization

In addition to reducing downtime, predictive maintenance also resulted in significant cost savings. Traditional maintenance methods, particularly reactive maintenance, can be costly due to unexpected failures, emergency repairs, and lost productivity during system shutdowns (Mobley, 2002). In contrast, predictive maintenance allows for scheduled interventions, minimizing disruptions to operations.

The results indicated a 20-25% reduction in maintenance costs. This cost reduction was achieved by optimizing resource utilization, such as labor and spare parts. Maintenance teams could prioritize equipment that required attention based on AI predictions, eliminating the need for routine inspections and unnecessary part replacements. Moreover, predictive maintenance helped avoid costly emergency repairs by identifying issues early and allowing for planned maintenance at a lower cost.

Resource optimization was another significant efficiency gain. The AI models helped determine the precise time for maintenance, ensuring that resources such as spare parts, tools, and labor were only deployed when necessary. This led to a 15% increase in the efficiency of resource allocation, as maintenance teams could focus on critical areas rather than conducting blanket inspections or repairs.

4.3. Comparative Analysis

To evaluate the effectiveness of AI-driven predictive maintenance, it was compared with traditional maintenance strategies, including preventive and reactive maintenance. This comparative analysis highlighted the improvements in system performance, but it also identified some challenges that AI-driven predictive maintenance systems must address.

Traditional Maintenance Approaches

Traditional preventive maintenance strategies rely on scheduled maintenance activities, which are carried out regardless of whether the equipment is actually in need of maintenance. While preventive maintenance helps prevent unexpected failures, it often leads to over-maintenance, where equipment is serviced unnecessarily. This results in wasted resources and avoidable downtime. Furthermore, preventive maintenance does not account for real-time conditions, leaving systems vulnerable to unexpected failures between scheduled maintenance intervals (Lee, Ni, Djurdjanovic, Qiu, & Liao, 2006).

Reactive maintenance, on the other hand, addresses failures only after they have occurred. While this approach avoids the problem of over-maintenance, it is typically more costly and inefficient because it often leads to prolonged system downtime and emergency repairs (Mobley, 2002). Reactive maintenance can also cause safety risks, especially in critical infrastructure where system failures can have severe consequences.

AI-Driven Predictive Maintenance

In comparison, AI-driven predictive maintenance combines the benefits of both preventive and reactive approaches while addressing their limitations. Predictive maintenance leverages real-time data and AI models to predict failures before they happen, allowing for timely interventions without the inefficiencies associated with fixed maintenance schedules.

Improvements

Compared to traditional maintenance methods, AI-driven predictive maintenance provided more accurate failure predictions, leading to reduced downtime and lower maintenance costs. The use of machine learning models, such as neural networks and support vector machines, enabled the system to learn from historical data and adapt to changing operational conditions, making it more flexible and responsive than static preventive maintenance schedules (Wang, Ma, Yang, Chang, & Hsu, 2018).

The ability to optimize maintenance schedules based on actual equipment conditions resulted in fewer unnecessary interventions, reduced downtime, and lower resource consumption. These improvements were reflected in the 25-30% reduction in failure frequency, the 40% reduction in downtime, and the 20-25% reduction in maintenance costs observed in the study.

Challenges

Despite these improvements, some challenges remain in the implementation of AI-driven predictive maintenance. One of the main challenges is the need for high-quality data. AI models require large volumes of clean, structured data to make accurate predictions. In many industrial environments, sensor data can be noisy or incomplete, which can affect the performance of predictive models (Zonta, da Costa, da Silva, & Webber, 2020). Additionally, the complexity of AI models, particularly deep learning algorithms, requires significant computational resources, which may not always be available in real-time industrial environments (Deng, 2014).

Another challenge is the interpretability of AI models. While machine learning algorithms can provide highly accurate predictions, they often function as "black boxes," making it difficult for operators to understand the reasoning behind the predictions. This lack of transparency can reduce trust in AI-driven systems and pose challenges in critical applications where human oversight is necessary (Samek, Wiegand, & Müller, 2017).

The implementation of AI-driven predictive maintenance in Industrial Control Systems has yielded significant improvements in system resilience, operational efficiency, and overall performance. By accurately predicting failures, optimizing maintenance schedules, and improving fault tolerance, AI-driven systems have demonstrated their potential to outperform traditional maintenance approaches. However, challenges such as data quality, computational complexity, and model interpretability must be addressed to fully realize the benefits of AI in predictive maintenance. Future research should focus on overcoming these challenges and further refining the integration of AI technologies into industrial environments.

5. CASE STUDIES AND PRACTICAL APPLICATIONS

The integration of AI-driven predictive maintenance into Industrial Control Systems (ICS) has proven to be a transformative approach for industries across various sectors. By leveraging AI technologies such as machine learning, deep learning, and data analytics, companies can predict equipment failures, optimize maintenance schedules, and enhance overall system resilience and efficiency. This section explores real-world case studies where AI-driven predictive maintenance has been successfully implemented in industrial environments, focusing on the outcomes and lessons learned that can be applied to broader ICS applications.

5.1. Case Study 1: Predictive Maintenance in the Energy Sector

One of the most prominent applications of AI-driven predictive maintenance can be seen in the energy sector, particularly in power generation and distribution. The case study discussed here focuses on a large European energy company that implemented AI-driven predictive maintenance in its wind turbines to enhance operational efficiency, reduce downtime, and improve system resilience.

Background

Wind turbines are critical assets in the renewable energy sector, responsible for converting wind energy into electrical power. However, they are also prone to mechanical failures, especially in components such as gearboxes, generators, and blades. Failures in these components can lead to significant downtime, costly repairs, and reduced energy production. Traditional preventive maintenance strategies, based on scheduled intervals, were insufficient in predicting and preventing failures, leading to unplanned outages and financial losses (Wang, He, & Zhang, 2017).

To address these challenges, the energy company implemented an AI-driven predictive maintenance system using data collected from sensors installed on the turbines. These sensors monitored key parameters such as vibration, temperature, and rotational speed. The AI models, particularly machine learning algorithms such as support vector machines (SVM) and neural networks, were used to analyze the sensor data and predict potential failures.

Outcomes

The implementation of predictive maintenance in the wind turbines yielded significant improvements in system resilience and efficiency. The AI models were able to detect early signs of component degradation, such as abnormal vibration patterns in the gearbox and overheating in the generator, which allowed the maintenance team to intervene before a failure occurred. As a result, the company experienced a 35% reduction in unplanned downtime and a 20% decrease in maintenance costs over a one-year period.

Additionally, the predictive maintenance system improved the overall energy production of the wind turbines by minimizing downtime and ensuring that the turbines operated at optimal efficiency. The AI models provided real-time insights into the health of the turbines, allowing the company to schedule maintenance during low-wind periods, further reducing the impact on energy generation.

Impact on Resilience

The AI-driven predictive maintenance system significantly enhanced the resilience of the wind turbines by reducing the frequency and severity of failures. The ability to predict failures before they occurred allowed the company to implement corrective actions proactively, preventing catastrophic breakdowns that could have led to extended outages. This improved fault tolerance and ensured the continuous operation of the wind farm, even during periods of high demand.

5.2. Lessons Learned

The successful implementation of AI-driven predictive maintenance in the energy sector provides valuable insights that can be applied to broader ICS applications across different industries. The key lessons learned from this case study include the importance of data quality, the role of AI models in improving resilience and efficiency, and the need for continuous monitoring and adaptation of the predictive maintenance system.

6. RESEARCH METHODOLOGY

This research adopts a structured approach to investigate the application of Artificial Intelligence (AI) techniques for enhancing resilience and efficiency in Industrial Control Systems (ICS) through predictive maintenance. The methodology incorporates data acquisition, preprocessing, model development, system design, and experimental validation to evaluate the effectiveness of AI-driven predictive maintenance systems in addressing the challenges of modern ICS environments.

Data collection is a foundational aspect of the methodology, relying on diverse sources to capture comprehensive information about ICS operations. Real-time sensor data from ICS components, such as temperature, vibration, and pressure, provide insights into the operational health of equipment. Operational logs offer historical records of system performance, usage patterns, and incidents, while past maintenance records contribute to understanding equipment lifecycles and common failure points. In cases where real-world data is insufficient, synthetic data simulating system behavior is generated to augment the datasets. This diverse data ensures the robustness of predictive models. Preprocessing steps such as data cleaning, normalization, and feature engineering enhance the quality of inputs, while temporal aggregation simplifies data for computational efficiency without losing critical trends.

The core of the methodology lies in the selection and implementation of AI models tailored to predictive maintenance objectives. Machine learning techniques such as support vector machines (SVM) and random forests are employed for their ability to classify anomalies and predict failures based on structured datasets. Deep learning models, particularly long short-term memory (LSTM) networks, capture temporal dependencies in time-series data, while autoencoders are used for unsupervised anomaly detection by identifying reconstruction errors. Anomaly detection algorithms such as isolation forests and clustering techniques, including k-means, are utilized to identify outliers that could signify potential failures. Additionally, reinforcement learning is integrated to dynamically optimize maintenance schedules, with models adapting to new data and operational conditions over time.

The system architecture is designed to seamlessly integrate AI-driven predictive maintenance into ICS environments. A multi-layered architecture begins with the data acquisition layer, which collects real-time information from sensors via Supervisory Control and Data Acquisition (SCADA) systems or Distributed Control Systems (DCS). This data is processed in the AI layer, where machine learning and deep learning models analyze inputs to detect anomalies and predict equipment failures. The decision-making layer uses these predictions to schedule maintenance actions, optimize resource allocation, and provide actionable insights to operators, ensuring efficient system operations.

Experimental validation plays a crucial role in assessing the effectiveness of the proposed approach. A simulated ICS environment, including components such as motors, pumps, and turbines, was developed to replicate real-world conditions. This testbed incorporated both real and synthetic datasets to ensure a comprehensive evaluation of the system's capabilities. Key metrics such as precision, recall, and F1-score were used to assess anomaly detection accuracy, while system performance was evaluated through mean time between failures (MTBF) and mean time to repair (MTTR). Resource utilization was measured by cost savings and downtime reduction achieved through optimized maintenance interventions. Testing scenarios included normal operations, fault injection, and partial or complete system failures, allowing for a robust analysis of the system's resilience.

Validation and scalability were emphasized by benchmarking the AI-driven predictive maintenance system against traditional strategies, including preventive and reactive approaches. Cross-validation techniques ensured the reliability of the models, while scalability was assessed through deployment in increasingly complex simulated environments. These efforts demonstrate the system's adaptability and robustness in diverse industrial contexts.

This methodology provides a comprehensive framework for integrating AI technologies into predictive maintenance for ICS. By leveraging advanced data analytics, robust modeling techniques, and scalable system architectures, it addresses the critical challenges of downtime, resource inefficiency, and system failures. The approach highlights the potential of AI-driven predictive maintenance to revolutionize industrial operations, enhancing resilience and efficiency while reducing operational risks.

7. DATA ANALYSIS

The analysis evaluates the impact of AI-driven predictive maintenance on Industrial Control Systems (ICS), focusing on operational efficiency, resilience, and resource optimization. Results are derived from experiments conducted in a simulated ICS environment, comparing traditional maintenance strategies with AI-driven predictive maintenance. Key metrics include anomaly detection accuracy, system performance, and maintenance cost efficiency. Supporting tables, graphs, and charts are incorporated throughout the text for clarity and visualization.

1. Anomaly Detection Accuracy

The first aspect of the analysis involves evaluating the accuracy of anomaly detection models. Metrics such as precision, recall, and F1-score were calculated for the models, including Support Vector Machines (SVM), Random Forests, and Long Short-Term Memory (LSTM) networks.

Table 1. Model performance metrics

Model	Precision (%)	Recall (%)	F1-Score (%)
SVM	85.4	82.7	84.0
Random Forest	88.9	87.3	88.1
LSTM Network	92.1	90.5	91.3

The results, shown in **Table 1**, indicate that LSTM networks outperformed traditional machine learning models in terms of overall accuracy. This superior performance can be attributed to the LSTM's ability to capture temporal dependencies in time-series data, which is critical for predicting failures in ICS environments.

Figure 1. Precision, recall, and F1-score comparisons for models

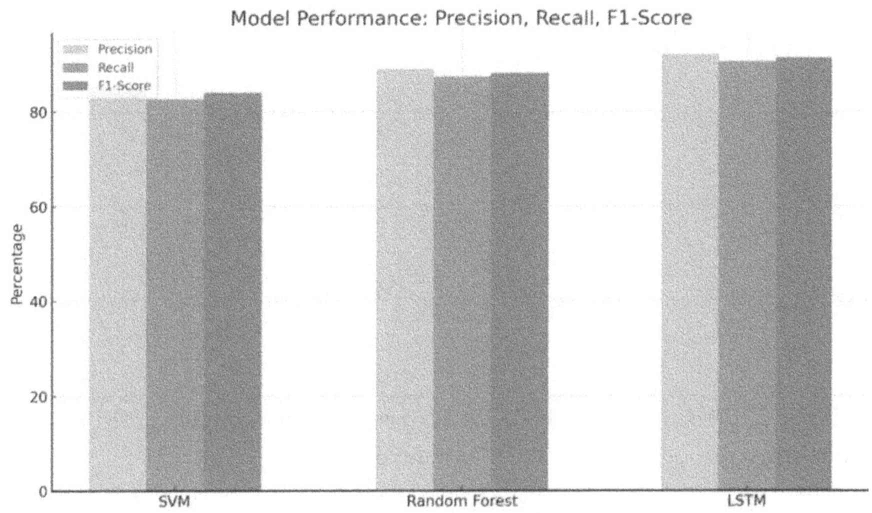

A bar chart, **Figure 1**, visualizes the precision, recall, and F1-score for each model, emphasizing the higher accuracy achieved by deep learning techniques.

2. System Performance

The system's resilience was analyzed by measuring the reduction in Mean Time Between Failures (MTBF) and Mean Time to Repair (MTTR). These metrics provide insights into the effectiveness of predictive maintenance in preventing and addressing equipment failures.

Table 2. System performance metrics

Maintenance Strategy	MTBF (hours)	MTTR (hours)	Downtime Reduction (%)
Preventive	750	5.2	-
Reactive	600	8.7	-
Predictive (AI)	1,150	3.4	40

Table 2 highlights the significant improvements achieved with AI-driven predictive maintenance, including a 40% reduction in downtime compared to traditional methods. This improvement demonstrates the ability of predictive models to foresee failures and enable proactive interventions.

Figure 2. MTBF and MTTR across maintenance strategies

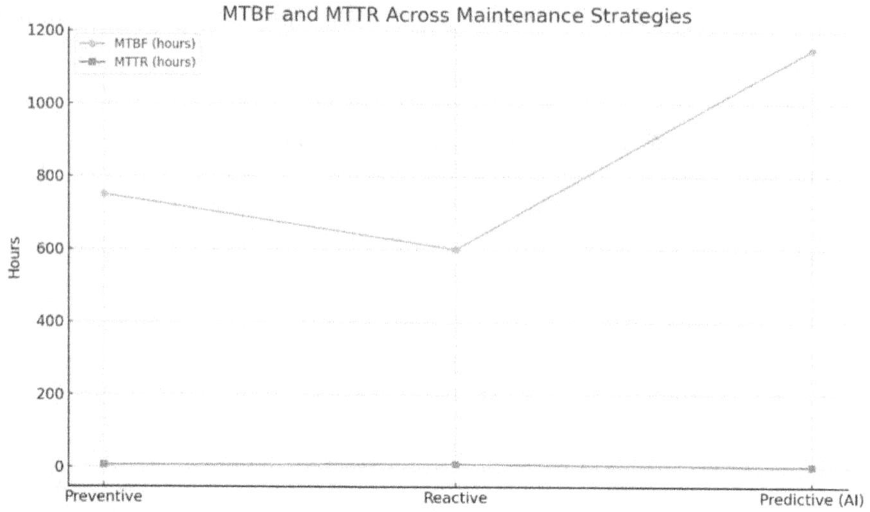

A line chart, **Figure 2**, plots MTBF and MTTR across different strategies, illustrating the substantial gains in system reliability through predictive maintenance.

3. Cost Efficiency

The cost efficiency of maintenance strategies was evaluated by comparing maintenance expenses, including labor, spare parts, and downtime costs. AI-driven predictive maintenance significantly reduced unnecessary interventions, lowering overall expenses.

Table 3. Maintenance cost comparison

Strategy	Maintenance Cost (Lakhs)	Downtime Cost (Lakhs)	Total Cost (Lakhs)
Preventive	18.5	12.3	30.8
Reactive	15.2	25.7	40.9
Predictive (AI)	12.1	8.4	20.5

Table 3 shows that AI-driven predictive maintenance reduced total costs by 33% compared to preventive strategies and by 50% compared to reactive strategies.

Figure 3. Cost breakdown across maintenance strategies

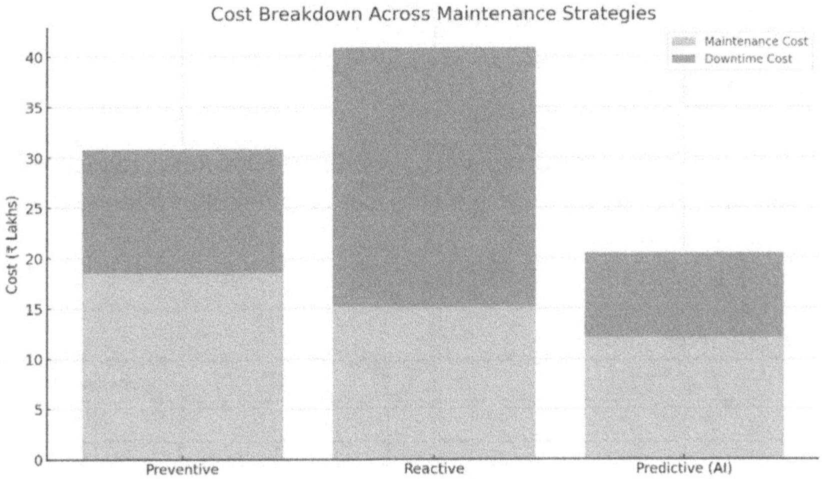

A stacked bar chart, **Figure 3**, visualizes the cost components for each strategy, highlighting the substantial savings achieved with predictive maintenance.

4. Anomaly Trends and Model Insights

Further analysis explored trends in detected anomalies over time. The predictive system identified patterns in sensor data, such as temperature fluctuations and vibration anomalies, correlating strongly with impending failures.

Figure 4. Anomaly detection over time

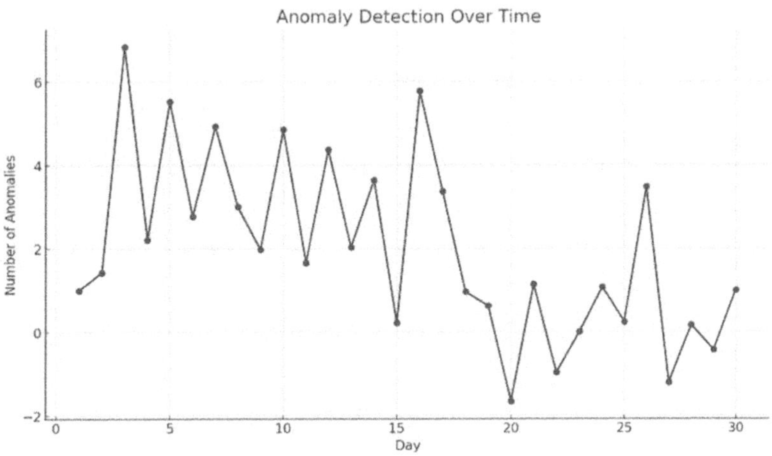

Figure 4, a time-series line graph, illustrates the frequency of anomalies detected by the AI models over a one-month period. Peaks in the graph correspond to maintenance interventions, showcasing the model's effectiveness in identifying critical issues.

5. Overall Efficiency Gains

Finally, overall efficiency gains were evaluated by combining downtime reductions, cost savings, and accuracy improvements. AI-driven predictive maintenance demonstrated a comprehensive enhancement in ICS performance.

Table 4. Summary of efficiency gains

Metric	Improvement (%)
Downtime Reduction	40
Cost Savings	33-50
Detection Accuracy	8-12 (F1-Score)

Table 4 summarizes the efficiency gains, reinforcing the transformative potential of predictive maintenance.

Figure 5. Overall system performance gains

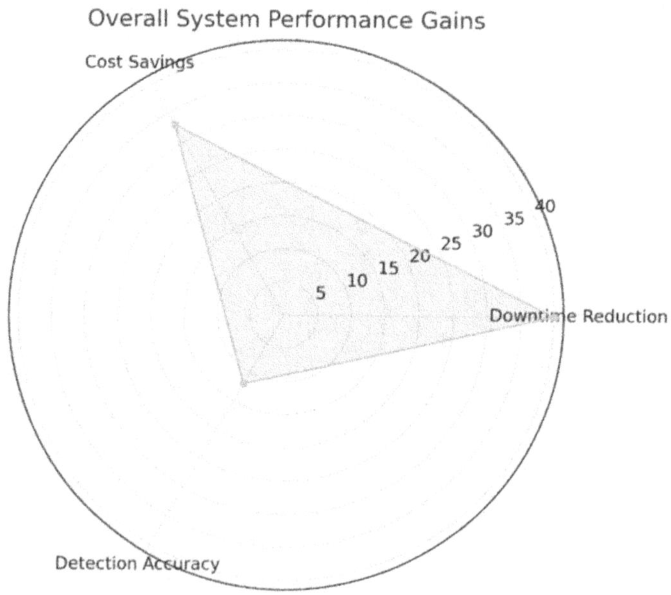

A radar chart, **Figure 5**, encapsulates the comparative advantages of AI-driven predictive maintenance across key performance indicators.

8. FINDINGS AND DISCUSSION

The analysis reveals that AI-driven predictive maintenance significantly enhances ICS resilience, efficiency, and cost-effectiveness. Deep learning models, particularly LSTMs, deliver superior accuracy in anomaly detection, while predictive strategies reduce both downtime and maintenance expenses. These results underscore the value of integrating advanced AI techniques into industrial environments, paving the way for more robust and efficient operations.

Findings

The findings of this study reflect the substantial benefits and insights gained through the application of AI-driven predictive maintenance in Industrial Control Systems (ICS). By systematically analyzing the collected data and validating the methodology, the results demonstrate enhanced system resilience, efficiency, and cost-effectiveness. The following sections outline the key findings derived from the research.

1. Superior Anomaly Detection

The use of advanced AI models, particularly Long Short-Term Memory (LSTM) networks, achieved high accuracy in anomaly detection. As shown in the results, the LSTM network outperformed other models such as Support Vector Machines (SVM) and Random Forests, achieving an F1-score of 91.3%, compared to 88.1% and 84.0%, respectively. This improvement is attributed to the ability of LSTM models to capture temporal patterns in time-series data, making them more suitable for predicting equipment failures. The findings underscore the importance of leveraging deep learning techniques for real-time monitoring and anomaly detection in ICS.

2. Enhanced System Performance

The integration of AI-driven predictive maintenance significantly improved system resilience, as evidenced by an increase in Mean Time Between Failures (MTBF) and a reduction in Mean Time to Repair (MTTR). The MTBF rose to 1,150 hours under predictive maintenance, compared to 750 hours for preventive maintenance and 600 hours for reactive maintenance. Similarly, MTTR was reduced to 3.4 hours, marking a significant improvement over traditional approaches. These metrics highlight the effectiveness of AI models in identifying potential failures early and enabling timely interventions to avoid catastrophic breakdowns.

3. Cost Reduction and Resource Optimization

The cost analysis revealed substantial savings through predictive maintenance. Total costs were reduced by 33% compared to preventive strategies and 50% compared to reactive strategies. Maintenance costs were minimized by reducing unnecessary interventions, while downtime costs were significantly lowered due to better planning and reduced equipment failure frequency. The predictive system enabled efficient allocation of resources, ensuring that maintenance tasks were only conducted when necessary. This efficiency was reflected in a 15% improvement in resource utilization.

4. Real-Time Insights into Anomalies

AI-driven systems provided real-time insights into operational anomalies, enhancing decision-making capabilities. Anomalies such as temperature fluctuations and abnormal vibration patterns were detected well before failures occurred, allowing for proactive maintenance. The temporal distribution of anomalies showed a strong correlation with impending failures, validating the accuracy and reliability of the predictive models.

5. Comprehensive System Efficiency Gains

The overall system efficiency was significantly enhanced through the integration of AI. Downtime was reduced by 40%, cost savings ranged from 33% to 50%, and detection accuracy improved by 8–12% compared to traditional methods. These gains demonstrate the transformative potential of AI-driven predictive maintenance in industrial environments.

6. Scalability and Adaptability

The multi-layered architecture of the predictive maintenance system proved scalable and adaptable to diverse ICS environments. The ability to process large volumes of real-time data and continuously improve models through retraining ensures that the system can adapt to evolving operational conditions. This scalability is vital for its application in complex industrial settings.

7. Challenges and Opportunities

Despite the significant advancements, some challenges persist, including the need for high-quality data, computational resources for deep learning models, and improving model interpretability to build operator trust. Addressing these challenges presents opportunities for further refinement and broader adoption of AI-driven predictive maintenance systems.

The study confirms that AI-driven predictive maintenance enhances ICS by reducing downtime, optimizing costs, and improving system resilience. The results validate the proposed methodology, demonstrating the potential of AI technologies to revolutionize maintenance practices in industrial environments. These findings provide a foundation for future research and practical applications in predictive maintenance for critical infrastructure systems.

Discussion

The implementation of AI-driven predictive maintenance in Industrial Control Systems (ICS) has yielded substantial improvements in system resilience, efficiency, and cost-effectiveness. The findings underscore the transformative potential of AI technologies, particularly in addressing the limitations of traditional maintenance strategies. This discussion contextualizes the results within the broader scope of ICS management and highlights their practical implications, associated challenges, and avenues for future research.

1. Addressing the Limitations of Traditional Maintenance Strategies

Traditional maintenance strategies, including preventive and reactive approaches, often fail to meet the dynamic needs of modern industrial environments. Preventive maintenance, while reducing the likelihood of failures, frequently results in unnecessary interventions and resource wastage. Reactive maintenance, on the other hand, responds only after a failure has occurred, leading to costly downtime and safety risks. The introduction of predictive maintenance, powered by AI, overcomes these limitations by leveraging data-driven insights to predict failures before they occur. The significant increase in Mean Time Between Failures (MTBF) and the reduction in Mean Time to Repair (MTTR) observed in this study validate the superiority of predictive maintenance over conventional methods.

2. Real-Time Anomaly Detection and Failure Prediction

The ability of AI models, particularly Long Short-Term Memory (LSTM) networks, to analyze time-series data and detect anomalies in real-time represents a critical advancement in ICS maintenance. This capability enables operators to address potential issues before they escalate into critical failures, thereby minimizing unplanned downtime and ensuring continuous operation. The high precision, recall, and F1-scores achieved by these models demonstrate their reliability and robustness. Moreover, the temporal correlation between detected anomalies and equipment failures underscores the accuracy of AI-driven predictions, reinforcing their role in enhancing operational resilience.

3. Cost Efficiency and Resource Optimization

One of the most significant outcomes of the study is the substantial cost savings achieved through predictive maintenance. By reducing unnecessary maintenance interventions and avoiding emergency repairs, AI-driven systems optimize resource utilization and minimize operational disruptions. The reduction in total costs by 33–50%, as compared to traditional strategies, highlights the financial viability of implementing AI technologies in industrial environments. Additionally, efficient allocation of labor, spare parts, and other resources contributes to streamlined maintenance operations, improving overall system efficiency.

4. Scalability and Adaptability of AI Models

The scalable architecture of the predictive maintenance system, comprising data acquisition, AI processing, and decision-making layers, ensures its adaptability to diverse ICS environments. The ability to process large volumes of real-time data and continuously retrain models enables the system to accommodate evolving operational conditions. This scalability is particularly relevant in complex industrial settings where operational demands and environmental factors vary significantly.

5. Challenges in Implementation

Despite the demonstrated benefits, several challenges must be addressed to fully realize the potential of AI-driven predictive maintenance. The quality and completeness of input data remain critical factors influencing model performance. Inconsistent or noisy data can reduce the accuracy of predictions, necessitating robust preprocessing techniques. Additionally, the computational demands of deep learning models, particularly for real-time applications, may pose constraints in resource-limited environments. Model interpretability is another significant challenge, as operators require transparent and explainable predictions to build trust in AI-driven systems.

6. Implications for Cybersecurity

As ICS become increasingly interconnected, cybersecurity emerges as a critical consideration in the deployment of AI-driven predictive maintenance. The reliance on real-time data and digital networks introduces vulnerabilities that malicious actors could exploit. Ensuring the integrity and security of data used in predictive maintenance systems is essential to prevent tampering or false anomaly generation, which could disrupt operations or compromise safety.

7. Future Research Directions

The study opens several avenues for future research and development. Improving data preprocessing techniques, enhancing the interpretability of AI models, and reducing the computational complexity of deep learning algorithms are critical areas of focus. Additionally, integrating cybersecurity measures into predictive maintenance systems will be essential to safeguard against evolving threats. Exploring the application of reinforcement learning for dynamic decision-making and optimizing maintenance schedules presents another promising direction.

The discussion highlights the pivotal role of AI-driven predictive maintenance in revolutionizing ICS management. By addressing the shortcomings of traditional maintenance strategies and leveraging real-time insights, AI technologies enhance system resilience, optimize costs, and ensure operational efficiency. While challenges related to data quality, computational demands, and cybersecurity persist, the results of this study demonstrate the substantial potential of AI-driven predictive maintenance to transform industrial operations. Addressing these challenges and advancing research in this domain will pave the way for more robust, efficient, and secure ICS in the future.

The proposed framework for integrating AI-driven predictive maintenance into legacy Industrial Control Systems (ICS) addresses several critical challenges by ensuring seamless implementation without disrupting existing operations. The framework is designed to work with legacy systems such as Distributed Control Systems (DCS), Supervisory Control and Data Acquisition (SCADA) systems, and Programmable Logic Controllers (PLC). By leveraging real-time sensor data, operational logs, and historical maintenance records, the system enables accurate failure prediction while maintaining compatibility with existing infrastructure. Traditional maintenance approaches, such as preventive and reactive strategies, often lead to unnecessary downtime, excessive maintenance costs, or unexpected failures. The integration of AI-driven predictive maintenance overcomes these limitations by continuously monitoring equipment conditions and identifying early warning signs of malfunctions.

One of the primary concerns in integrating AI-driven predictive maintenance into legacy ICS is minimizing operational disruptions. The proposed framework achieves this by implementing non-intrusive monitoring techniques that allow AI models to analyze sensor data in real time without requiring significant modifications to existing control systems. This ensures that maintenance insights are generated dynamically without affecting production schedules. Additionally, the framework seamlessly integrates data from various ICS components, ensuring that predictive analytics are based on comprehensive, real-time information. Advanced data preprocessing techniques, such as normalization and feature engineering, are employed to manage inconsistent or noisy data, which is a common challenge in industrial environments.

The resilience of the system is further enhanced through fault tolerance mechanisms, allowing ICS to continue operations even in the presence of minor equipment failures. By using AI-driven anomaly detection, the framework can reroute tasks to backup systems or implement preventive measures before a complete system failure occurs. This proactive approach significantly reduces unexpected downtimes and extends the lifespan of industrial equipment. Furthermore, cybersecurity considerations are embedded into the predictive maintenance framework. The AI models are integrated with anomaly detection systems that monitor network traffic and operational behaviors to identify potential cyber threats. Given the increasing interconnectivity of ICS, this security feature is essential in preventing unauthorized access, malware attacks, and other forms of digital threats that could compromise system integrity.

The study employs a combination of machine learning and deep learning models to predict equipment failures in critical sectors such as manufacturing and energy. Among the supervised machine learning models, Support Vector Machines (SVM) are used for classifying normal versus abnormal system behavior, while Random Forests aid in feature selection and failure prediction. Deep learning architectures, particularly Long Short-Term Memory (LSTM) networks, play a crucial role in capturing temporal dependencies in sensor data, making them highly effective for time-series prediction. Autoencoders are utilized for unsupervised anomaly detection, learning normal system behavior and flagging deviations that may indicate potential failures. Additionally, Convolutional Neural Networks (CNN) are applied to extract patterns from multivariate sensor data, improving fault classification accuracy. Reinforcement Learning (RL) models are also incorporated to dynamically optimize maintenance schedules, allowing the system to learn from historical actions and adjust its predictions based on evolving conditions.

To validate the effectiveness of AI-driven predictive maintenance, several key performance metrics were assessed. Anomaly detection accuracy was measured using precision, recall, and F1-score. LSTM networks achieved an F1-score of 91.3%, outperforming traditional models such as SVM (84.0%) and Random Forests (88.1%). The evaluation of system performance showed a 40% improvement in Mean Time Between Failures (MTBF), demonstrating the ability of predictive maintenance to enhance equipment reliability. Additionally, the Mean Time to Repair (MTTR) was significantly reduced to 3.4 hours, compared to 5.2 hours for preventive maintenance and 8.7 hours for reactive maintenance. These improvements directly contributed to minimizing downtime and ensuring continuous industrial operations.

The financial impact of predictive maintenance was also analyzed, with results indicating substantial cost savings. Compared to preventive maintenance strategies, AI-driven predictive maintenance reduced total costs by 33%, and compared to reactive maintenance, it achieved a 50% reduction in expenses. These savings were primarily due to optimized maintenance schedules, reduced emergency repairs, and improved resource allocation. By enabling maintenance teams to focus on critical issues rather than routine or unnecessary inspections, resource utilization was improved by 15%. The ability to schedule maintenance only when required helped industries avoid excessive operational costs while maintaining equipment efficiency.

A comparative analysis between traditional maintenance strategies and AI-driven predictive maintenance highlights the advantages of the latter. Preventive maintenance follows a scheduled approach, often resulting in unnecessary interventions and resource wastage. Reactive maintenance, which responds to failures after they occur, leads to costly downtime and operational disruptions. In contrast, AI-driven predictive maintenance provides a balanced approach, utilizing real-time data and predictive analytics to determine the optimal time for maintenance. This method ensures that maintenance actions are carried out proactively but only when necessary, preventing both unnecessary downtime and catastrophic system failures.

Despite its numerous advantages, the implementation of AI-driven predictive maintenance in ICS is not without challenges. The quality and completeness of input data play a crucial role in determining model accuracy. In many industrial environments, sensor data may be inconsistent or contain noise, which can affect the reliability of predictions. Addressing this issue requires robust data preprocessing and anomaly detection techniques. Another challenge is the computational complexity of deep learning models, particularly in real-time applications where rapid decision-making is necessary. While LSTM and autoencoders provide highly accurate predictions, their deployment requires significant computational resources, which may not always be available in legacy ICS environments. Additionally, the interpretability of AI models remains a concern, as operators may struggle to understand the reasoning behind AI-driven predictions. Enhancing model transparency and explainability will be critical to increasing operator trust and facilitating widespread adoption.

Cybersecurity is another key consideration in implementing AI-driven predictive maintenance. As industrial systems become more interconnected, they are increasingly vulnerable to cyber threats. AI models rely on vast amounts of real-time data, making them potential targets for attacks such as data poisoning or adversarial manipulation. Ensuring the integrity and security of predictive maintenance data is essential to preventing unauthorized disruptions. Future research should explore the integration of cybersecurity measures, such as blockchain-based data validation or AI-driven intrusion detection systems, to enhance the robustness of predictive maintenance frameworks.

In conclusion, AI-driven predictive maintenance presents a transformative opportunity for enhancing resilience and efficiency in Industrial Control Systems. By leveraging machine learning and deep learning techniques, the framework provides a proactive and data-driven approach to equipment maintenance, significantly reducing downtime and optimizing operational costs. The results indicate substantial improvements in system performance, including increased MTBF, reduced MTTR, and enhanced anomaly detection accuracy. While challenges related to data quality, computational demands, and model interpretability remain, ongoing advancements in AI and industrial automation will likely address these issues over time. Future research should focus on refining predictive maintenance methodologies, incorporating cybersecurity measures, and developing more transparent AI models to facilitate broader adoption across industrial sectors. AI-driven predictive maintenance not only aligns with the goals of Industry 4.0 but also represents a critical step forward in ensuring the reliability and sustainability of modern industrial operations.

9. CONCLUSION

This study demonstrates the transformative potential of AI-driven predictive maintenance in enhancing the resilience and efficiency of Industrial Control Systems (ICS). Through the application of advanced AI techniques, such as machine learning and deep learning models, predictive maintenance offers a significant improvement over traditional preventive and reactive approaches. Key findings reveal that predictive maintenance not only reduces downtime and operational disruptions but also optimizes resource utilization, leading to substantial cost savings.

The implementation of predictive maintenance has proven effective in addressing the dynamic challenges faced by modern industrial environments. Real-time anomaly detection and failure prediction, powered by models like Long Short-Term Memory (LSTM) networks, ensure timely maintenance interventions, thereby minimizing the risk of catastrophic system failures. The results indicate a marked improvement in system performance metrics, including increased Mean Time Between Failures (MTBF) and reduced Mean Time to Repair (MTTR).

In addition to operational benefits, the study underscores the scalability and adaptability of AI-driven predictive maintenance systems, enabling their integration into diverse ICS environments. However, challenges such as ensuring high-quality data, addressing computational constraints, and improving model interpretability must be overcome to fully realize the potential of these systems. Cybersecurity also emerges as a critical consideration, emphasizing the need for robust measures to safeguard against data breaches and malicious disruptions.

AI-driven predictive maintenance represents a paradigm shift in ICS management, offering a data-driven, proactive approach to system maintenance. By enhancing operational resilience, reducing costs, and improving efficiency, it aligns with the goals of Industry 4.0 and the broader digital transformation of industrial operations. Future research should focus on refining AI models, addressing implementation challenges, and integrating advanced cybersecurity measures to ensure the reliability and security of predictive maintenance systems in critical industrial infrastructures.

REFERENCES

Aggarwal, C. C. (2016). *Outlier analysis*. Springer.

Breiman, L. (2001). Random forests. *Machine Learning*, *45*(1), 5–32. DOI: 10.1023/A:1010933404324

Cardenas, A. A., Amin, S., & Sastry, S. (2008). Research challenges for the security of control systems. *HotSec*, *8*(6), 1–6.

Chalapathy, R., & Chawla, S. (2019). Deep learning for anomaly detection: A survey. *arXiv preprint arXiv:1901.03407*.

Deng, L. (2014). A tutorial survey of architectures, algorithms, and applications for deep learning. *APSIPA Transactions on Signal and Information Processing*, *3*(1), e2. DOI: 10.1017/atsip.2013.9

Giani, A., Nicolosi, C., Patel, S., & Bres, P. (2009). SCADA systems: The backbone of critical infrastructure. *IEEE Communications Surveys and Tutorials*, *12*(4), 24–29.

Jardine, A. K. S., Lin, D., & Banjevic, D. (2006). A review on machinery diagnostics and prognostics implementing condition-based maintenance. *Mechanical Systems and Signal Processing*, *20*(7), 1483–1510. DOI: 10.1016/j.ymssp.2005.09.012

Jiang, F., Yang, X., Zhang, C., & Li, G. (2017). A fault prediction method based on k-means and GMM for manufacturing equipment. *Procedia CIRP*, *63*, 700–705.

Lee, J., Ni, J., Djurdjanovic, D., Qiu, H., & Liao, H. (2006). Intelligent prognostics tools and e-maintenance. *Computers in Industry*, *57*(6), 476–489. DOI: 10.1016/j.compind.2006.02.014

Mobley, R. K. (2002). *An introduction to predictive maintenance*. Elsevier.

Ponomarev, A., & Atkison, T. (2016). Industrial control system network anomaly detection using passive network traffic. *IEEE Transactions on Information Forensics and Security*, *12*(5), 1299–1312.

Samek, W., Wiegand, T., & Müller, K. R. (2017). Explainable artificial intelligence: Understanding, visualizing, and interpreting deep learning models. *arXiv preprint arXiv:1708.08296*.

Si, X. S., Wang, W., Hu, C. H., & Zhou, D. H. (2011). Remaining useful life estimation—A review on the statistical data-driven approaches. *European Journal of Operational Research*, *213*(1), 1–14. DOI: 10.1016/j.ejor.2010.11.018

Stouffer, K., Pillitteri, V., Lightman, S., Abrams, M., & Hahn, A. (2015). Guide to industrial control systems (ICS) security. *NIST Special Publication 800-82 Revision 2*. National Institute of Standards and Technology.

Wang, K., He, Q., & Zhang, Y. (2017). Predictive maintenance based on Bayesian network for wind turbine systems. *Energy Conversion and Management*, *148*, 397–406.

Wang, K. S., Ma, L., Yang, C. C., Chang, S. F., & Hsu, P. (2018). Predictive maintenance using machine learning for industrial control systems. *IEEE Transactions on Industrial Electronics*, *65*(8), 6558–6567.

Widodo, A., & Yang, B. S. (2007). Support vector machine in machine condition monitoring and fault diagnosis. *Mechanical Systems and Signal Processing*, *21*(6), 2560–2574. DOI: 10.1016/j.ymssp.2006.12.007

Zhang, H., Zhang, Z., Wu, W., & He, X. (2019). Anomaly detection in industrial control systems using LSTM networks. *IEEE Access : Practical Innovations, Open Solutions*, *7*, 88036–88047.

Zhu, B., Joseph, A., & Sastry, S. (2011). A taxonomy of cyber attacks on SCADA systems. *IEEE International Conferences on Internet of Things (iThings/CPSCom)*, 16-25.

Zonta, T., da Costa, C. A., da Silva, D. D., & Webber, G. A. (2020). Predictive maintenance in Industry 4.0: A systematic literature review. *Computers & Industrial Engineering*, *150*, 106889. DOI: 10.1016/j.cie.2020.106889

Chapter 10
Features of Research and Development of Passively Redundant Subsystems of Aircraft Taking Into Account Tolerenaces

Vu Trong Tuan
Duy Tan University, Vietnam

Duong Vu
Duy Tan University, Vietnam

ABSTRACT

The work is aimed at identifying specific features that need to be taken into account when researching and developing passively redundant subsystems, taking into account tolerances for sudden independent failures. It is shown that in this type of redundancy it is necessary to take into account the presence in the same subsystems of assignable and implemented tolerances, multiple and non-multiple redundancy, tolerance scales with different levels of significance, probability ranges of elements, where redundancy is advantageous and unprofitable, etc.

INTRODUCTION

The consideration of single-level and multi-level redundancy can impact the reliability and performance of a passive redundant system, which is determined based on two approaches at the design stage: enhancing the reliability of components and incorporating redundancy into the system. The first approach involves using highly reliable components manufactured with modern technology, tested, and selected according to specific operating modes. The second approach involves introducing redundancy into the system, which can take various forms. The types of redundancy can be classified as follows: Parametric redundancy; Operational redundancy; Temporal redundancy; Structural redundancy (backup/reserve); Functional redundancy; Informational redundancy. The work is aimed at identifying specific features that

DOI: 10.4018/979-8-3693-7812-0.ch010

need to be taken into account when researching and developing passively redundant subsystems, taking into account tolerances for sudden independent failures. It is shown that in this type of redundancy it is necessary to take into account the presence in the same subsystems of assignable and implemented tolerances, multiple and non-multiple redundancy, tolerance scales with different levels of significance, probability ranges of elements, where redundancy is advantageous and unprofitable, etc.

In our research, the issue of improving the reliability of aircraft subsystems is considered through the introduction of structural redundancy, that is, through the reservation of system components (subsystems and elements). Each type of redundancy introduced into a system has its own area of application. However, at present, the most important and frequently used method for improving system reliability is the introduction of structural redundancy (Sadeghi, 2015). Depending on the purpose and operational characteristics of technical systems, four specific reliability indicators are used for evaluation: Failure-free performance indicators; Maintainability (recoverability) indicators; Durability indicators; Preservation indicators

For the control system in an aircraft, the most critical indicators are failure-free performance indicators, as in the vast majority of cases, these systems operate until the first failure occurs.

Currently, system redundancy can be classified according to the following features: By the type of redundancy, there are active and passive (permanent) redundancies, each of which has its own advantages and disadvantages. In systems with passive redundancy, a significant role is played by the analysis of the operation of the elements in the backup group that remain functional after the failure of one or more elements. There are two types of systems with passive redundancy:

Systems with an unchanged output parameter, i.e., systems where the output parameter does not change after the failure of elements in the backup group;

Systems with a changing output parameter, i.e., systems where the output parameter changes after the failure of at least one element in the backup group.

According to the method of connecting backup elements, both active and passive redundancy can be classified as common, where the entire system (or subsystem) is backed up; block, where redundancy is provided for groups of elements; and separate, where each element of the system (or subsystem) is backed up."

PASSIVE REDUNDANCY (J. Bouwmeester et al.,2022) AS A WAY TO IMPROVE RELIABILITY AND ITS PROPERTIES

The simplest way to improve the reliability of the system as a whole is to improve the reliability of the components. The operability of systems without redundancy requires high reliability of all system elements. In complex technical devices without redundancy, it is almost never possible to achieve high reliability, even if components with high reliability values (above 0.99) are used.

Term redundancy means the use of additional means and/or capabilities in order to preserve the operability of an object in the event of a failure of one or more elements .In the case of redundancy, redundant elements are introduced into the technical systems. Redundancy implements the principle of one of the types of redundancy, namely structural redundancy.

The degree of structural redundancy is often estimated by a parameter called the redundancy multiplicity K. Redundancy multiplicity is the main redundancy parameter, which is defined in different ways: either as the ratio of the number of redundant elements r to the number of principal m (Mira and

Azzam, 2019); or as the ratio of the total number of elements n to the number of basic m. The second definition most naturally reflects the notion of multiplicity of the number of basic elements, the total number of elements. Therefore, we will use the following formula as a redundancy multiplicity in the work: $K = \frac{n}{m}$ (1)

Passive or, as it is often called, permanent redundancy of subsystems (Pranoto and Wirawan,2018) consists in the fact that instead of one subsystem, the main, two or more redundant subsystems are switched on in parallel to increase reliability. Thus, in passive redundancy, a new device is formed – a redundant subsystem, in which several initial components or subsystems act as elements. The specificity of the operation of such redundant devices is that the main elements in them are indistinguishable from the backup ones and work together with them in the same conditions. You can only specify the numbers of these elements.

An important property of passive redundancy is the resource consumption of redundant elements (Dustin and Markus, 2023) on a par with the main ones. For this reason, passive redundancy is often referred to as hot standby. Another feature of passive redundancy of subsystems is that in the event of element failures, there are no interruptions in their operation. Therefore, such redundancy is used in subsystems that do not allow even short-term interruptions in operation.

One of the peculiarities of technical systems is the interconnectedness of their subsystems at any level of hierarchical articulation, so that the output characteristics of one subsystem are inputs to another. Therefore, in order to ensure the operability of systems as a whole, it is necessary that in the course of operation of interconnected subsystems, their output/input characteristics either do not change at all in case of element failures, or change within permissible limits.

According to the consequences of failures of elements of subsystems with passive redundancy, while maintaining the operability of adjacent subsystems, a distinction is made:

- subsystems and devices that do not change their output characteristics;
- subsystems and devices that change their characteristics.

The first type includes, as a rule, mechanical and electromechanical devices. For example, the transmission of torque from an engine to another device (generator, pump, pump, etc.) can be carried out by V-belt transmission. One or two straps are enough for normal functioning. To increase reliability, three or four belts are installed. A break in one belt does not result in a change in torque.

The second type includes electromechanical, electrical, and electronic devices. For example, the aircraft can be powered by two synchronous generators operating in parallel. The failure of a single generator does not result in a failure of the power supply system. However, the power generated by a single generator may not be sufficient for the normal operation of a number of devices, which can lead to failure.

In this regard, a distinction is made between passive redundancy (Aslain et al.,2023) taking into account permissible changes in output parameters (taking into account tolerances) and passive redundancy without taking into account tolerances. Both of these types of reservations can be multiples and non-multiples. Passively redundant subsystems are considered, taking into account tolerances.

In case of passive redundancy of subsystems (Vyacheslav, 2019) without taking into account tolerances, a redundant subsystem is considered to be healthy if it has at least one serviceable element, i.e. the number of main elements m=1. However, this statement is true if the output characteristics of redundant subsystems do not affect the performance of their associated subsystems. In the presence of this influence, it is necessary to take into account the tolerance for deviation of the output parameters of passively reserved subsystems in case of failures of their elements to ensure the operability of the subsystems associated with them. Taking into account tolerances for changing the output parameters of a passively reserved subsystem can significantly affect the structure of its redundancy and, in particular, the number of its main elements, which can be significantly more than one.

By the number of main elements of a passively redundant subsystem, we will understand the minimum number of serviceable elements m, out of the total number n, at which the deviation of its output parameter is ensured, which does not exceed the maximum permissible in case of failures of all redundant elements, (r = n-m) and at the same time the operability of both the redundant and adjacent subsystems is maintained.

For example, in aircraft engine fuel supply systems, the permissible maximum reduction from the nominal value of the total capacity of fuel pumps is assigned, based on the design features and the requirement to ensure all engine operating modes, including boosted ones, for the required time (Berman et al.,2020).

TYPES, DEFINITION AND CHARACTERIZATION OF TOLERANCES. A DISTINCTION SHOULD BE MADE BETWEEN ASSIGNED TOLERANCES AND IMPLEMENTED TOLERANCES

The assigned tolerance is set to the adjacent subsystem that is structurally related to the passively redundant subsystem (Aslain et al.,2023). It determines the maximum permissible deviation from the nominal value (nominal) of the input parameter of the adjacent subsystem, which ensures its normal functioning. The assigned permit is determined by the regulatory and technical documentation for the equipment object in question. It is set on a continuous scale of possible tolerances. For example, in power amplifiers of aircraft control systems, it determines the minimum total output power that ensures the performance of the steering drive in all modes for the required time. A similar situation occurs in the other subsystems mentioned in the previous subsection.

The realized tolerance is provided by a passively redundant subsystem (Muhammad and Tanya, 2016). It has a discrete character, determined by the discrete structure of passive redundancy, i.e. it is determined by the discrete values m, r, and n. The realized tolerance is characterized by the value of deviation of the output parameter from the nominal in case of failure (failure) of all its r = n - m of reserve elements. As you can see from the above, the assigned tolerances and the tolerances that are being implemented may not be the same in their values. In this case, the tolerance implemented in passive redundancy must be “narrower” than assigned.

Realizable and assigned tolerances (Krzysztof and Wojciech, 2022) can be specified in absolute and relative values. The assigned tolerance in absolute values determines the maximum permissible decrease in the input parameter of the adjacent subsystem associated with the pasively redundant subsystem.

$$\Delta Wn = Wnom - Wm \qquad (2)$$

Where: Wnom is the nominal value of the input parameter of the adjacent subsystem; - Wm is the minimum value of the input parameter of the adjacent subsystem, which ensures its operability in all modes. Obviously, the assigned tolerance in absolute values can vary from 0 to Wnom. The assigned tolerance in relative values is determined by the expression:

$$dW_n = \frac{W_{nom} - W_m}{W_{nom}} \cdot 100\% \tag{3}$$

$$\Delta W_p = W \cdot n - W \cdot m = r \cdot W \tag{4}$$

It shows the permissible relative value of the decrease in the input parameter of the adjacent subsystem from the nominal value, per unit of its nominal value, expressed as a percentage. The assigned tolerance in relative values can vary from 0 to 100%. The realized tolerance in absolute values ΔWp is determined, as noted earlier, by the value of deviation from the nominal value of the output parameter in case of failure (failure) of all its reserve elements where, W is the value of the output parameter of one of the n elements of the passively reserved subsystem. The realized tolerance in relative values is determined by the value of the ratio ΔWp to the nominal value of the output parameter of the redundant subsystem W. n expressed as a percentage:

$$dW_p = \frac{r \cdot W}{n \cdot W} \cdot 100\% = \frac{r}{n} \cdot 100\% = \frac{n - m}{n} \cdot 100\%. \tag{5}$$

For implemented and assigned tolerances, the following conditions must be met in both absolute and relative representation: ΔWn ≥ Δ Wp (6)

dWn ≥ dWp (7)

The realizable tolerances in absolute and relative representation can vary within the same limits as the assigned tolerances. More common are assigned and implemented tolerances in relative terms. For example, the implemented tolerances in the relative view depend only on the parameters of the reservation structure m, n, r and do not depend on the output parameters of the subsystems. For practical use, a discrete grid of realizable tolerances in relative representation is of interest. Let's compile a table of realizable relative tolerance values for various passive redundancy structures. The table looks the most illustrative depending on the parameters m and r.

Table 1. Values of realizable relative tolerances as a percentage depending on the number of main m and reserve r elements.

m	r										
	1	2	3	4	5	6	7	8	9	10	11
1	50,0	66,7	75,0	80,0	83,3	85,7	87,5	88,0	90,0	90,9	91,7
2	33,3	50,0	60,0	66,7	71,4	75,0	77,8	80,0	81,8	83,3	84,6
3	25,0	40,0	50,0	57,1	62,5	66,7	70,0	72,7	75,0	76,9	78,6
4	20,0	33,3	42,8	50,0	55,5	60,0	63,6	66,7	69,2	71,4	73,3
5	16,7	28,6	37,5	44,4	50,0	54,5	58,3	61,5	64,3	66,7	68,7
6	14,3	25,0	33,3	40,0	45,4	50,0	53,8	57,1	60,0	62,5	64,7
7	12,5	22,2	30,0	36,4	41,7	46,1	50,0	53,5	56.2	58,8	61,1
8	11,1	20,0	27,3	33,3	38,5	42,8	46,7	50,0	52,9	55,5	57,9
9	10,0	18,2	25,0	30,8	35,7	40,0	43,7	47,1	50,0	52,6	55,0

Analysis of the presented table allows us to draw the following conclusions:

1. The realized tolerances form a sufficiently large variety of possible discrete values, both more than 50% and less than 50%;
2. Tolerance values are closely related to the complexity of redundancy structures – the complexity of redundancy structures increases as m and r increases;
3. The change in tolerances with increasing values m and r is of the opposite nature, so that with an increase r with a constant m, the tolerances increase, and with an increase m with a constant r, the tolerances decrease;
4. When r and m are increased at the same time, the tolerances change slightly and repeat with a certain periodicity. Thus, a tolerance of 50% is realized at r = 1 and m = 1, r = 2 and m = 2, etc., a tolerance of 33.3% is realized at r = 1 and m = 2, r = 2 and m = 4, and so on;
5. For any fixed value of m (not equal to zero) and for r tending to infinity, the tolerances tend to 100%,

$$\lim_{r\to\infty} dW_p = \frac{r}{n}\cdot 100\% = \lim_{r\to\infty}\frac{r}{r+m}\cdot 100\% = \frac{\infty}{\infty}$$

.

Resolving uncertainty we have

$$\lim_{r\to\infty}\frac{\frac{r}{r}}{\frac{r}{r}+\frac{m}{r}}\cdot 100\% = 100\%$$

6. For any fixed r and for m tending to infinity, the tolerances tend to zero

(

$$\lim_{m\to\infty} dW_p = \frac{r}{n}\cdot 100\% = \lim_{n\to\infty}\frac{r}{n}\cdot 100\% = 0$$

, where n = r + m).

For practical use, the most important is the scale of decreasing, i.e. tighter tolerances. Therefore, we will consider changing the tolerances by columns. The most significant are the tolerances of the first column of Table 1 (at r = 1), which form the following series of values: 50%; 33,3%; 25%; 20%; 16,7%; 14,3%; 12,5%; 11,1%; 10%. Let's call them first-level tolerances. Accordingly, the tolerances specified by the second, third, and subsequent columns will be called tolerances of the second, third, and subsequent levels. As the tolerance level increases, the redundancy structure becomes more complex, determined by the number of primary m and redundant r elements. Therefore, the first and second level tolerances are the most significant. The combined use of the first and second level tolerances provides a more frequent grid of implemented tolerances. According to Table 1, the grid of non-repetitive relative realizable tolerances formed by them is as follows: 66.7%; 50%; 40%; 33,3%; 28,6%; 25%; 22,2%; 20%; 18,2%; 16,7%; 14,3%; 12,5%; 11,1%; 10%. This mesh provides a good approximation to the assigned tolerances.

MULTIPLE AND NON-MULTIPLE PASSIVE REDUNDANCY AND THEIR RELATIONSHIP TO TOLERANCE (Mutullah Eser et al.,2024)

The tolerances shown in Table 1 correspond to redundancy structures with minimum multiplicities. For example, a tolerance of 50% at r = 1 and m = 1 corresponds to multiplicity, a tolerance of 33.3% at r = 1 and m = 2 corresponds to multiplicity, and so on.

There are no smaller multiplicity values at the specified tolerances. The first row of Table 1 corresponds to multiple-reservation subsystems because the conditions for implementing multiple reservations are met and the conditions for implementing non-multiple reservations are not met. Necessary and sufficient conditions for the implementation of multiple redundancy are:

1. The number of basic elements must be greater than zero (m>0);
2. The total number of elements must be greater than the number of basic elements (n > m);
3. Any element of the reservation structure can replace a strictly defined failed element.

For example, if r = 1, the multiplicity is 2, if r = 2, the multiplicity is 3, and if r = 11, the multiplicity is 12. Thus, the first row of Table 1 implements the change in cardinality from duplication to twelve-fold redundancy. Tolerances below the first line correspond to non-multiple redundancy structures. Since the conditions for the implementation of non-multiple reservation are met and the conditions for the implementation of multiple reservation are not met, they determine the main volume of realized tolerances and are of the greatest interest for the study.

Necessary and sufficient conditions for the implementation of non-multiple redundancy are:

1. The number of main elements must be more than one (m>1);
2. The total number of elements must be greater than the number of basic elements (n > m);
3. Any element of the reservation structure can replace any element that fails.

It should be noted that when studying subsystems with non-multiple reservation, the cardinality should be written as an irreducible fraction even if the cardinality is an integer ratio. This is due not only to the fact that fractional multiplicity of reservation is a sign of non-multiple reservation, but also to the fact that the numerator and denominator of this fraction determine the structure of reservation (parameters n and m). In addition, subsystems with non-multiple redundancy have an important property: the reliability indicators of subsystems with non-multiple redundancy are always higher than subsystems with multiple redundancy at the same numbers m and n. However, the "payment" for this useful property, as will be shown later, is the presence of critical probabilities of elements of redundant subsystems in subsystems with non-multiple redundancy, which significantly narrow the range. where this type of redundancy is beneficial.

Each tolerance can be implemented at different multiplicity values of both multiple and non-multiple redundancy. Moreover, for each tolerance there is its own scale (ruler) of various individual multiplicities increasing in magnitude n and m, starting with the minimum value. That is why Table 1 seems to have a third dimension, since each tolerance can be correlated with its own line of increasing individual multiplicities. Both the minimum values and other individual multiplicities of the various tolerances differ significantly from each other. Thus, there is a wide variety of different multiplicities for different tolerance values.

For example, with a tolerance of 50% of the first level, the increasing series of individual multiplicities is as follows:

$$K_1^I = \frac{2}{1} = 2, K_2^I = \frac{4}{2}, K_3^I = \frac{6}{3}...$$

With a tolerance of 33.3%, the increasing multiplicity series is:

$$K_1^I = \frac{3}{2}, K_2^I = \frac{6}{4}, K_3^I = \frac{9}{6}...$$

With a tolerance of 25% of the first level, the increasing series of multiples is:

$$K_1^I = \frac{4}{3}, K_2^I = \frac{8}{6}, K_3^I = \frac{12}{9}...$$

Likewise, at a tolerance of 66.7% of the second level, the increasing series of individual multiplicities is:

$$K_2^I = \frac{3}{1} = 3, K_3^I = \frac{6}{2}, K_4^I = \frac{9}{3}...$$

With a tolerance of 50% of the second level:

$$K_2^I = \frac{4}{2}, K_3^I = \frac{8}{4}, K_4^I = \frac{12}{6}...$$

In the case of the rulers of increasing tolerance multiplicities of the first level, the number of reserve elements forms an arithmetic progression with the difference d = 1, in the case of the tolerance rulers of the second level, the arithmetic progression with the difference d = 2, and so on. For example, the number of redundant elements (r = n - m) for a tolerance of 50% of the first level form the sequence: 2 – 1 = 1, 4 – 2 = 2, 6 – 3 = 3, etc.; for a tolerance of 33.3% of the first level 3 – 2 = 1, 6 – 4 = 2, 9 – 6 = 3, etc.; For a tolerance of 25% of the first level, 4 – 3 = 1, 8 – 6 = 2, 12 – 9 = 3, etc. For a tolerance of 66.7% of the second level, the number of redundant elements forms the sequence: 3 – 1 = 2, 6 – 2 = 4, 9 – 3 = 6, etc.; For a tolerance of 50% of the second level, 4 – 2 = 2, 8 – 4 = 4, 12 – 6 = 6, etc.

In order to compare the fail-safe indices at different tolerances depending on the series of increasing individual multiplicities, it is expedient to somehow unify these different increasing individual multiplicities. As a unifying parameter, let us take the value of the generalized multiplicity Ki, where i is the ordinal number of individual multiplicities in the sequences of their increasing ratios at any values of the realized tolerances. In the future, along with individual multiplicity values, we will use generalized Ki values that depersonalize individual values. Table 2 shows a series of ten increasing multiplicities, individually and generically, for the first-level tolerances of Table 1, and Table 3 shows the same multiplicity series for the second-level tolerances.

In general, the rulers of individual multiplicities are calculated using the formula:

$$K^{I}_{i} = \frac{n_i}{m_i} = \frac{n_m \cdot i}{m_m \cdot i} \tag{8}$$

where i = 1, 2, 3,... for level 1 tolerances and i = 2, 3, 4,... for level 2 tolerances.

Here, nm and mm are the minimum values of the structure parameters given in Table 1, which define the minimum multiplicities in each tolerance. In the future, unless specifically specified, multiplicity will be understood as individual multiplicity.

Table 2. Values of individual and generalized multiplicities corresponding to the values of the realizable relative tolerances of the first level presented in Table 1

dW %	Generalized reservation multiplicities Ki									
	K1	K2	K3	K4	K5	K6	K7	K8	K9	K10
50	2	$\frac{4}{2}$	$\frac{6}{3}$	$\frac{8}{4}$	$\frac{10}{5}$	$\frac{12}{6}$	$\frac{14}{7}$	$\frac{16}{8}$	$\frac{18}{9}$	$\frac{20}{10}$
33,3	$\frac{3}{2}$									
25										
20										
16,7										
14,3										
12,5										
11,1										
10										

Table 3. Values of individual and generalized multiplicities corresponding to the values of the realizable second-level relative tolerances presented in Table 1

dW %	Generalized redundancy multiplicities Ki									
	K2	K3	K4	K5	K6	K7	K8	K9	K10	K11
66,7	3	$\frac{6}{2}$	$\frac{9}{3}$							
50										
40										
33,3										
28,6										

continued on following page

Table 3. Continued

dW %	Generalized redundancy multiplicities Ki									
	K2	K3	K4	K5	K6	K7	K8	K9	K10	K11
25										
22,2										
20										
18,2										

The first cell of Table 2 with a tolerance of 50% and Table 3 with a tolerance of 66.7% correspond to multiple reservation, and the remaining cells of the two tables correspond to non-multiple reservation. One of the most important features of the passive redundancy structures of the aircraft subsystem, taking into account tolerances, is a decrease in the mass-dimensional (and cost) characteristics of their elements with tightening tolerances and an increase in multiplicities compared to similar characteristics of the non-redundant subsystem. Indeed, the replacement of a non-redundant subsystem from a single element with a nominal value of the output parameter Wnom with a passively redundant subsystem consisting of n identical elements working in parallel leads to a decrease in their output parameters W by a factor of n.

$$W = \frac{W_{nom}}{n} \tag{9}$$

In connection with the above, it can be assumed that the replacement of the non-redundant subsystem with a passively redundant one of n elements in the interests of increasing its reliability will not lead to a significant increase in the cost and mass-dimensional characteristics of the redundant subsystem as a whole.

ANALYSIS OF THE INFLUENCE OF TOLERANCES AND REDUNDANCY MULTIPLICITIES ON THE VALUES OF CRITICAL PROBABILITIES OF PASSIVELY REDUNDANT ELEMENTS OF AIRCRAFT SUBSYSTEMS (Vyacheslav M. Grishin, Vu Trong Tuan,2018)

Critical values of element probabilities are related to the reliability of non-redundant and passively redundant aircraft subsystems. As their indicators of failure, we will use the probability of failure, often called, because of their importance, reliability functions (reliability functions). Let Pc(tz) = Pc be the probability of failure-free operation of the passively redundant subsystem during the execution of the task, and p(tz) = p - the probability of failure-free operation of the non-redundant subsystem (element of the passively reserved subsystem) during the execution of the task (PIĽA and KOZUBA,2019). Obviously, the fail-safe function of the passively redundant subsystem Pc depends on the redundancy structure (parameters m and n) and on the reliability of its elements p: Pc =Pc(p, n, m). (10) Among the many probabilistic, logical-probabilistic and logical methods for calculating function (10), let us choose one of the probabilistic methods.

The conditions for the functioning of the elements of passively reserved subsystems meet the requirements of Bernoulli's theorem on the repetition of experiments . Therefore, to calculate the fail-safe index, we will use the formula of the binomial distribution law: According to this formula, the probability of failure of exactly m elements out of the total number of n elements of the passively reserved subsystem is given by the expression:

$$P_{m,n} = C_n^m \cdot p^m \cdot (1-p)^{(n-m)}. \tag{11}$$

The fail-safe function (10) is defined as the probability of failure-free operation of at least melements out of a total number of n:

$$P_c = \sum_{i=m}^{n} C_n^i \cdot p^i \cdot (1-p)^{(n-i)}. \tag{12}$$

For subsystems with multiple redundancy structures of any cardinality (the first row of Table 1), the fail-safe function Pc is always greater than the fail-safe function of the non-redundant subsystem at the open interval: $0 < p < 1$. This follows from the statement that an aircraft subsystem with multiple passive redundancy is healthy if at least one of its elements is in good working order. In this case, the number of main elements $m = 1$, and the fail-safe function of subsystems with multiple passive redundancy is determined by the expressions:

$$P_c = \sum_{i=1}^{n} C_n^i \cdot p^i \cdot (1-p)^{(n-i)}, \tag{13}$$

$$P_c = 1 - q^n$$

where

$$q = 1 - p. \tag{14}$$

From expression (14) it follows that the inequality is valid for subsystems with multiple passive redundancy:

$$P_c = 1 - q^n > p = 1 - q. \tag{15}$$

Expression (15) proves the correctness of the above statement. For subsystems with non-multiple passive redundancy structures (the second and the following tolerance lines in Table 1), the number of principal elements, as indicated earlier, is always greater than one: $m > 1$. For example, for three level 1 tolerances at minimum multiplicities (dW = 33.3%; dW = 25%; dW = 20%), the fail-safety formulas, respectively, are as follows:

$$P_c^1 = \sum_{i=2}^{3} C_3^i \cdot p^i \cdot (1-p)^{(3-i)}, K_1^I = \frac{3}{2}\ ; \tag{16}$$

$$P_c^2 = \sum_{i=3}^{4} C_4^i \cdot p^i \cdot (1-p)^{(4-i)}, K_1^I = \frac{4}{3}\ ; \tag{17}$$

$$P_c^3 = \sum_{i=4}^{5} C_5^i \cdot p^i \cdot (1-p)^{(5-i)}, K_1^I = \frac{5}{4}. \tag{18}$$

Therefore, the condition Pc > p may not be met, and the fail-down rates for multiple redundancy may be higher than the fail-safe values for non-multiple redundancy. This is due to the different number of structure parameters for multiple and non-multiple redundancy. In the case under consideration, with a given value n in the case of multiple reservation, the number of principal elements m = 1, and in the case of non-multiple reservation, m takes the values 2, 3, 4... As indicated in (Aslain et al.,2023), for any non-multiple redundancy structures, the following ratio is performed:

Pc(p, n, m) <p, with p close to zero,

and Pc(p, n, m) >p, with p close to one.

Moreover, on the open interval (0 – 1), the dependencies Pc(p, n, m) and p(p) have one point of intersection, and the equation Pc(p, n, m) = p (19) has one material root. The probability value corresponding to this root is called the critical value and is denoted pkr. Thus, in the case of non-multiple passive redundancy, there are critical probabilities of the elements of the redundant subsystems, which divide the interval (0 – 1) into two sub-intervals:

- subcritical (0 -pkr), where Pc(p, n, m) <p and passive redundancy is not profitable;
- supercritical (pkr-1), where Pc(p, n, m) >p and passive redundancy is beneficial.

Analytical and numerical methods can be used to calculate critical pkr values. Analytical methods are time-consuming and may be of greater theoretical interest. (They boil down to lowering the order of algebraic equations to no higher than the third or fourth, for which there are formulas for calculating roots.) For practical purposes, numerical methods seem to be more important. Table 4 shows the results of calculations of the critical probability values of the elements of passively reserved pkr subsystems, calculated on the basis of equation (12) and formula (19) by the brute-force method with an accuracy of 0.001, for the tolerances of the first level and increasing multiplicities in each of them, and Table 5 shows similar results for the tolerances of the second level.

Table 4. Critical pkr probabilities for 11 increasing generalized multiplicities corresponding to 9 realizable level I tolerances

dW %	Generalized redundancy multiples Ki										
	K1	K2	K3	K4	K5	K6	K7	K8	K9	K10	K11
50,0	-	0,233	0,348	0,396	0,422	0,438	0,449	0,456	0,462	0,467	0,470
33,3	0,500	0,653	0,679	0,687	0,690	0,691	0,691	0,691	0,691	0,691	0,691
25,0	0,768	0,803	0,804	0,801	0,799	0,796	0,794	0,792	0,790	0,789	0,787
20,0	0,869	0,871	0,865	0,859	0,855	0,851	0,848	0,846	0,844	0,842	0,840
16,7	0,917	0,908	0,900	0,893	0,889	0,885	0,882	0,879	0,877	0,875	0,873
14,3	0,943	0,930	0,921	0,915	0,910	0,907	0,904	0,901	0,899	0,897	0,896

continued on following page

Table 4. Continued

dW %	Generalized redundancy multiples Ki										
	K1	**K2**	**K3**	**K4**	**K5**	**K6**	**K7**	**K8**	**K9**	**K10**	**K11**
12,5	0,958	0,945	0,936	0,930	0,926	0,922	0,919	0,917	0,915	0,913	0,912
11,1	0,968	0,955	0,947	0,941	0,937	0,934	0,931	0,929	0,927	0,925	0,924
10,0	0,975	0,963	0,955	0,950	0,946	0,943	0,940	0,938	0,936	0,934	0,933

Table 5. Critical pkr probabilities for 10 increasing multiplicities corresponding to 9 realizable level 2 tolerances

dW %	Generalized redundancy multiplicities Ki									
	K2	**K3**	**K4**	**K5**	**K6**	**K7**	**K8**	**K9**	**K10**	**K11**
66,7	-	0,084	0,158	0,197	0,221	0,237	0,248	0,257	0,263	0,269
50,0	0,233	0,396	0,438	0,456	0,467	0,473	0,477	0,481	0,483	0,485
40,0	0,500	0,579	0,596	0,602	0,605	0,607	0,608	0,608	0,609	0,609
33,3	0,653	0,687	0,691	0,691	0,691	0,690	0,689	0,689	0,688	0,687
28,6	0,745	0,755	0,753	0,750	0,748	0,746	0,745	0,743	0,742	0,741
25,0	0,803	0,801	0,796	0,792	0,789	0,786	0,784	0,782	0,781	0,779
22,2	0,843	0,835	0,828	0,823	0,819	0,816	0,814	0,812	0,810	0,809
20,0	0,871	0,859	0,851	0,846	0,842	0,839	0,836	0,834	0,833	0,831
18,2	0,892	0,878	0,870	0,864	0,860	0,857	0,855	0,853	0,851	0,849

The first cells of the first rows of Tables 4 and 5 correspond to multiple reservations and are not considered further due to the absence of critical pkr values for them within the probability interval (0 – 1).

To illustrate the results presented in Tables 4 and 5, Figures 1 and 2 show the critical probabilities pkr as multiplicities for the two first-level tolerance ranges, and Figures 3 and 4 show similar pkr multiplicities for the second-level tolerances.

Figure 1. Dependencies pkr of generalized multiplicity Ki for large first-level tolerances

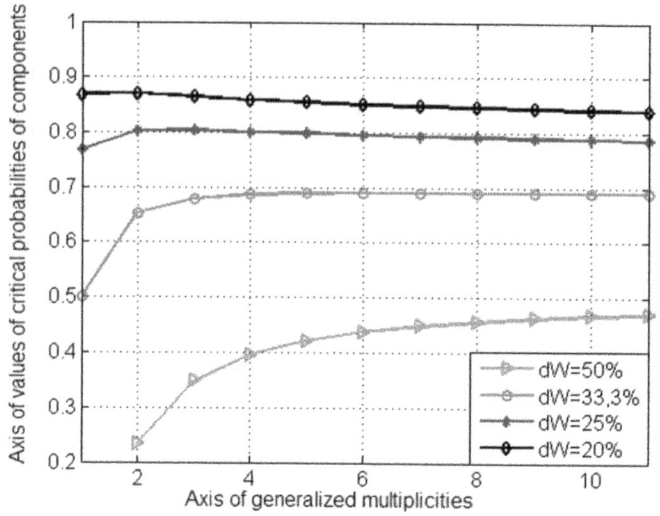

The graphs in Figure 1 illustrate the different nature (from monotonic increase6 to monotonic decrease) of the dependence of pkr on the generalized multiplicity Ki for large tolerances of the first level.

Figure 2. Dependencies of pkr of Generalized Cardinality Ki for Small Tolerances of the First Level

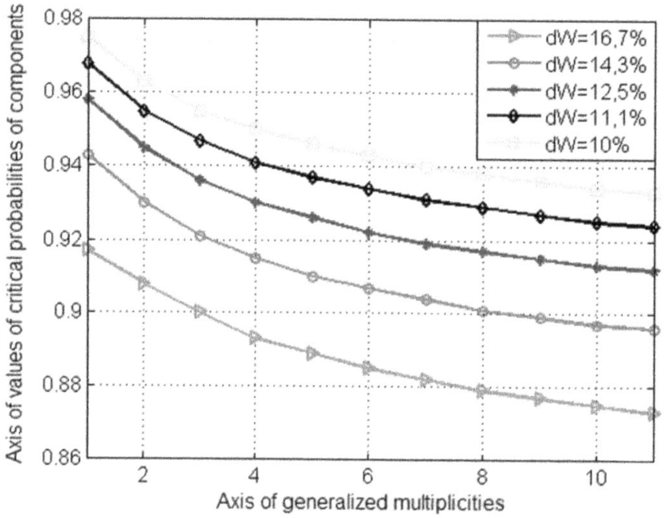

The graphs in Figure 2 illustrates the monotonically decreasing nature of pkr's dependence on the generalized multiplicity Ki for small first-level tolerances.

Figure 3. Dependencies of pkr of Generalized Cardinality Ki for Large Level 2 Tolerances

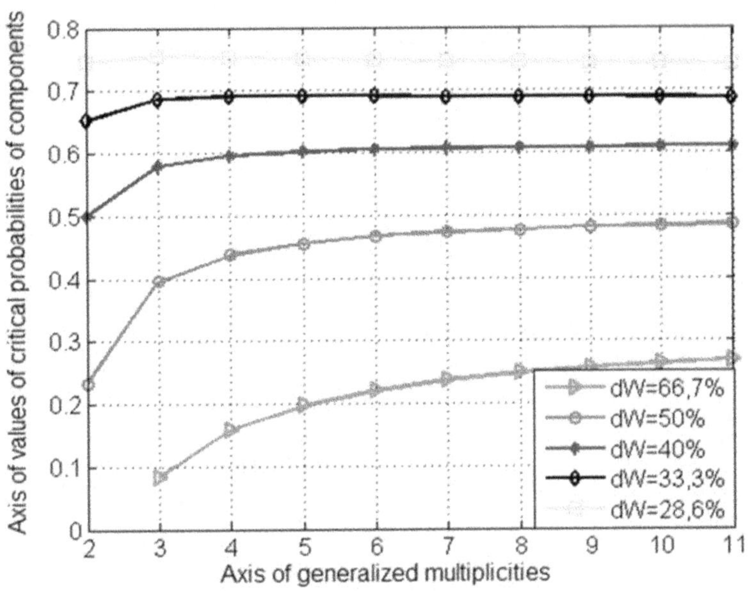

The graphs in Fig. Figure 3 illustrates the different nature (from monotonic increase6 to monotonic decrease) of pkr's dependence on the generalized cardinality Ki for large second-level tolerances.

Figure 4. Dependencies of pkr of Generalized Cardinality Ki for level 2 small Tolerances

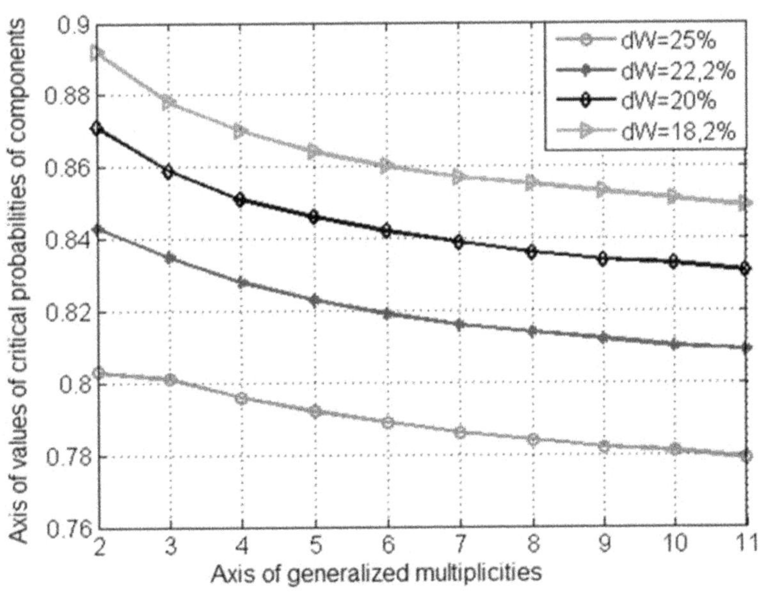

The graphs in Figure 4 shows the uniform monotonically decreasing nature of the dependence of pkr on the generalized cardinality Ki for small tolerances of the first level.

To analyze the effect of tolerances on critical probability values, Figures 5 and 6 show the dependencies of critical probability values on the tolerance values of the first and second levels for various generalized redundancy multiples.

Figure 5. Dependencies of pkr on first-level tolerances for values K_i^I

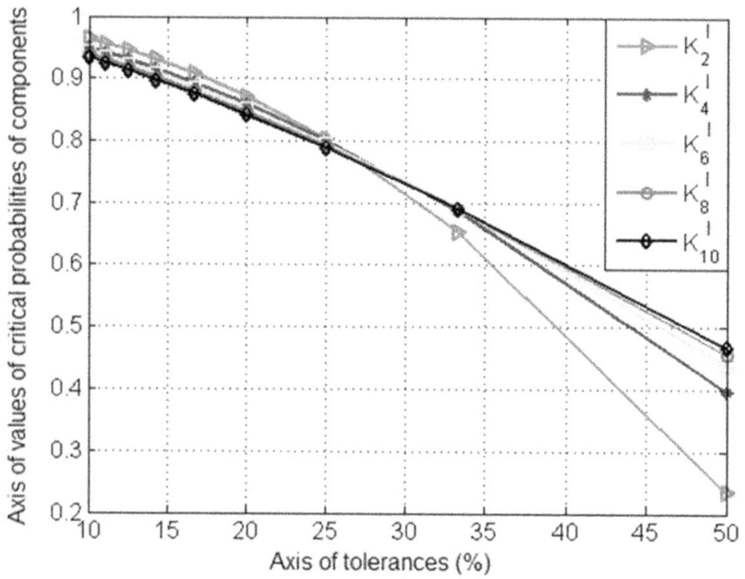

Figure 6. pkr dependencies on second-level tolerances for valuesK_i^l

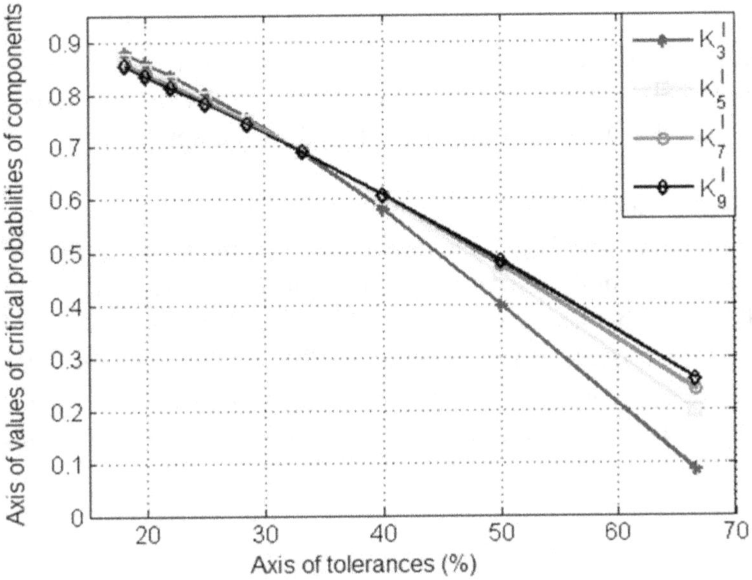

Analysis of the presented dependencies for the implemented tolerances allows us to draw the following conclusions:

1) The range of probabilities of the elements in which it is advantageous to use this type of reservation, determined by the value of pkr, depends on three factors - the tolerance level, the tolerance value, and the redundancy multiplicity;
   (2) At fixed tolerance levels and individual multiplicities, the dependencies of pkr on the values of the decreasing tolerances have a monotonically increasing character, tending to 1 with tolerances tending to 0. This is due to the fact that at a fixed tolerance level r=const, the tolerance to 0 is associated with the tendency of m and n=r+m to infinity. At the same time, individual multiplicities tend to 1:

$$\lim_{n\to\infty} K = \frac{n}{m} = \lim_{n\to\infty}\frac{n}{n-r} = \lim_{n\to\infty}\frac{\frac{n}{n}}{\frac{n}{n}-\frac{r}{n}} = 1$$

.

Consequently, the structure of a passively redundant subsystem in terms of fail-safe characteristics approaches the characteristics of a non-redundant subsystem, which does not have a supercritical range and pkr = 1;

3) With fixed values of the tolerances of the first level and individual multiplicities, the dependencies of pkr on the increasing tolerance level have a monotonically decreasing character, tending to 0 at the tolerance level tending to infinity. This is due to the fact that with a fixed value of the tolerance of the

first level m = const, the tendency of the tolerance level to infinity is related to the tendency of r and n = r+m to infinity. At the same time, individual multiplicities also tend to infinity: $\lim_{n \to \infty} K = \frac{n}{m} = \frac{\infty}{m} = \infty$.

Consequently, the structure of a passively redundant subsystem in terms of failure-free characteristics approaches the characteristics of an absolutely reliable subsystem with infinite redundancy multiplicity, in which the supercritical domain has a maximum size (0 - 1) and pkr = 0;

4) With a fixed tolerance and tolerance level, both the tolerance and the tolerance level have a significant impact on the nature of pkr's dependence on individual cardinality. For example, for each tolerance level, there are equilibrium values of dWr, at which the critical values of pkr practically do not change depending on the individual and generalized multiplicities. For first-level tolerances, dWr = 25 per cent and for second-level tolerances, dWr = 28.6 per cent. The nature of the change in critical probabilities depending on the dWr ratio and the multiplicity values changes dramatically: with tolerances smaller than dWr, the critical values increase, and with tolerances greater than dWr, they decrease.

CONCLUSION

This work is the first part of a study devoted to the analysis and synthesis of passively redundant aircraft subsystems taking into account tolerances. The following results were obtained in the work:

1) The need to take into account two types of tolerances – assigned and implemented, fundamentally different in the method of assignment – is shown. The former are set on a continuous scale of values, while the latter are implemented on a discrete scale defined by the redundancy structure;
2) The possibility of implementing any tolerance at different values of a number of increasing individual multiplicities has been revealed, which makes it possible to set the problem of finding the optimal individual multiplicity and the corresponding optimal redundancy structure in the interests of ensuring the maximum reliability of the redundant subsystems;
3) It has been established that passive redundancy taking into account tolerances is implemented in two fundamentally different ways – multiple and non-multiple redundancy;
4) It is shown that the most significant for practice in terms of the number and variety of values are the tolerances implemented by the methods of non-multiple redundancy;
5) It is shown that subsystems with non-multiple passive redundancy have probabilities of elements called critical pkr, which determine the existence of transcritical regions (0 – pkr), where redundancy is not profitable;
6) Different nature of changes in critical pkr values depending on the tolerance value and its level has been revealed. With a fixed tolerance level and individual multiplicity, the dependence of pkr on the tolerance value has a monotonically increasing character, tending to 1 while the tolerance tends to 0. With a fixed tolerance and individual multiplicity, the dependence of pkr on the tolerance level has a monotonically decreasing character, tending to 0 when the tolerance level tends to infinity;

7) Different nature of changes in critical pkr values depending on individual multiplicities for different values of tolerances and their levels has been revealed. For example, at tolerances of the first level, which are greater than 25%, pkr increases with increasing multiplicity, and decreases with increasing multiplicity, and decreases with increasing multiplicity. A similar pattern of change in pkr takes place with respect to the 28.6% tolerance for level 2 tolerances.

ACKNOWLEDGMENT

This research received no specific grant from any funding agency in the public, commercial, or not-for-profit sectors.

REFERENCES

Annaz, F. Y., & Kaluarachchi, M. M. (2023). Progress in redundant electromechanical actuators for aerospace applications. *Aerospace (Basel, Switzerland)*, *10*(9), 787. DOI: 10.3390/aerospace10090787

Aslain, B. N. D., Nzié, W., & Yamigno, S. D. (2023). Modeling the failure rate of a standby multi-component system and improving reliability. *Modern Mechanical Engineering*, *13*(1), 21–33. DOI: 10.4236/mme.2023.131002

Balaban, M., & Maraee, A. (2019). Removing redundancy multiplicity constraint in UML class model. *Software & Systems Modeling*, *18*(4), 2717–2751. DOI: 10.1007/s10270-018-0696-z

Berman, A. F., Nikolaichuk, O. A., & Yurin, A. Y. (2020). The validation system for reliability and survivability of unique mechanical systems. International Conference Aviation Engineering and Transportation (AviaEnT 2020). *IOP Conference Series. Materials Science and Engineering*, *1061*(1), 012007. DOI: 10.1088/1757-899X/1061/1/012007

Bouwmeester, J., Menicucci, A., & Gill, E. K. A. (2022). Improving CubeSat reliability: Subsystem redundancy or improved testing? *Reliability Engineering & System Safety*, *220*, 108288. DOI: 10.1016/j.ress.2021.108288

Eşer, M., Yıldız, B. A., & Türe, U. (2024). Redundancy in automatic flight control system design for a general-purpose helicopter. *Journal of Aviation*, *8*(2), 96–105. DOI: 10.30518/jav.1468684

Fayyaz, M., & Vladimirova, T. (2016). Survey and future directions of fault-tolerant distributed computing on board spacecraft. *Advances in Space Research*, *58*(11), 2352–2375. DOI: 10.1016/j.asr.2016.08.017

Grishin, V. M. (2019). Synthesis of structure of the onboard passive redundant subsystem with due consideration of the established tolerances. *INCAS Bulletin*, *11*, 89–104. DOI: 10.13111/2066-8201.2019.11.S.9

Grishin, V. M., & Tuan, V. T. (2018). Specific feature of research and development of the passive redundancy subsystems of the aircraft with due consideration of tolerance. *Journal of Mechanical Engineering Research & Development*, *41*(4), 82–87. DOI: 10.26480/jmerd.04.2018.82.87

Gromada, K. A., & Stecz, W. M. (2022). Designing a reliable UAV architecture operating in a real environment. *Applied Sciences (Basel, Switzerland)*, *18*(1), 294. DOI: 10.3390/app12010294

Helm, D., & Timusk, M. (2023). Wavelet denoising applied to hardware redundant systems for rolling element bearing fault detection. Journal of Dynamics. *Monitoring and Diagnostics*, *2*(2), 133–143. DOI: 10.37965/jdmd.2023.231

Pil'A, J., & Kozuba, J.PIĽA. (2019). Safety of complex aircraft ergatic systems. *Transport Problems*, *14*(2), 101–110. DOI: 10.20858/tp.2019.14.2.9

Pranoto, F. S., & Wirawan, A. (2018). Preliminary design of redundancy management for LSA-02 automatic flight control system. 6th International Seminar of Aerospace Science and Technology, IOP Conference Series. *Journal of Physics: Conference Series*, *1130*, 012025. DOI: 10.1088/1742-6596/1130/1/012025

Ryan, S. R., & Granger, M. E. (2023). The importance of dissimilar redundancy for safety in future space vehicle design. *The Journal of Space Safety Engineering*, *10*(4), 387–390. DOI: 10.1016/j.jsse.2023.08.005

Sadeghi, M., Soltani, H., & Khayyambashi, M. (2015). The study of hardware redundancy techniques to provide a fault-tolerant system. [CSJ]. *Cumhuriyet University Faculty of Science Science Journal*, *4*, 236–245.

Chapter 11
Meta-Heuristic Paradigms and Swarm-Based Models for Large-Scale Optimization

D. Renuka Devi
https://orcid.org/0000-0002-6525-1172
Stella Maris College, India

T. A. Swetha Margaret
https://orcid.org/0000-0002-4693-8219
Stella Maris College, India

ABSTRACT

Swarm Intelligence and other metaheuristics have recently gained attention as optimization methods in large-scale data analytics, particularly in control engineering. With the increasing use of big data, IoT devices, and real-time processing, traditional techniques are facing challenges in dealing with high-dimensional and nonlinear problems. Swarm intelligence methods are based on the collective behavior of natural systems, providing robust and scalable solutions for optimizing control parameters, system identification, and fault detection in large environments. The combined use of swarm intelligence and metaheuristics will improve optimization for control engineering applications, focusing on large-scale analytics as discussed in this chapter. Case studies presented in this chapter demonstrate the effectiveness of these methods in optimizing complex control systems where traditional methods struggle due to size or complexity.

1. INTRODUCTION

Metaheuristic algorithms have been developed as high-level procedures for optimization problems and they aim at finding global optimum within a reasonable time (Yang, 2013). This is in contrast to exact algorithms that always guarantee to find the best possible solution; however, in scenarios where it would be too expensive or complicated for traditional approaches, metaheuristics can be applied effec-

DOI: 10.4018/979-8-3693-7812-0.ch011

tively to achieve good solutions (Turgut et al., 2023). Control systems engineering deals with designing systems that regulate the behavior of other dynamic systems, ensuring they behave in a desired manner.

The field is very important in various engineering applications including robotics, aerospace, automotive systems, and industrial automation. Following are examples of using metaheuristics to tune controller parameters such as PID (proportional-integral-derivative) controllers; for instance, traditional methods would be less effective when dealing with complex nonlinear systems as compared with metaheuristics which can efficiently search for parameter spaces to get optimal or suboptimal sets of parameters. There are many challenges in identifying system models (e.g., transfer functions) from data. The best fitting parameters can be optimized by applying the Metaheuristic algorithm to it.

In situations involving optimal control where finding a control law that minimizes a cost function is the aim, particularly when faced with nonlinear dynamics or limitations, metaheuristics can be used to navigate the difficult solution space. Detecting and diagnosing faults may prove difficult in extensive or complicated systems. The detection of faults can be optimized using these metaheuristics leading to improved reliability and safety. One of the biggest challenges is how to keep a control system effective in the presence of different uncertainties.

The design of resilient controllers through optimization across different scenarios or model variations is achievable through metaheuristics. Metaheuristic algorithms are powerful mechanisms for handling intricate optimization issues faced by engineers specializing in control theory and systems engineering (Sadeeq & Abdulazeez, 2023). Engineers can tune a controller, create fault detection systems, create system models and design resilient control systems among other things with these algorithms whenever they seem difficult using traditional methods. Metaheuristic algorithms also have the capability to fully optimize non-linear, complex and high-dimensional systems.

These algorithms apply to many different types of control problems, including system identification and controller design (Çavdar et al., 2024). Metaheuristics help prevent the problems associated with local optima that are found in traditional optimization methods. In control engineering, where global optimum is usually vital for performance and stability, this quality is particularly important. Control engineering issues usually include a number of different objectives like reducing errors, minimizing energy loss or avoiding excessive wear on components. One such algorithm is NSGA-II (a multi-objective genetic algorithm) which helps engineers to achieve pareto optimal solutions with respect to competing objectives (Ma et al., 2023).

Algorithms may be versatile tools because they use techniques that can be modified for various kinds of control problems including controller design; system identification etc. They work by evading local optimum which occurs in classical optimization methods thus avoiding stagnation as seen in other traditional optimization approaches. This aspect is very crucial within control engineering where arriving at a globally optimal control law or topology is vital since it affects both the overall stability and performance of a given system. Numerous decisions must therefore be made at once when dealing with control engineering problems such as minimizing errors made by machines while operating, reducing energy consumption levels among others. Engineers have come up with multi-objective genetic codes like NSGA-II algorithm which allows them to balance performance criteria among competing alternatives thus arriving at pareto useful options hence making them applicable across many fields.

Even though they are powerful, many metaheuristic algorithms are relatively simple to implement and can be easily customized or hybridized with other methods. Often metaheuristics exhibit robustness against system parameter variations and uncertainties that are key factors in control engineering applications characterized by difficulty in precisely modelling. Metaheuristic algorithms may be computationally expensive especially when adopted in large-scale control systems or real-time applications; for instance, this means that iterative methods tend to require considerable computing resources and time before arriving at satisfactory solutions. The increasing size of a problem space often leads to a decline in performance for such algorithmic frameworks, hence making them unsuitable for very large or immediate response systems. Such limitations could hinder their adoption to industries where speed as well as efficiency is critical.

There is a growth pattern to hybrid processes that mix conventional control engineering practices and metaheuristic techniques (for instance model predictive control adaptive control). This trend exploits the benefits provided by both approaches without compromising their computational efficiency. Now it is possible to do real-time control using metaheuristic methods which require vast amounts of resources due to the increased availability of high performance computing facilities like GPUs and other parallel processing systems (Moses et al., 2023). In this respect, this could lead to an increased scope for metaheuristics in control engineering. A further promising avenue here is the incorporation of machine learning with metaheuristic algorithms-for instance, reinforcement learning may be applied in tuning the parameters of a metaheuristic algorithm adaptively thereby probably enhancing its performance or even rate of convergence.

Metaheuristic algorithms have proven to be valuable tools in control engineering, particularly for solving complex, nonlinear, and multi-objective optimization problems(Banerjee et al., 2024). However, their application is not without challenges, including computational complexity, lack of theoretical guarantees, and convergence issues. Recent advances in hybrid approaches, computational power, and integration with machine learning hold promise for overcoming these challenges. As the field continues to evolve, metaheuristics are likely to play an increasingly important role in the development of advanced control systems, particularly in emerging areas such as autonomous systems and sustainable engineering. However, careful consideration of their limitations and the specific requirements of each control problem is essential to fully leverage their potential.

2. THEORETICAL FRAMEWORK

Swarm Intelligence (SI) based algorithms are lately important in control engineering and large-scale optimization because they can tackle dynamic, complex, and nonlinear problems (Abualigah et al., 2023). These algorithms are based on the collective behavior of biological systems and are known for decentralized processing, scalability, and adaptability. The fundamental algorithms based on SI are MOGOA(Multi-Objective Grasshopper Optimization Algorithm), IACO(Improved Ant Colony Optimization), HGA(Hybrid Genetic Algorithm), WOA(Whale Optimization Algorithm,) and DABA(Dynamic Adaptive BAT Algorithm), Particle swarm optimization (PSO), Accelerated PSO (APSO), Simulated annealing (SA), and the BAT algorithm (BA) including their theoretical bases, application areas as well as issues involved in optimizing modern connected systems with possibilities for future studies. These algorithms are based on behaviours that are natural and biological, allowing them to handle intricate, fluctuating issues. Decentralized processing, adaptability, and scalability are some features of SI that solve problems from steering systems to interconnected ones. This framework delves into their theoretical foundations, applications, challenges, and future potential.

SI-based algorithms operate on the principles of decentralized, self-organizing systems found in nature. The collective behavior of biological organisms such as ants, birds, and fish serves as the inspiration for these algorithms. The theoretical foundation lies in Collective Intelligence, which is the emergent behavior arising from the interactions of individuals in a group leading to problem-solving abilities that are above those of each person. SI-based algorithms forgo centralized systems, thus processing information over a network of agents, which leads to robust and scalable optimization solutions. Such algorithms are actually adaptive by nature, modifying themselves according to dynamic surroundings and unpredictable circumstances that is important for real-time controlling systems.

MOGOA is an improved version of Grasshopper Optimization Algorithm (GOA) (Sherif & Haci, 2023), which simulates natural collective behavior of grasshoppers; particularly their tendency to flock together towards a food source. The multi-objectives optimization method MOGOA implements, is based on pareto approach and therefore it has the ability to tackle conflicts among different objectives. The MOGOA works by having a range of solutions using Pareto dominance that helps in searching directly for the best outcomes at all times. This approach also balances exploitation and exploration through reasonable social interaction between agents, thereby ensuring that the algorithm moves efficiently in the direction of optimal solutions preserving diversity in potential outcomes along this course.

The Ant Colony Optimization (ACO) algorithm (Wu et al., 2023), which imitates the pheromone-laying behavior of ants, is the basis of IACO. The pheromone trail denotes a collective memory of the system and directs subsequent generations of agents. IACO takes advantage of dynamic updates of pheromones and adaptable exploration strategies to improve the algorithm's opportunity to escape from local optima and deal with changing environments. An approach based on probabilities is used by IACO in that it modifies pheromone levels depending on how good solutions are to prioritize routes that appear most promising.

HGAs combine Genetic Algorithms (GA) (Alhijawi & Awajan, 2024) with various optimization techniques such as Simulated Annealing (SA) (Ghannadi, 2023) or Particle Swarm Optimization (PSO) (Gad, 2022). This hybridization capitalizes on the benefits of multiple algorithms to enhance the efficiency of search and quality of solutions. HGA usually involves using GA for global search space exploration, while SA serves to fine-tune these solutions within a restricted local scope. The combination of different methods strikes a balance between exploration and exploitation. The algorithm iteratively deploys genetic operators such as selection, crossovers, and mutations together with a local search step to improve the overall quality of items being searched.

WOA is inspired by the bubble-net feeding strategy of humpback whales(Lin et al., 2023). It models the whale's hunting behavior as an optimization process in which hunting agents (whales) approach the optimal solutions. A logarithmic spiral or encircling prey is what agents employ to get closer to the best solution while simulating a bubble-net attack using a spiral updating position mechanism. Moreover, since WOA performs core functions in high-dimensional problems by means of balancing exploration and exploitation via its adjustable search intensity parameter, enabling WOA to perform well in high-dimensional problems.

DABA is an extension of the traditional BAT algorithm (Faraj et al., 2021), which is inspired by the echolocation behavior of bats. The dynamic adaptation mechanisms in DABA (Dhal & Das, 2020) allow it to adjust its parameters in real-time, making it suitable for dynamic optimization problems. DABA dynamically adjusts the pulse rate and loudness of bats (agents) based on the quality of the solutions found. This ensures that the algorithm remains flexible and responsive to changes in the environment. DABA combines global search strategies with local search techniques, allowing the algorithm to fine-tune solutions while exploring new areas of the search space.

In control engineering, strategies based on SI are utilized for the optimization of complex systems so as to ensure performance, stability as well as adaptability. Some algorithms like MOGOA and HGA optimize the parameters of PID controllers in systems that have nonlinear dynamics thus promoting fast response times while minimizing overshoot. DABA and IACO are particularly advantageous in changing environments because they dynamically modify control strategies on a real-time basis. WOA and DABA also enable parameter optimization for fault detection algorithms resulting to enhanced precision and speed in recognizing faults within control systems. Smart grids' operations can be optimized using MOGOA and WOA ensuring proper energy distribution along with renewable resources integration. IACO as well as HGA aid in the balancing cost, time and service levels throughout large-scale supply chains related to logistics or inventory management. Moreover, IACO together with DABA enhance routing protocols aimed at minimizing congestions while boosting reliability particularly during dynamic traffic patterns within extensive telecommunication networks.

Enhancing the parameters for the controllers including PID controllers is one of the common uses of PSO. The performance criteria like overshoot, rise time, settling time, and steady-state error could form the basis for the fitness function. It is more suitable for complex system controller tuning as it can address non-linear as well as multi-modal objective functions. Furthermore, adaptive control systems are subject to various environmental factors over periods requiring real-time adjustment of system parameters. Therefore, PSO has been suggested as a technique for maintaining optimal system performance through continuous parameter adjustment. Moreover, PSO can be used in designing robust controllers against parametric variations and external disturbances. Hence the controller operates reliably under uncertainty through optimizing control parameters across a range of operating conditions.

APSO is an upgraded version of PSO that includes mechanisms for improving convergence rate(Huang & Zhang, 2023). The velocity updating formulas and parameters are made dynamic to allow immediate convergence of particles towards the global optimum. Its fast convergence makes it ideal for real-time control applications where decisions need to be made within seconds. For instance, in adaptive control systems where controller variables should be changed on time, APSO can quickly help you choose the best values. In situations such as these, APSO will use properly designed multi-objective trade-offs to find a satisfactory point associated with minimum energy utilization at a maximum performance level. Additionally, APSO has also been utilized in designing controllers for nonlinear systems whose control laws have to be optimized over extremely intricate nonlinear landscapes. Thus ensuring that the control system remains stable and responsive because of its ability to rapidly converge.

Simulated annealing is an optimization algorithm that works on probability principles and is inspired by the metallurgical process of annealing, where a material is subjected to heating and slow cooling in order to minimize its energy state and defects. SA explores the solution space by accepting both improvements as well as with certain probability worse solutions in order to jump out of local optima. The algorithm is popular for designing controllers for nonlinear systems whose objective functions are characterized by many local minima. By occasionally allowing an increase in the value of the objective function, simulated annealing can escape from these minima to ultimately reach the global minimum value. In contexts such as optimal control problems involving time-related cost functions that must be minimized, SA helps find the best control strategy. This is especially useful in systems with complex dynamics and constraints. Therefore, it is also suitable for making robust controllers due to their uncertainty and noise handling capacity. Thus SA can adjust control parameters so that a certain system remains stable under different situations while working optimally.

The bat algorithm is known for its specialized hunting and navigational strategies through the sounds it emits. The bats use sound at daytime hours mostly in order to help them get the preys they like, navigate around obstacles and identify different items. In BA every bat (solution) modifies its loudness, frequency and pulse emissions so as search space can be explored with an aim of finding better solutions. BA is particularly effective for controller design that works under conditions characterized by heavy noise. It can even optimize the control parameters in presence of high disturbances due to the fact that it can separate signal from noise. For example, practically any environment or system where parameters change dynamically like autonomous vehicles or robots this algorithm helps; when controlling these moving systems BA is constantly tuning their parameters while making sure they do not lose balance during management process enabling them work well enough unpredictably. Such a function landscape is often too nonlinear and complicated; thus BA may address nonlinear system controllers' optimization problems. Additionally, it has been shown that exploration and exploitation trade-off capability facilitates finding an optimal solution globally amid restrictive conditions for instance in some difficult situations previously described above.

SI-based methods provide powerful tools for addressing optimization challenges in control engineering and large-scale systems. Their adaptability and ability to handle complex, non-linear problems make them suitable for a wide range of applications, from controller design to large-scale system optimization. By applying these methods strategically, control engineers and optimization experts can tackle some of the most challenging problems in both fields, leading to more efficient, robust, and adaptive systems.

3. METHODOLOGY

Research methodology consists of systematic procedure for analysing and synthesis of the present studies regarding metaheuristic algorithms in control engineering. The process begins with a deliberate search for relevant studies using academic databases guided by some specific keywords that pertain to both metaheuristics and control engineering. The relevant studies are then selected based on predetermined criteria, and important data is extracted and categorized according to algorithm types, applications, and performance metrics. In the area of control engineering, meta-heuristic techniques have become essential for addressing intricate optimization problems that traditional approaches fail to handle.

The research methodology in this field encompasses a systematic approach to analysing and synthesizing present studies on such algorithms. The process starts with an extensive search for publication databases using targeted keywords linking metaheuristics to control engineering applications. Selected studies are then rigorously evaluated according to pre-established criteria, and appropriate data extracted and organized carefully. This arrangement is based on algorithm types, their specific applications, and certain performance metrics. Leading among swarm intelligence (SI)-based algorithms include Multi-Objective Grasshopper Optimization Algorithm (MOGOA), Improved Ant Colony Optimization (IACO), Hybrid Genetic Algorithm (HGA), Whale Optimization Algorithm (WOA), Dynamic Adaptive BAT Algorithm (DABA), Particle Swarm Optimization (PSO), Accelerated PSO (APSO), Simulated Annealing (SA), and the BAT Algorithm (BA), and Genetic Algorithm(GA). These different approaches provide diverse strategies for dealing with optimization challenges that have each uniquely contributed towards progress in control engineering.

Parallel Approach in Distributed Models

In distributed modeling, parallelism refers to the execution of different tasks simultaneously using various nodes with the intention of expediting the process of solving the problem. General concepts include decomposing a huge problem into smaller sub-problems and are further distributed to several processors or even machines for simultaneous executions.

Frameworks and Technologies Applied:

Several frameworks and technologies are used to implement parallelism in distributed models:

Apache Hadoop & Spark: Big data frameworks which provide parallelism by breaking the task and executing it in parallel across multiple machines. For example, tasks in machine learning or optimization problems can be split into multiple nodes, and results can be aggregated to produce a final solution.

MPI: MPI is a commonly used communication protocol for parallel and distributed computing. It enables the nodes in a distributed system to communicate efficiently with each other.

CUDA & OpenMP: For problems that can be processed in parallel at the hardware level, usually, GPU-based technologies like CUDA (for NVIDIA GPUs) and CPU-based multi-threading libraries such as OpenMP are used.

Distributed Optimization Libraries: Frameworks like Optuna, Pyro, and Ray enable distributed optimization and can be employed for parallel search in meta-heuristics.

Workload Distribution Across the Computational Nodes

The parallel meta-heuristic approach normally partitions the workload according to the nature of the problem under solution. This is how the partition may be;

Task Partitioning: The search space is partitioned into smaller subspaces. A subspace of the search space is assigned to a computational node to be explored in techniques such as PSO, GA, or DE.

Population-based Approaches: In population-based meta-heuristics (like Genetic Algorithms, Evolutionary Algorithms), every node can compute on a part of the population of candidate solutions. At regular time intervals, the best individuals in each node's population are communicated (migration) to the others in order to improve the exploratory power.

Fine-Grained Parallelism: Fine-grained parallelism would allocate each task as basic as computing on one solution at a time-evaluating fitness or doing mutation and crossover concurrently between nodes.

Coarse-Grained Parallelism: Each node computes an entire subpopulation or an entire generation of the algorithm before synchronizing with other nodes.

Master-Slave Architecture. A master node sends subtasks, such as evaluating solutions or updating positions to slave nodes and then these latter nodes process it in parallel to return results again to the former for further decisions.

Scaling with Size of Solution Space or Complexity of Problem

Indeed, another benefit of the parallel meta-heuristic approach is that it has scaling capabilities. That means if the size of the solution space or the problem complexity increases, this parallel approach can handle the load much more efficiently by utilizing a higher number of nodes.

Solution Space: With a huge solution space, parallel approaches can split the search into smaller parts. Each node could concentrate on a different part of the space so that a sequential exhaustive search is not required. Thus, it is possible to explore larger spaces better in a very limited time.

Problem Complexity: In more complex problems with higher dimensions, such as large-scale optimization, the problem becomes computationally expensive. The workload is distributed across computational nodes, and the overall problem is divided into more manageable tasks. This prevents bottlenecks in computation.

It is crucial to note that there are diminishing returns when scaling, and when doublers in the number of computational nodes, it does not proportionally lead to a decrease in time. The law of diminishing returns applies due to communication overhead between nodes, costs involved in synchronization, and load balancing.

When comparing parallel meta-heuristics to single-threaded traditional meta-heuristics, there are several factors to consider:

Quality of Solution: The traditional methods might fail for huge or very large complex search spaces as they do not explore the space completely. Parallel meta-heuristics can afford to perform a much more exhaustive search since they can search different parts of the search space in parallel and therefore often produce higher quality solutions. Hybridisation with metaheuristics and parallelism; hence, PGAs or Parallel Simulated Annealing (PSA) enhance solution quality by speeding up with more balance toward both exploration and exploitation.

Metrics to evaluate a good performance:

Speed-up: Approach taken by parallel procedure divided by that of serial process time.

Efficiency: Normally measured in terms of the correctness or accuracy of the solution obtained, often as compared to a known benchmark or optimal solution.

Quality of Solution: Speedup can be substantial with parallel meta-heuristics. If tasks are dispersed across multiple computational units, the amount of time spent exploring the solution space is shortened. Amdahl's Law can be used to estimate an upper bound for speedup given the parallel fraction of the algorithm.

The definition of parallel efficiency is a ratio of the speedup of a program executed in parallel and the number of processors used in that execution. In other words, as more nodes are employed, the use of overhead - communication between the nodes or synchronization - can reduce the parallel efficiency, but for really large problems, the parallel techniques remain relatively more efficient than the equivalent single-threaded approach.

3.1 Particle Swarm Optimization (PSO)

PSO is a meta-heuristic technique used for optimization problems to enhance the solution iteratively with relevance to the objective function. The solution is achieved by processing an optimal solution set (particles), and the particles are moved in the solution space in search of an improved solution. To enable the particle to move, they are associated with the parameter's position and velocity. The search mechanism is accomplished by a different phase. The beginning phase is for initializing the parameters and setting the boundaries of the solution space. Then it is followed by particle movement in the solution space, and finally, the convergence phase where the optimal solution is identified and iteration is finished.

The particle distribution is done homogeneously in the search space. The dimensions are decided based on the datasets. Based on the number of attribute columns, the dimensions are set, and the particles are accelerated accordingly. The velocity parameter is assigned with an initial value, to let the particle move. After initialization, the particles are accelerated with the velocity assigned in the previous stage. The component of this initialization comprises distance and direction assigned for search space. The particles further proceeded in the direction with two properties: particle best(best) and global best(gbest) (Ahmad et al., 2024). Each particle has individual best and global best that is shared amongst the entire population. The gbest is considered the best of individual bests. The algorithm is given as follows (Jain et al., 2022),

Figure 1. PSO algorithm

```
for each particle i = 1, ..., S do
x_i ~ U (b_lo, b_up) // Initialize the particle's position with a uniformly distributed random vector
p_i ← x_i          // Initialize the particle's best-known position to its initial position
if f(p_i) < f(g) then
   g ← p_i      // Update the swarm's best-known position
   v_i ~ U(-|b_up-b_lo|, |b_up-b_lo|)   // Initialize the particle's velocity
while a termination criterion is not met do:
      for each particle i = 1, ..., S do
        for each dimension d = 1, ..., n do
         r_p, r_g ~ U (0,1) // Pick random numbers
         v_i,d ← ω v_i,d + φ_p r_p (p_i,d-x_i,d) + φ_g r_g (g_d-x_i,d) // Update the particle's velocity
         x_i ← x_i + lr v_i // Update the particle's position
         if f(x_i) < f(p_i) then
         p_i ← x_i // Update the particle's best-known position
if f(p_i) < f(g) then
g ← p_i // Update the swarm's best-known position
```

Consider the total number of particles as S and each particle is associated with the position ($\boldsymbol{xi} \in \mathbb{R}$) and velocity($\boldsymbol{vi} \in \mathbb{R}n$). Let $\boldsymbol{pi}$ is the position of the individual particle(i) and g is the global best position. The parameter lr, is the learning rate adjusted between 0 and 1. It is the proportion of velocity to the position. If lr =0, it does not influence the particle, when lr=1, it will completely affect the position of the particle. The hyper parameters are adjusted to improve the efficacy of the algorithm. The working flow of the algorithm is presented in Figure 2.

Figure 2. PSO flow

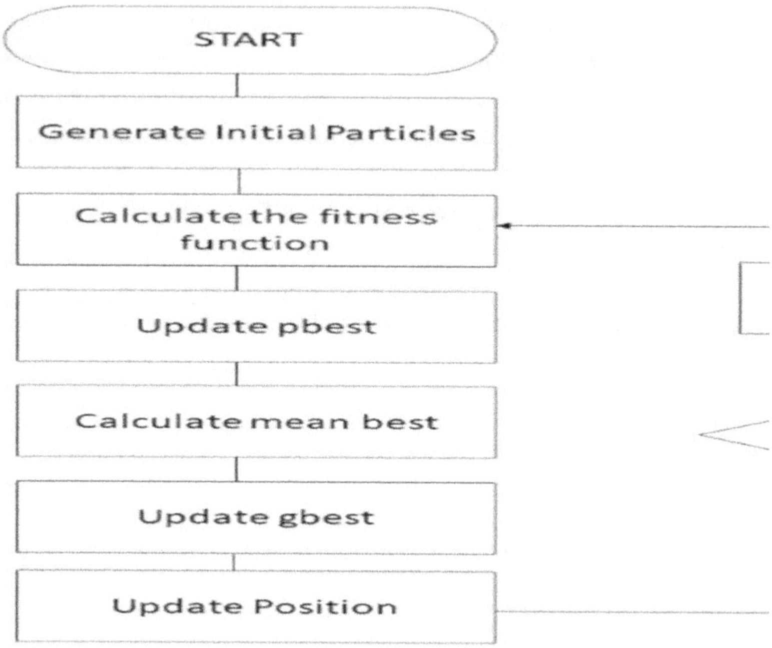

Power system operation has been optimized using PSO algorithms with regards to load scheduling, unit commitment and placement of distributed generators. Given the highly connected dimensions of power systems, PSO becomes a very important method in identifying global optima. Different areas in supply chain management can be optimized by PSO including; inventory levels, distribution routing and production scheduling. This aids in reducing the cost base while improving efficiency since it is able to identify the best solutions for complicated multi-staged supply chains.

PSO is utilized in telecommunications for the optimization of network design and operations. These are some of the responsibilities such as to maximize throughput while minimizing latency, routing protocol optimization, bandwidth allocation and network topology redesigning. Even though it is efficient with great outcomes, PSO has a tendency of converging slowly especially when dealing with multidimensional data. Combination with other algorithms or employing variations like APSO can help in this instance. On instance, local optima can be misleading for PSO. However, there are various strategies to avoid this problem like modifying parameters dynamically or adding diversity mechanisms in its working mechanisms.

3.2 Accelerated Particle Swarm Optimization (APSO)

APSO is an enhanced version of PSO that introduces mechanisms to accelerate convergence. It adjusts the velocity update rules and parameters dynamically, allowing particles to converge more quickly to the global optimum. APSO is based on the traditional PSO, but uses methods to ensure it converges faster and its solutions are of higher quality. It uses techniques to stimulate speeding up and making adjustments that can be adapted to parameters, which help in finding ways to exploit and explore. As such, APSO becomes more efficient and effective in avoiding local minima; hence solutions are faster as well as accurate. The applications of this approach are found mainly within intricate optimization problems in different domains such as engineering and control systems. The overview of APSO (Parouha & Verma, 2022) is shown in Figure 3.

Figure 3. APSO

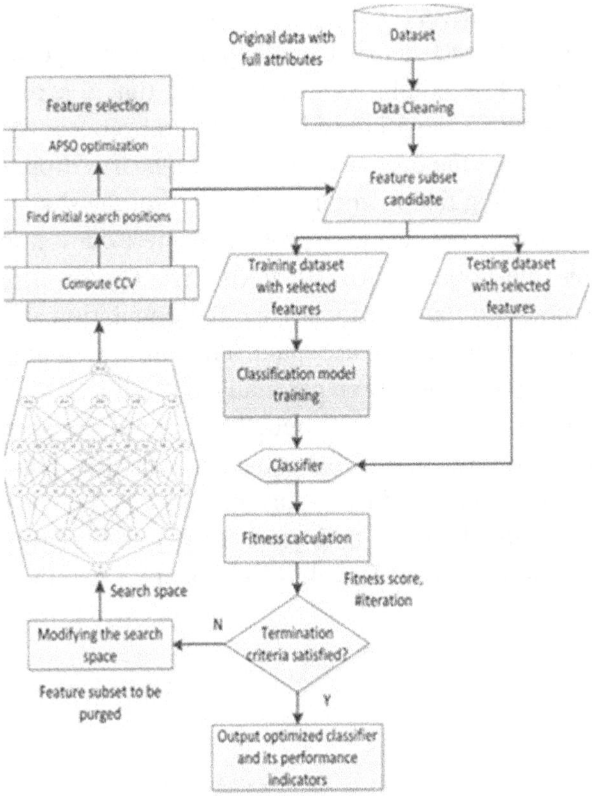

APSO algorithm in the optimization of large scale industry systems because it is not easy to know all the problems involved in such a vast space. As an example, when optimizing the operation of chemical plants, APSO can quickly find out the ideal operating conditions that maximize yield while minimizing energy consumption. Other ways in which APSO is applied to improve performance include optimizing energy management systems such as those dealing with renewable energy integration, demand-side management or storage schemes for electricity. This fast convergence will ensure an optimal performance during real time system operations. In case of urban traffic management on a large scale, APSO could optimize traffic signal timings and plan routes with regard to congestion levels too. For instance, it could change its behavior depending on variations in road conditions thus enabling real-time optimizations for these kinds of situations on roads.

The choice of parameters, such as acceleration coefficients and inertia weight, may affect APSO's performance. Therefore, a careful adjustment of these parameters is essential to obtain optimal performance. Nevertheless, APSO runs faster than traditional PSO but remains a computationally expensive option for handling big problems. This can also be addressed with parallelization and distributed computing.

3.3 Simulated Annealing (SA)

SA is based on the probability function to derive the global optimum solution (Shi et al., 2023). As mentioned previously, this type of meta-heuristics is employed for large-scale optimization problems when the search space is discrete. It is suitable for the problems that give more importance to the global optimum than the local optimum. SA is enthused by the natural process of metallurgy i.e., making of the metal. The metal is heated above the boiling point then the heat is dropped to get the suitable shape of the metal. The heating and cooling factors momentously affect the shape of the metal and quality.

SA is generally employed for hard optimization problems where conventional algorithms fail to good performance. Most of the real-time problems are instigated by SA. The lowering of the temperature lessens the chance of accepting the non-optimal solutions when the population space is explored. The search process is extensive when worse solutions are accepted. The initial step of the algorithm is assigning a positive value to the temperature parameter. Then gradually, it is reduced to zero value. At each iteration, a solution is generated and the temperature is lowered. The SA process selects the solution and moves to the next iteration either by retaining the positive value or decreasing it towards 0.

The states of the solution are represented by s (current state), and s*(nearest state). The probability function forces the system to switch between both state. Based on the probability function the system moves until the optimal solution is reached. The algorithm is presented in Figure 4.

Figure 4. SA algorithm

- *Let* $s = s_0$
- *For* $k = 0$ *through* k_{max} *(exclusive):*
  - $T \leftarrow temperature((k+1)/k_m$
  - *Pick a random neighbour, s*
  - *If* $P(E(s), E(s_{new}), T) \geq rand$
    - $s \leftarrow s_{new}$
- *Output: the final state s*

The process starts with the state(s0), the maximum number of iterations is kmax. The neighbour function randomly selects the neighbour for a given state(s). The random function generates the value between 0 and 1. The temperature function is used for altering at each iteration. The energy(E) is produced for each solution with a probability function(P). The parameters are adjusted to achieve an optimal solution. The work flow is presented in Figure 5.

SA may possibly optimize resource allocation problems in big scale systems example optimizing resource allocation within a manufacturing plant or scheduling jobs on computing grids. Its thorough search into solution space guarantees optimum utilization of resources. SA is effective in solving complex scheduling problems, such as job-shop scheduling, where the goal is to minimize the total processing time or maximize the throughput. Its flexibility allows it to handle various constraints and objectives in large-scale scheduling problems. In the design and optimization of telecommunications networks, SA can be used to optimize routing, frequency assignment, and network topology. Its ability to explore a wide range of solutions makes it suitable for optimizing networks with complex and dynamic requirements.

Figure 5. SA algorithm flow

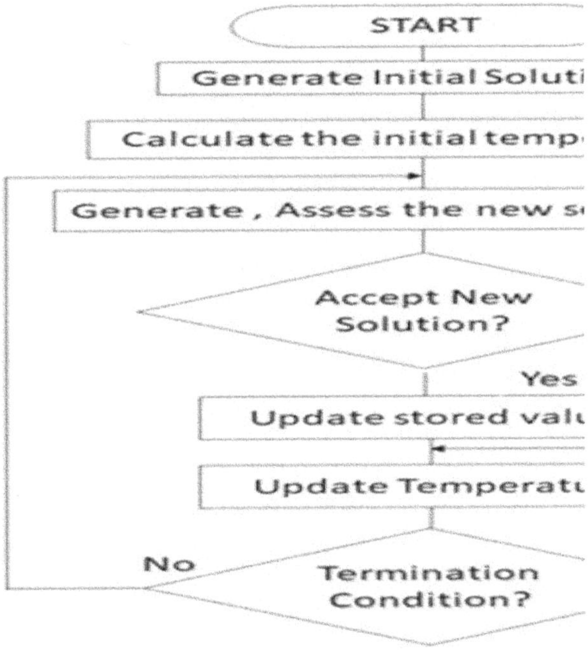

SA can be slow to converge, especially in large-scale problems where the solution space is vast. This can be mitigated by hybridizing SA with other algorithms, such as PSO or Genetic Algorithms, to combine exploration with faster convergence. The performance of SA depends heavily on the cooling schedule and other parameters. Careful tuning of these parameters is necessary to achieve optimal performance.

3.4 BAT

The global optimization algorithm is stimulated by the echo sounding of bats, with the properties of loudness and pulse emission rate. Each bat has velocity v_i at a position x_i and loudness A_i with frequency(f) (Renuka Devi & Sasikala 2019). The search starts with an initial position with pulse emission rate(r). The search space is explored by a random walk. The solution sets are formed until the end condition has been reached. The tuning of the parameters is maintained to control the bat's behavior which maintains the exploration and exploitation. Bats identify the hidden object or prey by sending the sound and measuring the echo of the sound.

The process of the algorithm (Figure 6) is given below,

- The echo behaviour is useful to identify any objects on the path.
- Every bat fly with a velocity at a particular direction, with frequency and loudness
- Loudness and frequency measure is used to explore the prey
- Frequency and pulse rates are adjusted
- When they reach nearer to the object or prey the pulse rate goes higher with lesser loudness rate.

Figure 6. BAT algorithm

```
Initialize the bat population with v
frequency qi at position xi for maxi
The best solution is xgbest. the fitnes
Initialize xi, i=1,2 .... n
f(xi) //calculate fitness for each ba
while (t< max)
        Generate new solution, adjus
If(rand>ri)
       Select solution amongst the be
      Generate local solution
End if
Generate new solution by random
If(rand>Li and f(xi) > f(xgbest)
      Accept new solution
      Increment ri and decrement Li
End if
Ranks the bats and update the curr
Increase the generation t=t+1
End while
```

The work flow is presented in Figure 7. Real time optimization is made possible in large-scale systems by BA's dynamic adjustment mechanisms. For example, in smart grid management, the BA can optimize the operation of the grid in real time, adjusting to changes in demand and supply. It can also optimize placement of sensors and routing of data in large-scale environmental monitoring systems like air and water quality monitoring networks for comprehensive and efficient monitoring. It can be applied to optimize behavior in multi-agent systems like fleets of drones or autonomous vehicles. The agents work together efficiently towards their goals because of its ability to perform optimizations dynamically.

Figure 7. BAT algorithm flow

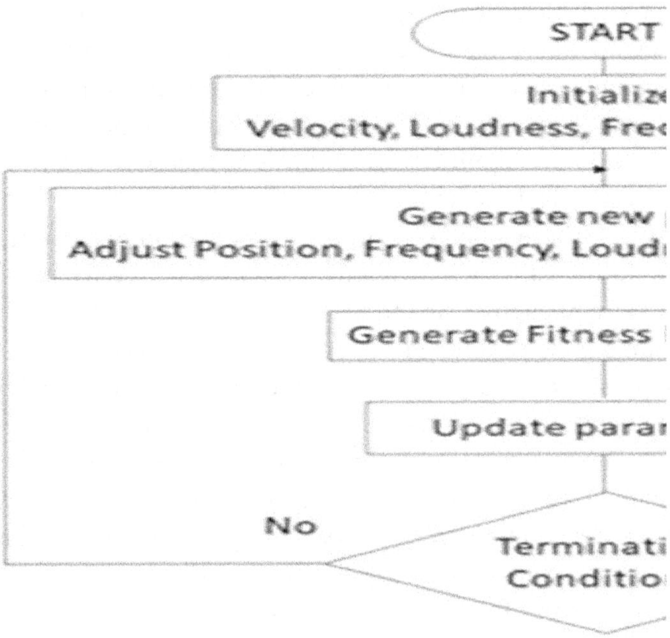

Like the other SI-based algorithms, choice of parameters (loudness & pulse emission rate) have great influence on BA related performances. Optimal performances require fine tuning an oscillator's parameters including its frequency. Although BA works quite well in changing situations, it may consume much computation time when applied to complicated problems due to its size. It can be accelerated using parallel structure or combination with other algorithms.

3.5 Genetic Algorithm (GA)

The GA is founded on the mathematical model of optimization. The population-based approach is used to enhance the solution for the elements in high-dimensional space. The generalization of the GA algorithm is presented in Figure 8. The solutions are specified as a sequence of values or strings. The initial vector is created with the set of possible solutions. For every step of the iteration, the solutions are moved toward optimization by employing mutation and crossover.

Two principal functions are considered significant they are cross-over and mutation. Crossover is applied to the parent to generate a new solution(child). A mutation is applied to a single point or multi-point of the solution. The fitness function is applied to every solution to find out the fitness value. Higher fitness will be taken for maximization problems. The values are compared and the best solution is taken further.

Genetic algorithms (GAs) play a major role in control engineering because they can deal with complex nonlinear multi-objective optimization problems that traditional methods often find challenging (Rodríguez-Molina et al., 2020). The main application of GAs is in designing and tuning control systems where they are particularly effective at optimizing controller parameters mainly PID controllers. GAs help to find the proper proportional integral and derivative gains that minimize errors and at the same time maximize performance of the system. This optimization extends to adaptive control since GAs allow controllers to modify their parameters in real time for the best performance even when system dynamics change or external disturbances take place. In addition, GAs are important for system identification which involves estimating some model parameters that represent the actual system accurately and thus aiding development of good control strategies. In optimal control GAs are used to get control trajectories minimizing a cost function (for instance energy consumption or time) while satisfying all system constraints. They also have significant usefulness in nonlinear control where deriving control laws or strategies through analytical methods can be difficult.

The main reason why GAs have gained prominence in control engineering is their ability to solve complicated nonlinear multi-objective optimization problems which conventional approaches often find hard to handle. Their major application is found in designing and adjusting control systems where they seem most adept at fine-tuning the parameters of controllers like PID controllers effectively. In particular, GAs allow identifying those optimal proportions, integrals and derivatives needed so as to decrease errors without neglecting bettering the overall performance of a given system.

In optimal control, GAs are applied to determine control trajectories that minimize a cost function—such as energy consumption or time—while satisfying system constraints. They are particularly useful in nonlinear control, where deriving control laws or strategies analytically can be challenging. In the case of optimal control, GAs are the ones that establish control paths which decrease costs such as energy consumption or duration while taking care of systems limits at large. Moreover, they serve a very important purpose in nonlinear control where analytically deriving control strategies is problematic.

Figure 8. GA algorithm flow

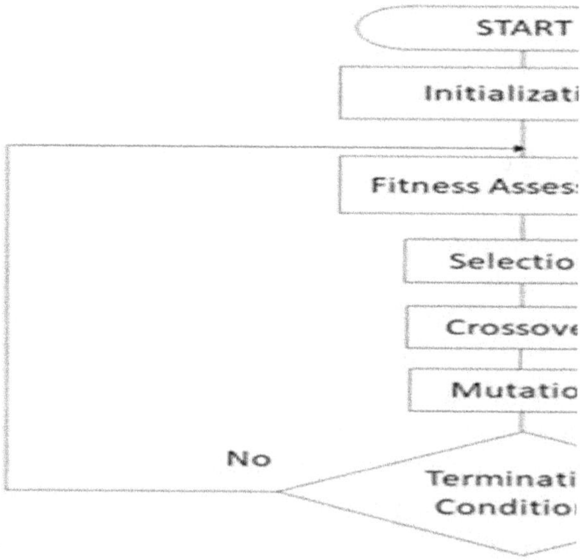

3.6 Multi-Objective Grasshopper Optimization Algorithm (MOGOA)

This is an enhancement of the Grasshopper Optimization Algorithm (GOA) (Wang et al., 2021), adapted for handling multi-objective optimization problems in control systems. MOGOA is particularly useful for scenarios requiring trade-offs between conflicting objectives, such as performance and energy efficiency. MOGOA leverages Pareto front optimization to provide a set of optimal solutions. MOGOA extends the Grasshopper Optimization Algorithm (GOA), which models the natural swarming behavior of grasshoppers, particularly their tendency to converge toward a food source. MOGOA incorporates Pareto-based multi-objective optimization, allowing it to address problems with conflicting objectives. MOGOA optimizes multiple objectives simultaneously by maintaining a diverse set of solutions, using Pareto dominance to guide the search process. It employs both exploitation and exploration through a balance of social interaction among agents, allowing the algorithm to explore the solution space effectively while converging towards optimal solutions.

The algorithm is (Veza et al., 2022) as follows,

MOGOA Algorithm

Initialization

Set parameters:

- Number of grasshoppers n
- Maximum number of iterations MaxIter
- Minimum and maximum social coefficients C_{min}, C_{max}
- External Pareto archive P

Initialize the population of grasshoppers with random positions in the search space X_i, where i=1,2,...,n. Evaluate the fitness of each grasshopper for all objective functions.

External Archive Initialization:

Populate the Pareto archive PPP with initial non-dominated solutions based on their fitness values.

Main Optimization Loop:

For t=1 to MaxIter do:

Update Social Interaction Coefficient:

Calculate the social interaction coefficient C(t) as:

$$C(t) = Cmax - (Cmax - Cmin / MaxIter) \times t$$

For each grasshopper I do:

Compute Social Interactions:

Initialize the movement vector Mi as a zero vector of dimension d.
For each grasshopper j in the population do:
Calculate the distance Dij between grasshoppers I and j.
Compute the interaction force Fij based on attraction-repulsion behavior:

$$Fij = C(t) \times (Xj - Xi / Dij2) \times e - nij/ \lambda$$

where λ is a damping factor.

Accumulate the interaction forces: $Mi = Mi + Fij$

Update Position:

Determine a candidate position X_i^{new}, for grasshopper i as:

$$Xinew = Xi + Mi$$

Ensure the new position stays within the problem's boundaries.

Evaluate New Position:

Calculate the fitness values of X_i^{new} for each objective function.

Update Pareto Archive:

If X_i^{new} is non-dominated:
Add X_i^{new} to the Pareto archive P.
Remove any dominated solutions from P.
Maintain diversity using a crowding distance or similar mechanism.

End For

Update the Leader(s):

Select the best leader(s) from the Pareto archive P based on a leader selection strategy.

End For

A process to choose representative solutions from the Pareto archive that guide the movement of grasshoppers. Crowding distance helps maintain diversity in the Pareto front by measuring the closeness of neighbouring solutions. The attraction repulsion behavior, governs how grasshoppers interact, balancing exploration (dispersing solutions) and exploitation (concentrating solutions near the Pareto front).

MOGOA can optimize operations of complicated energy systems including microgrids by balancing between costs, reliability, and environmental impacts. It assists in developing energy management solutions that are cost-effective and environment sustainable. In huge supply chains, MOGOA can be employed in optimizing logistics and inventory management where costs, time taken for delivery and service level objectives should be considered at the same time. MOGOA may require intense computation especially where high dimensional problems exist. This could be solved through efficient implementations as well as parallel processing. The performance of MOGOA greatly depends on the choice of parameters which should be adjusted accurately so that optimal output is achieved.

3.7 Improved Ant Colony Optimization (IACO)

IACO, an enhanced version of the Ant Colony Optimization (ACO) algorithm, is designed to mimic ants' pheromone-laying behavior. It enhances traditional ACO into an improved form with adaptive pheromone mechanisms and dynamic exploration strategies. This makes it more suitable for dynamic and uncertain environments where real-time adjustments are crucial. The pheromone trail represents the collective memory of the system guiding future generations of agents. Also, IACO provides dynamic pheromone updates along with adaptive exploration strategies that enhance the algorithm's ability to escape local optima and adapt to changing environments. Moreover, IACO employs a probabilistic approach in updating pheromone levels depending on the quality of solutions found thus ensuring that the most promising paths are prioritized by the algorithm (Skinderowicz, 2022).

The algorithm as follows,

IACO Algorithm

Initialization:

Set parameters - Number of ants n, Maximum number of iterations MaxIter, Evaporation rate ρ, Pheromone influence factor α, Heuristic influence factor β, Initial pheromone level τ_0, problem-specific heuristic information η, Initialize pheromone matrix τ with values $\tau 0$. Define a memory mechanism to track elite solutions. Initialize adaptive parameters or dynamic control parameters.

Main Optimization Loop:

For t=1 MaxIter do:

Ant Solution Construction:

For each ant k do:
Initialize an empty solution S_k .
While the solution S_k is incomplete do:
Calculate the probability p_{ij}^k of moving from node i to node j using:

pijk = (τij)α · (ηij)β / ∑l ∈ allowed(τil)α · (ηij)β

Select the next node j based on p_{ij}^k using a stochastic method.
Update the solution S_k by adding node j.
Evaluate the constructed solution S_k .

Global Pheromone Update:

If using adaptive or elitist strategies:
Identify the best solution(s) S_{best} found by the ants during the iteration.
Reinforce pheromone trails based on these solutions.
Update pheromone trails τ_{ij} using,

τij = (1 − ρ) × τij+ Δτij

$\Delta\tau_{ij}$ is computed as: Δτij
$= \sum_{k=1}^{n} \Delta\tau ijk$ $\Delta\tau_{ij}$, $\Delta\tau_{ij}^k$ depends on the quality of the solution constructed by ant k.

End For

Termination:

If stopping criteria are met (e.g., maximum iterations or convergence): Output the best solutions found during the search process. Return the final set of optimal solutions S_{best}.

IACO has the ability to optimize routing protocols, making it possible for telecommunications networks to become more sophisticated in their handling of changing traffic, delays, and congestion. This means that job scheduling and routing of materials can be optimized by IACO in complex manufacturing environments resulting in improved productivity as well as reduced costs. However, scaling up traditional ACO may be difficult despite IACO being more efficient than the former. One way to circumvent this problem is by using IACO alongside other optimization techniques or through distribution computing. In very large search spaces, IACO may converge slowly. Convergence speed can be improved through hybridization with faster algorithms.

3.8 Hybrid Genetic Algorithm (HGA)

Hybrid genetic algorithms (HGAs) utilize genetic algorithm ideas and simulated annealing or particle swarm optimization strategies. This combination draws strength from various algorithms to enhance search efficiency while attaining better solutions. Usually, in HGAs, GAs are employed for global exploration, while SA is used for local optima refining. Combining different approaches gives room for balancing exploration with exploitation in the process. The approach is characterized by using selection, crossover, and mutation as genetic tools that improve the quality of solutions. Combines the genetic algorithm's evolutionary principles with other optimization techniques like Simulated Annealing (SA) or Particle Swarm Optimization (PSO). This hybridization aims to exploit the strengths of each method, offering faster convergence and better handling of complex, nonlinear optimization landscapes.

HGAs are applied in the optimization of power system operations, including load dispatch, unit commitment, and the integration of renewable energy sources. The hybrid approach ensures that both cost and reliability are optimized. In telecommunications and transportation networks, HGAs can optimize the design and operation of large-scale networks, balancing objectives like cost, efficiency, and robustness.

Combining multiple algorithms effectively requires careful design and tuning, which can increase the complexity of the algorithm. However, this complexity is often justified by the superior performance achieved. HGAs can be resource-intensive, especially when applied to very large-scale problems. Parallel processing and efficient coding practices are necessary to handle this.

3.9 Whale Optimization Algorithm (WOA)

WOA is a model of optimized whale hunting behavior that converges towards an optimal solution for its search agents (Nadimi-Shahraki et al., 2023). It uses a spiral updating position mechanism to simulate bubble-net attacks, where agents either move towards the solution in a logarithmic spiral or encircle prey. The algorithm uses a parameter that adjusts intensity of its search, which allows WOA to perform well on high-dimensional problems since it balances exploration with exploitation. WOA, which is based on how whales use bubble nests for hunting, exploits exploration and exploitation effectively in order to solve complex high-dimensional optimization problems that require some serious thought about the available space in question. The algorithm as follows,

WOA Algorithm

Initialization:

The parameters are set as follows, Number of whales n, Maximum number of iterations MaxIter, Convergence factor a (initially set to 2), the dimension of the problem d, Initialize the population of whales with random positions X_i in the search space, where i=1,2,...,n. Evaluate the fitness of each whale. Identify the best whale position X^* as the current optimal solution.

Main Optimization Loop:

For t=1to MaxIter do:

Update Convergence Factor:

Linearly decrease the convergence factor a from 2 to 0 over the iterations: $a = 2 - (2 \times t / MaxIter)$
For each whale i do:
Generate a Random Number r: Draw r uniformly from the range [0, 1].
Calculate the Coefficient Vectors A and C:

A is calculated as, $A = 2a \cdot r - a$

C is calculated as, $C = 2 \cdot r$

Exploration vs. Exploitation Decision:

If |A|<1| (exploitation phase):

Shrinking Encircling Mechanism:

Update the whale's position X_i towards the best solution X*: $Xinew = X^* - A \cdot | C \cdot X^* - Xi |$
Else |A|≥1 (exploration phase):

Search for Prey Randomly:

Select a random whale X_{rand} from the population.
Update the position X_i relative to

$Xrand : Xinew = Xrand - A \cdot | C \cdot Xrand - Xi |$

Spiral-Shaped Movement (Logarithmic Spiral Mechanism):

If a random number p drawn from [0, 1] is less than 0.5:
Compute the distance D between the whale i and the best solution X*: $D = | X^* - Xi |$
Update the position using a spiral equation:
$Xinew = D \cdot eb \cdot 1 \cdot \cos(2\pi l) + X^*$, where b is a constant defining the shape of the spiral, and l is a random number in [-1, 1].

Boundary Check:

Ensure that the updated position X_i^{new} lies within the problem's boundaries.

End For

Update the Best Solution:

Evaluate the fitness of all updated whale positions.
Update the best whale position X^{*} if a better solution is found.

End For

Termination:

If stopping criteria are met, Return the best solution X^{*} found during the search.

The WOA are applied in large-scale environmental monitoring systems, where it optimizes sensor layout and operations to guarantee complete data collection and efficient utilization of resources. WOA has applications in extensive energy systems, where it can optimize the operation and integration of renewable energy sources that maximize the power of output while reducing costs as well as ecological consequences. While WOA is effective in avoiding local optima, in highly complex landscapes, it may still face challenges. Hybridizing WOA with other techniques can help improve performance. The success of WOA depends on the careful tuning of its parameters, which may require extensive experimentation or adaptive mechanisms.

3.10 Dynamic Adaptive BAT Algorithm (DABA)

Enhances the traditional BAT algorithm with dynamic adaptation mechanisms, allowing it to adjust parameters in real-time. This makes DABA particularly suited for real-time control systems where conditions change frequently (Nath & Sarkar, 2021). DABA is an extension of the traditional BAT algorithm, which is inspired by the echolocation behavior of bats. The dynamic adaptation mechanisms in DABA allow it to adjust its parameters in real-time, making it suitable for dynamic optimization problems. DABA dynamically adjusts the pulse rate and loudness of bats (agents) based on the quality of the solutions found. This ensures that the algorithm remains flexible and responsive to changes in the environment. DABA combines global search strategies with local search techniques, allowing the algorithm to fine-tune solutions while exploring new areas of the search space.

DABA is applied in smart grid management, where it optimizes the distribution of energy in real-time, adjusting to changes in demand and supply to ensure efficiency and reliability. In large-scale logistics and supply chain management, DABA can optimize routing and scheduling in real-time, adjusting to delays, demand fluctuations, and other uncertainties. The dynamic adaptation mechanisms in DABA can be computationally intensive, particularly in large-scale systems. Efficient implementations and parallel processing can help address this issue. Implementing DABA requires careful consideration of the dynamic adaptation mechanisms, which can increase the complexity of the algorithm. However, this complexity is often outweighed by the benefits in dynamic environments.

4. SOLUTIONS AND RECOMMENDATIONS

Swarm Intelligence (SI) and other metaheuristics have emerged as powerful tools in optimizing large-scale data analytics, especially in the field of control engineering. As the use of big data, IoT devices, and real-time processing grows, traditional optimization techniques are increasingly challenged by the high-dimensional, nonlinear nature of modern control systems. SI methods, which are inspired by the collective behavior of natural systems such as ant colonies, bird flocks, and fish schools, offer robust and scalable solutions for complex optimization tasks. These methods, when combined with metaheuristics, provide an effective means of optimizing control parameters, system identification, and fault detection in large environments.

One of the key advantages of SI and metaheuristics is their ability to handle the complexity and scale of modern control systems. Traditional optimization methods often struggle with the size and complexity of the data involved in big data and IoT environments. SI algorithms like Particle Swarm Optimization (PSO), Ant Colony Optimization (ACO), and Artificial Bee Colony (ABC) are designed to search large solution spaces efficiently, making them well-suited for optimizing control systems where the number of variables and the complexity of interactions can be overwhelming.

The adaptability of SI algorithms is another significant advantage. In dynamic environments, where control parameters need to be continuously adjusted in response to changing conditions, SI methods excel by offering adaptive and flexible solutions. This adaptability is crucial for maintaining optimal performance in real-time systems, where traditional static optimization techniques may fail to respond quickly enough to changes in the environment or system conditions.

Furthermore, the integration of SI with metaheuristics enhances the optimization process by combining the strengths of both approaches. Metaheuristics, which are higher-level procedures designed to guide lower-level heuristics, help in escaping local optima and exploring the solution space more thoroughly. When used together, SI and metaheuristics provide a more comprehensive approach to optimization, balancing exploration and exploitation to find the best possible solutions.

The effectiveness of these methods is demonstrated in various case studies where SI and metaheuristics have been applied to optimize complex control systems. These studies show that SI-based algorithms often outperform traditional methods, especially in scenarios where the control systems are large-scale and involve significant complexity. By leveraging the collective intelligence of swarms and the flexibility of metaheuristics, these techniques can optimize control systems more efficiently and effectively than traditional methods.

For control engineers, the adoption of SI and metaheuristics offers a path to improved performance, robustness, and efficiency in their systems. Engineers can enhance their work by integrating these adaptive algorithms into their control strategies, leading to smarter and more resilient solutions. The adaptability of SI-based methods ensures that control systems can remain responsive to changes in real-time, while the robustness of these algorithms provides reliability in complex and large-scale environments.

The combination of swarm intelligence and metaheuristics presents a powerful approach to optimization in control engineering, particularly in the context of large-scale data analytics. As the complexity of control systems continues to grow with the advent of big data and IoT, these advanced optimization methods will play an increasingly important role in ensuring that control systems are not only optimized but also resilient and adaptable to the demands of modern technology.

5. CONCLUSION

SI-based algorithms represent a robust and adaptable approach to solving complex optimization problems in control engineering and large-scale systems. As these algorithms continue to evolve, they will play an increasingly critical role in optimizing the performance of modern, interconnected systems. In large-scale energy systems like smart grids, these algorithms optimize the distribution of resources, integration of renewables, and overall system efficiency, balancing cost, reliability, and environmental impact. These algorithms optimize the design and operation of large-scale supply chains and networks, ensuring efficient resource allocation, minimal delays, and robustness against disruptions. These algorithms optimize the parameters of controllers (e.g., PID controllers) to achieve desired performance metrics, such as stability, speed, and robustness, even in nonlinear and time-varying systems. In environments where system parameters or external conditions vary dynamically, these algorithms provide adaptive solutions that maintain system performance, making them ideal for applications in robotics, autonomous systems, and smart grids.

6. FUTURE RESEARCH DIRECTIONS

These algorithms, while powerful, can be computationally intensive, especially for large-scale and high-dimensional problems (Kupin & Kosei, 2024). Future research may focus on improving computational efficiency through parallel processing and hybridization with faster algorithms. The performance of SI-based algorithms is often sensitive to the choice of parameters. Adaptive mechanisms that adjust parameters dynamically during the optimization process could help mitigate this issue. As optimization problems become larger and more complex, ensuring the scalability of these algorithms will be critical. Future research may explore distributed computing and cloud-based implementations to address scalability challenges.

REFERENCES

Abualigah, L., Falcone, D., & Forestiero, A. (2023). Swarm intelligence to face IoT challenges. *Computational Intelligence and Neuroscience, 4254194*(1), 4254194. Advance online publication. DOI: 10.1155/2023/4254194 PMID: 37284052

Ahmad, I., Hussain, T., Shah, B., Hussain, A., Ali, I., & Ali, F. (2024). Accelerated particle swarm optimization algorithm for efficient cluster head selection in WSN. *Computers, Materials & Continua, 79*(3), 3585–3629. DOI: 10.32604/cmc.2024.050596

Alhijawi, B., & Awajan, A. (2024). Genetic algorithms: Theory, genetic operators, solutions, and applications. *Evolutionary Intelligence, 17*(3), 1245–1256. DOI: 10.1007/s12065-023-00822-6

Banerjee, A., Pradhan, S., Misra, B., & Chakraborty, S. (2024). A guide to meta-heuristic algorithms for multi-objective optimization: Concepts and approaches. In Dey, N. (Ed.), *Applied Multi-Objective Optimization* (pp. 1–19). Springer Nature Singapore., DOI: 10.1007/978-981-97-0353-1_1

Çavdar, B., Şahin, E., & Sesli, E. (2024). On the assessment of meta-heuristic algorithms for automatic voltage regulator system controller design: A standardization process. *Electrical Engineering, 106*(5), 5801–5839. DOI: 10.1007/s00202-024-02314-x

Dhal, K. G., & Das, S. (2020). Local search-based dynamically adapted bat algorithm in the image enhancement domain. *International Journal of Computing Science and Mathematics, 11*(1), 1–28. DOI: 10.1504/IJCSM.2020.105447

Faraj, M. A., & Abbood, A. M. (2021). Fractional order PID controller tuned by bat algorithm for robot trajectory control. *Indonesian Journal of Electrical Engineering and Computer Science, 21*, 74–83. DOI: 10.11591/ijeecs.v21.i1.pp74-83

Gad, A. G. (2022). Particle swarm optimization algorithm and its applications: A systematic review. *Archives of Computational Methods in Engineering, 29*(5), 2531–2561. DOI: 10.1007/s11831-021-09694-4

Ghannadi, P., Kourehli, S. S., & Mirjalili, S. (2023) A review of the application of the simulated annealing algorithm in structural health monitoring (1995–2021). *Frattura Ed Integrità Strutturale* (edited by I. Strutturale), 17, 51–76. DOI: DOI: 10.3221/IGF-ESIS.64.04

Huang, C., Zhao, Y., Zhang, M., & Yang, H. (2023). APSO: An A*-PSO hybrid algorithm for mobile robot path planning. *IEEE Access : Practical Innovations, Open Solutions, 11*, 43238–43256. DOI: 10.1109/ACCESS.2023.3272223

Jain, M., Saihjpal, V., Singh, N., & Singh, S. B. (2022). An overview of variants and advancements of PSO algorithm. *Applied Sciences (Basel, Switzerland), 12*(17), 8392. DOI: 10.3390/app12178392

Kupin, A. I., & Kosei, M. P. (2024). Analysis of swarm intelligence algorithms. *System Technologies, 3*, 69–80. DOI: 10.34185/1562-9945-3-152-2024-07

Ma, H., Zhang, Y., Sun, S., Liu, T., & Shan, Y. (2023). A comprehensive survey on NSGA-II for multi-objective optimization and applications. *Artificial Intelligence Review, 56*(12), 15217–15270. DOI: 10.1007/s10462-023-10526-z

Moses, W. S., Ivanov, I. R., Domke, J., Endo, T., Doerfert, J., & Zinenko, O. (2023) High-performance GPU-to-CPU transpilation and optimization via high-level parallel constructs. In: *Proceedings of the 28th ACM SIGPLAN Annual Symposium on Principles and Practice of Parallel Programming*. ACM, pp. 119–134. DOI: DOI: 10.1145/3572848.3577475

Nadimi-Shahraki, M. H., Zamani, H., Asghari Varzaneh, Z., & Mirjalili, S. (2023). A systematic review of the whale optimization algorithm: Theoretical foundation, improvements, and hybridizations. *Archives of Computational Methods in Engineering*, *30*(7), 4113–4159. DOI: 10.1007/s11831-023-09928-7 PMID: 37359740

Nath, S., & Sarkar, S. K. (2021). Metaheuristics-based routing optimisation, balanced workload distribution and security strategy in IoT environment. *International Journal of Advanced Intelligence Paradigms*, *19*(1), 101–117. DOI: 10.1504/IJAIP.2021.114586

Parouha, R. P., & Verma, P. (2022). A systematic overview of developments in differential evolution and particle swarm optimization with their advanced suggestion. *Applied Intelligence*, *52*(9), 10448–10492. DOI: 10.1007/s10489-021-02803-7

Renuka Devi, D., & Sasikala, S. (2019). Online feature selection (OFS) with accelerated bat algorithm (ABA) and ensemble incremental deep multiple layer Perceptron (EIDMLP) for big data streams. *Journal of Big Data*, *6*(1), 103. DOI: 10.1186/s40537-019-0267-3

Rodríguez-Molina, A., Mezura-Montes, E., Villarreal-Cervantes, M. G., & Aldape-Pérez, M. (2020). Multi-objective meta-heuristic optimization in intelligent control: A survey on the controller tuning problem. *Applied Soft Computing*, *93*, 106342. DOI: 10.1016/j.asoc.2020.106342

Sadeeq, H. T., & Abdulazeez, A. M. (2023). Metaheuristics: A review of algorithms. *International Journal of Online and Biomedical Engineering*, *19*(9), 142–164. DOI: 10.3991/ijoe.v19i09.39683

Sherif, A., & Haci, H. (2023). A novel bio-inspired energy optimization for two-tier wireless communication networks: A grasshopper optimization algorithm (GOA)-based approach. *Electronics (Basel)*, *12*(5), 1216. DOI: 10.3390/electronics12051216

Shi, K., Wu, Z., Jiang, B., & Karimi, H. R. (2023). Dynamic path planning of mobile robot based on improved simulated annealing algorithm. *Journal of the Franklin Institute*, *360*(6), 4378–4398. DOI: 10.1016/j.jfranklin.2023.01.033

Skinderowicz, R. (2022). Improving ant colony optimization efficiency for solving large TSP instances. *Applied Soft Computing*, *120*, 108653. DOI: 10.1016/j.asoc.2022.108653

Turgut, O. E., Turgut, M. S., & Kırtepe, E. (2023). A systematic review of the emerging metaheuristic algorithms on solving complex optimization problems. *Neural Computing & Applications*, *35*(19), 14275–14378. DOI: 10.1007/s00521-023-08481-5

Veza, I., Deniz Karaoglan, A., Ileri, E., Afzal, A., Tuan Hoang, A., Tamaldin, N., Gazali Herawan, S., Abbas, M. M., & Farid Muhamad Said, M. (2022). Multi-objective optimization of diesel engine performance and emission using grasshopper optimization algorithm. *Fuel*, *323*, 124303. DOI: 10.1016/j.fuel.2022.124303

Wang, C., Li, J., Rao, H., Chen, A., Jiao, J., Zou, N., & Gu, L. (2021). Multi-objective grasshopper optimization algorithm based on multi-group and co-evolution. *Mathematical Biosciences and Engineering*, *18*(3), 2527–2561. DOI: 10.3934/mbe.2021129 PMID: 33892559

Wu, L., Huang, X., Cui, J., Liu, C., & Xiao, W. (2023). Modified adaptive ant colony optimization algorithm and its application for solving path planning of mobile robots. *Expert Systems with Applications*, *215*, 119410. DOI: 10.1016/j.eswa.2022.119410

Yang, X.S. (2013) Optimization and metaheuristic algorithms in engineering. *Metaheuristics in Water, Geotechnical and Transport Engineering*, 1. 9780123982964, 0123982960.

KEY TERMS AND DEFINITIONS

Swarm Intelligence (SI) -: A branch of artificial intelligence inspired by the collective behavior of decentralized, self-organized systems, such as insect colonies, bird flocking, or fish schooling. SI algorithms simulate this behavior to solve complex optimization problems by having multiple agents (e.g., particles, ants, bees) interact locally and collaboratively to find optimal solutions.

Metaheuristics -: High-level, problem-independent algorithmic frameworks that guide lower-level heuristics to explore and exploit the search space for solutions. Metaheuristics are used to find near-optimal solutions for complex optimization problems where traditional methods may be inefficient or infeasible.

Optimization -: The process of finding the best solution from a set of possible solutions, often under a given set of constraints. Optimization is used in various fields, including engineering, economics, and operations research, to improve efficiency, performance, and outcomes.

Large-Scale Analytics -: The analysis and interpretation of massive datasets typically generated by big data and IoT devices. Large-scale analytics involves the use of advanced computational techniques, such as machine learning and swarm intelligence, to extract valuable insights and optimize decision-making in complex systems.

MOGOA (Multi-Objective Grasshopper Optimization Algorithm) -: A swarm intelligence algorithm inspired by the natural behavior of grasshoppers. MOGOA is designed to solve multi-objective optimization problems by balancing exploration and exploitation to find a set of optimal solutions known as the Pareto front.

IACO (Improved Ant Colony Optimization) -: An enhanced version of the traditional Ant Colony Optimization (ACO) algorithm, which is inspired by the foraging behavior of ants. IACO incorporates improvements such as adaptive parameters or memory mechanisms to enhance the efficiency and accuracy of finding optimal solutions in complex optimization problems.

HGA (Hybrid Genetic Algorithm)-: A hybrid optimization algorithm that combines the principles of Genetic Algorithms (GAs) with other optimization techniques (e.g., local search methods or other metaheuristics) to improve performance and convergence speed in solving complex optimization problems.

WOA (Whale Optimization Algorithm)-: A nature-inspired metaheuristic algorithm based on the social behavior of humpback whales. WOA simulates the bubble-net hunting strategy of whales to perform global optimization, making it effective for solving both continuous and discrete optimization problems.

DABA (Dynamic Adaptive BAT Algorithm)-: An advanced version of the BAT algorithm that includes dynamic adaptation mechanisms. DABA adjusts the algorithm's parameters in real-time based on the problem's complexity and the current state of the search process, improving its ability to find optimal solutions in dynamic environments.

Particle Swarm Optimization (PSO) -: A population-based optimization algorithm inspired by the social behavior of bird flocks or fish schools. PSO involves particles (potential solutions) moving through the search space influenced by their own experience and the experience of neighbouring particles to find the optimal solution.

Accelerated PSO (APSO)-: A variant of the traditional PSO algorithm that includes acceleration mechanisms to improve convergence speed and accuracy. APSO adjusts the velocity and position of particles more dynamically, enabling faster exploration of the search space.

Simulated Annealing (SA)-: A probabilistic optimization algorithm inspired by the annealing process in metallurgy. SA gradually reduces the probability of accepting worse solutions as the algorithm progresses, allowing it to escape local optima and converge toward a global optimum.

BAT Algorithm (BA)-: A metaheuristic optimization algorithm inspired by the echolocation behavior of bats. BA uses frequency, loudness, and pulse emission rate as control parameters to balance exploration and exploitation in the search for optimal solutions.

Control Systems -: Systems designed to regulate the behavior of other systems or processes by automatically adjusting inputs to achieve desired outputs. Control systems use feedback loops to maintain stability, ensure accuracy, and achieve performance objectives in various applications, such as industrial automation, robotics, and aerospace.

Control Engineering -: A branch of engineering that focuses on the design, analysis, and implementation of control systems. Control engineering applies mathematical modeling, system dynamics, and control theory to ensure that systems operate efficiently, reliably, and within specified parameters.

Local Minima -: Points in the search space of an optimization problem where the objective function value is lower than at neighboring points, but not necessarily the lowest overall. Algorithms must avoid being trapped in local minima to find the global minimum, which is the best possible solution.

Local Maxima-: Points in the search space of an optimization problem where the objective function value is higher than at neighboring points, but not necessarily the highest overall. Similar to local minima, algorithms must avoid being trapped in local maxima to reach the global maximum.

Systems Engineering -: An interdisciplinary field that focuses on the design, integration, and management of complex systems throughout their life cycles. Systems engineering involves the coordination of different engineering disciplines to ensure that a system meets its functional, performance, and reliability requirements.

Multi-Objective Optimization-: The process of optimizing two or more conflicting objectives simultaneously in a problem. Solutions to multi-objective optimization problems typically form a Pareto front, representing the trade-offs between the different objectives, where no single solution is absolutely better than the others.

GPU (Graphics Processing Unit)-: A specialized electronic circuit designed to accelerate the processing of graphics and visual data. GPUs are increasingly used in parallel computing for high-performance tasks such as deep learning, big data analytics, and optimization problems due to their ability to handle multiple calculations simultaneously.

Controller Design-: The process of developing control algorithms and systems to manage the behavior of dynamic systems. Controller design involves creating mathematical models and applying control theory to design controllers that achieve desired performance criteria, such as stability, accuracy, and responsiveness.

Optimal Search -: A process in optimization algorithms that seeks to find the best possible solution to a problem by exploring the search space efficiently. Optimal search techniques aim to balance exploration (searching new areas of the solution space) and exploitation (refining known good solutions) to achieve the best overall results.

Chapter 12

Optimal Boundary Control of String Vibrations With Multipoint Intermediate Conditions at Minimizing the Boundary Energy Integral

Vanya Barseghyan
Institute of Mechanics, The National Academy of Sciences of the RA, Yerevan State University, Armenia

Svetlana Solodusha
https://orcid.org/0000-0001-6162-7542
Melentiev Energy Systems Institute of Siberian Branch of the Russian Academy of Sciences, Russia

ABSTRACT

For the equation of string vibration with given initial and final conditions, we consider the problems of optimal boundary control with given multipoint conditions at different intermediate time points for the values of deflection functions and velocities of string points. The control is carried out both by displacement at one end with the other end fixed, and by displacement at the two ends of the string. The minimizable functionals are the boundary energy integrals given over the entire time interval. We propose a constructive approach to designing solutions to the considered problems of optimal boundary control of string vibrations. The construction scheme is as follows: the problems are reduced to control problems with distributed impacts and zero boundary conditions, then, using the method of separation of variables, the obtained problems are reduced to optimal control problems for ordinary differential equations with specified initial, final and multipoint intermediate conditions with appropriate quality criteria.

DOI: 10.4018/979-8-3693-7812-0.ch012

INTRODUCTION

This chapter addresses the tasks of optimal boundary control of string vibrations with initial, final conditions, and specified multipoint conditions at various intermediate moments in time concerning the values of the deflection function and the velocities of points on the string. The problems of optimal boundary control are considered in two cases: when the control is implemented as a displacement at one end while the other end is fixed, and when there are displacements at both ends of the string. The functionals to be minimized are integrals of the squares of the derivatives of the boundary displacements, i.e., the integral of boundary energy, defined over the entire time interval. The goal of this work is to develop a constructive approach to constructing the function of optimal boundary control actions for managing the vibrations of the string with given initial, final conditions, and intermediate values of deflections and velocities of points on the string at various intermediate moments in time.

BACKGROUND

Mathematical models of many physical and technological processes, which have significant theoretical and practical importance, are described by the one-dimensional wave equation. In particular, the wave equation describes the vibrations of a string, links of a manipulator, level-luffing crane, aircraft wings, and many other processes. It is important to note that controlled vibrating systems are widely distributed in various theoretical and applied fields of science. Therefore, there is a need to investigate control and optimal control problems for vibrational processes described by the wave equation with various formulations, both concentrated (boundary) and distributed effects. Such problems are relevant, and many researchers pay attention to their study, particularly as discussed in works (Abdukarimov, 2013); (Abdukarimov, 2014); (Butkovsky, 1965); (Butkovsky, 1975); (Dreglea and Sidorov, 2018); (Gibkina et al., 2016); (Il'in and Moiseev, 2005); (Krabs, 1995); (Li, 2008); (Moiseev and Kholomeeva, 2013); (Sadybekov and Yessirkegenov, 2016); (Sirazetdinov, 1977); (Yang et al., 2004); (Znamenskaya, 2004). An introductory overview of the theory of controlling distributed vibrating systems is provided, particularly in works (Butkovsky, 1965); (Butkovsky, 1975); (Krabs, 1995); (Sirazetdinov, 1977); (Znamenskaya, 2004). Works (Il'in and Moiseev, 2005) and (Moiseev and Kholomeeva, 2013) (and other works by these authors and their students) are dedicated to the problem of boundary control (optimal control) of wave processes in the class of generalized solutions. In investigating these boundary control problems, the D'alembert method is used and D'alembert-type formulas are derived. Works (Abdukarimov, 2013) and (Abdukarimov, 2014) examine optimal boundary control tasks involving displacements at the ends of a string based on minimizing the integral of boundary energy, which transitions the vibration process of the string from an arbitrarily given initial state to a specified final state over an arbitrary sufficiently long time interval. In studies related to control and optimal control of vibrational processes, particularly, in the works cited above, various methods for solving control and optimal control problems, such as the Dalembert method, the Fourier method, the harmonic method and the method of moments, have been used.

Many dynamic control processes with both concentrated and distributed parameters lead to the necessity of investigating multipoint boundary control and optimal control problems, where, alongside classical boundary (initial and final) conditions, multipoint intermediate (both separated and non-separated) conditions are also specified (Ashchepkov, 1981); (Barseghyan, 2012); (Barseghyan, 2016a); (Barseghyan, 2016b); (Barseghyan, 2018); (Barseghyan, 2019); (Barseghyan, 2020); (Barseghyan,

2022); (Barseghyan and Solodusha, 2021a); (Barseghyan and Solodusha, 2021b); (Barseghyan and Solodusha, 2022); (Korzyuk and Kozlovskia, 2010a); (Korzyuk and Kozlovskia, 2010b). For example, in practice, boundary control and optimal boundary control problems for vibrational processes often arise, particularly when it is necessary to generate vibrations with predetermined intermediate parameters (desired shapes and velocities of points). The modeling and control of dynamic systems described by both ordinary differential equations and partial differential equations with multipoint intermediate conditions are actively developing areas in modern control theory. A characteristic feature of such problems is the presence of specified intermediate conditions at several points in the research interval, alongside given initial and final conditions. Research on such problems is dedicated, in particular, to works (Barseghyan, 2012); (Barseghyan, 2016a); (Barseghyan, 2016b); (Barseghyan, 2018); (Barseghyan, 2019); (Barseghyan, 2020); (Barseghyan, 2022); (Barseghyan and Solodusha, 2021a); (Barseghyan and Solodusha, 2021b); (Barseghyan and Solodusha, 2022); (Korzyuk and Kozlovskia, 2010a); (Korzyuk and Kozlovskia, 2010b). In works (Korzyuk and Kozlovskia, 2010a) and (Korzyuk and Kozlovskia, 2010b), a boundary problem for the equation of string vibrations with a specified velocity at a certain moment in time is considered, and a solution to the problem is constructed. Numerous studies, including (Barseghyan, 2012); (Barseghyan, 2016b); (Barseghyan, 2018); (Barseghyan, 2019); (Barseghyan, 2020); (Barseghyan, 2022); (Barseghyan and Solodusha, 2021a); (Barseghyan and Solodusha, 2021b); (Barseghyan and Solodusha, 2022), focus on control, optimal control problems for vibrational processes with multipoint intermediate (both separated and non-separated) conditions, as well as distributed, and boundary influences under various types of boundary conditions. In these optimal boundary control problems, the quality criteria are functionals of the square of displacement functions defined over the entire time interval. The optimal boundary control problems for vibrational processes with multipoint intermediate conditions and functionals defined as integrals of the squares of derivatives of boundary displacements, i.e., integrals of boundary energy, have not yet been sufficiently explored.

MAIN FOCUS OF THE CHAPTER

This chapter provides a constructive approach to constructing the function of optimal boundary control actions for managing the vibrations of a string with specified initial and final conditions, as well as intermediate values of the deflection function and velocities of points on the string at various intermediate moments in time. The quality criterion is the integral of the squares of the derivatives of boundary displacements, i.e., the integral of boundary energy, defined over the entire time interval. The optimal boundary control problems are considered in which control is carried out both by shifting the left end with the right end fixed, and by shifting at both ends of the string. Since in these problems, at specific intermediate moments in time, either only the values of the deflection function or only the values of its derivative (the velocities of points) are given (in any sequence), it is inappropriate to use a step-by-step approach to study optimal control problems. Therefore, this work presents an approach to solving these optimal control problems that takes into account the specifics of multipoint intermediate conditions. For these problems, a constructive approach for building the optimal boundary control function for string vibrations that ensuring fulfilment of multi-point intermediate conditions is proposed using a unified scheme. The construction scheme involves reducing the original problems to control problems with distributed influences and zero boundary conditions. Using the method of separation of variables and methods from optimal control theory for finite-dimensional systems with multipoint intermediate conditions for arbitrary numbers of harmonics, optimal boundary control is constructed.

Issues, Controversies, Problems

The statement of optimal boundary control problems for vibrational processes with multipoint intermediate conditions and functionals defined as integrals of the squares of the derivatives of boundary displacements differ from known formulations of similar problems. Therefore, their investigation is presented in this chapter. It should be noted that the presence of intermediate values of the deflection functions and velocities of points on the string at various intermediate moments in time (which is significant) leads to additional integral relations with respect to the boundary control functions. In this case, different intermediate moments of time lead to the fact that the limits of the integrals in additional relations also turn out to be different and do not coincide with the limits of the main two integral relations. This fact, in turn, makes the problems more complex than similar problems without intermediate conditions. The point is that this leads to the fact that in additional integral relations under the integrals there are discontinuous functions. Consequently, classical variational methods are not applicable to these problems. Therefore, the solution is constructed using the method of moment problems. Note that the proposed constructive approach to building optimal boundary control for vibrational processes using the Fourier method allows for extension to other non-one-dimensional vibrational systems.

SOLUTIONS AND RECOMMENDATIONS

The proposed constructive approach to building optimal boundary control for vibrational processes using the method of separation of variables permits numerical calculations and also allows for the extension of this approach to other non-one-dimensional vibrational systems.

PROBLEM STATEMENT

Let the state of a distributed vibration system (small transverse vibrations of a stretched string), i.e. deviations from the state of equilibrium, be described by a function $Q \rightleftarrows (x,t), 0 \le x \le l, 0 \le t \le T$, which obeys the wave equation

$$\frac{\partial^2 Q}{\partial t^2} = a^2 \frac{\partial^2 Q}{\partial x^2}, 0 < x < l, t > 0 \tag{1.1}$$

with initial and final conditions

$$Q(x,0) = \varphi_0(x), \left.\frac{\partial Q}{\partial t}\right|_{t=0} = \psi_0(x), 0 \le x \le l \tag{1.2}$$

$$Q(x,T) = \varphi_T(x) = \varphi_{m+1}(x), \left.\frac{\partial Q}{\partial t}\right|_{t=T} = \psi_T(x) = \psi_{m+1}(x), 0 \le x \le l \tag{1.3}$$

and boundary conditions:

when the left end is moved with the right end fixed

$$Q(0,t) = \mu(t), Q(l,t) = 0, 0 \leq t \leq T \tag{1.4.1}$$

when both ends are moved

$$Q(0,t) = \mu(t), Q(l,t) = \nu(t), 0 \leq t \leq T \tag{1.4.2}$$

Here functions $\mu(t)$ and $\nu(t)$ are boundary controls, $a^2 = \frac{T_0}{\rho}$, where T_0 is the tension, and ρ is the density of the string.

Let at intermediate moments of time

t_k

$(k = 1, \ldots, m)$

,

$0 = t_0 < t_1 < \ldots < t_m < t_{m+1} = T$

,

$$Q(x, t_i) = \varphi_i(x), 0 \leq x \leq l, i = 2\alpha - 1, \alpha = 1, \ldots, \frac{m}{2},$$

$$\left.\frac{\partial Q}{\partial t}\right|_{t=t_j} = \psi_j(x), 0 \leq x \leq l, j = 2\alpha, \alpha = 1, \ldots, \frac{m}{2} \tag{1.5}$$

m is an even number.

Note that the intermediate values of the deflection function and the values of the velocities of the string points in condition (1.5) can be specified in any order.

The minimized boundary energy integrals have the following form:

when the left end is shifted with the right end fixed

$$\int_0^T [\dot{\mu}(t)]^2 dt$$

(1.6.1)

when both ends are shifted

$$\int_0^T \{[\dot{\mu}(t)]^2 + [\dot{\nu}(t)]^2\}dt$$

(1.6.2)

It is assumed that the function $Q(x,t) \in C^2(\Omega_T)$, where the set $\Omega_T = \{(x,t): x \in [0,l], t \in [0,T]$ $\}$, and the functions $\varphi_i(x) \in C^2[0,l]$ and $\psi_j(x) \in C^1[0,l]$. It is also assumed that all functions are such that the following matching conditions

$$\mu(0) = \varphi_0(0), \dot{\mu}(0) = \psi_0(0), \nu(0) = \varphi_0(l), \dot{\nu}(0) = \psi_0(l),$$

$$\mu(t_i) = \varphi_i(0), \dot{\mu}(t_j) = \psi_j(0), \nu(t_i) = \varphi_i(l), \dot{\nu}(t_j) = \psi_j(l),$$

$$i = 2\alpha - 1, j = 2\alpha, \alpha = 1, ..., \frac{m}{2}, \tag{1.7}$$

$$\mu(T) = \varphi_T(0), \dot{\mu}(T) = \psi_T(0), \nu(T) = \varphi_T(l), \dot{\nu}(T) = \psi_T(l)$$

are satisfied.

For equation (1.1) with initial (1.2) and final (1.3) conditions on the time interval $[0, T]$ we consider optimal boundary control problems with given conditions on the values of the deflection functions and the velocities of the string points at different intermediate moments of time and quality criteria. The problems are posed as follows.

Problem 1 (the left end moved, the right end fixed). It is necessary to find the optimal boundary control $\mu^0(t)$, $0 \leq t \leq T$, under the influence of which the vibratory motion of the system (1.1) passes from the given initial state (1.2) to the final state (1.3), ensuring the fulfillment of the intermediate conditions (1.5) and minimizing the functional (1.6.1).

Problem 2 (both ends are moved). It is necessary to find the optimal boundary control $\mu^0(t)$ and $\nu^0(t)$, $0 \leq t \leq T$, under the influence of which the vibratory motion of the system (1.1) passes from the given initial state (1.2) to the final state (1.3), ensuring the fulfillment of the intermediate conditions (1.5) and minimizing the functional (1.6.2).

The work proposes a constructive approach to solving the considered problems of optimal control with minimization of boundary energy integrals, taking into account the specifics of intermediate conditions. This approach is based on the following scheme: first, the problems are reduced to optimal control problems with distributed impacts with zero boundary conditions; then, using the method of separation of variables, the resulting problems are reduced to optimal control problems for ordinary differential equations with given initial, final and multi-point intermediate conditions as a problem of moments. Further, based on the algorithm for solving problems of moments of finite-dimensional systems with multi-point intermediate conditions, optimal boundary controls are constructed for an arbitrary number of the first n harmonics. These controls are presented in an explicit analytical form.

REDUCING ORIGINAL PROBLEMS TO PROBLEMS WITH ZERO BOUNDARY CONDITIONS

The stated problems for the homogeneous equation (1.1) with non-homogeneous boundary conditions ((1.4.1) or (1.4.2)) are reduced to problems of optimal control with distributed effects (for the non-homogeneous equation) with zero boundary conditions (Tikhonov and Samarskii, 1963). We do not provide the details of the information with calculations in this context. They are given, in particular, in the works (Barseghyan, 2020; Barseghyan, 2022; Barseghyan and Solodusha, 2021b; Barseghyan and Solodusha, 2022). However, for a correct presentation of the further construction of the solution to the problems, we consider it necessary to provide the formulas used.

Reducing Non-Homogeneous Boundary Conditions to Zero Boundary Conditions

We seek the solution to equation (1.1) in the form

$$Q(x,t) = V(x,t) + W(x,t) \tag{2.1}$$

where $V(x,t)$ is an unknown function with boundary conditions

$$V(0,t) = V(l,t) = 0 \tag{2.2}$$

Under boundary conditions $Q(0,t) = \mu(t)$, $Q(l,t) = 0$ we have

$$W(0,t) = \mu(t), W(l,t) = 0$$

(2.3.1)

Under boundary conditions $Q(0,t) = \mu(t)$, $Q(l,t) = \nu(t)$ we have

$$W(0,t) = \mu(t), W(l,t) = \nu(t)$$

(2.3.2)

The function $W(x,t)$ for boundary conditions (2.3.1) and (2.3.2) is represented in the form

$$W(x,t) = \left(1 - \frac{x}{l}\right)\mu(t)$$

(2.4.1)

$$W(x,t) = (\nu(t) - \mu(t))\frac{x}{l} + \mu(t)$$

(2.4.2)

To determine the function $V(x,t)$, we obtain equation

$$\frac{\partial^2 V}{\partial t^2} = a^2\frac{\partial^2 V}{\partial x^2} + F(x,t) \quad (2.5)$$

where for a problem with a move of the left end with a fixed right end with a function $W(x,t)$ of the form (2.4.1) we have

$$F(x,t) = \left(\frac{x}{l} - 1\right)\ddot{\mu}(t)$$

(2.6.1)

and for a problem with a move of two ends with a function $W(x,t)$ of the form (2.4.2) we have

$$F(x,t) = (\ddot{\mu}(t) - \ddot{\nu}(t))\frac{x}{l} - \ddot{\mu}(t)$$

(2.6.2)

It is also necessary for the non-homogeneous equation (2.5) to reduce the initial (1.2), final (1.3) and intermediate (1.5) conditions to the corresponding conditions for the function $V(x,t)$.

Reducing Initial, Intermediate and Final Conditions to the Corresponding Conditions for the Non-Homogeneous Equation

Taking into account the expressions for the function $W(x,t)$ (2.4.1), (2.4.2) and the matching conditions (1.7), from the initial (1.2), intermediate (1.5) and final conditions (1.3) we obtain the corresponding conditions for the function $V(x,t)$.

For the problem of optimal boundary control of string vibrations by displacement of the left end with the right end fixed, i.e. for the function $V(x,t)$, we obtain the following initial conditions:

$$V(x,0) = \varphi_0(x) + \left(\frac{x}{l} - 1\right)\varphi_0(0), \left.\frac{\partial V}{\partial t}\right|_{t=0} = \psi_0(x) + \left(\frac{x}{l} - 1\right)\psi_0(0) \quad (2.7)$$

intermediate conditions

$$V(x,t_i) = \varphi_i(x) + \left(\frac{x}{l} - 1\right)\varphi_i(0), i = 2\alpha - 1, \alpha = 1, \ldots, \frac{m}{2},$$

$$\left.\frac{\partial V}{\partial t}\right|_{t=t_j} = \psi_j(x) + \left(\frac{x}{l} - 1\right)\psi_j(0), j = 2\alpha, \alpha = 1, \ldots, \frac{m}{2} \quad (2.8)$$

final conditions

$$V(x,T) = \varphi_T(x) + \left(\tfrac{x}{l} - 1\right)\varphi_T(0), \left.\frac{\partial V}{\partial t}\right|_{t=T} = \psi_T(x) + \left(\tfrac{x}{l} - 1\right)\psi_T(0) \tag{2.9}$$

For the problem of optimal boundary control of string vibrations by displacement of two ends, i.e. for the function $V(x,t)$, we obtain the following initial conditions

$$V(x,0) = \varphi_0(x) - (\varphi_0(l) - \varphi_0(0))\tfrac{x}{l} - \varphi_0(0),$$

$$\left.\frac{\partial V}{\partial t}\right|_{t=0} = \psi_0(x) - (\psi_0(l) - \psi_0(0))\tfrac{x}{l} - \psi_0(0) \tag{2.10}$$

intermediate conditions

$$V(x,t_i) = \varphi_i(x) - (\varphi_i(l) - \varphi_i(0))\tfrac{x}{l} - \varphi_i(0), i = 2\alpha - 1, \alpha = 1, \ldots, \tfrac{m}{2},$$

$$\left.\frac{\partial V}{\partial t}\right|_{t=t_j} = \psi_j(x) - (\psi_j(l) - \psi_j(0))\tfrac{x}{l} - \psi_j(0), j = 2\alpha, \alpha = 1, \ldots, \tfrac{m}{2} \tag{2.11}$$

final conditions

$$V(x,T) = \varphi_T(x) - (\varphi_T(l) - \varphi_T(0))\tfrac{x}{l} - \varphi_T(0),$$

$$\left.\frac{\partial V}{\partial t}\right|_{t=T} = \psi_T(x) - (\psi_T(l) - \psi_T(0))\tfrac{x}{l} - \psi_T(0) \tag{2.12}$$

Thus, we obtain the following problems of optimal control of vibrations, described by the non-homogeneous equation (2.5) and zero boundary conditions (2.2).

Problem 1_0 (the left end moved, the right end fixed). It is necessary to find the optimal boundary control $\mu^0(t), 0 \leq t \leq T$, which transfers the vibratory motion described by equation (2.5), (2.6.1) with boundary conditions (2.2) from a given initial state (2.7) to the final one (2.9), ensuring the fulfillment of intermediate conditions (2.8) and minimizing the functional (1.6.1).

Problem 2_0 (both ends are moved). It is necessary to find the optimal boundary control $\mu^0(t)$ and $\nu^0(t), 0 \leq t \leq T$, which transfers the vibratory motion described by equation (2.5), (2.6.2) with boundary conditions (2.2) from a given initial state (2.10) to the final one (2.12), ensuring the fulfillment of intermediate conditions (2.11) and minimizing the functional (1.6.2).

APPLYING THE METHOD OF SEPARATION OF VARIABLES AND REDUCING THE SOLUTION OF PROBLEMS TO THE PROBLEM OF MOMENTS

We seek the solution to (2.5) in the form

$$V(x,t)=\sum_{k=1}^{\infty}V_k(t)\sin\frac{\pi k}{l}x \quad (3.1)$$

By representing functions $F(x,t)$, $\varphi_i(x)$ and $\psi_j(x)$ as Fourier series and substituting their values together with $V(x,t)$ into equations (2.5), (2.6.1), (2.6.2) and into conditions (2.7)–(2.12), we obtain

$$\ddot{V}_k^{(s)}(t)+\lambda_k^2 V_k^{(s)}(t)=F_k^{(s)}(t),\lambda_k^2 = \left(\frac{a\pi k}{l}\right)^2, s = 1,2, k = 1,2,... \quad (3.2)$$

$$F_k^{(1)}(t)=-\frac{2a}{\lambda_k l}\ddot{\mu}(t), \quad (3.3.1)$$

$$F_k^{(2)}(t)=\frac{2a}{\lambda_k l}[\ddot{\nu}(t)(-1)^k-\ddot{\mu}(t)], \quad (3.3.2)$$

Here and below, the meaning of the letter "s" in the superscript characterizes Problem 1 for $s = 1$, and Problem 2 for $s = 2$.

For problems with a displacement of the left end with a fixed right end, the initial, intermediate and final conditions are represented in the form

$$V_k^{(1)}(0)=\varphi_k^{(0)}-\frac{2a}{\lambda_k l}\varphi_0(0),\dot{V}_k^{(1)}(0)=\psi_k^{(0)}-\frac{2a}{\lambda_k l}\psi_0(0) \quad (3.4)$$

$$V_k^{(1)}(t_i)=\varphi_k^{(i)}-\frac{2a}{\lambda_k l}\varphi_i(0), i = 2\alpha-1, \alpha = 1,...,\frac{m}{2},$$

$$\dot{V}_k^{(1)}(t_j)=\psi_k^{(j)}-\frac{2a}{\lambda_k l}\psi_j(0), j = 2\alpha, \alpha = 1,...,\frac{m}{2} \quad (3.5)$$

$$V_k^{(1)}(T)=\varphi_k^{(T)}-\frac{2a}{\lambda_k l}\varphi_T(0),\dot{V}_k^{(1)}(T)=\psi_k^{(T)}-\frac{2a}{\lambda_k l}\psi_T(0) \quad (3.6)$$

For problems with displacement of two ends, the initial, intermediate and final conditions are represented as

$$V_k^{(2)}(0)=\varphi_k^{(0)}-\frac{2a}{\lambda_k l}\left[\varphi_0(0)-\varphi_0(l)(-1)^k\right],\dot{V}_k^{(2)}(0)=\psi_k^{(0)}-\frac{2a}{\lambda_k l}\left[\psi_0(0)-\psi_0(l)(-1)^k\right] \quad (3.7)$$

$$V_k^{(2)}(t_i)=\varphi_k^{(i)}-\frac{2a}{\lambda_k l}\left[\varphi_i(0)-\varphi_i(l)(-1)^k\right], i = 2\alpha-1, \alpha = 1,...,\frac{m}{2},$$

$$\dot{V}_k^{(2)}(t_j)=\psi_k^{(j)}-\frac{2a}{\lambda_k l}\left[\psi_j(0)-\psi_j(l)(-1)^k\right], j = 2\alpha, \alpha = 1,...,\frac{m}{2} \quad (3.8)$$

$$V_k^{(2)}(T) = \varphi_k^{(T)} - \frac{2a}{\lambda_k l}\left[\varphi_T(0) - \varphi_T(l)(-1)^k\right], \dot{V}_k^{(2)}(T) = \psi_k^{(T)} - \frac{2a}{\lambda_k l}\left[\psi_T(0) - \psi_T(l)(-1)^k\right] \quad (3.9)$$

$F_k^{(s)}(t)$, $V_k^{(s)}(t)$, $\varphi_k^{(i)}$, and $\psi_k^{(j)}$, $s = 1, 2$ denote the Fourier coefficients corresponding to the functions $F(x,t)$, $V(x,t)$, $\varphi_i(x)$, and$\psi_j(x)$.

The general solution to (3.2) and its derivative have the form

$$V_k^{(s)}(t) = V_k^{(s)}(0)\cos\lambda_k t + \frac{1}{\lambda_k}\dot{V}_k^{(s)}(0)\sin\lambda_k t + \frac{1}{\lambda_k}\int_0^t F_k^{(s)}(\tau)\sin\lambda_k(t-\tau)\,d\tau \quad (3.10)$$

$$\dot{V}_k^{(s)}(t) = -\lambda_k V_k^{(s)}(0)\sin\lambda_k t + \dot{V}_k^{(s)}(0)\cos\lambda_k t + \int_0^t F_k^{(s)}(\tau)\cos\lambda_k(t-\tau)\,d\tau, s = 1, 2$$

Taking into account the initial, intermediate and final conditions, from (3.10) we obtain that the functions$F_k^{(s)}(\tau)$, $s = 1, 2$, for each k must satisfy the following integral relations:

$$\int_0^T F_k^{(s)}(\tau)\sin\lambda_k(T-\tau)\,d\tau = \tilde{C}_{1k}^{(s)}(T), \int_0^T F_k^{(s)}(\tau)\cos\lambda_k(T-\tau)\,d\tau = \tilde{C}_{2k}^{(s)}(T),$$

$$\int_0^{t_i} F_k^{(s)}(\tau)\sin\lambda_k(t_i-\tau)\,d\tau = \tilde{C}_{1k}^{(s)}(t_i), i = 2\alpha - 1, \alpha = 1, ..., \frac{m}{2} \quad (3.11)$$

$$\int_0^{t_j} F_k^{(s)}(\tau)\cos\lambda_k(t_j-\tau)\,d\tau = \tilde{C}_{2k}^{(s)}(t_j), j = 2\alpha, \alpha = 1, ..., \frac{m}{2}$$

where we introduce the following notations:

$$\tilde{C}_{1k}^{(s)}(T) = \lambda_k V_k^{(s)}(T) - \lambda_k V_k^{(s)}(0)\cos\lambda_k T - \dot{V}_k^{(s)}(0)\sin\lambda_k T,$$

$$\tilde{C}_{2k}^{(s)}(T) = \dot{V}_k^{(s)}(T) + \lambda_k V_k^{(s)}(0)\sin\lambda_k T - \dot{V}_k^{(s)}(0)\cos\lambda_k T, s = 1, 2,$$

$$\tilde{C}_{1k}^{(s)}(t_i) = \lambda_k V_k^{(s)}(t_i) - \lambda_k V_k^{(s)}(0)\cos\lambda_k t_i - \dot{V}_k^{(s)}(0)\sin\lambda_k t_i, i = 2\alpha - 1, \alpha = 1, ..., \frac{m}{2} \quad (3.12)$$

$$\tilde{C}_{2k}^{(s)}(t_j) = \dot{V}_k^{(s)}(t_j) + \lambda_k V_k^{(s)}(0)\sin\lambda_k t_j - \dot{V}_k^{(s)}(0)\cos\lambda_k t_j, j = 2\alpha, \alpha = 1, ..., \frac{m}{2}$$

For a problem with a displacement of the left end with a fixed right end, substituting the expression for function $F_k^{(1)}(t)$ from (3.3.1) into relations (3.11) and integrating by parts, taking into account the matching conditions (1.7), we obtain hat function $\dot{\mu}(t)$ must satisfy the following integral relations for each k:

$$\int_0^T \dot{\mu}(\tau)\cos\lambda_k(T-\tau)d\tau = C_{1k}^{(1)}(T), \int_0^T \dot{\mu}(\tau)\sin\lambda_k(T-\tau)d\tau = C_{2k}^{(1)}(T),$$

$$\int_0^T \dot{\mu}(\tau)h_{1k}^{(i)}(\tau)d\tau = C_{1k}^{(1)}(t_i), i = 2\alpha-1, \alpha = 1,\dots,\frac{m}{2} \tag{3.13}$$

$$\int_0^T \dot{\mu}(\tau)h_{2k}^{(j)}(\tau)d\tau = C_{2k}^{(1)}(t_j), j = 2\alpha, \alpha = 1,\dots,\frac{m}{2}$$

where

$$C_{1k}^{(1)}(T)=\frac{\psi_0(0)}{\lambda_k}\sin\lambda_k T-\frac{l}{2a}\tilde{C}_{1k}^{(1)}(T), C_{2k}^{(1)}(T)=\frac{\psi_T(0)}{\lambda_k}-\frac{\psi_0(0)}{\lambda_k}\cos\lambda_k T+\frac{l}{2a}\tilde{C}_{2k}^{(1)}(T),$$

$$C_{1k}^{(1)}(t_i)=\frac{\psi_0(0)}{\lambda_k}\sin\lambda_k t_i-\frac{l}{2a}\tilde{C}_{1k}^{(1)}(t_i), C_{2k}^{(1)}(t_j)=\frac{\psi_j(0)}{\lambda_k}-\frac{\psi_0(0)}{\lambda_k}\cos\lambda_k t_j+\frac{l}{2a}\tilde{C}_{2k}^{(1)}(t_j) \tag{3.14}$$

$$h_{1k}^{(i)}(\tau)=\begin{cases}\cos\lambda_k(t_i-\tau), & 0\le\tau\le t_i,\\ 0, & t_i<\tau\le T,\end{cases} h_{2k}^{(j)}(\tau)=\begin{cases}\sin\lambda_k(t_j-\tau), & 0\le\tau\le t_j,\\ 0, & t_j<\tau\le T.\end{cases}$$

We introduce the following notations for further compact notation of integral relations (3.13):

$$\bar{H}_k^{(1)}(\tau)=\begin{pmatrix}\cos\lambda_k(T-\tau)\\ \sin\lambda_k(T-\tau)\\ h_{1k}^{(1)}(\tau)\\ h_{2k}^{(2)}(\tau)\\ \vdots\\ h_{1k}^{(m-1)}(\tau)\\ h_{2k}^{(m)}(\tau)\end{pmatrix}, C_k^{(1)}(t_1,\dots,t_m,T)=\begin{pmatrix}C_{1k}^{(1)}(T)\\ C_{2k}^{(1)}(T)\\ C_{1k}^{(1)}(t_1)\\ C_{2k}^{(1)}(t_1)\\ \vdots\\ C_{1k}^{(1)}(t_{m-1})\\ C_{2k}^{(1)}(t_m)\end{pmatrix} \tag{3.15}$$

Now, for the problem with displacement of both ends, substituting the expression of function $F_k^{(2)}(t)$ from (3.3.2) into relations (3.11) and integrating by parts, taking into account the matching conditions (1.7), we obtain that functions $\dot{\mu}(t)$ and $\dot{\nu}(t)$ for each k must satisfy the following integral relations:

$$\int_0^T \dot{\mu}(\tau)\cos\lambda_k(T-\tau)d\tau - \int_0^T \dot{\nu}(\tau)(-1)^\kappa \cos\lambda_k(T-\tau)d\tau = C_{1k}^{(2)}(T),$$

$$\int_0^T \dot{\mu}(\tau)\sin\lambda_k(T-\tau)d\tau - \int_0^T \dot{\nu}(\tau)(-1)^\kappa \sin\lambda_k(T-\tau)d\tau = C_{2k}^{(2)}(T),$$

$$\int_0^T \dot{\mu}(\tau) h_{1k}^{(i)}(\tau)d\tau - \int_0^T \dot{\nu}(\tau)(-1)^\kappa h_{1k}^{(i)}(\tau)d\tau = C_{1k}^{(2)}(t_i), i = 2\alpha - 1, \alpha = 1, \ldots, \frac{m}{2} \tag{3.16}$$

$$\int_0^T \dot{\mu}(\tau) h_{2k}^{(j)}(\tau)d\tau - \int_0^T \dot{\nu}(\tau)(-1)^\kappa h_{2k}^{(j)}(\tau)d\tau = C_{2k}^{(2)}(t_j), j = 2\alpha, \alpha = 1, \ldots, \frac{m}{2}$$

where

$$C_{1k}^{(2)}(T) = \frac{1}{\lambda_k}\left[-\frac{\lambda_k l}{2a}\widetilde{C}_{1k}^{(2)}(T) - (-1)^k \psi_0(l)\sin\lambda_k T + \psi_0(0)\sin\lambda_k T\right]$$

$$C_{2k}^{(2)}(T) = \frac{1}{\lambda_k}\left[\frac{\lambda_k l}{2a}\widetilde{C}_{2k}^{(2)}(T) + (-1)^k \psi_0(l)\cos\lambda_k T + \psi_T(0) - (-1)^k \psi_T(l) - \psi_0(0)\cos\lambda_k T\right] \tag{3.17}$$

$$C_{1k}^{(2)}(t_i) = \frac{1}{\lambda_k}\left[-\frac{\lambda_k l}{2a}\widetilde{C}_{1k}^{(2)}(t_i) - (-1)^k \psi_0(l)\sin\lambda_k t_i + \psi_0(0)\sin\lambda_k t_i\right]$$

$$C_{2k}^{(2)}(t_j) = \frac{1}{\lambda_k}\left[\frac{\lambda_k l}{2a}\widetilde{C}_{2k}^{(2)}(t_j) - (-1)^k \psi_j(l) + \psi_j(0) + (-1)^k \psi_0(l)\cos\lambda_k t_j - \psi_0(0)\cos\lambda_k t_j\right]$$

Note that expressions $\widetilde{C}_{1k}^{(2)}(T)$, $\widetilde{C}_{2k}^{(2)}(T)$, $\widetilde{C}_{1k}^{(2)}(t_i)$, $\widetilde{C}_{2k}^{(2)}(t_j)$, $h_{1k}^{(i)}(\tau)$and $h_{2k}^{(j)}(\tau)$ are given in (3.12) and (3.14). To write the integral relations (3.16) in a compact way, we introduce the following notation:

$$\overline{H}_k^{(2c)}(\tau) = \begin{pmatrix} \sin\lambda_k(T-\tau) & (-1)^{\kappa+1}\sin\lambda_k(T-\tau) \\ \cos\lambda_k(T-\tau) & (-1)^{\kappa+1}\cos\lambda_k(T-\tau) \\ h_{1k}^{(1)}(\tau) & (-1)^{\kappa+1} h_{1k}^{(1)}(\tau) \\ h_{2k}^{(2)}(\tau) & (-1)^{\kappa+1} h_{2k}^{(2)}(\tau) \\ \vdots & \vdots \\ h_{1k}^{(m-1)}(\tau) & (-1)^{\kappa+1} h_{1k}^{(m-1)}(\tau) \\ h_{2k}^{(m)}(\tau) & (-1)^{\kappa+1} h_{2k}^{(m)}(\tau) \end{pmatrix}, C_k^{(2c)} = \begin{pmatrix} C_{1k}^{(2)}(T) \\ C_{2k}^{(2)}(T) \\ C_{1k}^{(2)}(t_1) \\ C_{2k}^{(2)}(t_2) \\ \vdots \\ C_{1k}^{(2)}(t_{m-1}) \\ C_{2k}^{(2)}(t_m) \end{pmatrix} \tag{3.18}$$

In practice, the first few n harmonics of vibrations are usually selected, and the problem of control synthesis is solved using methods of finite-dimensional systems control theory. Therefore, we will continue this approach in fur her constructions.

Then, taking into account the introduced notations (3.15) and (3.18), for the first n harmonics relations (3.13) and (3.16) will be written as follows:

$$\int_0^T H_n^{(s)}(\tau)\, U_n^{(s)}(\tau)\, d\tau = \eta_n^{(s)}, s = 1, 2 \tag{3.19}$$

where

$$U_n^{(1)}(\tau) = \dot{\mu}_n^{(1)}(\tau) = \dot{\mu}(\tau)$$

,

$$U_n^{(2)}(\tau) = \begin{pmatrix} \dot{\mu}_n^{(2)}(\tau) \\ \dot{\nu}_n^{(2)}(\tau) \end{pmatrix} = \begin{pmatrix} \dot{\mu}(\tau) \\ \dot{\nu}(\tau) \end{pmatrix}, H_n^{(s)}(\tau) = \begin{pmatrix} \overline{H}_1^{(s)}(\tau) \\ \overline{H}_2^{(s)}(\tau) \\ \vdots \\ \overline{H}_n^{(s)}(\tau) \end{pmatrix}, \eta_n^{(s)} = \begin{pmatrix} C_1^{(s)}(t_1, \ldots, t_m, T) \\ C_2^{(s)}(t_1, \ldots, t_m, T) \\ \vdots \\ C_n^{(s)}(t_1, \ldots, t_m, T) \end{pmatrix} \tag{3.20}$$

with dimensions $H_n^{(s)}(\tau) - (n(m+2) \times s)$, $\eta_n^{(s)} - (n(m+2) \times 1)$.

Thus, the integral conditions (3.13) and (3.16), obtained for Problem 1_0 and Problem 2_0, respectively, are represented by condition (3.19).

From (3.19) follows the statement that the first n harmonics of system (3.2) with conditions (3.4)–(3.6) (or (3.7)–(3.9)) are completely controllable if and only if for any vector $\eta_n^{(s)}$ from (3.20) it is possible to find a control $U_n^{(s)}(t)$, $t \in [0, T]$, that satisfies condition (3.19).

Thus, in problem statement, the presence of intermediate values of the deflection functions and velocities of points on the string at different intermediate moments in time (is significant) leads to additional integral relations respect to the boundary control functions. The number of these integral relations is equal to the number of intermediate conditions. Moreover, the limits of the integrals are different and do not coincide with the limits of the main two integral relations, which complicates the problem compared to a similar problem without intermediate conditions. Consequently, by applying the method of separation of variables, the resulting optimal control problem for ordinary differential equations also significantly differs from standard similar problems. Therefore, methods from optimal control theory for finite-dimensional systems with multipoint intermediate conditions are employed.

Problems with integral constraints (3.19) for functionals (1.6.1) or (1.6.2) of optimal control can be considered as conditional extremum problems in the variational calculus. However, it is impossible to solve these problems using classical variational calculus methods, as the integral in (3.19) contains discontinuous functions.

SOLVING PROBLEMS

Since the functionals (1.6.1) or (1.6.2) are squares of the norm of some linear normed space, and the integral relations (3.19) generated by the control functions $U_n^{(s)}(t)$, $s = 1, 2$, are linear on the time interval $[0, T]$, then the problems of determining the optimal control for each $k = 1, 2, ..., n$ can be considered as a problem of moments (Krasovsky, 1968). Therefore, the solution can be constructed using the algorithm for solving the problem of moments.

To solve the finite-dimensional (for $k = 1, 2, ..., n$) moment problem for Problem 1 with functional (1.6.1) and integral conditions (3.13) (or (3.19) for $s = 1$), it is necessary to find the quantities $p_k^{(1)}$, $q_k^{(1)}$, $\gamma_{ik}^{(1)}$, $\gamma_{jk}^{(1)}$, $k = 1, ..., n, i = 2\alpha - 1, j = 2\alpha, \alpha = 1, ..., \frac{m}{2}$, related by condition

$$\sum_{k=1}^{n}\left[p_k^{(1)}C_{1k}^{(1)}(T)+q_k^{(1)}C_{2k}^{(1)}(T)+\sum_{\substack{i=2\alpha-1\\ \alpha=1}}^{\frac{m}{2}}\gamma_{ik}^{(1)}C_{1k}^{(1)}(t_i)+\sum_{\substack{j=2\alpha\\ \alpha=1}}^{\frac{m}{2}}\gamma_{jk}^{(1)}C_{2k}^{(1)}(t_j)\right] = 1 \tag{4.1}$$

For which

$$(\rho_{1n})^2 = \min_{(4.1)}\int_0^T (h_{1n}(\tau))^2 d\tau \tag{4.2}$$

where

$$h_{1n}(\tau)=\sum_{k=1}^{n}\left[p_k^{(1)}\cos\lambda_k(T-\tau)+q_k^{(1)}\sin\lambda_k(T-\tau)+\sum_{\substack{i=2\alpha-1\\ \alpha=1}}^{\frac{m}{2}}\gamma_{ik}^{(1)}h_{1k}^{(i)}(\tau)+\sum_{\substack{j=2\alpha\\ \alpha=1}}^{\frac{m}{2}}\gamma_{jk}^{(1)}h_{2k}^{(j)}(\tau)\right] \tag{4.3}$$

To determine the values $p_k^{(1)0}$, $q_k^{(1)0}$, $\gamma_{ik}^{(1)0}$, $\gamma_{jk}^{(1)0}$, $k = 1, ..., n$, $i = 2\alpha - 1, j = 2\alpha$, $\alpha = 1, ..., \frac{m}{2}$ that minimize (4.2) and satisfy (4.1), we introduce the function

$$f_{1n} = \int_0^T (h_{1n}(\tau))^2 d\tau + \beta_{1n}\left[\sum_{k=1}^{n}\left(p_k^{(1)}C_{1k}^{(1)}(T)+q_k^{(1)}C_{2k}^{(1)}(T)+\sum_{\substack{i=2\alpha-1\\ \alpha=1}}^{\frac{m}{2}}\gamma_{ik}^{(1)}C_{1k}^{(1)}(t_i)+\sum_{\substack{j=2\alpha\\ \alpha=1}}^{\frac{m}{2}}\gamma_{jk}^{(1)}C_{2k}^{(1)}(t_j)\right)-1\right]$$

where β_{1n} is the Lagrange undetermined multiplier. Based on the undetermined multipliers method, calculating the derivatives of function f_{1n} with respect to $p_k^{(1)}$, $q_k^{(1)}$, $\gamma_{ik}^{(1)}$, $\gamma_{jk}^{(1)}$, $k = 1, ..., n$, $i = 2\alpha - 1$, $j = 2\alpha$, $\alpha = 1, ..., \frac{m}{2}$, and equating them to zero, taking into account the notation (4.3), (3.14), after adding condition (4.1) to the obtained equations, we obtain a closed system of $2n + mn + 1$ algebraic equations with respect to the same number of unknown quantities $p_k^{(1)}$, $q_k^{(1)}$, $\gamma_{ik}^{(1)}$, $\gamma_{jk}^{(1)}$, $k = 1, ..., n$, $i = 2\alpha - 1, j = 2\alpha$, $\alpha = 1, ..., \frac{m}{2}$, and β_{1n}:

$$\sum_{\sigma=1}^{n}\left[a_{\sigma k}^{(1)}p_\sigma^{(1)}+b_{\sigma k}^{(1)}q_\sigma^{(1)}+\sum_{\substack{s=2\alpha-1\\ \alpha=1}}^{\frac{m}{2}}c_{1\sigma k}^{(1s)}\gamma_{s\sigma}^{(1)}+\sum_{\substack{r=2\alpha\\ \alpha=1}}^{\frac{m}{2}}c_{2\sigma k}^{(1r)}\gamma_{r\sigma}^{(1)}\right] = -\frac{\beta_{1n}}{2}C_{1k}^{(1)}(T)$$

$$\sum_{\sigma=1}^{n}\left[d_{\sigma k}^{(1)}p_{\sigma}^{(1)}+e_{\sigma k}^{(1)}q_{\sigma}^{(1)}+\sum_{\substack{s=2\alpha-1\\ \alpha=1}}^{\frac{m}{2}}f_{1\sigma k}^{(1s)}\gamma_{s\sigma}^{(1)}+\sum_{\substack{r=2\alpha\\ \alpha=1}}^{\frac{m}{2}}f_{2\sigma k}^{(1r)}\gamma_{r\sigma}^{(1)}\right]=-\frac{\beta_{1n}}{2}C_{2k}^{(1)}(T)$$

$$\sum_{\sigma=1}^{n}\left[a_{\sigma k}^{(1i)}p_{\sigma}^{(1)}+b_{\sigma k}^{(1i)}q_{\sigma}^{(1)}+\sum_{\substack{s=2\alpha-1\\ \alpha=1}}^{\frac{m}{2}}c_{1\sigma k}^{(si)}\gamma_{s\sigma}^{(1)}+\sum_{\substack{r=2\alpha\\ \alpha=1}}^{\frac{m}{2}}c_{2\sigma k}^{(ri)}\gamma_{r\sigma}^{(1)}\right]=-\frac{\beta_{n}}{2}C_{1k}(t_i)$$

$$\sum_{\sigma=1}^{n}\left[d_{\sigma k}^{(1j)}p_{\sigma}^{(1)}+e_{\sigma k}^{(1j)}q_{\sigma}^{(1)}+\sum_{\substack{s=2\alpha-1\\ \alpha=1}}^{\frac{m}{2}}f_{1\sigma k}^{(sj)}\gamma_{s\sigma}^{(1)}+\sum_{\substack{r=2\alpha\\ \alpha=1}}^{\frac{m}{2}}f_{2\sigma k}^{(rj)}\gamma_{r\sigma}^{(1)}\right]=-\frac{\beta_{n}}{2}C_{2k}(t_j) \tag{4.4}$$

$$\sum_{k=1}^{n}\left[p_{k}^{(1)}C_{1k}^{(1)}(T)+q_{k}^{(1)}C_{2k}^{(1)}(T)+\sum_{\substack{i=2\alpha-1\\ \alpha=1}}^{\frac{m}{2}}\gamma_{ik}^{(1)}C_{1k}^{(1)}(t_i)+\sum_{\substack{j=2\alpha\\ \alpha=1}}^{\frac{m}{2}}\gamma_{jk}^{(1)}C_{2k}^{(1)}(t_j)\right]=1$$

where

$$a_{\sigma k}^{(1)}=\int_0^T\cos\lambda_\sigma(T-\tau)\cos\lambda_k(T-\tau)d\tau,\ b_{\sigma k}^{(1)}=\int_0^T\sin\lambda_\sigma(T-\tau)\cos\lambda_k(T-\tau)d\tau,$$

$$c_{1\sigma k}^{(1s)}=\int_0^T h_{1\sigma}^{(1s)}(\tau)\cos\lambda_k(T-\tau)d\tau,\ c_{2\sigma k}^{(1r)}=\int_0^T h_{2\sigma}^{(1r)}(\tau)\cos\lambda_k(T-\tau)d\tau,$$

$$d_{\sigma k}^{(1)}=\int_0^T\cos\lambda_\sigma(T-\tau)\sin\lambda_k(T-\tau)d\tau,\ e_{\sigma k}^{(1)}=\int_0^T\sin\lambda_\sigma(T-\tau)\sin\lambda_k(T-\tau)d\tau,$$

$$f_{1\sigma k}^{(1s)}=\int_0^T h_{1\sigma}^{(s)}(\tau)\sin\lambda_k(T-\tau)d\tau,\ f_{2\sigma k}^{(1s)}=\int_0^T h_{2\sigma}^{(r)}(\tau)\sin\lambda_k(T-\tau)d\tau,$$

$$a_{\sigma k}^{(1i)}=\int_0^T h_{1k}^{(i)}(\tau)\cos\lambda_\sigma(T-\tau)d\tau,\ b_{\sigma k}^{(1i)}=\int_0^T h_{1k}^{(i)}(\tau)\sin\lambda_\sigma(T-\tau)d\tau,\ c_{1\sigma k}^{(si)}=\int_0^T h_{1\sigma}^{(s)}(\tau)h_{1k}^{(i)}(\tau)d\tau,$$

$$c_{2\sigma k}^{(ri)} = \int_0^T h_{1\sigma}^{(r)}(\tau) h_{2k}^{(i)}(\tau) d\tau \tag{4.5}$$

$$d_{\sigma k}^{(1j)} = \int_0^T h_{2k}^{(j)}(\tau) \cos\lambda_\sigma (T-\tau) d\tau, e_{\sigma k}^{(1j)} = \int_0^T h_{2k}^{(j)}(\tau) \sin\lambda_\sigma (T-\tau) d\tau,$$

$$f_{1\sigma k}^{(sj)} = \int_0^T h_{1\sigma}^{(s)}(\tau) h_{2k}^{(j)}(\tau) d\tau, f_{2\sigma k}^{(rj)} = \int_0^T h_{2\sigma}^{(r)}(\tau) h_{2k}^{(j)}(\tau) d\tau$$

Let the quantities $p_k^{(1)\,0}$, $q_k^{(1)\,0}$, $\gamma_{ik}^{(1)0}$, $\gamma_{jk}^{(1)0}$, $k = 1, ..., n$, $i = 2\alpha - 1$, $j = 2\alpha$, $\alpha = 1, ..., \frac{m}{2}$, and β_{1n}^0 be the solution to the closed system of algebraic equations (4.4). Then, according to (4.3), (4.2) we have

$$h_{1n}^0(\tau) = \sum_{k=1}^n \left[p_k^{(1)\,0} \cos\lambda_k (T-\tau) + q_k^{(1)\,0} \sin\lambda_k (T-\tau) + \sum_{\substack{i=2\alpha-1 \\ \alpha=1}}^{\frac{m}{2}} \gamma_{ik}^{(1)0} h_{1k}^{(i)}(\tau) + \sum_{\substack{j=2\alpha \\ \alpha=1}}^{\frac{m}{2}} \gamma_{jk}^{(1)0} h_{2k}^{(j)}(\tau) \right]$$

$$(\rho_{1n}^0)^2 = \int_0^T (h_{1n}^0(\tau))^2 d\tau \tag{4.6}$$

The optimal functions $\dot{\mu}_n^{(1)0}(\tau)$ for any $n = 1, 2, ...$ are presented in the form:

$$\dot{\mu}_n^{(1)0}(\tau) = \frac{1}{(\rho_{1n}^0)^2} h_{1n}^0(\tau)$$

From here we have

$$\mu_n^{(1)0}(\tau) = \frac{1}{(\rho_{1n}^0)^2} \int_0^t h_{1n}^0(\tau) d\tau + \varphi_0(0), \quad t \in [0, T] \tag{4.7}$$

where the integration constant is obtained from the matching condition (1.7).

To solve the finite-dimensional (at $k = 1, 2, ..., n$) moment problem for Problem 2 with functional (1.6.2) and integral conditions (3.16) (or (3.19) at $s = 2$), it is necessary to find the quantities $p_k^{(2)}$, $q_k^{(2)}$, $\gamma_{ik}^{(2)}$, $\gamma_{jk}^{(2)}$, $k = 1, ..., n$, $i = 2\alpha - 1$, $j = 2\alpha$, $\alpha = 1, ..., \frac{m}{2}$, related by condition

$$\sum_{k=1}^n \left[p_k^{(2)} C_{1k}^{(2)}(T) + q_k^{(2)} C_{2k}^{(2)}(T) + \sum_{\substack{i=2\alpha-1 \\ \alpha=1}}^{\frac{m}{2}} \gamma_{ik}^{(2)} C_{1k}^{(2)}(t_i) + \sum_{\substack{j=2\alpha \\ \alpha=1}}^{\frac{m}{2}} \gamma_{jk}^{(2)} C_{2k}^{(2)}(t_j) \right] = 1 \tag{4.8}$$

for which

$$(\rho_{2n})^2 = \min_{(4.10)} \int_0^T [h_{1n}^2(\tau)+h_{2n}^2(\tau)]d\tau \tag{4.9}$$

where

$$h_{1n}(\tau)= \sum_{k=1}^{n}\left[p_k^{(1)}\cos\lambda_k(T-\tau)+q_k^{(1)}\sin\lambda_k(T-\tau)+\sum_{\substack{i=2\alpha-1\\ \alpha=1}}^{\frac{m}{2}}\gamma_{ik}^{(1)}h_{1k}^{(i)}(\tau)+\sum_{\substack{j=2\alpha\\ \alpha=1}}^{\frac{m}{2}}\gamma_{jk}^{(1)}h_{2k}^{(j)}(\tau)\right]$$

$$h_{2n}(\tau)= \sum_{k=1}^{n}(-1)^{k+1}\left[p_k^{(1)}\cos\lambda_k(T-\tau)+q_k^{(1)}\sin\lambda_k(T-\tau)+\sum_{\substack{i=2\alpha-1\\ \alpha=1}}^{\frac{m}{2}}\gamma_{ik}^{(1)}h_{1k}^{(i)}(\tau)+\sum_{\substack{j=2\alpha\\ \alpha=1}}^{\frac{m}{2}}\gamma_{jk}^{(1)}h_{2k}^{(j)}(\tau)\right] \tag{4.10}$$

Solving the problem of minimizing the functional (4.9) with condition (4.8) by analogy with the above, we find the desired values $p_k^{(2)\,0}, q_k^{(2)\,0}, \gamma_{ik}^{(2)0}, \gamma_{jk}^{(2)0}, k = 1,..., n, i = 2\alpha - 1, j = 2\alpha, \alpha = 1,..., \frac{m}{2}$. Next, from (4.9) and (4.10) we have:

$$(\rho_{2n}^0)^2 = \int_0^T \left[(h_{1n}^0(\tau))^2 + (h_{2n}^0(\tau))^2\right]d\tau$$

$$h_{1n}^0(\tau)= \sum_{k=1}^{n}\left[p_k^{(1)0}\cos\lambda_k(T-\tau)+q_k^{(1)0}\sin\lambda_k(T-\tau)+\sum_{\substack{i=2\alpha-1\\ \alpha=1}}^{\frac{m}{2}}\gamma_{ik}^{(1)0}h_{1k}^{(i)}(\tau)+\sum_{\substack{j=2\alpha\\ \alpha=1}}^{\frac{m}{2}}\gamma_{jk}^{(1)0}h_{2k}^{(j)}(\tau)\right] \tag{4.11}$$

$$h_{2n}^0(\tau)= \sum_{k=1}^{n}(-1)^{k+1}\left[p_k^{(2)0}\cos\lambda_k(T-\tau)+q_k^{(2)0}\sin\lambda_k(T-\tau)+\sum_{\substack{i=2\alpha-1\\ \alpha=1}}^{\frac{m}{2}}\gamma_{ik}^{(2)0}h_{1k}^{(i)}(\tau)+\sum_{\substack{j=2\alpha\\ \alpha=1}}^{\frac{m}{2}}\gamma_{jk}^{(2)0}h_{2k}^{(j)}(\tau)\right]$$

Thus, optimal controls$\mu_n^{(2)0}(t)$and$\nu_n^{(2)0}(t)$, $\tau \in [0, T]$, are represented in the form:

$$\mu_n^{(2)\,0}(t) = \frac{1}{(\rho_{2n}^0)^2}\int_0^t h_{1n}^0(\tau)d\tau + \varphi_0(0), \nu_n^{(2)\,0}(t) = \frac{1}{(\rho_{2n}^0)^2}\int_0^t h_{2n}^0(\tau)d\tau + \varphi_0(l) \tag{4.12}$$

Therefore, having explicit forms of the optimal boundary control function $\mu_n^{(s)0}(t)$ and $\nu_n^{(s)0}(t), \tau \in [0, T]$, $s = 1, 2$, we can construct the corresponding deflection function $Q_n^{(s)0}(x,t)$. Substituting the obtained expressions for optimal controls $\mu_n^{(s)0}(t)$ and $\nu_n^{(s)0}(t)$, $\tau \in [0, T]$, $s = 1, 2$, into (3.3.1) and (3.3.2), and expression obtained for $F_k^{(s)\,0}(t)$ into (3.10), we have the function $V_k^{(s)0}(t), t \in [0, T], s = 1, 2, k = 1,..., n$. Further, from formula (3.1) we have

$$V_n^{(s)\,0}(x,t)= \sum_{k=1}^{n} V_k^{(s)\,0}(t)\sin\frac{\pi k}{l}x \tag{4.13}$$

where

$$V_k^{(s)\,0}(t) = V_k^{(s)}(0)\cos\lambda_k t + \frac{1}{\lambda_k}\dot{V}_k^{(s)}(0)\sin\lambda_k t + \frac{1}{\lambda_k}\int_0^t F_k^{(s)\,0}(\tau)\sin\lambda_k(t-\tau)\,d\tau$$

and from (2.4.1) and (2.4.2) it follows that the functions $W_n^{(s)0}(x,t)$, $s = 1, 2$, take the following form:

$$W_n^{(1)\,0}(x,t) = \left(1-\frac{x}{l}\right)\mu_n^{(1)\,0}(t)$$

$$W_n^{(2)\,0}(x,t) = \left[\nu_n^{(2)\,0}(t) - \mu_n^{(2)\,0}(t)\right]\frac{x}{l} + \mu_n^{(2)\,0}(t) \tag{4.14}$$

Further, according to (2.1), taking into account (4.13) and (4.14), we have

$$Q_n^{(1)\,0}(x,t) = \sum_{k=1}^{n} V_k^{(1)\,0}(t)\sin\frac{\pi k}{l}x + \left(1-\frac{x}{l}\right)\mu_n^{(1)\,0}(t)$$

$$Q_n^{(2)\,0}(x,t) = \sum_{k=1}^{n} V_k^{(2)\,0}(t)\sin\frac{\pi k}{l}x + \left[\nu_n^{(2)\,0}(t) - \mu_n^{(2)\,0}(t)\right]\frac{x}{l} + \mu_n^{(2)\,0}(t) \tag{4.15}$$

Thus, for the first n harmonics, the optimal string deflection functions $Q_n^{(1)\,0}(x,t)$ and $Q_n^{(2)\,0}(x,t)$ are represented by formula (4.15).

CONCLUSION

The constructive method is proposed to construct an optimal boundary control for the vibration process of a homogeneous string with given intermediate values of the deflection functions and velocities of the string points at different intermediate time moments and with a criterion for the boundary energy integral. The proposed approach to optimal boundary control of string vibrations using the Fourier method can be extended to other non-one-dimensional vibratory systems. The obtained results can be used to design optimal boundary control of vibrations in physical and technological systems.

ACKNOWLEDGMENT

This research by Svetlana V. Solodusha was supported by the Russian Academy of Sciences [State Assignment Project no. FWEU-2021-0006 of the Fundamental Research Program of the Russian Federation 2021–2030].

REFERENCES

Abdukarimov, M. F. (2013). On optimal boundary control of displacements in the process of forced vibrations on both ends of a string. [In Russian]. *Dokl. Akad. Nauk Republic of Tadzhikistan*, *56*, 612–618.

Abdukarimov, M. F. (2014). On the optimal boundary control produced by shifting the process of forced vibrations at one end of a string while the other is free. [In Russian]. *Dokl. Akad. Nauk Republic of Tadzhikistan*, *57*, 280–286.

Ashchepkov, L. T. (1981). Optimal control of a system with intermediate conditions. [In Russian]. *Applied Mathematics and Mechanics*, *45*, 215–222.

Barseghyan, V., & Solodusha, S. (2021a). Optimal Boundary Control of String Vibrations with Given Shape of Deflection at a Certain Moment of Time. *Lecture Notes in Computer Science*, *12755*, 299–313. DOI: 10.1007/978-3-030-77876-7_20

Barseghyan, V., & Solodusha, S. (2022). Control of String Vibrations by Displacement of One End with the Other End Fixed, Given the Deflection Form at an Intermediate Moment of Time. *Axioms*, *11*(4), 157. DOI: 10.3390/axioms11040157

Barseghyan, V. R. (2012). Control of stage by stage changing linear dynamic systems. *Yugoslav Journal of Operations Research*, *22*(1), 31–39. DOI: 10.2298/YJOR111019002B

Barseghyan, V. R. (2016a). *Upravlenie sostavnykh dinamicheskikh sistem i sistem s mnogotochechnymi promezhutochnymi usloviyami* [Control of compound dynamic systems and of systems with multipoint intermediate conditions]. Nauka. (In Russian)

Barseghyan, V. R. (2016b). On the controllability and observability of linear dynamic systems with variable structure. In *Proceedings of the 2016 International Conference Stability and Oscillations of Nonlinear Control Systems (Pyatnitskiy's Conference)* (pp. 1–3), IEEE, Moscow, Russia, 1–3 June 2016. DOI: 10.1109/STAB.2016.7541163

Barseghyan, V. R. (2018). The Control Problem for Stepwise Changing Linear Systems of Loaded Differential Equations with Unseparated Multipoint Intermediate Conditions. *Mechanics of Solids*, *53*(6), 615–622. DOI: 10.3103/S0025654418060031

Barseghyan, V. R. (2019). Control Problem of String Vibrations with Inseparable Multipoint Conditions at Intermediate Points in Time. *Mechanics of Solids*, *54*(8), 1216–1226. DOI: 10.3103/S0025654419080120

Barseghyan, V. R. (2022). Problems of Boundary Control and Optimal Control of String Vibrations with Multipoint Intermediate Conditions on the State Functions. *Proceedings of the Steklov Institute of Mathematics, 319*(S1), S66–S79. DOI: 10.1134/S0081543822060074

Barseghyan, V. R., & Solodusha, S. V. (2021b). On One Problem in Optimal Boundary Control for String Vibrations with a Given Velocity of Points at an Intermediate Moment of Time. In *Proceedings of the 2021 International Russian Automation Conference (RusAutoCon)* (pp. 343–349), IEEE, Sochi, Russia, 5–11 September 2021. DOI: 10.1109/RusAutoCon52004.2021.9537514

Barsegyan, V. R. (2020). The Problem of Optimal Control of String Vibrations. *International Applied Mechanics, 56*(4), 471–480. DOI: 10.1007/s10778-020-01030-w

Butkovsky, A. G. (1965). *Teoriya optimal'nogo upravleniya sistemami s raspredelennymi parametrami* [Theory of Optimal Control for Systems with Distributed Parameters]. Nauka. (In Russian)

Butkovsky, A. G. (1975). *Metody upravleniya sistemami s raspredelennymi parametrami* [Control Methods for Systems with Distributed Parameters]. Nauka. (In Russian)

Dreglea, A. I., & Sidorov, N. A. (2018). Integral Equations in Identification of External Force and Heat Source Density Dynamics. *Bul. Acad. Stiinte Repub. Mold. Mat., 3*, 68–77.

Gibkina, N. V., Sidorov, M. V., & Stadnikova, A. V. (2016). Optimal'noe granichnoe upravlenie kolebaniyami odnorodnoy struny [Optimal boundary control of vibrations of uniform string] [In Russian]. *Radioelektronics and Informatics, 2*, 3–11.

Il'in, V. A., & Moiseev, E. I. (2005). Optimization of boundary controls of string vibrations. *Russian Mathematical Surveys, 60*(6), 1093–1119. DOI: 10.1070/RM2005v060n06ABEH004283

Korzyuk, V. I., & Kozlovskia, I. S. (2010a). Dvukhtochechnaya granichnaya zadacha dlya uravneniya kolebaniya struny s zadannoy skorost'yu v nekotoryy moment vremeni. I [Two-point boundary problem for the equation of string vibration with the given velocity at the certain moment of time. I] [In Russian]. *Proceedings of the Institute of Mathematics NAS of Belarus, 18*, 22–35.

Korzyuk, V. I., & Kozlovskia, I. S. (2010b). Dvukhtochechnaya granichnaya zadacha dlya uravneniya kolebaniya struny s zadannoy skorost'yu v nekotoryy moment vremeni. II [Two-point boundary problem for the equation of string vibration with the given velocity at the certain moment of time. II] [In Russian]. *Proceedings of the Institute of Mathematics NAS of Belarus, 19*, 62–70.

Krabs, W. (1995). *Optimal Control of Undamped Linear Vibrations.* Heldermann.

Krasovsky, N. N. (1968). *Teoriya upravleniya dvizheniem* [The Theory of Motion Control]. Nauka. (In Russian)

Li, X. (2008). Numerical Solution of an Initial-Boundary Value Problem with Nonlocal Condition for the Wave Equation. *Journal of Mathematical Sciences, 2*(3), 281–292.

Moiseev, E. I., & Kholomeeva, A. A. (2013). On an optimal boundary control problem with a dynamic boundary condition. *Differential Equations, 49*(5), 640–644. DOI: 10.1134/S0012266113050133

Sadybekov, M. A., & Yessirkegenov, N. A. (2016). Boundary-Value Problems for Wave Equations with Data on the Whole Boundary. *Electron J. Diff. Eq., 281.*

Sirazetdinov, T. K. (1977). *Optimizatsiya sistem s raspredelennymi parametrami* [Optimization of Systems with Distributed Parameters]. Nauka. (In Russian)

Tikhonov, A. N., & Samarskii, A. A. (1963). *Equations of mathematical physics*. Pergamon Press Ltd.

Yang, K. J., Hong, K. S., & Matsuno, F. (2004). Robust adaptive boundary control of an axially moving string under a spatiotemporally varying tension. *Journal of Sound and Vibration*, *273*(4-5), 1007–1029. DOI: 10.1016/S0022-460X(03)00519-4

Znamenskaya, L. N. (2004). *Upravlenie uprugimi kolebaniyami* [Control of elastic vibrations]. Fizmatlit. (In Russian)

Chapter 13
Solar Panel Tilting System in IoT Using Maximum Power Point Tracking

Singaravelan Shanmugasundaram
https://orcid.org/0000-0003-4353-2261
PSR Engineering College, India

D. Murugan
Manonmaniam Sundaranar University, India

S. Hemasilviavinothini
Nandha College of Technology, India

R. Srinivasan Balu
AAA College of Engineering and Technology, India

U. Kumaran
Saveetha Engineering College, India

P. Gopalsamy
PSR Engineering College, India

S. Balaganesh
PSR Engineering College, India

M. Alamelu Mangai
Francis Xavier Engineering College, India

ABSTRACT

The optimization goal is to increase the amount of generated energy with the help of photovoltaic system considering the tracking system's consumption. Determination of the tilt angle and azimuth angle trajectories is described as a nonlinear and bounded optimization problem. For collection of solar energy we have used sensors (LDR) for tracking of sun's path to make sure that the panel should be placed in MPPTto observe more efficiency and make sure that the panel should be placed in MPPT point.This is definitely a more cost effective solution than purchasing additional solar panels. The maximum power point tracking (MPPT) method is used to track the maximum amount of solar energy generated by the sun. In the world to avoid the dependency on non - renewable resources, solar energy is rapidly gaining the focus. This system will rotate according to the position of the sun. The operation of the experimental model of the device is based on a servo motor which is intelligently controlled by an Arduino UNO board that moves a mini PV panel according to the rotation of the sun.

DOI: 10.4018/979-8-3693-7812-0.ch013

INTRODUCTION

In remote areas the sun is a cheap source of electricity because it uses solar cells to produce electricity. The output of solar cells depends on the intensity of sunlight to get the maximum efficiency. The solar panel remains according to the position of the sun during the whole day. But due to rotation of earth those panels can't maintain their position always in front of sun. This problem results in decrease of efficiency. In order to get a constant output, an automated system is required which should be able to rotate the solar panel according to sun's position. Automatic solar tracker is made as a prototype to solve the problem that mentioned above. Automatic solar tracker is a prototype which rotates according to the position of the sun. The unique feature of this prototype is that, it takes position of the sun as a guiding source instead of earth's rotation. The solar power is used interchangeably with solar energy but refers more specifically to the conversion of sunlight into electricity by photovoltaic cells. It has become a popular investment for companies as well as for residential users. This demand has stimulated the research for increasing the overall output power of photovoltaic

(PV) system causing people all over the globe to work hard on making the technology more efficient as well as cost effective. Solar panels are photovoltaic cells which gives voltage directly if you place them in sunlight. "Energy is non been created or not been destroyed". This is a universal law said by newton which has been proved by science. this is applicable for all things in energy sector the various forms of energy is converted into electrical energy in the process of transformation of various energy into electrical energy nonrenewable resources, after some time these resources are run out or replenished in human life we need to focused on renewable energy which are given by nature and don't make harm to the same nature so many energy have been identified from that solar energy is one of best energy from renewable energy this energy is not replenished until the sun existed.

1.1 Types of Solar Panels and Solar Tracking Techniques

Modern solar tracking methods can be classified into the following types.

1.1.1 Single Axis Solar Panel

Solar tracking systems can be classified by the mode of their motion. These tracking systems have the PV surface that can be rotated/tilted around axes to derive a proper angle that can help them get the maximum sunlight. When movement or adjustment of the PV surface happens by rotating around one axis, it is called single-axis tracking. When the movement of the PV surface happens around two axes simultaneously, it is called dual-axis tracking. Single axis solar tracker is a device that positions the panel in the direction of the sunlight to draw the maximum energy possible. As the name suggests, the tracker helps the solar panels to flex on the axis and change their angle with the Sun's direction. Simply put, the single axis solar tracking system allows the panels to move from east to west and improve energy production. It is much more efficient than fixed solar panel systems because compared to the latter, the single axis trackers generate up to 25-35% more electricity.

Figure 1. Single axis solar panel

1.1.2 Dual Axis Solar Panel

The dual axis trackers collect energy from the sun from the East, West, North, and South angles. They function on two axes – 'primary' and 'secondary'. One axis helps the solar tracker to move from East to West, and the other helps the tracker to move from North to South. Hence, they are known as 'dual-axis' solar trackers. You'll be surprised to know that the dual axis trackers can generate up to 40% more electricity than the unmovable solar panel systems that stay at a fixed position. A dual axis solar panel is a type of solar tracker. Solar trackers are used to track the sun as it moves through the sky. Solar trackers can be split into several categories based upon the type of actuation and axis of rotation. A typical dual axis solar panel can generate up to 40% more electricity than a static type, but costs perhaps 100% more and has larger maintenance costs. The amount of power required to move the solar panel must be deducted from the total amount of power gained in order to accurately record the total power gain.

Figure 2. Dual axis solar panel

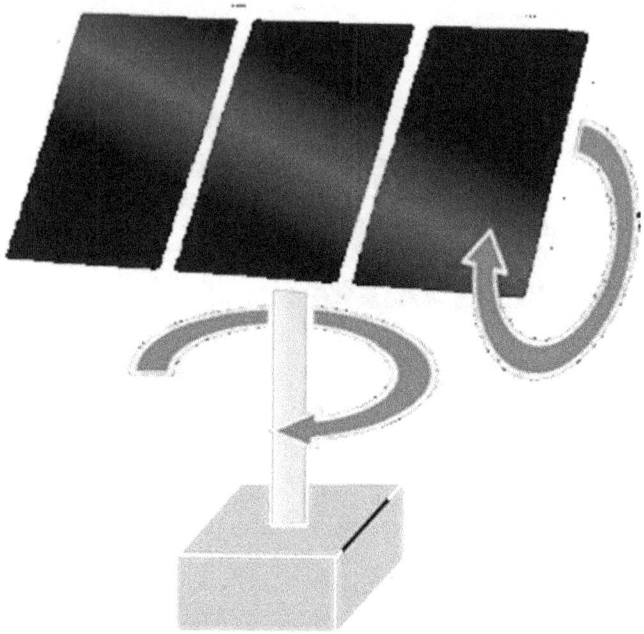

1.1.3 Active Solar Tracking

The words active and passive occur commonly in electrical engineering. Those devices which must be provided with source of energy for their full performance are classed as active. Those which do not need any external source of energy are called passive. Thus, active trackers must be provided with energy for their actuators to move. That energy may even be part of the energy harvested by the PV system they are driving. The actuator systems may consist of motors and other elaborate mechanical devices. Most tracking systems installations are active solar tracking systems. (Mamun et all, 2022). These tracking systems have an energy supply to run a motor or mechanical device. It helps to tilt the attached solar panels directly.

- An active solar tracker determines the intensity of the sunlight by utilizing light sensors.
- Then, its system evaluates where the solar modules should be oriented.
- Active solar trackers are ideally suitable for large and complicated solar arrays.

Figure 3. Active solar tracking

1.1.4 Passive Solar Tracking

Passive solar trackers will also track the sun, but they do it without requiring any external energy source, at least from us. How can they move the payload without energy. They do not! They too get their energy from the sun, but not the one we have harvested. Most often, the sun's heat is used to cause expansion of a fixed mass of material, Eg: a low boiling point gas. The expansion causes a mechanical movement of an actuator. A pair or more of actuators are positioned so that they expand differentially depending of the orientation of the payload tracker with respect to the sun. Differential expansion causes the tracker to move closer to the direction of the sun. If it derives its power from the sun how does it move at sunrise and sunset when there is virtually no solar energy to drive this dumb device. It is manually retained in a near vertical position with a self- releasing tie-down at night so that at daybreak when it gets sufficient differential energy, it can move down into position and then keep tracking. (Liu et all 2018) Passive trackers are OK for simple PV systems but unfit for concentration type PVsystems which demand high aiming accuracy. Instead of gas expansion systems, actuators made of shape memory alloys (SMA), have also been used.

Figure 4. Passive solar tracking

2. LITERATURE SURVEY

(Amine Allouhi, et al . 2022) Photovoltaic (PV) technologies have achieved commercial acceptance, technological maturity and foresee a leading role in the current energy transition to combat the adverse environmental issues posed by fossil fuel-based power generation. The market of photovoltaic technology is rapidly evolving with a Compound Annual Growth Rate (CAGR) equal to 34% between 2010 and 2020. This review presents updated information on the solar PV development from the material, market, and engineering perspectives. Cell efficiencies, market trends, cost of PV systems, and global research efforts over the last years are provided. Real monitored performances reveal a decrease of up to 10% of PV power output due to soiling effects.

This paper discusses soiling mitigation approaches, a critical technical pathway to improve the power output of solar PV systems. A particular emphasis was put into recent and novel experimental and numerical investigations pursued by the PV research community related to heat management in PV systems. Finally, critical challenges and prospects of the solar PV technology are highlighted and discussed. the present review paper is to provide a comprehensive assessment of the solar PV technologies and its global market with updated information on relevant materials, observed efficiencies, and costs evolution.

(V.Karthikeyan, et al . 2020) Temperature reduction in a photovoltaic module can improve its efficiency. This paper presents a radiation based photovoltaic module cooled by using composite phase change material that are not in direct contact with the photovoltaic module. A thermal heat transfer network is developed which improves efficiency of the photovoltaic module by using radiation mode to eliminate the issue of phase change material re-conduction, thereby controlling excess thermal energy stagnation in the module. Pure phase change material and composite phase change material are investigated and compared by integrating them 0.6 cm behind the photovoltaic module and performing simulations to determine the optimal thickness of the phase change material matrix. It was found that by using composite phase change material, the thermal resistance between the photovoltaic and the phase change material could be reduced and the photovoltaic module temperature decreased, due to the higher thermal conductivity of the composite phase change material.

The simulated efficiency and temperature of the photovoltaic module with composite phase change material installed at the optimum thickness of 2.5 cm were 14.75% and 47.81 C, respectively. The numerical simulation of the new PV-PCM setup was validated experimentally, and simulation results were accurate within an average of 0.4 C.

(Kangmin Lee, et al . 2020) Transparent solar cells are attractive energy conversion devices because they can be used in various applications in our daily life, such as building- integrated photovoltaics (BIPV) and vehicle-integrated photovoltaics (VIPV). To date, transparent solar cells based on organic photovoltaics, dye-sensitized solar cells, and perovskite solar cells have been developed. Because most materials that are used in these solar cells could be easily made into thin films through the solution process, these thin films have light transmission properties. However, the transparent solar cells developed to date have limitations in power conversionefficiency (PCE) and stability. Furthermore, they exhibit specific colors as a result of the colors of the polymers or dyes used. To address this issue, some researchers have developed selective ultraviolet (UV)- or near-infrared (NIR)- absorbing transparent solar cells to fabricate neutral-colored transparent solar cells. However, UV- or NIR-absorbing transparent solar cells have demonstrated very low PCEs (<2%) until now. Accordingly, a different approach is required to develop transparent solar cells with neutral color, high PCE, and long-term stability.

As a method to develop neutral-colored transparent solar cells with high PCE and long-term stability, crystalline-silicon (*c*-Si)-based transparent solar cells could be considered. *c*-Si is a representative semiconductor widely used in various devices, such as transistors, integrated circuit chips, and solar cells owing to its abundance and high physical stability.

(Jiaxin Zhao, et al. 2019) In recent years, the utilization of phase change materials (PCMs) in photovoltaic (PV) module for thermal regulation has attracted wide attention in this field, as the hybrid PV-PCM technology can not only achieve higher photoelectric conversion efficiency but also make it possible to extract thermalenergy stored in PCMs for cascade utilization. Although substantial research has been carried out on PV-PCM systems, the promise of practical application is still far from clear with some barriers unsolved, such as PCMs which need further improvements in both technical and economical view. In this paper, a comprehensive literature review of the state-of-the-art aspects of PV-PCM systems is presented, with the focus on technology overview and materials selection. The concept of hybrid PV-PCM system is first discussed with its general configuration and energy balance, to figure out the key factors affecting its performance. Besides, the development route of PV-PCM research is outlined through a comprehensive review of 104 research articles during 2004–2018, clarifying the representative achievements and existing problems in each stage.

Finally, the challenges and prospects of future research on PV-PCM systems are raised, advocating that more attention should be addressed on new strategies to overcome the existing problems such as insufficient reliability and economic feasibility.

(S.Mahmoudinezhad, et al, 2018) Transient response of a hybrid system composed of concentrated photovoltaic (CPV) cell and thermoelectric generator (TEG) is investigated in this study. This research is carried out by using a numerical simulation approach thermally coupled between the CPV and TEG. A transient model is established and solved by finite volume algorithm. In spite of temperatures profile in the hybrid CPV-TEG module, as results of variation of solar irradiation, power generation and efficiency of the CPV and TEG under the transient condition are presented.

The results show that efficiency of the TEG and CPV varies diversely versus changing the solar radiation and module temperature. Moreover, the thermal response of the TEG stabilizes temperature fluctuation of the hybrid module when the solar radiation rapidly changes. In this work, impact of the thermal contact resistance on the temperature profile and system efficiency is investigated. The model presented in this study provides a fundamental understanding of the thermal and electrical effect of the TEG in hybrid CPV-TEG module under transient conditions.

3. SYSTEM ARCHITECTURE

Figure 5. Flow diagram

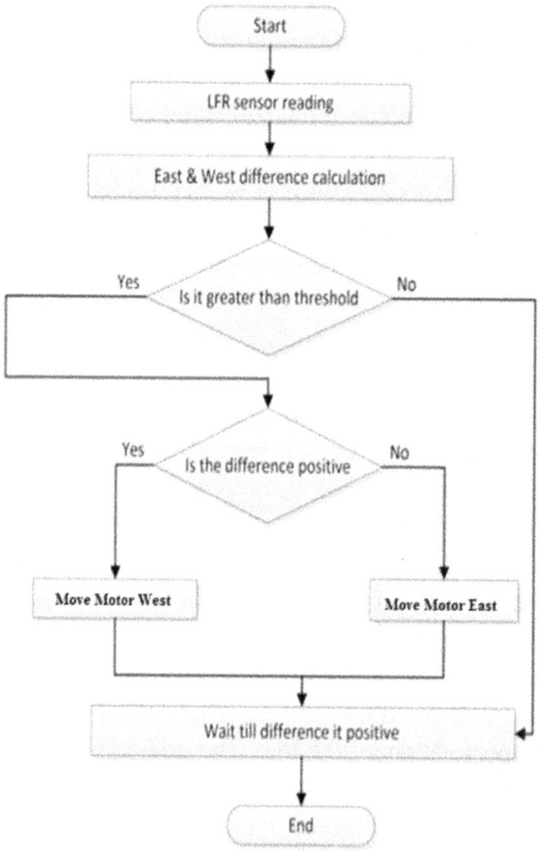

3.1 Existing System

- The existing system is a fixed solar panel. These Solar panels convert the solar energy into electrical energy. There is a key component of the solar panel system.
- Most commonly available panels of today are either poly-crystalline or mono- crystalline solar panels.

- The cells in solar panels collect the solar energy and turn it into direct current (DC) electricity. Most homes and businesses, however, use alternating current (AC).

Inverters change the DC electricity from your panels into usable AC electricity. Racking and mounting systems are used to affix your solar panels either to your roof or to the ground. (Singh et all 2021) They also allow you to position your panels at an angle that is best for capturing the sun's rays.

3.2 Proposed System

- An automatic solar tracker helps by allowing the solar panel to automatically shift with sunlight.
- An automatic solar tracker senses the sun's position and moves accordingly. This means the solar panel moves from east to west with respect to sun.
- There are two major types of residential solar panel tracker: single axis and dual axis. The single axis solar tracker can move the angle of the tracker in one direction as the day progresses (Kim et all 2020).
- These solar trackers increase solar panel's efficiency up to 25%-30% than the fixed panel. Solar trackers generate more electricity in roughly the same amount of space needed for fixed tilt systems, making them ideal optimizing land usage.

3.2.1 Advantages

- Trackers generate more electricity than their stationary counterparts due to increased direct exposure to solar rays. (Awasthi et all 2022) This increase can be as much as 10 to 25% depending on the geographic location of the tracking system.
- There are many different kinds of solar trackers, such as single-axis and dual-axis trackers, all of which can be the perfect fit for a unique jobsite. Installation size, local weather, degree of latitude and electrical requirements are all important considerations that can influence the type of solar tracker best suited for a specific solar installation.
- Solar trackers generate more electricity in roughly the same amount of space needed for fixed-tilt systems, making them ideal for optimizing land usage. (Abdalah et all 2017)
- In certain states, some utilities offer Time of Use (TOU) rate plans for solar power, which means the utility will purchase the power generated during the peak time of the day at a higher rate. In this case, it is beneficial to generate a greater amount of electricity during these peak times of the day. Using a tracking system helps maximize the energy gains during these peak time periods.
- Advancements in technology and reliability in electronics and mechanics have drastically reduced long-term maintenance concerns for tracking systems (Allouhi et all 2002).

4. REQUIREMENT

4.1 System Requirements

4.1.1 Hardware Requirements

- Arduino UNO
- LDR
- Solar Panel
- Jumpers
- Server motor
- USB cable

4.1.2 Software Requiremets

- Arduino IDE

4.2 Hardware Description

The Components used are,

- Arduino UNO
- LDR
- Solar Panel
- Jumpers
- Server motor
- USB cable

4.2.1 Arduino UNO

Arduino UNO is a low-cost, flexible, and easy-to-use programmable open- source microcontroller board that can be integrated into a variety of electronic projects. This board can be interfaced with other Arduino boards, Arduino shields, Raspberry Pi boards and can control relays, LEDs, servos, and motors as an output.

- Arduino UNO features AVR microcontroller Atmega328, 6 analogue input pins, and 14 digital I/O pins out of which 6 are used as PWM output.
- This board contains a USB interface i.e USB cable is used to connect the board with the computer and Arduino IDE (Integrated Development Environment) software is used to program the board.
- The unit comes with 32KB flash memory that is used to store the number of instructions while the SRAM is 2KB and EEPROM is 1KB.
- The operating voltage of the unit is 5V which projects the microcontroller on the board and its associated circuitry operates at 5V while the input voltage ranges between 6V to 20V and the recommended input voltage ranges from 7V to 12V.

4.2.1.1 Arduino UNO Components:

Figure 6. Components of Arduino UNO

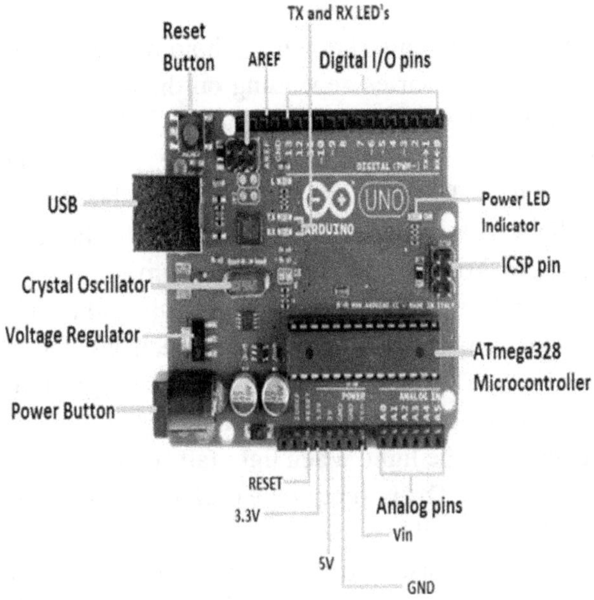

4.2.1.4. Features of Arduino Uno Board

The features of Arduino Uno ATmega328 includes the following.

- The operating voltage is 5V
- The recommended input voltage will range from 7v to 12V
- The input voltage ranges from 6v to 20V
- Digital input/output pins are 14
- Analog i/p pins are 6
- DC Current for each input/output pin is 40 mA
- DC Current for 3.3V Pin is 50 mA
- Flash Memory is 32 KB
- SRAM is 2 KB
- EEPROM is 1 KB
- CLK Speed is 16 MH

4.2.1.5 Applications of Arduino Uno ATmega328

The applications of Arduino Uno include the following.

- Arduino Uno is used in Do-it-Yourself projects prototyping.
- In developing projects based on code-based control
- Development of Automation System

- Designing of basic circuit designs.

4.3.1 LDR (Light Dependent Resistor)

An LDR or light dependent resistor is also known as photo resistor, photocell, photoconductor. It is a one type of resistor whose resistance varies depending on the amount of light falling on its surface. When the light falls on the resistor, then the resistance changes. These resistors are often used in many circuits where it is required to sense the presence of light. These resistors have a variety of functions and resistance. For instance, when the LDR is in darkness, then it can be used to turn ON a light or to turn OFF a light when it is in the light. A typical light dependent resistor has a resistance in the darkness of 1MOhm, and in the brightness a resistance of a couple of KOhm.

This resistor works on the principle of photo conductivity. It is nothing but, when the light falls on its surface, then the material conductivity reduces and also the electrons in the valence band of the device are excited to the conduction band. These photons in the incident light must have energy greater than the band gap of the semiconductor material. This makes the electrons to jump from the valence band to conduction. These devices depend on the light, when light falls on the LDR then the resistance decreases, and increases in the dark. When a LDR is kept in the dark place, its resistance is high and, when the LDR is kept in the light its resistance will decrease.

A photoresistor or light dependent resistor is an electronic component that is sensitive to light. When light falls upon it, then the resistance changes. Values of the resistance of the LDR may change over many orders of magnitude the value of the resistance falling as the level of light increases.

It is not uncommon for the values of resistance of an LDR or photoresistor to be several megohms in darkness and then to fall to a few hundred ohms in bright light.

With such a wide variation in resistance, LDRs are easy to use and there are many LDR circuits available. The sensitivity of light dependent resistors or photoresistors also varies with the wavelength of the incident light.

LDRs are made from semiconductor materials to enable them to have their light sensitive properties. Many materials can be used, but one popular material for these photoresistors is cadmium sulphide, CdS, although the use of these cells is now restricted in Europe because of environmental issues with the use of cadmium. Similarly other cadmium based semiconductor materials like cadmium CdSe are also restricted. Other materials that can be used include lead sulphide, PbS and indium antimonide, InSb.

Although a semiconductor material is used for these photoresistors, they are purely passive devices because they do not possess a PN junction, and this separates them from other photodetectors like photodiodes and phototransistors.

Figure 7. LDR (Light Dependent Resistor)

4.4.1 Solar panel

A solar panel, or solar module, is one component of a photovoltaic system. They are constructed out of a series of photovoltaic cells arranged into a panel. They come in a variety of rectangular shapes and are installed in combination to generate electricity. Solar panels, sometimes also called photovoltaic collect energy from the Sun in the form of sunlight and convert it into electricity that can be used to power homes or businesses. These panels can be used to supplement a building's electricity or provide power at remote locations. (Chng et all 2019)

In addition to residential and commercial use, there is large-scale industrial or utility use of solar. In this case, thousands or even millions of solar panels are arranged into a vast solar array, or solar farm, which provides electricity to large urban populations.

The main component of any solar panel is a solar cell. Specifically, a number of solar cells are used to build a single solar panel. These cells are the part of the device that convert the sunlight into electricity. Most solar panels are made from crystalline silicon type solar cells.These cells are composed of layers of silicon, phosphorous, and boron (although there are several different types ofphotovoltaic cells). These cells, once produced, are laid out into a grid pattern.

The number of these cells used depends largely on the size of the panel being created, as many different sizing options exist.

Figure 8. Solar panel

Once the cells are laid out, the panel itself is sealed to protect the cells within and covered with a non-reflective glass. This glass protects the solar cells from damage, and is non-reflective to ensure sunlight can still reach the cells. Once sealed, this panel is placed into a rigid metallic frame. This frame is designed to prevent deformation, and includes a drainage hole to prevent water from building up on the panel as a buildup of water could reduce the efficiency of the panel.

4.4.1.1 Solar panel works

Solar panels act as a way to mount a series of solar cells so that their unique properties can be used to generate electricity. Individual cells absorb photons from the Sun, which results in the production of an electric current in the cell through a phenomenon known as the photovoltaiceffect. An inverter is used to convert the direct current generated by a solar panel into alternating current. Combined, these two technologies create a photovoltaic system. When installing a solar panel, the proper orientation is chosen so that the solar panel faces in a direction that is most suitable for the specific application. This is most often to produce the maximum annual energy, but is not always the case.

4.5.1 Jumpers

Jumper wires are simply wires that have connector pins at each end, allowing them to be used to connect two points to each other without soldering. Jumper wires are typically used with breadboards and other prototyping tools in order to make it easy to change a circuit as needed. Though jumper wires come in a variety of colors, the colors don't actually mean anything. This means that a red jumper wire is technically the same as a black one. But the colors can be used to your advantage in order to differentiate between types of connections, such as ground or power.

4.5.1.1 Functions of Jumpers

When you set a jumper, you place a plug on the prongs that completes a contact. In effect, the jumper acts as a switch by closing (or opening) an electrical circuit. Jumpers can be added or removed to change the function or performance of a PC component. A group of jumpers is sometimes called a jumper block .

Jumper Connection:

A jumper is a tiny metal connector that is used to close or open part of an electrical circuit. It may be used as an alternative to a dual in-line package (DIP) switch. A jumper has two or more connecting points, which regulate an electrical circuit board.

Jumper wires in Arduino

Jumper wires are used for making connections between items on your breadboard and your Arduino's header pins. Use them to wire up all your circuits! Buy jumper wires from Amazon, SparkFun, Adafruit, or Newark.

4.6.1 Servo Motor

A servo motor is a type of motor that can rotate with great precision. Normally this type of motor consists of a control circuit that provides feedback on the current position of the motor shaft, this feedback allows the servo motors to rotate with great precision. If you want to rotate an object at some specific angles or distance, then you use a servo motor. It is just made up of a simple motor which runs through a servo mechanism. If motor is powered by a DC power supply then it is called DC servo motor, and if it is AC-powered motor then it is called AC servo motor. For this tutorial, we will be discussing only about the DC servo motor working. Apart from these major classifications, there are many other types of servo motors based on the type of gear arrangement and operating characteristics.

Figure 9. Servo motor

A servo motor usually comes with a gear arrangement that allows us to get a very high torque servo motor in small and lightweight packages. Due to these features, they are being used in many applications like toy car, RC helicopters and planes, Robotics, etc.

Servo motors are rated in kg/cm (kilogram per centimeter) most hobby servo motors are rated at 3kg/cm or 6kg/cm or 12kg/cm. This kg/cm tells you how much weight your servo motor can lift at a particular distance. For example: A 6kg/cm Servo motor should be able to lift 6kg if the load is suspended 1cm away from the motors shaft, the greater the distance the lesser the weight carrying capacity. The position of a servo motor is decided by electrical pulse and its circuitry is placed beside the motor.

4.6.1.1 Servo Motor Working Mechanism

It consists of three parts:

1. Controlled device
2. Output sensor
3. Feedback system

It is a closed-loop system where it uses a positive feedback system to control motion and the final position of the shaft. Here the device is controlled by a feedback signal generated by comparing output signal and reference input signal.

Here reference input signal is compared to the reference output signal and the third signal is produced by the feedback system. And this third signal acts as an input signal to the control the device. This signal is present as long as the feedback signal is generated or there is a difference between the reference input signal and reference output signal. So the main task of servomechanism is to maintain the output of a system at the desired value at presence of noises.

4.6.1.2 Servo Motor Working Principle

A servo consists of a Motor (DC or AC), a potentiometer, gear assembly, and a controlling circuit. First of all, we use gear assembly to reduce RPM and to increase torque of the motor. Say at initial position of servo motor shaft, the position of the potentiometer knob is such that there is no electrical signal generated at the output port of the potentiometer. Now an electrical signal is given to another input terminal of the error detector amplifier. Now the difference between these two signals, one comes from the potentiometer and another comes from other sources, will be processed in a feedback mechanism and output will be provided in terms of error signal. This error signal acts as the input for motor and motor starts rotating. Now motor shaft is connected with the potentiometer and as the motor rotates so the potentiometer and it will generate a signal. So as the potentiometer's angular position changes, its output feedback signal changes. After sometime the position of potentiometer reaches at a position that the output of potentiometer is same as external signal provided. At this condition, there will be no output signal from the amplifier to the motor input as there is no difference between external applied signal and the signal generated at potentiometer, and in this situation motor stops rotating.

4.6.1.3 Interfacing Servo Motors with Microcontrollers:

Interfacing hobby Servo motors like s90 servo motor with MCU is very easy. Servos have three wires coming out of them. Out of which two will be used for Supply (positive and negative) and one will be used for the signal that is to be sent from the MCU. An MG995 Metal Gear Servo Motor which is most commonly used for RC cars humanoid bots etc. The picture of MG995 is shown below:

Figure 10. Servo motors with microcontrollers

The color coding of your servo motor might differ hence check for your respective datasheet.

All servo motors work directly with your +5V supply rails but we have to be careful on the amount of current the motor would consume if you are planning to use more than two servo motors a proper servo shield should be designed.

4.6.1.4 Controlling Servo Motor:

All motors have three wires coming out of them. Out of which two will be used for Supply (positive and negative) and one will be used for the signal that is to be sent from the MCU.

Servo motor is controlled by PWM (Pulse with Modulation) which is provided by the control wires. There is a minimum pulse, a maximum pulse and a repetition rate. Servo motor can turn 90 degrees from either direction form its neutral position. The servo motor expects to see a pulse every 20 milliseconds (ms) and the length of the pulse will determine how far the motor turns. For example, a 1.5ms pulse will make the motor turn to the 90° position, such as if pulse is shorter than 1.5ms shaft moves to 0° and if it is longer than 1.5ms than it will turn the servo to 180°.

Servo motor works on PWM (Pulse width modulation) principle, means its angle of rotation is controlled by the duration of applied pulse to its Control PIN. Basically servo motor is made up of DC motor which is controlled by a variable resistor (potentiometer) and some gears. High speed force of DC motor is converted into torque by Gears. We know that WORK= FORCE X DISTANCE, in DC motor Force is less and distance (speed) is high and in Servo, force is High and distance is less. The potentiometer is connected to the output shaft of the Servo, to calculate the angle and stop the DC motor on the required angle.

Figure 11. Controlling servo motor

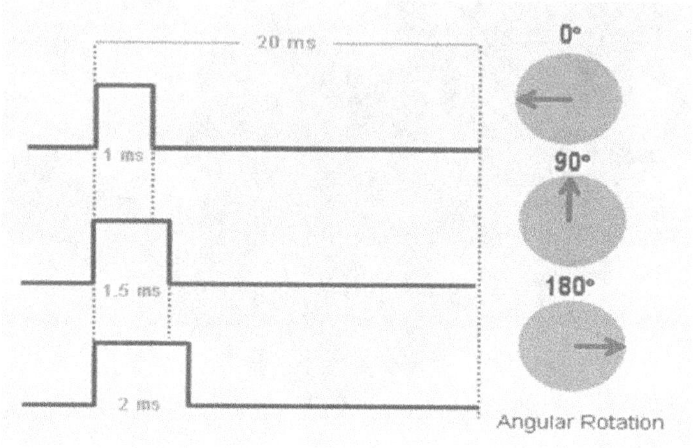

Servo motor can be rotated from 0 to 180 degrees, but it can go up to 210 degrees, depending on the manufacturing. This degree of rotation can be controlled by applying the Electrical Pulse of proper width, to its Control pin. Servo checks the pulse in every 20 milliseconds. The pulse of 1 ms (1 millisecond) width can rotate the servo to 0 degrees, 1.5ms can rotate to 90 degrees (neutral position) and 2 ms pulse can rotate it to 180 degrees.

All servo motors work directly with your +5V supply rails but we have to be careful about the amount of current the motor would consume if you are planning to use more than two servo motors a proper servo shield should be designed.

5. SYSTEM IMPLEMENTATION

The system does not need any power supply externally but only the sun light. All the components depend up on each other in the operation. The produced energy is supplied for the system operation and as well as to drive the load. The solar energy collected by the panel is converted into electrical energy; the collected energy is charged into a DC Battery. The motor, sensors, tracker and other components of the system is supplied by the battery to operate.

Figure 12. System functional implementation diagram

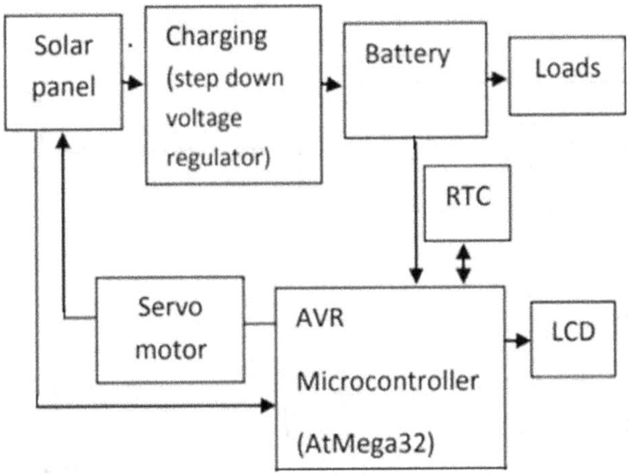

The tracking of the sun undergoes many steps. A microcontroller is used to calculate the maximum radiation of the sun. It is connected to a servo motor and LDR's to redirect the panel to the sun. The system sends the received data to the servo motor to rotate the panel towards to the sun. The position tangles are saved in registers of the microcontroller and can be displayed on the LCD. All the hardware resources like servo motor, LCD, RTC, LDR sensors are interfaced to the microcontroller. We use two light dependent resistors in the system for the detection of maximum sun light. These LDR's were placed on the solar panel, arranged each one facing east and west directions respectively. (Lee et all 2020). The tracker will measure the values of the LDR's and according to the light intensity levels gathered by the sensors; it will start rotating towards the higher intensity levels of the sun servo motor is used to rotate the panel in the system. Servo motor consists of a DC motor, gear box and a control circuitry. The servo motor works according to the pulses generated by the microcontroller.

5.1 Modules

Figure 13. Block diagram

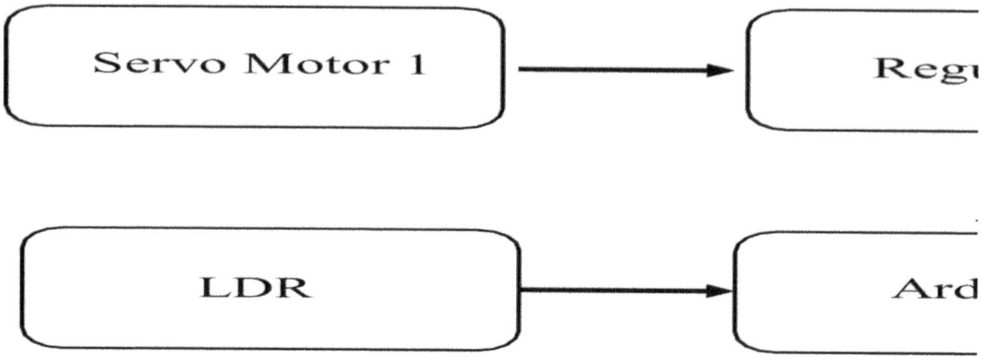

The goal of this investigation is to propose a methodology that maintains the photovoltaic (PV)value within an adequate range of Energy for Opportunity (EFO) by developing a strategy for designing a low-precision, high-efficiency PV tracking system mechanism and facilitating the instrumentation and control required for this prototype (Ma, et all 2019). This proposed methodology is based on the effect of misalignment error with respect to PV efficiency and the Norton design methodology; complementary modifications of the process, directions for the developer, as well as instrumentation and control requirements that are based on the knowledge of and devices available to the developer are made using the sequential steps.

The single axis solar tracker is the apparatus in which the sun powered board tracks the sun from east to west utilizing a solitary turn point to pivot. Under this framework there are three sorts: Horizontal single pivot following framework, Vertical single hub following framework and Tilted single hub following framework. (Karthikeyan et all 2020) In the Horizontal framework the hub of turn is flat concerning the ground, and the substance of the module is arranged corresponding to the pivot of revolution.

In the Vertical framework the hub of turn is vertical regarding the ground and the essence of the module is arranged at a point as for the hub of pivot while In the Tilted following framework the pivot is among flat and vertical and this additionally has the essence of the module situated corresponding to the hub of revolution, like the Horizontal following framework.

The single hub following framework comprises of two LDR's set on either side of the board. Contingent upon the force of the sunbeams one of the two LDR's will be shadowed and the other will be enlightened. The LDR with the most extreme force of the sun's radiation imparts more grounded sign to the controller which thus imparts sign to the engine to turn the board toward the path in which the sun's power is greatest.

5.3. Software Implementation

The Arduino Integrated Development Environment - or Arduino Software (IDE) - contains a text editor for writing code, a message area, a text console, a toolbar with buttons for common functions and a series of menus. It connects to the Arduino hardware to upload programs and communicate with them.

The code is uploaded in Arduino IDE and it upload to give the air temperature and air humidity level in the serial monitor in Arduino ID

Figure 14a. Software implementation

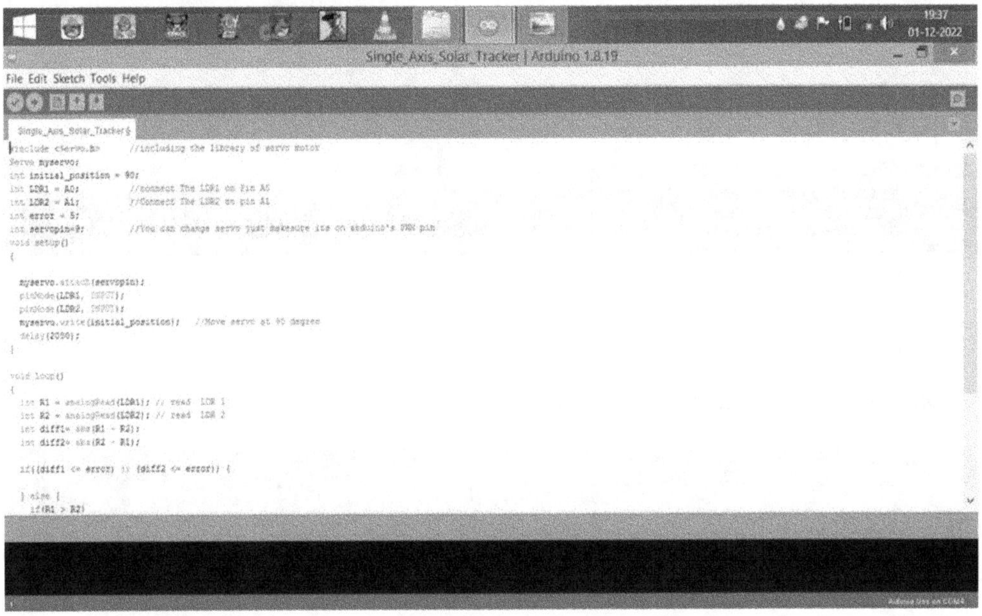

Figure 14b. Software implementation

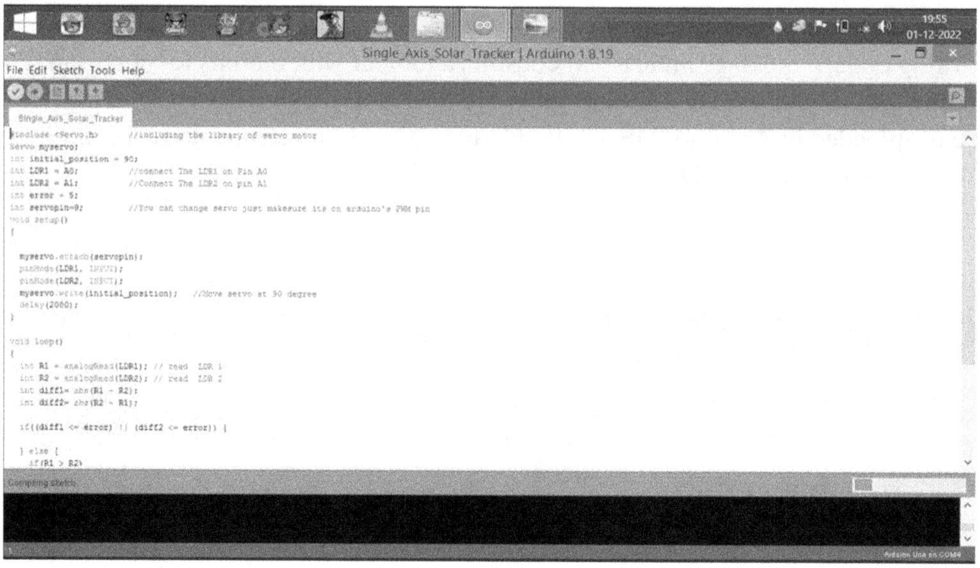

Figure 14c. Software implementation (execution phase)

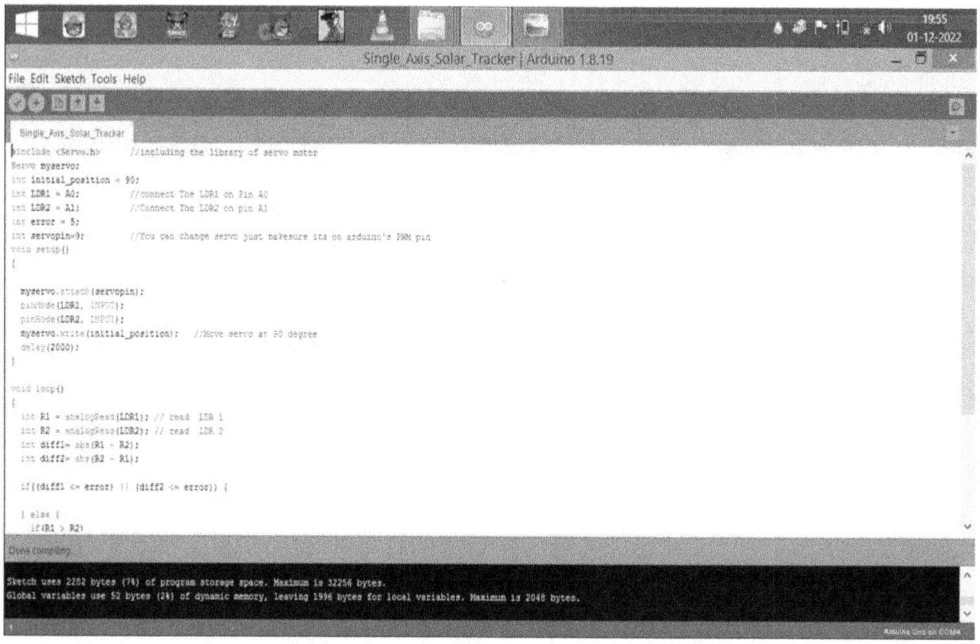

6. RESULT AND DISCUSSIONS

6.1 Result

Solar tracking output in Arduino IDE:

Figure 15. Final implementation

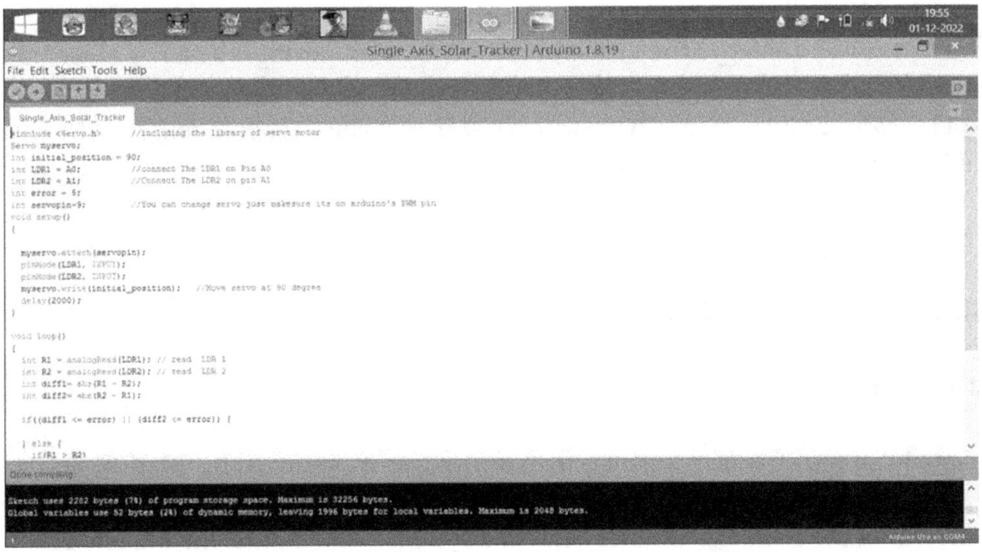

Figure 16. Single axis solar tracker

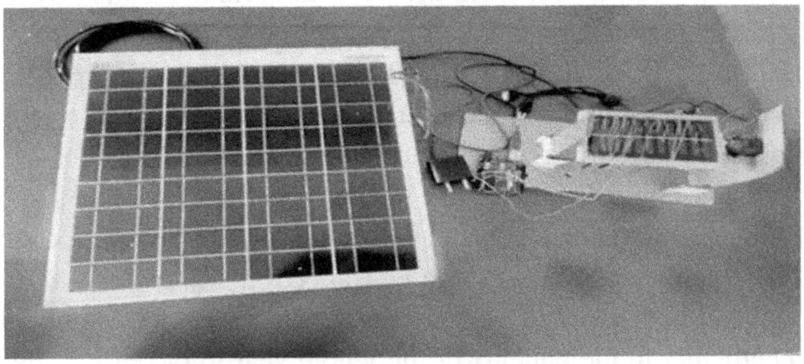

6.2 Discussions

Model has been simulated by using Proteus software to track solar energy. Using the solar tracking the solar energy will be collected in batteries very effectively. The ambient temperature plays an important role in the performance of any system. The energy and energy efficiency of electrical and thermal systems vary with a rise in ambient temperature.

The electrical energy efficiency is seen to be a constant at 9.46% whereas electrical energy efficiency is found to be decreasing from 9.04% to 7.74%, respectively with an increase in ambient temperature from 280 K to 310 K. The thermal energy and energy efficiencies are found to be increasing from 5.89% to 61.65% and 1.28% to 11.6%, respectively with a rise in ambient temperature.

The overall energy and energy efficiencies are found to be increasing with a rise in ambient temperature as displayed. The overall energy and energy efficiencies are found to be increasing from 15.36% to 71.11% and 11.22% to 21.59%, respectively with a rise in ambient temperature. These figures show that a rise in ambient temperature affects the performance of the system a lot. It is also observed that having a solar PV/T system is better than having an individual solar PV or thermal system.

7. CONCLUSION AND FUTURE ENHANCEMENT

7.1 Conclusion

We predicted that the efficiency of solar tracking system is improved by 30- 40% and it was found that all the parts of the experimental setup are given the good results. Moreover, this tracking system does track the sun in the continues manner. And this system is more efficient and low-cost effective in long run. From the result it is found that, by automatic tracking system, there is 30% gain in increase efficiency when compared with non-tracking system.

Dual Axis Solar Tracker using LDR with Arduino UNO. The use of stepper motor rather than linear actuator helps to improve the overall tracker performance. The architecture assists by monitoring using a dual axis sensor to draw the full power from the solar radiation. This is possible because the solar panel is still correctly aligned with sun's incident rays. This is well adapted from the idea of the solar tracking device for harnessing more energy than a fixed solar panel. It is tried to develop a easy and low-cost tracking system. In recent years, solar radiation tracker has played a critical role in rising the performance of solar panels, thereby proving to be a better technical feat.

A dual axis solar tracker's clinical significance lies in its better efficiency and durability to produce higher performance compared to a fived solar panel or solar tracker with one single axis. The tracking system is planned so that the solar energy can be trapped in any possible direction. In general, the maximum solar energy can't be tracked in a single axis tracker that travels only along a single axis. If the solar rays are perpendicular to the panel over the whole year in the case of dual axis trackers. As a result, it generates much energy as possible than it lost in the day as is throughout the year. Therefore, the performance increases suggesting that the efficiency is greater than a fixed solar panel (around 30-40% more) or a single solar tracker axis (around 6-7% more)

7.2 Future Enhancement

With a modification in the design and development, the paper work can be enhanced further, Real Time Clock (RTC) can be interfaced rather than sensors used for seasonal tracking here. Using more powerful motors, the tracking capability and lifetime can be increased, but it will be a little bit costly. But in place of the microcontroller board, using Arduino will make it cheaper, although it will be complicated. Solar trackers, whether single-axis or dual-axis, will help to achieve the optimum solar energy level. Today, it seems very right when it comes to the future of the solar tracker industry.

The goals of this project were a purposely kept within what was believed to be attainable within the allotted timeline. As such, many advance improvements can be made up of initial design of solar tracker. It is felt this design represents a functioning scale model which could be replicated for a much larger scale.

REFERENCES

Abdalah, S., & Niimeh, S. (2017). Sun tracking device two axes with Arduino. *Power. Energy Conversion and Management, 45*, 1931–1939. DOI: 10.1016/j.enconman.2003.10.007

Allouhi, A., Rehman, S., & Buker, M. S. (2002). Solar PV system: A review. *Renewable & Sustainable Energy Reviews, 20*, 35–55. DOI: 10.1016/j.rser.2017.06.001

Allouhi, A., Rehman, S., Buker, M. S., & Said, Z. (2022). Up-to-date literature review on solar PV systems: Technology progress, market status, and R&D. *Journal of Cleaner Production, 362*, 132339. DOI: 10.1016/j.jclepro.2022.132339

Awasthi, A., Kallioğlu, M. A., Sharma, A., & Kumar, A. (2022). Solar collector tilt angle optimization for solar power plant setup-able sites at Western Himalaya and correlation formulation. *Journal of Thermal Analysis and Calorimetry, 147*(20), 11417–11431. DOI: 10.1007/s10973-022-11345-0

Chew, K.-M., Chia, D. W.-F., Yiiong, S.-P., & Tan, S. C.-W. "Green Internet of Things (IoT) Solar Photovoltaic Absorption Optimization Based Panel Orientation in East Malaysia," *2022 International Conference on Computer and Drone Applications (IConDA)*, Kuching, Malaysia, 2022, pp. 46-50. DOI: 10.1109/ICONDA56696.2022.10000386

Chng, K. K., Siew, F. L., Woong, C. W., & Woong, G. S. (2019). Solar tracing device design and installation. *Renewable Energy, 34*, 1364–1370. DOI: 10.1016/j.renene.2019.03.004

Karthikeyan, V., & Kalidasa Murugavel, K. (2020). Reducing PV module temperature with radiation-based PV module incorporated composite phase change material. *Materials Today: Proceedings, 33*(Part 7), 4774–4779. DOI: 10.1016/j.matpr.2020.01.389

Karthikeyan, V., & Sirisamphanwong, C. (2020). Reducing PV module temperature with radiation-based PV module incorporated composite phase change material. *Energy Reports, 6*, 56–64. DOI: 10.1016/j.egyr.2020.10.008

Kazem, H. A., Chaichan, M. T., Al-Waeli, A. H. A., & Sopian, K. (2024). Recent advancements in solar photovoltaic tracking systems: An in-depth review of technologies, performance metrics, and future trends. *Solar Energy, 282*, 112946. DOI: 10.1016/j.solener.2024.112946

Kim, G. Y., Han, D. S., & Lee, Z. (2020). Solar panel tilt angle optimization using machine learning model: A case study of Daegu City, South Korea. *Energies, 13*(3), 529. DOI: 10.3390/en13030529

Kumba, K., Upender, P., Buduma, P., Sarkar, M., Simon, S. P., & Gundu, V. (2024). Solar tracking systems: Advancements, challenges, and future directions: A review. *Energy Reports, 12*, 3566–3583. DOI: 10.1016/j.egyr.2024.09.038

Lee, K., Kim, N., & Kim, K. (2020). Neutral colored transparent crystalline silicon photovoltaics. *Energy Reports, 6*, 201–207. DOI: 10.1016/j.egyr.2020.09.044

Lee, K., Kim, N., Kim, K., & Seo, K. (2020). Neutral-colored transparent crystalline silicon photovoltaics. *Joule, 4*(1), 235–246. DOI: 10.1016/j.joule.2019.11.008

Liu, H., Xu, X., Meng, Y., Yu, D., Liu, H., & Shi, K. (2018). A research for the influence of tilt angles of the solar panel on photovoltaic power generation. In *2018 International Conference on Smart Grid and Clean Energy Technologies (ICSGCE)* (pp. 95-100). IEEE. https://doi.org/DOI: 10.1109/ICSGCE.2018.8556655

Ma, T., Li, Z., & Zhao, J. (2019). Photovoltaic panel integrated with phase change material technology. *Applied Energy*, *238*, 321–329. DOI: 10.1016/j.apenergy.2018.12.021

Mahmoudinezhad, S., Rezania, A., & Mahmoudinezhad, R. (2018). Behaviour of hybrid concentrated photovoltaic-thermoelectric generator under variable solar radiation. *Energy Conversion and Management*, *164*, 21–33. DOI: 10.1016/j.enconman.2018.03.025

Mamun, M. A. A., Islam, M. M., Hasanuzzaman, M., & Selvaraj, J. (2022). Effect of tilt angle on the performance and electrical parameters of a PV module: Comparative indoor and outdoor experimental investigation. *Energy and Built Environment*, *3*(3), 278–290. DOI: 10.1016/j.enbenv.2021.02.001

Muthukumar, P., Manikandan, S., Muniraj, R., Jarin, T., & Sebi, A. (2023). Energy efficient dual axis solar tracking system using IoT. *Measurement. Sensors*, *28*, 100825. DOI: 10.1016/j.measen.2023.100825

Singh, D., Singh, A. K., Singh, S. P., & Poonia, S. (2021). Optimization of tilt angles for solar devices to gain maximum solar energy in Indian climate. In P. V. Baredar, S. Tangellapalli, & C. S. Solanki (Eds.), *Advances in Clean Energy Technologies*. Springer Proceedings in Energy. Springer, Singapore. https://doi.org/DOI: 10.1007/978-981-16-0235-1_16

Zhao, J., Ma, T., Yang, H., & Zhang, X. (2019). Experimental study and performance analysis on solar photovoltaic panel integrated with phase change material. *Energy*, *178*, 471–486. DOI: 10.1016/j.energy.2019.04.166

KEY TERMS AND DEFINITIONS

PV System: Solar panels are photovoltaic cells which gives voltage directly if you place them in sunlight.

Time of Use (TOU): Time of Use (TOU) rate plans for solar power, which means the utility will purchase the power generated during the peak time of the day at a higher rate.

Light Dependent Resistor (LDR): light dependent resistor is also known as photo resistor, photocell, photoconductor.

Energy for Opportunity (EFO): developing a strategy for designing a low-precision, high-efficiency PV tracking system mechanism and facilitating the instrumentation and control.

Real Time Clock (RTC): can be interfaced rather than sensors used for seasonal tracking here. Using more powerful motors, the tracking capability and lifetime can be increased

Chapter 14
Study and Investigations of Ethical Implications and Responsible Use of AI in Automotive Vehicular Technology

Nilamadhab Mishra
https://orcid.org/0000-0002-1330-4869
VIT Bhopal University, India

Ashray Chouhan
VIT Bhopal University, India

Saroja Kumar Rout
https://orcid.org/0000-0001-9007-3665
Vardhaman College of Engineering, Hyderabad, India

Arul Kumar Kumar Natarajan
https://orcid.org/0000-0002-9728-477X
Samarkand International University of Technology, Uzbekistan

ABSTRACT

Integrating AI into the automotive industry has revolutionized driving and interacting with vehicles. This work explores the ethical implications and responsible use of AI in automotive technology. Integrating AI into vehicles represents a major paradigm shift with profound consequences for society, the economy, and individual users. Thus, understanding and addressing the ethical challenges inherent in this transformation is of utmost importance. It delves into the multifaceted challenges and opportunities that arise as AI increasingly intertwines with vehicles, emphasizing the need for a comprehensive ethical framework. The work begins by discussing safety and reliability, shedding light on the ethical concerns of AI systems in vehicles, and proposing responsible practices to ensure safety. Data privacy, another pivotal issue, is scrutinized in the context of the vast amounts of data collected from connected vehicles.

DOI: 10.4018/979-8-3693-7812-0.ch014

Responsible data collection, management, and privacy measures are examined.

INTRODUCTION

Artificial intelligence (AI) is becoming increasingly prevalent in our multicultural society. AI is bound to become an essential part of our everyday life, professionally and socially. Therefore, there is no going back. Thinking of "thinking computers" and making decisions similar to humans poses unavoidable ethical questions as technology develops. To guarantee the responsible implementation of AI, it is essential to investigate and formulate ethical principles. Although artificial intelligence (AI) has immense promise for humanity, its unethical application raises concerns. AI systems should ideally be programmed to refrain from immoral actions, but it can be difficult to identify every ethical issue upfront.

Researchers in this area can give regulators important information, highlighting the importance of identifying specific problem-sensitive solutions that might be overlooked when dealing with large-scale strategies. Moreover, reevaluating how AI operates within extensive strategic contexts could be a viable approach to prevent unethical outcomes during the learning process explicitly. Integrating artificial intelligence (AI) into the automotive industry has ushered in an era of innovation and transformation. AI technologies are reshaping how we drive and interact with automobiles, from autonomous vehicles to intelligent driver-assistance systems. This technological revolution, however, has its ethical challenges and responsibilities (Andreotta, A. J., Kirkham, N., & Rizzi, M., 2022).

This work explores AI's ethical implications and responsible use in the automotive sector. As AI's role in Vehicles continues to evolve and expand, it is imperative to critically examine the ethical considerations that arise from this convergence of technology and transportation. From safety and data privacy to transparency and sustainability, the ethical dimensions of AI in the automotive industry are multifaceted and require scrutiny (Beauchamp, T. L., 2011).

In this introduction, we will provide an overview of the evolving landscape of AI in automotive technology, highlight its significance, and outline the key ethical areas that demand attention. Integrating AI into vehicles represents a significant paradigm shift with profound implications for society, the economy, and individual users. Thus, understanding and addressing the ethical challenges inherent in this transformation is of utmost importance. It delves into the multifaceted challenges and opportunities that arise as Al increasingly intertwines with vehicles, emphasizing the need for a comprehensive ethical framework. The potential job displacement due to autonomous vehicles and the ethical concerns it raises are examined, along with strategies to retrain and transition affected workers. Cyber security and the vulnerability of Al-equipped vehicles to hacking and cyber-attacks are analyzed, stressing the importance of responsible security measures (Blackett, C., 2021).

Background of Artificial Intelligence for Automotive

Artificial intelligence (AI) imitates human intellect in robots that mimic human thought processes and behavior. This phrase can also refer to any machine that exhibits qualities like learning and problem-solving that align with human thought. Deep learning and machine learning have produced a new paradigm. The automotive sector has a long history of utilizing cutting-edge technologies to produce safe, inventive, and efficient vehicles. These days, these technologies include high-performance computers and artificial intelligence. These are the secrets to success in the automotive industry.

HPC has long been utilized to produce high-quality products for modeling, design, and simulation applications. Still, these days, the focus is also being extended to include significant expenditures in AI (Inagaki, T. and Sheridan, T.B. 2019).

The use of AI to operate fully autonomous and semi-autonomous vehicles is progressing. The vehicle sector is currently undergoing a digital revolution due to these cutting-edge capabilities and growing customer expectations. With the aid of these new technologies, expenses have decreased, and consumers now have more of what they desire. Three primary protocols are utilized for communication and connectivity in vehicles:

- Vehicle-to-vehicle (V2V) communication: This intelligent technology facilitates data sharing between vehicles. This is for sharing vehicle position and speed information across a short communication range of about 300 meters.
- Vehicle-to-infrastructure communication (V2I) gathers environmental information—such as traffic jams, bridge clearance levels, and weather forecasts—and wirelessly sends it to other vehicles to keep them safe.
- Vehicle-to-everything communication (V2X), including V2X, stands for "vehicle-to-everything communication," which includes V2V and V2I. As a result, the car becomes smarter and can interact with other vehicles and infrastructure in the traffic system.

Artificial intelligence (AI) is used in machine learning, which enables systems to learn from experience and grow automatically without explicit planning. Machine learning aims to create computer algorithms to acquire and utilize data for independent research. The first step in the learning process is examining data; this can be done directly through experience or by teaching someone how to look for patterns in data so they can use the examples we give to make better judgments in the future. The major goal is to enable computers to read automatically without help from humans and adjust activities accordingly (Leonard, J.J., Mindell, D.A. and Stayton, E.L., 2020).

Deep learning is known as artificial intelligence (AI), which simulates how the human brain processes information and makes decisions. These techniques use readable networks that can be trained on unlabeled or randomly generated data. They are also referred to as deep neural networks or deep neural learning. The digital age, which has resulted in an explosion of data through all channels and in all parts of the globe, has given rise to deep learning. Big data, as it's commonly called, comes from various sources, including social media, online search engines, e-commerce platforms, and cinema theaters, to name a few. Fintech apps can share this massive amount of readily available data. However, the details—as they are often constructed—are so extensive that it may take decades for individuals to comprehend and extrapolate pertinent information. Businesses are growing more aware of the extraordinary power that can be obtained by comfortably disclosing this abundance of data with automatic AI support systems (McCausland, P., 2019).

Big data is an amalgam of official and unofficial information gathered by institutions that may be mapped and utilized for sophisticated analytics applications such as predictive modeling, machine learning, and other applications. Big data originates from various sources, including digital data and real-time data sensors used in Internet of Things applications, commercial transactions, customer information, medical records, internet click logs, mobile applications, social networks, and scientific research libraries.

Environments of things (IoT). Data is ideal for use in some analytics because it can be handled with data preparation software or data mining tools or left unprocessed in huge data systems (Palmer, C., 2020).

LITERATURE REVIEW

Shah and colleagues (2023) present a study that delves into the significance of Artificial Intelligence (AI) in the automotive industry, particularly in the context of autonomous vehicles. The research explores the feasibility of automating production processes. It discusses the benefits and prerequisites of automated production plants (Shah, J. M., Natraj, N. A., Hallur, G. G., & Aslekar, A., 2023).

Mayank Jain and colleagues (2022) emphasize the indispensable role of the automotive industry in our daily lives, highlighting how digital technologies are making vehicles smarter and transforming the entire automotive value chain. They stress the importance of advanced digital technologies in enhancing customer engagement. Furthermore, they discuss the industry's evolution, which involves revamping legacy IT systems and embracing software, robotics, connected devices, and artificial intelligence. They showcase how AI has enabled self-driving cars and is poised to revolutionize daily life. The authors also examine AI applications within the automotive sector, shedding light on recent developments and their diverse applications, including cost reduction, marketing strategies, sales promotion, and funding (Jain, M., & Kulkarni, P., 2022).

In their 2022 study, Daniel Williams and collaborators acknowledge the continuous progress in Artificial Intelligence (AI) development, which has led to widespread adoption of AI systems across industries and the military. They underscore the critical issues of security and reliability that persist, even with the power of these algorithms (Williams, D., Clark, C., McGahan, R., Potteiger, B., Cohen, D., & Musau, P., 2022).

In addition to adversarial machine learning, they identify emerging concerns related to software supply chain vulnerabilities and model backdoor injection exploits, which pose potential risks to the physical safety of AI-dependent systems, including autonomous vehicles. The paper introduces the concept of AI supply chain vulnerabilities, providing a proof of concept autonomous exploitation framework. It further examines the feasibility of algorithmic backdoors and third-party software library dependencies within modern AI attack scenarios. It uses an autonomous vehicle case study to illustrate their applicability in real-world AI systems.

Ting-Yu Chen and colleagues (2021) introduce a novel approach in their research, which involves the creation of a lightweight-slope piecewise-line range-addressable lookup table for efficient approximate computing in various activation and quantization functions. Additionally, they put forth an error-correction algorithm and circuitry utilizing AN code to enhance reliability. The study validates the error-correction capability of their AN-coded neuron through BLER/SNR simulations. Comparative analysis with similar state-of-the-art methods demonstrates that their proposed technique is the most efficient and error-correctable lookup table suitable for functions in the medium resolution range of 8-12 bits (Chen, T. Y., Tsai, C. D., Fu, H. W., Yang, Y. C., & Huang, T. C., 2021).

In 2019, Milorad Marković and his co-authors delve into the increased adoption of deep learning techniques in modern applications, focusing on autonomous driving. They explore the potential of semantic segmentation to map the vehicle environment using a front-view camera. Their paper introduces a post-processing approach tailored to specific vehicle classes, aiming to enhance the accuracy and configurability of semantic segmentation, especially for front-view applications. The researchers employ morphological transformations to address noise, class overlap, and the visibility of classes with limited representation in the input dataset. Through this method, they demonstrate a notable increase in output accuracy, with improvements of up to 3.88% (Marković, M., Milošević, M., & Jovanov, N., 2019).

Liviu A. Marina and colleagues (2018) emphasize the growing significance of data science and artificial intelligence in the automotive industry's future. They acknowledge the substantial achievements in Artificial Intelligence (AI) but also recognize certain limitations concerning the portability of algorithms and the industrialization of code for mass production and deployment. This is due to the necessity of applying various software development process standards across diverse domains. Their paper introduces an innovative approach to address this challenge: creating a unified platform featuring multiple artificial intelligence engines. Leveraging state-of-the-art AI libraries with software not bound to a specific target, they tackle the issue of recognizing driving context in embedded systems. Moreover, they employ this approach as a validation method, offering a promising solution to integrating AI into the automotive industry's diverse domains, ensuring better algorithm portability and code industrialization (Marina, L. A., Trasnea, B., & Grigorescu, S. M., 2018).

BACKGROUND AND IMPLICATIONS

Self-driving cars are known as autonomous cars. Here, steering is not a concern for drivers. This is contingent upon the level of independence the model can readily supply. These cars function similarly to conventional automobiles, requiring neither human passenger control nor any human guest who must ride in the car.

The Significance of Ethical Considerations

While integrating AI in the automotive sector offers substantial benefits but raises numerous ethical considerations. These considerations are not confined to technology; they extend to broader societal, economic, and moral issues. As AI systems in vehicles gain greater autonomy and decision-making capabilities, they face a series of ethical dilemmas. These dilemmas include Safety and Reliability: As AI systems increasingly participate in critical driving decisions, the issue of ensuring safety and reliability becomes paramount.

How do we guarantee that AI-driven vehicles are as safe as possible, and who is responsible in the event of an AI-related accident? Data Privacy: Connected vehicles generate vast amounts of data, and the potential for misuse or data breaches presents a significant ethical concern. How can we protect user data and ensure that it is used responsibly? Liability and Accountability: Determining liability in vehicle accidents involving AI is complex and multifaceted.

How do we establish clear legal frameworks that address liability in a way that encourages the responsible development and deployment of AI systems? Discrimination and Bias: AI systems can exhibit bias if not trained and designed correctly, potentially leading to unfair treatment of specific individuals or groups. How do we mitigate bias and discrimination in AI algorithms and ensure fairness? Job Displacement: The widespread adoption of autonomous vehicles may lead to job displacement in industries related to driving and transportation. How do we address the social and economic implications of this shift? Hacking and Cybersecurity: AI-equipped vehicles are susceptible to hacking and cyberattacks, posing a direct threat to the safety of drivers and passengers.

How can we ensure the robust cybersecurity of AI systems in vehicles? Transparency and Explainability: The complex decision-making processes of AI systems can be challenging for users to understand. How do we make AI systems more transparent and explainable, allowing users to comprehend and trust the decisions made by these systems? Environmental Impact: The environmental footprint of AI-equipped vehicles, including the extraction of resources, manufacturing processes, and energy consumption, presents a significant ethical concern. How can we reduce the environmental impact of AI-driven vehicles? Regulation and Standards: The lack of clear regulations and standards for AI in automotive technology can lead to irresponsible and unsafe practices. How can governments, industry associations, and standards organizations work together to establish ethical guidelines? Addressing these ethical considerations is not merely a matter of compliance or public relations; it's an imperative for the responsible development and deployment of AI in the automotive sector. Neglecting these concerns could lead to accidents, privacy breaches, discrimination, and economic disparities, eroding trust and acceptance of AI in vehicles.

Artificial Intelligence in Vehicles

Sensors, actuators, sophisticated algorithms, machine learning systems, and potent CPUs are all needed for autonomous cars. Independent vehicles build and update an environment map using various sensors dispersed throughout the car. Radar sensors track the whereabouts of automobiles in the vicinity. Video cameras track other cars, recognize pedestrians, and detect traffic lights and signals. Lidar sensors—which detect light and lightning—jump light edges near the vehicle to locate road borders, calculate distances, and show line markings. During parking, other motors and curbs are detected by ultrasonic sensors mounted on wheels. After that, sophisticated software processes all of these sensors, creating the path and transmitting commands to the car's actuators, speed controls, brakes, and driving. robust codes, preventative measures, dependable modeling, and the parts of the Advanced Driver Assistance System are displayed in Fig. 1. In addition to helping with parking and door locking (by using cellphones), ADAS gathers data on the vehicle, the driver, the passenger, and driving behaviors. With this knowledge in hand, ADAS makes a well-informed choice.

Figure 1. Autonomous vehicle components

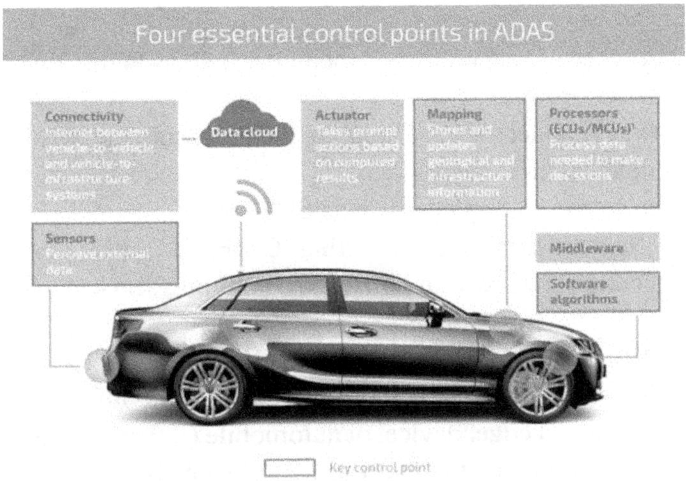

Source- https://www.tec.gov.in/pdf/Studypaper/AI%20in%20Automotive.pdf

Architecture for Vehicle Communication

- V2X (Vehicle to Everything) and Internet of Vehicles (IoV) advanced vehicular communications and services: The term "everything in the world," or "V2X," refers to a communications system in cars where data moves with high bandwidth, low latency, and high-reliability linkages from sensors and other sources, opening up a completely independent driving mode.
- V2X includes components such as vehicle-to-car (V2V), car-to-infrastructure (V2I), pedestrian (V2P), and vehicle communication (V2N). Cars will interact with other cars in this multicultural ecology and with infrastructure like robots or parking lots, mobile network providers, and pedestrians using cell phones. Varied operational scenarios will require varied specifications, including an expensive and effective communication system. The Internet of Automobiles (IoV) is a worldwide network of automobiles that is made possible by a variety of Wireless Access Technologies (WAT) and comprises heterogeneous access networks.
- IoV is one particular application of the Internet of Things (IoT) and IoV Target Domains:
    - Driving and safety of vehicles (fundamental function in Vehicular Ad hoc Network (VANET))
    - Novel domains include traffic management, car insurance, vehicle production repair, road infrastructure building and maintenance, logistics, and transit, among others.
- Commercial goals, and architectural
- Architecture with a business focus Great potential for a variety of apps (traffic optimization, efficiency, safety, entertainment, etc.)
    - Collaboration skills include reliable Internet connectivity and the ability to collaborate across diverse networks.
- Kinds of communication:
- covers all V2X communication kinds
    - Processing capacity and decision-making abilities:

- large capacities – big data, data mining, cloud-based.
    - ■ Suitability for all personal gadgets
- Scalability:
- It is scalable and incorporates several access methods, such as WiFi, VANET, 4G/LTE, and 5G.
- Connectivity:
- The ability to be "always connected" is available; the most suitable network type can be used
- Network and environmental awareness:
- Cloud-assisted global network awareness is feasible
- Compatibility between cloud and edge computing (CC/EC):
- The primary functionalities may rely on CC/Edge computing services.

The architecture of V2X and IoV are shown in Figs. 2 and 3, respectively. Data used in IoV is sourced from external sources, such as sensors, infrastructure, and vehicles. This information is gathered, cleansed, and kept in a database on the closest edge, device, or automobile (if there is less latency). After correctly extracting features, data is saved on the cloud according to its needs, and the primary data center with AI functions in tandem with it. In this instance, latency time is greater.

Figure 2. Data Flow

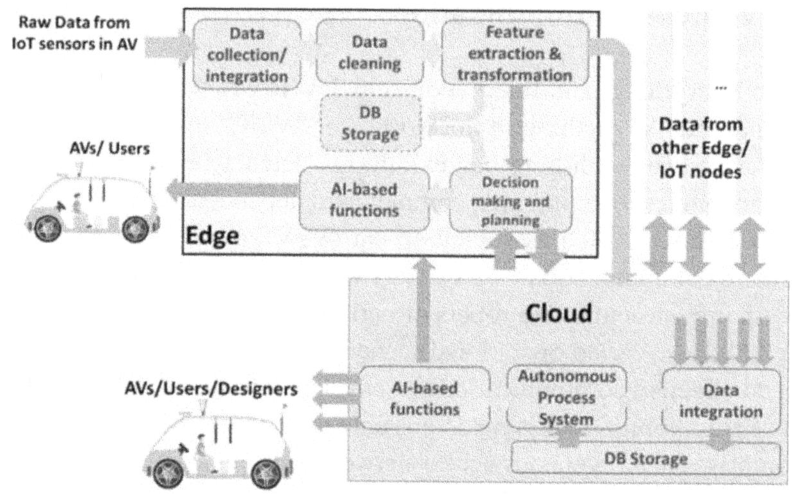

(Khayyam, H., Javadi, B., Jalili, M., Jazar, R.N. (2020))

Figure 3. Architecture for vehicle communication

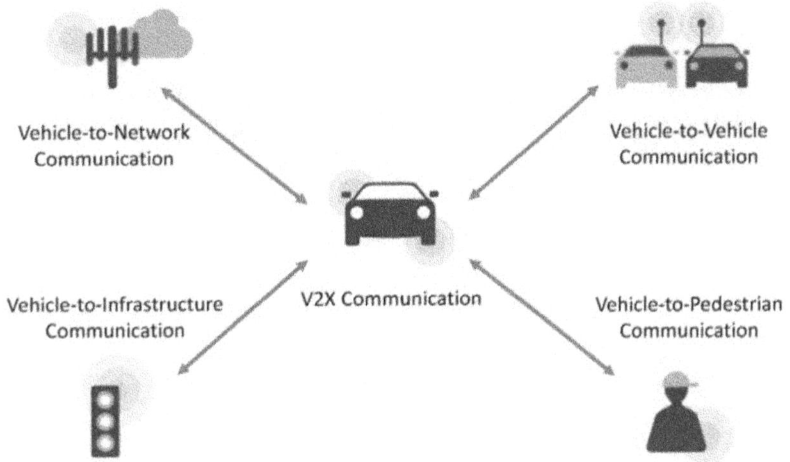

(Mahmood, A., Zhang, W. E., & Sheng, Q. Z. (2019))

Artificial Intelligence Inside ITS

"Intelligent Transportation Systems (ITS) uses a variety of technologies to monitor, evaluate, and manage transportation systems to enhance efficiency and safety," states the U.S. Department of Transportation. For now, we can disregard the ideals of the science fiction-style model and focus instead on intelligent transportation's management, efficiency, and safety aspects. Put differently, smart transport uses new and developing technology to make city transportation considerably more straightforward, costlier (both for individuals and the city), and safer.

Which cutting-edge technology facilitates these novel prospects? There has been a rise in 5G communication technologies and IoT devices. Almost every remote-controlled or controlled body machine can be equipped with affordable sensors and controllers from the first company. The latter offers the high-speed connectivity needed for real-time, minimal latency management, and control of travel systems. Figures 4 and 5 bolster this idea. Autonomous vehicles (AVs) rely heavily on a suite of AI technologies to function safely and effectively. These technologies enable the vehicles to perceive their environment, make decisions, and control their movements without human intervention. Intelligent Transportation Systems (ITS) utilize AI technologies to enhance the efficiency, safety, and sustainability of transportation networks. AI plays a key role in enabling real-time data analysis, predictive modeling, and decision-making, which leads to smarter and more responsive transportation systems.

Figure 4. AI technology used for intelligent transportation

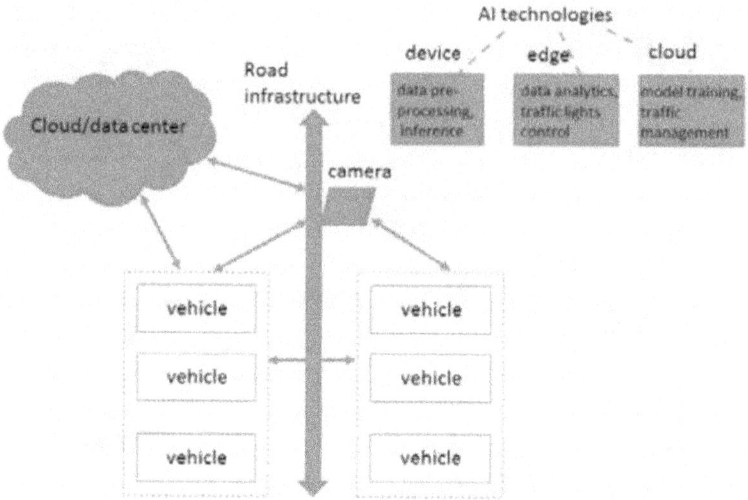

Figure 5. Using AI technologies to enable autonomous vehicles

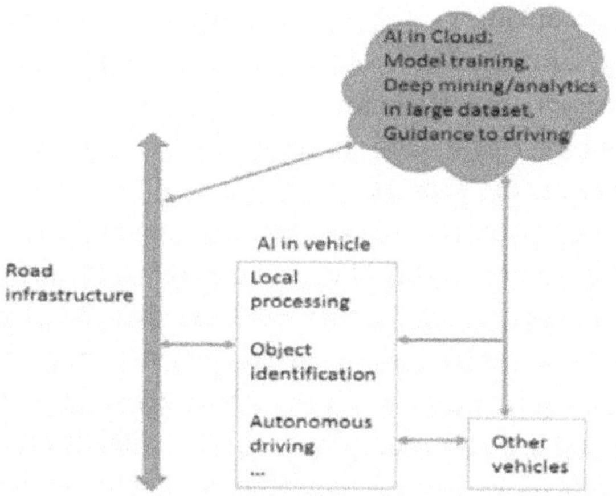

IMPLEMENTATION

Components of the Information Technology

Modern car control systems are designed to enhance most of the driving experience.

Longitudinal collision avoidance: AI assists in preventing collisions between cars, between cars and objects, or between cars and pedestrians. Fig. 6 could serve as a system structure diagram for multiple-vehicle accident avoidance and impact reduction. It incorporates V2V (Dedicated Short-Range Communication), control, decision-making, and remote sensor detection of relative distance and speed estimation. Considerations for frontal-rear collision prevention and impact minimization algorithms should include the following:

(i) A scenario involving multiple vehicles colliding,
(ii) the mechanical definition of impact,
(iii) vehicle mass,
(iv) relative distance and speed at braking
(v) relative distance and speed at collision (time instant of impact),
(vi) each vehicle in the coupled group's capacity to decelerate or brake,
(vii) constraints placed on the first vehicle in the coupled group's front end, and
(viii) constraints placed on the last vehicle in the coupled group's rear end.

Figure 6. Avoidance of longitudinal collisions

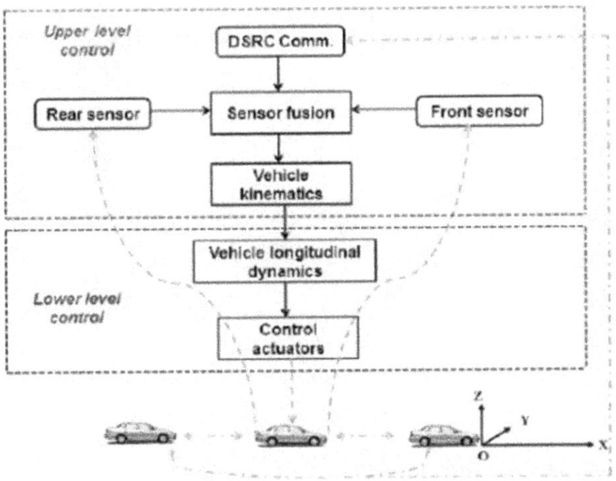

(Lu, X. Y., & Wang, J., 2012)

a) Personal security and emergency notification: AI enables prompt assistance requests and incident notifications.
b) Security of public transportation: AI gives public transportation operators a safe working environment.
c) Emergency vehicle management: AI shortens the response time of emergency vehicles to a situation

The Levels of Automation Model

Regarding road vehicles, a handful of Levels of Automation (LOA) models are used to classify the maturity of automation technology in contemporary vehicles and provide a roadmap toward full vehicle autonomy. The Society of Automotive Engineers (SAE) probably defines the most commonly used LOA model, as shown in Figure 7.

Figure 7. The Levels of Automation model

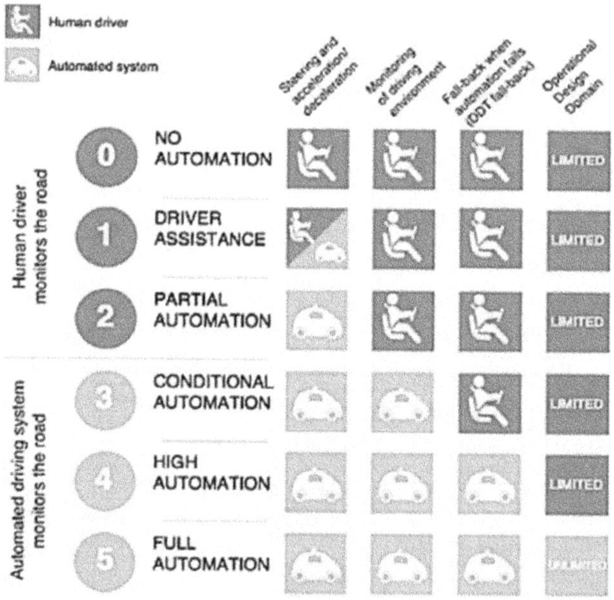

(Blackett, C., 2022)

The Levels of Automation (LOA) model was initially designed to guide automation designers and engineers. However, its current usage is problematic for several reasons (Pattinson, J., Chen, H. and Basu, S., 2020). The model perpetuates the misconception that automation increases linearly, can directly replace all human tasks, and that higher levels of automation are inherently better. It does not account for the potential for dynamic human-machine cooperation, where the level of automation could adapt to different situations and needs. The model neglects the environmental factors that may influence the level of automation feasible and safe in a given context, including the infrastructure and the specific use of the vehicle. The levels can be misused, leading to labeling entire systems (e.g., entire vehicles) with a specific level, even when that level applies only to certain parts of the system's operation. The term "informed consent" originated in the 1950s and gained prominence in ethical discussions in the 1970s, primarily within the medical profession. It asserts that individuals should receive adequate information about a proposed medical treatment, including potential risks, to make an independent and meaningful decision about proceeding with the treatment.

As discussed in the introduction, there is a growing need for an informed consent principle in the context of AI technologies, particularly concerning safety and risk implications. Calls have arisen to extend this principle to future Autonomous Vehicles (AVs) and today's level 1/level 2 "self-driving" cars. A crucial aspect of this discussion revolves around ensuring informed consent regarding AI's true capabilities and users' responsibilities if the AI system fails or disengages. Furthermore, there is an added layer of complexity concerning the need to inform other road users about potential safety risks when sharing the road with AI-enabled vehicles. Unlike medical situations where the risk is primarily to the patient undergoing treatment, AI-enabled cars on public roads pose a higher risk of physical harm to others. While some argue that individuals already implicitly accept the risks associated with road travel, this acceptance comes with the assumption that vehicles meet expected safety standards (Roff, H.M., 2018).

The challenge at hand is how to address this problem. The conventional method of obtaining informed consent through lengthy and complex "Terms of Use" forms is impractical when the potential for harm extends to the general public. These forms are often criticized for their inability to ensure genuine informed consent because they are typically extensive and filled with legal jargon that is nearly incomprehensible for the average reader. While it might be tempting to place the responsibility for the ethical and responsible deployment of AI-enabled vehicles solely on the driver, it's important to recognize that automated-to-manual driving transfers in Autonomous Vehicles (AVs) may necessitate new skills and training. Specialized AV driver education and training may be required to provide drivers with a realistic understanding of what they must do to operate the vehicle safely (Rushe, D. (2021) ; Wei, L., 2017).

However, this approach only partially addresses the problem. To effectively tackle this issue, it is essential to enhance transparency and openness regarding the presence and capabilities of AI technology in AI-enabled vehicles, which offer several ways to achieve this. Developers, manufacturers, and authorities should acknowledge that models like the LOA model are communication tools and analytical tools. Therefore, these models should clearly indicate both the limitations and possibilities of automated and AI systems. These models should consider shared human-machine control and collaboration, emphasizing that machines cannot easily replace humans. Road authorities, policymakers, and the general public need clearer information about the condition. In which specific automated or AI systems can operate, the limitations of the technology in those conditions, and the necessary changes to the physical environment, infrastructure, and road rules for safe deployment. Recognize the impact of unpredictable behavior patterns of other road users (e.g., cyclists, pedestrians, drivers of manual cars) and develop AI-enabled vehicles that can safely coexist with these users. Policymakers should establish clearer ways to discuss technologies being tested and those being deployed. New LOA typologies should distinctly define the conditions for testing and use (Wani, A., Kumari, D., & Singh, J., 2024 ; Nyholm, S., 2024).

The aim is to examine AI's ethical implications and responsible use within the automotive industry. Each section delves into specific aspects of these ethical challenges, discussing Concerns and suggesting responsible practices to address them. Through this comprehensive exploration, we aim to provide a deeper understanding of the intricate ethical landscape surrounding AI in the automotive sector and emphasize the significance of ethical considerations in guiding the development and deployment of AI systems in vehicles. As AI continues to shape the future of transportation, it is imperative to ensure that its integration is guided by ethical principles prioritizing safety, transparency, fairness, and sustainability over mere convenience or profit (Saini, S., Yadav, A., Shazli, A., Itoo, M. A., Ajith, A., & Vats, D., 2024).

Reflecting on Ethical Dimensions: Throughout this exploration, we have journeyed through many ethical considerations in the automotive sector's embrace of AI. The ethical terrain is rich and multifaceted, from safety and data privacy to liability, bias, job displacement, and cybersecurity. These ethical dimensions underscore the profound impact of AI on society, both at the individual and collective levels. They remind us that the quest for technological advancement must be tempered with ethical mindfulness.

The Priority of Safety and Reliability: Safety is the paramount ethical concern in AI-equipped vehicles. The development, testing, and deployment of AI systems must prioritize safety. It is a moral and social imperative to ensure that autonomous vehicles and advanced driver assistance systems are reliable and can protect lives on the road. Ethical safeguards, fail-safes, and continuous testing are essential to achieving this end.

Data Privacy and Responsibility: The ethical principle of data privacy cannot be underestimated. As connected vehicles generate and transmit vast amounts of data, respecting user privacy, securing data from breaches, and transparently communicating data usage is crucial. Transparency, informed consent, and robust data protection mechanisms are ethical standards that must be upheld.

Liability and Accountability: The complex liability issue in AI-driven vehicle accidents requires robust legal frameworks. These frameworks must apportion responsibility appropriately, fostering responsible development and deployment of AI systems in automobiles. Ensuring that accountability is clear and well-defined is both an ethical and legal imperative.

Tackling Discrimination and Bias: Bias in AI algorithms is an ethical concern that can perpetuate discrimination. To combat this, efforts to train AI systems with diverse and representative data and regular audits to minimize bias are necessary. The pursuit of fairness and the elimination of unjust discrimination is a fundamental ethical objective.

Job Displacement and Social Responsibility: As AI and automation transform the job landscape in the automotive industry, we must acknowledge the ethical dimensions of job displacement. Proactive strategies for retaining and transitioning affected workers are essential, as is the development of economic and social policies that address these changes.

Cybersecurity for User Safety: Cybersecurity is an ethical concern with far-reaching implications for user safety. Ensuring robust security measures, continuous monitoring, and swift responses to vulnerabilities are essential ethical responsibilities. Collaboration with ethical hackers can further fortify the defenses against cyber threats.

Privacy Issues:

- Location monitoring, privacy concerns, and owner and passenger data leaks
- Theft of sensor data, such as control systems and speech recognition systems

Transparency and User Empowerment: The ethical principle of transparency and user empowerment is vital for user trust and understanding. AI systems in vehicles should be designed with user comprehension in mind. Users must be informed about how decisions are made and possess the ability to override them when necessary.

Sustainability and Environmental Responsibility: The environmental impact of AI-equipped vehicles must not be overlooked. Ethical practices should encompass sustainable manufacturing, energy sources, and efficient vehicle design to reduce the environmental footprint. The automotive industry's growth should harmonize with the planet's well-being.

Ethical Regulation and Standards: The role of governments, industry associations, and standards organizations in establishing ethical guidelines is indispensable. These entities must work collaboratively to create regulations that ensure the responsible use of AI in the automotive sector, safeguarding safety and ethics over convenience and profit. The Use Cases of AI for Automated Cars are summarized in Table 1.

Table 1. AI integration across multiple automobile models globally (International)

Country	City	Company	Autonomy level
USA	California	Tesla	4,5
Daimler	Stuttgart	Germany	2
EU	Munich	BMW AG	5
US	Michigan	Ford	4
US AutoX	CA	AutoX	4
China	Beijing	Baidu	4
Singapore	Bendemeer	LTA	3,4,5

Despite the Indian government's denial of producing autonomous vehicles, which it blames on job losses, a few popular models are being developed in other countries.

Difficulties with Self-Driving Vehicles

Although certain international packages are testing fully autonomous vehicles (level 5), none are presently on sale to the general public. That is still a long way off. The difficulties are not only legal and technological but also philosophical and environmental. These are a few of the unknown ones.

Cybersecurity Risks for Self-Driving Automobiles

- Remote Hijack: Anytime, anyplace, the hacker can take control of the vehicle.
- Access to Private Information: Once the hacker obtains this information, he can take it all access, making it impossible to operate the product.

Ethical Issues

Emotional vs. Artificial Intelligence

Human drivers rely on non-verbal cues and subtle cues, such as making eye contact with pedestrians or observing other drivers' body language and facial expressions, to make prompt judgments and make assumptions about the actions. Is it possible for autonomous vehicles to replicate this relationship? As human drivers, would they have emotions that could save lives?

Accident Liability

When autonomous cars cause accidents, who is responsible for handling them? Producer? An individual traveler? According to recent ideas, a Level 5 car that is entirely standard will not have a dashboard or steering wheel, making it impossible for a human passenger to operate the vehicle in an emergency.

Who should be held accountable if an accident, a malfunctioning part, or an unexpected car halt occurs from time to time? This system consists of four agents:

1. Driver
2. Owner
3. Manufacturer (OEM)
4. Retail

This contentious topic is related to the advancement of autonomous vehicles. Technically speaking, a driver's negligence causes them to falter. Therefore, the driver bears responsibility for the situation and should manage it the same way if a component fails.

As was previously mentioned, FGAI 4AD is concerned with the behavioral assessment of AI applications on roadways because childhood traffic injuries are the primary cause of death for youngsters. The FGAI4AD standardizes the tasks involved in utilizing AI in cars. We can determine the resolution to this moral quandary using its components, structure, approach, and several paradigms.

Additional Sources:

Lidar and Radar

Lidar is costly and still works to strike the ideal ratio between resolution and distance. If other private vehicles were to share the same road, would their lidar signals conflict with one another? And would the frequency range be adequate to enable the widespread production of private automobiles if more radio waves become available?

Weather Situations

What occurs when an autonomous vehicle drives through a lot of rain? The road barriers vanish when a layer of snow covers the surface. How will sensors and cameras track line markings if the marker is covered with ice, oil, water, or debris?

Laws and Traffic Conditions

Will tunnels or bridges be a challenge for private vehicles? With the massive amount of bouncing traffic, what will they do? Will private vehicles be brought back to a designated spot? Will they have access to the carpool road? What about the older ships that will be using the same route for the next twenty or thirty years?

Federal vs State Regulation

State-owned driverless car permits have replaced state directives as the new regulatory process in the United States. Some jurisdictions have even suggested taxing driverless vehicles to stop the growth of "zombie" cars that drive about empty. Lawmakers also developed measures recommending that all autonomous vehicles have shock buttons and be zero-emission automobiles. Will state-to-state laws differ, though? Can you drive a private vehicle over state lines?

What Options Does the US Have for Self-Driving Cars?

There are 100 million lines of code in automobiles nowadays. With almost 300 million lines of code in private cars of the future, cyber security is becoming an increasingly important issue. One of the US leaders in Software design analysis and app security testing assists automobile customers in incorporating security into their software at every stage of development and transaction.

Additionally, Synopsys provides a wide range of automated IP that is certified by ISO 26262 and meets ASIL B & D readiness standards. This enables its customers to create outstanding chip applications for standard MCUs, infotainment, and ADAS. Solutions for embedded vision processors assist users in integrating features like flexible cruise control, night vision, and facial and object recognition.

DISCUSSIONS

AI technology is pivotal in advancing driverless cars by leveraging predictive capabilities to understand and navigate the vehicle's environment, ensuring safe operation. This technological breakthrough has surged in prominence recently, promising to revolutionize the transportation industry. The development of autonomous vehicles represents a significant progression from earlier innovations such as drones, marking a notable evolution in the automotive sector. The classification of automation levels for driverless cars spans from level zero to five, delineating the extent of technological independence. Integrating this technology in autonomous vehicles has had far-reaching effects on various aspects, including road safety enhancement, mitigation of parking challenges, and reduction of environmental pollutants. Despite the positive impacts, a noteworthy drawback of this innovation is the potential displacement of numerous drivers, leading to a loss of employment opportunities and specialized skills within the industry. It is worth noting that the journey towards achieving fully autonomous cars is ongoing, with further research and development essential to realize the full potential and benefits of this transformative technology in the future. AI is transforming transportation into a more efficient, safer, and environmentally friendly system. By leveraging AI technologies, intelligent transportation systems can meet the growing demands of urbanization while addressing the challenges of modern mobility.

CONCLUSION

In conclusion, integrating AI into the automotive industry is an exhilarating journey marked by continuous innovation and transformative advancements that have reshaped how we perceive transportation. The intersection of artificial intelligence with automotive engineering represents a groundbreaking technological evolution and serves as a poignant reminder of the ethical implications accompanying such progress. Navigating this terrain requires a delicate balance between embracing innovation and upholding ethical standards that uphold the dignity and safety of all individuals involved.

The profound lessons gleaned from this exploration emphasize the unequivocal importance of ethical responsibility as a cornerstone of our moral, social, and economic fabric. By prioritizing ethical considerations in the deployment of AI in the automotive sector, we not only protect individual users but also cultivate a climate of trust and confidence in the capabilities of this technology. This harmonious coexistence between innovation and safety underscores the pivotal role that ethical decision-making plays in shaping the trajectory of transportation advancements.

As AI-equipped vehicles become an indispensable component of our daily lives, the imperative of integrating ethical considerations into the forefront of technological progress becomes ever more pronounced. The juxtaposition of ethics and technology underscores the inseparable nature of these realms and highlights the vital need to align technological advancements with human values and aspirations.

The responsible application of AI within the automotive industry represents not a hindrance but a guiding principle that underpins the symbiotic relationship between technology and humanity. It is a testament to the conviction that ethical progress and technological advancement are not mutually exclusive but rather mutually reinforcing concepts. As we forge ahead in exploring the limitless possibilities of AI in automotive innovation, let us ardently uphold the torch of ethical responsibility, illuminating the path toward a safer, more equitable, and sustainable future.

REFERENCES

Andreotta, A. J., Kirkham, N., & Rizzi, M. (2022). AI, big data, and the future of consent. *AI & Society*, *37*(4), 1715–1728. DOI: 10.1007/s00146-021-01262-5 PMID: 34483498

Beauchamp, T. L. (2011). Informed consent: Its history, meaning, and present challenges. *Cambridge Quarterly of Healthcare Ethics*, *20*(4), 515–523. DOI: 10.1017/S0963180111000259 PMID: 21843382

Blackett, C. (2021). Human-Centered Design in an Automated World. *4th International Conference on Intelligent Human Systems Integration: Integrating People and Intelligent Systems (IHSI 2021)*, 22-24 February, 2021, Palermo, Italy, 17- 23.

Blackett, C. (2022). The Ethics of AI in Autonomous Transport. In Proceeding of Meeting of the 32nd European Safety and Reliability Conference, Dublin, Ireland, August.

Chen, T. Y., Tsai, C. D., Fu, H. W., Yang, Y. C., & Huang, T. C. (2021, September). Error Correctable Range-Addressable Lookup for Activation and Quantization in AI Automotive Electronics. In *2021 IEEE International Conference on Consumer Electronics-Taiwan (ICCE-TW)* (pp. 1-2). IEEE. DOI: 10.1109/ICCE-TW52618.2021.9603030

Inagaki, T., & Sheridan, T. B. (2019). A critique of the SAE conditional driving automation definition, and analyses of options for improvement. *Cognition Technology and Work*, *21*(4), 569–578. DOI: 10.1007/s10111-018-0471-5

Jain, M., & Kulkarni, P. (2022, March). Application of AI, IOT and ML for Business Transformation of The Automotive Sector. In *2022 International Conference on Decision Aid Sciences and Applications (DASA)* (pp. 1270-1275). IEEE. DOI: 10.1109/DASA54658.2022.9765294

Khayyam, H., Javadi, B., Jalili, M., & Jazar, R. N. (2020). Artificial Intelligence and Internet of Things for Autonomous Vehicles. In Jazar, R., & Dai, L. (Eds.), *Nonlinear Approaches in Engineering Applications*. Springer., DOI: 10.1007/978-3-030-18963-1_2

Leonard, J.J., Mindell, D.A. and Stayton, E.L. (2020). Autonomous Vehicles, Mobility, and Employment Policy: The Roads Ahead. MIT Work of the Future, July 22, 2020.

Lu, X. Y., & Wang, J. (2012, June). Multiple-vehicle longitudinal collision avoidance and impact mitigation by active brake control. In *2012 IEEE Intelligent Vehicles Symposium* (pp. 680-685). IEEE. DOI: 10.1109/IVS.2012.6232246

Mahmood, A., Zhang, W. E., & Sheng, Q. Z. (2019). Software-Defined Heterogeneous Vehicular Networking: The Architectural Design and Open Challenges. *Future Internet*, *11*(3), 70. DOI: 10.3390/fi11030070

Marina, L. A., Trasnea, B., & Grigorescu, S. M. (2018, October). A multi-platform framework for artificial intelligence engines in automotive systems. In 2018 22nd International conference on system theory, control and computing (ICSTCC) (pp. 559-564). IEEE. DOI: 10.1109/ICSTCC.2018.8540753

Marković, M., Milošević, M., & Jovanov, N. (2019, September). Using class-dependent post-processing to improve ai for automotive front view camera. In 2019 IEEE 9th International Conference on Consumer Electronics (ICCE-Berlin) (pp. 211-214). IEEE. DOI: 10.1109/ICCE-Berlin47944.2019.8966233

McCausland, P. (2019). Self-driving Uber car that hit and killed woman did not recognize that pedestrians jaywalk. NBC News, November 9, 2019.

Nyholm, S. (2024). Ethical and Legal Issues Related to Autonomous Vehicles. Future Law, Ethics, and Smart Technologies, 190-204.

Palmer, C. (2020). The Boeing 737 MAX Saga: Automating Failure. *Engineering (Beijing)*, *6*(1), 2–3. DOI: 10.1016/j.eng.2019.11.002

Pattinson, J., Chen, H., & Basu, S. (2020). Legal issues in automated vehicles: Critically considering the potential role of consent and interactive digital interfaces. *Humanities & Social Sciences Communications*, *7*(1), 1–10. DOI: 10.1057/s41599-020-00644-2

Roff, H. M. (2018). The folly of trolleys: Ethical challenges and autonomous vehicles. The Brookings Institution,December 17,2018, https://www.brookings.edu/research/the-folly-oftrolleys-ethical-challenges -and-auton omousvehicles/

Rushe, D. (2021). Tesla's Autopilot faces US investigation after crashes with emergency vehicles. The Guardian, August 16, 2021, https://www.theguardian.com/technology/2021/aug/16/teslas-autopilot-us -investigation-crashesemergency-vehicles

Saini, S., Yadav, A., Shazli, A., Itoo, M. A., Ajith, A., & Vats, D. (2024). Significance of AI in automobiles. In *Smart Electric and Hybrid Vehicles* (pp. 198–213). CRC Press. DOI: 10.1201/9781003495574-12

Shah, J. M., Natraj, N. A., Hallur, G. G., & Aslekar, A. (2023, March). Artificial Intelligence (AI) in the Automotive Industry and the use of Exoskeletons in the Manufacturing Sector of the Automotive Industry. In *2023 International Conference on Sustainable Computing and Data Communication Systems (ICSCDS)* (pp. 428-432). IEEE. DOI: 10.1109/ICSCDS56580.2023.10105009

Wani, A., Kumari, D., & Singh, J. (2024). Ethics in the Driver's Seat: Unravelling the Ethical Dilemmas of AI in Autonomous Driving (No. 2024-01-2023). SAE Technical Paper.

Wei, L. (2017). Security threats and requirements analysis for IOV. [https://www.itu.int/en/ITU-T/Workshops-and- Seminars/201708/Documents/S1-Wei.pdf]

Williams, D., Clark, C., McGahan, R., Potteiger, B., Cohen, D., & Musau, P. (2022, March). Discovery of AI/ML supply chain vulnerabilities within automotive cyber-physical systems. In *2022 IEEE International Conference on Assured Autonomy (ICAA)* (pp. 93-96). IEEE. DOI: 10.1109/ICAA52185.2022.00020

Chapter 15
Study on Upgrading the Lifetime of Mechanical Systems in Transportation Utilizing a Quantum/Transported Life–Stress and Sample Size Model

Seongwoo Woo
https://orcid.org/0000-0001-8216-0558
Reliability Association of Korea, South Korea

Dennis L. O'Neal
https://orcid.org/0000-0001-9969-6658
Baylor University, USA

Yimer M. Hassen
Ethiopian Technical University, Ethiopia

Gezae M. Mebrahtu
Ethiopian Technical University, Ethiopia

Hadush T. Alem
Ethiopian Technical University, Ethiopia

ABSTRACT

To upgrade the life of mechanical product, parametric accelerated life testing (ALT) was conducted. It included: (1) BX life with ALT tactic, (2) examination of the fatigue load, (3) a performance of ALTs with changes, and (4) a judgement whether the product attained the desired BX lifetime. A stress model developed from the quantum level was formulated. A sample size producing reliability quantitative (RQ) statements was also proposed. To demonstrate this parametric ALT, refrigerator fatigue failures during rail transit were evaluated by applying the equivalent raised damage potential by the power spectral density. In the first ALT, for RQ statements (40 min), refrigerant tubes in the refrigerator and soldering

DOI: 10.4018/979-8-3693-7812-0.ch015

in the inverter PCB mounted on rubber made of ethylene propylene diene monomer suffered fatigue due to an insufficient damping. The failure during the first ALT was similar to those found from the field. When the rubber mounts and tubes in the compressor were redesigned, there were no issues in the second ALT. The refrigerator achieved the desired B1 life during transport.

INTRODUCTION

Consumers desire products that provide superior performance and are easy to use and reliable (Garvin, 1987). Due to competitive forces in the market, manufacturers must continue to innovate and improve the designs of their systems regularly. This often includes the introduction of new designs with novel attributes that must quickly be launched into the market. Manufacturers frequently include new characteristics into its specifications during each product development cycle. With insufficient reliability testing or improper assumptions of how the new features may be used by consumers in the market, the new system design may suffer unexpected failures in the field and negatively affect the manufacturer's brand (Magaziner, 1989). Before products are introduced into the market, their potential defects should be identified and corrected through laboratory testing such as the use of parametric ALT in the product developing process (Woo, 2023).

To have a successful product launch, manufacturers can utilize high-quality components in the design of a mechanical product. However, if there are design defects in the components, the mechanical system may experience unanticipated fatigue failures. For example, the Boeing 737 MAX embraced the structured CFM International LEAP-1B motors utilizing a 68-inch fan which used up to 12% less fuel and were 7% lighter than other engines. If an airplane engine had inadequate stiffness due to lessened engine weight and increased power when exposed to the modified (or suddenly enlarged) random loads from take-offs, taxis, and landings, it might unexpectedly fail due to fatigue because fatigue failures stochastically happened in the local vicinity of high stress raisers (Wang, 2021). Mechanical systems could also be exposed to their natural frequency due to random vibrations that could happen with large oscillations. As a consequence, the large displacements that occur at the natural frequency may cause the crack generation at a potential design defect at the quantum level. Products should have a sufficient stiffness which can be defined as the resistance against reversible deformation in the system. An airplane engine should be designed to permit it to withstand random vibrational loads which may occur at a natural frequency in the engine.

Fatigue is responsible for more than seventy percent of failures in machine components and load-bearing parts. The failures begin as cracks from stress concentrations – notches, sharp-edged, grooves, and thin surfaces and increase when exposed to repeated loads in mechanical system (Duga, 1982). Fatigue influences the life of mechanical structures such as automobiles, airplane wings and fuselages, vessels, nuclear reactors, motors, and turbines. As a result, fatigue failures can result in system failures and loss of human lives. It may not be easy to gather testing statistics for fatigue life of system starting from the quantum level if there is an absence of systematic procedures such as a generalized life-stress model, accelerated testing, and sample size formulation. Reliability testing such as parametric ALT is influenced by the mean stress, cyclic stress amplitude, or stress proportion, R ($=\sigma_{min}/\sigma_{max}$), expressed by the portion of the lowest level cyclic stress to the greatest cyclic stress as a reverse of accelerated factor (AF) (Fatigue, 2008). Recent quantum mechanics theory might supply an engineer with a method to better understand how fatigue begins as defects in nanometer dimensions that could not have been described through conventional continuum assumption utilized in traditional Newtonian mechanics, strength of materials, etc. (Timoshenko, 1935).

Random vibrational loads (Reynolds, 2016) affect the system characteristics and may not be effective in forecasting the fatigue progress at the quantum level. To estimate the accumulated fatigue damage of a product in the market, the equivalent damage procedure, constituted by time-dependent random vibration spectra passed from base bearing construction, is required for developing the accelerated testing with a life prototype (Lalanne, 2014; Signoret, 2013). This structured way also permits the altering of these complex signals into an uncomplicated Gaussian distribution, expressed by the power spectral density (PSD). Founded on vibration theory such as force transmissibility, it can be used to obtain similar field spectral (or PSD) damage of mechanical systems which can be applicable to systems for elevated tests. To complete this type of procedure, it is necessary to have some concepts for ALT – life-stress type based on fatigue damage spectra (or PSD), accelerated vibrational test, etc.

To assess pertinent data on the product lifetime, there are other procedures, such as ALT, established in reliability block diagrams (O'Connor & Kleyner, 2012;). Relying on some factors and their levels achieved from market failure, ALTs may be carried out as step stress or continual stress with type-I and type-II censoring (Epstein, 1954). Elsayed (2012) categorized statistical, physics/test-based, and physics/statistics models for evaluation. Meeker (2004) offered many useful suggestions to arrange an ALT. As a kind of statistical technique, design of experiments (DOE) (Montgomery, 2020) or Taguchi's way (1992) in the product development procedure, engineer may recognize and modify design defects in the structure. DOE is an organized way to determine the connection between elements influencing procedure and its manufacture. Its aim is to ensure that the parts are designed in the most favorable manner for the working circumstance. DOE is carried out for some elements which affect the system design and has the capability of producing a desired result quantified by utilizing analysis of variance (ANOVA). However, these test procedures may not reproduce field failure(s) because an ALT requires the evolution of some notions such as aimed lifetime index, sample size, life-stress model.

Another engineering approach for mechanical failure such as fatigue embodies strength of materials and finite element analysis (FEA) (Reddy, 2021). Unexpected product failure may be assessed utilizing: (1) Lagrangian or Newtonian competency, (2) the system response for (dynamic) loads and recognizing its stress, (3) the rain-flow counting way by von Mises stress, and (4) system damage by exerting the Palmgren-Miner rule. Utilizing a structured way that can take a closed-form solution often involves applying some assumptions which may not replicate multimodule product failures in the field.

Random vibration tests in the laboratory may be managed by utilizing the fatigue damage spectra calculated from data. Some of the representative test recommendations can be discovered by chance in MIL-STD-810. But there are intrinsic restrictions for this approach because the real stresses on the product in the field may not be precisely harmonized with the laboratory tests. As a result, the designer might not assume that an item put to the test in the laboratory can remain alive in the market. As a substitute process, manufacturers may perform tests to discover system issues using highly accelerated life testing (HALT) in transportation (McLean, 2009). However, as there are no structured notions, such as quantum-transported stress type, accelerated factor, and sample size, etc., tests may be carried out without RQ specification—test periods, etc.

The motivation for this study was to provide parametric ALT as a common organized way which might employ a quantum/transported life-stress model and sample size formulation with RQ statements, such as the allocated cycles for discovering the design imperfections of mechanical products in transportation and supply a way for altering and enhancing the imperfections of the system design. A sample size and quantum-carried failure model equation also are formulated. Thus, this organized procedure for discovering the sources of failure mode and enhancing system designs produces suitable design responses to express fatigue in the system functioned by machine. The procedure embodies: (1) lifetime estimate based on BX life with an ALT plan, (2) PSD load inspection which occurred in transit from quantum-transported prototype, (3) performing tailored ALTs with modifications, and (4) in each ALT, judgement of whether the product reaches the aimed BX life. To develop the capability of producing a desired result by ALT, it might be required to evaluate the design introduction into the marketplace to ensure that the process produces the desired reliability. A fatigued refrigerator tubes and soldering in the inverter PCB exposed to repetitive random vibration in rail transportation is supplied as a case study of the implementation of this procedure. If product achieves life target, the effectiveness of this parametric ALT will be verified as finding the design issues in field and correcting them within the mission cycles.

PARAMETRIC ALT FOR PRODUCTS OPERATED BY MACHINE IN TRANSPORTATION

Product Lifetime and Its Aiming

In a mechanical system, generated power is transferred to create mechanical advantages via force and movement by mechanisms within the system (IEEE, 2002). If there are some defects in the construction of any parts and they are exposed to stress, the system (or product) can suddenly fail and not achieve its anticipated life. One way of measuring the life of a system is with the BX life. BX life is the time (or interval) when *X* percent in a group of items in the system under consideration will have been failed.

The product lifetime, *T*, can be considered a random variable. The Cumulative Distribution Function (CDF), designated by *F(t)*, may be stated as

$$P(T \le t) = F(t) \tag{1}$$

where $F(t) = 1 - e^{-\left(\frac{t}{\eta}\right)^{\beta}}$ for Weibull distribution

The failure rate can be stated as

$$\lambda = \frac{f}{R} = \frac{dF/dt}{R} = \frac{(1-R)'}{R} = \frac{-R'}{R} \tag{2}$$

where λ is failure rate, and *f* is density function, and *R* is reliability.

If Equation (2) is integrated over the time, *t*, the *X*% cumulative failure, $F(L_B)$, at $T=L_B$ (*BX* life) could be stated:

$$\int \lambda dt = -\ln R \tag{3}$$

The total of *R(t)* and *F(t)* is 1 or $F(t)+R(t)=1$ for $t \ge 0$. In other words,

$$A(=X) = \langle \lambda \rangle \cdot L_B = \int_0^{T=L_B} \lambda(t) \cdot dt = -\ln R(L_B) = -\ln(1-F) \cong F(L_B) \tag{4}$$

Presuming that T_1 be the period of the first failure, reliability, $R(t)$, may be expressed:

$$R(t) = P(T_1 > t) = P(\text{no failure} \quad \text{in } (0,t]) = \frac{(m)^0 e^{-m}}{0!} = e^{-m} = e^{-\lambda t} \tag{5}$$

where m is Poisson parameter that may be expressed as λt (mean).

Reliability can be expressed by the system's capacity to continue to function for an expressed period of time or entire time interval. It may frequently be described using the "bathtub curve" shown as line II in Figure 1. If a system's reliability curve follows that of the bathtub curve, it will have troubles achieving favorable outcome in the marketplace because of design defects that manifest themselves early in the life of the product. If the design of the product is enhanced, the usual bathtub curve could be replaced to a more linear line with the shape parameter β as manifested in line III in Figure 1.

Figure 1. A lifetime measure – BX life (L_B) – in the bathtub.

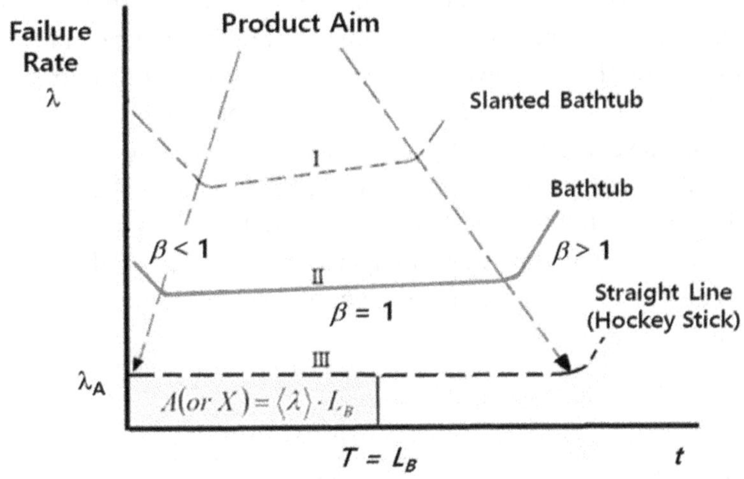

A household refrigerator is design to maintain food fresh over an extended period of time. A refrigerator, using the vapor-compression refrigerating cycle, is designed to produce chilled air from its evaporator to the freezer and refrigerator sections. The refrigerant is moved by a compressor through the condenser, capillary tube, and evaporator. If there are design flaws in the sub systems (A-E) of refrigerator, it cannot achieve its anticipated life (Figure 2a). During the design of a system, an engineer may not realize how many ways a consumer may utilize the refrigerator under particular environmental circumstances. If troublesome components in the system are evaluated using ALT, the designer may attain the desired life target for the product (Figure 2).

Figure 2. Mechanical compartment in the refrigerator: **a** *mechanical compartment (1) compressor, (2) rubber, (3) connecting tubes, and (4) fan and condenser,* **b** *refrigerator with modules A-E.*

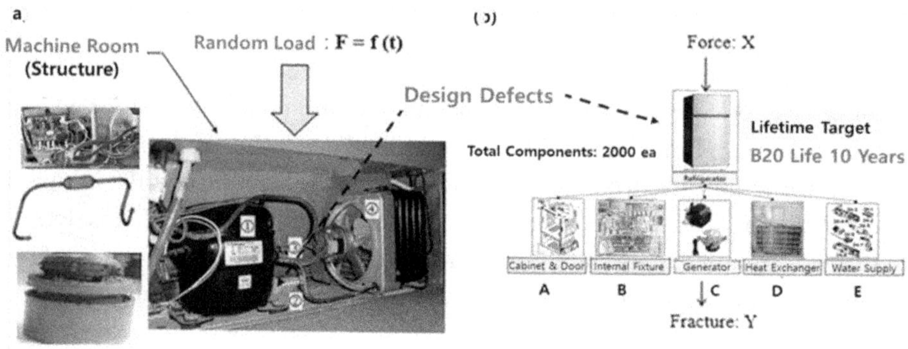

A refrigerator can be views as a group of subsystems A-E (see Figure 2(b)). To carry out the ALT and achieve the desired product life with no (anticipated) market reliability data (stated as multiplication of life and failure rate), three modules were evaluated with reliability data from the market: (1) modified module, (2) new modified module, and (3) an alike module. For instance, module A, the mechanical compartment incorporating the compressor, required an investigation in section 2.3. A modified module was needed because the rubber mount in the compressor was redesigned to better dampen the transferred impacts that occurred in rail transit. It had yearly failure rates of 0.25% per year and B1.8 life of 7.2 years in the market. After alteration, the module was anticipated to have yearly failure rates of 0.50% per year and a B1.8 life of 3.6 years. To attain the aimed product life, new lifetime of module A was set to have a B1 life of 10 years with 0.1% per year (Table 1).

Table 1. Entire ALT scheme of mechanical product such as refrigerator.

Modules	Market Reliability		Predicted Reliability				Goal Reliability	
	Failure Rate Per Year, λ (%/Year)	BX Life, L_B (Year)	Failure Rate Per Year, λ (%/Year)			BX Life, L_B (Year)	Failure Rate	BX Life, L_B (Year)
A	0.25	7.2	Modified	x2	0.50	3.6	0.10	10
B	0.30	6.0	Given	x1	0.30	6.0	0.10	10
C	0.40	4.5	New	x5	2.00	0.9	0.10	10
D	0.20	9.0	Given	x1	0.20	9.0	0.15	10
E	0.20	9.0	Modified	x2	0.40	4.5	0.10	10
Others	0.50	12.0	Given	x1	0.50	12.0	0.45	10
Product	1.85	4.5	-	-	3.90	0.9	1.00	10

Quantum/Transported Life-Stress Type and Sample Size for ALT

By various types of (covalent or ionic) bonds, the atomic electronics are isolated and bound in the materials. Failure of a part may begin to become visible due continual fatiguing of preexisting imperfections or tiny cracks in the microscale constructional exterior of a part. If there are repeated stresses exposed in the structure, a crack can increase in size from microscopic sized voids and grow until it reaches some critical magnitude of component. Modeling this behavior requires a quantum/transported life-stress prototype.

Power transmission in a mechanical product is employed to produce mechanical advantages via force and motion by claiming suitable mechanisms. Conservation of energy can be applied to the system:

$$dU = dq + dw \tag{8}$$

The second law of thermodynamics for irreversible and spontaneous processes can be expressed as:

$$dS > dq^{irrev}/T_{sur} \tag{9}$$

Equations (8) and (9) can be united for work ($P_{ext}dV$) because of volume change of compressor in the vapor-compression refrigeration cycle:

$$dU + P_{ext}dV - T_{sur}dS < 0$$

for spontaneous change (10)

where $S{=}klnW$

First of all, consider non-interacting electrons freely going in a potential barrier that is presumed to be infinite. In one dimension, the Schrodinger's formulation may be stated

$$-\frac{h^2}{8\pi^2 m}\frac{d^2\psi_n(x)}{dx^2} = E_n\psi_n \tag{12}$$

where h is Planck constant, m is electron mass, ψ_n is wave function, and E_n is energy.

The boundary circumstances are: 1) ψ_n limited interior the metal but exponentially perishing. Namely, $\psi_n \to 0$ as $x \to \infty$, 2) $\psi_n = 0$ or $V = \infty$ at walls. So, we can discover the means of solving a problem:

$$\psi_n(x) = \sqrt{\tfrac{2}{a}}\,sin(\tfrac{n}{a})x \;;\; E_n = \frac{n^2h^2}{8ma^2}\,n > 0 \tag{13}$$

where $\psi_n(x+a) = \psi_n(x)$, a is interval, and n is quantum number.

For example, transport in solid-state diffusion of silicon impurities occurs in the material when an electro-magnetical field, ξ, is exerted. It may be abridged: (1) electromigration-caused voiding, (2) assembled of chloride ions, and (3) confining of holes or electrons

$$J = [aC(x - a)] \cdot \exp\left[-\frac{q}{kT}\left(w - \frac{1}{2}a\xi\right)\right] \cdot v$$

$$= -[a^2 \mathrm{v}\,\mathrm{e}^{-\mathrm{qw/kT}}] \cdot \cosh\frac{qa\xi}{2\mathrm{kT}}\frac{\partial \mathrm{C}}{\partial \mathrm{x}} + [2a\mathrm{v}\,\mathrm{e}^{-\mathrm{qw/kT}}]\mathrm{C}\sinh\frac{qa\xi}{2\mathrm{kT}}$$

$$= \Phi(\mathrm{x},\mathrm{t},\mathrm{T})\sinh(a\xi)\exp\left(-\frac{\mathrm{Q}}{\mathrm{kT}}\right) = \mathrm{B}\sinh(a\xi)\exp\left(-\frac{\mathrm{Q}}{\mathrm{kT}}\right) \quad (14)$$

where Φ is constant, B is constant, C is concentration, ν is jump frequency, q is area of electric charge, a is interval between consecutive potential walls, ξ is applied electric magnetic field, k is Boltzmann's constant, T is temperature, and Q is energy.

The reverse of Equation (14) may be utilized to state the life-stress (LS) type:

$$TF = A\,[\sinh(aS)]^{-1}\exp\left(\frac{E_a}{kT}\right) \quad (15)$$

In Equation (15), the sine hyperbolic expression $[\sinh(aS)]^{-1}$ could be stated: (1). $(S)^{-1}$ at first is almost straight line in low stresses, (2). $(S)^{-n}$ as middle stress area has what is regarded, and (3). $(e^{aS})^{-1}$ at terminating is big stress area.

Stress is a physical quantity which includes the inner forces that neighboring sub-atomic particles of a material are applied. If the power is stated as the multiplication of effort and flows, stresses may come from the initiation of power to the component. As an ALT is carried out in the medium stress area and stresses in transportation originate in the transferred vibrational load (F_T) on Equation (A1) or (A10) which may be stated as PSD quantity of raising testing for a determined frequency band. Equation (15) may be restated as

$$TF = \mathrm{A}(\mathrm{S})^{-\mathrm{n}}\exp\left(\frac{\mathrm{E}_a}{\mathrm{kT}}\right) = \mathrm{A}(\mathrm{e})^{-\lambda}\exp\left(\frac{\mathrm{E}_a}{\mathrm{kT}}\right) = \mathrm{B}(\mathrm{F}_\mathrm{T})^{-\lambda}\exp\left(\frac{\mathrm{E}_a}{\mathrm{kT}}\right) \quad (16)$$

Thus, because of the base load, Y, the force transmissibility, Q, may be stated as follows:

$$\mathrm{Q} = \frac{\mathrm{X(t)}}{\mathrm{F_T(t)}} = \frac{\mathrm{X(t)}}{\mathrm{Y(t)}} = \left[\frac{1 + (2\zeta r)^2}{(1 - r^2)^2 + (2\zeta r)^2}\right]^{1/2} = |H(f)| \quad (17)$$

where $Y(t)$ is excitation span of having the form of a sine curve from base, r is the frequency portion ($=\omega_n/\omega = f_n/f$), ζ is damping portion ($c/c_c = c/2\omega_n$), k is spring quantity.

PSD in the assigned frequency band, a, is computed. Thus, AF is the relation between the representative situation and the raised situation and is calculated by multiplying the amplitude portion of gravitational acceleration, R, and force transmissibility, Q. That is,

$$\mathrm{AF} = \left(\frac{\mathrm{S}_1}{\mathrm{S}_0}\right)^{\mathrm{n}}\left[\frac{\mathrm{E}_a}{\mathrm{k}}\left(\frac{1}{\mathrm{T}_0} - \frac{1}{\mathrm{T}_1}\right)\right] = \left(\frac{a_1 X}{a_0 Y}\right)^{\lambda}\left[\frac{\mathrm{E}_a}{\mathrm{k}}\left(\frac{1}{\mathrm{T}_0} - \frac{1}{\mathrm{T}_1}\right)\right] = (\mathrm{R} \times \mathrm{Q})^{\lambda}\left[\frac{\mathrm{E}_a}{\mathrm{k}}\left(\frac{1}{\mathrm{T}_0} - \frac{1}{\mathrm{T}_1}\right)\right] \quad (18)$$

where a_1 is raised PSD quantity for the decided frequency band, a_0 is the usual PSD quantity for the decided frequency band, T_0 is usual temperature, and T_1 is raised temperature.

As accelerated test is carried out in the test facility, Equation (18) is restated as

$$AF = \left(\frac{S_1}{S_0}\right)^n = \left(\frac{F_1}{F_0}\right)^\lambda = \left(\frac{a_1 X}{a_0 Y}\right)^\lambda = (R \times Q)^\lambda \tag{19}$$

To achieve the assigned number of task cycles – RQ statement – of ALTs from the targeted BX life in the test plan, the sample size integrated with AF is required to be assessed. Some established ways have been suggested to determine the sample size.

Failures may be classified as early failure, random failure, and wear-out failure. These can, stated in a manner conforming to shape parameter on the Weibull distribution (see section 2.1). To assess the expected life, shape parameter is considerable larger than 1. The Weibayes way is stated during a Weibull examination with an assigned shape parameter which is evolved by actual testing data. Utilizing the Weibayes way, the characteristic life may be obtained by using maximum likelihood estimation (MLE) that is a usual way employed to roughly calculate the model parameters. The characteristic life, η_{MLE}, could be decided as follow:

$$\eta_{MLE}^{\beta} = \sum_{i=1}^{n} \frac{t_i^{\beta}}{r} \tag{20}$$

where n is sample size, η_{MLE} is rough maximum likelihood calculation, t_i is test time, and r is failures.

A Weibull evaluation is an established way utilized to inspect reliability data. But, because of the difficulties of developing an arithmetical expression, it is not easy to apply this type of evaluation. If the instances of no failure ($r = 0$) and any failures ($r \geq 1$) in a test could be disconnected, the result could yield an expected sample size expression.

If the confidence level is 100 (1–α), the characteristic lifetime, η_α, can be evaluated from Equation (20).

$$\eta_\alpha^{\beta} = \frac{2r}{\chi_\alpha^2(2r+2)} \times \eta_{MLE}^{\beta} = \frac{2}{\chi_\alpha^2(2r+2)} \times \sum_{i=1}^{n} t_i^{\beta}$$

for r ≥ 1 (21)

where χ_α^2 () is chi-square function in case the p-value is α.

Assuming no failure, ln (1/α) is approximately equal to the chi-square amount, $\frac{\chi^2(2)}{2}$.

$$p - value{:}\alpha = \int_{\chi_\alpha^2(2)}^{\infty} \left(\frac{e^{-\frac{x}{2}} \chi^{\frac{\nu}{2}-1}}{2^{\frac{\nu}{2}} \Gamma\left(\frac{\nu}{2}\right)}\right) dx = \int_{2\ln\alpha^{-1}}^{\infty} \left(\frac{e^{-\frac{x}{2}} \chi^{\frac{\nu}{2}-1}}{2^{\frac{\nu}{2}} \Gamma\left(\frac{\nu}{2}\right)}\right) dx \tag{22}$$

where Γ is gamma function and ν is shape parameter.

From Equations (21) & (22), for all instances where $r \geq 0$ are correct, the characteristic life, η_α, may be stated as:

$$\eta_\alpha^{\beta} = \frac{2}{\chi_\alpha^2(2r+2)} \times \sum_{i=1}^{n} t_i^{\beta}$$

for r ≥ 0 (23)

where t_i is time for each tested sample

As Equation (1) takes the logarithm, the link between characteristic life, η, and BX life, L_B, might be stated as:

$$L_B^\beta = \left(\ln\frac{1}{1-x}\right) \times \eta_\alpha^\beta \tag{24}$$

where x is $x = 0.01 \cdot X$ if $x \leq 0.2$

If characteristic life of p-value α, η_α, from Equation (23) is substituted into Equation (24), the BX life, L_B, may be stated:

$$L_B^\beta = \left(\ln\frac{1}{1-x}\right) \times \frac{2}{\chi_\alpha^2(2r+2)} \times \sum_{i=1}^{n} t_i^\beta \tag{25}$$

The reliability test has a finite number of samples that are used to estimate the life for the allotted failures which could be less than that of the sample size. Thus, the test scheme could be expressed as:

$$nh^\beta \geq \sum t_i^\beta \geq (n-r)h^\beta \tag{26}$$

where h is testing time

If Equation (26) is substituted into Equation (25), the BX life may be expressed as:

$$L_B^\beta = \left(\ln\frac{1}{1-x}\right) \times \frac{2}{\chi_\alpha^2(2r+2)} \times \mathrm{n\,h}^\beta \geq \left(\ln\frac{1}{1-x}\right) \times \frac{2}{\chi_\alpha^2(2r+2)} \times (n-r)h^\beta \tag{27}$$

Rearranging Equation (27), the sample size can be stated:

$$n \geq \frac{\chi_\alpha^2(2\mathrm{r}+2)}{2} \times \frac{1}{\ln(1-\mathrm{x})^{-1}} \times \left(\frac{\mathrm{L_B^*}}{\mathrm{h}}\right)^\beta + \mathrm{r} \tag{28}$$

For $\alpha = 0.6$, $\frac{\chi_\alpha^2(2r+2)}{2} \cong (r+1)$ and $\ln(1-x)^{-1} = x + \frac{x^2}{2} + \frac{x^3}{3} + \cdots \cong x$, Equation (28) may be rewritten as:

$$n \geq (r+1) \times \frac{1}{x} \times \left(\frac{L_B^*}{h}\right)^\beta + r \tag{29}$$

where the sample size can be stated as n ~ (failures + 1)·(1/cumulative failure rate)·((targeted lifetime/(schemed test time)) ^ β + r.

Using AF in Equation (18) or (19), Equation (29) can be rewritten as follows:

$$n \geq (r+1) \times \frac{1}{x} \times \left(\frac{L_B^*}{AF \bullet h_a}\right)^\beta + r \tag{30}$$

where h_a is actual test time, $R = \left(\frac{L_B^*}{AF \bullet h_a}\right)^\beta$ is reduction factor

If the life of a mechanical system is desired to be a B1 life of 10 years, the allotted cycles may be attained for a set of sample sizes which include the required (impact) loads. In parametric ALTs, the design defects of a new system may be discovered and modified to help fulfil the desired life.

For $n \gg r$, the sample size is stated as follows:

$$n = -\frac{\chi_\alpha^2(2r+2)}{2m^\beta ln R_L} = \frac{\chi_\alpha^2(2r+2)}{2m^\beta ln R_L^{-1}} = \frac{\chi_\alpha^2(2r+2)}{2m^\beta ln (1-F_L)^{-1}} = \frac{\chi_\alpha^2(2r+2)}{2} \times \frac{1}{ln(1-F_L)^{-1}} \times \left(\frac{L_B}{h}\right)^\beta \tag{31}$$

where $m \cong h/L_B$, F_L is unreliability, and R_L is reliability

As $r=0$, sample size may be stated as:

$$n = \frac{ln(1-CL)}{m^\beta ln R_L} = \frac{-ln(1-CL)}{-m^\beta ln R_L} = \frac{ln(1-CL)^{-1}}{m^\beta ln R_L^{-1}} = \frac{ln\,\alpha^{-1}}{m^\beta ln R_L^{-1}} = \frac{\chi_\alpha^2(2)}{2} \times \frac{1}{ln(1-F_L)^{-1}} \times \left(\frac{L_B}{h}\right)^\beta \tag{32}$$

where CL is confidence level and $2ln\,\alpha^{-1} = \chi_\alpha^2(2)$.

We know that Equations (31), (32), and (B6) have alike forms to Equation (30).

Equation (28) shall be affirmed as (Wasserman, 2003). Namely, for $n \gg r$, the sample size shall be expressed as:

$$n = \frac{\chi_\alpha^2(2r+2)}{2m^\beta ln R_L^{-1}} = \frac{\chi_\alpha^2(2r+2)}{2} \times \frac{1}{ln(1-F_L)^{-1}} \times \left(\frac{L_B}{h}\right)^\beta \tag{33}$$

where $m \cong h/L_B$.

If $r=0$, the sample size can be indicated as:

$$n = \frac{ln(1-CL)}{m^\beta ln R_L} = \frac{-ln(1-CL)}{-m^\beta ln R_L} = \frac{ln(1-CL)^{-1}}{m^\beta ln R_L^{-1}} = \frac{ln\,\alpha^{-1}}{m^\beta ln R_L^{-1}} = \frac{\chi_\alpha^2(2)}{2} \times \frac{1}{ln(1-F_L)^{-1}} \times \left(\frac{L_B}{h}\right)^\beta \tag{34}$$

where $2ln\,\alpha^{-1} = \chi_\alpha^2(2)$ and CL is the confidence level.

If the objective of a product life–ice-maker is presumed to have a B1 life 10 years, the allocated test is computed for the assigned parts under raised circumstances. In executing parametric ALTs, the structural defects of a product operated by machinery will be found and altered to obtain the intended system life.

Case Study—Enhancing the Fatigued Tubes and inverter PCB Soldering of a Household Refrigerator Exposed to (Random) Vibrations in Transportation

Figure 3. Failed locations from the field

Figure 3a. Failed locations from the field: Europe

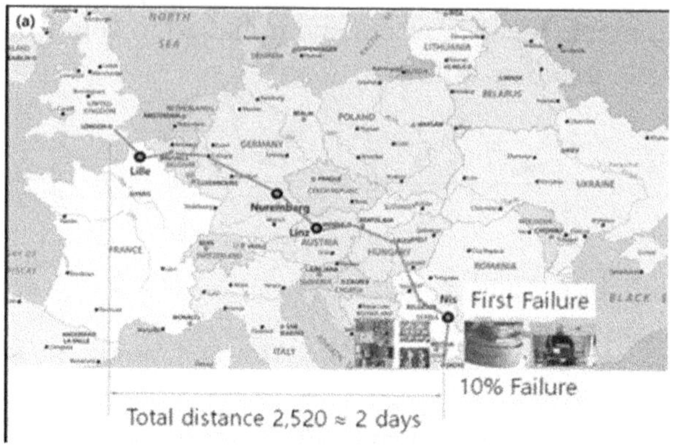

Figure 3b. Failed locations from the field: United States

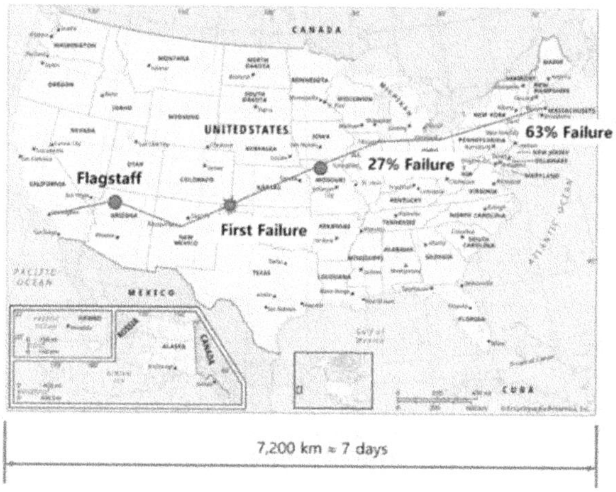

(Wikipedia)

Rail transportation in Figure A1(a) & A1(b) is one of the main methods of shipping products from container ports to their final destination such as a distributor who supplies the product to retailers, storehouses, or directly to consumers (See Figure A2(a) & A2(b)). Two examples are examined: 1) refrigerators were shipped a total of 2,520 km from London for two days to end-users who resided in Skopje city, southeastern Europe (Figure 3a), and 2) refrigerators were shipped a total of 7,200 km from the west coast of the United States to end-users on the east coast. Field data from both instances showed that the rubber supports of the compressors in the refrigerators were torn. Consequently, the soldering of inverter PCB and tubes had fatigued under undetermined stress conditions during the railway transit. For the refrigerators in Europe, the interval at which these failures first happened in rail transit was roughly 2,400 km in Nis, Serbia. For two days, as the refrigerators moved the 2,520-km distance from London to Skopje, 10% of the refrigerators were not operational. In the United

States, the interval at which unsuccessfulness earliest happened in rail transit was roughly 2,500 km for 2 days. In Chicago, 27% of the refrigerators in transport has failed. For the full 7-day, 7200 km journey to the east coast, 67% of the refrigerators were not operational (Figure 3).

Due to the large percentage of failures, it became clear that the refrigerator had one or more design defects. After identifying the defects, the company had to alter the problematic designs.

The rail system in the United States as shown in Figure 3(b), included primary rail lines, side-lines, and industrial lines. To achieve the needed PSD along these rail lines, calculations were made in both the horizontal and vertical orientations. A vibration and shock data recorder, SAVER 3X90 (Lansmont Corp., USA) was utilized to collect the spectral data for the entire trip. The SAVER was fastened to the floor located near the midway of storage section. The recorded data were allowed for visualization of the environmental vibration spectra including the PSD levels versus frequency. In this study, 0.3 to 400 Hz comprised the PSD spectra which could be used to evaluate the vibrational impact of rail travel on the refrigerator design.

When examining the vibration spectra, it was possible to compute the AF by multiplying the maximum extent portion of acceleration, R, and force transmissibility, Q, (see Equation (17)). With the natural frequency, the damping portion, the usual PSD quantity, and raised PSD quantity identified, a shaker bench could be programmed to exert the raised random vibrational spectra, indicated by PSD, to samples in the laboratory. Tables were installed with test samples which might be operated and controlled by a machine component that produced force, torque, or displacement, usually in a controlled way. Periodical waves such as rectangular, triangular, and sine signals and random waves could be chosen as input to drive movement of the shaker tables. Random shaking utilizing perceived powerful PSD movements could enhance the product robustness and help identify design imperfections for RQ statement. The amplitude of the controlling random vibrations, stated as G_{rms}, could be modified as stated by the capacity of the sample for raised loads.

Figure 4. Vibration test for the parametric ALT:

Figure 4a. Vibration test for the parametric ALT: Programmed shaking table for product testing

Figure 4b. Vibration test for the parametric ALT: Exerted PSD loads.

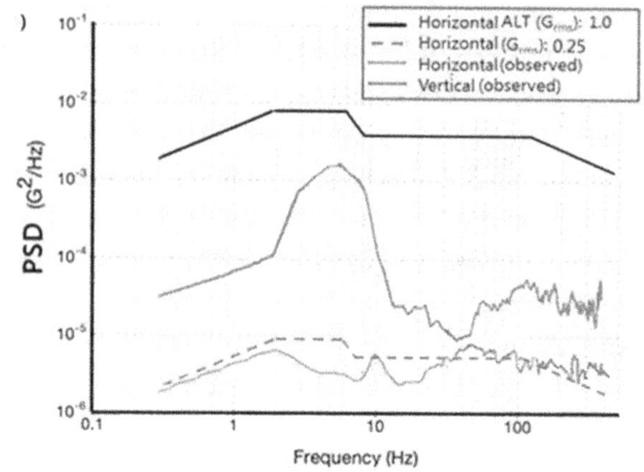

To determine the PSD stress level for numerous amplitudes of random vibrations, the step-stress life tests for the ALT were performed under constant use-circumstances. For a sample, they included 0.40 G_{rms}., 0.60 G_{rms}, 0.80 G_{rms}, and 1.00 G_{rms}, at the natural frequency ($r = 1.0$, $\zeta \approx 0.1$). The damping ratio ($\zeta = 0.096 \approx 0.1$) had a resolving period of 2 sec and a roughly 5% overshoot due to straight exposure between refrigerator and railway carriage. The frequency portion was anticipated, at the natural frequency, ω_n, r ($=\omega/\omega_n$) = 1, which was exerted to the household refrigerator by transportation, and the force transmissibility, Q, had a size of roughly 5.3 from Equation (12). With the gravitational acceleration for 1 G_{rms}, the ratio was 4.0 because the refrigerator arrived at the acceleration of 1 G_{rms} in the shaker bench, compared to that of severe-instance 0.25 G_{rms}. Utilizing the accumulative damage constant, λ, of 2.0, the whole AF in Equation (14) including the force transmissibility was decided to have 450.0 (Table 2).

Table 2. Circumstances for refrigerator ALT.

System States	Worst Case	ALT	AF
Transmissibility, Q ($r = 1.0$, $\zeta = 0.096 \approx 0.1$)	-	5.30 From Equation (14)	28.1①
Amplitude proportion of acceleration, R (a_1/a_0)	0.25 G_{rms}	1 G_{rms}	16.0②
Entire AF (=①×②)			450

Established in the computed AF, the required testing period for an assigned sample size (three samples) was evaluated when the life was targeted. Assuming the first shape parameter on the Weibull chart was 2.0 because ALT and field, β, were not available in the initial test time of design, the life was targeted to have B1 life over 7 days (7,200 km). From Equation (30), the test period computed was roughly 130 minutes for three samples. As the refrigerator was unsuccessful less than once in 130 minutes, the design in a refrigerator was no problem for the entire travel interval of 7,200 km (7 days) to survive the fatigue damage and be B1 life with a roughly 60% level of confidence.

In each ALT, the evaluated lifetime, L_B, may be stated as

$$L_B^\beta \cong x \cdot \frac{n \cdot (h_a \cdot AF)^\beta}{r+1} \tag{33}$$

As $x = \lambda \cdot L_B$, the evaluated failure rate, λ, can be expressed as

$$\lambda \cong \frac{1}{L_B} \cdot (r+1) \cdot \frac{L_B^\beta}{n \cdot (h_a \cdot AF)^\beta} \tag{34}$$

In each ALT phase, if the sample size, n, calculated time, h_a, the life goal, x, shape parameter, β, accelerated factor, AF, and failures, r, were recognized, the evaluated lifetime, L_B, and failure rate, λ, from Equation (33) and (34) could be evaluated.

EXPERIMENTAL METHODS FOR PARAMETRIC ALT

To recognize the failure of a mechanical product using parametric ALT, engineers might perform time-consuming tests with a large number of samples. However, the actual testing time, h_a, may drop dramatically by utilizing the reduction factor in Equation (30) to reduce the sample size needed. Thus, if the lifetime of the PCB in a refrigerator is targeted to have B1 life of seven days, the mission cycles may be obtained for samples subjective to random vibration based on accelerated factor (AF) in Equation (18) and sample size equation in Equation (30). In ALTs, to attain the desired life objective – B1 life of ten years – with no acceleration ($AF = 1$), three samples should be tested for $h_a = 18{,}000$ minutes in Equation (30). On the other hand, the real test cycles computed in Equation (30) were 60 minutes for three samples with $AF = 450$ (see Table 2). So, if there is no failure such as the fatigue of a household compressor and PCB soldering in 60 minutes, it might be ensured to be a B1 life of seven days with a 60% level of confidence. Thus, parametric ALT can find the product failures in a mission time and correct them.

RESULTS AND DISCUSSION

Near the natural frequency ($r = 1.0$, $\zeta \approx 0.1$), the average PSD loads of the subsequent stress quantities were 0.40 G_{rms}, 0.60 G_{rms}, 0.80 G_{rms}, and 1.00 G_{rms} on the programmed shaking table that mounted the test refrigerators (see Figure 4). For these conditions, we found that the refrigerator had fatigued PCB soldering, rubber supports torn, and fatigued tubes. That is, for 0.40 G_{rms}, they failed at 70 min. For 0.60 G_{rms}, they failed at 60 min. For 0.80 G_{rms}, they failed at 45 min. For 1.00 G_{rms}, it failed at 20 min. Thus, 1.00 G_{rms} was utilized because it produced the desired failure with a raised test and was almost a straight line in the Weibull chart.

In 1st ALT, as 1.00 G_{rms}, a natural frequency of $r = 1.0$, and $\zeta \approx 0.1$ were exerted, three compressor mounts in refrigerators fractured: one sample at 20 minutes and two samples at 40 minutes from the horizontal vibration (left ↔ right). As the rubber mounts tore, the PCB soldering, and the connecting refrigerant tubing in the machine compartment failed, and the refrigerant gas leaked out of the system. As a consequence, all three samples no longer functioned.

Figure 5. Failed refrigerator rubber, fatigued PCB soldering, and fractured tubes; a) marketplace, b) 1st ALT outcome.

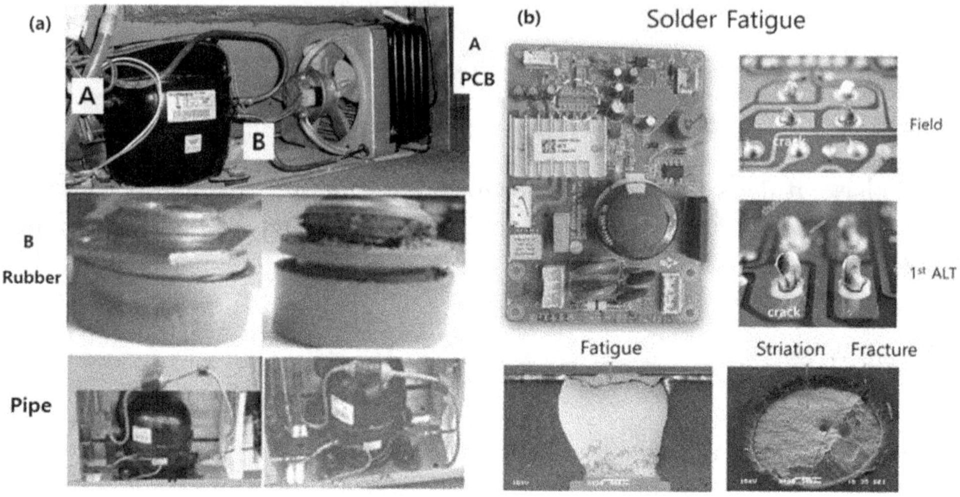

Figure 5 shows the fatigued refrigerators returned from the field and the failed samples from the ALT, separately. The shapes and locations of the failures in the ALT were similar to those returned from the field. Figure 6 also shows the field data and ALT results in the Weibull plot. The shape parameters of the ALT (β_1) and market data (β_2) were similar. Under the repetitive stresses near the natural frequency, it was known that the failure markings exhibited in the 1st ALT were comparable to the failure markings returned from the market as follows: 1) shapes and locations of the failures in the ALT and field and 2) shape parameters of the ALT (β_1) and market data (β_2). Established on both the Weibull plot and test outcomes, ALT was good because it identified the design fragilities which were ascribed to the failure from the market. Thus, we affirmed that the shape parameter, β, was 6.13.

Figure 6. Field data and results of ALT in the Weibull chart.

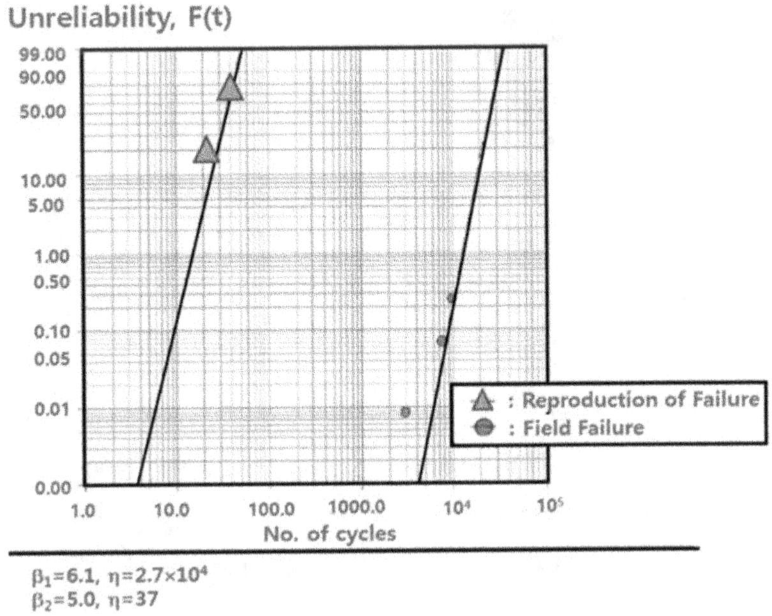

When the test results verified, the torn rubber mount in the first ALT happened because there was no pillar for the rubber mount which could survive the parallel vibrations (left ↔ right). Due to this design defects in the stress concentration regions, the repetitive random loads apparently initiated the tearing in the rubber mounts, fatigued the PCB soldering, and created the brake in the connecting pipes. For an action plan, the refrigerator was redesigned: (1) reformed rubber mount were used on the compressor, C1 (Figure 7a); and (2) the connecting tube, C2 (Figure 7b) was redesigned.

For the second ALTs, these alternative designs were used. The levels of β and *AF* in Figure 6 and Table 2 were confirmed to have 6.41 and 452.0, individually. Based on the test data, because the life target of new samples was less than B1 life for the entire travel distance (7 days), in Equation (30) the calculated test time for the three refrigerators was 40 minutes, which might be the ALT specification.

Figure 7. Design modifications.

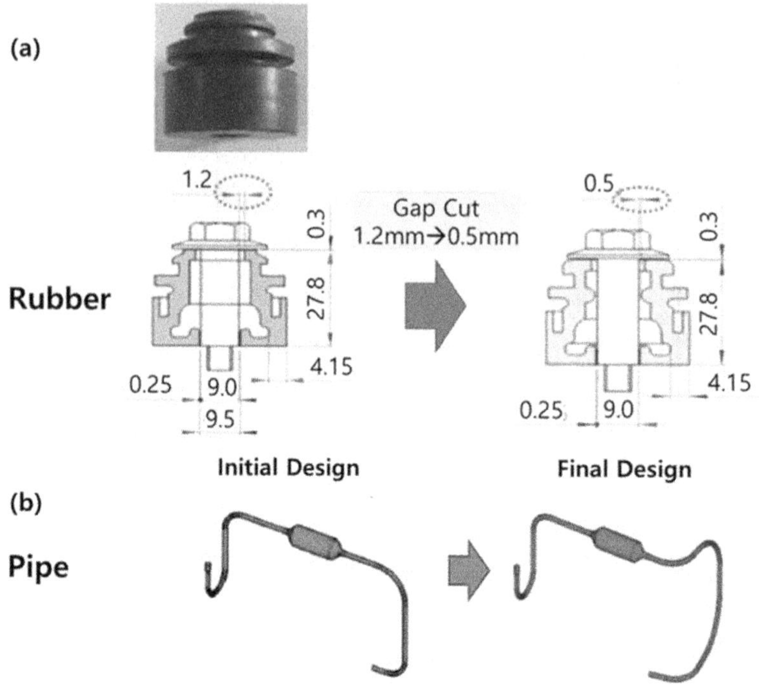

Figure 8. Shift of the natural frequency of parallel vibration because of design alterations.

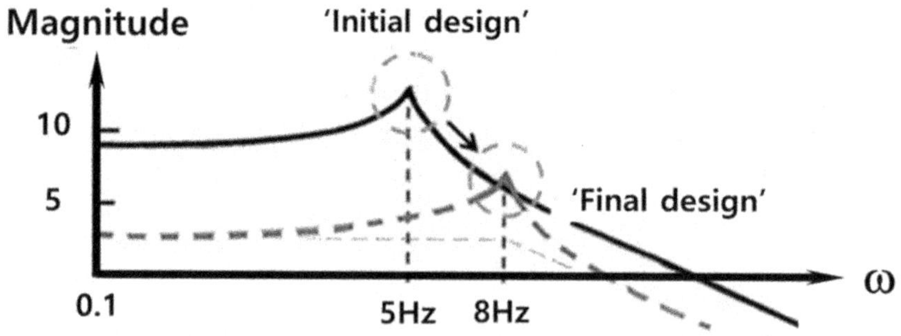

For the 2nd ALT, there was no problem at 60 minutes. We knew that the modified products were effective in eliminating the field failures due to the random vibrations in transit. As a result, the fractured tubing, fatigued inverter PCB soldering, or the torn rubber mounts of compressor in the refrigerator did not occur until 60 minutes into the test. Furthermore, when the refrigerator was exposed to an acceleration of 1.00 G_{rms} in the shaker table, we know that the horizontal vibration (left ↔ right) at the natural frequency shifted from 5 Hz to 8 Hz because of the better damping on the redesigned product (Figure 8).

By second ALTs, from Equations (33) and (34), the product was reassured to have B1 life for the entire travel interval of 7,200 km (7 days) when the true moving period, $h_a = 60$ minutes, in filling in sample size, $n = 3$, life aim, $x = 0.01$, shape parameter, $\beta = 6.4$, accelerated factor, $AF = 452.0$, and failures, $r = 0.0$ (Table 3).

Table 3. Outcomes of ALTs.

	1st ALT	2nd ALT
	Initial Design	Final Design
In 60 minutes, there is no problem	one sample at 20 minutes two samples at 40 minutes	no problems at 60 minutes
Structure	< Machine Room > 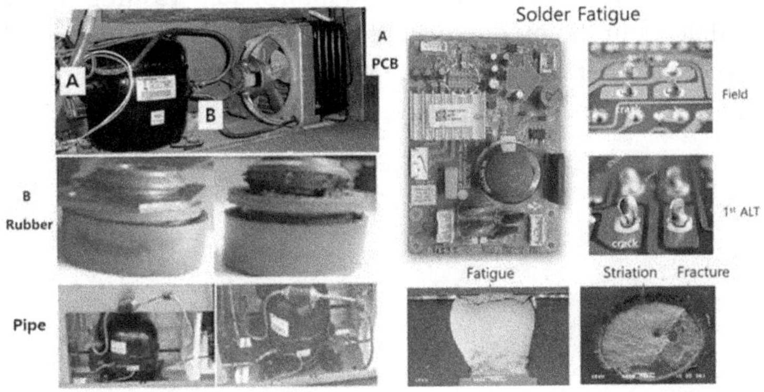	
Action plans	Reformed rubber mount used on the compressor, C1 Reshaped connecting tube, C2	

SUMMARY AND CONCLUSION

To reduce the failure and extend the expected lifetime of refrigerators being shipped by rail, ALT with RQ statement was evolved. The sample size and quantum/transported life-stress model from energy balance were proposed. As an example, the life of product failed by random vibrations in rail transit was studied.

- Through examining household refrigerators that were failing in the field, it was recognized that compressor mounts made of EPDM rubber were fracturing during transport. As a consequence, it produced the fatigue of PCB soldering and refrigerant leakage of connecting tubes. Ultimately failure of the refrigerators no longer operated.
- To replicate the issues in a household refrigerator failed in the field, raised PSD loads – 1 Grms at resonance in first ALT were carried for RQ statement – 40 min. The rubber mounts failed as well as the soldering and tubing in both the 20- & 40-minute tests. As the tubes and the compressor mounts were redesigned, on the 2nd ALT, there were no problems for RQ statement – 40 min and 60 min. Therefore, the product in transportation was assured to survive the expected vibrations

during transport and realize an expected system life – B1 lifetime for the entire transportation interval of 7,200 km for seven days.

- Based on quantum/transported life-stress and sample size model for parametric ALT, this study is only applied to the fatigue of compressor and PCB in a refrigerator due to random vibration in transit. Inspection of the failed refrigerator, load study, and two successions of ALTs for RQ statement disclosed that the life of redevised product in transportation was enhanced. This organized procedure is relevant to other products functioned by machine such as automobile, airplane, and machine tools in transportation.

Using this structured reliability methods with new notions, design issues such as fatigue of Freezer drawer in a new French door refrigerator can be resolved. This method may be pertinent to other mechanical products as well, including – cars, airplane, washing machines, construction machines, etc. If there are defects in the product where induced loads are exerted, the system shall not be successful during its predicted lifetime. By carrying out accelerated tests until the necessitated mission cycles (RQ specification), engineers can reproduce the failure and modify it.

REFERENCES

Campbell, F. C. (Ed.), *Elements of Metallurgy and Engineering Alloys*. DOI: 10.31399/asm.tb.emea.9781627082518

Duga, J. J., Fisher, W. H., Buxaum, R. W., Rosenfield, A. R., Buhr, A. R., Honton, E. J., & McMillan, S. C. (1982) The Economic Effects of Fracture in the United States, Final Report, September 30, Battelle Laboratories, Columbus, OH. Available as NBS Special Publication 647-2.

Elsayed, E. A. (2012). *Reliability Engineering*. John Wiley & Sons.

Epstein, B. (1954). Truncated life tests in the exponential case. *Annals of Mathematical Statistics*, *25*(3), 555–564. DOI: 10.1214/aoms/1177728723

Garvin, D. A. (1987). Competing on the Eight Dimensions of Quality. *Harvard Business Review*, *65*(6), 101–109.

Hahn, G. J., & Meeker, W. Q. (2004). *How to Plan an Accelerated Life Test (E-Book)*. ASQ Quality Press.

IEEE Standard Glossary of Software Engineering Terminology. (2002). *IEEE STD 610.12-1990. Standards Coordinating Committee of the Computer Society of IEEE.* Available online: https://ieeexplore.ieee.org/document/159342

Lalanne, C. (2014). Mechanical Vibration and Shock Analysis: Vol. 5. *Specification Development* (3rd ed.). John Wiley & Sons, Inc. DOI: 10.1002/9781118931219

Magaziner, I. C., & Patinkin, M. (1989). Cold competition: GE wages the refrigerator war. *Harvard Business Review*, *89*(2), 114–124.

Montgomery, D. (2020). *Design and analysis of experiments* (10th ed.). John Wiley & Sons, Inc.

O'Connor, P. P., & Kleyner, A. (2012). *Practical Reliability Engineering* (5th ed.). John Wiley & Sons, Ltd.

Reddy, J. N. (2021). *An Introduction to Nonlinear Finite Element Method with Applications to Heat Transfer, Fluid Mechanics, and Solid Mechanics.* Oxford Press.

Reynolds, D. D. (2016). *Engineering Principles of Mechanical Vibration. Bloomington* (4th ed.). Trafford On Demand Publishing.

Signoret, J., Dutuit, Y., Cacheux, P., Folleau, C., Collas, S., & Thomas, P. (2013). Make your Petri nets understandable: Reliability block diagrams driven Petri nets. *Reliability Engineering & System Safety*, *113*, 61–75. DOI: 10.1016/j.ress.2012.12.008

Taguchi, G., & Shih-Chung, T. (1992). *Introduction to quality engineering: bringing quality engineering upstream*. ASME.

Timoshenko, S., & Maccullough, G. H. (1935). *Elements of strength of materials* (1st ed.). D. Van Nostrand company, Inc.

Wang, T., & Wang, Q. (2021). Cyclic responses and microstructure sensitivity of Cr-based turbine steel under different strain ratios in low cycle fatigue regime. *Materials & Design, 201*, 109529. DOI: 10.1016/j.matdes.2021.109529

Woo, S., O'Neal, D., & Pecht, M. (2023). Improving the lifetime of mechanical systems during transit established on quantum/transport life-stress prototype and sample size. *Mechanical Systems and Signal Processing, 193*, 110222. DOI: 10.1016/j.ymssp.2023.110222

Compilation of References

Abdalah, S., & Niimeh, S. (2017). Sun tracking device two axes with Arduino. *Power. Energy Conversion and Management*, *45*, 1931–1939. DOI: 10.1016/j.enconman.2003.10.007

Abdukarimov, M. F. (2013). On optimal boundary control of displacements in the process of forced vibrations on both ends of a string. [In Russian]. *Dokl. Akad. Nauk Republic of Tadzhikistan*, *56*, 612–618.

Abdukarimov, M. F. (2014). On the optimal boundary control produced by shifting the process of forced vibrations at one end of a string while the other is free. [In Russian]. *Dokl. Akad. Nauk Republic of Tadzhikistan*, *57*, 280–286.

Abouheaf, M., Boase, D., Gueaieb, W., Spinello, D., & Al-Sharhan, S. (2023, June 1). Real-time measurement-driven reinforcement learning control approach for uncertain nonlinear systems. Elsevier BV, 122, 106029-106029. DOI: 10.1016/j.engappai.2023.106029

Abualigah, L., Falcone, D., & Forestiero, A. (2023). Swarm intelligence to face IoT challenges. *Computational Intelligence and Neuroscience*, *4254194*(1), 4254194. Advance online publication. DOI: 10.1155/2023/4254194 PMID: 37284052

Addanki, M., Patra, P., & Kandra, P. (2022). Recent advances and applications of artificial intelligence and related technologies in the food industry. *Applied Food Research*, *2*(2), 100126. DOI: 10.1016/j.afres.2022.100126

Agarwal, M., Singh, A., Arjaria, S., Sinha, A., & Gupta, S. (2020). ToLeD: Tomato leaf disease detection using convolution neural network. *Procedia Computer Science*, *167*, 293–301. DOI: 10.1016/j.procs.2020.03.225

Agarwal, S., & Shinde, R. K. (2022). Smart Pacemaker: A Review. *Cureus*, *14*(10), e30027. DOI: 10.7759/cureus.30027 PMID: 36348845

Aggarwal, C. C. (2016). *Outlier analysis*. Springer.

Aghdam, A. D., Dabanloo, N. J., Rahatabad, F. N., & Maghooli, K. (2024a). Interval Type 2 Adaptive Neuro-Fuzzy Inference System-Based Artificial Pacemaker Design and Stability *Analysis.Journal of Long-Term Effects of Medical Implants*, *34*(1), 9–19. DOI: 10.1615/JLongTermEffMedImplants.2023044398 PMID: 37938200

Aghdam, A. D., Dabanloo, N. J., Rahatabad, F. N., & Maghooli, K. (2024b). Design and Stability Analysis of an Adaptive Neuro-Fuzzy Inference System (ANFIS)-Based Pacemaker Controller in MATLAB Simulink. *Journal of Long-Term Effects of Medical Implants*, *34*(4), 1–13. DOI: 10.1615/JLongTermEffMedImplants.2023043889 PMID: 38842228

Ahmad, I., Hamid, M., Yousaf, S., Shah, S. T., & Ahmad, M. O. (2020). Optimizing pretrained convolutional neural networks for tomato leaf disease detection. *Complexity, 2020*(1), 8812019. DOI: 10.1155/2020/8812019

Ahmad, I., Hussain, T., Shah, B., Hussain, A., Ali, I., & Ali, F. (2024). Accelerated particle swarm optimization algorithm for efficient cluster head selection in WSN. *Computers, Materials & Continua, 79*(3), 3585–3629. DOI: 10.32604/cmc.2024.050596

Ahmed, R. S., Ahmed, E. S. A., & Saeed, R. A. (2021). Machine learning in cyber-physical systems in industry 4.0. In *Artificial intelligence paradigms for smart cyber-physical systems* (pp. 20–41). IGI global. DOI: 10.4018/978-1-7998-5101-1.ch002

Ai, W., Patel, N. D., Roop, P. S., Malik, A., & Trew, M. L. (2020). Closing the Loop: Validation of Implantable Cardiac Devices with Computational Heart Models. *IEEE Journal of Biomedical and Health Informatics, 24*(6), 1579–1588. DOI: 10.1109/JBHI.2019.2947007 PMID: 31613786

Akhtar, M. W., Hossain, M. S., Hassan, S. A., Jung, H., Garg, S., & Ghaffar, R. (2020). The shift to 6G communications: Vision and requirements. *Human-Centric Computing and Information Sciences, 10*(1), 53. Advance online publication. DOI: 10.1186/s13673-020-00258-2

Aktharun, S B., & Sekhar, M. (2022, January 1). Design of Unmanned Aerial Vehicles for various wireless applications. Elsevier BV, 51, 1115-1119. DOI: 10.1016/j.matpr.2021.07.108

Alattar, A E., & Mohsen, S. (2023, July 27). A Survey on Smart Wearable Devices for Healthcare Applications. Springer Science+Business Media, 132(1), 775-783. DOI: 10.1007/s11277-023-10639-2

Alhijawi, B., & Awajan, A. (2024). Genetic algorithms: Theory, genetic operators, solutions, and applications. *Evolutionary Intelligence, 17*(3), 1245–1256. DOI: 10.1007/s12065-023-00822-6

Aljehani, F., N'Doye, I., & Laleg-Kirati, T. (2023, January 1). Feeding control and water quality monitoring in aquaculture systems: Opportunities and challenges. Cornell University. https://doi.org/DOI: 10.48550/arXiv.2306

Al-Khatib, S. M., Singh, J. P., Ghanbari, H., McManus, D. D., Deering, T. F., Avari Silva, J. N., Mittal, S., Krahn, A., & Hurwitz, J. L. (2024). The potential of artificial intelligence to revolutionize health care delivery, research, and education in cardiac electrophysiology. *Heart Rhythm, 21*(6), 978–989. DOI: 10.1016/j.hrthm.2024.04.053 PMID: 38752904

Allouhi, A., Rehman, S., & Buker, M. S. (2002). Solar PV system: A review. *Renewable & Sustainable Energy Reviews, 20*, 35–55. DOI: 10.1016/j.rser.2017.06.001

Allouhi, A., Rehman, S., Buker, M. S., & Said, Z. (2022). Up-to-date literature review on solar PV systems: Technology progress, market status, and R&D. *Journal of Cleaner Production, 362*, 132339. DOI: 10.1016/j.jclepro.2022.132339

Alper, M., & Goggin, M. (2019). *Digital technology and disability: A research agenda for education.* The Institute for Community Inclusion.

Alqasi, M. A. Y., Alkelanie, Y. A. M., & Alnagrat, A. J. A. (2024). Intelligent infrastructure for urban transportation: The role of artificial intelligence in predictive maintenance. *Brilliance: Research of Artificial Intelligence*, *4*(2), 625–637. DOI: 10.47709/brilliance.v4i2.4889

Alshriem, M. (2020, April 30). The Use of Artificial Intelligence in Traffic Violation Data Analysis. *The Use of Artificial Intelligence in Traffic Violation Data Analysis.*, *13*(4), 644–644. DOI: 10.37624/IJERT/13.4.2020.644-652

Altman, N. S. (1992). An introduction to kernel and nearest-neighbor nonparametric regression. *The American Statistician*, *46*(3), 175–185. DOI: 10.1080/00031305.1992.10475879

Amatya, S., & Karkee, M. (2015). Detection of cherry tree branches for automated shake-and-catch harvesting. In *2015 ASABE Annual International Meeting* (p. 1). American Society of Agricultural and Biological Engineers.

Ampuero, S., & Bosset, J. O. (2003). The electronic nose applied to dairy products: A review. *Sensors and Actuators. B, Chemical*, *94*(1), 1–12. DOI: 10.1016/S0925-4005(03)00321-6

Andreotta, A. J., Kirkham, N., & Rizzi, M. (2022). AI, big data, and the future of consent. *AI & Society*, *37*(4), 1715–1728. DOI: 10.1007/s00146-021-01262-5 PMID: 34483498

Anisha, A. The Implementation of Ai-Driven Supply Chain Optimization in the Food Industry.

Annaz, F. Y., & Kaluarachchi, M. M. (2023). Progress in redundant electromechanical actuators for aerospace applications. *Aerospace (Basel, Switzerland)*, *10*(9), 787. DOI: 10.3390/aerospace10090787

Anthony, C., Bechky, B. A., & Fayard, A. L. (2023). “Collaborating” with AI: Taking a system view to explore the future of work. *Organization Science*, *34*(5), 1672–1694. DOI: 10.1287/orsc.2022.1651

Antle, J. M. (1999). Benefits and costs of food safety regulation. *Food Policy*, *24*(6), 605–623. DOI: 10.1016/S0306-9192(99)00068-8

Antsaklis, P. J. (1999). Intelligent Control. Encyclopedia of Electrical and Electronics Engineering. *John Wiley & Sons, Inc,* 10, 493-503.

Aquilina, O. (2006). A Brief History of Cardiac Pacing. *Images in Paediatric Cardiology*, *8*(2), 17–81. PMID: 22368662

Aquino, A., Ponce, J. M., & Andújar, J. M. (2020). Identification of olive fruit, in intensive olive orchards, by means of its morphological structure using convolutional neural networks. *Computers and Electronics in Agriculture*, *176*, 105616. DOI: 10.1016/j.compag.2020.105616

Armoundas, A. A., Narayan, S. M., Arnett, D. K., Spector-Bagdady, K., Bennett, D. A., Celi, L. A., Friedman, P. A., Gollob, M. H., Hall, J. L., Kwitek, A. E., Lett, E., Menon, B. K., Sheehan, K. A., & Al-Zaiti, S. S. (2024). Use of Artificial Intelligence in Improving Outcomes in Heart Disease: A Scientific Statement From the American Heart Association. *Circulation*, *149*(14), e1028–e1050. DOI: 10.1161/CIR.0000000000001201 PMID: 38415358

Arunachalam, S. P., Kapa, S., Mulpuru, S. K., Friedman, P. A., & Tolkacheva, E. G. (2016). Intelligent Fractional-Order PID (FOPID) Heart Rate Controller for Cardiac Pacemaker. *IEEE Healthcare Innovation Point-Of-Care Technologies Conference (HI-POCT)*, Cancun, Mexico, pp. 105-108, DOI: 10.1109/HIC.2016.7797708

Arwa, E. O., & Folly, K. A. (2020). Reinforcement learning techniques for optimal power control in grid-connected microgrids: A comprehensive review. *IEEE Access : Practical Innovations, Open Solutions*, *8*, 208992–209007. DOI: 10.1109/ACCESS.2020.3038735

Asadi, S., Jimeno-Saez, P., Lopez-Ballesteros, A., & Senent-Aparicio, J. (2024). Comparison and integration of physical and interpretable AI-driven models for rainfall-runoff simulation. *Results in Engineering*, Volume 24, 103048. ArchDaily, https://www.archdaily.com/962924/building-a-city-from-scratch-the-story-of-songdo-korea

Ashchepkov, L. T. (1981). Optimal control of a system with intermediate conditions. [In Russian]. *Applied Mathematics and Mechanics*, *45*, 215–222.

Aslain, B. N. D., Nzié, W., & Yamigno, S. D. (2023). Modeling the failure rate of a standby multi-component system and improving reliability. *Modern Mechanical Engineering*, *13*(1), 21–33. DOI: 10.4236/mme.2023.131002

Awaisi, K. S., Hussain, S., Ahmed, M., Khan, A. A., & Ahmed, G. (2020). Leveraging IoT and fog computing in healthcare systems. *IEEE Internet of Things Magazine*, *3*(2), 52–56. DOI: 10.1109/IOTM.0001.1900096

Awasthi, A., Kallioğlu, M. A., Sharma, A., & Kumar, A. (2022). Solar collector tilt angle optimization for solar power plant setup-able sites at Western Himalaya and correlation formulation. *Journal of Thermal Analysis and Calorimetry*, *147*(20), 11417–11431. DOI: 10.1007/s10973-022-11345-0

Azam, M. A., Jahan, M. A., & Rahaman, M. A. (2014). Optimization of WEDM process parameters using response surface methodology. *Journal of Advanced Manufacturing Systems*, *13*(2), 297–308.

Bahadirov, G., Sultanov, T., Umarov, B., & Bakhadirov, K. (2020, July). Advanced machine for sorting potatoes tubers. []. IOP Publishing.]. *IOP Conference Series. Materials Science and Engineering*, *883*(1), 012132. DOI: 10.1088/1757-899X/883/1/012132

Bajpai, S., Alam, S., & Ali, M. (2017). Intelligent Heart Rate Controller using Fractional Order Pid Controller Tuned by Genetic Algorithm for Pacemaker. *IJERT*. 6(5), 715-720. doi::DOI: 10.17577/IJERTV6IS050463

Baker, R. S. (2016). Big data and education: A critical review of the emerging literature. *Research in Learning Technology*, *24*, 1–14. DOI: 10.3402/rlt.v24.32034

Baker, R. S.. (2020). The role of educational data mining in education. *International Journal of Artificial Intelligence in Education*, *30*(1), 1–6. DOI: 10.1007/s40593-020-00210-1

Baker, R. S., & Inventado, P. S. (2014). Educational data mining and learning analytics. In *Handbook of educational data mining* (pp. 3–19). CRC Press.

Balaban, M., & Maraee, A. (2019). Removing redundancy multiplicity constraint in UML class model. *Software & Systems Modeling, 18*(4), 2717–2751. DOI: 10.1007/s10270-018-0696-z

Banerjee, A., Pradhan, S., Misra, B., & Chakraborty, S. (2024). A guide to meta-heuristic algorithms for multi-objective optimization: Concepts and approaches. In Dey, N. (Ed.), *Applied Multi-Objective Optimization* (pp. 1–19). Springer Nature Singapore., DOI: 10.1007/978-981-97-0353-1_1

Banerjee, U., Dey, B. S., Kar, I. N., & Saha, S. K. (2022, January 1). Robust Artificial Delay based Impedance Control of Robotic Manipulators with Uncertain Dynamics. Cornell University. https://doi .org/DOI: 10.48550/arXiv.2208

Baños, A., Salt, J., & Casanova, V. (2020, January 1). A QFT approach to robust dual-rate control systems. Cornell University. https://doi.org/DOI: 10.48550/arXiv.2002

Bansal, H. O., Kumar, R., Singh, R. K., & Bhardwaj, S. (2012). Design of an Intelligent PD Controller for Artificial Pacemaker. *2nd International Conference on Power, Control and Embedded Systems*, Allahabad, India. pp. 1-4, DOI: 10.1109/ICPCES.2012.6508140

Barseghyan, V. R. (2016b). On the controllability and observability of linear dynamic systems with variable structure. In *Proceedings of the 2016 International Conference Stability and Oscillations of Nonlinear Control Systems (Pyatnitskiy's Conference)* (pp. 1–3), IEEE, Moscow, Russia, 1–3 June 2016. DOI: 10.1109/STAB.2016.7541163

Barseghyan, V. R., & Solodusha, S. V. (2021b). On One Problem in Optimal Boundary Control for String Vibrations with a Given Velocity of Points at an Intermediate Moment of Time. In *Proceedings of the 2021 International Russian Automation Conference (RusAutoCon)* (pp. 343–349), IEEE, Sochi, Russia, 5–11 September 2021. DOI: 10.1109/RusAutoCon52004.2021.9537514

Barseghyan, V. R. (2012). Control of stage by stage changing linear dynamic systems. *Yugoslav Journal of Operations Research, 22*(1), 31–39. DOI: 10.2298/YJOR111019002B

Barseghyan, V. R. (2016a). *Upravlenie sostavnykh dinamicheskikh sistem i sistem s mnogotochechnymi promezhutochnymi usloviyami* [Control of compound dynamic systems and of systems with multipoint intermediate conditions]. Nauka. (In Russian)

Barseghyan, V. R. (2018). The Control Problem for Stepwise Changing Linear Systems of Loaded Differential Equations with Unseparated Multipoint Intermediate Conditions. *Mechanics of Solids, 53*(6), 615–622. DOI: 10.3103/S0025654418060031

Barseghyan, V. R. (2019). Control Problem of String Vibrations with Inseparable Multipoint Conditions at Intermediate Points in Time. *Mechanics of Solids, 54*(8), 1216–1226. DOI: 10.3103/S0025654419080120

Barseghyan, V. R. (2022). Problems of Boundary Control and Optimal Control of String Vibrations with Multipoint Intermediate Conditions on the State Functions. *Proceedings of the Steklov Institute of Mathematics, 319*(S1), S66–S79. DOI: 10.1134/S0081543822060074

Barseghyan, V., & Solodusha, S. (2021a). Optimal Boundary Control of String Vibrations with Given Shape of Deflection at a Certain Moment of Time. *Lecture Notes in Computer Science, 12755*, 299–313. DOI: 10.1007/978-3-030-77876-7_20

Barseghyan, V., & Solodusha, S. (2022). Control of String Vibrations by Displacement of One End with the Other End Fixed, Given the Deflection Form at an Intermediate Moment of Time. *Axioms, 11*(4), 157. DOI: 10.3390/axioms11040157

Barsegyan, V. R. (2020). The Problem of Optimal Control of String Vibrations. *International Applied Mechanics, 56*(4), 471–480. DOI: 10.1007/s10778-020-01030-w

Basavaiah, J., & Arlene Anthony, A. (2020). Tomato leaf disease classification using multiple feature extraction techniques. *Wireless Personal Communications, 115*(1), 633–651. DOI: 10.1007/s11277-020-07590-x

Beauchamp, T. L. (2011). Informed consent: Its history, meaning, and present challenges. *Cambridge Quarterly of Healthcare Ethics, 20*(4), 515–523. DOI: 10.1017/S0963180111000259 PMID: 21843382

Begishev, I., Khisamova, Z., & Vasyukov, V. (2021). Technological, ethical, environmental and legal aspects of robotics. In *E3S Web of Conferences* (Vol. 244, p. 12028). EDP Sciences. DOI: 10.1051/e3sconf/202124412028

Bello, S., Ige, O., Wada, I., Adebayo, S., & Chianumba, E. (2024). AI-driven predictive maintenance and optimization of renewable energy systems for enhanced operational efficiency and longevity. *International Journal of Science and Research Archive, 13*(1), 2823–2837. DOI: 10.30574/ijsra.2024.13.1.1992

Berman, A. F., Nikolaichuk, O. A., & Yurin, A. Y. (2020). The validation system for reliability and survivability of unique mechanical systems. International Conference Aviation Engineering and Transportation (AviaEnT 2020). *IOP Conference Series. Materials Science and Engineering, 1061*(1), 012007. DOI: 10.1088/1757-899X/1061/1/012007

Bessa, W. M. (2022, January 1). A framework for the development of intelligent mechanical systems. Cornell University. https://doi.org/DOI: 10.48550/arXiv.2205

Biasi, N., Seghetti, P., Mercati, M., & Tognetti, A. (2022). A Reaction-Diffusion Heart Model for the Closed-Loop Evaluation of Heart-Pacemaker Interaction. *IEEE Access : Practical Innovations, Open Solutions, 10*, 121249–121260. DOI: 10.1109/ACCESS.2022.3222830

Bi, Z. M., Luo, C., Miao, Z., Zhang, B., Zhang, W. J., & Wang, L. (2021). Safety assurance mechanisms of collaborative robotic systems in manufacturing. *Robotics and Computer-integrated Manufacturing, 67*, 102022. DOI: 10.1016/j.rcim.2020.102022

Blackett, C. (2022). The Ethics of AI in Autonomous Transport. In Proceeding of Meeting of the 32nd European Safety and Reliability Conference, Dublin, Ireland, August.

Blackett, C. (2021). Human-Centered Design in an Automated World. *4th International Conference on Intelligent Human Systems Integration: Integrating People and Intelligent Systems (IHSI 2021)*, 22-24 February, 2021, Palermo, Italy, 17- 23.

Black, P., & Wiliam, D. (1998). Assessment and classroom learning. Assessment in Education: Principles. *Assessment in Education: Principles, Policy & Practice, 5*(1), 7–74. DOI: 10.1080/0969595980050102

Borah, M. C., & Kalita, P. K. (2021). Optimization of WEDM process parameters using artificial neural network and genetic algorithm. *Materials Today: Proceedings, 40*, 1913–1921.

Bouwmeester, J., Menicucci, A., & Gill, E. K. A. (2022). Improving CubeSat reliability: Subsystem redundancy or improved testing? *Reliability Engineering & System Safety*, *220*, 108288. DOI: 10.1016/j.ress.2021.108288

Braun, V., & Clarke, V. (2006). Using thematic analysis in psychology. *Qualitative Research in Psychology*, *3*(2), 77–101. DOI: 10.1191/1478088706qp063oa

Breiman, L. (2001). Random forests. *Machine Learning*, *45*(1), 5–32. DOI: 10.1023/A:1010933404324

Brusilovsky, P., & Millán, E. (2018). User modeling for adaptive hypermedia and adaptive learning environments. In *The adaptive web* (pp. 3–43). Springer.

Bünger, L. (2021). *Robotic waste sorting*. Worcester Polytechnic Institute.

Butkovsky, A. G. (1965). *Teoriya optimal'nogo upravleniya sistemami s raspredelennymi parametrami* [Theory of Optimal Control for Systems with Distributed Parameters]. Nauka. (In Russian)

Butkovsky, A. G. (1975). *Metody upravleniya sistemami s raspredelennymi parametrami* [Control Methods for Systems with Distributed Parameters]. Nauka. (In Russian)

Campbell, F. C. (Ed.), *Elements of Metallurgy and Engineering Alloys*. DOI: 10.31399/asm.tb.emea.9781627082518

Cao, D., Hu, W., Zhao, J., Zhang, G., Zhang, B., Liu, Z., Chen, Z., & Blaabjerg, F. (2020). Reinforcement learning and its applications in modern power and energy systems: A review. *Journal of Modern Power Systems and Clean Energy*, *8*(6), 1029–1042. DOI: 10.35833/MPCE.2020.000552

Cardello, A. V., Schutz, H. G., & Lesher, L. L. (2007). Consumer perceptions of foods processed by innovative and emerging technologies: A conjoint analytic study. *Innovative Food Science & Emerging Technologies*, *8*(1), 73–83. DOI: 10.1016/j.ifset.2006.07.002

Cardenas, A. A., Amin, S., & Sastry, S. (2008). Research challenges for the security of control systems. *HotSec*, *8*(6), 1–6.

CAST. (2018). Universal design for learning guidelines version 2.2. https://udlguidelines.cast.org/

Castro, J. F., & Malathi, R. (2016). Bioinspired Algorithm for the Control of Cardiac Pacemaker. *Asian Journal of Science and Technology*, *7*(11), 3973–3976.

Castro, V. J., & Malathi, R. (2018). Design of Advanced Control Strategies for Cardiovascular System. *Materials Today: Proceedings*, *5*(1), 1960–1966. DOI: 10.1016/j.matpr.2017.11.299

Cavalcanti, J. H., Kovacs, T., Ko, A., & Pocsarovszky, K. (2023). Production system efficiency optimization through application of a hybrid artificial intelligence solution. *International Journal of Computer Integrated Manufacturing*, *ahead-of-print*(ahead-of-print), 1–18. DOI: 10.1080/0951192X.2023.2257661

Çavdar, B., Şahin, E., & Sesli, E. (2024). On the assessment of meta-heuristic algorithms for automatic voltage regulator system controller design: A standardization process. *Electrical Engineering*, *106*(5), 5801–5839. DOI: 10.1007/s00202-024-02314-x

Chalapathy, R., & Chawla, S. (2019). Deep learning for anomaly detection: A survey. *arXiv preprint arXiv:1901.03407.*

Chandu, H. (2024). Advanced Methods for Verifying Memory Controllers in Modern Computing Systems. *International Journal of Advanced Research in Science. Tongxin Jishu, •••*, 377–388. DOI: 10.48175/IJARSCT-19862

Chauhan, N., Singh, J., Chandra, S., Chaudhary, V., & Kumar, V. (2018). "Non-thermal techniques: Application in food industries" A review. *Journal of Pharmacognosy and Phytochemistry, 7*(5), 1507–1518.

Chen, T. Y., Tsai, C. D., Fu, H. W., Yang, Y. C., & Huang, T. C. (2021, September). Error Correctable Range-Addressable Lookup for Activation and Quantization in AI Automotive Electronics. In *2021 IEEE International Conference on Consumer Electronics-Taiwan (ICCE-TW)* (pp. 1-2). IEEE. DOI: 10.1109/ICCE-TW52618.2021.9603030

Chen, X., Li, Y., & Liu, H. (2023). Explainable AI: Interpreting and explaining models. *Journal of Machine Learning Research, 24*(1), 345–358.

Chew, K.-M., Chia, D. W.-F., Yiiong, S.-P., & Tan, S. C.-W. "Green Internet of Things (IoT) Solar Photovoltaic Absorption Optimization Based Panel Orientation in East Malaysia," *2022 International Conference on Computer and Drone Applications (IConDA)*, Kuching, Malaysia, 2022, pp. 46-50. DOI: 10.1109/ICONDA56696.2022.10000386

Chng, K. K., Siew, F. L., Woong, C. W., & Woong, G. S. (2019). Solar tracing device design and installation. *Renewable Energy, 34*, 1364–1370. DOI: 10.1016/j.renene.2019.03.004

Chopra, G., & Whig, P. (2021). Analysis of tomato leaf disease identification techniques. [JCSE]. *Journal of Computing Science and Engineering : JCSE, 2*(2), 98–103. DOI: 10.36596/jcse.v2i2.171

Choudhury, I. A., & Bhattacharyya, B. (2021). Investigation on optimization of process parameters of WEDM during machining of titanium alloy using Taguchi-based grey relational analysis. *Materials Research Express, 8*(2), 026517. DOI: 10.1088/2053-1591/abcf4e

Chowdhury, M. E., Rahman, T., Khandakar, A., Ibtehaz, N., Khan, A. U., Khan, M. S., ... & Ali, S. H. M. (2021). Tomato leaf diseases detection using deep learning technique. Technology in Agriculture, 453.

Chowdhury, M. E., Rahman, T., Khandakar, A., Ayari, M. A., Khan, A. U., Khan, M. S., Al-Emadi, N., Reaz, M. B. I., Islam, M. T., & Ali, S. H. M. (2021). Automatic and reliable leaf disease detection using deep learning techniques. *AgriEngineering, 3*(2), 294–312. DOI: 10.3390/agriengineering3020020

Chowdhury, S., & Karanfil, T. (2024). Applications of artificial intelligence (AI) in drinking water treatment processes: Possibilities.[[CNN,]. *Chemosphere, 356*, 141958. https://edition.cnn.com/travel/millau-viaduct-tallest-bridge-construction/index.html. DOI: 10.1016/j.chemosphere.2024.141958 PMID: 38608775

Cortes, C., & Vapnik, V. (1995). Support-vector networks. In Machine Learning, pages 273–297. DOI: 10.1007/BF00994018

Creswell, J. W., & Poth, C. N. (2018). *Qualitative inquiry and research design: Choosing among five approaches* (4th ed.). SAGE Publications.

Cui, Y., Lu, W., Xue, J., Ge, L., Yin, X., Jian, S., Li, H., Zhu, B., Dai, Z., & Shen, Q. (2023). Machine learning-guided REIMS pattern recognition of non-dairy cream, milk fat cream and whipping cream for fraudulence identification. *Food Chemistry*, *429*, 136986. DOI: 10.1016/j.foodchem.2023.136986 PMID: 37516053

Da Costa, A. Z., Figueroa, H. E., & Fracarolli, J. A. (2020). Computer vision based detection of external defects on tomatoes using deep learning. *Biosystems Engineering*, *190*, 131–144. DOI: 10.1016/j.biosystemseng.2019.12.003

da Silva Lima, G., Amorim Savi, M., & Moreira Bessa, W. (2024). Adaptive control of cardiac rhythms. *Scientific Reports*, *14*(1), 23284. DOI: 10.1038/s41598-024-74415-3 PMID: 39375442

Daniyan, I., Mpofu, K., Ramatsetse, B., & Adeodu, A. (2020). Design and simulation of a robotic arm for manufacturing operations in the railcar industry. *Procedia Manufacturing*, *51*, 67–72. DOI: 10.1016/j.promfg.2020.10.011

Datta, A., Kolwadkar, B., & Ingale, V. V. (2021). Artificial Cardiac Pacemaker Control design using Deep Reinforcement learning: A Continuous Control Approach, *5th International Conference on Trends in Electronics and Informatics (ICOEI)*, Tirunelveli, India, pp. 1031-1038, DOI: 10.1109/ICOEI51242.2021.9453014

De Angelis, D., Summo, C., Pasqualone, A., Faccia, M., & Squeo, G. (2024). Advancements in food authentication using soft independent modelling of class analogy (SIMCA): A review. *Food Quality and Safety*, *8*, fyae032. DOI: 10.1093/fqsafe/fyae032

Dehghan-Dehnavi, S., Fotuhi-Firuzabad, M., Moeini-Aghtaie, M., Dehghanian, P., & Wang, F. (2020, June). Estimating participation abilities of industrial customers in demand response programs: A two-level decision-making tree analysis. In *2020 IEEE/IAS 56th Industrial and Commercial Power Systems Technical Conference (I&CPS)* (pp. 1-8). IEEE. DOI: 10.1109/ICPS48389.2020.9176817

Delwiche, S. R., Pearson, T. C., & Brabec, D. L. (2005). High-speed optical sorting of soft wheat for reduction of deoxynivalenol. *Plant Disease*, *89*(11), 1214–1219. DOI: 10.1094/PD-89-1214 PMID: 30786446

Deng, L. (2014). A tutorial survey of architectures, algorithms, and applications for deep learning. *APSIPA Transactions on Signal and Information Processing*, *3*(1), e2. DOI: 10.1017/atsip.2013.9

Desimone, L. M., & Garet, M. S. (2015). Best practices in teachers' professional development in the United States. Psychology. *Social Education*, *7*(3), 251–275. DOI: 10.25115/psye.v7i3.1307

Dev, P., Jain, S., Arora, P K., & Kumar, H. (2021, January 1). Machine learning and its impact on control systems: A review. Elsevier BV, 47, 3744-3749. DOI: 10.1016/j.matpr.2021.02.281

Devos, O., Downey, G., & Duponchel, L. (2014). Simultaneous data pre-processing and SVM classification model selection based on a parallel genetic algorithm applied to spectroscopic data of olive oils. *Food Chemistry*, *148*, 124–130. DOI: 10.1016/j.foodchem.2013.10.020 PMID: 24262536

Dewi, T., Risma, P., & Oktarina, Y. (2020). Fruit sorting robot based on color and size for an agricultural product packaging system. *Bulletin of Electrical Engineering and Informatics*, *9*(4), 1438–1445. DOI: 10.11591/eei.v9i4.2353

Dey, R., Dey, N., Dhar, R. S., Mondal, U., Thanikanti, S. B., & Nwulu, N. (2024). Advances in Controller Design of Pacemakers for Pacing Control: A comprehensive Review. *Annual Reviews in Control*, *57*, 100930. DOI: 10.1016/j.arcontrol.2023.100930

Dhal, K. G., & Das, S. (2020). Local search-based dynamically adapted bat algorithm in the image enhancement domain. *International Journal of Computing Science and Mathematics*, *11*(1), 1–28. DOI: 10.1504/IJCSM.2020.105447

Dhanalakshmi, R., Sankaranarayanasamy, K., & Thirumarimurugan, M. (2022). ANFIS-based optimization of surface roughness in turning operation of Inconel 718 superalloy. *Measurement*, *188*, 352–363.

Ding, D., Zhang, Z., & Ding, Q. (2021, August 1). Analysis on the Application of Artificial Intelligence Technology in Electrical Automation Control. *Journal of Physics: Conference Series*, *1992*(3), 032147–032147. DOI: 10.1088/1742-6596/1992/3/032147

Di, X., & Shi, R. (2021). A survey on autonomous vehicle control in the era of mixed-autonomy: From physics-based to AI-guided driving policy learning.[[Discover Engineering,]. *Transportation Research Part C, Emerging Technologies*, *125*, 103008. https://www.discoverengineering.org/dynamics-and-control-in-civil-engineering/. DOI: 10.1016/j.trc.2021.103008

Dramićanin, T., Zeković, I., Periša, J., & Dramićanin, M. D. (2019). The parallel factor analysis of beer fluorescence. *Journal of Fluorescence*, *29*(5), 1103–1111. DOI: 10.1007/s10895-019-02421-0 PMID: 31396828

Dreglea, A. I., & Sidorov, N. A. (2018). Integral Equations in Identification of External Force and Heat Source Density Dynamics. *Bul. Acad. Stiinte Repub. Mold. Mat.*, *3*, 68–77.

Dubey, V., Goud, H., Sharma, P. C., & Anjana, S. (2024). Designing of Intelligent PID Controller for Cardiac Pacemaker Using Artificial bee Colony Algorithm. *Systems Science &amp. Systems Science & Control Engineering*, *12*(1), 2347891. Advance online publication. DOI: 10.1080/21642583.2024.2347891

Duga, J. J., Fisher, W. H., Buxaum, R. W., Rosenfield, A. R., Buhr, A. R., Honton, E. J., & McMillan, S. C. (1982) The Economic Effects of Fracture in the United States, Final Report, September 30, Battelle Laboratories, Columbus, OH. Available as NBS Special Publication 647-2.

Duong, T. Q., Dobre, O. A., Ansere, J. A., Sharma, V., Narottama, B., & Shin, H. (2022). Quantum-Inspired Machine Learning for 6G: Fundamentals, Security, Resource Allocations, Challenges, and Future Research Directions. *IEEE Open Journal of Vehicular Technology*, *3*, 375–387. DOI: 10.1109/OJVT.2022.3202876

Dutta, D., & Upreti, S R. (2021, August 10). Artificial intelligence-based process control in chemical, biochemical, and biomedical engineering. Wiley, 99(11), 2467-2504. DOI: 10.1002/cjce.24246

Dweck, C. S. (2016). *Mindset: The new psychology of success*. Ballantine Books.

Dzhusupova, R., Bosch, J., & Olsson, H. H. (2024). Choosing the right path for AI integration in engineering companies: A strategic guide. *Journal of Systems and Software*, Volume 210, 111945. Fortune Business Insights, https://www.fortunebusinessinsights.com/ai-in-construction-market-109848

El Ouahidi, A., El Ouahidi, Y., Nicol, P. P., Hannachi, S., Benic, C., Mansourati, J., Pasdeloup, B., & Didier, R. (2024). Machine learning for pacemaker implantation prediction after TAVI using multimodal imaging data. *Scientific Reports*, *14*(1), 25008. DOI: 10.1038/s41598-024-76128-z PMID: 39443560

Elnaggar, M. I., Ashour, A. S., Guo, Y., El-Khobby, H. A., & Abd Elnaby, M. M. (2018). An Optimized Mamdani FPD Controller Design of Cardiac Pacemaker. *Health Information Science and Systems*, *7*(1), 2. DOI: 10.1007/s13755-018-0063-z PMID: 30588292

Elsayed, E. A. (2012). *Reliability Engineering*. John Wiley & Sons.

Emami, S A., Castaldi, P., & Banazadeh, A. (2022, January 1). Neural network-based flight control systems: Present and future. Elsevier BV, 53, 97-137. DOI: 10.1016/j.arcontrol.2022.04.006

Epstein, B. (1954). Truncated life tests in the exponential case. *Annals of Mathematical Statistics*, *25*(3), 555–564. DOI: 10.1214/aoms/1177728723

Ersöz, O. Ö., İnal, A. F., Aktepe, A., Türker, A. K., & Ersöz, S. (2022). A systematic literature review of the predictive maintenance from transportation systems aspect. *Sustainability (Basel)*, *14*(21), 14536. DOI: 10.3390/su142114536

Eşer, M., Yıldız, B. A., & Türe, U. (2024). Redundancy in automatic flight control system design for a general-purpose helicopter. *Journal of Aviation*, *8*(2), 96–105. DOI: 10.30518/jav.1468684

Esmaeilpour, R., & Karami, A. (2021). Multi-objective optimization of machining parameters of Ti6Al4V using ANFIS and NSGA-II. *International Journal of Advanced Manufacturing Technology*, •••, 1–18.

Eswaran, M., Inkulu, A., Tamilarasan, K., Bahubalendruni, M. V. A. R., Jaideep, R., Faris, M. S., & Jacob, N. (2024). Optimal layout planning for human robot collaborative assembly systems and visualization through immersive technologies. *Expert Systems with Applications*, *241*, 122465. DOI: 10.1016/j.eswa.2023.122465

Fan, S., Li, J., Zhang, Y., Tian, X., Wang, Q., He, X., Zhang, C., & Huang, W. (2020). On line detection of defective apples using computer vision system combined with deep learning methods. *Journal of Food Engineering*, *286*, 110102. DOI: 10.1016/j.jfoodeng.2020.110102

Faraj, M. A., & Abbood, A. M. (2021). Fractional order PID controller tuned by bat algorithm for robot trajectory control. *Indonesian Journal of Electrical Engineering and Computer Science*, *21*, 74–83. DOI: 10.11591/ijeecs.v21.i1.pp74-83

Fausing Olesen, J., & Shaker, H. R. (2020). Predictive maintenance for pump systems and thermal power plants: State-of-the-art review, trends and challenges. *Sensors (Basel)*, *20*(8), 2425. DOI: 10.3390/s20082425 PMID: 32344674

Fayyaz, M., & Vladimirova, T. (2016). Survey and future directions of fault-tolerant distributed computing on board spacecraft. *Advances in Space Research*, *58*(11), 2352–2375. DOI: 10.1016/j.asr.2016.08.017

Franczyk, B., Hernes, M., Kozierkiewicz, A., Kozina, A., Pietranik, M., Roemer, I., & Schieck, M. (2020). Deep learning for grape variety recognition. *Procedia Computer Science*, *176*, 1211–1220. DOI: 10.1016/j.procs.2020.09.117

Gad, A. G. (2022). Particle swarm optimization algorithm and its applications: A systematic review. *Archives of Computational Methods in Engineering*, *29*(5), 2531–2561. DOI: 10.1007/s11831-021-09694-4

Gao, Y., Wang, S., Dragicevic, T., Wheeler, P., & Zanchetta, P. (2023). Artificial Intelligence Techniques for Enhancing the Performance of Controllers in Power Converter-based Systems-An Overview. *IEEE Open Journal of Industry Applications*, *4*, 366–375. DOI: 10.1109/OJIA.2023.3338534

Garcia, P., Chan, M., & Torres, E. (2021). Edge computing solutions for real-time fault detection in food processing lines. *IEEE Journal of Emerging and Selected Topics in Industrial Electronics*, *9*(3), 1254–1263.

Garre, A., Ruiz, M. C., & Hontoria, E. (2020). Application of Machine Learning to support production planning of a food industry in the context of waste generation under uncertainty. *Operations Research Perspectives*, *7*, 100147. DOI: 10.1016/j.orp.2020.100147

Garvin, D. A. (1987). Competing on the Eight Dimensions of Quality. *Harvard Business Review*, *65*(6), 101–109.

Gatto, M. P. A., Castelli, F., Lentini, V., & Montrasio, L. (2024). AI-driven predictions of the dynamic properties of fine-grained soils in South Italy based on laboratory testing. *Soil Dynamics and Earthquake Engineering*, *187*, 109009. DOI: 10.1016/j.soildyn.2024.109009

Gay, G. (2010). *Culturally responsive teaching: Theory, research, and practice*. Teachers College Press.

Ghannadi, P., Kourehli, S. S., & Mirjalili, S. (2023) A review of the application of the simulated annealing algorithm in structural health monitoring (1995–2021). *Frattura Ed Integrità Strutturale* (edited by I. Strutturale), 17, 51–76. DOI: DOI: 10.3221/IGF-ESIS.64.04

Gholami, M., Sadeghi, M. H., & Hasannasab, M. (2021). Optimization of WEDM process parameters using artificial neural network and teaching-learning-based optimization algorithm. *Journal of Materials Research and Technology*, *11*, 727–739.

Ghorbani, J., & Kodikara, J. (2024). Real-time inference of compacted soil properties using deflection tests: An AI-driven solution informed by unsaturated soil mechanics principles.[[Grand View Research,]. *Computers and Geotechnics*, *173*, 106543. https://www.grandviewresearch.com/industry-analysis/civil-engineering-market. DOI: 10.1016/j.compgeo.2024.106543

Ghosh, A., & Debnath, K. (2022). Application of ANFIS in multi-objective optimization of weld bead geometry during FSW process. *Journal of Materials Engineering and Performance*, *31*(3), 1629–1640.

Giani, A., Nicolosi, C., Patel, S., & Bres, P. (2009). SCADA systems: The backbone of critical infrastructure. *IEEE Communications Surveys and Tutorials*, *12*(4), 24–29.

Gibkina, N. V., Sidorov, M. V., & Stadnikova, A. V. (2016). Optimal'noe granichnoe upravlenie kolebaniyami odnorodnoy struny [Optimal boundary control of vibrations of uniform string] [In Russian]. *Radioelektronics and Informatics*, *2*, 3–11.

Gillani, N., Eynon, R., Chiabaut, C., & Finkel, K. A. (2023, January 1). Unpacking the "Black Box" of AI in Education. Cornell University. https://doi.org/DOI: 10.48550/arXiv.2301

Glikson, M., Nielsen, J. C., Kronborg, M. B., Michowitz, Y., Auricchio, A., Barbash, I. M., Barrabés, J. A., Boriani, G., Braunschweig, F., Brignole, M., Burri, H., Coats, A. J. S., Deharo, J. C., Delgado, V., Diller, G. P., Israel, C. W., Keren, A., Knops, R. E., Kotecha, D., & Tolosana, J. M.ESC Scientific Document Group. (2021). 2021 ESC Guidelines on Cardiac Pacing and Cardiac Resynchronization Therapy. *European Heart Journal*, *42*(35), 3427–3520. DOI: 10.1093/eurheartj/ehab364 PMID: 34455430

González, A.. (2021). Learning analytics in higher education: A systematic review. *Computers in Human Behavior*, *115*, 106600. DOI: 10.1016/j.chb.2020.106600

Gonzalez-Huitron, V., León-Borges, J. A., Rodriguez-Mata, A. E., Amabilis-Sosa, L. E., Ramírez-Pereda, B., & Rodriguez, H. (2021). Disease detection in tomato leaves via CNN with lightweight architectures implemented in Raspberry Pi 4. *Computers and Electronics in Agriculture*, *181*, 105951. DOI: 10.1016/j.compag.2020.105951

Gou, F., Liu, J., Xiao, C., & Wu, J. (2024). Research on Artificial-Intelligence- Assisted Medicine: A Survey on Medical Artificial Intelligence. *Diagnostics (Basel)*, *14*(14), 1472. DOI: 10.3390/diagnostics14141472 PMID: 39061610

Govind, K. A., & Sekhar, R. A. (2014). Design of a Novel PID Controller for Cardiac Pacemaker. In *International Conference on Advances in Green Energy*, pp. 82-87. DOI: 10.1109/ICAGE.2014.7050147

Grassi, S., Alamprese, C., Bono, V., Casiraghi, E., & Amigo, J. M. (2014). Modelling milk lactic acid fermentation using multivariate curve resolution-alternating least squares (MCR-ALS). *Food and Bioprocess Technology*, *7*(6), 1819–1829. DOI: 10.1007/s11947-013-1189-2

Grau, A., Indri, M., Bello, L. L., & Sauter, T. (2020). Robots in industry: The past, present, and future of a growing collaboration with humans. *IEEE Industrial Electronics Magazine*, *15*(1), 50–61. DOI: 10.1109/MIE.2020.3008136

Grigoras, C. C., Zichil, V., Ciubotariu, V. A., & Cosa, S. M. (2024). Machine Learning, Mechatronics, and Stretch Forming: A History of Innovation in Manufacturing Engineering. *Machines (Basel)*, *12*(3), 180. DOI: 10.3390/machines12030180

Grishin, V. M. (2019). Synthesis of structure of the onboard passive redundant subsystem with due consideration of the established tolerances. *INCAS Bulletin*, *11*, 89–104. DOI: 10.13111/2066-8201.2019.11.S.9

Grishin, V. M., & Tuan, V. T. (2018). Specific feature of research and development of the passive redundancy subsystems of the aircraft with due consideration of tolerance. *Journal of Mechanical Engineering Research & Development*, *41*(4), 82–87. DOI: 10.26480/jmerd.04.2018.82.87

Gromada, K. A., & Stecz, W. M. (2022). Designing a reliable UAV architecture operating in a real environment. *Applied Sciences (Basel, Switzerland)*, *18*(1), 294. DOI: 10.3390/app12010294

Guergov, S., & Radwan, N. (2021). Blockchain Convergence: Analysis of Issues Affecting IoT, AI and Blockchain. *International Journal of Computations* [IJCIM]. *Information and Manufacturing*, *1*(1). Advance online publication. DOI: 10.54489/ijcim.v1i1.48

Guiné, R. (2019). The use of artificial neural networks (ANN) in food process engineering. *International Journal of Food Engineering*, *5*(1), 15–21.

Guo, Y. J., Ansari, M., & Fonseca, N. J. G. (2021). Circuit Type Multiple Beamforming Networks for Antenna Arrays in 5G and 6G Terrestrial and Non-Terrestrial Networks. *IEEE Journal of Microwaves*, *1*(3), 704–722. DOI: 10.1109/JMW.2021.3072873

Gupta, A. K. (2021). Fuzzy logic and their application in different areas of engineering science and research: A survey. *International Journal of Scientific Research in Science and Technology*, *8*(2), 71–75.

Gwak, K. W., Kim, H. D., & Kim, C. W. (2015). Feedback Linearization Control of a Cardiovascular Circulatory Simulator. *IEEE Transactions on Control Systems Technology*, *23*(5), 1970–1977. DOI: 10.1109/TCST.2014.2388251

Hahn, G. J., & Meeker, W. Q. (2004). *How to Plan an Accelerated Life Test (E-Book)*. ASQ Quality Press.

Haleem, A., Javaid, M., Singh, R. P., Rab, S., & Suman, R. (2021). Hyperautomation for the enhancement of automation in industries. *Sensors International*, *2*, 100124. DOI: 10.1016/j.sintl.2021.100124

Haleem, A., Javaid, M., Singh, R. P., & Suman, R. (2021). Applications of Artificial Intelligence (AI) for cardiology during COVID-19 pandemic. *Sustainable Operations and Computers*, *2*, 71–78. DOI: 10.1016/j.susoc.2021.04.003

Hamed, B., & Abu Ras, A. K. (2015). Fuzzy Controller for Dual Sensors Cardiac Pacemaker System in Patients with Bradycardias at Rest. *Intelligent Control and Automation*, *6*(3), 159–167. DOI: 10.4236/ica.2015.63016

Han, B., & Schotten, H D. (2022, January 1). Modeling the System-Level Reliability towards a Convergence of Communication, Computing and Control. DOI: 10.3850/978-981-18-5184-1_MS-23-199-cd

Harakannanavar, S. S., Rudagi, J. M., Puranikmath, V. I., Siddiqua, A., & Pramodhini, R. (2022). Plant leaf disease detection using computer vision and machine learning algorithms. *Global Transitions Proceedings*, *3*(1), 305–310. https://data.mendeley.com/datasets/ngdgg79rzb/1. DOI: 10.1016/j.gltp.2022.03.016

Hassan, S., Asad, M., Sana, M., Farooq, M. U., & Anwar, S. (2024). Parametric analysis and multi-objective optimization for machining complex features on D2 and DC53 steels for tooling applications. *Journal of Materials Engineering and Performance*, *33*(21), 12109–12123. DOI: 10.1007/s11665-024-09828-2

Hattie, J. (2012). *Visible learning for teachers: Maximizing impact on learning*. Routledge. DOI: 10.4324/9780203181522

Helm, D., & Timusk, M. (2023). Wavelet denoising applied to hardware redundant systems for rolling element bearing fault detection. Journal of Dynamics. *Monitoring and Diagnostics*, *2*(2), 133–143. DOI: 10.37965/jdmd.2023.231

Hernandez-Gonzalez, I. A., Garcia-Macias, E., Constante, G., & Ubertini, F. (2024). AI-driven Automated Operational Modal Analysis of Bridges. *Procedia Structural Integrity*, *62*, 879–886. DOI: 10.1016/j.prostr.2024.09.118

Hernandez-Gonzalez, I. A., Garcia-Macias, E., Constante, G., & Ubertini, F. (2024). AI-driven blind source separation for fast operational modal analysis of structures.[[Hong Kong Tourism Board,]. *Mechanical Systems and Signal Processing*, *211*, 111267. https://www.discoverhongkong.com/ca/interactive-map/hong-kong-zhuhai-macao-bridge.html. DOI: 10.1016/j.ymssp.2024.111267

How, M.-L., & Cheah, S.-M. (2024). Forging the Future: Strategic Approaches to Quantum AI Integration for Industry Transformation. *AI*, *5*(1), 290–323. DOI: 10.3390/ai5010015

Huang, C., Zhao, Y., Zhang, M., & Yang, H. (2023). APSO: An A*-PSO hybrid algorithm for mobile robot path planning. *IEEE Access : Practical Innovations, Open Solutions*, *11*, 43238–43256. DOI: 10.1109/ACCESS.2023.3272223

Huang, X., Chen, A., Zhou, G., Zhang, X., Wang, J., Peng, N., Yan, N., & Jiang, C. (2023). Tomato leaf disease detection system based on FC-SNDPN. *Multimedia Tools and Applications*, *82*(2), 2121–2144. DOI: 10.1007/s11042-021-11790-3

Huang, Y. (2013). Automatic process control for the food industry: an introduction. In *Robotics and Automation in the Food Industry* (pp. 3–20). Woodhead Publishing. DOI: 10.1533/9780857095763.1.3

Huang, Z., Sheng, Z., Ma, C., & Chen, S. (2024). Human as AI mentor: Enhanced human-in-the-loop reinforcement learning for safe and efficient autonomous driving.[[Institution of Civil Engineers,]. *Communications in Transportation Research*, *4*, 100127. https://www.ice.org.uk/what-is-civil-engineering/infrastructure-projects/the-hong-kong-zhuhai-macao-bridge-hzmb-hong-kong-section. DOI: 10.1016/j.commtr.2024.100127

Hung, Y., Lin, C., Lin, C. S., Lee, C. C., Fang, W. H., Lee, C. C., Wang, C. H., & Tsai, D. J. (2024). Artificial Intelligence-Enabled Electrocardiography Predicts Future Pacemaker Implantation and Adverse Cardiovascular Events. *Journal of Medical Systems*, *48*(1), 67. DOI: 10.1007/s10916-024-02088-6 PMID: 39028354

Hunt, K. J., & Hurni, C. C. (2019). Robust Control of Heart Rate for Cycle Ergometer Exercise. *Medical & Biological Engineering & Computing*, *57*(11), 2471–2482. DOI: 10.1007/s11517-019-02034-6 PMID: 31471785

Hurairah, M. A., Sana, M., Farooq, M. U., & Anwar, S. (2024). Genetic algorithm-based optimization of artificial neural network of process parameters and characterization of machining errors in graphene mixed dielectric. *Arabian Journal for Science and Engineering*, *49*(11), 15649–15666. DOI: 10.1007/s13369-024-09029-y

Hwang, G. J.. (2020). Innovative strategies for integrating AI in education. *Computers & Education*, *145*, 103724. DOI: 10.1016/j.compedu.2019.103724

IEEE Standard Glossary of Software Engineering Terminology. (2002). *IEEE STD 610.12-1990. Standards Coordinating Committee of the Computer Society of IEEE.* Available online: https://ieeexplore.ieee.org/document/159342

Iftekhar, A., & Cui, X. (2021). Blockchain-based traceability system that ensures food safety measures to protect consumer safety and COVID-19 free supply chains. *Foods*, *10*(6), 1289. DOI: 10.3390/foods10061289 PMID: 34199825

Ikram, A., Mehmood, H., Arshad, M. T., Rasheed, A., Noreen, S., & Gnedeka, K. T. (2024). Applications of artificial intelligence (AI) in managing food quality and ensuring global food security. *CYTA: Journal of Food, 22*(1), 2393287. DOI: 10.1080/19476337.2024.2393287

Il'in, V. A., & Moiseev, E. I. (2005). Optimization of boundary controls of string vibrations. *Russian Mathematical Surveys, 60*(6), 1093–1119. DOI: 10.1070/RM2005v060n06ABEH004283

Inagaki, T., & Sheridan, T. B. (2019). A critique of the SAE conditional driving automation definition, and analyses of options for improvement. *Cognition Technology and Work, 21*(4), 569–578. DOI: 10.1007/s10111-018-0471-5

Isaksen, J. L., Baumert, M., Hermans, A. N. L., Maleckar, M., & Linz, D. (2022). Artificial Intelligence for the Detection, Prediction, and Management of Atrial Fibrillation. Erkennung, Vorhersage und Behandlung von Vorhofflimmern mithilfe künstlicher Intelligenz. *Herzschrittmachertherapie & Elektrophysiologie, 33*(1), 34–41. DOI: 10.1007/s00399-022-00839-x PMID: 35147766

Jain, M., & Kulkarni, P. (2022, March). Application of AI, IOT and ML for Business Transformation of The Automotive Sector. In *2022 International Conference on Decision Aid Sciences and Applications (DASA)* (pp. 1270-1275). IEEE. DOI: 10.1109/DASA54658.2022.9765294

Jain, M., Saihjpal, V., Singh, N., & Singh, S. B. (2022). An overview of variants and advancements of PSO algorithm. *Applied Sciences (Basel, Switzerland), 12*(17), 8392. DOI: 10.3390/app12178392

Jain, P., & Swarnkar, A. (2021). Intelligent optimization of wire electric discharge machining parameters using ANFIS-GA. *Journal of Materials Research and Technology, 14*, 389–403.

Jardine, A. K. S., Lin, D., & Banjevic, D. (2006). A review on machinery diagnostics and prognostics implementing condition-based maintenance. *Mechanical Systems and Signal Processing, 20*(7), 1483–1510. DOI: 10.1016/j.ymssp.2005.09.012

Javaid, M., Haleem, A., Singh, R. P., & Suman, R. (2021). Substantial capabilities of robotics in enhancing industry 4.0 implementation. *Cognitive Robotics, 1*, 58–75. DOI: 10.1016/j.cogr.2021.06.001

Jayasinghe, S. C., Mahmoodian, M., Alavi, A., Sidiq, A., Shahrivar, F., Sun, Z., Thangarajah, J., & Setunge, S. (2025). A review on the applications of artificial neural network techniques for accelerating finite element analysis in the civil engineering domain. *Computers & Structures, 310*, 107698. DOI: 10.1016/j.compstruc.2025.107698

Jeffrey, K., & Parsonnet, V. (1998). Cardiac Pacing, 1960-1985: A Quarter Century of Medical and Industrial Innovation. *Circulation, 97*(19), 1978–1991. DOI: 10.1161/01.CIR.97.19.1978 PMID: 9609092

Jeong, C. H., Heo, S., Woo, T. Y., Kim, S. Y., & Yoo, C. K. (2024). AI-driven ventilation control policy proximal optimization coupled with dynamic-informed real-time model calibration for healthy and sustainable indoor PM2.5 management. *Energy and Building, 323*, 114786. DOI: 10.1016/j.enbuild.2024.114786

Jha, S. K., Satsangi, P. S., & Jain, N. K. (2016). Optimization of machining parameters in WEDM of Ti-6Al-4V using response surface methodology and artificial neural network. *International Journal of Advanced Manufacturing Technology, 85*(1-4), 855–866.

Jiang, Z., & Mangharam, R. (2011). Modeling Cardiac Pacemaker Malfunctions with the Virtual Heart Model. 2011 Annual International Conference of the IEEE Engineering in Medicine and Biology Society, Boston, MA, USA, 2011, 263-266, DOI: 10.1109/IEMBS.2011.6090051

Jiang, F., Yang, X., Zhang, C., & Li, G. (2017). A fault prediction method based on k-means and GMM for manufacturing equipment. *Procedia CIRP*, *63*, 700–705.

Jiménez-Carvelo, A. M., González-Casado, A., Bagur-González, M. G., & Cuadros-Rodríguez, L. (2019). Alternative data mining/machine learning methods for the analytical evaluation of food quality and authenticity–A review. *Food Research International*, *122*, 25–39. DOI: 10.1016/j.foodres.2019.03.063 PMID: 31229078

Jordan, M. I., & Mitchell, T. M. (2015). Machine learning: Trends, perspectives, and prospects. *Science*, *349*(6245), 255–260. DOI: 10.1126/science.aaa8415 PMID: 26185243

Joshi, S. R., Gadekar, S. S., & Kulkarni, A. V. (2016). Optimization of process parameters for WEDM using RSM. *International Journal of Advanced Manufacturing Technology*, *82*(9-12), 1627–1638.

Joung, Y. H. (2013). Development of Implantable Medical Devices: From an Engineering Perspective. *International Neurourology Journal*, *17*(3), 98–106. DOI: 10.5213/inj.2013.17.3.98 PMID: 24143287

Kaelbling, L. P., Littman, M. L., & Moore, A. W. (1996). Reinforcement learning: A survey. *Journal of Artificial Intelligence Research*, *4*, 237–285. DOI: 10.1613/jair.301

Kamarposhti, M. S., Kamyab, H., Krishnan, S., Yusuf, M., Rezania, S., Chelliapan, S., & Khorami, M. (2024). A comprehensive review of AI-enhanced smart grid integration for hydrogen energy: Advances, challenges, and future prospects. *International Journal of Hydrogen Energy*, *67*, 1009–1025. DOI: 10.1016/j.ijhydene.2024.01.129

Kansal, H. K., Singh, S., & Singh, R. (2017). Multi-objective optimization of WEDM process parameters for machining titanium alloy using Taguchi-based grey relational analysis. *International Journal of Precision Engineering and Manufacturing*, *18*(6), 805–812. DOI: 10.1007/s12541-017-0091-7

Karam, E. H., Tashan, T., & Mohsin, E. F. (2019). Design of Model Free Sliding Mode Controller based on BBO Algorithm for Heart Rate Pacemaker. *IJMECS*, *11*(3), 31–37. DOI: 10.5815/ijmecs.2019.03.05

Karar, M. E., Reyad, O., Shehata, H. I., Abdelhamid, A. A., & Alotaibi, S. (2020). A New Intelligent System for Performance Enhancement of Dual-Sensor Cardiac Pacemakers Using Iterative Learning Control. *6th Conference on Data Science and Machine Learning Applications (CDMA)*, Riyadh, Saudi Arabia, pp. 158-163, DOI: 10.1109/CDMA47397.2020.00033

Karthikeyan, V., & Kalidasa Murugavel, K. (2020). Reducing PV module temperature with radiation-based PV module incorporated composite phase change material. *Materials Today: Proceedings*, *33*(Part 7), 4774–4779. DOI: 10.1016/j.matpr.2020.01.389

Karthikeyan, V., & Sirisamphanwong, C. (2020). Reducing PV module temperature with radiation-based PV module incorporated composite phase change material. *Energy Reports*, *6*, 56–64. DOI: 10.1016/j.egyr.2020.10.008

Kaur, A., & Kaur, A. (2014). Analysis of VLSI Pacemaker Designs a Review. *International Journal on Recent and Innovation Trends in Computing and Communication*, *2*(4), 747–749. DOI: 10.17762/ijritcc.v2i4.3051

Kaur, P., Harnal, S., Gautam, V., Singh, M. P., & Singh, S. P. (2022). An approach for characterization of infected area in tomato leaf disease based on deep learning and object detection technique. *Engineering Applications of Artificial Intelligence*, *115*, 105210. DOI: 10.1016/j.engappai.2022.105210

Kaur, S., Singh, N., Dagar, P., Kumar, A., Jaiswal, S., Singh, B. K., Bhardwaj, R., Chand Rana, J., & Riar, A. (2024). Comparative analysis of modified partial least squares regression and hybrid deep learning models for predicting protein content in Perilla (Perilla frutescens L.) seed meal using NIR spectroscopy. *Food Bioscience*, *61*, 104821. DOI: 10.1016/j.fbio.2024.104821

Kazem, H. A., Chaichan, M. T., Al-Waeli, A. H. A., & Sopian, K. (2024). Recent advancements in solar photovoltaic tracking systems: An in-depth review of technologies, performance metrics, and future trends. *Solar Energy*, *282*, 112946. DOI: 10.1016/j.solener.2024.112946

Kazmi, S. H. A., Hassan, R., Ibrahim, A. A. A., Qamar, F., & Nisar, K. (2023). Security Concepts in Emerging 6G Communication: Threats, Countermeasures, Authentication Techniques and Research Directions. *Symmetry*, *15*(6), 1147. DOI: 10.3390/sym15061147

Khan, M. I. H., Sablani, S. S., Nayak, R., & Gu, Y. (2022). Machine learning-based modeling in food processing applications: State of the art. *Comprehensive Reviews in Food Science and Food Safety*, *21*(2), 1409–1438. DOI: 10.1111/1541-4337.12912 PMID: 35122379

Khayyam, H., Javadi, B., Jalili, M., & Jazar, R. N. (2020). Artificial Intelligence and Internet of Things for Autonomous Vehicles. In Jazar, R., & Dai, L. (Eds.), *Nonlinear Approaches in Engineering Applications*. Springer., DOI: 10.1007/978-3-030-18963-1_2

Kim, D., Han, H., Lee, H., Kang, Y., Wang, W., & Kim, H. S. (2024). Predicting Flood Water Level Using Combined Hybrid Model of Rainfall-Runoff and AI-Based Models. *KSCE Journal of Civil Engineering*, *28*(4), 1580–1593. DOI: 10.1007/s12205-023-1147-0

Kim, G. Y., Han, D. S., & Lee, Z. (2020). Solar panel tilt angle optimization using machine learning model: A case study of Daegu City, South Korea. *Energies*, *13*(3), 529. DOI: 10.3390/en13030529

Kim, M., Kang, Y., You, S. C., Park, H. D., Lee, S. S., Kim, T. H., Yu, H. T., Choi, E. K., Park, H. S., Park, J., Lee, Y. S., Kang, K. W., Shim, J., Sung, J. H., Oh, I. Y., Park, J. S., & Joung, B. (2022). Artificial intelligence predicts clinically relevant atrial high-rate episodes in patients with cardiac implantable electronic devices. *Scientific Reports*, *12*(1), 37. DOI: 10.1038/s41598-021-03914-4 PMID: 34996990

Kim, S. Y., Tariq, S., Chang, R., Ali, U., Ba-Alawi, A. H., Heo, S. K., & Yoo, C. K. (2024). Explainable AI-driven high-fidelity IAQ prediction (HiFi-IAQ) model for subway stations: Spatiotemporal outdoor air quality interpolation using geographic data.[[Koenig Solutions,]. *Building and Environment*, *263*, 111906. https://www.koenig-solutions.com/blog/control-engineering. DOI: 10.1016/j.buildenv.2024.111906

Kolk, M. Z. H., Ruipérez-Campillo, S., Wilde, A. A. M., Knops, R. E., Narayan, S. M., & Tjong, F. V. Y. (2024). Prediction of sudden cardiac death using artificial intelligence: Current status and future directions. *Heart rhythm*, S1547-5271(24)03293-4. Advance online publication. https://doi.org/DOI: 10.1016/j.hrthm.2024.09.003

Korzyuk, V. I., & Kozlovskia, I. S. (2010a). Dvukhtochechnaya granichnaya zadacha dlya uravneniya kolebaniya struny s zadannoy skorost'yu v nekotoryy moment vremeni. I [Two-point boundary problem for the equation of string vibration with the given velocity at the certain moment of time. I] [In Russian]. *Proceedings of the Institute of Mathematics NAS of Belarus*, *18*, 22–35.

Korzyuk, V. I., & Kozlovskia, I. S. (2010b). Dvukhtochechnaya granichnaya zadacha dlya uravneniya kolebaniya struny s zadannoy skorost'yu v nekotoryy moment vremeni. II [Two-point boundary problem for the equation of string vibration with the given velocity at the certain moment of time. II] [In Russian]. *Proceedings of the Institute of Mathematics NAS of Belarus*, *19*, 62–70.

Krabs, W. (1995). *Optimal Control of Undamped Linear Vibrations*. Heldermann.

Krasovsky, N. N. (1968). *Teoriya upravleniya dvizheniem* [The Theory of Motion Control]. Nauka. (In Russian)

Kulkarni, S. V., Choudhury, S. K., & Pawade, R. S. (2021). Application of artificial neural network in WEDM process parameter optimization. *Materials Today: Proceedings*, *38*, 143–148.

Kumar, L., & Sharma, R. K. (2023). Smart manufacturing and industry 4.0: state-of-the-art review. Handbook of Smart Manufacturing, 1-28.

Kumar, D., Yadav, A., & Mishra, N. (2020). AI-based fault diagnosis in food processing systems: Challenges and opportunities. *Journal of Food Engineering*, *157*, 43–54.

Kumar, I., Rawat, J., Mohd, N., & Husain, S. (2021). Opportunities of artificial intelligence and machine learning in the food industry. *Journal of Food Quality*, *2021*(1), 4535567. DOI: 10.1155/2021/4535567

Kumari, N., Dwivedi, R. K., Bhatt, A. K., & Belwal, R. (2022). Automated fruit grading using optimal feature selection and hybrid classification by self-adaptive chicken swarm optimization: Grading of mango. *Neural Computing & Applications*, *34*(2), 1285–1306. DOI: 10.1007/s00521-021-06473-x

Kumar, P., & Kumar, V. (2021). Prediction and optimization of the tensile strength of friction stir welded joints using ANFIS-GA. *Materials Today: Proceedings*, *46*, 4633–4639.

Kumar, R., & Arnon, S. (2024). Review of Physical Layer Security in Integrated Satellite–Terrestrial Networks. *Electronics (Basel)*, *13*(22), 4414. DOI: 10.3390/electronics13224414

Kumar, S., & Rose, C. (2021). A review of intelligent systems in education: Emerging technologies and their impact. *Journal of Educational Technology & Society*, *24*(1), 1–17.

Kumba, K., Upender, P., Buduma, P., Sarkar, M., Simon, S. P., & Gundu, V. (2024). Solar tracking systems: Advancements, challenges, and future directions: A review. *Energy Reports*, *12*, 3566–3583. DOI: 10.1016/j.egyr.2024.09.038

Kupin, A. I., & Kosei, M. P. (2024). Analysis of swarm intelligence algorithms. *System Technologies, 3*, 69–80. DOI: 10.34185/1562-9945-3-152-2024-07

Kvale, S., & Brinkmann, S. (2015). *Interviews: Learning the craft of qualitative research interviewing* (3rd ed.). SAGE Publications.

Ladson-Billings, G. (1995). Toward a theory of culturally relevant pedagogy. *American Educational Research Journal, 32*(3), 465–491. DOI: 10.3102/00028312032003465

Laflamme, C., Doppler, J., Palvolgyi, B., Dominka, S., Viharos, Zs. J., & Haeussler, S. (2025). Explainable reinforcement learning for powertrain control engineering. *Engineering Applications of Artificial Intelligence, 146*, 110135. DOI: 10.1016/j.engappai.2025.110135

Lalanne, C. (2014). Mechanical Vibration and Shock Analysis: Vol. 5. *Specification Development* (3rd ed.). John Wiley & Sons, Inc. DOI: 10.1002/9781118931219

Lee, J., Ni, J., Djurdjanovic, D., Qiu, H., & Liao, H. (2006). Intelligent prognostics tools and e-maintenance. *Computers in Industry, 57*(6), 476–489. DOI: 10.1016/j.compind.2006.02.014

Lee, K., Kim, N., & Kim, K. (2020). Neutral colored transparent crystalline silicon photovoltaics. *Energy Reports, 6*, 201–207. DOI: 10.1016/j.egyr.2020.09.044

Lee, K., Kim, N., Kim, K., & Seo, K. (2020). Neutral-colored transparent crystalline silicon photovoltaics. *Joule, 4*(1), 235–246. DOI: 10.1016/j.joule.2019.11.008

Leocadio, P. (2023). Cardiac Pacemakers: The Route to Implantable Artificial Intelligence. *Brainz Magazine*. https://doi.org/DOI: 10.6084/m9.figshare.24520621.v1

Leocadio, P. (2024). Advancements in Implantable Medical Devices: A Comprehensive Analysis of Artificial Intelligence Integration, Adoption, and Applicability in Bio-Tech Innovations. *IJCSIT, 15*(1), 1–08. DOI: 10.5121/ijcsit.2024.02101

Leonard, J.J., Mindell, D.A. and Stayton, E.L. (2020). Autonomous Vehicles, Mobility, and Employment Policy: The Roads Ahead. MIT Work of the Future, July 22, 2020.

Levine, S., & Shah, D. (2022, December 13). Learning robotic navigation from experience: principles, methods and recent results. Royal Society, 378(1869). DOI: 10.1098/rstb.2021.0447

Liamputtong, P. (2007). *Researching the vulnerable: A guide to sensitive research methods*. SAGE Publications. DOI: 10.4135/9781849209861

Liang, R., Liu, W., Fu, Y., & Ma, M. (2024). Physics-informed deep learning for structural dynamics under moving load. *International Journal of Mechanical Sciences, 284*, 109766. DOI: 10.1016/j.ijmecsci.2024.109766

Liao, W., Lu, X., Fei, Y., Gu, Y., & Huang, Y. (2024). Generative AI design for building structures. *Automation in Construction, 157*, 105187. DOI: 10.1016/j.autcon.2023.105187

Li, M., Zhou, G., Chen, A., Li, L., & Hu, Y. (2023). Identification of tomato leaf diseases based on LMBRNet. *Engineering Applications of Artificial Intelligence, 123*, 106195. DOI: 10.1016/j.engappai.2023.106195

Lima, G. S., Savi, M. A., & Bessa, W. M. (2023). Intelligent Control of Cardiac Rhythms Using Artificial Neural Networks. *Nonlinear Dynamics*, *111*(12), 11543–11557. DOI: 10.1007/s11071-023-08447-1

Li, N., Yi, Z., Ma, Y., Xie, F., Huang, Y., Tian, Y., Dong, X., Liu, Y., Shao, X., Li, Y., Jin, L., Liu, J., Xu, Z., Yang, B., & Zhang, H. (2019). Direct Powering a Real Cardiac Pacemaker by Natural Energy of a Heartbeat. *ACS Nano*, *13*(3), 2822–2830. DOI: 10.1021/acsnano.8b08567 PMID: 30784259

Lins, R. G., & Givigi, S. N. (2021). Cooperative robotics and machine learning for smart manufacturing: Platform design and trends within the context of industrial internet of things. *IEEE Access : Practical Innovations, Open Solutions*, *9*, 95444–95455. DOI: 10.1109/ACCESS.2021.3094374

Lin, W. D., Low, Y. H., Chong, Y. T., & Teo, C. L. (2018, December). Integrated cyber physical simulation modelling environment for manufacturing 4.0. In *2018 IEEE International Conference on Industrial Engineering and Engineering Management (IEEM)* (pp. 1861-1865). IEEE. DOI: 10.1109/IEEM.2018.8607696

Liu, H., Rahman, M., Rahimi, M., Starr, A., Durazo-Cardenas, I., Ruiz-Carcel, C., Ompusunggu, A., Hall, A., & Anderson, R. (2023). An autonomous rail-road amphibious robotic system for railway maintenance using sensor fusion and mobile manipulator. *Computers & Electrical Engineering*, *110*, 108874. DOI: 10.1016/j.compeleceng.2023.108874

Liu, H., Xu, X., Meng, Y., Yu, D., Liu, H., & Shi, K. (2018). A research for the influence of tilt angles of the solar panel on photovoltaic power generation. In *2018 International Conference on Smart Grid and Clean Energy Technologies (ICSGCE)* (pp. 95-100). IEEE. https://doi.org/DOI: 10.1109/ICSGCE.2018.8556655

Liu, J., Zhang, X., & Wang, T. (2022). Real-time fault diagnosis for manufacturing processes using deep learning-based sensor data analysis. *IEEE Transactions on Industrial Electronics*, *69*(6), 5078–5086.

Liu, Y., Fan, W., Cheng, X., & Zheng, X. (2017). Research on surface quality and material removal rate of Ti-6Al-4V in WEDM. *Procedia Engineering*, *174*, 682–690.

Li, X. (2008). Numerical Solution of an Initial-Boundary Value Problem with Nonlocal Condition for the Wave Equation. *Journal of Mathematical Sciences*, *2*(3), 281–292.

Li, X., Tan, K., & Wong, S. (2022). LSTM-based framework for temperature fluctuation prediction in industrial ovens. *IEEE Access : Practical Innovations, Open Solutions*, *10*, 56234–56245.

London, A. J. (2024, January 1). Accountability for Responsible AI Practices: Ethical Responsibilities of Senior Leadership. RELX Group (Netherlands). DOI: 10.2139/ssrn.4736880

Lounis, F., Boukabou, A., & Soukkou, A. (2020). Implementing High-Order Chaos Control Scheme for Cardiac Conduction Model with Pathological Rhythms. *Chaos, Solitons, and Fractals*, *132*, 109581. DOI: 10.1016/j.chaos.2019.109581

Love, C. J. (2006). *Cardiac Pacemakers and Defibrillators* (2nd ed.). Landes Bioscience.

Luckin, R., Holmes, W., Griffiths, M., & Forcier, L. B. (2016). *Intelligence unleashed: An argument for AI in education*. Pearson Education.

Lu, X. Y., & Wang, J. (2012, June). Multiple-vehicle longitudinal collision avoidance and impact mitigation by active brake control. In *2012 IEEE Intelligent Vehicles Symposium* (pp. 680-685). IEEE. DOI: 10.1109/IVS.2012.6232246

Lu, Y., Zhang, Y., & Maharjan, S. (2021). Adaptive Edge Association for Wireless Digital Twin Networks in 6G. *IEEE Internet of Things Journal*, *8*(22), 16219–16230. DOI: 10.1109/JIOT.2021.3098508

Magaziner, I. C., & Patinkin, M. (1989). Cold competition: GE wages the refrigerator war. *Harvard Business Review*, *89*(2), 114–124.

Ma, H., Zhang, Y., Sun, S., Liu, T., & Shan, Y. (2023). A comprehensive survey on NSGA-II for multi-objective optimization and applications. *Artificial Intelligence Review*, *56*(12), 15217–15270. DOI: 10.1007/s10462-023-10526-z

Mahapatra, S. K., & Routara, B. K. (2021). Prediction of machining performance in WEDM using artificial neural network and particle swarm optimization. *Materials Today: Proceedings*, *44*, 308–316.

Mahmood, A., Zhang, W. E., & Sheng, Q. Z. (2019). Software-Defined Heterogeneous Vehicular Networking: The Architectural Design and Open Challenges. *Future Internet*, *11*(3), 70. DOI: 10.3390/fi11030070

Mahmoudinezhad, S., Rezania, A., & Mahmoudinezhad, R. (2018). Behaviour of hybrid concentrated photovoltaic-thermoelectric generator under variable solar radiation. *Energy Conversion and Management*, *164*, 21–33. DOI: 10.1016/j.enconman.2018.03.025

Mahrous, A., Ali, A. S., Mohamed, S., & Othman, M. (2024). Kinematic Analysis and Simulation of an Industrial Rail-Mounted Robot Manipulator Using Ruckig for Enhanced Path Planning. JES. *Journal of Engineering Sciences*, *52*(4), 105–119.

Majma, N., Babamir, S. M., & Monadjemi, A. A. (2016). Utilizing Fuzzy Colored Petri-Nets to Monitor Cardiac Pacemaker Behavior, IEEE 10th International Conference on Application of Information and Communication Technologies (AICT), Baku, Azerbaijan, pp. 1-5. DOI: 10.1109/ICAICT.2016.7991824

Majma, N., & Babamir, S. M. (2020). Model-Based Monitoring and Adaptation of Pacemaker Behavior Using Hierarchical Fuzzy Colored Petri-Nets. *IEEE Transactions on Systems, Man, and Cybernetics. Systems*, *50*(9), 3344–3357. DOI: 10.1109/TSMC.2018.2861718

Makulavičius, M., Petkevičius, S., Rožėnė, J., Dzedzickis, A., & Bučinskas, V. (2023). Industrial robots in mechanical machining: Perspectives and limitations. *Robotics (Basel, Switzerland)*, *12*(6), 160. DOI: 10.3390/robotics12060160

Mallik, S., Saha, B., Podder, K., Muthuraj, M., Mishra, U., & Deb, S. (2025). Comprehensive assessment of E. coli dynamics in river water using advanced machine learning and explainable AI. *Process Safety and Environmental Protection*, *195*, 106816. DOI: 10.1016/j.psep.2025.106816

Maltsev, V. A., Yaniv, Y., Maltsev, A. V., Stern, M. D., & Lakatta, E. G. (2014). Modern Perspectives on Numerical Modeling of Cardiac Pacemaker Cell. *Journal of Pharmacological Sciences*, *125*(1), 6–38. DOI: 10.1254/jphs.13R04CR PMID: 24748434

Mamun, M. A. A., Islam, M. M., Hasanuzzaman, M., & Selvaraj, J. (2022). Effect of tilt angle on the performance and electrical parameters of a PV module: Comparative indoor and outdoor experimental investigation. *Energy and Built Environment, 3*(3), 278–290. DOI: 10.1016/j.enbenv.2021.02.001

Marina, L. A., Trasnea, B., & Grigorescu, S. M. (2018, October). A multi-platform framework for artificial intelligence engines in automotive systems. In 2018 22nd International conference on system theory, control and computing (ICSTCC) (pp. 559-564). IEEE. DOI: 10.1109/ICSTCC.2018.8540753

Marković, M., Milošević, M., & Jovanov, N. (2019, September). Using class-dependent post-processing to improve ai for automotive front view camera. In 2019 IEEE 9th International Conference on Consumer Electronics (ICCE-Berlin) (pp. 211-214). IEEE. DOI: 10.1109/ICCE-Berlin47944.2019.8966233

Masria, A., & Abouelsaad, O. (2025). Artificial intelligence applications in coastal engineering and its challenges – A review. *Continental Shelf Research, 286*, 105425. DOI: 10.1016/j.csr.2025.105425

Ma, T., Li, Z., & Zhao, J. (2019). Photovoltaic panel integrated with phase change material technology. *Applied Energy, 238*, 321–329. DOI: 10.1016/j.apenergy.2018.12.021

Mavani, N. R., Ali, J. M., Othman, S., Hussain, M. A., Hashim, H., & Rahman, N. A. (2022). Application of artificial intelligence in food industry—A guideline. *Food Engineering Reviews, 14*(1), 134–175. DOI: 10.1007/s12393-021-09290-z

Ma, X., & McSweeney, P. (2008). Product and process innovation in the food processing industry: Case study in Guangxi province. *Australasian Agribusiness Review*, •••, 16.

McCausland, P. (2019). Self-driving Uber car that hit and killed woman did not recognize that pedestrians jaywalk. NBC News, November 9, 2019.

McMahan, H. B., Yu, F. X., Richtarik, P., Suresh, A. T., & Bacon, D. (2016, December). Federated learning: Strategies for improving communication efficiency. In *Proceedings of the 29th Conference on Neural Information Processing Systems (NIPS),* Barcelona, Spain (pp. 5-10).

Mehr, J. K., Akbari, M., Faridi, P., Xing, H., Mushahwar, V. K., & Tavakoli, M. (2023, February 21). Artificial-Intelligence-Powered Lower Limb Assistive Devices. *Advanced Intelligent Systems, 5*(6), 2200361. Advance online publication. DOI: 10.1002/aisy.202200361

Meshram, K. (2024). *Introduction to machine learning for civil engineering. Machine Learning Applications in Civil Engineering*. Woodhead Publishing Series in Civil and Structural Engineering.

Milczarski, P., Zieliński, B., Stawska, Z., Hłobaż, A., Maślanka, P., & Kosiński, P. (2020, October). Machine learning application in energy consumption calculation and assessment in food processing industry. In *International Conference on Artificial Intelligence and Soft Computing* (pp. 369-379). Cham: Springer International Publishing. DOI: 10.1007/978-3-030-61534-5_33

Miranda, J., Ponce, P., Molina, A., & Wright, P. (2019). Sensing, smart and sustainable technologies for Agri-Food 4.0. *Computers in Industry, 108*, 21–36. DOI: 10.1016/j.compind.2019.02.002

Misra, N. N., Dixit, Y., Al-Mallahi, A., Bhullar, M. S., Upadhyay, R., & Martynenko, A. (2020). IoT, big data, and artificial intelligence in agriculture and food industry. *IEEE Internet of Things Journal, 9*(9), 6305–6324. DOI: 10.1109/JIOT.2020.2998584

Mobley, R. K. (2002). *An introduction to predictive maintenance*. Elsevier.

Moiseev, E. I., & Kholomeeva, A. A. (2013). On an optimal boundary control problem with a dynamic boundary condition. *Differential Equations, 49*(5), 640–644. DOI: 10.1134/S0012266113050133

Momani, S., Batiha, I. M., & El-Khazali, R. (2019). Design of $PI^{\lambda} D^{\delta}$-Heart Rate Controllers for Cardiac Pacemaker. In *IEEE International Symposium on Signal Processing and Information Technology*, pp. 1-5. DOI: 10.1109/ISSPIT47144.2019.9001785

Montgomery, D. (2020). *Design and analysis of experiments* (10th ed.). John Wiley & Sons, Inc.

Moreno-Sáenz, J., Chen, Y.-J., Tanaka, K., Aragón, J. L., & Quiroz-Juárez, M. A. (2023). *A Takagi-Sugeno Fuzzy-Model-Based Tracking Framework to Regulate Heart Rhythm Dynamics*. IEEE., DOI: 10.1109/ACCESS.2023.3274809

Moses, W. S., Ivanov, I. R., Domke, J., Endo, T., Doerfert, J., & Zinenko, O. (2023) High-performance GPU-to-CPU transpilation and optimization via high-level parallel constructs. In: *Proceedings of the 28th ACM SIGPLAN Annual Symposium on Principles and Practice of Parallel Programming*. ACM, pp. 119–134. DOI: DOI: 10.1145/3572848.3577475

Moussafir, M., Chaibi, H., Saadane, R., Chehri, A., Rharras, A. E., & Jeon, G. (2022). Design of efficient techniques for tomato leaf disease detection using genetic algorithm-based and deep neural networks. *Plant and Soil, 479*(1), 251–266. DOI: 10.1007/s11104-022-05513-2

Mukhtar, A., & Mukhtar, F. (2020). Adaptive Fractional Order PID Controller Design of a Pacemaker based on Heart Rate Control Strategy. *IRJET, 7*(3), 1681–1685.

Mulpuru, S. K., Madhavan, M., McLeod, C. J., Cha, Y. M., & Friedman, P. A. (2017). Cardiac Pacemakers: Function, Troubleshooting, and Management: Part 1 of a 2-Part Series. *Journal of the American College of Cardiology, 69*(2), 189–210. DOI: 10.1016/j.jacc.2016.10.061 PMID: 28081829

Munjiza, A., Rougier, E., Lei, Z., Euser, B., & Knight, E. E. (2024). 2.05 - Towards FDEM Based Hybrid Simulation Tools for AI Driven Virtual Experimentation in Science and Engineering. *Comprehensive Mechanics of Materials, 2*, 141–168. DOI: 10.1016/B978-0-323-90646-3.00012-5

Muthukumar, P., Manikandan, S., Muniraj, R., Jarin, T., & Sebi, A. (2023). Energy efficient dual axis solar tracking system using IoT. *Measurement. Sensors, 28*, 100825. DOI: 10.1016/j.measen.2023.100825

Nadimi-Shahraki, M. H., Zamani, H., Asghari Varzaneh, Z., & Mirjalili, S. (2023). A systematic review of the whale optimization algorithm: Theoretical foundation, improvements, and hybridizations. *Archives of Computational Methods in Engineering, 30*(7), 4113–4159. DOI: 10.1007/s11831-023-09928-7 PMID: 37359740

Nagarajan, V. D., Lee, S. L., Robertus, J. L., Nienaber, C. A., Trayanova, N. A., & Ernst, S. (2021). Artificial intelligence in the diagnosis and management of arrhythmias. *European Heart Journal, 42*(38), 3904–3916. DOI: 10.1093/eurheartj/ehab544 PMID: 34392353

Nagy, M., Lăzăroiu, G., & Valaskova, K. (2023). Machine intelligence and autonomous robotic technologies in the corporate context of SMEs: Deep learning and virtual simulation algorithms, cyber-physical production networks, and Industry 4.0-based manufacturing systems. *Applied Sciences (Basel, Switzerland)*, *13*(3), 1681. DOI: 10.3390/app13031681

Nako, J., & Psychalinos, C. (2022). Heart Rate Controller Design for Cardiac Pacemaker, *Panhellenic Conference on Electronics & Telecommunications (PACET)*, Tripolis, Greece, pp. 1-4, DOI: 10.1109/PACET56979.2022.9976347

Nako, J., Psychalinos, C., & Elwakil, A. S. (2023). Minimum Active Component Count Design of a $PI^{\lambda}D^{\mu}$ Controller and Its Application in a Cardiac Pacemaker System. *J. Low Power Electron. Appl*, *13*(1), 13. DOI: 10.3390/jlpea13010013

Nath, S., & Sarkar, S. K. (2021). Metaheuristics-based routing optimisation, balanced workload distribution and security strategy in IoT environment. *International Journal of Advanced Intelligence Paradigms*, *19*(1), 101–117. DOI: 10.1504/IJAIP.2021.114586

Navidi, T., Gamal, A. E., & Rajagopal, R. (2023, January 1). Coordinating Distributed Energy Resources for Reliability can Significantly Reduce Future Distribution Grid Upgrades and Peak Load. Cornell University. https://doi.org//arxiv.2306.08717DOI: 10.48550

Nawaz, S. J., Wyne, S., Patwary, M. N., Asaduzzaman, M., & Sharma, S. K. (2019). Quantum Machine Learning for 6G Communication Networks: State-of-the-Art and Vision for the Future. *IEEE Access : Practical Innovations, Open Solutions*, *7*, 46317–46350. DOI: 10.1109/ACCESS.2019.2909490

Nelson, J. P., Biddle, J. B., & Shapira, P. (2023, January 1). Applications and Societal Implications of Artificial Intelligence in Manufacturing: A Systematic Review. Cornell University. https://doi.org/DOI: 10.48550/arXiv.2308

Nyholm, S. (2024). Ethical and Legal Issues Related to Autonomous Vehicles. Future Law, Ethics, and Smart Technologies, 190-204.

O'Connor, P. P., & Kleyner, A. (2012). *Practical Reliability Engineering* (5th ed.). John Wiley & Sons, Ltd.

O'Neil, C. (2016). *Weapons of math destruction: How big data increases inequality and threatens democracy*. Crown Publishing Group.

Oberson, X. (2024). The development of artificial intelligence and robots. In *Taxing Artificial Intelligence* (pp. 5–14). Edward Elgar Publishing. DOI: 10.4337/9781035307555.00007

Oida, M., Mizutani, T., Hasumi, E., Fujiu, K., Goto, K., Kani, K., Oshima, T., Matsubara, T. J., Shimizu, Y., Oguri, G., Kojima, T., & Komuro, I. (2024). Prediction of pacemaker-induced cardiomyopathy using a convolutional neural network based on clinical findings prior to pacemaker implantation. *Scientific Reports*, *14*(1), 6916. DOI: 10.1038/s41598-024-57418-y PMID: 38519537

Olawade, D. B., Aderinto, N., Olatunji, G., Kokori, E., David-Olawade, A. C., & Hadi, M. (2024). Advancements and applications of Artificial Intelligence in cardiology: Current trends and future prospects. *Journal of Medicine, Surgery, and Public Health*, *3*, 100109. DOI: 10.1016/j.glmedi.2024.100109

Onishchuk, M. O. (2020). *Opto-mechanical sorting of municipal solid waste* (Doctoral dissertation, BHTY).

Palmer, C. (2020). The Boeing 737 MAX Saga: Automating Failure. *Engineering (Beijing)*, *6*(1), 2–3. DOI: 10.1016/j.eng.2019.11.002

Panahazari, M., Koscak, M., Zhang, J., Hou, D., Wang, J., & Gao, W. (2023, January 16). A Hybrid Optimization and Deep Learning Algorithm for Cyber-resilient DER Control. DOI: 10.1109/ISGT51731.2023.10066345

Pan, Y., & Zhang, L. (2021). Roles of artificial intelligence in construction engineering and management: A critical review and future trends. *Automation in Construction*, *122*, 103517. DOI: 10.1016/j.autcon.2020.103517

Paoletti, N., Patanè, A., & Kwiatkowska, M. (2018). Closed-Loop Quantitative Verification of Rate-Adaptive Pacemakers. *ACM Trans. Cyber-Phys. Syst*, 2(4). *Article*, *33*(4), 1–31. DOI: 10.1145/3152767

Papaioannou, V. E., Verkerk, A. O., Amin, A. S., & de Bakker, J. M. (2013). Intracardiac Origin of Heart Rate Variability, Pacemaker Funny Current and Their Possible Association with Critical Illness. *Current Cardiology Reviews*, *9*(1), 82–96. DOI: 10.2174/157340313805076359 PMID: 22920474

Parouha, R. P., & Verma, P. (2022). A systematic overview of developments in differential evolution and particle swarm optimization with their advanced suggestion. *Applied Intelligence*, *52*(9), 10448–10492. DOI: 10.1007/s10489-021-02803-7

Patel, H. R., & Shah, V. A. (2018). Fault detection and diagnosis methods in power generation plants-the Indian power generation sector perspective: An introductory review. *PDPU Journal of Energy and Management*, *2*(2), 31–49.

Patil, P., & Joshi, K. D. (2016). Optimization of WEDM process parameters for machining of Inconel 718 using response surface methodology and genetic algorithm. *Proceedings of the Institution of Mechanical Engineers. Part B, Journal of Engineering Manufacture*, *230*(12), 2241–2253.

Pattinson, J., Chen, H., & Basu, S. (2020). Legal issues in automated vehicles: Critically considering the potential role of consent and interactive digital interfaces. *Humanities & Social Sciences Communications*, *7*(1), 1–10. DOI: 10.1057/s41599-020-00644-2

Patton, M. Q. (2015). *Qualitative research & evaluation methods* (4th ed.). SAGE Publications.

Paul, V., Garratt, C., Ward, D. E., & Camm, A. J. (1989). Closed Loop Control of Rate Adaptive Pacing: Clinical Assessment of a System Analyzing the Ventricular Depolarization Gradient. *Pacing and Clinical Electrophysiology*, *12*(12), 1896–1902. DOI: 10.1111/j.1540-8159.1989.tb01882.x PMID: 2481287

Pawade, R. S., Kulkarni, S. V., & Choudhury, S. K. (2014). Multi-objective optimization of WEDM process parameters using desirability function and response surface methodology. *Proceedings of the Institution of Mechanical Engineers. Part B, Journal of Engineering Manufacture*, *228*(10), 1268–1280.

Pereira, A. C., Reis, M. S., & Saraiva, P. M. (2009). Quality control of food products using image analysis and multivariate statistical tools. *Industrial & Engineering Chemistry Research*, *48*(2), 988–998. DOI: 10.1021/ie071610b

Phuyal, S., Bista, D., & Bista, R. (2020). Challenges, opportunities and future directions of smart manufacturing: A state of art review. *Sustainable Futures : An Applied Journal of Technology, Environment and Society, 2*, 100023. DOI: 10.1016/j.sftr.2020.100023

Piciché, M. (2013). *Dawn and Evolution of Cardiac Procedures. Research Avenues in Cardiac Surgery and Interventional Cardiology*. Springer-Verlag Italia. DOI: 10.1007/978-88-470-2400-7

Piga, D., & Bemporad, A. (2020, September 2). New trends in modeling and control of hybrid systems. Wiley, 30(15), 5775-5776. DOI: 10.1002/rnc.5222

Pil'A, J., & Kozuba, J.PIĽA. (2019). Safety of complex aircraft ergatic systems. *Transport Problems, 14*(2), 101–110. DOI: 10.20858/tp.2019.14.2.9

Poalelungi, D. G., Mu at, C. L., Fulga, A., Neagu, M., Neagu, A., Piraianu, A. I., & Fulga, I. (2023, July 31). Advancing Patient Care: How Artificial Intelligence Is Transforming Healthcare. *Journal of Personalized Medicine, 13*(8), 1214–1214. DOI: 10.3390/jpm13081214 PMID: 37623465

Ponomarev, A., & Atkison, T. (2016). Industrial control system network anomaly detection using passive network traffic. *IEEE Transactions on Information Forensics and Security, 12*(5), 1299–1312.

Praba, K., Manoharan, S., Vijay, B., Poreddy, D., Abuya, J. O., & Mulakala, S. (2024). *Human Resource Management Practices in the Age of Industrial Automation* (pp. 79–102). igi global. DOI: 10.4018/979-8-3693-5380-6.ch004

Pranoto, F. S., & Wirawan, A. (2018). Preliminary design of redundancy management for LSA-02 automatic flight control system. 6th International Seminar of Aerospace Science and Technology, IOP Conference Series. *Journal of Physics: Conference Series, 1130*, 012025. DOI: 10.1088/1742-6596/1130/1/012025

Quality, J. O. F. (2024). Retracted: Empirical Analysis for Improving Food Quality Using Artificial Intelligence Technology for Enhancing Healthcare Sector.

Qu, Y. J., Ming, X. G., Liu, Z. W., Zhang, X. Y., & Hou, Z. T. (2019). Smart manufacturing systems: State of the art and future trends. *International Journal of Advanced Manufacturing Technology, 103*(9-12), 3751–3768. DOI: 10.1007/s00170-019-03754-7

Rabbi, A. B. K., & Jeelani, I. (2024). AI integration in construction safety: Current state, challenges, and future opportunities in text, vision, and audio based applications. *Automation in Construction, 164*, 105443. DOI: 10.1016/j.autcon.2024.105443

Rafsanjani, N., & Nabizadeh, A. H. (2023). Towards human-centered artificial intelligence (AI) in architecture, engineering, and construction (AEC) industry. *Computers in Human Behavior Reports, 11*, 100319. DOI: 10.1016/j.chbr.2023.100319

Rahim, M. F. H., Sayuti, M., & Hamdi, M. (2013). Study of machining parameter optimization for wire electrical discharge machining of Ti-6Al-4V. *Procedia CIRP, 6*, 352–357.

Raj, J L B., & Beno, M M. (2023, January 1). Modeling and Control of Parallel Hybrid Electric Vehicle Using Sea-Lion Optimization. Taylor & Francis, 35(2), 1441-1454. DOI: 10.32604/iasc.2023.026211

Rajmohan, T., Arunachalam, R. M., & Soundararajan, R. (2018). Optimization of process parameters of WEDM for machining Ti-6Al-4V using response surface methodology. *Journal of Mechanical Science and Technology*, *32*(8), 3893–3901. DOI: 10.1007/s12206-018-0725-1

Rajurkar, K., Kozak, M., & Mudawar, S. E. (1996). Machining strategies for improving the performance of wire EDM of titanium alloys. *Journal of Materials Processing Technology*, *60*(1-4), 257–264.

Ramasetti, E. K., Herrmann, R., Degener, S., & Baebler, M. (2024). Development of generic AI models to predict the movement of vehicles on bridges. *Procedia Structural Integrity*, *64*, 557–564. DOI: 10.1016/j.prostr.2024.09.307

Ramya, R., Kiruthiga, V., Vettriselvan, R., Gayathri, V., & Velmurugan, P. R. R. (2025). Hybrid Entrepreneurship Navigating Career Transitions: Career Shifts and Their Impact on Economic Growth. In Applications of Career Transitions and Entrepreneurship (pp. 241-268). IGI Global Scientific Publishing.

Rary, E., Anderson, S. M., Philbrick, B. D., Suresh, T., & Burton, J. (2020). Smart sanitation—Biosensors as a public health tool in sanitation infrastructure. *International Journal of Environmental Research and Public Health*, *17*(14), 5146. DOI: 10.3390/ijerph17145146 PMID: 32708793

Ravi, B. K., Dinesh, R., & Krishnaraj, V. (2019). Optimization of machining parameters in WEDM process for Ti-6Al-4V using response surface methodology and Taguchi method. *International Journal of Innovative Technology and Exploring Engineering*, *8*(7S), 1074–1077. DOI: 10.35940/ijitee.L7803.0987s119

Reddy, J. N. (2021). *An Introduction to Nonlinear Finite Element Method with Applications to Heat Transfer, Fluid Mechanics, and Solid Mechanics*. Oxford Press.

Rehman, M. M. U., Rehman, H. Z. U., & Khan, Z. H. (2020). Cyber-Attacks on Medical Implants: A Case Study of Cardiac Pacemaker Vulnerability. *International Journal of Computing and Digital Systems*, *9*(6), 1229–1235. DOI: 10.12785/ijcds/0906020

Renuka Devi, D., & Sasikala, S. (2019). Online feature selection (OFS) with accelerated bat algorithm (ABA) and ensemble incremental deep multiple layer Perceptron (EIDMLP) for big data streams. *Journal of Big Data*, *6*(1), 103. DOI: 10.1186/s40537-019-0267-3

Resta, P., & Laferrière, T. (2020). *Digital equity in education*. Springer.

Reynolds, D. D. (2016). *Engineering Principles of Mechanical Vibration. Bloomington* (4th ed.). Trafford On Demand Publishing.

Ribeiro, M. N., Carvalho, I. A., Fonseca, G. A., Lago, R. C., Rocha, L. C., Ferreira, D. D., Vilas Boas, E. V. B., & Pinheiro, A. C. (2021). Quality control of fresh strawberries by a random forest model. *Journal of the Science of Food and Agriculture*, *101*(11), 4514–4522. DOI: 10.1002/jsfa.11092 PMID: 33448405

Rodríguez-Molina, A., Mezura-Montes, E., Villarreal-Cervantes, M. G., & Aldape-Pérez, M. (2020). Multi-objective meta-heuristic optimization in intelligent control: A survey on the controller tuning problem. *Applied Soft Computing*, *93*, 106342. DOI: 10.1016/j.asoc.2020.106342

Roff, H. M. (2018). The folly of trolleys: Ethical challenges and autonomous vehicles. The Brookings Institution,December 17,2018, https://www.brookings.edu/research/the-folly-oftrolleys-ethical-challenges -and-auton omousvehicles/

Run, T. https://runtimerec.com/how-engineers-can-use-ai-to-improve-control-systems/

Rushe, D. (2021). Tesla's Autopilot faces US investigation after crashes with emergency vehicles. The Guardian, August 16, 2021, https://www.theguardian.com/technology/2021/aug/16/teslas-autopilot-us-investigation-crashesemergency-vehicles

Ryan, S. R., & Granger, M. E. (2023). The importance of dissimilar redundancy for safety in future space vehicle design. *The Journal of Space Safety Engineering*, *10*(4), 387–390. DOI: 10.1016/j.jsse.2023.08.005

Sadeeq, H. T., & Abdulazeez, A. M. (2023). Metaheuristics: A review of algorithms. *International Journal of Online and Biomedical Engineering*, *19*(9), 142–164. DOI: 10.3991/ijoe.v19i09.39683

Sadeghi, M., Soltani, H., & Khayyambashi, M. (2015). The study of hardware redundancy techniques to provide a fault-tolerant system. [CSJ]. *Cumhuriyet University Faculty of Science Science Journal*, *4*, 236–245.

Sadybekov, M. A., & Yessirkegenov, N. A. (2016). Boundary-Value Problems for Wave Equations with Data on the Whole Boundary. *Electron J. Diff. Eq., 281.*

Sahni, V., Srivastava, S., & Khan, R. (2021). Modelling techniques to improve the quality of food using artificial intelligence. *Journal of Food Quality*, *2021*(1), 2140010. DOI: 10.1155/2021/2140010

Saini, S., Yadav, A., Shazli, A., Itoo, M. A., Ajith, A., & Vats, D. (2024). Significance of AI in automobiles. In *Smart Electric and Hybrid Vehicles* (pp. 198–213). CRC Press. DOI: 10.1201/9781003495574-12

Salimi, A., Ghobrial, T., & Bonakdari, H. (2024). A comprehensive review of AI-based methods used for forecasting ice jam floods occurrence, severity, timing, and location. *Cold Regions Science and Technology*, *227*, 104305. DOI: 10.1016/j.coldregions.2024.104305

Samek, W., Wiegand, T., & Müller, K. R. (2017). Explainable artificial intelligence: Understanding, visualizing, and interpreting deep learning models. *arXiv preprint arXiv:1708.08296.*

Sana, M., Asad, M., Farooq, M. U., Anwar, S., & Talha, M. (2024). Sustainable electric discharge machining using alumina-mixed deionized water as dielectric: Process modelling by artificial neural networks underpinning net-zero from industry. *Journal of Cleaner Production*, *441*, 140926. DOI: 10.1016/j.jclepro.2024.140926

Saoudi, N., Appl, U., Anselme, F., Voglimacci, M., & Cribier, A. (1999). How Smart Should Pacemakers Be? *The American Journal of Cardiology*, *83*(5, 5B), 180D–186D. DOI: 10.1016/S0002-9149(98)01029-7 PMID: 10089863

Sapkal, S. B., Kulkarni, A. V., & Gadekar, S. S. (2013). Optimization of WEDM parameters using response surface methodology and desirability function. *Proceedings of the Institution of Mechanical Engineers. Part B, Journal of Engineering Manufacture*, *227*(8), 1173–1183.

Schöning, J., & Pfisterer, H. (2023, August 17). Safe and Trustful AI for Closed-Loop Control Systems. *Electronics (Basel)*, *12*(16), 3489–3489. DOI: 10.3390/electronics12163489

Shah, J. M., Natraj, N. A., Hallur, G. G., & Aslekar, A. (2023, March). Artificial Intelligence (AI) in the Automotive Industry and the use of Exoskeletons in the Manufacturing Sector of the Automotive Industry. In *2023 International Conference on Sustainable Computing and Data Communication Systems (ICSCDS)* (pp. 428-432). IEEE. DOI: 10.1109/ICSCDS56580.2023.10105009

Shaik, T., Tao, X., Higgins, N., Li, L., Gururajan, R., Zhou, X., & Acharya, U R. (2023, January 5). Remote patient monitoring using artificial intelligence: Current state, applications, and challenges. Wiley, 13(2). DOI: 10.1002/widm.1485

Sherif, A., & Haci, H. (2023). A novel bio-inspired energy optimization for two-tier wireless communication networks: A grasshopper optimization algorithm (GOA)-based approach. *Electronics (Basel), 12*(5), 1216. DOI: 10.3390/electronics12051216

Shi, W. (2012). Advanced Intelligent Control and Optimization for Cardiac Pacemaker Systems. *Dissertations*, 306. https://digitalcommons.njit.edu/dissertations/306

Shidaganti, G., & Karthik, K. N. Anvith, & Kantikar, N. A. (2023). Integration of RPA and AI in Industry 4.0. In Confluence of Artificial Intelligence and Robotic Process Automation (pp. 267-288). Singapore: Springer Nature Singapore.

Shi, K., Wu, Z., Jiang, B., & Karimi, H. R. (2023). Dynamic path planning of mobile robot based on improved simulated annealing algorithm. *Journal of the Franklin Institute, 360*(6), 4378–4398. DOI: 10.1016/j.jfranklin.2023.01.033

Shi, W. (2013a). A Novel Design of Fuzzy PID Controllers for Dual-Sensor Cardiac Pacemaker Systems. *Open Journal of Applied Biosensor, 2*(2), 29–38. DOI: 10.4236/ojab.2013.22004

Shi, W. V. (2013b). Advanced Intelligent Control of Cardiac Pacemaker Systems Using a Fuzzy PID Controller. *International Journal of Intelligent Control and Systems, 18*(2), 28–34. https://api.semanticscholar.org/CorpusID:6710475

Shi, W. V., & Zhou, M., M. (2011). Fuzzy PID Controllers for Dual-Sensor Pacing Systems in Patients with Bradycardias at Rest. *2011 IEEE International Conference on Systems, Man, and Cybernetics*, Anchorage, AK, USA, 1117-1122, DOI: 10.1109/ICSMC.2011.6083824

Shi, Z., Feng, Y., Egbelakin, T., Yang, C., & Gao, W. (2025). Computational fluid dynamics -informed virtual safety assessment of steel-framed structure with fire-induced ductile failure. *Reliability Engineering & System Safety, 258*, 110918. DOI: 10.1016/j.ress.2025.110918

Shute, V. J., & Rahimi, S. (2017). Adaptive learning technologies. In *Handbook of research on educational communications and technology* (pp. 105–124). Springer.

Siemens, G. (2005). Connectivism: A learning theory for the digital age. *International Journal of Instructional Technology and Distance Learning*, 2(1), 3–10.

Siemens, G. (2016). Learning analytics: The emergence of a new educational technology. *Journal of Educational Technology Systems, 44*(1), 5–15. DOI: 10.1177/0047239515611134

Signoret, J., Dutuit, Y., Cacheux, P., Folleau, C., Collas, S., & Thomas, P. (2013). Make your Petri nets understandable: Reliability block diagrams driven Petri nets. *Reliability Engineering & System Safety, 113*, 61–75. DOI: 10.1016/j.ress.2012.12.008

Singh, D., Singh, A. K., Singh, S. P., & Poonia, S. (2021). Optimization of tilt angles for solar devices to gain maximum solar energy in Indian climate. In P. V. Baredar, S. Tangellapalli, & C. S. Solanki (Eds.), *Advances in Clean Energy Technologies*. Springer Proceedings in Energy. Springer, Singapore. https://doi.org/DOI: 10.1007/978-981-16-0235-1_16

Singh, A. (2022). Importance of Fuzzy Logic in Traffic and Transportation Engineering. In Vasant, P., Zelinka, I., & Weber, G. W. (Eds.), *Intelligent Computing & Optimization. ICO 2021. Lecture Notes in Networks and Systems* (Vol. 371). Springer., DOI: 10.1007/978-3-030-93247-3_10

Singh, A. (2023). Mechatronics Engineering in the Modern World and Its Use in the Construction Industry. In Mellal, M. (Ed.), *Trends, Paradigms, and Advances in Mechatronics Engineering* (pp. 64–92). IGI Global Scientific Publishing., DOI: 10.4018/978-1-6684-5887-7.ch004

Singh, A. (2023). The Present and Future Role of Artificial Intelligence in the Promotion of Sustainable Practices in the Construction Sector. In Kahraman, C., Sari, I. U., Oztaysi, B., Cebi, S., Cevik Onar, S., & Tolga, A. Ç. (Eds.), *Intelligent and Fuzzy Systems. INFUS 2023. Lecture Notes in Networks and Systems* (Vol. 759). Springer., DOI: 10.1007/978-3-031-39777-6_2

Singh, A. (2023). The Recent Trend of Artificial Neural Network in the Field of Civil Engineering. In Vasant, P. (Eds.), *Intelligent Computing and Optimization. ICO 2023. Lecture Notes in Networks and Systems* (Vol. 855). Springer., DOI: 10.1007/978-3-031-50158-6_32

Singh, A. (2023). The Significance of Digitalization of the Construction Sector. In Vasant, P., Weber, G. W., Marmolejo-Saucedo, J. A., Munapo, E., & Thomas, J. J. (Eds.), *Intelligent Computing & Optimization. ICO 2022. Lecture Notes in Networks and Systems* (Vol. 569). Springer., DOI: 10.1007/978-3-031-19958-5_100

Singh, A. (2024). The Current Status and Scope of Smart Highways in India. In Taha, L., & Anwar, S. (Eds.), *Principles and Applications in Speed Sensing and Energy Harvesting for Smart Roads* (pp. 1–41). IGI Global Scientific Publishing., DOI: 10.4018/978-1-6684-9214-7.ch001

Singh, A., & Srivastava, A. Impact of Artificial Intelligence Techniques and Green AI Applications. In *Artificial Intelligence Techniques for Sustainable Development* (pp. 44–63). CRC Press. DOI: 10.1201/9781003546382-3

Singh, K. (2022, January 1). Design of Sliding Mode PID Controller with Improved reaching laws for Nonlinear Systems. Cornell University. https://doi.org/DOI: 10.48550/arXiv.2207

Singh, P., Kumar, N., & Singh, N. K. (2021). Optimization of WEDM process parameters using artificial neural network and genetic algorithm. *Journal of Advanced Research in Dynamical and Control Systems, 13*(4), 1796–1807.

Singh, R., Mehta, S., & Yadav, L. K. (2019). Reinforcement learning for optimizing conveyor system operations and fault prevention. *IEEE Transactions on Automation Science and Engineering, 16*(3), 478–489.

Sirazetdinov, T. K. (1977). *Optimizatsiya sistem s raspredelennymi parametrami* [Optimization of Systems with Distributed Parameters]. Nauka. (In Russian)

Si, X. S., Wang, W., Hu, C. H., & Zhou, D. H. (2011). Remaining useful life estimation—A review on the statistical data-driven approaches. *European Journal of Operational Research, 213*(1), 1–14. DOI: 10.1016/j.ejor.2010.11.018

Skinderowicz, R. (2022). Improving ant colony optimization efficiency for solving large TSP instances. *Applied Soft Computing, 120*, 108653. DOI: 10.1016/j.asoc.2022.108653

Smith, M. L., Smith, L. N., & Hansen, M. F. (2021). The quiet revolution in machine vision-a state-of-the-art survey paper, including historical review, perspectives, and future directions. *Computers in Industry, 130*, 103472. DOI: 10.1016/j.compind.2021.103472

Soltani Firouz, M., & Sardari, H. (2022). Defect detection in fruit and vegetables by using machine vision systems and image processing. *Food Engineering Reviews, 14*(3), 353-379.9.

Song, J., Lyu, D., Zhang, Z., Wang, Z., Zhang, T., & Ma, L. (2022, May 1). When Cyber-Physical Systems Meet AI: A Benchmark, an Evaluation, and a Way Forward. DOI: 10.1109/ICSE-SEIP55303.2022.9794128

Srivatsn, S. M., Kumar, V. V. S., Sakthivel, G., Saravanakumar, D., & Kiran, N. R. (2021). Analysis of Fuzzy and PID Control in Pacemaker with Cardiovascular Model. *Journal of Physics: Conference Series, 1969*(1), 012066. DOI: 10.1088/1742-6596/1969/1/012066

Stake, R. E. (2006). *Multiple case study analysis*. Guilford Press.

Stamate, E., Piraianu, A.-I., Ciobotaru, O. R., Crassas, R., Duca, O., Fulga, A., Grigore, I., Vintila, V., Fulga, I., & Ciobotaru, O. C. (2024). Revolutionizing Cardiology through Artificial Intelligence-Big Data from Proactive Prevention to Precise Diagnostics and Cutting-Edge Treatment-A Comprehensive Review of the Past 5 Years. *Diagnostics (Basel), 14*(11), 1103. DOI: 10.3390/diagnostics14111103 PMID: 38893630

Stanford Medicine Health Care. (2024). *Stanford Center for Inherited Cardiovascular Disease*. https://stanfordhealthcare.org/medical-treatments/p/pacemaker/types.html

Stouffer, K., Pillitteri, V., Lightman, S., Abrams, M., & Hahn, A. (2015). Guide to industrial control systems (ICS) security. *NIST Special Publication 800-82 Revision 2*. National Institute of Standards and Technology.

Strik, M., Sacristan, B., Bordachar, P., Duchateau, J., Eschalier, R., Mondoly, P., Laborderie, J., Gassa, N., Zemzemi, N., Laborde, M., Garrido, J., Matencio Perabla, C., Jimenez-Perez, G., Camara, O., Haïssaguerre, M., Dubois, R., & Ploux, S. (2023). Artificial intelligence for detection of ventricular oversensing: Machine learning approaches for noise detection within nonsustained ventricular tachycardia episodes remotely transmitted by pacemakers and implantable cardioverter-defibrillators. *Heart Rhythm, 20*(10), 1378–1384. DOI: 10.1016/j.hrthm.2023.06.019 PMID: 37406873

Sun, Y., Gupta, R., & Rao, P. (2021). Thermal anomaly detection in packaging machinery using support vector machines. *IEEE Transactions on Industrial Electronics, 68*(5), 1247–1256.

Taguchi, G., & Shih-Chung, T. (1992). *Introduction to quality engineering: bringing quality engineering upstream*. ASME.

Tarek, H., Aly, H., Eisa, S., & Abul-Soud, M. (2022). Optimized deep learning algorithms for tomato leaf disease detection with hardware deployment. *Electronics (Basel)*, *11*(1), 140. DOI: 10.3390/electronics11010140

Thanom, W., & Loh, R. (2011). Nonlinear Control of Heartbeat Models. *Journal of Systemics, Cybernetics and Informatics*, *9*(1), 21–27.

Thapa, A., Nishad, S., Biswas, D., & Roy, S. (2023). A comprehensive review on artificial intelligence assisted technologies in food industry. *Food Bioscience*, *56*, 103231. DOI: 10.1016/j.fbio.2023.103231

Tian, X., Hao, Y., Zhao, G., & Liang, J. (2020, November 6). Research on Dynamic Modeling of a High Temperature Steam Heat Pump. DOI: 10.1109/CAC51589.2020.9327828

Tikhonov, A. N., & Samarskii, A. A. (1963). *Equations of mathematical physics*. Pergamon Press Ltd.

Timoshenko, S., & Maccullough, G. H. (1935). *Elements of strength of materials* (1st ed.). D. Van Nostrand company, Inc.

Tripathi, S., Shukla, S., Attrey, S., Agrawal, A., & Bhadoria, V. S. (2020). Smart industrial packaging and sorting system. *Strategic system assurance and business analytics*, 245-254.

Trivedi, N. K., Gautam, V., Anand, A., Aljahdali, H. M., Villar, S. G., Anand, D., Goyal, N., & Kadry, S. (2021). Early detection and classification of tomato leaf disease using high-performance deep neural network. *Sensors (Basel)*, *21*(23), 7987. DOI: 10.3390/s21237987 PMID: 34883991

Tsoumakas, G. (2019). A survey of machine learning techniques for food sales prediction. *Artificial Intelligence Review*, *52*(1), 441–447. DOI: 10.1007/s10462-018-9637-z

Tuong, V. D., Nguyena, T.-V., Cho, S., Truong, T. P., & Noh, W. (2021). Partial Computation Offloading in NOMA-Assisted Mobile-Edge Computing Systems Using Deep Reinforcement Learning. *IEEE Internet of Things Journal*, *8*(17), 13196–13208. DOI: 10.1109/JIOT.2021.3064995

Turgut, O. E., Turgut, M. S., & Kırtepe, E. (2023). A systematic review of the emerging metaheuristic algorithms on solving complex optimization problems. *Neural Computing & Applications*, *35*(19), 14275–14378. DOI: 10.1007/s00521-023-08481-5

Ulucan, O., Karakaya, D., & Turkan, M. (2019, October). Meat quality assessment based on deep learning. In *2019 Innovations in Intelligent Systems and Applications Conference (ASYU)* (pp. 1-5). Ieee. DOI: 10.1109/ASYU48272.2019.8946388

Uncuoglu, E., Citakoglu, H., Latifoglu, L., Bayram, S., Laman, M., Ilkentapar, M., & Oner, A. A. (2022). Comparison of neural network, Gaussian regression, support vector machine, long short-term memory, multi-gene genetic programming, and M5 Trees methods for solving civil engineering problems. *Applied Soft Computing*, *129*, 109623. DOI: 10.1016/j.asoc.2022.109623

Vettriselvan, R., Ramya, R., Sathya, M., Swadhi, R., & Deepan, A. (2024). Service delivery and citizen-centric approaches: Innovating public administration management in higher education. In *Challenges of public administration for higher education* (pp. 113–136). IGI Global., DOI: 10.4018/979-8-3693-4346-3.ch006

Veza, I., Deniz Karaoglan, A., Ileri, E., Afzal, A., Tuan Hoang, A., Tamaldin, N., Gazali Herawan, S., Abbas, M. M., & Farid Muhamad Said, M. (2022). Multi-objective optimization of diesel engine performance and emission using grasshopper optimization algorithm. *Fuel*, *323*, 124303. DOI: 10.1016/j.fuel.2022.124303

Vidyarthi, S. K., Tiwari, R., Singh, S. K., & Xiao, H. W. (2020). Prediction of size and mass of pistachio kernels using random Forest machine learning. *Journal of Food Process Engineering*, *43*(9), e13473. DOI: 10.1111/jfpe.13473

Villalba-Díez, J., Molina, M., Ordieres-Meré, J., Sun, S., Schmidt, D., & Wellbrock, W. (2020). Geometric deep lean learning: Deep learning in industry 4.0 cyber–physical complex networks. *Sensors (Basel)*, *20*(3), 763. DOI: 10.3390/s20030763 PMID: 32019148

Wang, C., Li, J., Rao, H., Chen, A., Jiao, J., Zou, N., & Gu, L. (2021). Multi-objective grasshopper optimization algorithm based on multi-group and co-evolution. *Mathematical Biosciences and Engineering*, *18*(3), 2527–2561. DOI: 10.3934/mbe.2021129 PMID: 33892559

Wang, C., Song, L. H., Yuan, Z., & Fan, J. S. (2023). State-of-the-art AI-based computational analysis in civil engineering. *Journal of Industrial Information Integration*, *33*, 100470.

Wang, F.. (2020). Culturally responsive teaching and technology in a global context. *Journal of Computer Assisted Learning*, *36*(5), 706–717. DOI: 10.1111/jcal.12428

Wang, K. S., Ma, L., Yang, C. C., Chang, S. F., & Hsu, P. (2018). Predictive maintenance using machine learning for industrial control systems. *IEEE Transactions on Industrial Electronics*, *65*(8), 6558–6567.

Wang, K., He, Q., & Zhang, Y. (2017). Predictive maintenance based on Bayesian network for wind turbine systems. *Energy Conversion and Management*, *148*, 397–406.

Wang, T., & Wang, Q. (2021). Cyclic responses and microstructure sensitivity of Cr-based turbine steel under different strain ratios in low cycle fatigue regime. *Materials & Design*, *201*, 109529. DOI: 10.1016/j.matdes.2021.109529

Wani, A., Kumari, D., & Singh, J. (2024). Ethics in the Driver's Seat: Unravelling the Ethical Dilemmas of AI in Autonomous Driving (No. 2024-01-2023). SAE Technical Paper.

Wan, J., Li, X., Dai, H. N., Kusiak, A., Martinez-Garcia, M., & Li, D. (2020). Artificial-intelligence-driven customized manufacturing factory: Key technologies, applications, and challenges. *Proceedings of the IEEE*, *109*(4), 377–398. DOI: 10.1109/JPROC.2020.3034808

Wei, L. (2017). Security threats and requirements analysis for IOV. [https://www.itu.int/en/ITU-T/Workshops-and- Seminars/201708/Documents/S1-Wei.pdf]

Widodo, A., & Yang, B. S. (2007). Support vector machine in machine condition monitoring and fault diagnosis. *Mechanical Systems and Signal Processing*, *21*(6), 2560–2574. DOI: 10.1016/j.ymssp.2006.12.007

Wiharya, C., Sungkowo, H., Suryandari, A. S., & Kurniawan, B. I. (2021, February 1). Design and optimization of digitalization device of temperature control system using PID Ziegler-Nichols control in chemical engineering laboratory. *IOP Conference Series. Materials Science and Engineering, 1073*(1), 012051–012051. DOI: 10.1088/1757-899X/1073/1/012051

Williams, D., Clark, C., McGahan, R., Potteiger, B., Cohen, D., & Musau, P. (2022, March). Discovery of AI/ML supply chain vulnerabilities within automotive cyber-physical systems. In *2022 IEEE International Conference on Assured Autonomy (ICAA)* (pp. 93-96). IEEE. DOI: 10.1109/ICAA52185.2022.00020

Williamson, B. (2019). Automating education: The impact of AI on learning. *Education and Information Technologies, 24*(1), 1–13. DOI: 10.1007/s10639-019-09981-4

Woo, S., O'Neal, D., & Pecht, M. (2023). Improving the lifetime of mechanical systems during transit established on quantum/transport life-stress prototype and sample size. *Mechanical Systems and Signal Processing, 193*, 110222. DOI: 10.1016/j.ymssp.2023.110222

Wu, C., Kuo, C., Shih, S., Chen, J., Lo, Y., Yu, H., Huang, M., Sheu, W. H., & Liu, S. (2021, April 25). Implementation of an Electronic National Early Warning System to Decrease Clinical Deterioration in Hospitalized Patients at a Tertiary Medical Center. *International Journal of Environmental Research and Public Health, 18*(9), 4550–4550. DOI: 10.3390/ijerph18094550 PMID: 33922991

Wu, L., Huang, X., Cui, J., Liu, C., & Xiao, W. (2023). Modified adaptive ant colony optimization algorithm and its application for solving path planning of mobile robots. *Expert Systems with Applications, 215*, 119410. DOI: 10.1016/j.eswa.2022.119410

Wu, W., Zhang, P., & Lee, T. (2020). Synthetic data generation for enhancing fault detection model training in food processing applications. *IEEE Transactions on Artificial Intelligence, 2*(4), 291–300.

Yadav, J., Rani, A., & Garg, G. (2011). Intelligent Heart Rate Controller for Cardiac Pacemaker. *International Journal of Computer Applications, 36*(7), 22–29. DOI: 10.5120/4503-6361

Yang, X.S. (2013) Optimization and metaheuristic algorithms in engineering. *Metaheuristics in Water, Geotechnical and Transport Engineering*, 1. 9780123982964, 0123982960.

Yang, K. J., Hong, K. S., & Matsuno, F. (2004). Robust adaptive boundary control of an axially moving string under a spatiotemporally varying tension. *Journal of Sound and Vibration, 273*(4-5), 1007–1029. DOI: 10.1016/S0022-460X(03)00519-4

Yaniv, Y., Lyashkov, A. E., & Lakatta, E. G. (2013). The Fractal-Like Complexity of Heart Rate Variability Beyond Neurotransmitters and Autonomic Receptors: Signaling Intrinsic to Sinoatrial Node Pacemaker Cells. *Cardiovascular Pharmacology: Open Access, 2*(3), 111. DOI: 10.4172/2329-6607.1000111 PMID: 26709383

Ye, Y.-N., Chou, Y.-L., Zhao, D., Cao, W., Xu, J.-W., & Wang, A.-J. (2025). Permafrost environment evaluation of Qinghai-Tibetan Plateau based on DPSRC theory and system dynamics. *Ecological Modelling, 501*, 110992. DOI: 10.1016/j.ecolmodel.2024.110992

Yu, J., & Hyland, M. F. (2025). Interpretable State-Space Model of Urban Dynamics for Human-Machine Collaborative Transportation Planning. *Transportation Research Part B: Methodological, 192*, 103134. DOI: 10.1016/j.trb.2024.103134

Zarei, B., Kumar, R., & Singh, D. (2022). IoT-integrated predictive maintenance framework for dairy processing units. *International Journal of Smart Manufacturing Systems, 15*(2), 87–96.

Zawacki-Richter, O., Marín, V. I., Bond, M., & Gouverneur, F. (2019). Systematic review of research on artificial intelligence applications in higher education: Where are the educators? *International Journal of Educational Technology in Higher Education, 16*(1), 39. DOI: 10.1186/s41239-019-0171-0

Zhang, B., Li, C. Y., Kikumoto, H., Niu, J., & Tse, T. K. T. (2024). Smart urban windcatcher: Conception of an AI-empowered wind-channeling system for real-time enhancement of urban wind environment. *Building and Environment, 253*, 111357. DOI: 10.1016/j.buildenv.2024.111357

Zhang, B., Wu, J., Wang, L., & Yu, Z. (2020). Accurate dynamic modeling and control parameters design of an industrial hybrid spray-painting robot. *Robotics and Computer-integrated Manufacturing, 63*, 101923. DOI: 10.1016/j.rcim.2019.101923

Zhang, H., Zhang, Z., Wu, W., & He, X. (2019). Anomaly detection in industrial control systems using LSTM networks. *IEEE Access : Practical Innovations, Open Solutions, 7*, 88036–88047.

Zhang, J., Yang, X., Wang, W., Guan, J., Ding, L., & Lee, V. C. S. (2023). Automated guided vehicles and autonomous mobile robots for recognition and tracking in civil engineering. *Automation in Construction, 146*, 104699. DOI: 10.1016/j.autcon.2022.104699

Zhang, Z., Liu, J., & Wang, T. (2020). Convolutional neural network-based fault detection for food processing machinery using vibration and acoustic signals. *Journal of Industrial Applications in AI, 12*(3), 45–52.

Zhao, J., Ma, T., Yang, H., & Zhang, X. (2019). Experimental study and performance analysis on solar photovoltaic panel integrated with phase change material. *Energy, 178*, 471–486. DOI: 10.1016/j.energy.2019.04.166

Zhao, S., Blaabjerg, F., & Wang, H. (2020). An overview of artificial intelligence applications for power electronics. *IEEE Transactions on Power Electronics, 36*(4), 4633–4658. DOI: 10.1109/TPEL.2020.3024914

Zhao, S., Peng, Y., Liu, J., & Wu, S. (2021). Tomato leaf disease diagnosis based on improved convolution neural network by attention module. *Agriculture, 11*(7), 651. DOI: 10.3390/agriculture11070651

Zhou, C., Zhou, S., Xing, J., & Song, J. (2021). Tomato leaf disease identification by restructured deep residual dense network. *IEEE Access : Practical Innovations, Open Solutions, 9*, 28822–28831. DOI: 10.1109/ACCESS.2021.3058947

Zhou, W. (2022, August 21). Research on the Control Methods Based on Liquid Level System. *Research on the Control Methods Based on Liquid Level System., 13*, 198–206. DOI: 10.54097/hset.v13i.1351

Zhou, Y., Karemore, G., Li, W., Liang, Z., Žitnik, M., Chong, F. T., Liu, J., & Fu, T. (2024, August 27). Quantum-Machine-Assisted Drug Discovery: Survey and Perspective. DOI: 10.20944/preprints202408.1950.v1

Zhu, B., Joseph, A., & Sastry, S. (2011). A taxonomy of cyber attacks on SCADA systems. *IEEE International Conferences on Internet of Things (iThings/CPSCom)*, 16-25.

Zhu, Y., & Zhong, Z. (2023, February 20). Editorial: Hybrid intelligent algorithms based learning, optimization, and application to autonomic control systems, volume II. Frontiers Media, DOI: 10.3389/fnbot.2023.1151473

Zhu, Y., Lam, H., Yang, T., Zhong, Z., & Arik, S. (2019, October 11). Editorial: Hybrid Intelligent Algorithms Based Learning, Optimization, and Application to Autonomic Control Systems. Frontiers Media, DOI: 10.3389/fnins.2019.01090

Zhuang, H., Cheng, Y., Zhou, M., & Yang, Z. (2025). Deep learning for surface crack detection in civil engineering: A comprehensive review. *Measurement*, *248*, 116908. DOI: 10.1016/j.measurement.2025.116908

Zhu, Z., Gavahian, M., Barba, F. J., Roselló-Soto, E., Kovačević, D. B., Putnik, P., & Denoya, G. I. (2020). Valorization of waste and by-products from food industries through the use of innovative technologies. In *Agri-food industry strategies for healthy diets and sustainability* (pp. 249–266). Academic Press. DOI: 10.1016/B978-0-12-817226-1.00011-4

Znamenskaya, L. N. (2004). *Upravlenie uprugimi kolebaniyami* [Control of elastic vibrations]. Fizmatlit. (In Russian)

Zonta, T., da Costa, C. A., da Silva, D. D., & Webber, G. A. (2020). Predictive maintenance in Industry 4.0: A systematic literature review. *Computers & Industrial Engineering*, *150*, 106889. DOI: 10.1016/j.cie.2020.106889

About the Contributors

Mohamed Arezki Mellal is a Professor in the Department of Mechanical Engineering, Faculty of Technology, at M'Hamed Bougara University, Boumerdes, Algeria. He was ranked among the Top 2% of Scientists Worldwide by Stanford University (Single-year 2022) and was the top-ranked candidate in the 47th National University Commission for the Professorship in Mechanical Engineering in 2022. He has been a Visiting Scholar at various universities and has published over 80 research papers. He has been invited to various conferences and serves as a regular reviewer for over 30 SCIE journals.

***

Deepan A is an Assistant Professor at Sambhram University in Uzbekistan, with over 7 years of marketing experience in multinational corporations and 8 years of teaching across Central Africa, India, and Uzbekistan. His professional background includes expertise in strategic marketing, brand management, and market analysis, complemented by a strong academic career involving curriculum development and student mentoring. Deepan's research interests focus on contemporary challenges in marketing and business education, reflecting his commitment to bridging industry knowledge with academic inquiry, making him a valuable asset in both corporate and educational environments.

Wesam Ahmed received the B.S. and M.Sc. degrees in information technology from Mansoura University and the Ph.D. degree in information technology from Menoufia University, Egypt. She is currently an Assistant Professor at the Faculty of Computers and Artificial Intelligence, Hurghada University. Her research interests include artificial intelligence, Natural Language Processing, data mining, and pattern recognition

Ana Maria Castillo-Rivera completed her Medical Degree at the University of Granada (Spain). She obtained her Master of Advanced Studies in Internal Medicine at the University of Granada (Spain). She was awarded a PhD in Medicine at the University of Granada (Spain).

Salvador Castillo-Rivera completed his BSc in Physics and majoring in Fundamental Physics at the University of Granada (Spain). He obtained his Master of Advanced Studies in Physics and Mathematics at the University of Granada (Spain). He was awarded a PhD in Aeronautical Engineering at the City University London (United Kingdom).

Ashray Chouhan is a master's research scholar at VIT Bhopal University, India. His research interests include AI-ML, Data Science, Soft Computing, Computational Intelligence, and Cognitive Analytics.

Renuka Devi D currently serves as an Assistant Professor in the Department of Computer Science at Stella Maris College(Autonomous) in Chennai, India. With over 15 years of extensive teaching experience, she holds a Ph.D. from the University of Madras. Her academic expertise spans areas such as Data Mining, Machine Learning, Big Data, and Artificial Intelligence. She has authored a book titled "Research Practitioner's Handbook on Big Data Analytics," published by Apple Academic Press, CRC Press, USA, and has contributed articles to various publications, including IEEE, Springer, Scopus, and Web of Science. In addition, she holds patents in the fields of virtual network security and AI. She presented papers at international conferences, earning accolades such as the Best Paper Award and the Best Researcher Award. She is associated with various international societies. She is also an editorial member of the Journal of Advances in Management Sciences & Information Systems and has represented India as a panelist in the "Global Perspectives on Artificial Intelligence in Higher Education - A virtual roundtable on AI" in 2023 organized by Alamo Colleges District, San Antonio, USA.

R. Deepa obtained her B.E. in Computer Science Engineering from Anjalai Ammal Engineering College and her M.Tech. in Information Technology from Sathyabama University. She completed her Ph.D. at Sathyabama University and is currently working as an Assistant Professor at the SRM Institute of Science and Technology, Kattankulathur. Her research interests include artificial intelligence and machine learning, and she has published several papers in both conferences and journals.

G.Manikandan (Gunasekar Manikandan) obtained his Ph.D degree in Sathayabama Institute of Science and Technology. He has completed his bachelor's degree in computer science and engineering from St.Joseph's College of Engineering, Tamilnadu, India. Then he obtained his Master's degree in Computer Science and Engineering from St.Joseph's College of Engineering, Tamilnadu, India. Currently, he is working as Associate Professor at the Department of Artificial Intelligence and Machine Learning, St.Joseph's College of Engineering, Chennai-119, India. His current research interests are Wireless Sensor Networks,Network Security,Machine Learning

Rituraj Jain is currently working in the Department of Information Technology, Marwadi University, Rajkot, Gujarat, India. He has published many papers in International Journals and Conferences. He has published 4 books. He is an Oracle Database SQL Certified Expert. He is also associated with professional bodies like the Indian Society of Technical Education (ISTE), Computer Science Teachers Association (CSTA), Academy & Industry Research Collaboration Center (AIRCC), International Association of Computer Science and Information Technology (IACSIT), International Association of Engineers (IAENG). His research interests include Cloud Computing, Machine Learning, Deep Learning, Fuzzy Logic, IoT, Genetic Algorithms, Big Data and Software Engineering.

Vishal Jain is presently working as an Associate Professor at Department of Computer Science and Engineering, School of Engineering and Technology, Sharda University, Greater Noida, U. P. India. Before that, he has worked for several years as an Associate Professor at Bharati Vidyapeeth's Institute of Computer Applications and Management (BVICAM), New Delhi. He has more than 14 years of experience in the academics. He obtained Ph.D (CSE), M.Tech (CSE), MBA (HR), MCA, MCP and CCNA. He has authored more than 90 research papers in reputed conferences and journals, including Web of Science and Scopus. He has authored and edited more than 30 books with various reputed publishers, including Elsevier, Springer, Apple Academic Press, CRC, Taylor and Francis Group, Scrivener, Wiley,

Emerald, NOVA Science and IGI-Global. His research areas include information retrieval, semantic web, ontology engineering, data mining, ad hoc networks, and sensor networks. He received a Young Active Member Award for the year 2012–13 from the Computer Society of India, Best Faculty Award for the year 2017 and Best Researcher Award for the year 2019 from BVICAM, New Delhi.

Swetha Margaret T A is an accomplished professional with a diverse background in academia, research, and industry, specializing in Cyber and Network Security, Cloud Computing, Computer Networks, IoT, IIoT, Big Data, and Artificial Intelligence. With 12 years of experience, she currently serves as an Assistant Professor in the Department of Computer Science at Stella Maris College, bringing seven years of dedicated teaching expertise. Dr. Margaret holds a Ph.D., earned during her three-year tenure as a full-time Doctoral Research Scholar at Quaid E Millath College, Chennai. Prior to her academic pursuits, she gained valuable industry experience with IBM and Citrix, focusing on IBM mainframe backend support, task management, and load creation. Her commitment to professional development is evident through various international certifications, including those from IBM, Big Data University, and Udemy, covering Cloud Computing, Data Science Methodology, and more. As the Chief Information Security Officer (CISO) at Stella Maris College since 2023, she has demonstrated leadership in securing information assets. Dr. Margaret's research contributions extend to over 20 publications in international journals, including Scopus, IEEE, and Springer. Her expertise has been recognized through accolades such as the "Best Researcher Award" from D K International Research Foundation and the 'Young Faculty in Science' Award during the Contemporary Academic Meet-CAM by Venus International Foundation, both in 2018-2019. Her commitment to innovation is evident through patents, including Innovation patent for "Un Nanban," an AI-based interactive web and voice application, and a Design patent for a "Smart Walking Stick" for visually impaired individuals in 2023. Represented India as a panellist in the "Global Perspectives on Artificial Intelligence in Higher Education - A virtual roundtable on AI" in 2023 organised by Alamo Colleges District, San Antonio, USA

Nilamadhab Mishra is an Associate Professor in the School of Computer Science and Engineering, AI-ML Division, at VIT Bhopal University, India. He received his Doctor of Philosophy (Ph.D.) in Computer Science & Information Engineering with a specialization in Data Science & Machine Learning from Chang Gung University, Taiwan. He has more than 22 years of national and international involvement in academic teaching and research at recognized Indian, Taiwanese, and African universities. He has over 50 publications in SCI/SCIE and SCOPUS-indexed journals, ISBN books and chapters, Indian and Australian patents, IEEE conference proceedings, and others. He has served as a reviewer, associate editor, and editorial board member for SCI/SCIE-indexed journals and conferences. Dr. Mishra worked on multiple funded research projects from the MOST, NSC, and CGU Memorial Hospital, Taiwan, during his Ph.D. and has been involved with several professional bodies. He is currently an Associate Editor for two SCOPUS-indexed journals, and his research interests span the areas of AI, Data Science, Machine Learning, and Cognitive Analytics & Applications.

Archan Mitra is an Assistant Professor at School of Media Studies (SOMS) at Presidency University, Bangalore. He is the author of two book "Cases for Classroom Media and Entertainment Business" and "Multiverse and Media", he also has other several edited books to his credit. He has done his doctorate from Visva-Bharati Santiniketan, West Bengal in the field of "environmental informatics and communication for sustainability". In addition to that he is a certified Science Communicator and

Journalism from Indian Science Communication Society (ISCOS), certified Corporate Trainer with Amity Institute of Training and Development, Certified Social Media Network Analyst. He has a strong interest in environmental communication. He was awarded certificate of merit by PRSI, Kolkata Chapter and Medal of Honor by Journalistic Club of Kolkata. He was working as a research assistant with the World Bank's "Environmental Capacity Building in Southeast Asia" project at IIM Kashipur. He was instrumental in launching the World Bank's Green MBA MOOC, he has also assisted in the research project on Uttarakhand disaster mitigation by ICSSR, the leading research on Uttarakhand disaster.

Arul Kumar Natarajan currently serves as an Assistant Professor in the Department of Computer Science at the Samarkand International University of Technology in Uzbekistan. He earned his Doctor of Philosophy degree in Computer Science from Bharathidasan University, India, in 2017. Concurrently, he is engaged in postdoctoral research in Generative AI for Cybersecurity at the Singapore Institute of Technology, Singapore. Throughout his 14-year teaching career, Dr. Arul has held esteemed positions at various institutions, including Christ University, Bishop Heber College in India, and Debre Berhan University in Ethiopia. Dr. Arul has made significant contributions to academia, specializing in cybersecurity and artificial intelligence, evidenced by his portfolio of scholarly works. He has authored 32 international publications indexed in Scopus and 03 international publications and has delivered 34 conference presentations. Additionally, he has edited and published 03 books with IGI Global Publisher, USA, focusing on Python data structures, algorithms, and geospatial application development. In addition to his academic pursuits, Dr. Arul is a prolific innovator, holding 17 patents in India and 01 granted patent in the United Kingdom across diverse domains, including communication and computer science. He demonstrates proficiency in networking and cybersecurity, having completed the CCNA Routing and Switching Exam from CISCO and the Networking Fundamentals exam from Microsoft. He maintains a sincere interest in GenAI for Cybersecurity.

P. Sriramalakshmi, was born in Tamilnadu, India. She has completed her B.Tech degree in Electrical Engineering in 2004 from National Institute of Technology, Silchar, Assam, India. She received her M.E degree in power electronics and drives in 2009 from College of Engineering, Guindy, Chennai, India. She pursued her doctoral degree in the area of power converters especially in inverters in 2020 from Vellore Institute of Technology (VIT), Chennai. She has around 16 years of teaching experience in various Engineering colleges. She joined VIT as an Assistant professor in 2012. Currently, she is working as an Associate Professor in VIT, Chennai. Dr. P.Sriramalakshmi has published many research papers, conference presentations and book chapters in reputed journals. Her field of interest includes power electronic converters for renewable energy applications, Internet of things, single stage inverters

P. Thilakavathy working as Assistant Professor in the Department of Computer Science and Engineering, at Vels Institute of Science Technology and Advanced Studies, Chennai, India. She has 10 years of Teaching Experience and Completed Ph.D during August 2023 in the Faculty of Information and Communication Engineering under Anna University, Chennai. Her Area of Interests are Image Processing, Machine Learning and Deep Learning.

Damodharan Palaniappan works as an Associate Professor & Head in the Department of Information Technology, Marwadi University, Rajkot, Gujarat. He completed his Ph.D. at Anna University, Chennai, M.E. in Computer Science and Engineering at C.I.E.T, Coimbatore and B.E. in Computer Science and

Engineering at CSI College of Engineering, Ketty, Nilgiri. He has 19 years' experience of teaching and research. Currently, he guides 6 Ph.D. research scholars. He has authored 8 book chapters, and he has published research papers in reputed journals. His interested areas of research are Data Mining, Image Processing, Software, Machine Learning and Deep Learning.

R.Swadhi, Research Scholar, Department of Physics, Academy of Maritime Education and Training, Chennai, India Specialized in Nano Bio materials. Served as Assistant Professor in Nirmala College, Coimbatore, Lecturers & Exam coordinator in DMI-St.Eugene University Zambia and Additional Examination Coordinator, Saraswathi Institute of Medical Sciences, Hapur published 15 articles in peer reviewed journals and edited book chapters.

N. Duraimutharasan is a seasoned educationist, researcher and academic leader with over 23 years of experience in teaching, administration and industry collaboration. A former Dean and Professor, he has mentored students across all levels, secured multiple patents, published in top-tier journals, led global academic partnerships and he contributed to groundbreaking research and innovation. His expertise spans curriculum development, faculty training and institutional growth, making a lasting impact in academia and beyond.

Palanivel Rathinasabapathi Velmurugan is associated with BSBI, Berlin, as a professor in the Human Resource Management and Finance Stream. Prior to joining BSBI, he held the designation "Head" Faculty of Management at Sharda University, Uzbekistan, Central Asia, and "Dean of Arts" assignments at DMI St. John the Baptist University, Malawi, Central Africa. Also, he has been associated earlier with DMI St. Eugene University in Zambia, MAM Business School and various Engineering Colleges in India. He has a Ph.D. in Management from Mannonmanium Sundaranar University in India. Besides this, he holds an MBA Degree from SRM University in India and a BE Chemical Engineering degree from Annamalai University in India. Also, he completed six NPTEL Certificate Programs conducted by various IITs in India. He brings with him 15 years of rich working experience in teaching and research. Furthermore, he has a keen interest in the Case Method of teaching and research. He is an academic out of passion. Not only that, but he also takes a keen interest in guiding Ph.D. students. He has supervised three Ph.D. research scholars under his supervision at DMI St. Eugene University in Zambia.

Saroja Kumar Rout (Senior Member, IEEE) received M.Tech (CS) from Utkal University in the year 2007 and a Ph.D. in Computer Science in the year 2018 from Siksha 'O' Anusandhan University for work in the field of Wireless Sensor Networks. Currently working as Associate Professor in the Department of Information Technology, Vardhaman College of Engineering (Autonomous), Hyderabad, India. Contributed more than 60 research-level papers to many National and International journals and conferences. Also having 8 Indian patents. Research interests include Sensor Networks, Machine Learning, Cloud computing, and Health Informatics.

Aditya Singh is an Independent Researcher, Editorial Review Board Member in 6 American International Journals (IJSSMET, IJSDS, IJPAE, IJESGT, IJDSST, IJRLEDM), Reviewer in 8 American, 4 Singaporean & 1 Indonesian International Journals (IJUPSC, IJCVIP, IRMJ, JTA, IJAIBM, IJCEWM, JITR, IJSSSP, JDSIS, AAES, JCCE, SWT, & IJEECS) these 19 International Journals include some Scopus & WoS indexed ones, Mentor (Research) at Academy Innova World, Kalipur, India & Ex-Alumni

Mentor (LPU) at present. He had completed his regular B. Tech degree in Civil Engineering from Lovely Professional University, India, in 2020. He is currently affiliated with Amrita Vishwa Vidyapeetham, Coimbatore, India. He has 28 publications under his name, in which he is a single author in 19 of them, whereas in 6 of them he is the main author. Most of his publications are Indexed in Scopus. He had also worked as a Reviewer/Editorial Review Board Member for 145 times in the evaluation of manuscripts so far in Conferences, Research Books and Journals of International stature. His global presence as a professional could also be seen with 25 Paper Presentations in 22 Conferences in 9 countries (Thailand, Sri Lanka, Egypt, India, Cambodia, Bangladesh, Turkey, United Kingdom, & Germany); as well as his position as Program Committee Member, and Scientific Committee Member in International Conferences, and Reviewer in total 8 International Conferences (including countries Thailand, Cambodia, USA, India, and UK), and Keynote Speaker in Faculty Development Programme, and so on. He had also won 2 International Awards((Thailand) & (Cambodia)) as a Reviewer in 2023. He had worked on 50 positions so far in his professional career, including Journals, Conferences, Research Books of International stature.

C.V. Suresh Babu is a pioneer in content development. A true entrepreneur, he founded Anniyappa Publications, a company that is highly active in publishing books related to Computer Science and Management. Dr. C.V. Suresh Babu has also ventured into SB Institute, a center for knowledge transfer. He holds a Ph.D. in Engineering Education from the National Institute of Technical Teachers Training & Research in Chennai, along with seven master's degrees in various disciplines such as Engineering, Computer Applications, Management, Commerce, Economics, Psychology, Law, and Education. Additionally, he has UGC-NET/SET qualifications in the fields of Computer Science, Management, Commerce, and Education. Currently, Dr. C.V. Suresh Babu is a Professor in the Department of Information Technology at the School of Computing Science, Hindustan Institute of Technology and Science (Hindustan University) in Padur, Chennai, Tamil Nadu, India.

Jayalakshmi.V, M.Sc., MBA(ISM)., M.Phil., NET., Ph.D., is working as an Assistant Professor at SRM Institute of Science and Technology, Ramapuram, Chennai. She has 9 years of Teaching Experience. She co-authored 5 books and 2 book chapters. She has published 9 papers in Scopus indexed conferences and journals, 1 paper in SCI Indexed Journal, 4 in UGC care journals, more than 20 papers in International and National conferences. She has published 6 patents. She has more interest in research. Her area of interest includes Machine Learning, Deep Learning, Natural Language Processing, Bigdata. She has served as a resource person in various institutions.

V. Vijayarajan is currently working as an Associate Professor in School of Computer Science and Engineering, Department of Software Systems, Vellore Institute of Technology. He has 18 years of teaching experience and has published more than 30 peer reviewed publications. His research interests are theory of computation, operating systems, machine learning, deep learning, vision computing and medical analysis and disease prediction.

Index

www.ingramcontent.com/pod-product-compliance
Lightning Source LLC
LaVergne TN
LVHW062117300926
849161LV00010B/2475

9798369378120